# PL/I
# Structured
# Programming

# PL/I
# Structured
# Programming

## THIRD EDITION

Joan K. Hughes

**John Wiley & Sons**

New York • Chichester • Brisbane • Toronto • Singapore

Copyright © 1973, 1979, 1986, by John Wiley & Sons, Inc.

All rights reserved.   Published simultaneously in Canada.

Reproduction or translation of any part of
this work beyond that permitted by Sections
107 and 108 of the 1976 United States Copyright
Act without the permission of the copyright
owner is unlawful.   Requests for permission
or further information should be addressed to
the Permissions Department, John Wiley & Sons.

*Library of Congress Cataloging in Publication Data:*

Hughes, Joan Kirkby.
   PL/I structured programming.

   Includes index.
   1.  PL/I (Computer program language)   2.  Structured programming.   I. Title.

QA76.73.P25H83      1986       005.13′3       86-18
ISBN 0-471-83746-6

Printed in the United States of America

10 9 8 7 6 5

# About the Author

**Joan Kirkby Hughes** is the author of four college textbooks in the computer programming field. She has taught a number of computer-related courses to both management and nonmanagement personnel in leading companies in Southern California. In addition, she has taught at the community college level and served as conference leader at the Industrial Relations Center at California Institute of Technology in Pasadena. She has an extensive background in technical education, having been an IBM data processing instructor at one of IBM's Los Angeles Education Centers. While at IBM she developed education guides, video packages, and programmed instruction (PI) materials — all used by IBM on a nationwide basis.

Joan Hughes began her career as a programmer for the Bunker-Ramo Corporation, and has data processing experience that spans three generations of computing equipment. She is currently the president of Execudata, Inc., a microcomputer software development company that she founded in 1979 to supply turn-key systems to the real estate and property management industries.

## IN APPRECIATION

To my husband, Bill, and my dear children, John and Jenny, for their love and support.

Special appreciation is extended to Marcia Rybak, systems consultant, for her capable programming and editing assistance. Her attention to detail and willingness to pursue excellence is commendable. Recognition is also extended to Tom Butoryak of Litton Industries for handling the running of computer programs as well as the text preparation of the index in its final form.

# Preface

## TO THE READER

PL/I is a powerful language that can be used to solve both business and scientific problems. In this text, the PL/I language is presented in as simple and logical a manner as possible. Features that help you grasp the material are incorporated. For example, checkpoint questions are interspersed throughout each chapter to determine your comprehension and understanding. (The answers are in Appendix A.) A detailed *index* is provided so that you can quickly reference a technical point or locate the answer to a question. If you are new to the field of computers, you will find the *glossary* in Appendix E helpful in looking up the definitions of new terms. The section on *debugging techniques* in each chapter will help you to code and test your programs. Each chapter provides a *case study* and other PL/I programs that were compiled using IBM's OS PL/I Optimizing Compiler and executed under the MVS operating system on an IBM 3081.

## TO THE INSTRUCTOR

It is almost universally agreed that the best approach for beginning programming students is a "structured approach." In this way, students learn proper programming techniques from the beginning, before bad habits are developed. The techniques that comprise *structured programming* are stressed throughout the text.

PL/I is so comprehensive that a 1000-page book could be written and some things would still be left unsaid. I decided to present *List-Directed I/O* in Chapter 1 so that students could—after reading only the first chapter of this book—actually code a complete (though simple) PL/I program that would compile and execute. Getting students involved in *doing* at an early stage of a class gets their attention, their interest, and their commitment to the subject. The material is organized on a "need to know" basis.

Chapter 2, "Top–Down Programming—Internal and External Procedures," describes the concept of programming by first defining the criteria of good programs. The *basic* structures are described in detail. Then pseudocode and stepwise refinement are introduced as alternatives to program flowcharting. The mechanics of subroutines and functions are introduced in this important chapter and covered in detail along with recursive programming in Chapter 4.

*Stream I/O* is presented before *record I/O* because that is how it is taught in many colleges today. Arrays are presented when the iterative DO is presented; structures are discussed in the chapter dealing with record I/O, because the need for structures arises when using the RECORD form of I/O.

Other material in this edition includes a section on *list processing*, which contains a case study with a binary tree (Chapter 9), and a section on VSAM file structure (Chapter 10), as well as ISAM and REGIONAL data sets.

The chapters are mostly modular and self-contained, so you can teach according to your own sequence of topics and assign reading that is not in the sequence of this book. For example, there would be little if any loss of continuity if you taught record I/O before stream I/O.

There is a Teacher's Manual for this text. It consists of a number of visual aids suitable for making overhead transparencies for use in the classroom. It also contains suggested laboratory problems for each chapter in the book. The manual is available from the publisher.

**Joan K. Hughes**

# Contents

**CHAPTER**

1 Introduction to PL/I   **1**
2 Top-Down Structured Programming   **31**
3 Data Types and Data Manipulation   **77**
4 Subroutines and Functions   **141**
5 Logical Testing   **179**
6 DOs and Arrays   **227**
7 File Declarations and Stream I/O   **275**
8 Record I/O, Structures, Pictures   **327**
9 Storage Classes and List Processing   **387**
10 File Processing   **435**

**APPENDIX**

A Answers to Checkpoint Questions   **499**
B Built-in Functions   **519**
C PL/I Language Comparison Charts   **527**
D Data Formats   **585**
E Glossary of PL/I Terms   **597**

**INDEX 615**

# CHAPTER 1

# Introduction to PL/I

This is a book about Programming Language/One. PL/I (note the Roman numeral, I) is a language suited to developing *systems* and *applications* programs because it can be effectively used to write *structured programs.*

In structured programming, attention is directed to form and organization. To draw an analogy, artists through the ages have expressed their creativity through form and structure. Poets may express themselves in iambic pentameter or rhyming couplets. Composers may create a song or a symphony, but the song is of the form A, A, B, A and the symphony has four movements. And so it is with programmers. They will express logical solutions to computing problems using structure and form. The creativity of programming is the challenge of writing programs that are clear, understandable, and error free. As you read this text, you will learn not only how to write PL/I programs that are highly reliable, but also how to write programs that are easy to read and easy to modify.

## WRITING A PL/I PROGRAM

Writing any computer program involves several steps or phases. Once the problem is defined (which is not always an easy task), then the logical solutions should be thoroughly thought out and expressed in the form of a *program flowchart* or **pseudocode.** To illustrate, assume that a program is to compute the average of five exam grades. To do this, the exam marks — say 100, 90, 80, 70, and 90 — are represented on some form of external storage medium capable of being read or input by the computer. A magnetic disk is one of today's most common forms of external storage. A computer terminal's keyboard is another means of providing data directly to a computer program. (Historically, the punched card was the most widely used form of external storage.) Once the five values are input, they must be summed and divided by five to give the grade-point average or mean. Here are the program steps expressed as a flowchart:

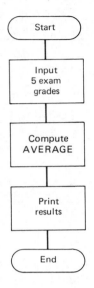

As an alternative to program flowcharting, a technique that is gaining acceptance today is that of expressing the logical solution in **pseudocode.** Pseudocode is not a programming language nor are there any rules as to how it should be written. Pseudocode, in its most abstract form, is simply a statement of the problem to be solved. For example:

Find grade-point average

This is a very general statement of the problem. However, even this problem requires more specific steps in its logical solution. To make the problem statement more specific, the pseudocode is rewritten to specify more precisely the steps the computer must take in solving the problem. For example:

Input 5 exam values
Compute grade-point average
Output (print) results

This is a *refinement* or further clarification of the first statement, *find grade-point average.* As the program steps become more specific, pseudocode begins to resemble the computer language in which you are coding. For example, in PL/I, the keywords GET and PUT may be used to specify input and output operations, respectively. The pseudocode solution could take this form:

GET 5 values
Compute grade-point average
PUT results
END

The pseudocode words that are typically written in uppercase letters are the **keywords** from the programming language in which the pseudocode is ultimately coded.

Notice that an END statement is added to indicate the end of the program. When each pseudocode statement roughly corresponds to one PL/I programming language statement, the refinement process stops and you are ready to code your PL/I program. This technique is discussed in more detail in Chapter 2. What is important now is that pseudocode can be in whatever form makes sense to you. First, general statements expressing program logic are written. In the final version, pseudocode resembles—but doesn't match—PL/I statements.

## Coding a Program

As an introduction to PL/I programming, let us code the grade-point average program. It is good programming practice to begin your PL/I program with comments. For example:

/* PROGRAM TO COMPUTE GRADE AVERAGE FROM 5 EXAM MARKS */

As you can see, a PL/I comment line begins with /* and ends with */. Comments, which have no effect on the execution of a program, generally may appear anywhere in a PL/I program. Although comments may be embedded within a PL/I statement wherever blanks are allowed, it is recommended that *embedded* comments be kept to a minimum. Comments that merely echo the code are of little value to the developer or subsequent reader of a program. Typically, a paragraph or two of comments should precede a block of code (i.e., a procedure) describing that procedure's name, function, and input/output devices:

```
/*************************************************************************/
/*   PROGRAM NAME: AVERAGE                                              */
/*   DESCRIPTION:    CALCULATE THE AVERAGE GRADE FROM 5 EXAM MARKS      */
/*   INPUT:          SYSTEM INPUT                                       */
/*   OUTPUT:         PRINTER                                            */
/*************************************************************************/
```

Comments are not PL/I statements; thus, the *first* PL/I statement in the program is the PROCEDURE statement:

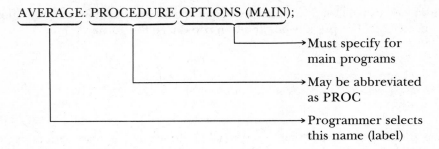

AVERAGE: PROCEDURE OPTIONS (MAIN);

→ Must specify for main programs

→ May be abbreviated as PROC

→ Programmer selects this name (label)

All PL/I statements terminate with a semicolon (;). The name affixed to the PROCEDURE statement (AVERAGE in the previous example) is called a **label.** The label is separated from the rest of the PL/I statement by a colon (:) and may or may not appear on a separate line.

The label is typically coded on the same line with the PROCEDURE statement indented a few spaces. The PROCEDURE statement is not executable. It is simply a way of telling the computer that this statement marks the beginning of a block of PL/I statements. The PROCEDURE statement must always be labeled.

A distinction is made here between *main* procedures and *subprogram* procedures that, while different, also begin with a PROCEDURE statement but without the OPTIONS (MAIN). For example:

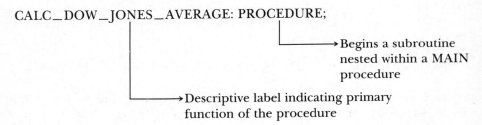

CALC_DOW_JONES_AVERAGE: PROCEDURE;

→ Begins a subroutine nested within a MAIN procedure

→ Descriptive label indicating primary function of the procedure

Following the PROCEDURE OPTIONS (MAIN) statement, the statement to input the data (examination marks) is specified. This is accomplished with the statement

GET LIST (A, B, C, D, E);

The five input values must be separated from each other by a blank or comma. When the GET statement is executed, the five values (100, 90, 80, 70, 90) are read into the computer and assigned correspondingly to the **variables** named A, B, C, D, and E. Thus, A contains the value 100, B the value 90, C the value 80, and so on. Variables are names representing data; they are names to which data items are assigned.

The next programming step is to compute the sum. This is accomplished by the assignment statement

$$SUM = \underbrace{A + B + C + D + E;}_{\text{Expression}}$$

Arithmetic assignment statement

The equal sign (=) is the *assignment symbol* and denotes the assignment statement. The assignment statement does not necessarily represent equality. The operation means "Assign the value of the expression on the right of the assignment symbol (=) to the variable on the left of the assignment symbol."

After the sum is calculated, it must be divided by 5 to give the average.

AVERAGE_GRADE = SUM / 5;

The slash (/) indicates a divide operation. The quotient is assigned to the variable called AVERAGE_GRADE.

The final step is that of printing the results. This is accomplished with the statement

PUT LIST ('AVERAGE GRADE IS', AVERAGE_GRADE);

This statement generates output to a system printer and looks like this:

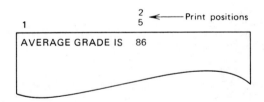

Why print position 1 and then 25? Data items printed with a PUT LIST statement are automatically aligned on predetermined *tab positions*. These positions for IBM PL/I implementations are typically 1, 25, 49, 73, 97, and 121, an interval of 24 positions. (It is possible that in your installation these predetermined tab positions may not match the positions stated.) In the PUT LIST statement, two data items were output:

1. 'AVERAGE GRADE IS'
2. The contents of the identifier called AVERAGE_GRADE

Notice how 'AVERAGE GRADE IS' is surrounded with single quotation marks in the PUT LIST statement; however, on output, the single quote marks are removed before they are printed. This data item is a *character-string constant*. A **character-string** is a group of **alphameric characters** used as a single data item. A **constant** is an arithmetic data item or string data item that does not have a name and whose value cannot change. Thus, 'AVERAGE GRADE IS' is a character-string constant, and the value 5 in the assignment statement previously introduced is an arithmetic decimal constant. Remember, string constants are surrounded by single quote marks; arithmetic constants are not surrounded by any punctuation marks.

Logically, the grade-point program is finished. The physical end of the program is indicated by an END statement. For program readability, the END statement contains the label of the procedure it is ending. For example:

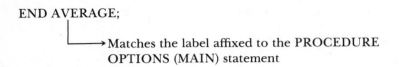

END AVERAGE;

        →Matches the label affixed to the PROCEDURE
          OPTIONS (MAIN) statement

Here, then, is the complete program:

```
/*      PROGRAM TO COMPUTE GRADE AVERAGE FROM 5 EXAM MARKS                 */
/**************************************************************************/
/*  PROGRAM NAME: AVERAGE                                                  */
/*  DESCRIPTION:     CALCULATE THE AVERAGE GRADE FROM 5 EXAM MARKS         */
/*  INPUT:             SYSTEM INPUT                                        */
/*  OUTPUT:            PRINTER                                             */
/**************************************************************************/
AVERAGE:   PROCEDURE OPTIONS(MAIN);

    GET LIST(A,B,C,D,E);
    SUM = A + B + C + D + E;
    AVERAGE__GRADE = SUM / 5;
    PUT LIST('AVERAGE GRADE IS',AVERAGE__GRADE);

END AVERAGE;
```

## CHECKPOINT QUESTIONS

**1.** True or false? There are specific rules as to how pseudocode should be written.

**2.** Define a program *constant* and give two examples.

**3.** How are comments specified in a PL/I program and where should they be specified?

**4.** What must you consider when naming PROCEDUREs?

### Compiling a Program

At this point, you are ready to key your program onto a diskette (or perhaps cards) or enter it directly into the computer through a terminal.

After keying, a PL/I program is ready to be **compiled.** This is a translation process in which your PL/I program statements are converted into the binary language "understood" by the computer.

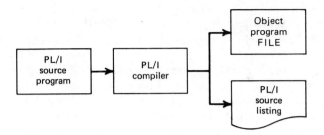

Typically, the binary object program is placed on a disk, waiting to be link edited and then loaded into *main storage* where it will be executed. The source listing consists of a printout of your PL/I statements along with any diagnostic messages from the compiler.

The process of compiling a program and executing it in the computer's main storage takes place through instructions to the computer's operating system program. The instructions are referred to as Job Control Language (JCL) or operating system "commands." JCL statements surround your source program and its data to indicate which is the program to be compiled and which is the data file (or files) to be processed. JCL is unique to each type of computer; sometimes it is even unique to a given computer installation. Contact your instructor or someone in the computer lab for the JCL or operating system commands you need to compile and execute PL/I programs.

A number of PL/I compilers are provided in the industry today. In addition to IBM, other computer manufacturers such as Digital Equipment Corporation (DEC), Data General, and Honeywell provide PL/I compilers. Software firms, such as Digital Research, who provide PL/I for microcomputers (PL/I, subset G) are another source of compilers. Cornell University has also developed a PL/I compiler for use by students in colleges across the country. The PL/I compiler is called PL/C[1] and runs under IBM operating systems.

Although the various implementations of PL/I have a great deal of similarity with respect to their language capabilities, a number of small details or restrictions set them apart from each other. Appendix C compares the capabilities of the various compilers. This text addresses the *full language* capabilities of PL/I as specified by the American National Standards Institute (ANSI).

### Debugging a Program

Debugging a program is the process of removing known errors from your program. For example, when you first compile a program, chances are you will make

---

[1] Cornell University also has an interactive version of PL/C called PL/CT. It is completely compatible with PL/C, but permits the use of an individual terminal rather than a card reader and line printer.

some syntax mistakes such as forgetting a semicolon or omitting a necessary PL/I keyword. The compiler will note these errors for you; the errors must then be corrected. The PL/I compiler indicates the severity of the errors it encounters. You will have to recompile a program until there are no more *Errors* or *Severe Errors*. In addition to these types of errors, there are *Informatory* and *Warning* messages from the compiler letting you know about some assumption or compiler action taken.

Once compile-time errors have been removed, you may experience problems in getting your program to run the way you intended. These are errors resulting from the logic of your program. You know they are errors because the visual output does not look as you had intended. For example, the printed values may be wrong, missing, or skewed across the printer page.

PL/I offers a wide variety of debugging aids that will be discussed throughout this text. One common aid is a program trace feature called CHECK. A *program trace* is a printout of the computer results after each PL/I statement is executed. Use the CHECK feature when it is not obvious to you as to "what went wrong."

To call for this trace feature, affix the keyword CHECK enclosed in parentheses, preceding the label on your PROCEDURE statement. For example:

        (CHECK):
        AVERAGE: PROCEDURE OPTIONS(MAIN);
              .
              .
              .
        END AVERAGE;

Notice how the parenthesized word CHECK is followed by a colon. Once you have located your program logic errors, CHECK should be removed. That is why, incidentally, it was coded on a separate line. When you correct your source code, all you have to do is remove that specific line.

By preceding a procedure with a CHECK prefix, you can receive a printout of all program variables when they change values. In addition, the names of subroutines called will also be printed. The output is in the form of assignment statements to the system line printer. If your program outputs to the same printer file, then that output will be intermixed with the output from CHECK as is the case with the grade-point average program.

In the following grade-point average program,

```
/*     PROGRAM TO COMPUTE GRADE AVERAGE FROM 5 EXAM MARKS        */
/********************************************************************/
/*   PROGRAM NAME:   AVERAGE                                      */
/*   DECRIPTION:     CALCULATE THE AVERAGE GRADE FROM 5 EXAM MARKS */
/*   INPUT:          SYSTEM INPUT                                 */
/*   OUTPUT:         PRINTER                                      */
/********************************************************************/
1  (CHECK):
   AVERAGE: PROCEDURE OPTIONS(MAIN);

2     GET LIST(A,B,C,D,E);
3     SUM = A + B + C + D + E;
```

```
4        AVERAGE_GRADE = SUM / 5;
5        PUT LIST('AVERAGE GRADE IS',AVERAGE_GRADE);

6   END AVERAGE;
```
└──Source program statement numbers generated by the
    PL/I compiler.

the output from CHECK includes the data value input or computed followed by
the program statement number producing the result:

```
A= 8.50000E+01;

B= 7.60000E+01;

C= 9.50000E+01;

D= 8.80000E+01;

E= 9.80000E+01;

SUM= 4.42000E+02;

AVERAGE_GRADE= 8.83999E+01;
AVERAGE GRADE IS           8.83999E+01
```

The printed format of items A, B, C, D, and E is in **floating-point** which is
explained later in this chapter.

For large programs, the output from CHECK could be voluminous. If you are
only interested in tracing the output of a limited number of program variables,
then these variables may be listed in parentheses following the keyword CHECK.
For example:

    (CHECK(A,B,SUM)):
    AVERAGE: PROCEDURE OPTIONS(MAIN);
        .
        .
    END AVERAGE;

CHECK may also precede any PL/I statement within the procedure, in which case
only the results from that statement will be output. For example:

    AVERAGE: PROCEDURE OPTIONS(MAIN);
        .
        .
    (CHECK): SUM = A + B + C + D + E;
        .
        .
    END AVERAGE;

## Testing a Program

Testing a program is different from debugging a program. *Testing*, the last phase
of your program development effort, involves proving the program's correct-

ness. Programs must be correct to be useful. To prove the program's validity, a variety of sets of test data must be developed and run with the debugged program. Typically, the data items for debugging a program are selected by the programmer. Test data, however, should be determined by someone other than the programmer who developed the program. With this approach, there is an increased likelihood that the program will be more thoroughly tested, and therefore greater confidence in the program's reliability generated. It is recommended that test data be prepared *before* the program is coded by a programmer.

The coding and testing of JCL should also be done before the program is coded and debugged. Then, when the program is ready to be debugged, the programmer does not have to be concerned with possible JCL errors and data file references in that JCL. To test the JCL simply create a *program stub*. A program stub is a skeleton of a total program. It contains whatever minimal code is necessary to indicate that the program was, in fact, executed. Here is an example of a program stub:

---

AVERAGE: PROCEDURE OPTIONS [MAIN];
    PUT LIST ('PROGRAM TO COMPUTE AVERAGE');
END AVERAGE;

---

The only statement in this program was a PUT LIST to indicate that the program did go into execution. The message PROGRAM TO COMPUTE AVERAGE on the printed output is proof of this.

## CHECKPOINT QUESTIONS

**5.** Distinguish between *source* and *object* programs.

**6.** Explain *compilation* and *execution*.

**7.** What is the purpose of JCL?

**8.** What is the difference between *debugging* and *testing?*

**9.** Why would a program trace be used? How is it activated in PL/I?

**10.** What is a program stub?

## PL/I LANGUAGE COMPONENTS

### Character Sets

There are 60 characters in the PL/I language. They include:

> *Extended alphabet of 29 characters*
> $ @ # A B C D E F G H I J K L
> M N O P Q R S T U V W X Y Z

*Ten decimal digits*

0 1 2 3 4 5 6 7 8 9

*21 special characters*

| | |
|---|---|
| Blank | |
| Equal or assignment symbol | = |
| Plus sign | + |
| Minus sign | − |
| Asterisk or multiply symbol | * |
| Slash or divide symbol | / |
| Left parenthesis | ( |
| Right parenthesis | ) |
| Comma | , |
| Point or period | . |
| Single quotation mark or apostrophe | ' |
| Percent symbol | % |
| Semicolon | ; |
| Colon | : |
| NOT symbol (or ^ or ˜)[2] | ¬ |
| AND symbol | & |
| OR symbol (or ! or /)[2] | \| |
| "Greater than" symbol | > |
| "Less than" symbol | < |
| Break (underscore) | _ |
| Question mark | ? |

The question mark, in most PL/I compilers, has no specific use in the language.

Special characters may be combined to create other symbols; for example, <= means "less than or equal to" and ¬= means "not equal to." The combination ** denotes exponentiation ($X**2$ means $X^2$, $X**3$ means $X^3$). Blanks are not permitted in such character combinations. For example:

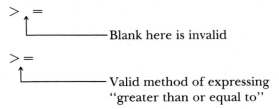

A special 48-character set is also available as an alternative to the 60-character set. This 48-character set is provided as a convenience to the programmer and is used instead of the 60-character set if some of the special characters (>, %, ;, :, etc.) are not graphically available on the printer on which the source program is

[2] If the keyboard you are using does not have the NOT (¬) or the OR (|) symbol, the compiler may allow ! or / as substitute symbols for the OR operation and ^ (CTRL) or ˜ (tilde) for the NOT operation.

listed.  If you write programs using punctuation from the 60-character set, but the printer on which the source program is being listed does not have the proper characters, certain symbols will not print.  For example:

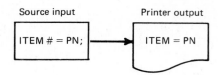

Note that it is not an "error" when the ; or # is not printed.  It presents a problem while debugging your PL/I program because you have to resort to displaying source code to verify that certain characters have indeed been entered.  In this situation, it is usually easier if you use the 48-character set.

Figure 1.1 illustrates how various punctuation marks and operations are expressed in each of the character sets.  The small b in the 48-character set symbols (bGTb) indicates that a blank must appear at that place.  Note that @, #, ?, and the break character (_) are not available in the 48-character set.  When using the 48-character set, the special operators CAT, NE, NL, NG, GT, GE, LT, LE, NOT, OR, AND, and PT are *reserved* keywords that must be surrounded by one or more blanks and cannot be used by the programmer for any other purpose.

## Identifiers

The general term **identifiers** is given to names of data (AVERAGE_GRADE, A, B, C, D, and E in the grade-point average program), names of **procedures** (AVERAGE in the same program), names of **files** (there were no explicitly defined files in that program), labels of PL/I **statements** (only the PROCEDURE statement was labeled), and **keywords** (such as GET or PUT).

**Keywords** constitute the vocabulary that makes up the PL/I language.  When keywords are used in proper context, they have a specific meaning.  (Appendix C provides a list of keywords available for various PL/I compilers.)  With respect to formatting, keywords are generally separated from each other by a blank.  Your common sense is the best guide to following this rule.  For example, GET and LIST are two PL/I keywords.  Common sense tells us that

GETLIST (A,B,C);

is not as clear and readable as

GET LIST (A,B,C);

*When in doubt, use blanks.*

An identifier for *data names,* **statement labels,** and **internal procedure** *names* may be from 1 to 31 alphabetic characters (A – Z, !, #, $), numeric digits (0 – 9), and break (_) characters.  (Note that in PL/I, the characters @, #, and $ are defined as alphabetic.)  The break character is the same as the typewriter underline

| Explanation | 60-character set | 48-character set |
|---|---|---|
| Alphabetic letters | A through Z<br>$<br>@<br># | A through Z<br>$<br>Not available<br>Not available |
| Numeric digits | 0123456789 | 0123456789 |
| Punctuation<br>  Period<br>  Comma<br>  Single quote<br>  Parentheses<br>  Colon<br>  Semicolon | .<br>,<br>'<br>( )<br>:<br>; | .<br>,<br>'<br>( )<br>..<br>,. |
| Arithmetic | + − * / ** | + − * / ** |
| Special<br>  Blank<br>  Break<br>  Percent<br>  Question mark<br>  Concatenation<br>  Equal<br>  Greater than<br>  Greater than or equal<br>  Less than<br>  Less than or equal<br>  Not less than<br>  Not greater than<br>  Not equal<br>  Not<br>  Or<br>  And<br>  Points to | <br>_<br>%<br>?<br>‖<br>=<br>><br>>=<br><<br><=<br>¬<<br>¬><br>¬=<br>¬<br>\|<br>&<br>−> | <br>Not available<br>/ /<br>Not available<br>bCATb<br>=<br>bGTb<br>bGEb<br>bLTb<br>bLEb<br>bNLb<br>bNGb<br>bNEb<br>bNOTb<br>bORb<br>bANDb<br>bPTb |

FIGURE 1.1  Expressing punctuation and operations in 60- and 48-character sets.

character.  It can be used within a data name, such as GROSS_PAY, to improve readability.  A hyphen cannot be used because it would be treated as a minus sign.

The first character of an identifier must be alphabetic, and there may be no embedded blanks within the name.  Select names that state the function the identifier serves.  For example:

NET_INCOME_BEFORE_TAXES    ACCOUNT_NO
CLIENT_NAME                BALANCE_FORWARD

A procedure with an OPTIONS (MAIN) is an *external* procedure.  Names of **external procedures** and **files** are a maximum of seven or eight characters, depending on which computer and operating system you are using.

One way to select file names is to identify which major application the file relates to. For example, accounts receivable files would begin with AR, accounts payable files with AP, or payroll files with PR. The remaining five characters imply the function. Some examples follow:

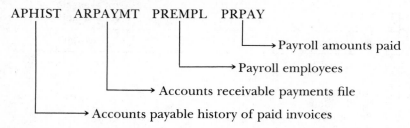

APHIST  ARPAYMT  PREMPL  PRPAY

→ Payroll amounts paid

→ Payroll employees

→ Accounts receivable payments file

→ Accounts payable history of paid invoices

The break or underscore character (\_), the #, and the @ may not be used in file names or external procedure names even though they are allowed for other identifiers within your program.

In PL/I there are two types of procedures: **external,** whose names must be known to the operating system, and **internal,** those nested within an external procedure. Internal procedures, discussed in more detail in the next chapter, may have names up to 31 characters long. A procedure with the option MAIN is one type of external procedure; subprograms[3] are the other type of external procedure (Chapter 4). The limitation of seven or eight characters applies to external procedures but not internal procedures.

### Statement Format

PL/I statements take the general form

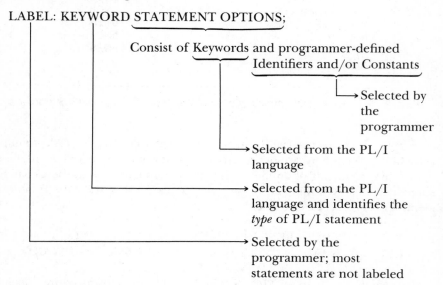

LABEL: KEYWORD STATEMENT OPTIONS;

Consist of Keywords and programmer-defined Identifiers and/or Constants

→ Selected by the programmer

→ Selected from the PL/I language

→ Selected from the PL/I language and identifies the *type* of PL/I statement

→ Selected by the programmer; most statements are not labeled

[3] An external subprogram is compiled separately from the main program. It is stored in a library on disk and is retrieved when needed by a main program.

For example:

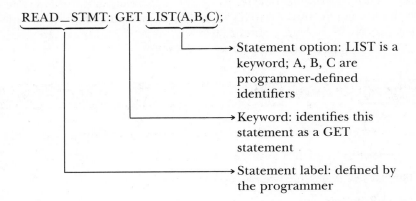

READ_STMT: GET LIST(A,B,C);

Statement option: LIST is a keyword; A, B, C are programmer-defined identifiers

Keyword: identifies this statement as a GET statement

Statement label: defined by the programmer

PL/I is said to be free-form; that is, a statement may contain blanks as needed to improve readability of the source program. A PL/I statement may be continued across several lines. For example:

One PL/I statement { Second line (A,B,C,D,E); First line GET LIST

Or, one line may contain several PL/I statements. For example:

GET LIST(A,B,C,D,E); SUM = A + B + C + D + E;

The reason that more than one statement may appear on a line is that a semicolon (;) terminates a PL/I statement. If a programmer inadvertently omits a semicolon at the end of a PL/I statement, thereby causing two statements to "run" together, the compiler may flag the combined statements as being in error. Sometimes the compiler can detect where the semicolon should appear and insert one for you. Flagged errors of this and other types are referred to as *compiler diagnostics.*

Because PL/I is free-form, no special coding sheets are required. The following is the accepted IBM standard for typing programs:

| | |
|---|---|
| Position 1 | Reserved for use by the operating system. |
| Positions 2–72 | May contain one or more PL/I statements or part of a statement. |
| Positions 73–80 | May contain program identification name and/or a sequence number; the compiler, however, does not check for consecutive order of sequence numbers. |

For program readability, no more than one statement should appear on one line. In many cases, it is desirable to divide a statement into smaller parts and code on separate lines using indentation to highlight logical grouping of code. Positions or spaces selected for indenting should be fixed at a specific number. In this text, an *indentation unit* of three spaces is used.

## CHECKPOINT QUESTIONS

**11.** What characters other than A through Z are considered alphabetic in PL/I?

**12.** Define *identifier* and give examples.

**13.** What is a *keyword?* What are *reserved keywords?*

**14.** Which of the following are valid data names?

(a) 1STMT           (d) VALUE-1

(b) #_OF_ITEMS    (e) LIST

(c) SOCIAL SECURITY

### PL/I Constants

A **constant** is a data item that does not have a name and whose value cannot change in a program. In the grade-point average program, you saw the two most com-

| Type | Example | When to use |
|---|---|---|
| Decimal fixed-point | 12.75 | Commercial and scientific applications |
| Decimal floating-point | 0.1275E+2 | Scientific applications |
| Character-string | 'ABCD' | More common in commercial applications but often needed in scientific computing as well |
| Bit-string | '1'B | Program switches or flags in scientific or commercial programs |
| Binary fixed-point | 1B | For nonoptimizing compilers where program efficiency is of paramount concern |
| Binary floating-point | 0.110011E+48B | Highly specialized applications (typically scientific) |

FIGURE 1.2   PL/I constants.

mon types of PL/I constants:

- Fixed decimal (the divisor, 5).
- Character string ('AVERAGE GRADE IS').

Actually there are six types of PL/I constants, but for the most part you will only need to use two or three of these in your programs. The six types depicted in Figure 1.2 are provided as an overview of data types. The last two data constant types in this figure are not covered in this text because of their limited use.

**Decimal Fixed-Point Constants.** These consist of one or more decimal digits and, optionally, a decimal point. If no decimal point appears, then the data item is an integer. Some examples are:

$$180 \quad 3.1415 \quad +52.98 \quad -100 \quad 0.0003$$

Decimal fixed-point constants are widely used in almost all programs.

**Decimal Floating-Point Constants.** These constants are written using exponential notation (or E-notation). This is explained as follows (where X represents any decimal digit):

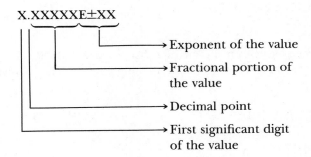

For example, a value of 86 in decimal floating-point could look like this:

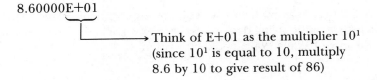

In the previous example, the E+01 *floats* the decimal point to the right 01 places so that the value is 86.

Decimal floating-point constants do not have to be coded in the format just explained. In fact, this format is more typically found on printed output.

Some examples of decimal floating-point constants, along with their decimal fixed-point equivalents, are given as follows:

| Decimal floating-point constant | Decimal fixed-point equivalent |
|---|---|
| 12.E+05 or 12E5 | 1200000. |
| 3141593E−6 | 3.141593 |
| .1E−07 | .00000001 |
| −45E+11 | −4500000000000. |
| 84E | 84 |

On IBM implementations, the range of decimal floating-point exponents is approximately $10^{-78}$ to $10^{+75}$.

Decimal floating-point data items are used in scientific applications (engineering, physics, astronomy) or math-related business applications such as statistics or simulation.

**Character-String Constants.** These constants are **alphameric** data items that may include any of the up to 256 characters recognized by the computer system. Any blank included in a character-string is considered part of and is included in the count of the length of the string. When written in a program, character-string constants must be enclosed in single quote marks. For example:

'THE ROAD NOT TAKEN'
'DR. STRETCH, CHIROPRACTOR'
'10600 DEERING AVE.'

If an apostrophe is needed within the character-string constant, it must be written as two single quotation marks with no intervening blanks. The following constant

'SHAKESPEARE''S HAMLET'

is stored inside the computer as

S H A K E S P E A R E ' S   H A M L E T

It is also possible to specify a **repetition factor** for string constants. This feature is useful when a *pattern* in the string data exists. For example, the character-string constant for the city of Walla Walla could be written

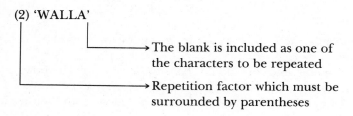

(2) 'WALLA'

→ The blank is included as one of the characters to be repeated

→ Repetition factor which must be surrounded by parentheses

and gives the following character-string with a length of 12 characters:

| W | A | L | L | A |  | W | A | L | L | A |  |
|---|---|---|---|---|---|---|---|---|---|---|---|

Here is an example of the DECLARE statement and an assignment statement that assigns a character constant to the variable declared:

```
DECLARE NAME CHAR (20);
NAME = 'JENNIFER HUGHES';
```

| J | E | N | N | I | F | E | R |  | H | U | G | H | E | S |  |  |  |  |  |
|---|---|---|---|---|---|---|---|---|---|---|---|---|---|---|---|---|---|---|---|

The name JENNIFER HUGHES is less than 20 characters, which is the length declared for NAME. In this case, unused positions of the variable are padded on the right with blanks. (The DECLARE statement is used to specify the attributes of the variable called NAME.)

**Bit-String Constants.** These constants are written in a program as a series of binary digits enclosed in single quote marks and followed by the letter B. Bit-strings are valuable for general use as *indicators* or *flags*. They can be set to 1 or 0 and then tested later in the program. Bit-strings are increasingly used in information retrieval because many "yes" or "no" answers can be recorded as a bit-string in a relatively small area. Here are some examples of bit-string constants:

```
'1'B
'11111010110001'B
(64)'0'B
```

The number in parentheses preceding the last example is a repetition factor specifying that the following bit or bits are to be repeated the specific number of times. The example shown would result in a string of 64 binary zeros.

Bit-strings are not used in calculations. Instead, bit-strings are used in a program to indicate whether or not certain conditions exist (yes or no, 1 or 0, true or false). Bit-strings can also be used as a compact method of describing characteristics. For example, assume a television and movie casting agency is using a computer to keep track of the thousands of Hollywood "bit part" actors (pardon the pun) available for movie and television work. When the studio has determined its requirements for "extras," that request is sent to the casting agency. On what basis does the agency select the actors to fill the request? Or when a request for a particular type of actor or actress comes to the agency, how does the agency select from the thousands of possible actors the right person for the part? One method would be to describe the various talents (comedy, heavy dramatic) and characteristics (age, hair color, height) of the actors or actresses in terms of bit-strings.  For example:

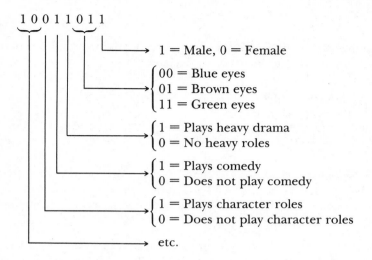

These bit-strings could be stored on tape or disk files.  When a request for a certain acting type is made, a bit-string of the desired characteristics is defined. Using this bit pattern as a guide, the files of bit-strings can be easily searched by a PL/I program for the person who most closely resembles the desired characteristics.  You can see from the above example that a lot of information about a person can be compacted into a small "space."  Large companies, having computerized their personnel records, use the method of coding bit-strings to describe employees' job skills, education, work experience, etc.

**Binary Fixed-Point and Binary Floating-Point Constants.**  These constants are beyond the scope of an introductory text on PL/I.  Their use is limited; many professional PL/I programmers never use them.  Binary fixed-point **variables** will be discussed later; binary fixed-point **constants** aren't generally needed because it is easier to express their equivalents in decimal.

## CHECKPOINT QUESTION

**15.** Identify each of the following constants, using the proper PL/I term (e.g., fixed-point decimal):

(a)  101

(b)  '101'

(c)  101E

(d)  '101'B

## LIST-DIRECTED I/O

### List-Directed Input

List-directed data transmission is the first form of input/output discussed because it is easy to learn (thereby allowing you to start writing PL/I programs quickly). Although it would not often be used in production-type jobs, it can be a useful debugging or program checkout tool.

In the grade-point average program, the input statement

GET LIST (A,B,C,D,E);

causes data to be read from the system input device, which is typically a diskette reader or perhaps a card reader. For this type of input, each data value must be separated by a delimiter such as a blank. For example, the five values could be keyed into one line:

```
100 90 80 70 90
```

Because the data can be separated by one or more blanks, each value could be keyed on a separate line:

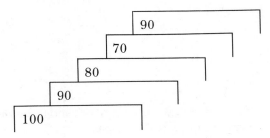

The input data could be *separated by commas* and blanks. For example:

```
100, 90,80,70, 90
```

Or, input data could be separated by commas only. For example:

```
100,90,80,70,90
```

Notice there is no comma following the last data item in the input **stream.** The term **stream** is used because in list-directed input or output data transmission, data items are treated as one *continuous* stream of characters. In understanding this concept, it might be helpful to think of the data characters in an input stream as being on a conveyor belt. A number of characters — perhaps decimal digits — will be "taken" off the conveyor belt and assigned to the appropriate variable by the GET LIST statement. Just how many digits are combined and assigned to one variable is determined by the blank or comma that separates each data item in the stream. Thus, characters are read (i.e., the conveyor belt is moved) until a blank or comma is encountered. That group of characters would then make up one data item. Assuming the information is keyed into separate lines when there are no more characters on one line, then the next line would be input, and the "conveyor belt" analogy would continue. Another way of looking at the stream concept is to imagine taping all the lines of input end to end:

As a further illustration of the stream concept, assume the values from the grade-point average program are keyed in the following manner,

    100 90 80 70 90

and we write the statement:

    GET LIST (A,B,C);

Here, of course, A will take on the value of 100, B the value of 90, and C the value of 80. Now, assume the next statement in the PL/I program is:

    GET LIST (D,E);

The variable D will take on the value 70, and E the value 90. For the previous GET LIST, a new line was not read because there were still some values contained on the first line. In other words, the record, punched card, or print line is an *artificial boundary,* as seen by PL/I. Another way the five values from a single line could have been read is:

    GET LIST(A);
    GET LIST(B);
    GET LIST(C);
    GET LIST(D);
    GET LIST(E);

Although the previous method takes longer to code, it illustrates stream data transmission. Note also that there is no space implied between lines. For example, if a data item ended in the last physical position of one line, the next line in the input stream must have a blank or comma in position 1 to separate the previous data item from the next in the stream.

A feature of the GET LIST is the COPY option. By adding the keyword COPY to the input statement, the data will be "echoed" on the system printer. For example,

GET LIST (A,B,C,D,E) COPY;

causes the values in A, B, etc., to appear on the printout at the predetermined tab positions. This feature could be useful in the debugging phase or testing phase of your program.

Any type of PL/I constant may appear in the input stream for list-directed input. For example:

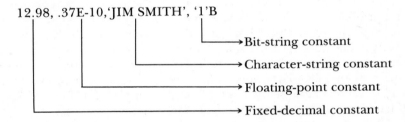

12.98, .37E-10,'JIM SMITH', '1'B

→ Bit-string constant

→ Character-string constant

→ Floating-point constant

→ Fixed-decimal constant

If a character-string constant appears in the input stream and is read using a GET LIST statement, then the identifier in the GET statement should be described as containing character data. The DECLARE statement is used to specify an identifier as having the attribute CHARACTER. For example, to read 'WALLA WALLA', the following would be coded:

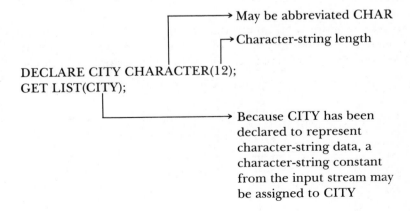

→ May be abbreviated CHAR

→ Character-string length

DECLARE CITY CHARACTER(12);
GET LIST(CITY);

→ Because CITY has been declared to represent character-string data, a character-string constant from the input stream may be assigned to CITY

Data must be in the form of PL/I constants so that the input routine activated when the GET is executed will recognize the type of data being read.

### List-Directed Output

Because PL/I constants may be data items in the PUT LIST statement, the statements

    PUT LIST (50, 'ABC',123,127);
    PUT LIST (23,86,87);

give us this output:

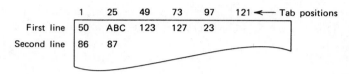

In PUT LIST, the stream concept still applies. The data items specified for output are printed beginning at predetermined tab positions. Notice how the first data item in the second PUT LIST statement is printed on the first line with data items from the first PUT LIST statement. From this you can see that a PUT statement does not necessarily cause data to be printed on a new line. Output begins wherever that last output ended. Notice that nothing is printed in tab position 121. This is because the default line size for a PUT LIST is 120 positions. It has been shown that the IBM default tab positions are 1, 25, 49, 73, 97, and 121. How, then, does one output to a print position beyond 120 if the line size for PUT LIST is 120 maximum positions? The answer is that certain attributes or characteristics are assumed for the output file (e.g., the printer) associated with the PUT LIST statement. One of these characteristics is that the line size is 120 positions. As will be seen later, it is possible to define a file whose line size is greater than 120 print positions, in which case tab position 121 would be used in the list-directed printed output (assuming the printer has more than 120 print positions).

Sometimes it is desired to print information in a specified tab position without printing in the tab positions that precede it. This can be accomplished by specifying a character-string of a blank to the preceding tab positions. For example:

    PUT PAGE LIST (' ', ' ', 'WEEKLY ACTIVITY REPORT');

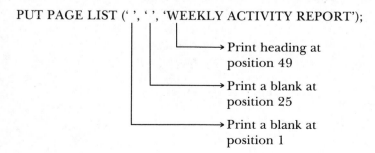

Constants, variables, or expressions may be specified as **data items** in a PUT LIST statement. For example:

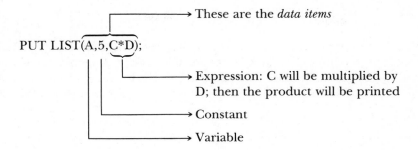

Assume it is desired to print one value on one line and a second value on the next line. This can be accomplished through the PAGE and/or SKIP options. The PAGE option causes the paper in the printer to advance to the top of a new page. The SKIP option causes the paper to be advanced the number of lines specified. If the number of lines is not explicitly stated, a SKIP (1) is assumed.

Whenever a PUT LIST is *first* executed in your program, there is an automatic skip to a new page on the printer. Thereafter you must specify the *printer control options* as your program logic dictates. For example:

```
PUT PAGE    LIST('ABC');   /* START A NEW PAGE             */
PUT SKIP     LIST(123);     /* SKIP ONE LINE BEFORE PRINT  */
PUT SKIP(2) LIST (127);    /* SKIP TWO LINES BEFORE PRINT */
```

A SKIP (0) causes a suppression of the line feed. For example, suppose it is desired to print a heading on a new page and underline that heading (e.g., STANLEY P. SMERSCH & ASSOCIATES). These statements would accomplish it:

```
PUT PAGE    LIST('STANLEY P. SMERSCH & ASSOCIATES');
PUT SKIP(0) LIST((31)'_');/* A REPETITION FACTOR OF 31 */
    /* UNDERSCORE CHARACTERS IS SPECIFIED */
```

Since SKIP (0) prevents advancing of the paper in the printer, we simply go back to the beginning of the line on which the previous information was printed. Using the break character in the second PUT statement causes the heading to be underlined.

The LINE option may be used to indicate the line of the page on which you would like information printed. For example:

```
PUT PAGE LINE (10) LIST (A,B,C);
```

This indicates that a new page should be started and that the values of A, B, and C be printed starting on line 10 of that new page. It is also possible to write

PUT LINE (10) PAGE LIST (A,B,C);

The effect is the same as in the previous example. This is because when PAGE and LINE are specified in the same PUT statement, there is a hierarchy governing which option is exercised first. The order of priority is PAGE first, then LINE.

The PAGE, SKIP, and LINE options may also appear by themselves. For example:

```
PUT PAGE;        /* START A NEW PAGE                   */
PUT SKIP (2);    /* SKIP TWO LINES                     */
PUT LINE (15);   /* SET CURRENT LINE COUNTER TO 15 */
```

In this example, there is a comment about the *current line counter*. This is an internal counter provided by PL/I for keeping track of vertical spacing on the line printer. Every time a line is printed during the execution of your PL/I object program, the line counter is automatically incremented by one. When the value in the line counter reaches a predetermined maximum, it is reset and the process begun again for a new page. The maximum value for the line count is a system standard that is defined at each computer installation, or that may be specified through a special option called PAGESIZE (to be explained later).

List-directed I/O is one of three forms of STREAM I/O. The other two forms are edit-directed and data-directed I/O, which are discussed in Chapter 7. As an example of using GET and PUT LIST as well as the arithmetic symbols presented in this chapter, let's look at a small program to compute the area of a triangle, given the base and height where

$$\text{Area} = \frac{1}{2} \text{ Base} \times \text{Height}$$

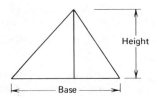

Also, find the area of a second triangle where only the lengths of the sides are known. The formula is

$$\text{Area} = \sqrt{S(S - A)(S - B)(S - C)}$$

where A, B, and C are the triangle's sides and

$$S = \frac{A + B + C}{2}$$

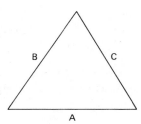

To find the square root of a value is to raise it to a half power. For example:

AREA = RESULT**.5;

└──→ Double asterisks denote exponentiation

Here is the PL/I program:

```
/* COMPUTE THE AREAS OF TRIANGLES USING 2 DIFFERENT ALGORITHMS        */
/**********************************************************************/
/*   PROGRAM NAME:   AREA                                             */
/*   DESCRIPTION:    CALCULATE THE AREA OF 2 DIFFERENT TRIANGLES USING */
/*                   2 DIFFERENT FORMULAS.                            */
/*                      FORMULA 1:   AREA = 1/2 BASE * HEIGHT         */
/*                      FORMULA 2:   (S*(S-A)*(S-B)*(S-C))**.5        */
/*                   WHERE S = SUM OF ALL SIDES / 2;   A, B, C ARE THE */
/*                   SIDES OF THE TRIANGLE.                           */
/*   INPUT:          SYSTEM INPUT                                     */
/*   OUTPUT:         PRINTER                                          */
/**********************************************************************/
1   AREA: PROCEDURE OPTIONS(MAIN);

2      GET   LIST(BASE,HEIGHT,SIDE1,SIDE2,SIDE3);

3      AREA_TRIANGLE1 = BASE / 2 * HEIGHT;
4      PUT PAGE LIST('AREA OF TRIANGLE 1 IS', AREA_TRIANGLE1);

5      SUM = (SIDE1 + SIDE2 + SIDE3) / 2;
6      AREA_TRIANGLE2 = (SUM*(SUM-SIDE1)*(SUM-SIDE2)*(SUM-SIDE3))**.5;
7      PUT SKIP LIST('AREA OF TRIANGLE 2 IS', AREA_TRIANGLE2);

8   END AREA;
```

Notice that the GET LIST statement reads all data in one statement. Observe also, the printer control options PAGE and SKIP. What would the output look like had they not been used?

## CHECKPOINT QUESTIONS

**16.** In list-directed input, what form must the input values take and how may they be separated?

**17.** Can we tell, from the following statements, just how many lines containing data will be read?

> GET LIST (A,B,C);
> GET LIST (D,E);

**18.** What does the COPY option of the GET statement accomplish?

**19.** Indicate the tab positions at which each of the data items would be printed when the following two statements are executed in sequential order in a program:

> PUT LIST (5,10,15);
> PUT LIST ('THIS IS SOME FUN AND MARKS THE END OF JOB',
>       '09/09/99');

## SUMMARY

**Character Sets:** There are 60 characters in the PL/I language.  They include an extended alphabet of 29 characters, 10 decimal digits, and 21 special characters. Special characters may be combined to create other symbols.

**Identifiers:** Names of data, procedures, files, labels of PL/I statements, and keywords are all given the general term **identifiers.**  An identifier for data names, internal procedures, and statement labels may be from 1 to 31 alphabetic characters (A – Z, @, #, $), numeric digits (0 – 9), and break (_) characters, providing that the first character is alphabetic and there are no embedded blanks.  Names of external procedures and files may be a maximum of seven or eight characters.

**Statement Format:** PL/I is said to be free-form; that is, a statement may contain blanks to improve readability of the source program.  Select an indentation value (e.g., two or three spaces) as a standard for *all* of your PL/I programs.

**PL/I Constants:** These constants may appear not only in the input or output streams for GET or PUT but also in PL/I program statements.  For example:

> J = K + 25;
> PUT LIST(J * 100);

The types of constants are as follows:

**1.** Decimal fixed-point: 3.14159, −5280, 45.3.

**2.** Decimal floating-point: 12E5, +12E+05, 84E, −76E+7, 3E−17.

**3.** Character-string: 'DR. SPITZ, DOG TRAINER',(2)'TOM'.

**4.** Bit-string: '1'B, '01011'B, (32)'0'B.

**5.** Binary fixed-point: 10110B, 111B, −101B.

**6.** Binary floating-point: 11011E3B, 10110.1EB.

**Pseudocode:** Pseudocode is an alternative to program flowcharting.  There are no specific rules as to how it should be written—just use whatever language makes sense to you. The process of solving a problem via pseudocode is an iterative one. First, general steps are written. The next iteration involves more detailed pseudocode statements. In the last iteration, pseudocode may closely resemble PL/I code. At that point, pseudocode is ready for translation by you to a PL/I language program.

**Program Debugging and Testing:** Debugging is the process of removing known errors from a program. Testing involves proving the program's correctness. Sets of test data should be developed by someone other than the programmer who coded the program or the analyst who designed the program. Ideally, test data is developed before the program is coded.

**PL/I Comments:** A comment begins with /* and ends with */. Because the compiler takes the first line of your PL/I program and prints that information at the top of every page of output of the source listing, it is a good practice to have a meaningful first line comment heading your source program statements.

**The PROCEDURE Statement:** The PROCEDURE statement tells the compiler that this statement marks the beginning of the block of PL/I statements. There are two types of procedures: external and internal.

**The END Statement:** This statement is used to mark the physical end of a procedure and may also be used to end a procedure logically.

**The Assignment Statement:** The value of the expression on the right of the = is assigned (moved) to the variable on the left of the = symbol. Examples are:

```
GROSS_PAY = HOURS * RATE;
COUNT     = COUNT + 1;
```

**List-Directed I/O:** Input data may be separated by a comma or one or more blanks. The input data is in the form of *valid* PL/I constants (e.g., 'ABC', 12.5, 57E). Output is to tab positions 1, 25, 49, 73, and 97. Examples are:

```
GET LIST (A,B,C);
GET LIST (A,B,C) COPY;
PUT LIST (A * B);
PUT SKIP LIST (X,Y,Z);
PUT PAGE LIST ('HEADING');
```

**PAGE, SKIP, and LINE Options:** The PAGE option causes the paper in the line printer to advance to the top of a new page. The SKIP option causes the paper in the line printer to be advanced the number of lines specified (e.g., PUT SKIP (2);). A SKIP (0) causes a suppression of the line feed. The LINE option may be used to indicate the line of the page on which you would like information to be printed (e.g., PUT PAGE LINE (10);). The order of priority is PAGE first, then SKIP, then LINE.

# CHAPTER 2

# Top-Down Structured Programming

This chapter introduces the *top-down* design of a program and coding of a problem using basic **structures.** This chapter also presents some PL/I statements needed to write complete programs. You will learn enough to be able to use the statements. Then, in subsequent chapters, more technical details will be presented about these statements.

In beginning to think about programming, it is important to understand the goals or criteria of a good program. First, *it must correctly solve the problem it is intended to solve.* Often, this goal is not achieved for a variety of reasons — a primary one being *communication.* In a data processing installation, there are two basic groups: the DP organization and the user departments. Typically, the user department — the accounting department or the personnel department, for example — goes to the DP department and requests that a new application be developed or that a major modification be implemented into existing programs. The user must communicate the department's needs to the DP professional. This is often difficult for users because they are not trained in "computerese" nor do they realize that *all* conditions must be anticipated at the planning stages. The DP professional does not fully understand the application or just what all the conditions are that could arise. The DP professional tries to determine what it is the users need and, in some cases, tries to tell the users just what it is they need. You can see how a problem in communication evolves and how the resulting program product may not solve the problem it was intended to solve. A partial solution to the problem lies in the DP professional and the user department members working together, reviewing the work output from each phase of a program development effort.

A second criterion of a good program is that *it must be reliable.* No significant program can ever be proven to be completely error free. This is because the variety of combinations of test data required to test a program *completely* is almost infinite. So, because of cost and time, we settle for something less than perfection. However, when a program is developed from the top down and is coded as a structured program, there is greater confidence in the reliability of the program. This confidence is based on experience. Installations developing programs using the newer methods have found that these programs have fewer errors at the end of a year's use than do comparable programs in which these methods were not used.

A third criterion (or goal) of a good program is that *it must be easy to read and easy to maintain.* Programs are written to be read. In the past, good programmers were often thought to be those who could write clever and tricky code that ran in the least amount of computer storage and in the shortest amount of time. Typically, once a program was put into production, the clever and tricky code had to be maintained by another programmer — usually a junior person not as skilled in programming. (The *maintenance* of a program involves removing subsequent errors that may be found and altering the code to reflect changes to the program's specifications due to changing needs.) Today, maintenance costs run anywhere from 2 to 1 to 20 to 1 to as much as 100 to 1 over development costs. Thus, in an effort to minimize costs, it is essential that easy-to-read and easy-to-maintain programs be developed.

How this is achieved is discussed throughout the book. However, here are a few basic things to keep in mind as you begin to write PL/I programs:

**1.** Use as meaningful data names as possible. Code QUANTITY_ON_HAND not QOH, ENERGY not E, MASS not M.

**2.** Use a data name for one purpose only. Do not, for example, let TABLE_OF_PRICES contain retail prices in one part of a program and later — even though no longer needed for retail prices — contain discount prices in another part of the same program.

**3.** Have the program code read from "top" to "bottom." Do not use branch instructions (e.g., the GOTO statement in PL/I) that cause the reader to "jump" around in the program, as illustrated in Figure 2.1. These programs are referred to as BS ("bowl of spaghetti") programs. Their logic is difficult to follow, making the program almost impossible to maintain.

**4.** Given two alternatives — clever code versus clearer code that may take a few more instructions or more execution time — opt for the *clearer code.*

**5.** *Remember:* Programs are written to be read by other people.

## CHECKPOINT QUESTIONS

**1.** Name three criteria of good programs.

**2.** Define program maintenance.

**3.** What is the primary disadvantage of traditional "bowl of spaghetti" programs?

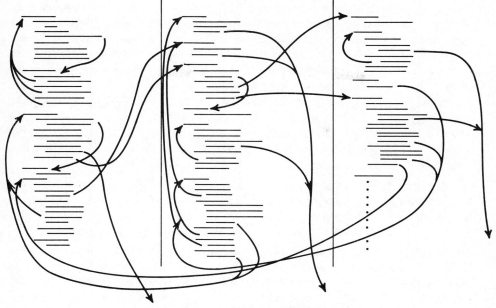

FIGURE 2.1   The bowl of spaghetti.

## TOP-DOWN DEVELOPMENT

The criteria of good programs have been discussed. Now, let us consider *how* to develop programs that meet these criteria. As a vehicle for presenting the techniques, an inventory control application is used. The application is simplified to emphasize top-down development rather than the method of controlling inventory.

Before computers, companies typically kept records on the flow of items in their inventories on cards in tub files. Clerks would enter changes in "quantities on hand" on these cards as goods were either sold (issues) or received (receipts). They were supposed to notice when a certain item fell below a minimum number of items to be kept in inventory and see that additional quantities were reordered. Financial and business management people need to know about the status of inventory because too many items housed on shelves ties up capital, too few items results in lost sales. Finding the proper balance is still a major concern of business today. With the widespread use of computers now, most companies with more than $1 million yearly gross sales and/or with more than 2500 active items in their inventories have computerized the control of that inventory. Let us look at how a basic inventory control system might be implemented using a computer. After examining the application, the logic and some of the PL/I statements needed to code two of the programs in that application will be presented.

Figure 2.2 shows a chart (similar to a company organization chart) in which four major functions for inventory control are depicted:

**1. Create master file:** In converting from a manual system, the *source data* (e.g., the data recorded on cards in the tub file system) must be encoded into a machine-processable form. Historically, the punched card was the most common medium. Today, the punched card is replaced by other forms such as a diskette. Typically, *loading* (i.e., writing records onto) the master file is a one-time operation. Once created, the file will be modified and updated.

**2. Transaction processing:** When items are purchased by customers, the record of this activity becomes a *transaction*. Transaction processing, then, is updating the master file to reflect the various business activities that have taken place. For example, posting ISSUES (items sold) and RECEIPTS (items received into inventory) are two types of transaction processing.

**3. Reorder analysis:** When the number of items in inventory falls below a specified amount (called the *reorder point*), it is time to replenish the stock. This aspect of reordering can be complex, depending on the techniques used to determine just *when* and *how much* to reorder (called the *economical order quantity*).

**4. Management reporting:** Because computers can generate printed output at relatively high speeds, there is a tendency to generate reports that may be of limited value to management simply because *all* data items are printed—not just selected relevant items. Management often complains that it must look through hundreds of pages of output just to find the one piece of information it needs. Today, it is not uncommon to see a company "drowning in *data* but starved for *information*." A report needs to contain data essential to understanding the report; its value, however, comes from the *information* supplied. The exceptions, the changing activities, are particularly important types of information. For example, in determining just how a warehouse should stock its goods, it would be useful for the warehouse manager to know not only the quantities on hand (data) but also the top 200 most active items (information). Active items could be placed nearer the loading dock, thereby saving extra steps to the back of the warehouse when goods are to be taken from inventory.

The four functions in Figure 2.2 could be four programs in the inventory control system. When coded in a programming language, some of these pro-

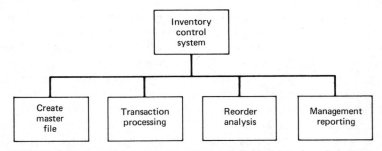

FIGURE 2.2  Inventory control system subdivided into four functions.

grams could be fairly large (more than 200 executable statements). There are some problems to having large programs:

- They are often difficult for trainees and inexperienced programmers to program.
- They are more difficult to test exhaustively.
- They are more difficult to modify.
- They are less likely to be reusable for other related applications.

Thus, it is desirable to subdivide large programs into smaller modules. An example is shown in Figure 2.3. A *module* is one external procedure (e.g., a separate compilation). Thus, as used here, a **program** consists of one or more external procedures or modules. In Figure 2.3, the CREATE MASTER FILE program is small enough that it need not be further subdivided. Observe, however, that the other programs are subdivided. These modules may be thought of as subfunctions of functions that precede them on the hierarchy chart. The term *hierarchy* is used because there is a hierarchical relationship to the major functions and their subfunctions depicted in the chart.

What is meant by the word **function**? *It is the change that takes place from the time the module is entered until it completes its action.* It is the transformation of input to the module to output from the module that occurs when the module is executed. Ideally, each module should perform exactly *one* function and perform *all* of that function. The concept of *one module: one function* is the key to a well-adjusted program. Functions should be describable in one sentence. For example:

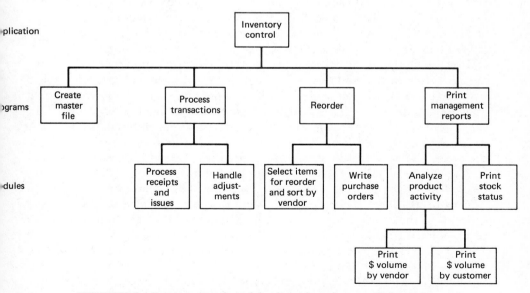

FIGURE 2.3   Programs and modules in an inventory control system.

- Load master file.
- Compute weekly pay.
- Invert matrix.
- Print stock status report.

Returning to Figure 2.3, note that each box in this chart could represent some program code with the exception of the naming of the application at the top of the chart. For example, PRINT MANAGEMENT REPORTS could be a small module that invokes or calls the other modules immediately below it on the chart (e.g., ANALYZE PRODUCT ACTIVITY and PRINT STOCK STATUS). Again, ANALYZE PRODUCT ACTIVITY could be a small module that calls either or both of the modules on its immediately lower level.

Note that a hierarchy chart differs from a flowchart. The flowchart shows logic, the sequence in which operations will be carried out. The hierarchy chart does not show decision-making logic or flow of execution; it shows what needs to be done. In other words, the flowchart shows *procedure*, the hierarchy chart, *function*. An advantage of the hierarchy chart is that it allows you to concentrate on defining *what* needs to be done in a program *before* you decide *how* it is to be done. It also groups related functions together, which is a key to good program design.

To create a hierarchy chart, start at the top and work your way down (hence the term **top-down design**). Top-down program design is based on the idea of *levels of abstraction* becoming levels of modules in a program. One definition of *abstract*, as a noun, is "a summary." In a sense, this is what each higher level module is — a summary of subfunctions on lower levels. For example, the abstraction *accounts receivable* is useful for those who wish to communicate generally without having to reference specifically invoicing, cash receipts, paid transactions, or customer statements. The terms *invoicing*, etc., are lower levels of abstraction. These levels of abstraction, then, become the levels of modules in a program.

Because hierarchy charts do not show data flow, order of execution, or when and how often each module will be invoked, there is no order of execution implied by placing modules within a given level. People tend to think in a left-to-right manner, and there is no harm in arranging the boxes in that fashion. (Certainly, there would be no point to placing them intentionally in a different order.) The logic determining the control of the frequency and order of execution is "inside" the boxes. That is, logic is shown in program flowcharts for each of the boxes.

If the lines don't show order of execution, what do they show? They show **flow of control.** Each module is invoked by the one above it and when completed returns to its caller. It is, therefore, subordinate to the module above it and superior to those below it. To draw an analogy with the organization chart, it receives *orders* from its *boss* and reports back to the *boss* the outcome of its action. To complete that action it may need to invoke one or more of its subordinate modules before it can report back.

Flow of control proceeds along the vertical lines connecting the modules in the hierarchy chart. This means that any module can invoke another module at a lower level and has control returned to it when the lower-level module is completed. To ensure this vertical movement, here are some guidelines:

**1.** A module must return to its caller.

**2.** The same module may appear more than once in the hierarchy chart at the appropriate levels. Recurring modules should be identified, typically with vertical lines added to the box.

Of course, when the module is actually coded, it appears only once in the collection of modules that makes up the program.

**3.** A module may call another module immediately below the level on which it appears; it may not call another module on the same or higher level. (However, a module may call itself, as in the case of *recursive programming*.) If, for example, module A needs to call module C in the following diagram,

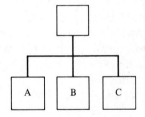

then module C can be shown as a recurring module:

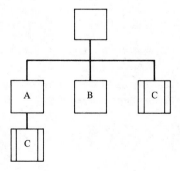

**4.** Major decision making should be placed at as high a level as possible. Typically, the top module (first level) contains the main decisions of a program. The top module is a synopsis of the entire program.

The advantage of the hierarchy chart showing flow of control is that when it is time to modify a program, it is easier to determine the impact of a program change. For example, in the following chart,

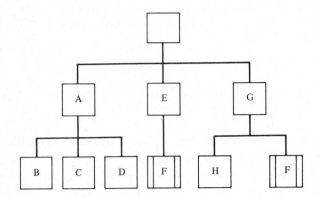

assume that module F is to be modified. What other modules must be studied to determine the impact of the change? E and G must be examined because they call F. It would not be necessary to study A, B, C, or D because they are not logically related to what is accomplished by F. In traditional "bowl of spaghetti" programs, it was often difficult to make a program change because the "rippling" effect of a modification could not be determined with absolute certainty.

It is not expected, with this brief overview of hierarchy charts, that you will be able to construct the complex hierarchy charts of the type needed for full application design. The hierarchical concept and the *one module: one function* concept have been presented because they are some of the newer methods being used in computer installations today. The primary advantage of the hierarchy chart is that once modules have been defined in this hierarchical relationship, the modules can be coded and tested in a top-down manner. Coding and testing higher-level modules before lower modules have the advantage of pointing out logic flaws sooner. Hierarchy charts also have these advantages:

**1.** When reading a program, it is easier to follow the logic if the hierarchy chart has been studied first.

**2.** When changing a program, it is easier to pinpoint which modules must be modified if the hierarchy chart has been examined before the program code.

## CHECKPOINT QUESTIONS

**4.** What is a program flowchart? What does it depict?

**5.** What is a hierarchy chart? What does it show?

**6.** Define *function* and relate it to module development.

## STRUCTURED PROGRAMMING

This section describes the **structures** you will use in expressing logical solutions to computing problems.

The term **structured programming** is used in two ways. In the general sense, it is used to refer to the whole evolution that is taking place in programming methods. Thus, the term refers to a number of disciplines — such as top-down development, the team approach, structured walk-throughs, and programming — in which there are few or no GOTOs because only the basic structures are used. In a more narrow sense, structured programming is the coding of a problem in which the basic structures that are sufficient for solving *any* computing problem are used.

There are three basic structures or forms in which logic may be expressed in a structured program. Each structure has a name: **sequence, choice,** and **repetition.** These structures (or *constructs,* as they are sometimes called) are explained via flowchart symbols. A complete program is a combination of these basic structures.

### Symbols

**Process Box.** This symbol represents an operation. It consists of a rectangle with one control path leading into it and one leading out.

The operation *a* may be a single executable instruction such as a GET statement. Or the operation could represent a number of logic structures forming a subprocedure or subroutine. Although pictured here as flowing from left to right, *any* of the symbols may be drawn in a top-to-bottom fashion as well.

**Decision Symbol.** This symbol specifies a test operation:

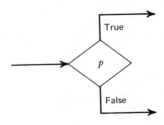

It consists of the standard decision box and is characterized by one control path leading in and two paths leading out. The specification *p* (for predicate) represents a test to be performed. One or the other output path (but not both) is taken as a result of the test.

**Collector Symbol.** This symbol is represented by a circle where control paths converge:

No operation is performed; the symbol is simply a junction that typically has two entries and one exit. Usually, there is no symbol written in the circle.

**Connector Lines.** These lines represent the passing of control from one of the above symbols to another in the direction of the arrow:

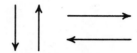

### Sequence Structure

The sequence structure is represented by two process symbols:

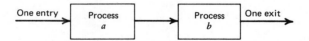

Each process box represents an operation; the flow of control is from one operation to the next. For example:

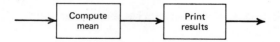

One frequent use of the sequence structure is to represent a subroutine or subprogram. For example:

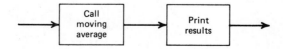

The subroutine or subprogram to compute a moving average is PL/I code that is *out-of-line*. That is, the actual coding for the *moving average* function resides elsewhere in computer storage *not* contiguous to the *call* statement or *print results* function. Control may pass out-of-line as long as control is returned to the next sequential step.

## Choice Structure

The choice structure is also called an IF-THEN-ELSE. It indicates a test and one of two alternative paths taken depending on the results of the test.

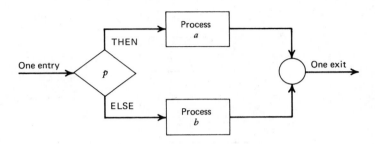

The symbol $p$ indicates that any logical expression may be specified for the test. Logical expressions are covered in Chapter 5. Logical expressions are generally combinations of data names and the logical operators $(=, >, <, \neg)$. For example:

QTY $\_$ ON $\_$ HAND > MINIMUM $\_$ QTY
DATA $\_$ INPUT $\_$ ERROR = YES

When the logical expression is tested, it must be capable of being resolved into a true/false condition. For example, the expression

AMT $\_$ DUE < 0

can be resolved into a true/false situation. If the AMT $\_$ DUE is negative, then a "true" condition exists and the THEN branch will be executed; if AMT $\_$ DUE is zero or positive, then the ELSE branch will be performed.

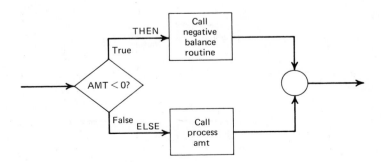

Each of the paths (the THEN clause and the ELSE clause) leads to a common merge point so that processing continues in a forward direction regardless of which path is taken. The decision paths may be labeled true/false, yes/no, on/off, etc.

It may be that for one of the results of the test there is no action to be performed. In that case, only one of the process blocks would be included. For example:

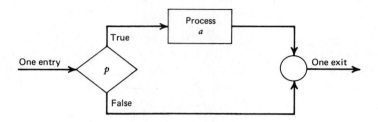

Or the process box for which there is no action may be shown but labeled *null*.

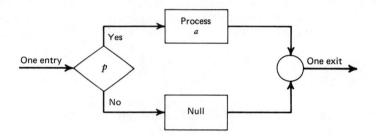

As with the sequence structure, the process block can represent as many statements as desired. Or it may be replaced by another structure such as another IF-THEN-ELSE structure:

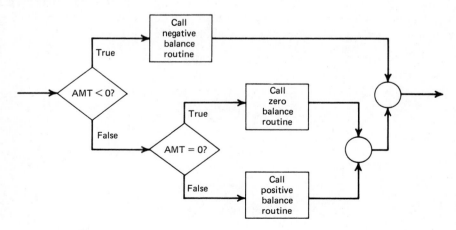

The previous example is called a *nested* IF-THEN-ELSE. It is possible to nest IF-THEN-ELSEs to any depth. However, readability decreases when the nesting exceeds more than three or four levels.

**7.** Draw a sequence structure(s) to read 10 data items, print the data items, call a subroutine to compute standard deviation, and then print the results.

**8.** Draw the choice structure that shows a test for a customer's credit limit. If the customer's order amounts to a value less than or equal to the credit limit, fill the order (i.e., print a sales order).

**9.** Draw the choice structure for this set of conditions: If over credit limit but pay record is OK, fill order; otherwise, print a message for the sales department indicating order is rejected.

### Repetition — DO-WHILE

It is important to see how the DO-WHILE structure works because it provides the repetitive execution or **loop** control that is the essence of computer programming. For example, if a program is written to compute weekly pay of an employee, the same basic set of program instructions can be executed to compute Don Anderson's pay, then Rich Berman's pay, then Chris Cole's pay, and so on. This is a loop operation because the program loops back again and again to compute pay for each subsequent employee on the payroll.

Here is the DO-WHILE structure:

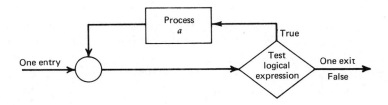

The flow passes through the merge point to the decision symbol. Here a logical expression is evaluated: if it is *true,* the *process* represented is executed and the expression is evaluated again. This iterative operation continues as long as the expression tested is true. When it becomes *false,* there is an exit from the structure.

The structure is explained as:

"DO (that is, execute statements in the process box)
WHILE the logical expression specified is true."

There are two key items to remember about the DO-WHILE:

**1.** During the execution of the process box, the control variable affecting the test must be modified—otherwise the program would be in an endless loop. For example, in the PL/I method of expressing this structure,

DO WHILE (X > 0);

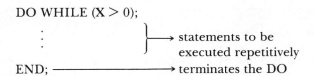

                         statements to be
                         executed repetitively

END;                  → terminates the DO

X must be set to zero or negative within the loop operation; otherwise there would be no method for leaving the loop. If you have had some programming experience, you might think that a GOTO statement could be used to leave the loop. For example, in nonstructured programs, the following might have been coded:

DO WHILE (X > 0);
   ⋮

   IF X = 0
      THEN GO TO SOME_WHERE_ELSE;
   ⋮

END;

Recall, however, that *bowl of spaghetti* programs are to be avoided because they detract from program readability and ease of maintenance. The GOTO as used here contributed to the "BS" program. In the previous example, the IF statement isn't needed because inherent in the DO-WHILE is the test provided by the IF.

**2.** It is possible that the statements within the DO may never be executed. This occurs because the condition to be tested may be *false* initially. For example:

GET LIST(X);        /* ASSUME X = 0 */
DO WHILE (X > 0);
   ⋮

END;

Because the expression controlling the loop is tested *first* (before the process is ever executed), the process statements following the DO are not executed because the expression tested (X > 0) is false.

### GOTOless Programming

For some time, writing programs that contained GOTO statements has been considered "harmful." As mentioned earlier, the uncontrolled use of the GOTO statement detracts from program readability and maintainability. Using the basic structures just defined, it is possible to write PL/I programs that have no GOTO statements. For this reason, structured programming is sometimes referred to as *GOTOless programming*. However, this is too narrow a definition and impossible in some programming languages. The point is, *the elimination of the GOTO is a by-product of expressing program logic using only these structures.*

## The Structured Theorem

It has been proved that the **sequence, choice** (IF-THEN-ELSE), and **repetition** (DO-WHILE) structures are all that are needed to solve any logic problem. The proof is based on a theoretical foundation defined by Böhm and Jacopini and is something that you, as a programmer, won't need to know. However, to explain it generally, the proof may be demonstrated by converting each part of a program to one or more of the three basic structures — leaving the remaining parts of the program smaller than before. By sufficient repetitions, the remaining unstructured portion of the program can be reduced until it is nonexistent or not needed. Thus, the result of this process is an equivalent program that needs only the basic structures. (It is not intended, however, that structured programs be written first in an unstructured manner and then converted to a structured form using the method just described.)

The proof applies only to proper programs. A *proper program* has these characteristics:

1. It has one entry point.
2. It has one exit point.
3. It has no dead (unreachable) code.
4. It has no infinite loops.

Why use only these structures? The primary advantage is that the logic flow of a program will be from *top to bottom*. That is, specified program statements will be executed in the order in which they appear in the source program listing. Of course, some blocks of code will be *skipped over* (as in the case of the IF-THEN-ELSE), but the branching will always be in a forward manner. This forward direction of program logic makes a program easier to read when it must be modified.

Another advantage is that of *uniformity*. Anyone who is familiar with the basic structures is in a better position to understand a program's logic more quickly. A final advantage to many programmers is *reduced errors* in their programs. A structured approach to programming seems to point up potential logic errors earlier in the program development effort.

Although sequence, IF-THEN-ELSE, and DO-WHILE are all that are needed to code any computer problem, several additional structures have been defined, including DO-UNTIL and CASE. Using these additional structures provides for greater programming convenience without detracting from the goal of program readability.

**10.** Draw the repetition and sequence structures to sum the numbers from 1 to 100.

**11.** List the characteristics of a proper program.

**12.** Given the following code, what will be printed?

```
GET LIST (A,B);        /* ASSUME A=5, B=5 */
DO WHILE (A > B);
    A   = A * .5;
    SUM = A + B;
    PUT LIST (SUM);
END;
```

## DEVELOPING A PROGRAM

Now that top-down development and structured programming have been presented, let us use these two techniques in the development of a PL/I program.

Returning to an earlier example — the inventory control system — consider the CREATE MASTER FILE program depicted in Figure 2.3. Creating the master file might involve inputting inventory information interactively from a computer terminal or keyboard. Or, for some computer systems, it might involve reading information from data encoded on punched cards. Then, that information is written into a master file, which is typically disk storage. In addition to creating the master file, two types of printed output are generated as shown in Figure 2.4. The STOCK LISTING is a copy of data written onto the master file. It is needed so that information written onto the master file may be visually verified. The EXCEPTION LISTING is provided when the program notes errors in the data from the input file. This is called *data validation*. For example, if the part number or item number is supposed to be an all-numeric value, then the

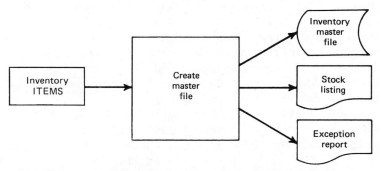

FIGURE 2.4   Data flow in the CREATE MASTER FILE program.

data validation routine could test each character of the item number to be sure that it is a numeric character. This test is needed because it is possible for a data entry operator to key inadvertently a letter instead of a digit. This error can be detected by your program, providing you code the logic for that test. In a *batch system,* the input data in error is not written into the master file — the error noted appears on an EXCEPTION REPORT so that the input can be corrected later and reentered into the system. In an *on-line system,* the invalid data is immediately rejected. The data entry operator has two choices: (1) correct.the data immediately or, (2) set aside the data entry inventory item in question and process later after valid data has been obtained. In the on-line system, the EXCEPTION REPORT is not needed. However, another printout is usually generated instead — an INVENTORY ITEM LIST of data entered during this session on the computer terminal. In this way, the data entry operator (or preferably someone else) can sight verify the computer printout with the source document from which data was entered.

### Program Hierarchy Chart

Usually hierarchy charts are most useful for showing a system and its component **programs.** The same approach can be used at the module level. Now, however, each box in the hierarchy chart represents a *segment* of that module. In the CREATE MASTER FILE program (Figure 2.3), because it will contain relatively few PL/I executable statements (e.g., less than 60), a further decomposition into modules is not needed. Thus, in this **program** there is only one *module.* The term program and its associated segments will be used for the CREATE MASTER FILE function because it is one program of one module. Later, in this chapter's case study, the function of PRINT STOCK STATUS REPORT will be referred to as a module (because it is one of several modules in the PRINT MANAGEMENT REPORTS program) with its associated segments. A *segment,* as used here, is a logical subdivision of one external procedure or module. For example, in Figure 2.5, the CREATE MASTER FILE program may be divided into several segments.

The top segment is called the *nucleus* of the module. The nucleus provides an overview or snapshot of the basic logic of the entire module. The lower-level segments are subfunctions of the major function — CREATE MASTER FILE.

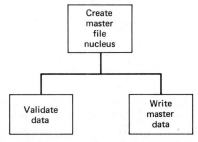

FIGURE 2.5   Program hierarchy chart with three segments.

| Segment | Subfunctions |
|---|---|
| Nucleus | Initialize<br>Read input records |
| Validate data | Test specified fields for validity<br>If error, write exception message<br>Set error indicator on/off |
| Write master data | Write disk master record<br>If disk I/O error, write exception message<br>Write copy of disk record on printer |

FIGURE 2.6   Segments and their subfunctions in the File Create program.

From this hierarchy chart, you can see the flow of control. That is, the top segment calls either the VALIDATE DATA segment or the WRITE MASTER DATA segment — or both. Neither of the two lower-level segments calls the other. (If one did call the other, the segments would be arranged differently in the chart.) To *call* a segment is to invoke or activate that block of code. "Calling" a segment is the process of transferring control to that block of code. When the called segment is logically finished, it must return to its "caller." That a module or segment returns to its caller is a *ground rule* we must always follow. This is a sound programming technique — one that simplifies program maintenance once the program is put into production.

Figure 2.6 describes the subfunctions for each of the segments in the file-create program. As you study this figure, note that there is no one correct way to solve a problem. This solution is simply one method of visualizing how the problem may be solved. Notice how a "top-down" approach to problem solving is being illustrated. Right now, we are only concerned with logical *subfunctions* of the file-create **function.** We are not concerned with *how* each segment will carry out the subfunctions; that comes later.

## Program Switches

One of the logical steps that usually occurs in almost every program or module nucleus is initialization. This could involve clearing to zero those data names into which values are to be accumulated. For example:

$$SUM = 0;$$
$$\vdots$$
$$SUM = SUM + VALUE;$$

Had SUM not been initialized to zero at the beginning of the program, then an incorrect total could result when VALUE was accumulated into SUM.

Program switches or indicators are another type of data item that are typically initialized in the program's nucleus. **Program switches** are the key to top-down structured programming. The term *switch* was probably selected in the early days of programming because of the public's general knowledge of trains. Switching a train to one of several tracks depends on where the train is to travel and whether or not there is a train coming in the opposite direction. In other words, a station-master could pull a "switch" that would cause a mechanism in the track to move, thereby causing the train to travel down one set of tracks or another. In a sense, your program logic must accomplish the same thing. For example, the nucleus in our file-create program handles the basic loop operation of reading records until an end-of-file condition is detected. (The end-of-file is designated by a special marker. Typically for disk files the end-of-file is indicated by a designation of file size in the disk's directory.)

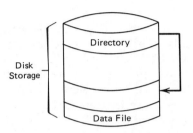

As long as there are more records in the disk file, your program's logic is to travel down the path that handles data validation and writing records. When the end-of-file is detected, the program's logic must travel down a different path— that of some wrap-up activity such as printing an end-of-job message. The end-of-file switch determines which logic path is traveled.

Why are program switches necessary in programming? Switches are a convenient method of recording (i.e., "remembering") what has happened in a program. At one point in a program, after a series of computations, for example, a switch may be set. Actually, the status of this indicator is needed later in the program, so the switch will be tested at that point.

The nucleus transfers control to the WRITE MASTER DATA segment. However, if errors in an input record have been detected, then the WRITE MASTER DATA segment must not be invoked, lest invalid records be output to the master disk file. This situation creates the need for another program switch—a *data error switch*. This switch is turned ON by the VALIDATE DATA segment when an error is found and turned OFF when there are no errors. The status (ON/OFF) of the switch is tested by the nucleus to determine whether or not the WRITE MASTER DATA segment is called.

It is up to you to decide what switches are needed and their meaning. You could select the data name

DATA_VALIDATION_SWITCH

and assign it a status of OK or NOT＿OK.   On the other hand, the data name

DATA＿ERROR

could be selected and be in either the YES or NO condition.   What is important is that you select meaningful names that truly describe the *function* of that program switch and that a switch be used for only one purpose.   Use the appropriate names to initialize program switches.   For example:

```
DATA＿ERROR    = NO;   /* YES AND NO ARE LOGICAL */
MORE＿RECORDS = YES;   /* VARIABLES WHOSE BOOLEAN */
                      /* STATUS MAY BE 0 OR 1 */
```

## Program Organization

Each segment in the hierarchy chart (Figure 2.5) corresponds to a PL/I procedure.   The top segment is an external procedure.   It contains the OPTIONS (MAIN) option in its PROCEDURE statement.   VALIDATE DATA and WRITE MASTER DATA are internal procedures **nested** within the external procedure (Figure 2.7).   Figure 2.8 shows the equivalent PL/I program code.   Notice how the two lower-level segments are indicated, first with a label and then with a PROCEDURE statement *without* the option MAIN.   There is a corresponding END statement for each PROCEDURE statement.   Thus, there are three END statements because there are three PROCEDURE statements.

The nested procedures, whose names may be up to 31 characters, are invoked by a CALL from the top segment.   For example:

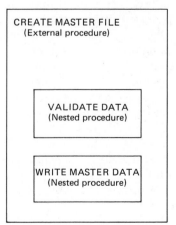

FIGURE 2.7   An external procedure with two internal procedures.

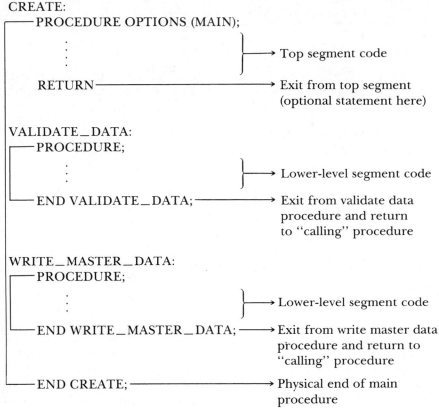

FIGURE 2.8   The PL/I implementation of Figure 2.7.

```
        CALL VALIDATE_DATA;
        CALL WRITE_MASTER_DATA;
```

*Procedures are invoked by CALLs; they are never "fallen into."* The only way to execute the procedure blocks being discussed here is to CALL them.

In developing a larger program, segments could initially be coded as *stubs* to check out your overall program logic. The stubs (i.e., segments) contain whatever minimal code is needed to execute the nucleus. Again, this is a top-down approach to programming because the details of program logic in each of the segments are being deferred. Once the overall logic is verified, the program code for each of the segment stubs can be added. An approach in which you "code a little" and "test a little" is the best way to proceed in developing programs. Stubs should stay stubs until the *calling* modules are fully debugged.

**13.** Explain *program switch.*

**14.** Write the PL/I statements (PROCEDUREs, ENDs, etc.) for a main program, called LIST, and one nested procedure called PRINT_HEADING. Each procedure is a stub containing a PUT LIST indicating a "got here" message.

### Expressing the Logical Solution

Basic data processing can be illustrated as a three-step procedure:

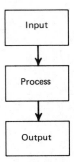

Generally, *input* refers to reading one record, *process* being the computations performed, and **output** the writing of processed results. The three steps are repeated for each record in the file. To diagram the repetitive reading and writing of records, a structured flowchart is given in Figure 2.9. The sequence and DO-WHILE structures accomplish the reading and writing of multiple records in a sequential file. DO-WHILE provides the basic loop capability.

The program begins by initializing the MORE_RECORDS indicator or program switch to the status of ON. Then the first record in the input file is read. The system input routine handling the read operation causes the physical input of specified data and then tests to see if an end-of-file has been detected. If it has, the MORE_RECORDS indicator will be turned OFF. Since there are many indicators in a program, how does the system input routine know which one of your program indicators to turn OFF? This is handled through a PL/I statement called ON ENDFILE in which you specify the indicator's name that is to be reset. This will be discussed in detail in the PL/I implementation section of this chapter.

Now that the overall logic is defined, we are ready to expand the boxes in the flowchart in Figure 2.9 that require further clarification. This is the *refinement* process first introduced in Chapter 1. Again, we move from the general to the more specific. The box

```
Process
   a
```

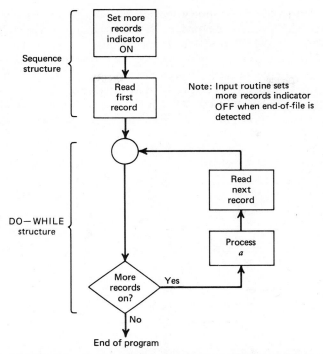

FIGURE 2.9   Structured flowchart for repetitive input/output.

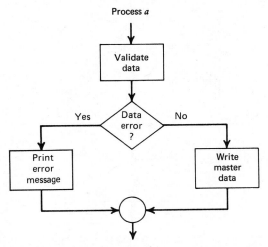

FIGURE 2.10   Expansion of process *a* from Figure 2.9.

may be expanded to the steps shown in Figure 2.10. The VALIDATE DATA segment is invoked. The test of a program switch is made to determine whether or not the WRITE MASTER DATA segment should be invoked. Then the next record in the input file is read. By the process of replacement, we could redraw the flowchart for the nucleus as shown in Figure 2.11. The refinement process —expanding those boxes that require further clarification—continues for the two remaining segments: VALIDATE DATA and WRITE MASTER DATA. These refinements are shown in Figures 2.12 and 2.13. Note that further expan-

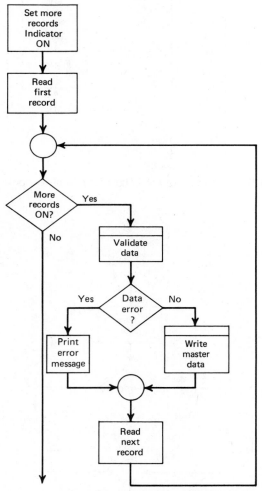

FIGURE 2.11    Combined program logic from Figures 2.9 and 2.10.

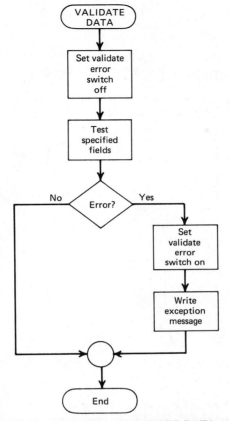

FIGURE 2.12   Expansion of VALIDATE DATA segment.

sions may still be needed.   For example, the process

```
┌──────────┐
│ Test     │
│ fields   │
│          │
└──────────┘
```

in the VALIDATE DATA segment might require further clarification by flow-charting its expansion on another page.   A technique for indicating that there is a flowchart expansion for a process box is a figure with an additional horizontal line:

```
┌──────────┐
├──────────┤
│ Test     │
│ fields   │
└──────────┘
```

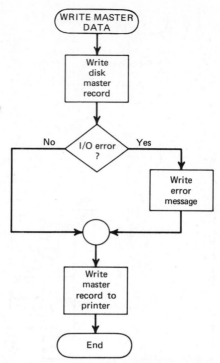

FIGURE 2.13    Expansion of WRITE MASTER DATA segment.

One method of expressing the logical solution to a problem is to use the
flowchart.   A flowchart should read from top to bottom and/or left to right.   It
should be a combination of the basic structures just described, although for large
problems some people have difficulty in expressing structured logic in flowchart
form.    For this reason, an alternative method is often used.    The method is
**pseudocode** and was briefly introduced in Chapter 1.   In using pseudocode, you
express the same logic as you would in a flowchart; however, you do not have to
draw all the boxes.    This has the advantages of saving time and not limiting
wording by the size of the box.   Again, you would use a number of pieces of paper
as you first expressed the general solution to the problem followed by the details
related to each segment.   In pseudocode, use words to describe the function of
flowchart boxes or program structures.   Consider pseudocode for the DO-
WHILE structure.   The flowchart lines tell you the range of the DO-WHILE, but
in pseudocode you need to use an END or END-DO to indicate the range limit.
For example:

DO-WHILE there are more records
    .
    .
    .
END-DO

For the choice structure, IF is followed by the THEN clause and can be expressed as follows:

    IF data error = no
        Write master data

It isn't necessary to write the word THEN (unless you wish to) because it is implied that the statements following the IF are related to the THEN path. *Notice how statements are indented to show logical structuring.* To express an IF-THEN-ELSE structure, the following might be written:

    IF end-of-file = no
        CALL process record
    ELSE
        CALL end-of-job routine

In this case, the ELSE lines up with the IF. Another format is to show both the keywords THEN and ELSE indented with their respective clauses:

    IF end-of-file = no
        THEN CALL process record
        ELSE CALL end-of-job routine

Now let us develop the same problem, this time using pseudocode. Here is the top segment:

    Read first record
    DO WHILE more records switch is on
        Validate data
        IF data error switch is on
            print error message
        ELSE
            write master record
        Read next record
    END-DO

Notice how the code within the DO-WHILE is indented—again to show the logical structuring of the program. This helps the reader of a program to identify quickly all statements that are within the range of the DO-WHILE.

## CHECKPOINT QUESTION

**15.** On a sheet of paper write the pseudocode logic for the VALIDATE DATA and WRITE MASTER DATA segments (see Figures 2.12 and 2.13).

Two techniques for expressing the logical solution in a top-down fashion to any computer problem have been presented. Which method — flowcharts or pseudocode — should you use? Either one. Pseudocode is gaining in widespread use over traditional program flowcharts.

## PL/I IMPLEMENTATION

Now let us look at the PL/I statements that could be coded for the file-create program. Using the basic logic depicted in Figure 2.11, we begin with the assignment statement needed to initialize the MORE_RECORDS program switch.

> MORE_RECORDS = YES;

At the coding stage you do not code in precisely the same wording as expressed in the flowchart or pseudocode stage. For program readability, use 'YES' and 'NO' for the program switch initialization.

A DECLARE statement is needed for those data names to which character- or bit-strings are assigned. Thus, the MORE_RECORDS program switch must be declared to have the BIT attribute of length one:

> DECLARE MORE_RECORDS    BIT(1);

In addition, DECLARE statements are needed to define and initialize the variables YES and NO to their respective values of 1 and 0:

> DECLARE NO    BIT(1) INITIAL ('0'B);
> DECLARE YES   BIT(1) INITIAL ('1'B);

Another initialization step is the ON ENDFILE statement. This statement tells the system input routine what to do *when* the end-of-file is encountered. For example:

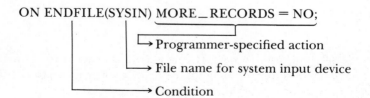

Note that the programmer-specified action *does not* take place until the end-of-file condition is detected. The ENDFILE statement is an initialization step because you only need to tell the system *once* what action is to be taken when the end-of-file condition is detected for the specified file. The name SYSIN is the name of the file for which the end-of-file action is to be taken. The file name is required because there may be more than one input file in a program for which the end-of-file condition could occur.   For example:

```
ON ENDFILE (TIMECRD)
    MORE_TRANSACTIONS = NO;
ON ENDFILE (PAYMAST)
    MORE_MASTER_RECS = NO;
```

The file name SYSIN is the name of the standard PL/I default input file.   It is typically associated with a sequential disk file.   All input/output operations must refer either *explicitly* or *implicitly* to the name of a file.   (The file name is, in turn, associated via JCL with a physical data set on some storage medium.)   In Chapter 1, you saw the statement

```
GET LIST (A,B,C,D,E);
```

Another way to code this statement, explicitly coding the file name, is

```
GET FILE (SYSIN) LIST (A,B,C,D,E);
```

The initialization steps, then, up to reading the first record, could be coded as follows:

```
DECLARE MORE_RECORDS    BIT(1);
DECLARE NO              BIT(1) INITIAL ('0'B);
DECLARE YES             BIT(1) INITIAL ('1'B);
ON ENDFILE (SYSIN)
    MORE_RECORDS = NO;
MORE_RECORDS = YES;
GET FILE (SYSIN) LIST (INVENTORY_RECORD);
```

Now we are ready to move into the basic program loop operation.   It is fortunate that PL/I provides a statement identical in wording to the DO-WHILE structure.   Here is an example:

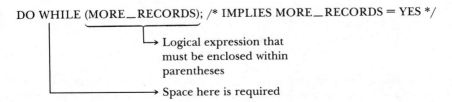

The DO WHILE statement says, in effect, "do, that is execute, the following code *while* the expression in parentheses is *true*."

The end of the DO-WHILE is indicated by an END statement. For example:

```
DO WHILE (MORE_RECORDS);
    .
    .
    .
END;
```

When the END statement matching the DO-WHILE is encountered, that is the signal to loop back to the beginning of the DO-WHILE. The test of the logical expression for a true condition is performed again. If MORE_RECORDS still = YES(true), then the statements within the range of the DO are again executed.

The end-of-file condition controls the execution of the statements following the DO. When end-of-file is encountered, MORE_RECORDS is set = NO(false). On the next iteration, the logical expression following the DO-WHILE is no longer true. The transfer of control is now to the statement immediately following the END statement terminating the DO-WHILE.

Within the DO-WHILE, the code for the entire nucleus can be coded. For example:

```
DO WHILE (MORE_RECORDS);
    CALL VALIDATE_DATA;
    IF DATA_ERROR
        THEN PUT SKIP LIST ('DATA ERROR==>',
            INVENTORY_RECORD);
        ELSE CALL WRITE_MASTER_DATA;
    GET FILE (SYSIN) LIST (INVENTORY_RECORD);
END;
```

The CALL to the VALIDATE_DATA procedure is followed by the IF statement. The IF statement takes this general form (it is covered more thoroughly later):

```
IF expression = true
    THEN action if condition tested is true
    ELSE action if condition tested is false
```

If the ELSE clause is not required, only IF and THEN are used. How you actually format the IF statement is flexible: the method shown here has been found to be convenient and readable.

The segments VALIDATE DATA and WRITE MASTER DATA would be

coded as nested procedures as shown in Figure 2.8. Initially (during the first stage of program checkout) these nested procedures can be coded as stubs.

The nucleus is shown in Figure 2.14 and the stubs are shown in Figure 2.15. In order to compile and execute this program correctly, a DECLARE statement must be added. The DECLARE statement is used to identify the program data names and their associated attributes. (An attribute is a descriptive property.) For example, the data name INVENTORY_RECORD has been defined as being a character-string 75 characters long. The program switches MORE_RECORDS and DATA_ERROR are character-strings, each three characters long. Data types are covered in detail in the next chapter.

```
/*    CREATE MASTER INVENTORY FILE FROM SOURCE DATA                    */
/***********************************************************************/
/*                                                                     */
/* PROGRAM NAME: CREATE                                                */
/*                                                                     */
/* DESCRIPTION:    THIS PROGRAM CREATES THE MASTER INVENTORY FILE      */
/*                 FROM SOURCE DATA.  INPUT DATA IS VALIDATED AND       */
/*                 VALID DATA IS DISPLAYED ON THE PRINTER AND WRITTEN   */
/*                 TO THE INVENTORY FILE.                              */
/*                                                                     */
/* INPUT:          INVENTORY ITEMS                                     */
/*                                                                     */
/* OUTPUT:         INVENTORY MASTER FILE                               */
/*                 STOCK LIST                                          */
/*                 EXCEPTION REPORT                                    */
/*                                                                     */
/***********************************************************************/
CREATE:  PROCEDURE OPTIONS(MAIN);
    DECLARE DATA_ERROR                 BIT(1);
    DECLARE INVENTORY_RECORD           CHARACTER(25);
    DECLARE MORE_RECORDS               BIT(1);
    DECLARE NO                         BIT(1)        INITIAL('0'B);
    DECLARE YES                        BIT(1)        INITIAL('1'B);


    ON ENDFILE(SYSIN)
       MORE_RECORDS = NO;

/***********************************************************************/
/*                                                                     */
/*  PROGRAM NUCLEUS                                                    */
/*                                                                     */
/***********************************************************************/

    MORE_RECORDS = YES;
    GET FILE (SYSIN) LIST (INVENTORY_RECORD);
    DO WHILE (MORE_RECORDS);
       CALL VALIDATE_DATA;
       IF DATA_ERROR
          THEN PUT SKIP LIST ('DATA ERROR==>',INVENTORY_RECORD);
          ELSE CALL WRITE_MASTER_DATA;
       GET FILE(SYSIN)LIST(INVENTORY_RECORD);
    END;
```

FIGURE 2.14 Nucleus of CREATE MASTER FILE program—first page of source listing.

```
/**********************************************************************/
/*                                                                    */
/* THIS SEGMENT SETS AN INDICATOR TO EITHER A YES OR NO STATUS        */
/* SIGNALING WHETHER OR NOT THE INPUT DATA IS VALID.                 */
/*                                                                    */
/**********************************************************************/

VALIDATE_DATA:  PROCEDURE;
   PUT SKIP LIST('VALIDATE_DATA: PROCEDURE');
   DATA_ERROR = NO;
END VALIDATE_DATA;

/**********************************************************************/
/*                                                                    */
/* THIS SEGMENT WRITES DATA ONTO A FILE CALLED 'INVEN'.              */
/* IT ALSO PRINTS THE RECORD ON THE LINE PRINTER.                    */
/*                                                                    */
/**********************************************************************/

WRITE_MASTER_DATA:  PROCEDURE;
   PUT SKIP LIST('WRITE_MASTER_DATA: PROCEDURE');
   PUT SKIP LIST(INVENTORY_RECORD);
END WRITE_MASTER_DATA;

END CREATE;
```

FIGURE 2.15   Two stubs in CREATE MASTER FILE program—second page of source listing.

## CHECKPOINT QUESTIONS

**16.** Modify the flowchart in Figure 2.11 to count the number of valid records written into the master file.   Print the total record count as part of the end-of-job message.

**17.** Write a program to read records and list them on the printer.   Use the file name SYSIN for the input file.

### DEBUGGING TECHNIQUES

The techniques presented in this chapter emphasize the importance of developing overall logic and primary functions first, deferring details until the end.   This refinement process is applied first to the program as a whole, then to each module, and finally to each lower-level segment of the program.   The use of program stubs aids in the analysis of the program; program stubs also help in the debugging stage.

The nucleus of the program should be coded first.   Each segment needed by the nucleus is programmed with only the minimal code required so that the nucleus may be tested.   Those *stubs* should include some confirmation that the segment was reached.   For example, a line or two could be printed specifying the name of the segment and the contents of key identifiers.   Values that the segment may calculate could be provided by simple assignment statements.

Avoid "throwaway" code.   If possible, code statements that ultimately would be used in the program. For example, if a report is to be prepared, the actual report heading could be coded.

The nucleus then is submitted for testing. In this way testing begins earlier and each segment is tested nearer the time it was coded, when the logic is still fresh in mind. With a top-down approach, logic flaws are detected earlier, before lower-level segments are coded, thus avoiding recoding. **Coding** and *testing* are overlapping phases of the development effort. One doesn't code the program first in its entirety and then test for flaws.

Even when correct results are returned, more than one test may be required. If the stubs are returning results in the form of switch settings, one run will be required to return an "on" setting, another to return a setting of "off."

As each successive segment is tested, it is necessary to provide data that cause each path of that segment to be executed. In the first phase of a problem solution, creative effort is concentrated on *what* needs to be done. The variables that the program encounters determine the functions to be performed. For example, different record types may be read, different files created or updated, or exceptions encountered. The variety of conditions that the program handles are defined more and more specifically as the refinement process continues. Eventually all variations should be tested.

During the analysis phase you determine how to handle all the alternatives, choices, and varieties of processing. At this time a written list of all variations to be tested should be prepared. When designing tests, try to

**1.** Exercise every line of code.

**2.** Exercise every logic path.

**3.** Test every function (or subfunction).

This "To-Be-Tested" list is used to prepare test data and then checked off during debugging. This helps to avoid that common error of "forgetting" to test a routine.

For example, if the quantity-on-hand is compared to the quantity-on-order, then test cases of quantity-on-hand being less than on-order, equal to on-order, and greater than on-order must all be prepared. If a report is prepared to identify exceptions, what should be done if there are no exceptions, one exception, or many exceptions must be determined and tested. Combinations of conditions must also be considered. If an operation is controlled by the result of testing for A equal to B *and* X equal to Y, four conditions must be tested:

$$A = B \text{ with } X = Y$$
$$A = B \text{ with } X \neq Y$$
$$A \neq B \text{ with } X = Y$$
$$A \neq B \text{ with } X \neq Y$$

In a complicated program the list of tests will be long. But if it is prepared when your concentration is still on the logic and not on translating that logic to code, there is less likelihood that necessary tests will be overlooked or unnecessary tests included. Be sure to retain the complete set of test data and sample results so that when modifications are made, the set may be rerun and any undesirable changes inadvertently made can be spotted.

Of course, you can only anticipate conditions of which you are aware. Following the debugging stage, you test with "live" data — that is, data gathered from actual business transactions or scientific experiments, projects, etc.

This chapter has presented techniques to help achieve the goals of a good program, one of which was a program that is easy to read and easy to maintain. The first maintenance job is performed by you, the creator of the program. During the debugging and testing states, you will probably modify your original code to make the program run correctly. You will be the first to benefit from your own efforts to make your program code easy to modify.

## CASE STUDY: STOCK REORDER REPORT

An important part of an inventory control application is examining stock on hand to determine which items need to be reordered. Many factors go into determining the proper level of inventory for each item. For example, average usage, the amount of time required for delivery, and seasonal load requirements are considered in determining the *reorder point* (i.e., the level of stock on hand that should initiate a reorder). Manufacturer's case lot requirements, quantity discounts, and shipping costs are the types of things that determine the *economical-order-quantity* (i.e., how much would be reordered).

In this simplified reorder analysis, it is assumed that the reorder point and the economical-order-quantity have already been determined for each item of inventory. These values and other product information have been recorded in an inventory data file. The program shown here reads the inventory data records and prints a reorder analysis report.

Analysis of the program logic is shown by both structured flowcharts and pseudocode to illustrate the two techniques. Both methods use the refinement process.

**Problem Statement.** Data records containing product number, product description, quantity-on-hand, reorder point, and economical-order-quantity are to be read. Product number, product description, and quantity-on-hand are printed for each item. If the quantity-on-hand is less than the reorder point, then the economical-order-quantity is also to be printed. After all records have been read the message END OF REPORT is to be printed.

**Problem Analysis.** Figure 2.16 shows the basic program logic. Figure 2.17 shows the refinement of one box in Figure 2.16: this is the PRINT box. In Figure 2.16, note that processing is to continue as long as the read operation results in a record being read. A program switch MORE_RECORDS is initialized to ON. It is to be turned OFF when the end-of-file is detected. The ON ENDFILE

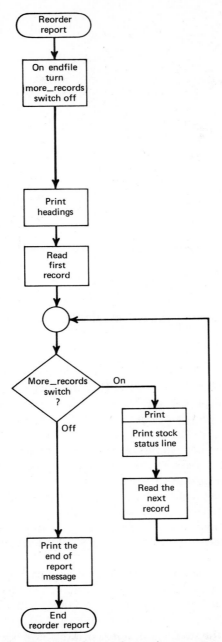

FIGURE 2.16   Flowchart for stock reorder report—case study.

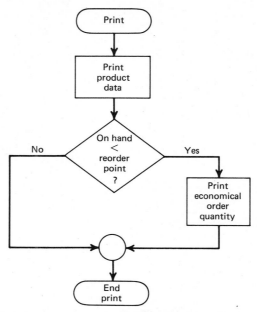

FIGURE 2.17    Expansion of PRINT box from Figure 2.16.

statement need only be specified once — as an initialization step — in a program. It does not matter whether the ENDFILE statement precedes or follows the initialization step that presets the MORE_RECORDS switch.   The important thing is that these two program actions be specified before any input statement is coded.

For purposes of simplicity in this case study, headings are printed at the top of the first page only.   Typically, 60 lines of printed output will fit on one computer printout page.   In stream output, when the maximum number of lines allowed for a printer page has been reached, there is an automatic skip to a new page.   In this way, printing on the perforation of the continuous form is avoided.   However, headings are not automatically printed on subsequent pages.   To print headings on every page of printed output, as is the usual case, then you code that logic in the program.

The main logic is developed in the first flowchart, Figure 2.16.   An initial record is read and then the main loop is entered.   The process of printing a stock line and reading a record continues until the MORE_RECORDS switch is turned off, when the ON ENDFILE condition occurs.

The details of how the stock status line is printed have been deferred, as shown in Figure 2.17.   In this figure the PRINT routine includes printing the basic program data, comparing the quantity-on-hand and reorder point, and possibly printing the economical-order-quantity.

Figure 2.18 develops the same logic but uses pseudocode to express it.   The flowchart has the advantage of a more pictorial visual display of the program

REORDER REPORT
      ON ENDFILE turn more_records switch off
      print report and column headings
      GET first record
      DO-WHILE more_records switch is on
          CALL print routine
          READ next record
      END-DO
      print 'End of Report'
      RETURN
PRINT
      print the basic portion of the inventory stock data record
         (product #, description, and quantity-on-hand)
      IF the quantity-on-hand is less than the reorder point
      THEN print the economical-order-quantity
      END PRINT
END REORDER REPORT

FIGURE 2.18  Pseudocode solution for stock reorder report case study.

structures; however, the pseudocode allows more leniency in describing the operations. Also, by eliminating boxes, more logic may be shown in a smaller amount of space. Note that indentation is used to indicate the structures present.

**Program Techniques Used in the Case Study.** Figure 2.19 shows a compiled program listing. The program begins with comments statements describing the program's function. The compiler picks up the first comments statement in a program and prints that statement as header information at the top of every page of the program listing. This is why a general comment was selected. Following the comments, notice the overall spacing of the source program. This spacing is done to improve program readability. Logical sections of code are separated from each other by blocks of comments.

There are several ways to separate logical sections of code:

**1.** As you are entering your program, simply insert the desired number of blank lines as a means of "forcing" extra space on the output listing.

**2.** Most PL/I compilers provide keywords to achieve spacing on the source listing. One keyword is SKIP. SKIP, as in the case of the SKIP option in a PUT LIST, simply causes the specified number of lines on the output page to be skipped. It must be coded with a percent symbol (%) preceding the word. A blank following the percent symbol is optional. Typically, the %SKIP[1] is coded

---

[1] The MACRO or INCLUDE option must be specified in the *PROCESS statement or indicated as a PARM parameter in IBM's OS EXEC job control statement for the %SKIP or %PAGE control statements to work.

```
      /* CHAPTER TWO CASE STUDY -- STOCK REORDER REPORT                       */
      /*********************************************************************/
      /*                                                                   */
      /*   PROGRAM NAME:   STOCK                                            */
      /*                                                                   */
      /*   DESCRIPTION:    THIS PROGRAM READS THE INVENTORY FILE FOR PRODUCT */
      /*                   NUMBER, DECRIPTION, AND QUANTITY ON HAND.  IF THE */
      /*                   QUANTITY ON HAND IS BELOW THE REORDER POINT, THEN */
      /*                   PRINT THE QUANTITY TO REORDER (CALLED THE        */
      /*                   ECONOMICAL ORDER QUANTITY).  PRINT THE PRODUCT   */
      /*                   NUMBER, DESCRIPTION, QUANTITY ON HAND AND THE     */
      /*                   ECONOMICAL ORDER QUANTITY ON THE REPORT.         */
      /*                                                                   */
      /*   INPUT:          INVENTORY FILE                                   */
      /*                                                                   */
      /*   OUTPUT:         STOCK REORDER REPORT                             */
      /*                                                                   */
      /*********************************************************************/
 1    STOCK:   PROCEDURE OPTIONS(MAIN);
 2       DECLARE DESCRIPTION                   CHARACTER   (20);
 3       DECLARE ECONOMICAL_ORDER_QUANTITY     FIXED DECIMAL (5);
 4       DECLARE MORE_RECORDS                  BIT         (1)  INITIAL('1'B);
 5       DECLARE NO                            BIT         (1)  INITIAL('0'B);
 6       DECLARE PRODUCT_NO                    CHARACTER   (8);
 7       DECLARE QUANTITY_ON_HAND              FIXED DECIMAL (5);
 8       DECLARE REORDER_POINT                 FIXED DECIMAL (5);

 9       ON ENDFILE(SYSIN)
            MORE_RECORDS = NO;


      /*********************************************************************/
      /*                                                                   */
      /*   PROGRAM NUCLEUS                                                  */
      /*                                                                   */
      /*********************************************************************/
10       CALL PRINT_HEADING;
11       GET FILE (SYSIN) LIST
            (PRODUCT_NO,DESCRIPTION,QUANTITY_ON_HAND,
             REORDER_POINT,ECONOMICAL_ORDER_QUANTITY);

12       DO WHILE (MORE_RECORDS);
13          CALL PRINT_DETAIL_LINE;
14          GET FILE (SYSIN) LIST
               (PRODUCT_NO,DESCRIPTION,QUANTITY_ON_HAND,
                REORDER_POINT,ECONOMICAL_ORDER_QUANTITY);
15       END;

16       PUT SKIP (3) LIST ('END OF REPORT');
      /*********************************************************************/
      /*                                                                   */
      /*   PRINT DETAIL LINE ON REPORT                                      */
      /*                                                                   */
      /*********************************************************************/
17    PRINT_DETAIL_LINE:   PROCEDURE;
18       PUT SKIP LIST (PRODUCT_NO,DESCRIPTION,QUANTITY_ON_HAND);
19       IF QUANTITY_ON_HAND < REORDER_POINT
            THEN PUT LIST (ECONOMICAL_ORDER_QUANTITY);
20    END PRINT_DETAIL_LINE;


      /*********************************************************************/
      /*                                                                   */
      /*   PRINT THE REPORT HEADING                                         */
      /*                                                                   */
      /*********************************************************************/
21    PRINT_HEADING:   PROCEDURE;
22       PUT LIST (' ','TRIM AND GYM EQUIPMENT CORPORATION');
23       PUT SKIP (3) LIST
            ('PRODUCT NO.','DESCRIPTION','QUANTITY','ECONOMICAL');
24       PUT SKIP LIST
            (' ',' ','ON HAND','ORDER QUANTITY');
25       PUT SKIP;
26    END PRINT_HEADING;

27    END STOCK;
```

FIGURE 2.19   Source listing for stock reorder report.

starting in position 2.   Because it is a PL/I statement, it must be terminated with a semicolon.   Here are some examples:

```
%SKIP;      OR   %SKIP(1);
%SKIP(2);
%SKIP(3);
```

Another keyword that facilitates the spacing of a source program for improved readability is PAGE.   It is useful for causing a program's or module's segments to be printed on separate pages of the source listing.   It is simply coded as:

```
%PAGE;
```

**3.** Use ASA carriage control characters in position 1.   See appropriate *PL/I Programmer's Guide* reference manual description for *source margins* (SOURCE or SM).

Notice in the overall picture of the program that each source statement is preceded with a statement number.   This statement number is generated by the PL/I compiler and inserted for your visual inspection on the output listing.   Because a PL/I statement, particularly in structured programming, spans several lines, only those lines on which a new statement begins are numbered.   It is always a good idea, in the debugging phase of your program, to inspect these statement numbers to be sure that the compiler has numbered these statements as you think they should be numbered.   For example, if a semicolon were inadvertently omitted from one statement, the statement immediately following is typically considered part of the preceding line.   Many times the compiler can determine when a missing semicolon should be inserted.   It will insert the missing semicolon and print an "E" level message[2] that a semicolon has been assumed at a given point.   Other times, particularly within the DECLARE statement, the missing semicolon can be disastrous from the standpoint of the number of diagnostics generated by the compiler.   Here the compiler cannot determine where the intended semicolon belongs.   Instead, it does the best it can with the information provided; usually a number of error messages are printed that may not make sense to you.   These error messages will often clear up when the DECLARE statement with the missing semicolon is corrected.   From a debugging point of view, then, it is essential that you *first* inspect the DECLARE statement or statements to be sure that the compiler has interpreted the syntax as you intended.

Following is an explanation of the statements in the program:

**Statements 2 – 8:** The DECLARE statement items are specified at the beginning of the source program.   Notice how the data names appear in column form and in alphabetical order.   Each identifier and its attributes are declared separately for ease of reference.

---

[2] See Chapter 1, page 8, for a definition of the various error message levels.

**Statement 9:** The ON ENDFILE statement specifies that the MORE_ RECORDS indicator be set to "NO" when the end-of-file condition occurs.

**Statement 10:** Calls the PRINT_HEADING subroutine.

**Statement 11:** The initial GET, causing the first record to be read, is specified. Sometimes the list items specified in parentheses following the keyword LIST appear on the same line as the GET, and at other times these list items appear on subsequent lines. Either syntax approach is acceptable. The approach taken here is that if all of the list items will not fit on the same line as the GET, then the entire list is started on a new line and overflows to subsequent lines if necessary.

**Statement 12:** The DO WHILE statement for the main program loop is specified. Remember when coding the DO WHILE to enclose the *condition tested* in parentheses. The inadvertent omission of parentheses causes the compiler to print a diagnostic.

**Statements 13–14:** These source statements are indented three spaces from the DO in which they are nested. The indenting of the logic code within DOs improves program readability. Within the DO-WHILE the print segment is called. After printing a record, the next record is read.

**Statement 15:** This statement marks the end of the DO-WHILE. Notice how it is "lined up" in the same column as its matching DO.

**Statement 16:** An end-of-job message is printed. A skip of three lines is specified before the message END OF REPORT is printed.

**Statement 17:** PRINT_DETAIL_LINE is the name of the internal or nested procedure. If this segment were larger than is shown here, it probably would have been best to "force" this procedure to print on a new page through the %PAGE statement. However, because this nested procedure is short, the procedure is printed on the same page as the nucleus.

**Statement 18:** Three data items are specified for output: PRODUCT_NO, DESCRIPTION, and INPUT_ON_HAND. Notice that it is necessary to specify the SKIP option in the PUT LIST so that each line item starts a new line in the output report.

**Statement 19:** An IF statement is specified in which the QUANTITY_ ON_HAND is compared with the REORDER_POINT. If it is time to reorder a given item, then the ECONOMICAL_ORDER_QUANTITY is printed. This value is output in the PUT LIST statement following the THEN clause.

**Statement 20:** This marks the end of the PRINT_DETAIL_LINE. Notice how the name of the procedure follows the END. This END statement represents both the logical and physical end of the nested procedure. It causes a *return* to the calling program—in this case, the top segment. This

| RODUCT NO. | DESCRIPTION | QUANTITY ON HAND | ECONOMICAL ORDER QUANTITY |
|---|---|---|---|
| 23457R | BARBELLS | 742 | |
| 24842W | TRAMPOLINES | 57 | 100 |
| 74287F | BALANCE BEAMS | 5 | |
| 84314G | EXERCYCLES | 235 | |
| 11847E | SLANT BOARDS | 1048 | |
| 88331F | JOGGING TREADMILL | 17 | 12 |
| 48219E | ROPE BODY EXERCISER | 2054 | |
| 12934Y | SUN LAMP | 7453 | |
| 99434Y | MASSAGE ROLLER | 19 | 24 |
| 14345B | REDUCING BELT | 896 | 250 |
| 81942L | MATS | 4800 | |

ND OF REPORT

**FIGURE 2.20**

nested procedure has the characteristics of a proper program — one entry and one exit.

**Statements 21 – 22:** Figure 2.20 shows sample output from the program. The first line of this report refers to the name of a sample company. Notice how

## TRIM AND GYM EQUIPMENT CORPORATION

appears starting in the second tab position on the output listing. Now look at Statement 22 (in Figure 2.19) and observe how this output is accomplished. The first item in the PUT LIST statement is a character-string of one blank character followed by a comma, followed by the company's name. The blank character-string is output to the first tab position, thereby causing the company name to appear at the second tab position. Note also that the first PUT to a given printer output file automatically causes the information specified to print starting at the beginning of a new page.

**Statements 23 – 24:** These statements cause the next two heading lines to print. Notice again, in Statement 24, how two character-strings of one blank each have to be output to "force" the column headings ON HAND and ORDER QUANTITY to print in the tab positions 3 and 4.

**Statement 25:** This statement causes one line to be skipped following the heading lines. Notice that it is not necessary to include the word LIST in this type of PUT statement.

**Statement 27:** This marks the physical end of the source program. Although the procedure's name is not required, it is good programming practice to include the name of the procedure to which this END statement corresponds.

## SUMMARY

**Good Program:** A good program should do the following:

1. Correctly solve the problem it is intended to solve.
2. Be reliable and as free from errors as possible.
3. Be easy to read and easy to maintain.

To achieve easy-to-read and easy-to-maintain programs:

1. Use as meaningful data names as possible.
2. Use a data name for one purpose only.
3. Have the program code read from top to bottom.
4. Use clear code rather than clever code.

Large programs should be subdivided into smaller modules because large programs are 1) difficult to program, 2) difficult to test exhaustively, 3) difficult to modify, and 4) less likely to be reusable in other applications.

**Proper Program:** A proper program has these characteristics:

1. One entry point.
2. One exit point.
3. No dead (unreachable) code.
4. No infinite loops.

**Top-Down Programming:** A program consists of one or more external procedures or modules. A module is one external procedure (e.g., a separate compilation). A module's function is the change that takes place from the time the module is entered until it completes its action. A module's function should be described in one sentence. The concept of "one module: one function" is the key to a well-designed program. The logical relationships between functions, modules, and the program are depicted in a hierarchy chart.

**Hierarchy Chart:** A hierarchy chart shows function—what needs to be done rather than how it is to be done. It groups related functions together and makes it easier to determine the impact of a program change. To create a hierarchy chart, start at the top and work down (top-down design). The lines on a hierarchy chart show flow of control. Any module can invoke another module at a lower level and has a control returned to it. A module must return to its caller. The same module may appear more than once in the hierarchy chart. Recurring modules are shown at the appropriate levels where they are called and are usually depicted as a box with vertical lines added.

A module may call another module *immediately* below but not on the same or higher level. Major decision making should be placed at as high a level as possible. Hierarchy charts are used to define a *system* and its component *programs*. Another level at which these charts are useful is in the definition of a program and its component segments.

**Program Hierarchy Chart:** Each box in the hierarchy chart represents a *segment* of that module. A segment is a logical subdivision of one external procedure or module. The top segment is called the *nucleus* of the module: it provides an overview of the basic logic of the entire module. The lower-level segments are the subfunctions of the major function. "Calling" a segment is the process of transferring control to that block of code. A module or segment must return to its caller.

**Procedures:** Each segment in a program hierarchy chart corresponds to a PL/I procedure. Nested procedures are internal procedures written first with a label and then with a PROCEDURE statement without the option MAIN. There is a corresponding END statement for each procedure statement. Procedures are invoked by CALLS. In developing a large program, segments could initially be coded as *stubs*. This is a top-down approach to programming because the details of program logic in each of the segments are being deferred.

**Structured Programming:** There are three basic structures or constructs in which logic may be expressed in a structured program.

**1.** The *Sequence* structure is represented by two process symbols, each box representing an operation. The flow of control is from one operation to the next. The operation may be out-of-line — that is, elsewhere in computer storage — as long as control is returned to the next sequential step.

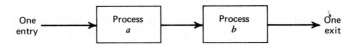

**2.** The *Choice* structure (IF-THEN-ELSE) indicates a test is to be made and one of two alternative paths taken depending on the results of the test. The test must be resolved into a true or false condition.

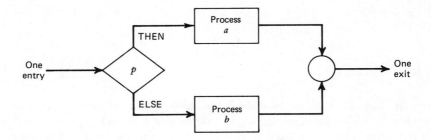

**3.** One *Repetition* structure is called the DO-WHILE. It consists of a collector symbol, a decision symbol, and a process symbol. It is an iterative operation that continues as long as the expression tested is true. During the execution of the process box, the control variable affecting the test must be modified so that an exit from the loop is possible. If the condition tested is false initially, then the statements within the DO-WHILE are never executed.

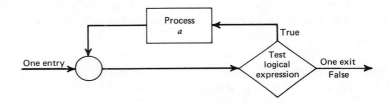

Advantages of structured programs are:

**1.** The flow of logic will be from top to bottom, making the program easier to read;

**2.** Uniformity — anyone who is familiar with the basic structures will more quickly understand a program's logic;

**3.** Reduced errors — potential logic errors are pointed up earlier.

**GOTOless Programming:** Eliminating the GOTO is a by-product of expressing program logic using only the three basic structures.

**Expressing the Logical Solution:** The logical solution to a problem may be expressed using flowcharts, which contain combinations of the three basic structures. The refinement process consists of expanding those boxes that require further clarification. A process box that is further refined by an additional flowchart is often depicted as a box with a horizontal line added.

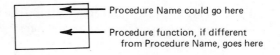

Pseudocode uses words to describe the functions of the program structures. Statements are indented to show logical structuring.

**Program Switches:** A switch is a programming technique that allows the program to "remember" what has happened so that the logic path the program will take may be altered when needed. This is usually setting an indicator to ON or OFF and then testing the status of that indicator at some other point in the program. Meaningful names should be selected and the switch should be used for only one purpose.

**ON ENDFILE:** The ON ENDFILE statement tells the system input routine what to do when the end-of-file is encountered. A file name is required because there may be more than one input file for which the end-of-file condition could occur. All input-output operations must refer either *explicitly* or *implicitly* to the name of a file. The ENDFILE statement is an initialization step because you only need to tell the system *once* what action is to be taken when the end-of-file condition is detected for the specified file.

**DO WHILE:** The DO WHILE statement says, in effect, "*do* — that is, execute — the following code while the expression in parentheses is *true*." When the END statement matching the DO WHILE is encountered, there is a "loop back" to the beginning of the DO WHILE. The test of the condition (determining whether or not the code following the DO WHILE will be executed) is performed *first*. Thus, the code within the range of the DO may or may not be performed.

**IF Statement:** The IF statement is used when a test is to be made between alternatives. For example:

```
/* **************************************************************** /
/*   SIMPLE IF                                                  */
/* **************************************************************** /
IF BALANCE > 0 THEN COMMENT = 'CREDIT';            /* OR */
IF BALANCE > 0 THEN
   COMMENT = 'CREDIT';
/* **************************************************************** /
/*   COMPOUND IF
/* **************************************************************** /
IF A = B THEN
   X = 1;
ELSE
   X = 2;                                          /* OR */
IF A = B
   THEN X = 1;
   ELSE X = 2;
```

# CHAPTER 3

# Data Types and Data Manipulation

Goethe once wrote: "What is not fully understood is not possessed." His remark is particularly appropriate to your study of PL/I data types, for if you fully understand the different types of data provided in PL/I, then you will possess a solid foundation on which to build your knowledge of programming.

There are a variety of ways of representing data inside the hardware of a computer. The implementation of PL/I for a specific computer—i.e., the PL/I compiler—will adapt the PL/I data types to the specific data formats of that particular computer.

Internal representation of data is the part of a computer language that is related to a specific computer—the computer on which the program is to be executed. It will be easier for you to understand the various PL/I data types if you can visualize how these data types are represented in storage. For this reason the IBM computers are referenced. If you are unfamiliar with these systems' data formats, you may wish to consult Appendix D for a discussion of IBM data formats.

The "working title" used during the development of this chapter was "Beauty and the Beast." The *beautiful* part of PL/I is the wide variety of data types it offers; the *beastly* part is fully understanding why and when to use each type. Every effort has been made to make this topic easy for you. However, experience has shown that a beginning programming student will have the most difficulty with this topic.

As you study each data type, be sure you know why it is provided, how much computer storage it requires, and when it should be used. After mastering data types, the benefits to you are fourfold:

- You should have greater confidence in your understanding of computing in general and PL/I in particular.
- You will avoid errors caused by using the wrong data types.
- You will be able to write programs with a higher level of proficiency.
- You should have more fun with programming.

## CHECKPOINT QUESTIONS

1. The term *byte* is an acronym for —————— —————— .

2. How many bytes constitute a *word*?  A *halfword*?

3. How many bytes are required to represent 2050 in packed decimal?

4. In which data formats may arithmetic be performed directly?

If you answered these questions correctly, then congratulations on knowing data formats and/or studying Appendix D.

An overview of the IBM data formats and the PL/I terminology used to describe these data formats are shown in Figure 3.1.

The statement used to define the various data types *explicitly* is the DECLARE statement.  All data names, in the absence of the DECLARE statement, have an *implied* data type.  Data names beginning with the letters I through N (for INteger) represent whole numbers only.  (The data format is fixed-point binary.)  Data names beginning with the letters A through H, O through Z, and the symbols @, #, and $ are assumed to be in the short-form floating-point format.  For example, in the following code,

```
A = 100;
B = 91;
SUM = A + B;
MEAN = SUM/2;
```

the decimal values 100 and 91 are converted to floating-point notation and stored in the identifiers A and B.  They are added together and the sum (1.91E+02) is stored in the floating-point identifier, SUM.  SUM is divided by 2, yielding a quotient of 9.55 E+01 (95.5 in decimal).  When this result is assigned to MEAN, however, only the integer portion of the number is retained.  In this case, the .5 would be dropped.

Of course, having variable names that represent only whole numbers can work to our advantage.  Suppose it is desired to give the average as a whole number, but rounded off.  That is, if the average's fraction is .5 or more, round up to the next whole number so that a calculated average of 95.5 would be 96 on the printout.

| | IBM data format | When to use | When not to use | PL/I attributes | Storage requirements |
|---|---|---|---|---|---|
| Coded arithmetic data | Packed decimal | Commercial applications | | FIXED DECIMAL | Two digits per byte plus sign |
| | Fixed-point | Commercial or scientific applications | For decimal fractions | FIXED BINARY | Halfword or fullword |
| | Floating-point | Scientific applications | When $ and ¢ accuracy is needed | FLOAT DECIMAL FLOAT BINARY | Fullword, doubleword, or two doublewords |
| Numeric character data | Zoned decimal | In stream or record output for editing arithmetic data; in record I/O for describing data that are in character form but arithmetic in nature | Avoid, if possible, use in computations | PICTURE | One digit per byte |
| Logical data | Character | Alphameric descriptions (names, addresses, part numbers, employee numbers, etc.) | Arithmetic operations | CHARACTER or PICTURE | One character per byte |
| | Bit | Program switches; Boolean operations | Arithmetic operations | BIT | One byte |

FIGURE 3.1   Data types overview.

This could be accomplished by the statement:

$$MEAN = SUM/2 + .5;$$

The expression is computed in such a manner that intermediate results allow for mixed numbers to be retained.   When the result is assigned to MEAN, the fractional part is then **truncated** (dropped).

A number of keywords presented in this chapter may be abbreviated.   Here are the keywords and their abbreviations:

| | |
|---|---|
| BINARY | BIN |
| CHARACTER | CHAR |
| COMPLEX | CPLX |
| DECLARE | DCL |
| DECIMAL | DEC |
| INITIAL | INIT |

**5.** Indicate which identifiers default to fixed-point binary and which default to floating-point:

      MEAN   SUM   ALPHA   PAGE   LINE_COUNT

**6.** What data formats are suitable for arithmetic computations (use the IBM terminology)?

**7.** Given: A = 10.75; B = 2.9; C = 123.4; What will I, J, and K contain after the following statements are executed (assuming all the identifiers are implicitly declared)?

      I  = A;
      J  = B;
      K = C;

## THE DECLARE STATEMENT

The DECLARE statement is needed in a number of instances:

**1.** When the programmer does not wish to use the data formats that are assigned by the compiler by default *(implicitly declared)*.

**2.** When information is supplied to the compiler that an identifier represents an array or a structure (called **data aggregates**).

**3.** When input or output files are explicitly declared within the PL/I program.

    DECLARE statements may appear anywhere following the PROCEDURE statement. It is common to find DECLARE statements grouped together at the beginning of a PL/I program. It is not necessary for a DECLARE to precede the declared variable's use in a PL/I statement.

### Base and Scale Attributes

Here is an example of a DECLARE statement:

    DECLARE PRICE DECIMAL FIXED(5,2);

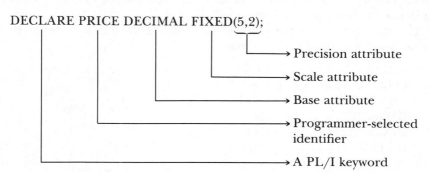

                      → Precision attribute

                      → Scale attribute

                      → Base attribute

                      → Programmer-selected identifier

                      → A PL/I keyword

A DECLARE statement always begins with the keyword DECLARE as its statement identifier. Its statement body contains one or more variables and a description of the characteristics of the value to be stored in each variable. The words used to describe the characteristics of data are called **attributes.** In the preceding DECLARE statement, the variable name is PRICE. It is declared to have the *base attribute* DECIMAL, the *scale attribute* FIXED, and the *precision attribute* (5,2). Another way in which the preceding statement could be written is

DECLARE PRICE FIXED DECIMAL (5,2);

where the keywords FIXED and DECIMAL are reversed. Most attributes may appear in any sequence as long as the precision attribute follows either the base or the scale attribute. Attributes are separated by one or more blanks. The identifier PRICE has been described as fixed decimal (i.e., packed decimal). There are five decimal positions, of which three are integers and two are decimals or fractional digits.

When an identifier has its attributes described in a DECLARE statement, it is said to be declared *explicitly.* When a variable name begins with the letters I through N and is simply used in a program without appearing in a DECLARE statement, the variable is said to be declared *implicitly.* The implied attributes are FIXED BINARY (15). An identifier beginning with any alphabetic letter other than I through N and not described in a DECLARE statement is *implicitly* declared to have the attributes DECIMAL FLOAT (6).

One of the biggest problems for the beginning PL/I programmer is failing to realize that if the base, scale, and precision of data items are not declared, the compiler will assume certain attributes by default. Often, these **default** assumptions are not the ones the programmer desired.

More than one variable name may be specified in a DECLARE statement; however, it is not recommended.

Variable names may be grouped by the type of attributes they possess and perhaps in alphabetic order within each set of attributes. For example:

DECLARE INTEREST_DUE     FIXED DECIMAL (7,2);
DECLARE PRINCIPAL_DUE    FIXED DECIMAL (7,2);
DECLARE RATE             FIXED DECIMAL (3,3);

Notice how the attributes are coded in columnar form, spaced farther over from the data names. In many installations, this is the preferred format for writing a DECLARE's **scalar** data items. A **scalar variable** is a single data item as contrasted with a **data aggregate,** which is an array or structure.

## Precision Attribute

The precision attribute specifies the number of significant digits of data and/or the decimal or binary point alignment. The precision of a variable is either attributed by default or it is declared along with the base and/or scale; it is never specified alone.  It must follow either (or both) the base or scale in the declaration.  For example:

DECLARE VALUE FIXED DECIMAL(7,2);

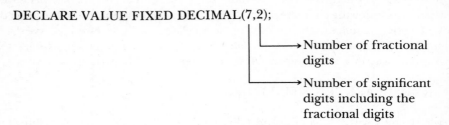

In the example, VALUE may contain up to a *seven*-digit number, of which *two* are fractional.  Thus, its form may be stated as

XXXXX.XX

where X represents any decimal digit.  If there are no fractional digits, then you may omit the comma and second digit of the precision attribute.  For example,

DECLARE QUANTITY FIXED DECIMAL (5);

is equivalent to

DECLARE QUANTITY FIXED DECIMAL (5,0);

Precision is never specified alone.  Thus, if the FIXED scale and DECIMAL base attributes are omitted, the statement

DECLARE QUANTITY (5,0);

becomes an *invalid precision* declaration.

For floating-point data, declare only the number of significant digits.  For example:

DCL PI FLOAT DECIMAL (6);
PI = 3.14159;

Do not specify fractions in the precision attribute for floating-point data.  For example,

DCL PI FLOAT DECIMAL (6,5); /* ERROR */

is invalid.

It is important to understand that if the base attribute is decimal, then the precision is expressed in terms of the number of *decimal* digits.  For a binary base, the precision is specified in terms of the number of *binary* digits or bits. In the following example,

```
DECLARE RECORD_COUNT    FIXED BINARY (15);
DECLARE PI              FLOAT BINARY (31);
```

a precision of 15 or 31 is the *number of bits* in the data item. You must understand the binary number system in order to specify enough precision for a binary base identifier. For example, the maximum decimal value that may be contained in 15 bits is 32,767.[1] If RECORD_COUNT in the previous example were to exceed this value, then a larger precision should be declared. Typically, fixed binary data items are declared to have either 15 or 31 bits of precision because fixed-point binary data always require two or four bytes depending on the precision. Note that there are 16 bits in two bytes and 32 bits in four bytes; however, the maximum precision is 15 or 31 bits, respectively. An extra bit position is required for the sign and is not counted when determining the required precision.

It is possible to specify a fraction for FIXED BINARY values. For example:

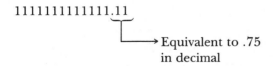

```
DECLARE BETA    FIXED BINARY (15,2);
```
Two bits constitute the fractional portion

What is being specified here is the presence of a *binary* point and the number of bits for the binary fraction. Thus, the maximum binary value that could be represented in BETA is this:

```
1111111111111.11
```
Equivalent to .75 in decimal

Internally, there is no difference between FLOAT DECIMAL (6) and FLOAT BINARY (31) data items. For this reason, some subset compilers do not give you FLOAT DECIMAL attributes.

## CHECKPOINT QUESTIONS

**8.** If you do not declare attributes for variable names (i.e., programmer-defined identifiers), what does the PL/I compiler do about it?

**9.** Where may DECLARE statements appear in your program?

[1] See Figure D.4 in Appendix D for a table of binary powers of two.

**10.** What purposes does the DECLARE statement serve?

**11.** Does ALPHA require more computer storage than BETA in the following example?

    DCL ALPHA    FIXED DECIMAL (7);
    DCL BETA     FIXED DECIMAL (6);

## Mode Attribute

Mode specifies whether a variable has the REAL or COMPLEX attribute. If the mode is not declared, REAL is assumed. Either mode may be declared for variables.

The following information is of value only to those who have the need to use complex quantities in their programming solutions of various problems. Thus, if the expression

$$8 + 2i$$

where $i$ is $\sqrt{-1}$

has no meaning to you, you will not miss anything by skipping to the next section of this chapter. In the *complex* mode, an arithmetic data item has two parts: a real part and a signed imaginary part.

There are no complex constants in PL/I. A complex value is obtained by a real constant and an imaginary constant. An imaginary constant is written as a real constant of any type followed by the letter I. Here are some examples:

    15I
    7.14E10I

Each of these is considered to have a real part of zero.

A complex value with a nonzero real part is represented in the following form:

    [+|−] real constant [+|−] imaginary constant

Thus, a complex value could be written as

    46 + 2I
          └──────→ alphabetic letter
                   indicating imaginary
                   constant

The keyword attribute for declaring a complex variable is COMPLEX.

    DCL PRIMITIVE_ROOT FLOAT DECIMAL (6) COMPLEX;

A complex variable may have any of the attributes valid for the different types of *real* arithmetic data. Each of the base, scale, and precision attributes applies to both fields.

DCL X COMPLEX FLOAT DEC (6);
DCL Y COMPLEX FIXED DEC (5);

The standard arithmetic operations are provided for complex data. For example, assume X, Y, SUM, DIFF, PRODUCT, QUOTIENT, and POWER have the attribute COMPLEX.

```
GET LIST (X,Y);
SUM        = X + Y;
DIFF       = X - Y;
PRODUCT    = X * Y;
QUOTIENT   = X / Y;
POWER      = X**3;
```

## Partially Declared Identifiers

We have seen that the characteristics of arithmetic data are described with three basic attributes: **base, scale,** and **precision.** It is possible to make a partial declaration of variables. To declare partially a variable name is to specify one of the following:

**1.** The base: DCL A DECIMAL;   DCL B BINARY;
**2.** The scale: DCL C FIXED;      DCL D FLOAT;
**3.** The base and precision: DCL AA DECIMAL(16);   DCL BB BINARY(53);
**4.** The scale and precision: DCL CC FIXED(9,2);      DCL DD FLOAT(16);

The chart in Figure 3.2 summarizes the defaults that are taken for partially declared variables. Note that when you specify only the base (BINARY or DECI-

| Declared attributes | Default attributes |
| --- | --- |
| DECIMAL FIXED | (5,0) |
| DECIMAL FLOAT | (6) |
| BINARY FIXED | (15,0) |
| BINARY FLOAT | (21) |
| DECIMAL | FLOAT (6) |
| BINARY | FLOAT (21) |
| FIXED | DECIMAL (5,0) |
| FLOAT | DECIMAL (6) |
| None—initial character I–N | BINARY FIXED (15) |
| None—initial character A–H, O–Z, @, #, $ | DECIMAL FLOAT (6) |

FIGURE 3.2   Default attributes for partially declared identifiers.

MAL), the **scale** defaults to FLOAT and the **precision** to 21 for BINARY or 6 for DECIMAL. In other words, when you write

DECLARE STRESS_FACTOR DECIMAL;

it is equivalent to

DECLARE STRESS_FACTOR DECIMAL FLOAT (6);

When you specify only the **scale** (FIXED or FLOAT), the **base** will default to DECIMAL and the **precision** to 5,0 for FIXED or 6 for FLOAT. Thus, when you write

DECLARE VOLUME FIXED;

it is equivalent to

DECLARE VOLUME FIXED DECIMAL (5);

or

DECLARE VOLUME FIXED DECIMAL (5,0);

Precision may not be specified alone.

### String Data Attributes

Logical data items in PL/I are referred to as **string** data. A *string* is a sequence of characters or bits that is treated as a single data item. In referring to string data, the term *length* is used. (The term **precision** refers only to arithmetic data.) The length is the number of characters or bits a data item is to contain. For example:

DECLARE MORE_RECORDS BIT(1);

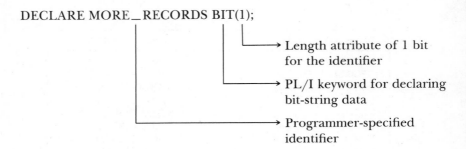

Length attribute of 1 bit for the identifier

PL/I keyword for declaring bit-string data

Programmer-specified identifier

The way to handle program switches is through the use of identifiers that have the BIT attribute. To establish indicators related to the programming of I/O operations, declare those identifiers with the BIT attribute. For example:

```
DCL MORE_RECORDS    BIT(1);
DCL NO              BIT(1) INIT ('0'B);
DCL YES             BIT(1) INIT ('1'B);
ON ENDFILE(SYSIN)
    MORE_RECORDS = NO;
MORE_RECORDS = YES;
```

Notice that names YES and NO were selected, given the BIT(1) attribute, and initialized to the corresponding bit-string (a '1'B for yes and a '0'B for no). The MORE_RECORDS indicator is initialized with an assignment statement because that indicator is changed during program execution.

MORE_RECORDS = YES takes the contents of YES ('1'B) and moves it to the bit-string variable, MORE_RECORDS. Correspondingly, MORE_RECORDS = NO causes '0'B to be moved to the bit-string variable. The indicator will most likely be tested in a DO WHILE statement:

```
DO WHILE(MORE_RECORDS);
   .
   .
   .
END;
/* AT THIS POINT, MORE_RECORDS INDICATOR = NO */
```

In declaring CHARACTER data, be sure to specify a length attribute long enough to hold the anticipated length of the largest string assigned to the variable name. For example, in an inventory application, the description of various parts ranges in length from 4 to 23 characters. However, 98% of the descriptions are less than 20 characters, so it is decided to abbreviate the few descriptions that exceed 20 characters. In this case, the following is coded:

```
DCL ITEM_DESCRIPTION    CHAR(20);
```

Character-string data items are padded with blanks on the right if the assigned constant is *shorter* than the declared length. If the constant is *longer* than the declared length, then truncation to the right of the data occurs. Similarly, bit-strings are padded on the right with zeros if the assigned constant is shorter than the declared length. If the constant is longer, then truncation on the right also occurs.

## VARYING Attribute

It has been illustrated that when a smaller character-string is assigned to a larger character-string field, there is padding on the right with blanks. There may be some instances, however, when it is not desired to have this padding with blanks.

A string value is not extended with blanks when it is assigned to a character-string variable that has the VARYING attribute.   To illustrate:

DCL NAME CHAR(20) VARYING;

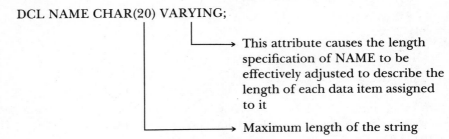

This attribute causes the length specification of NAME to be effectively adjusted to describe the length of each data item assigned to it

Maximum length of the string

In the previous example, NAME so far has a length of zero (called a **null string**) because no character-string has been assigned to it.   When the statement

NAME = 'SANDY L. KIRKBY';

is executed, NAME will have a length of 15 because there are 15 characters in the character-string constant.   If the statement

NAME = 'SANDY';

is specified, NAME now has a length of 5.   If the statement

NAME = ' '; /* NULL STRING */

which contains no characters, is assigned to NAME, the length becomes zero again.   Incidentally, the character-string constant ' ', or one with a repetition factor of zero, is called a **null string** because it contains no characters.
     The VARYING attribute may be specified for identifiers that have the CHARACTER or BIT attribute.   Truncation occurs if the length of an assigned string exceeds the maximum length declared for the varying-length string variable.   For example:

DCL X        BIT(4) VARYING;
X = '11001'B;   /* X = '1100'B */

The rightmost bit in the string constant was truncated when assigned to X.

### The DEFINED Attribute

The DEFINED attribute is a very useful feature of PL/I.   How it works is introduced here, but the many uses of this attribute are illustrated throughout the remainder of this book.   The DEFINED attribute, which may be abbreviated DEF, allows you to equate two or more different names to the same storage area.   In addition, one of the names being declared may represent either all or part of the same storage as that assigned to the other.   For example, the statements

DCL NAME    CHAR(20) INITIAL ('JOHN WILLIAM HUGHES');
DCL FIRST    CHAR(4) DEFINED NAME;

would produce the following storage layout:

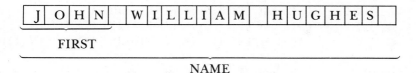

In this example, NAME and FIRST occupy the same storage area. However, FIRST will be equated only to the four leftmost characters (i.e., it will be left-justified in the NAME field) of the string inasmuch as FIRST has a length attribute of four. NAME is the *base identifier;* this is the variable name to which other variable names are equated or "defined." The PL/I term for this function is *overlay-defining.* You may only specify the INITIAL attribute for the base identifier. Also, the base identifier must be equal to or greater than any of the other variables that are overlay-defined on it. Finally, more than one item may be overlay-defined on a base identifier. For example:

DCL A CHAR (10),
     B CHAR (5) DEF A,
     C CHAR (8) DEF A;

Here is an ILLEGAL example of overlay-defining:

DCL A CHAR (10),
     B CHAR (8) DEF A,
     C CHAR (5) DEF B; /* ILLEGAL */

In this case, B can overlay-define A, but C cannot overlay-define B. The base identifier cannot have the DEFINED attribute. To accomplish what was intended in the illegal statement, we can code

DCL C CHAR (5) DEF A;

Following is a list of possible base identifiers and the type of items that may be overlay-defined on them.

| Base identifier | Defined item |
| --- | --- |
| A coded arithmetic variable | A coded arithmetic variable of the *same* base, scale, and precision |
| Character-string | A bit-string or character-string |
| Bit-string | A bit-string or character-string |

## The POSITION Attribute

The POSITION attribute may be specified in overlay-defining of bit and character-strings. For example:

```
DECLARE LIST   CHARACTER (40),
     A_LIST    CHARACTER (10) DEFINED LIST,
     B_LIST    CHARACTER (20) DEFINED LIST POSITION (21),
     C_LIST    CHARACTER (10) DEFINED LIST POSITION (11);
```

In this example of overlay-defining, A_LIST refers to the first ten characters of LIST, B_LIST refers to the twenty-first through fortieth characters of LIST, and C_LIST refers to the eleventh through twentieth characters of LIST.

## The INITIAL Attribute

An identifier may be set to an initial value by adding the INITIAL attribute to the DECLARE statement.

```
DECLARE AMT FIXED DECIMAL (7,2) INITIAL (24.50);
```

The DECLARE statement is not an executable statement. Therefore, when the value of a variable is initialized through the use of the INITIAL attribute (assigning 24.50 in the previous example), this is done once only — and done before any of the PL/I executable statements in the procedure are performed by the computer, regardless of where the DECLARE statement appears in a PL/I procedure.

Another method for assigning values to a variable is to use the assignment statement. For example:

```
AMT = 24.50;
```

This is an executable statement. AMT is set to 24.50 when the statement is encountered in program execution. Under certain circumstances, using the INITIAL attribute to initialize a variable to a predetermined value can result in greater program efficiency than if the assignment statement is used to initialize a variable. To accomplish this efficiency, another attribute must be added to the DECLARE statement, STATIC.

```
DCL AMT FIXED DECIMAL(7,2) INITIAL(24.50) STATIC;
```

STATIC is a storage class explained in Chapter 9. The constant specified after the keyword INITIAL must be enclosed in parentheses and expressions are not allowed.

```
DCL PAGE_CT FIXED BINARY (15) INITIAL (0);
```

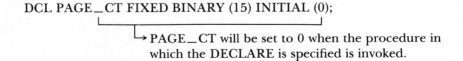

&rarr; PAGE_CT will be set to 0 when the procedure in which the DECLARE is specified is invoked.

The INITIAL attribute may be specified for either BIT or CHARACTER data as well. For example:

DECLARE HEADING        CHARACTER (22)    INITIAL
           ('WEEKLY ACTIVITY REPORT');
DECLARE DATA_ERROR    BIT (1)            INITIAL ('0'B);

The string constants must be enclosed in single quote marks within the parentheses and a B must follow bit-string constants.

As mentioned, there are two ways to initialize identifiers:

**1.** Use the INITIAL attribute in the DECLARE statement.

**2.** Use an assignment statement.

When should you use the INITIAL attribute and when should you use the assignment statement? For consistency and improved readability of a program, here are two guidelines:

**1.** For program constants, use meaningful data names and initialize them in the DECLARE statement. For example:

DECLARE PI            FLOAT DECIMAL (6) INITIAL (3.14159);
DCL SQ_FT_PER_ACRE    FIXED DEC (5) INIT (43560);

**2.** For program variables and indicators, DECLARE them *but* initialize them with assignment statements in the executable code section of the PL/I procedure. In the following example,

DCL DATA_ERROR       BIT(1);
DCL INPUT_ERROR      BIT(1);
DCL MORE_RECORDS    BIT(1);
DCL NO               BIT(1)    INIT('0'B);
DCL YES             BIT(1)    INIT('1'B);

NO and YES are program constants, given meaningful names. Their values never change; hence, they are initialized in the DECLARE. The other three indicators are initialized via assignment statements because it is possible that their values may change during the execution of the program.

**12.** Using the chart in Figure 3.2, what are the base, scale, and precision attributes for the following partially declared identifiers?

(a)    DCL ALPHA;                 (c)    DCL COUNT DECIMAL;
(b)    DCL UNIT_PRICE            (d)    DCL INPUT;
       FIXED (7,2);

| (e) | DCL DELTA FLOAT (6); | (g) | DCL HELP BINARY; |
| (f) | DCL PAGE# BINARY FIXED; | (h) | DCL TOTAL_AMT FIXED; |

**13.** What value will be placed into each of the following identifiers?

| (a) | DCL A | FIXED DECIMAL (5,2); | A = 12345; |
| (b) | DCL B | FIXED BINARY; | B = 32768; |
| (c) | DCL C | FIXED DECIMAL; | C = 43.76; |
| (d) | DCL D | FIXED DECIMAL (4,2); | D = 123.45; |
| (e) | DCL ANAME | BIT(8) | INIT ('11'B); |
| (f) | DCL BNAME | BIT(3) | INIT ('11011'B); |
| (g) | DCL SONG | CHAR(12) | INIT ('MISSISSIPPI MUD'); |

**14.** Match the following constants with their PL/I attributes:

| (a) | '011000'B | (1) | FIXED DECIMAL (5,2) |
| (b) | 01011101B | (2) | FIXED BINARY (8) |
| (c) | 01011101 | (3) | DECIMAL FLOAT (3) |
| (d) | '5' | (4) | CHARACTER (5) |
| (e) | 34.5E2 | (5) | BINARY FLOAT (5) |
| (f) | 101.11 | (6) | DECIMAL FIXED (8) |
| (g) | 101.11B | (7) | CHARACTER (1) |
| (h) | 'ABCDE' | (8) | BINARY FIXED (5,2) |
| (i) | 101.11E3 | (9) | BIT (6) |
| | | (10) | DECIMAL FLOAT (5) |
| | | (11) | BIT (8) |
| | | (12) | NO-MATCH |

## PL/I DATA ATTRIBUTES

Because you may wish to reference the following section at a later time, pertinent facts and examples of DECLARE statements are given for each data type.

### FIXED DECIMAL

DATA FORMAT NAME:    packed decimal

| Type of data: | coded arithmetic |
| Default precision: | 5 decimal digits (99999.) |
| Maximum precision: | 15 decimal digits (999,999,999,999,999.) |

### Examples

```
DECLARE GROSS_SALES    FIXED DEC(7);
DECLARE BASE_COMM      FIXED DEC(9,2) INIT(24.00);
DECLARE NET_SALES      FIXED DEC;
     /* NET_SALES IS FIXED DECIMAL(5) */
```

Note in the following examples how a number will be altered to fit the declared precision (whether intended or not):

```
DCL HOUR_1 FIXED DEC(3,1) INIT(42.6);
   /* HOUR_1 = 42.6      */
DCL HOUR_2 FIXED DEC(5,2) INIT(42.6);
   /* HOUR_2 = 042.6     */
DCL HOUR_3 FIXED DEC(1,1) INIT(42.6);
   /* HOUR_3 = .6        */
DCL HOUR_4 FIXED DEC(3,2) INIT(42.6);
   /* HOUR_4 = 2.60      */
DCL HOUR_5 FIXED DEC(7,4) INIT(42.6);
   /* HOUR_5 = 042.6000 */
DCL HOUR_6 FIXED DEC(5,0) INIT(42.6);
   /* HOUR_6 = 00042.    */
```

**Comments.** FIXED DECIMAL is the type of data that commercial programmers most often use because it provides the capability needed for monetary calculations. It is more efficient to declare the precision of fixed decimal data as an odd number (5,7,9, etc.) of digits. An even number of digits requires the same amount of storage as the next higher number of digits, but the PL/I compiler will have to generate additional code to ensure that the leftmost half byte always contains a zero. Several terms in PL/I refer to this data type:

FIXED,   FIXED DECIMAL,   or   DECIMAL FIXED

This format is used to represent mixed numbers (e.g., 12.98), fractions (0.035), or whole numbers (144).

## FIXED BINARY

DATA FORMAT NAME:     fixed-point

Type of data:         coded arithmetic
Default precision:    15 bits (equivalent to 32,767 in decimal)
Maximum precision:    31 bits (equivalent to 2,147,483,647 in decimal)

### Examples

```
DCL ECONOMICAL_ORDER_QUANTITY  FIXED BIN(15);
DCL MAXIMUM                     FIXED BIN(31)
                                   INIT(2147483647);
DCL DELTA                       FIXED BIN(31,6);
```

**Comments.** Generally, instructions that perform arithmetic operations on FIXED BINARY data have a faster execution time than instructions that operate on other data types. Thus, fixed-point binary data should be used whenever execution time of a program is a primary consideration. This does not apply, however, to converting, repeatedly, binary data to characters for output.

Variables that begin with the letters I through N default to FIXED BINARY (15). Decimal constants are typically used to initialize fixed-point binary identifiers. The values are converted to binary by the PL/I processor (compiler). If the binary precision is less than or equal to 15 bits, two bytes of storage are used for the data item; otherwise, four bytes of storage are used. Integers, fractions, or mixed numbers may be specified. This format may be used to represent mixed numbers, whole numbers, or fractions. Note that many decimal fractions do not have an exact representation in binary. For example, 0.1 in decimal may only be represented in binary as an approximation; on the other hand, 0.5 may be represented exactly in binary.

## FLOAT DECIMAL

| DATA FORMAT NAME: | floating-point |
| --- | --- |
| **Type of data:** | coded arithmetic |
| **Default precision:** | 6 decimal digits |
| **Maximum precision:** | 16 decimal digits (33 in the OS PL/I Optimizing and Checkout Compilers) |
| **Range of Exponent:** | $10^{-78}$ to $10^{+75}$ |

### Examples

| | | |
| --- | --- | --- |
| DCL FORCE | FLOAT DEC(6); | |
| DCL INTERVAL | DEC(6); | |
| DCL VARIANCE | FLOAT (6); | |
| DCL LIGHT_YEAR | FLOAT DEC(16) | INIT(6E+12); |
| DCL MILE | FLOAT DEC | INIT(5280); |

**Comments.** Because of the range of the exponent of floating-point data, scientific programmers find this data format useful for working with very large or very small numbers that do not require more than 16 digits of accuracy. Identifiers that begin with anything other than I through N will default to FLOAT DECIMAL (6). Notice in the first DECLARE statement that there are several ways of specifying this type of data. Notice, also, that fixed-point decimal constants (e.g., 5280) or floating-point decimal constants (e.g., 6E+12) may be used to initialize floating-point identifiers. Floating-point data items are not suitable for commercial programs where dollar and cents accuracy is required.

## FLOAT BINARY

| DATA FORMAT NAME: | floating-point |
| --- | --- |
| **Type of data:** | coded arithmetic |
| **Default precision:** | 21 bits (1,048,576 in decimal) |

| Maximum precision: | 53 bits (109 in OS PL/I Optimizing and Checkout Compilers) |
| Range of Exponent: | $2^{-260}$ to $2^{+252}$ |

## Examples

| DCL A | FLOAT BINARY; |
| DCL B | BINARY FLOAT; |
| DCL C | BINARY; |
| DCL D | BIN(21); |
| DCL E | FLOAT BIN; |
| DCL F | FLOAT BIN(21); |
| | /* A,B,C,D,E, AND F ARE EQUIVALENT */ |
| DCL ALPHA | BINARY    INIT(101101E5B); |
| | /* ALPHA=10110100000 */ |
| DCL BETA | FLOAT BIN(53)   INIT(10011E+72B); |

**Comments.** In main storage, there is no difference between the format of FLOAT DECIMAL data and FLOAT BINARY data. The difference exists externally for the convenience of the programmer. Usually, the FLOAT BINARY data format is used only in specialized areas such as where the programmer desires to control the number of bits of precision generated when decimal fractions are converted to binary fractions. To draw an analogy, we know that the decimal fraction ⅓ is a continuing fraction (0.33333333333 on to infinity). Perhaps, for computation purposes, you only want to use the value 0.33. You are *controlling* the number of digits of precision by using two decimal digits to represent or approximate ⅓. The same situation can occur in working with binary data. For example, in its binary equivalent, the decimal number ¹⁄₁₀ will be a continuing fraction. If the programmer so desires, he or she may indicate the precision that ¹⁄₁₀ is to have for purposes of a specific computation. Just as we said that two decimal digits would be used to approximate ⅓, we could also say that, through the use of FLOAT BINARY (12), only 12 bits will be used to approximate the decimal fraction ¹⁄₁₀.

## BIT

| DATA FORMAT NAME: | bit (bits are stored from 1 to 8 bits per byte) |
| Type of data: | logical |
| Default length: | none |
| Maximum length: | 8000 bits for constants |
| | 32767 bits for variables |

## Examples

| DCL ITEM | BIT(9)   INIT('111100001'B); |
| DCL PATTERN | BIT(16)   INIT((8)'10'B); |
| | /* PATTERN   = '1010101010101010'B */ |

DCL SYMPTOMS    BIT(8)      INIT('0011'B);
                         /* SYMPTOMS = '00110000'B              */

**Comments.** Bit-string constants are enclosed in single quote marks followed by a B.

 Bit-string data items are assigned from left to right in the field, as are character-string data. Thus, if a smaller bit-string is assigned to a larger field, there is padding on the right with zeros. If a bit-string is larger than the field to which it is being assigned, then the leftmost bits only (as many as will fit) are assigned. In other words, those on the right in bit-string data are truncated. Do not confuse a bit-string with a binary arithmetic data item. Bit-strings are not usually used in calculations. Instead, they may be used to represent a combination of related facts or events or as single bits indicating whether or not certain conditions exist (yes or no, 1 or 0, true or false).

## CHARACTER

DATA FORMAT NAME: character

  Type of data:  alphameric
  Default length:  none
  Maximum length:  1000 characters for constants
         32767 characters for variables

### Examples

```
DCL DESCRIPTION          CHAR(20);
DCL TITLE                CHAR(25)
    INIT('BOOK STATUS REPORT');
DCL PART_NUMBER          CHAR(9);
DCL CUSTOMER_NAME        CHAR(15);
CUSTOMER_NAME = 'VILLAGE SMITHIES';
```

**Comments.** In the declaration for the identifier TITLE, padding on the right with blanks occurs. In the declaration for the identifier CUSTOMER_NAME, truncation occurs. Because string data items are moved in a left-to-right manner, the final S is dropped from VILLAGE SMITHIES when that constant is assigned to the identifier CUSTOMER_NAME.

 It is recommended that you avoid arithmetic operations on data having the CHARACTER attribute, even though in some compilers it is possible to perform arithmetic operations on this data type.

### A Sample Program

Let us look at a program in which a number of PL/I data attributes are used. Assume it is desired to print an Inventory Audit Report:

```
                    VALUE  OF  INVENTORY  REPORT

PART  NUMBER              COST              QUANTITY              TOTAL  COST

1001                    20.00                 30                   600.00
2104                     7.30                 30                   219.00
4030                     1.05                150                   157.50
3035                    17.50                  2                    35.00
2200                     1.45                 10                    14.50

                    TOTAL  VALUE  OF  INVENTORY                   1026.00

                    NUMBER  OF  RECORDS  PROCESSED                    5
```

Each data item in the input stream is separated by a blank. The input items are as follows:

| Item# | Cost | Qty |
|-------|-------|-----|
| '1001' | 20.00 | 030 |
| '2104' | 07.30 | 030 |
| '4030' | 01.05 | 150 |
| '3035' | 17.50 | 000 |
| '2200' | 01.45 | 010 |

As each set of data is read using a GET LIST statement, the program calculates the *extension* by multiplying PRICE times QUANTITY. The TOTAL value of the inventory is accumulated and printed at the end of the report. The solution is shown in Figure 3.3.

## THE ASSIGNMENT STATEMENT

You will be using the assignment statement often because it specifies arithmetic and logical operations and/or causes data to be *moved* from one storage area to another.

Here is an example of an arithmetic assignment statement:

TOTAL_COST = COST * QUANTITY;

In this type of PL/I statement, the system computes the expression on the right side of the assignment symbol (=) and *assigns* the result to the variable TOTAL-_COST, on the left. The equal (=) sign in the arithmetic assignment statement means *replace the value of the variable on the left of the assignment symbol with the value of the expression on the right of the assignment symbol.* The arithmetic assignment statement is not an algebraic equation, although it looks like one in the preceding example. This is because the assignment symbol is identical to the equal sign. However,

N = N − 1;

```
/*   GENERATE THE INVENTORY AUDIT REPORT                                */
/**********************************************************************/
/*                                                                    */
/* PROGRAM NAME: AUDIT                                                 */
/*                                                                    */
/* DESCRIPTION:   THIS PROGRAM READS THE ENTIRE FILE OF INVENTORY      */
/*                RECORDS AND COMPUTES THE VALUE OF THE ITEMS          */
/*                ON HAND.                                             */
/*                                                                    */
/* INPUT:         INVENTORY FILE                                       */
/*                                                                    */
/* OUTPUT:        INVENTORY AUDIT REPORT                               */
/*                                                                    */
/*                                                                    */
/**********************************************************************/
AUDIT:  PROCEDURE OPTIONS(MAIN);
    DECLARE COUNT             FIXED DECIMAL(5)   INITIAL(0);
    DECLARE TOTAL_COST        FIXED DECIMAL(7,2);
    DECLARE ITEM#             CHARACTER(4);
    DECLARE MORE_RECORDS      BIT(1)             INITIAL('1'B);
    DECLARE NO                BIT(1)             INITIAL('0'B);
    DECLARE COST              FIXED DECIMAL(5,2);
    DECLARE QUANTITY          FIXED DECIMAL(3);
    DECLARE TOTAL             FIXED DECIMAL(7,2) INITIAL(0);

    ON ENDFILE(SYSIN)
       MORE_RECORDS = NO;
/**********************************************************************/
/*                                                                    */
/*   PROGRAM NUCLEUS                                                   */
/*                                                                    */
/**********************************************************************/
   CALL PRINT_HEADING;
   GET LIST (ITEM#,COST,QUANTITY);

   DO WHILE (MORE_RECORDS);
      COUNT      = COUNT + 1;
      TOTAL_COST = COST * QUANTITY;
      TOTAL      = TOTAL + TOTAL_COST;
      PUT SKIP LIST (ITEM#,COST,QUANTITY,TOTAL_COST);
      GET LIST (ITEM#,COST,QUANTITY);
   END;

   PUT SKIP (2) LIST (' ','TOTAL VALUE OF INVENTORY',TOTAL);
   PUT SKIP (2) LIST (' ','NUMBER OF RECORDS PROCESSED',COUNT);
/**********************************************************************/
/*                                                                    */
/*            PRINT REPORT HEADING                                     */
/*                                                                    */
/**********************************************************************/
PRINT_HEADING:  PROCEDURE;
   PUT LIST((18)' '||'V A L U E   O F   I N V E N T O R Y'
                 ||'   R E P O R T');
   PUT SKIP (2);
   PUT SKIP LIST ('PART NUMBER','    COST','QUANTITY','TOTAL COST');
   PUT SKIP (2);
END PRINT_HEADING;

END AUDIT;
```

FIGURE 3.3   Value of Inventory Report.

is a valid arithmetic assignment statement. Clearly in this example, the statement is not an equation.

**Expressions** specify a computation and appear to the right of the assignment symbol in an assignment statement. A **variable** is a term used to indicate a quantity that is referred to by name. A name is classified as a variable because it can take on different values during the execution of a program, whereas a constant is restricted to one value. In PL/I when we want to compute new values, we combine variables and constants together into expressions. The actual arithmetic operations performed on the data variables are indicated by operators.

There is a form of the assignment statement where more than one identifier (variable name) may appear to the left of the assignment symbol:

A,B,C = 0;

This statement causes A, B, and C each to be assigned a value of zero. Any value or expression may appear to the right of the assignment symbol in this type of statement.

## Arithmetic Operations

The PL/I symbols for the five basic arithmetic operations are:

| Symbol | Operation |
|--------|-----------|
| ** | Exponentiation |
| * | Multiplication |
| / | Division |
| + | Addition |
| − | Subtraction |

Multiplication must always be indicated with the asterisk(*) operator. Thus, multiplication in the algebraic expression

$(a + b)(c + d)$

is written in PL/I as

$(A + B) * (C + D)$

Here are some rules regarding arithmetic expressions:

*Rule 1:* The order in which arithmetic operations are performed is:
1 *Exponentiation* (raising a number to a power, moving from right to left in an expression).
2 *Multiplication or division* (whichever appears first, moving from left to right in an expression).
3 *Addition or subtraction* (whichever appears first, moving from left to right in the expression).

*Rule 2:* Parentheses are used in expressions to affect the order of arithmetic operations. They serve the same function as parentheses and brackets in algebraic equations. *When parentheses are specified, the expression within the parentheses will be evaluated first, starting with the innermost pair of parentheses* and solving according to the hierarchy established previously in Rule 1.

It is important to understand how the use of parentheses can affect the order in which arithmetic operations are performed. For example, in the expression

$A + B/C$

the order of execution is:

**1.** Divide B by C.
**2.** Add A to the quotient.

However, if the expression

$(A + B) / C$

were given, the order of operations is:

**1.** Add A to B.
**2.** Divide sum by C.

In some cases, the use of parentheses does not change the order of arithmetic operations in an expression. For example:

$A * B + C$

is the same as

$(A * B) + C$

A good rule to follow is: when in doubt about the order of arithmetic operations, use parentheses. Specifying *extra* parentheses to clarify the order of operations — perhaps just for *documentation* purposes — is valid.

*Rule 3:* A **prefix operator** is an operator that precedes, and is associated with, a single operand. The prefix operators in PL/I are

|     |          |
| --- | -------- |
| ¬   | Not      |
| +   | Positive |
| −   | Negative |

Prefix operators are contrasted with **infix operators,** which specify a specific operation such as addition, subtraction, multiplication, etc. For example:

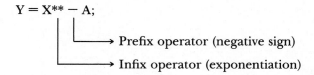

$Y = X** - A;$

↳ Prefix operator (negative sign)

↳ Infix operator (exponentiation)

In the above statement, X is raised to the $-A$ power. *When prefix operations are indicated in an expression, they are performed before infix operations.* The prefix operators do not have to be separated from the infix operators with parentheses as is the restriction in other high-level languages. For example, the PL/I statement

$Y = X** - A;$

would have to be written in other languages (e.g., FORTRAN) that contain a similar type of arithmetic statement as

$Y = X**(-A)$

Prefix operations are performed on the same level as exponentiation.

*Rule 4: Any expression or element may be raised to a power and the power may have either a positive or negative value.* For example:

```
X**2
(X+5)**3
X**−A
```

*The exponent itself may be an expression:*

$X**(J*2)$

*Rule 5: If two or more operators of the highest priority appear in the same expression, the order of priority of those operators is from right to left.* In the expression

$-A**2$

the order of operations is:

**1.** Exponentiation.
**2.** Negation.

As a further example, in the expression

$-A**-Y$

the order of operations is:

**1.** Negation (−Y).

**2.** Exponentiation (A**−Y).

**3.** Negation.

The expression

A**B**C

is evaluated in PL/I as

A**(B**C)

**15.** What does the = symbol mean in an arithmetic assignment statement?

**16.** In the PL/I statement,

Y = A + B/C;

identify the following:

(a)  Operation symbol(s)
(b)  Expression(s)
(c)  Arithmetic assignment statement(s)

**17.** What function(s) do parentheses serve in arithmetic expressions?

**18.** Indicate the order in which arithmetic operations will be performed in the following expressions:

(a)  A * X + B * X        (c)  X**2/Y**2
(b)  ((A * X) + B) * X     (d)  −Y * B

## Concatenation

In PL/I there is a special operation that facilitates manipulation of string data. The operation is called **concatenate** and is indicated by two consecutive stroke[2] marks. It means "to join together" string (character or bit) data. For example:

```
FIRST_NAME    = 'JOHN ';
LAST_NAME     = 'SMITH';
FULL_NAME     = FIRST_NAME || LAST_NAME;      /* JOHN SMITH */
FULL_NAME     = LAST_NAME || ',' || FIRST_NAME; /* SMITH, JOHN */
```

---

[2] The stroke character is a vertical bar as opposed to the slash, which is a diagonal line. In some compilers, !! or // is used to denote concatenation.

```
ZONE          = '1100'B;
DIGIT         = '0001'B;
EBCDIC_CODE = ZONE || DIGIT; /*  '11000001'B                    */
```

As another illustration, assume that a heading is to be printed on a report that contains lines 80 characters long. The heading is

PAYROLL REGISTER

and it is desired to center the heading above the printout. This could be accomplished by having 32 leading blanks, followed by the literal data:

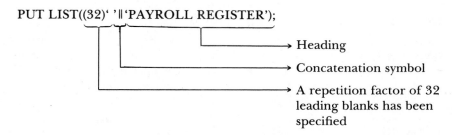

PUT LIST((32)' '||'PAYROLL REGISTER');

→ Heading

→ Concatenation symbol

→ A repetition factor of 32 leading blanks has been specified

In the following example, notice the use of the repetition factor and concatenation to center the heading WEEKLY ACTIVITY REPORT in the middle of a 120 print position line. Only the leading 49 blanks had to be specified. To the right of the literal heading, blanks are automatically padded or filled in.

```
DCL PRINT_LINE   CHAR (120);
PRINT_LINE = (49)' ' || 'WEEKLY ACTIVITY REPORT';
```

Suppose it is desired to write the bit-string constant

11111111111111110000000000000000

where there are 16 ones and 16 zeros in one string. Using the repetition factor and the concatenation operator allows us to write the PL/I constant as follows:

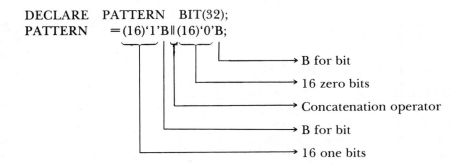

```
DECLARE   PATTERN   BIT(32);
PATTERN   = (16)'1'B || (16)'0'B;
```

→ B for bit

→ 16 zero bits

→ Concatenation operator

→ B for bit

→ 16 one bits

| Levels | 60-character set | 48-character set |
|---|---|---|
| 1 | prefix +, prefix −, **, ¬ | prefix +, prefix −, **, NOT |
| 2 | *, / | *, / |
| 3 | infix +, infix − | infix +, infix − |
| 4 | ‖ | CAT |
| 5 | >=, >, ¬=, =, <, <=, ¬<, ¬> | GE, GT, NE, =, LT, LE, NL, NG |
| 6 | & | AND |
| 7 | \| | OR |

FIGURE 3.4　Complete hierarchy of PL/I operations.

## Hierarchy of PL/I Operations

Various PL/I operations have been introduced. Because any number of operations may be specified in an expression, it is necessary to establish a *priority* in which these operations take place so that we may predict the results of expressions. The hierarchy of these operations is summarized in Figure 3.4.

## CHECKPOINT QUESTION

**19.** Consider the following sequence of arithmetic assignment statements to be executed in the order they are written. After each statement has been executed, show the current values of the variables A, B, and C, assuming each was originally zero.

|  | A | B | C |
|---|---|---|---|
| A = 5; | _____ | _____ | _____ |
| B = −A; | _____ | _____ | _____ |
| C = A / B; | _____ | _____ | _____ |
| C = C + 2; | _____ | _____ | _____ |
| B = B * B + C; | _____ | _____ | _____ |
| A = A**2 − B; | _____ | _____ | _____ |
| B = B − C + A; | _____ | _____ | _____ |
| C = B * C; | _____ | _____ | _____ |
| B = B / 2; | _____ | _____ | _____ |
| A = C / B + 12; | _____ | _____ | _____ |

## BUILT-IN FUNCTIONS

Built-in functions are subprograms supplied as part of the PL/I language. A number of programming tasks are common to many programs. In scientific computing, it might be the square root function; in business applications, it could be obtaining the system date for printing on reports. Rather than having each programmer "reinvent the wheel" — that is, code and debug basic functions — a number of functions common to a wide variety of applications have been identified, coded, debugged, and provided as an extension of PL/I. Built-in functions should be taught as a "running thread" throughout the study of PL/I. Consequently, they will be introduced here with various functions presented throughout the text as the need for them arises. Built-in functions have the attribute BUILTIN.

A **function** produces a new value for each value or set of values it receives. Graphically, the function of producing square roots can be pictured as follows:

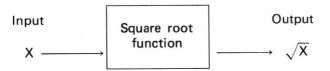

Some functions require more than one input value in order to produce an output value. The motion of an airplane can be described by a complicated function requiring basically four input values:

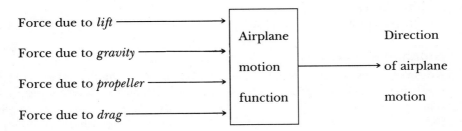

Functions, regardless of the number of input values or **arguments,** always produce a single value.

We invoke a PL/I function by using its name. For example, SQRT is the name of the PL/I built-in function that performs the action of computing square roots. Arguments (the values to be input to a function) are specified by a value or a list of the argument values separated by commas and enclosed in parentheses following the function name.

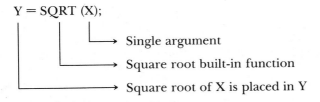

A reference to a PL/I built-in function will cause that function to be performed on the argument values, resulting in the function value. The value *returned by* the function logically replaces the function reference in any expression. Most functions require arguments.  However, some functions return a value that is independent of everything else in the program and, hence, do not require an argument.  An example is the DATE function.  When we use a function requiring no arguments, it is a good idea (indeed, it is required with some compilers) to declare that name explicitly as having the attribute BUILTIN.  For example:

DECLARE DATE BUILTIN;

Because a reference to such a function looks so much like a variable, it is preferred to state explicitly that we always want DATE to stand for the value returned by the BUILTIN function.

Built-in functions are classified according to the PL/I features they are intended to serve.  These classes include:

Arithmetic
Mathematical
Array-handling
String-handling
Condition-handling
Storage control
Miscellaneous

## Arithmetic Functions

Arithmetic functions facilitate the manipulation of arithmetic data.  They are useful in testing a value (SIGN, ABS, CEIL, FLOOR, MOD), determining a given relationship between several values (MIN, MAX), or modifying a given value (ROUND, TRUNC).  Figure 3.5 defines these functions — with the exception of ROUND and MOD, described in the following paragraphs.

## Round

This function rounds a given value at a specified digit and pads spare digit positions with zeros.  For example, if the argument is 8.77 and it is desired to round to the first fractional digit, the result would be 8.80.  There are two arguments to this function:

ROUND(m,n)

Second argument

First argument

**First Argument.**  This is the value to be rounded.  It must be a coded arithmetic or decimal picture data item.  It may be an element expression or array name representing the value (or values, in the case of an array).  If the value to be rounded is negative, its *absolute* value is rounded, but its sign remains unchanged.

| Built-in function | Purpose | Example |
|---|---|---|
| ABS | Finds the absolute value of a given quantity | X = −3.714;<br>Y = ABS (X);   /* Y = 3.714 */<br>X = +7.47;<br>Y = ABS (X);   /* Y = 7.47 */ |
| CEIL | Finds *smallest* integer greater than or equal to argument | X = 3.32;<br>Y = CEIL (X);   /* Y = 4.00 */<br>Y = FLOOR (X);   /* Y = 3.00 */ |
| FLOOR | Finds *largest* integer that does not exceed the argument | X = −3.32<br>Y = CEIL (X);   /* Y = −3.00 */<br>Y = FLOOR (X); /* Y = −4.00 */<br>X = 6.00;<br>Y = CEIL (X);   /* Y = 6.00 */<br>Y = FLOOR (X);   /* Y = 6.00 */ |
| MIN | Finds smallest value from two or more arguments | X = 100;<br>Y = 32.76;<br>Z = −6;<br>W = MIN (X,Y,Z);   /* W = −6 */ |
| MAX | Finds largest value for two or more arguments | W = MAX (X,Y,Z);   /* W = 100 */ |
| TRUNC | Changes fractional part of an argument to zero | DCL (X,Y) DECIMAL FIXED (3,2);<br>X = 3.32;<br>Y = TRUNC (X);   /* Y = 3.00 */<br>X = −3.32;<br>Y = TRUNC (X);   /* Y = −3.00 */ |
| SIGN | Determines the sign of a value and returns a FIXED BINARY (15)<br>result of:  1 for positive argument<br>          0 for zero argument<br>        −1 for negative argument | X = 123;<br>I = SIGN (X);   /* I = 1 */<br>X = −175;<br>I = SIGN (X);   /* I = −1 */<br>X = 0;<br>I = SIGN (X);   /* I = 0 */ |

FIGURE 3.5  Some PL/I arithmetic built-in functions.

**Second Argument.** The second argument, called "n," specifies the digit at which the value is to be rounded. It may be unsigned or signed. If n is positive, rounding occurs at the nth digit to the right of decimal (or binary) point in the first argument; if n is zero, rounding occurs at the first digit to the left of the decimal (or binary) point in the first argument; if n is negative, rounding occurs at the (nth + 1) digit to the left of the decimal (or binary) point in the first argument. For example:

```
DCL X          FIXED DEC (7,4);
DCL Y          FIXED DEC (7,4);
X = 123.7261;
Y = ROUND(X,3);   /*  Y NOW IS   123.7260 */
Y = ROUND(X,2);   /*  Y NOW IS   123.7300 */
Y = ROUND(X,1);   /*  Y NOW IS   123.7000 */
Y = ROUND(X,0);   /*  Y NOW IS   124.0000 */
X = -123.7261;
Y = ROUND(X,2);   /*  Y NOW IS  -123.7300 */
Y = ROUND(X,0);   /*  Y NOW IS  -124.0000 */
Y = ROUND(X,-1); /*  Y NOW IS  -120.0000 */
X = 9.9999;
Y = ROUND(X,0);   /*  Y NOW IS 10.0000     */
```

Generally, only fixed-point values would be rounded using the ROUND function. Floating-point values, for practical purposes, would not be rounded using this function. (The usual practice is to round floating-point values just before output. This rounding is automatically done in stream output.) Should the first argument to the ROUND function be in floating-point format, the second argument of ROUND is ignored, and the rightmost bit in the internal floating-point representation of the expression's value is set to 1 if it is 0. If the rightmost bit is 1, it is left unchanged. If the first argument is a character- or bit-string, the returned value is the same string unmodified.

### MOD

The MOD function extracts the remainder resulting from the division of the first argument by the second argument. The value returned is the smallest number that must be subtracted from the first argument in order to make it exactly divisible by the second argument. This means that if the first argument is positive, the returned value is the remainder resulting from a division of the first argument by the second. For example, MOD (29,6) returns the value 5:

$$
\begin{array}{r}
4 \\
6\overline{)29} \\
\underline{24} \\
+5 \quad \text{Remainder}
\end{array}
$$

If the first argument is negative, the returned value is the *modular* equivalent of this remainder. Thus, MOD(−29,6) will return the value 1:

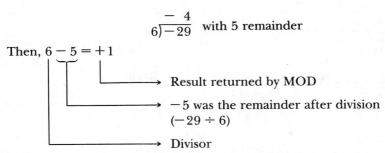

$$6\overline{)-29}\quad\text{with 5 remainder}$$

Then, $6 - 5 = +1$

→ Result returned by MOD

→ $-5$ was the remainder after division $(-29 \div 6)$

→ Divisor

When the MOD function is used with fixed arguments of different scale factors, the results may be truncated. It is an error if the second argument is zero.

## Mathematical Functions

Because this chapter has dealt with the assignment statement, mathematical functions should be logically presented here for the scientific programmer. These functions are listed in Figure 3.6. The functions operate on arguments in the floating-point scale. Generally, if an argument is not in floating-point, it will be converted to floating-point before the function is invoked.

The functions shown in Figure 3.6 include a reference to the results returned. For some functions, error conditions occur if invalid arguments are specified (e.g., a negative argument to the square root function). Typically, an error message with an identification code as to the nature of the error will be printed and the program terminated.

An argument to a mathematical built-in function may be a single value, an expression, or an array name. (Arrays and array-handling functions are covered in Chapter 6.)

## DATE and TIME

Along with several others, DATE and TIME are classified as *miscellaneous* built-in functions. These functions are discussed now because they are useful and easy to understand. Here are the explanations of each function:

```
DCL GREGORIAN   CHAR (6);
GREGORIAN = DATE;
```

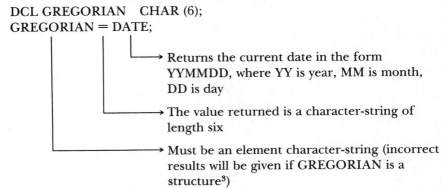

→ Returns the current date in the form YYMMDD, where YY is year, MM is month, DD is day

→ The value returned is a character-string of length six

→ Must be an element character-string (incorrect results will be given if GREGORIAN is a structure[3])

[3] Structures and the reason for incorrect results are explained in Chapter 8. See index entry "DATE error in a structure" for page reference.

| Function reference | Value returned for REAL arguments | Error conditions |
|---|---|---|
| ACOS (x) | Inverse (arc) cosine in radians $0 <= ACOS (x) <= pi$ | Error if ABS (x) <= 1 |
| ASIN (x) | Inverse (arc) sine in radians $-pi/2 <= ASIN (x) <= pi/2$ | Error if ABS (x) <= 1 |
| ATAN (x) | arctan (x) in radians $-(pi/2) < ATAN (x) < (pi/2)$ | |
| ATAN (x,y) | arctan (x/y) in radians arctan (x/y) for y > 0 pi/2 for y = 0 and x > 0 | Error if x = 0 and y = 0 |
| ATAND (x) | arctan (x) in degrees $-90 < ATAND (x) < 90$ | |
| ATAND (x,y) | arctan (x/y) in degrees 180/pi * ATAN (x,y) | Error if x = 0 and y = 0 |
| ATANH (x) | tanh $^{1}$(x) | Error if ABS (x) $\geq$ 1 |
| COS (x) x in radians | cos (x) | |
| COSD (x) x in degrees | cos (x) | |
| COSH (x) | cosh (x) | |
| ERF (x) | $\dfrac{2}{\sqrt{\pi}} \displaystyle\int_0^x e^{-t^2}\, dt$ | |
| ERFC (x) | 1 − ERF (x) | |
| EXP (x) | e | |
| LOG (x) | $\log_e (x)$ | Error if x $\leq$ 0 |
| LOG10 (x) | $\log_{10} (x)$ | Error if x $\leq$ 0 |
| LOG2 (x) | $\log_2 (x)$ | Error if x $\leq$ 0 |
| SIN (x) x in radians | sine (x) | |
| SIND {x) x in degrees | sine (x) | |
| SINH (x) | sinh (x) | |
| SQRT (x) | $\sqrt{x}$ | Error if x < 0 |
| TAN (x) x in radians | tan (x) | |
| TAND (x) x in degrees | tan (x) | |
| TANH (x) x in radians | tanh (x) | |

FIGURE 3.6  Mathematical built-in functions.

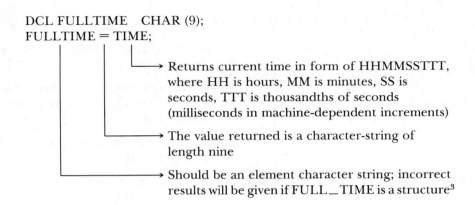

```
DCL FULLTIME   CHAR (9);
FULLTIME = TIME;
```

Returns current time in form of HHMMSSTTT, where HH is hours, MM is minutes, SS is seconds, TTT is thousandths of seconds (milliseconds in machine-dependent increments)

The value returned is a character-string of length nine

Should be an element character string; incorrect results will be given if FULL_TIME is a structure[3]

When these functions are used, they should be explicitly declared to have the BUILTIN attribute. For example:

```
DECLARE (DATE, TIME) BUILTIN;
```

## String-Handling Functions

**SUBSTR.** This function derives its name from the words *SUBSTRing,* meaning that the function is designed to manipulate smaller parts of a larger character or bit string. SUBSTR may be used on identifiers that have either the CHARACTER or BIT attribute (and in some cases, the PICTURE attribute).

The DATE built-in function returns the date in the form of YYMMDD. However, we would like to have the date printed in the form of MM/DD/YY. Thus, it is necessary to extract substrings YY, MM, and DD, not only for the purposes of concatenating the slashes, but also to rearrange the subfields within the date character-string.

To begin, we declare items and retrieve the date as follows:

```
DCL DATE      BUILTIN;
DCL DAY       CHAR(2);
DCL MONTH     CHAR(2);
DCL TODAY     CHAR(6);
DCL YEAR      CHAR(2);
TODAY = DATE; /* INVOKE BUILTIN FUNCTION */
```

To extract the month from the TODAY character-string, the substring built-in function would be invoked in the following way:

MONTH = SUBSTR (TODAY,3,2);

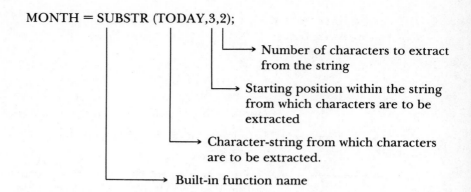

→ Number of characters to extract from the string

→ Starting position within the string from which characters are to be extracted

→ Character-string from which characters are to be extracted.

→ Built-in function name

SUBSTR has three arguments:

**1.** The character or bit string from which to extract data.

**2.** The starting position in the string (positions are numbered from left to right, starting with 1 as the first position).

**3.** The number of characters to extract from the string.

Assume that TODAY_EDITED is a character-string of length 8. Observe how SUBSTR and concatenation can be used to retrieve and rearrange fields to give the date in the edited form MM/DD/YY:

```
MONTH        = SUBSTR(TODAY,3,2);
DAY          = SUBSTR(TODAY,5,2);
YEAR         = SUBSTR(TODAY,1,2);
TODAY_EDITED = MONTH || '/' || DAY || '/' || YEAR;
```

To recap, then, the format of this highly used function is as follows:

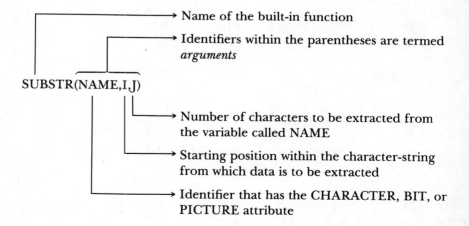

→ Name of the built-in function

→ Identifiers within the parentheses are termed *arguments*

SUBSTR(NAME,I,J)

→ Number of characters to be extracted from the variable called NAME

→ Starting position within the character-string from which data is to be extracted

→ Identifier that has the CHARACTER, BIT, or PICTURE attribute

The arguments may be constants, variable names, or expressions. The position of the arguments is critical. For example,

SUBSTR (NAME,1,2)

is *not* equivalent to

SUBSTR (NAME,2,1)

Function references can be used as arguments to other functions. For example,

MONTH = SUBSTR (DATE,3,2);

⌐_____→ Built-in function reference as an
argument to SUBSTR, another
built-in function

When a function name appears as an argument to another function, the function argument is invoked *before* the "outer" function is invoked. Thus, DATE is invoked before SUBSTR. When DATE is invoked, the result (YYMMDD) replaces the function reference.

**Pseudovariables.** A pseudovariable is a built-in function name appearing as a receiving field. This means that the function reference may be specified to the left of the assignment symbol as if it were a variable. It may also be specified as a list item in a GET statement. Several built-in function names may be used as pseudovariables. For example, SUBSTR, when used as a built-in function, returns a string that is a substring of the first argument to the function. When used as a function, SUBSTR represents the value of the substring. SUBSTR may also be used as a pseudovariable if, for example, we want to *store* a value in the substring of another string. In other words, we want to designate a part of a string as the *receiving field* in an assignment statement. For example:

DCL EDIT_DATE   CHAR (14) INIT ('DATE: 03/14/88');
SUBSTR(EDIT_DATE,7,2) = '12'; /* CHANGE MONTH 03 TO */
                      /* MONTH 12          */

By using SUBSTR in this manner, we designate a substring of the variable EDIT-_DATE to be the receiving field of an assignment statement. SUBSTR is not a function when we use it in this way; it is called a pseudovariable. Here is an example of using SUBSTR as a pseudovariable in a GET statement:

DCL MESSAGE   CHAR(40);
GET LIST (SUBSTR(MESSAGE,20,10));

Here, the characters input were placed into positions 20 through 29 of the character-string identifier, MESSAGE. The other positions of the character-string are unchanged.

Only a few built-in functions may be used as psuedovariables, of which SUBSTR is one. Others will be noted when the specific built-in function is discussed.

**BIT.** This function converts a coded arithmetic data item or character-string to a bit-string. The argument may be a single value, an expression, or an array name. The length of the resulting bit-string is determined by the argument supplied. For example:

```
DCL NUMBER   FIXED BIN(31);
ITSY_BITS = BIT(NUMBER); /* ITSY_BITS = BIT-STRING OF */
                         /* LENGTH 32                 */
```

The variable ITSY_BITS will be set to a string length of 32 because a fixed binary data item of 31 bits also has a sign bit.

It is also possible to supply two arguments to the BIT function, in which case the second argument is a decimal integer **constant** specifying the length of the resulting bit-string. For example:

```
ITSY_BITS = BIT(NUMBER,15); /* ITSY_BITS = BIT-STRING */
                            /* OF LENGTH 15          */
```

**CHAR.** This function converts a given value to a character-string.

```
DCL A        FIXED DEC (5)   INIT (175);
DCL B        FIXED BIN (15)  INIT (16500);
DCL C        CHAR(5);
C = CHAR(A);         /* C = '  175' */
C = CHAR(B);         /* C = '16500' */
```

Another form of the CHAR function, in which two arguments may be specified, follows:

CHAR (x,n)

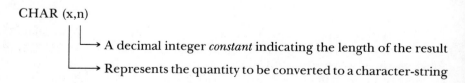

→ A decimal integer *constant* indicating the length of the result

→ Represents the quantity to be converted to a character-string

Note that CHAR may not be used on POINTER variables.

**LENGTH.** This function finds the length of a given bit- or character-string. It is useful in determining the length of string data items that have the VARYING attribute. The argument, however, need not represent a character- or bit-string. If it does not, it is converted before the function is invoked to a character-string if the argument has the decimal base, or a bit-string if the argument has a binary base. The LENGTH function returns a result with the attributes FIXED BINARY (15).

```
DCL NAME        CHAR(30) VARYING;
NAME = 'MAVIS   KIRKBY';
LTH   = LENGTH(NAME);      /* LTH = 12 */
```

**INDEX.** This function searches a string for a specified bit or character configuration. If the configuration is found, the starting location of the leftmost configuration within the string is returned. If the configuration does not exist, the value returned will be zero. The result returned has the attributes BINARY FIXED (15). The arguments to INDEX are described as follows:

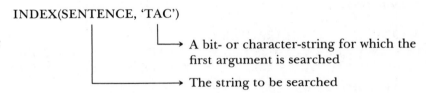

INDEX(SENTENCE, 'TAC')

⟶ A bit- or character-string for which the first argument is searched

⟶ The string to be searched

These arguments may be bit-string, character-string, binary coded arithmetic, decimal picture, or array names. If neither argument is a bit-string, or if only one argument is a bit-string, both arguments are converted to character-strings. If both arguments are bit-strings, no conversion is performed. Binary coded arithmetic arguments are converted to bit-string; decimal picture arguments are converted to character-string before the above conversions are performed.

### Examples

```
DCL SENTENCE   CHAR(40);
SENTENCE = 'THE DOG CHASED THE TAC'; /* CAT IS MISSPELLED */
START    = INDEX(SENTENCE,'TAC');
SUBSTR(SENTENCE,START,3) = 'CAT';          /* SENTENCE NOW    */
                /* CONTAINS THE CORRECT SPELLING OF CAT.     */
SENTENCE = 'CONSTELLATION';
START    = INDEX(SENTENCE,'E');     /* START = 6     */
START    = INDEX(SENTENCE,'L');     /* START = 7     */
START    = INDEX(SENTENCE,'P');     /* START = 0     */
```

**REPEAT.** This function takes a given string value and forms a new string consisting of the string value concatenated with itself a specified number of times. The arguments are described as follows:

REPEAT (m,n)

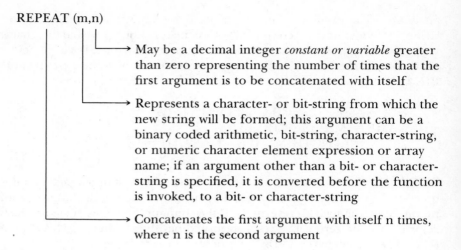

→ May be a decimal integer *constant or variable* greater than zero representing the number of times that the first argument is to be concatenated with itself

→ Represents a character- or bit-string from which the new string will be formed; this argument can be a binary coded arithmetic, bit-string, character-string, or numeric character element expression or array name; if an argument other than a bit- or character-string is specified, it is converted before the function is invoked, to a bit- or character-string

→ Concatenates the first argument with itself n times, where n is the second argument

### Examples

```
DCL CITY             CHARACTER (12);
CITY = (2) 'WALLA ';              /* CITY = 'WALLA WALLA '   */
CITY = REPEAT('WALLA ',2);       /* CITY = 'WALLA WALLA '   */

DCL ITSY_BIT      BIT(3);
DCL BIGGER_BIT   BIT(15);
ITSY_BIT = '101'B;
BIGGER_BIT = REPEAT(ITSY_BIT,5);/* BIGGER_BIT =            */
                                /* '101101101101101'B      */
```

**TRANSLATE.** This function substitutes one character with another character or one bit with another bit. There are three arguments to this function:

TRANSLATE (S,R,P)

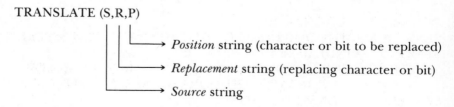

→ *Position* string (character or bit to be replaced)

→ *Replacement* string (replacing character or bit)

→ *Source* string

To illustrate the translation that takes place, the following example is given:

```
DCL SOURCE        CHARACTER (5);
DCL TARGET        CHARACTER (5);
DCL NEW_VALUE   CHARACTER (1);
DCL OLD_VALUE   CHARACTER (1);
```

```
SOURCE      = '+1234';
OLD_VALUE = '+';
NEW_VALUE = '  ';
```

└──→ If a '+' sign appears in the source string,
     replace it with a blank

When the TRANSLATE function is invoked, for example,

TARGET = TRANSLATE(SOURCE,NEW_VALUE,OLD_VALUE);

if SOURCE = '+1234', then TARGET = ' 1234'.

The *replacement* and *position* strings may contain as many characters as it is desired to have substituted.

### Example

```
DCL STARTING_VALUE        CHAR(10);
DCL RESULT                CHAR(10);
DCL REPLACEMENT_CHAR   CHAR(1);
DCL CURRENT_CHAR         CHAR(1);
CURRENT_CHAR       = ' ';
REPLACEMENT_CHAR = '0';
STARTING_VALUE      = '  12 34';
RESULT = TRANSLATE(STARTING_VALUE,REPLACEMENT_CHAR,
/* CURRENT_CHAR); RESULT = '0012003400' */
```

The following example is a practical application of the use of DATE and TIME built-in functions in which the system date and time are arguments to the TRANSLATE function that causes the editing of date and time.

```
DCL EDIT_DATE   CHAR(8);
DCL EDIT_TIME   CHAR(8);
DCL DATE             BUILTIN;
DCL TIME             BUILTIN;
DCL TRANSLATE    BUILTIN;
EDIT_DATE = TRANSLATE('MO/DA/YR',DATE,'YRMODA');
EDIT_TIME = TRANSLATE('HR:MN:SE',TIME,'HRMNSE');
```

└──→ Built-in functions

└──→ "Mask" to edit date and time

**VERIFY.** This function examines two strings to verify that each character or bit in the first string is represented in the second string, returning a fixed binary value of 0 if this is the case; otherwise, the value returned is the position of the first character in the first string that is not represented in the second string.

### Examples

```
DCL TEST_VALUE   CHAR (5);
DCL DIGITS         CHAR (10) INIT ('0123456789');
TEST_VALUE = '01234';
NON_DIGIT  = VERIFY(TEST_VALUE,DIGITS); /* NON_DIGIT = 0 */
TEST_VALUE = '123.4';
NON_DIGIT  = VERIFY(TEST_VALUE,DIGITS); /* NON_DIGIT = 4 */
TEST_VALUE = '973  ';
NON_DIGIT  = VERIFY(TEST_VALUE,DIGITS); /* NON_DIGIT = 4 */
```

### A Program Illustrating Character-String Processing

PL/I provides powerful character-string handling capabilities as illustrated in the program in Figure 3.7 that turns a negative sentence into a positive sentence. Interaction with this program could produce the following type of dialogue:

```
WHAT'S UP?    NOTHING IS UP.
ACTUALLY,   SOMETHING IS UP.

WHAT'S UP?    TOM, I WILL NEVER DO THAT AGAIN.
ACTUALLY, THAT'S AN INTERESTING IDEA.
ACTUALLY,   TOM, I WILL ALWAYS DO THAT AGAIN.

WHAT'S UP?    THIS IS NOT FUN.
ACTUALLY,   THIS IS FUN.

WHAT'S UP?    NOBODY CARES AND IT'S NONE OF YOUR BUSINESS.
ACTUALLY, THAT'S AN INTERESTING IDEA.
ACTUALLY,   SOMEBODY CARES AND IT'S ALL OF YOUR BUSINESS.
```

The program solution involves placing negative words such as "never" or "none" in a table (called an array in PL/I) and the corresponding positive word in a second table.  For example:

|  | NEGATIVE | POSITIVE |
|---|---|---|
| (1) | never | always |
| (2) | none | all |
| (3) | nothing | something |
| (4) | not | |
| (5) | no | some |

Arrays are explained in Chapter 5.   In examining the program here to convert negative sentences to positive sentences, note that two arrays are declared: POSITIVE(5) and NEGATIVE(5).   The 5 in parentheses is the number of elements in the array as specified in the DECLARE statement:

DECLARE POSITIVE(5)          CHARACTER(10) VARYING;

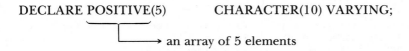

an array of 5 elements

When referring to an element of the array, the array name plus a subscript reference is used:

POSITIVE(ARRAY_INDEX)

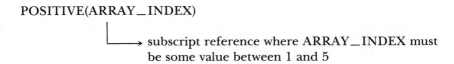

subscript reference where ARRAY_INDEX must be some value between 1 and 5

The arrays of words, then, give this program its "vocabulary."   The word *never* becomes *always;* the word *not* is replaced with a blank or empty string.   The program constructs a sentence up to 254 characters long by concatenating each word (input via GET LIST) on the end of the sentence.   The SUBSTR built-in function is used to test for a period at the end of the input sentence.   The VERIFY built-in function is used to ensure that the input sentence consists only of letters, blanks, and a period.   If characters other than an alphabetic character, blanks, or period are found, the program responds with

ACTUALLY, THAT'S AN INTERESTING IDEA.

On each iteration, the program uses the INDEX built-in function to search for the next negative word.   The SUBSTR function is used with concatenation to construct the new *positive* form of the sentence.   Here is the program:

## CHECKPOINT QUESTIONS

**20.** Select the item(s) that apply to the term *argument.*

(a)   The value operated on by a built-in function.
(b)   The result returned by a built-in function.
(c)   The value input to a built-in function.

**21.** True or false?   Built-in functions may return one or more results.

**22.** True or false?   All functions require arguments.

**23.** When must the BUILTIN attribute be explicitly declared?

```
/*   CHANGE A PESSIMIST TO AN OPTIMIST                                    */
/************************************************************************/
/*   PROGRAM NAME: OPTIMST                                               */
/*                                                                      */
/*   DECRIPTION:     THIS PROGRAM DEMONSTRATES PL/I CHARACTER STRING     */
/*                   PROCESSING BY TURNING A NEGATIVE SENTENCE INTO      */
/*                   A POSITIVE ONE.                                     */
/*                                                                      */
/*   INPUT:          SYSTEM INPUT                                        */
/*                                                                      */
/*   OUTPUT:         PRINTER                                             */
/*                                                                      */
/************************************************************************/
OPTIMST:  PROCEDURE OPTIONS(MAIN);
    DECLARE   ARRAY_INDEX        FIXED BINARY(15,0);
    DECLARE   MORE_RECORDS       BIT(1)              INITIAL ('1'B);
    DECLARE   NEGATIVE (5)       CHARACTER(8) VARYING
        INITIAL (' NEVER',
                 ' NONE',
                 ' NOTHING',
                 ' NOT',
                 ' NO');
    DECLARE   NO                 BIT (1)             INITIAL ('0'B);
    DECLARE   POSITIVE (5)       CHARACTER(10) VARYING
        INITIAL (' ALWAYS',
                 ' ALL',
                 ' SOMETHING',
                 '',
                 ' SOME');
    DECLARE   SENTENCE           CHARACTER(254) VARYING;
    DECLARE   START_OF_WORD      FIXED BINARY(15,0);
    DECLARE   VALID_CHARACTERS   CHARACTER(28)
        INITIAL ('ABCDEFGHIJKLMNOPQRSTUVWXYZ. ');
    DECLARE   WORD               CHARACTER(32) VARYING;

    DECLARE   INDEX              BUILTIN;
    DECLARE   LENGTH             BUILTIN;
    DECLARE   SUBSTR             BUILTIN;
    DECLARE   VERIFY             BUILTIN;

    ON ENDFILE (SYSIN)
        MORE_RECORDS = NO;

/************************************************************************/
/*                                                                      */
/*   PROGRAM NUCLEUS                                                     */
/*                                                                      */
/************************************************************************/

    SENTENCE = ' ';
    DO WHILE (MORE_RECORDS);
        DO WHILE(SUBSTR(SENTENCE,LENGTH(SENTENCE))¬='.');
            GET LIST(WORD);
            SENTENCE = SENTENCE || ' ' || WORD;
        END;
        PUT SKIP(2) LIST ('WHAT''S UP?  ' || SENTENCE);
        IF VERIFY(SENTENCE,VALID_CHARACTERS) > 0
            THEN PUT SKIP LIST('ACTUALLY, THAT''S AN INTERESTING IDEA.');
        ARRAY_INDEX = 1;
        DO WHILE (ARRAY_INDEX <= 5);
            START_OF_WORD = INDEX(SENTENCE,NEGATIVE(ARRAY_INDEX));
            IF START_OF_WORD ¬= 0
                THEN SENTENCE = SUBSTR(SENTENCE,1,START_OF_WORD - 1)
                                || POSITIVE(ARRAY_INDEX)
                                || SUBSTR(SENTENCE,START_OF_WORD +
                                   LENGTH(NEGATIVE(ARRAY_INDEX)));
            ARRAY_INDEX = ARRAY_INDEX + 1;
        END;
        PUT SKIP LIST ('ACTUALLY, ' || SENTENCE);
        GET LIST (WORD);
        SENTENCE = ' ' || WORD;
    END;
END OPTIMST;
```

FIGURE 3.7   Character-string manipulation.

**24.** On what types of data does SUBSTR operate?

(a) Arithmetic.
(b) Character-string.
(c) Bit-string.

**25.** Mathematical built-in functions operate on what type of data?

(a) Fixed-point binary.
(b) Fixed-point decimal.
(c) Floating-point.

## DATA CONVERSIONS

A computer cannot do arithmetic operations on two values having unlike data formats. Likewise, logical operations cannot be performed on unlike string data. Therefore, when mixed data types appear in an arithmetic expression, the PL/I compiler automatically inserts the appropriate instructions to cause one of the data items to be converted to the data format of the other. The rules for these conversions are:

**1.** If the **base** of the data items differs, DECIMAL is converted to BINARY.

**2.** If the **scale** of the data items differs, FIXED is converted to FLOAT.

**3.** If CHARACTER and BIT are specified, then BIT is converted to CHARACTER, a 1 bit becoming a character 1, a zero bit becoming a character 0.

Here are the conventions PL/I follows when different data types are specified in expressions:

Arithmetic[4] to CHARACTER: The value of the internal coded arithmetic data item is converted to a character-string, the length of which depends on the precision of the arithmetic data. Any decimal point, negative sign, or decimal fraction in the source appears in the resulting character-string.

CHARACTER to arithmetic: The character-string must contain only valid numeric characters; i.e., digits, and optionally a decimal point and a sign. There may be surrounding but no embedded blanks.

Arithmetic to BIT: The absolute arithmetic value is converted to a binary integer with a length of the target bit-string. The binary integer, without a sign, is then treated as a bit-string.

BIT to arithmetic: The bit-string is interpreted as an unsigned binary integer.

CHARACTER to BIT: The character-string should contain the characters 1 and 0 only; the character 1 becomes a bit 1 and the character 0 becomes the bit 0.

---

[4] Arithmetic refers to any coded arithmetic data item (FIXED, FLOAT, FIXED BINARY, etc.).

| Values to be operated on | Conversion that takes place | Comments |
|---|---|---|
| DCL A FIXED DEC,<br>B FLOAT DEC;<br>Y=A+B; | A is converted to FLOAT DEC | Scale is different; thus,<br>FIXED → FLOAT |
| DCL C FIXED DEC,<br>D FIXED BIN;<br>I=C*D; | C is converted to FIXED BIN | Base is different; thus,<br>DECIMAL → BINARY |
| DCL E FIXED DEC,<br>F FLOAT BIN;<br>Z=E/F; | E is converted to FLOAT BIN | Both base and scale are different; thus,<br>FIXED → FLOAT<br>DECIMAL→ BINARY |
| DCL G FIXED DEC,<br>H FIXED DEC;<br>R=G−H; | None | Base and scale are already the same |
| DCL K CHAR(13),<br>I CHAR(5),<br>J BIT(8);<br>K=I‖J; | J is converted to<br>CHARACTER(8) | String data formats are different; thus,<br>BIT → CHARACTER<br>before concatenation is performed |

FIGURE 3.8 · Examples of data conversions that take place in mixed expressions.

**BIT to CHARACTER:** The bit 1 becomes the character 1; the bit 0 becomes the character 0.

Figure 3.8 shows examples of data conversions in mixed expressions. You should avoid arithmetic operations on mixed data types.

The complete set of PL/I operations has been presented (see Figure 3.3) for use in expressions in assignment statements and other PL/I statements such as the IF statement. Built-in functions, supplied as part of the PL/I language, have also been introduced. Now let us look at a PL/I program that prints a backlog report as shown in Figure 3.9. This report is prepared from the open-order file of the Waterway Marine Supply Company. The report shows sales order number, customer name, promised delivery date, and the total order amount. The promised delivery data is to be compared to today's date. If today's date is greater than the promised date, the order is to be identified by printing the word "DELINQUENT." The purpose of this problem is to use the built-in functions DATE, TRANSLATE, and SUBSTR as well as concatenation.

Each input record contains sales order number, customer number (not to be printed on the report, but must be read), customer name, promised delivery date, and total order amount as follows:

| ORDER# | CUST# | NAME | DELIVERY DATE | ORDER TOTAL |
|--------|-------|------|---------------|-------------|
| 12864 | 86425 | 'SHIP & SHORE' | '070476' | 2054.75 |
| 18744 | 29341 | 'WHITECAP CORP.' | '103180' | 35.25 |
| 18746 | 97824 | 'THE STARTING LINE' | '091476' | 775.00 |
| 20243 | 77538 | 'BOW & STERN INC.' | '010188' | 5488.27 |
| 20307 | 11302 | 'THE WEATHER HELM' | '021492' | 126.00 |

The PL/I solution to this problem is shown in Figure 3.10. Recall the Inventory Report presented earlier in this chapter. It was a more primitive solution to the same type of problem that is being solved here. The program loops until the end-of-file condition is detected. Notice how the ON ENDFILE statement sets the MORE_RECORDS indicator OFF. Notice also the attributes of this indicator. The indicators MORE_RECORDS and NO are initialized to their corresponding values via the INIT attribute. The DATE and SUBSTR built-in functions are invoked in the INITIALIZATION procedure. The IF statement compares today's date with the input record date. Notice how the year within the delivery date is extracted first and then concatenated with the month and day. This is necessary to ensure proper comparison between years, then months, then days.

```
                          WATERWAY MARINE SUPPLY COMPANY        08/01/87
                                  BACKLOG REPORT


ORDER NUMBER    CUSTOMER NAME        DELIVERY DATE    ORDER TOTAL

  12864         SHIP & SHORE           08/04/87         2054.75
  18744         WHITECAP CORP          10/31/87           35.25
  18746         THE STARTING LINE      04/11/87          775.00
  20243         BOW & STERN INC.       04/12/87         5488.27    DELINQUENT
  20307         THE WHEATHER HELM      02/14/88          126.00    DELINQUENT
```

**FIGURE 3.9**

```
      /*                      BACKLOG REPORT                               */
      /*******************************************************************/
      /*                                                                 */
      /*  PROGRAM NAME: BACKLOG                                           */
      /*                                                                 */
      /*  DESCRIPTION:   THIS PROGRAM READS THE OPEN ORDER FILE AND COMPARES */
      /*                 THE PROMISED DELIVERY DATE TO TODAY'S DATE.  IF  */
      /*                 TODAY'S DATE IS GREATER THAN THE PROMISED DATE THE */
      /*                 ORDER IS MARKED DELINQUENT.  ALL ORDERS ARE PRINTED */
      /*                 ON THE OUTPUT REPORT.                            */
      /*                                                                 */
      /*  INPUT:         OPEN ORDER FILE                                  */
      /*                                                                 */
      /*  OUTPUT:        OUTPUT REPORT                                    */
      /*                                                                 */
      /*******************************************************************/
 1    BACKLOG: PROC OPTIONS(MAIN);

 2       DCL CUSTOMER#                   FIXED DEC (5,0);
 3       DCL DELIVERY_DATE              CHAR(6);
 4       DCL EDIT_DATE                  CHAR(8);
 5       DCL MORE_RECORDS               BIT(1)        INIT('1'B);
 6       DCL NAME                       CHAR(20);
 7       DCL NO                         BIT(1)        INIT('0'B);
 8       DCL ORDER_TOTAL                FIXED DEC (7,2);
 9       DCL ORDER#                     FIXED DEC (5,0);
10       DCL TODAY                      CHAR(6);
11       DCL TODAYS_DAY                 CHAR(2);
12       DCL TODAYS_MONTH               CHAR(2);
13       DCL TODAYS_YEAR                CHAR(2);

14       DCL (DATE,TRANSLATE)           BUILTIN;

15       ON ENDFILE(SYSIN)
            MORE_RECORDS = NO;
      /*******************************************************************/
      /*                                                                 */
      /*  PROGRAM NUCLEUS                                                 */
      /*                                                                 */
      /*******************************************************************/
16       CALL INITIALIZATION;
17       GET LIST(ORDER#,CUSTOMER#,NAME,DELIVERY_DATE,ORDER_TOTAL);
18       DO WHILE(MORE_RECORDS);
19          EDIT_DATE = TRANSLATE('MO/DA/YR',DELIVERY_DATE,'MODAYR');
20          PUT SKIP LIST(ORDER#,NAME,'   ' || EDIT_DATE,ORDER_TOTAL);
21          IF TODAY > SUBSTR(DELIVERY_DATE,5,2)||
                        SUBSTR(DELIVERY_DATE,1,2)||
                        SUBSTR(DELIVERY_DATE,4,2)
               THEN PUT LIST('DELINQUENT');

22          GET LIST(ORDER#,CUSTOMER#,NAME,DELIVERY_DATE,ORDER_TOTAL);

23       END;


      /*******************************************************************/
      /*                                                                 */
      /*  GET TODAY'S DATE AND INITIALIZE HEADINGS                       */
      /*                                                                 */
      /*******************************************************************/
24    INITIALIZATION:  PROC;

25       TODAY        = DATE;
26       TODAYS_MONTH = SUBSTR(DATE,3,2);
27       TODAYS_DAY   = SUBSTR(DATE,5,2);
28       TODAYS_YEAR  = SUBSTR(DATE,1,2);

29       PUT LIST((38)' '||'WATERWAY MARINE SUPPLY COMPANY'||(10)' '
                  ||TODAYS_MONTH||'/'||TODAYS_DAY||'/'||TODAYS_YEAR);
30       PUT SKIP LIST((46)' '||'BACKLOG REPORT');
31       PUT SKIP(2) LIST('ORDER NUMBER','CUSTOMER NAME',
                  'DELIVERY DATE','ORDER TOTAL');
32       PUT SKIP(1);

33    END INITIALIZATION;

34    END BACKLOG;
```

FIGURE 3.10

**26.** Indicate which of the following are true and which are false:

(a) Mixed data types may appear in an expression in PL/I.

(b) A computer cannot do arithmetic operations on two values having unlike data formats.

(c) If CHARACTER and BIT are specified in the same expression, CHARACTER will be converted to BIT.

**27.** What does the SIGN built-in function accomplish?

**28.** What result does the ABS built-in function return?

**29.** True or false? Arithmetic operations on mixed data types are not allowed in PL/I.

## DEBUGGING

This section gives you some steps that, when followed, will help in the speedy and successful elimination of errors from your program.

When your program is compiled, the PL/I compiler prints a source listing of your program and, if requested through the *PROCESS statement, other information that is most useful. One valuable tool is the *attribute and cross-reference table*. An example of this table is shown in Figure 3.11. It is the attribute listing for the Stock Reorder Report Case Study in Chapter 2 (Figure 2.19, page 68).

Develop the habit of examining this table early in the debugging phase of your program. Following is a description of specific items to understand in this table. Notice that there are three major columns in this table: DCL NO., IDENTIFIER, and ATTRIBUTE AND CROSS-REFERENCE TABLE.

### DCL NO. Column

In the DCL NO. column, the number of the declare statement is specified. For identifiers implicitly declared (i.e., identifiers not appearing in a DECLARE statement), a string of asterisks is printed indicating that default attributes apply. This string of asterisks can be the key to the successful debugging of your program. Typically, in a structured approach to debugging, all identifiers should be explicitly declared as an aid to the reader of the program.

In this example, some asterisks do appear in this column. As we begin to inspect the next column, we will see that the compiler's assumptions are in fact those that we wanted.

### IDENTIFIER Column

In the IDENTIFIER column, *all* programmer-defined identifiers are listed in alphabetic order. You should be sure to scan this list to verify that only those names you intended to use are present. Sometimes a data entry error is made in

ATTRIBUTE AND CROSS-REFERENCE TABLE (FULL)

| DCL NO. | IDENTIFIER | ATTRIBUTES AND REFERENCES |
|---|---|---|
| 2 | DESCRIPTION | AUTOMATIC UNALIGNED CHARACTER (20)<br>11,14,18 |
| 3 | ECONOMICAL_ORDER_QUANTITY | AUTOMATIC ALIGNED DECIMAL FIXED (5,0)<br>11,14,19 |
| 4 | MORE_RECORDS | AUTOMATIC UNALIGNED INITIAL BIT (1)<br>1,12<br>9 |
| 5 | NO | AUTOMATIC UNALIGNED INITIAL BIT (1)<br>1,9 |
| 17 | PRINT_DETAIL_LINE | ENTRY RETURNS(DECIMAL /* SINGLE */ FLOAT (6))<br>13 |
| 21 | PRINT_HEADING | ENTRY RETURNS(DECIMAL /* SINGLE */ FLOAT (6))<br>10 |
| 6 | PRODUCT_NO | AUTOMATIC UNALIGNED CHARACTER (8)<br>11,14,18 |
| 7 | QUANTITY_ON_HAND | AUTOMATIC ALIGNED DECIMAL FIXED (5,0)<br>11,14,18,19 |
| 8 | REORDER_POINT | AUTOMATIC ALIGNED DECIMAL FIXED (5,0)<br>11,14,19 |
| 1 | STOCK | EXTERNAL ENTRY RETURNS(DECIMAL /* SINGLE */ FLOAT (6)) |
| ******** | SYSIN | EXTERNAL FILE<br>9,11,14 |
| ******** | SYSPRINT | EXTERNAL FILE PRINT<br>16,18,19,22,23,24,25 |

FIGURE 3.11

which an intervening blank is inserted in the middle of an identifier. For example,

QUANTITY_ON_HAND

might have been inadvertently keyed as

QUANTITY_ ON_HAND

This situation could cause the compiler to treat the intended identifier as two separate identifiers: QUANTITY_ and ON_HAND. Thus, you would see both of these names in the IDENTIFIER column listing rather than the one intended.

## ATTRIBUTES and REFERENCES Column

In the ATTRIBUTES and REFERENCES column, the attributes for the corresponding identifiers are listed. You will recognize some of the attribute keywords. Some keywords, however, have not yet been explained in this text. Such keywords as AUTOMATIC, ALIGNED, and UNALIGNED are default attributes. These will be discussed later.

Notice the ENTRY attribute for the identifier PRINT_HEADING. Recall from Figure 2.19 that PRINT_HEADING is the **entry name** of the nested procedure. Moving on down to the identifier STOCK, notice that it also has the ENTRY attribute, but is further identified with the attribute EXTERNAL. STOCK is EXTERNAL because the name of this procedure must be known to programs outside (i.e., external to) this program. For example, it is the operating system that will locate this procedure and transfer control to it so that it may be executed.

Both ENTRY names also have some arithmetic attributes [e.g., DECIMAL FLOAT (6)]. These arithmetic attributes are not significant for these types of programs. There is one situation when a specific type of subprogram (a *function subprogram*) returns a value that has the attributes assigned to the subprogram's name. Only in this case should the attributes of the procedure name be taken into consideration in your programming task.

SYSIN and SYSPRINT are the default names of the files communicated with when a GET or PUT is issued. Notice that these file names are given the attributes EXTERNAL and FILE. SYSPRINT is an output file to the line printer, as specified by the attribute PRINT.

Immediately following each line in which the attributes are listed we see a line of statement numbers, inserted because the cross-reference option was requested (via *PROCESS statement). These are the numbers of the source statements in which the corresponding identifiers were used. The statement numbers are particularly useful when modifying a program. Assume, for example, you wish to change the attributes of a given identifier. It would be important to inspect all statements in which this identifer appears in assessing the impact of the change on the program.

The first three steps to debugging any program should be:

**1.** Inspect the source listing. Is the program within positions 2 through 72? (Anything inadvertently placed in position 1 or positions 73 to 80 will be ignored by the PL/I compiler.) Is the source listing spaced on the printer page in a way that enhances program readability? (The statements %SKIP and %PAGE can be inserted in subsequent runs of your program providing the MACRO or IN-CLUDE option is in effect for the compilation.

**2.** Eliminate diagnostic messages. Following the source listing will be the compiler diagnostic messages produced for the compilation. Recall that some compiler-detected errors actually cause other diagnostics to be generated by the compiler. Thus, when debugging from a long list of errors, attempt to clean up the known errors first, then recompile your program and repeat the process, if necessary. Informatory (I) and Warning (W) messages should be removed although some programmers do not eliminate them if they agree with the options assumed by the compiler. Any E-level (Error) and S-level (Severe) errors must be removed from the source program.

**3.** Read the attribute and cross-reference table to determine that every identifier has the attributes you intended. It is this step that is most often bypassed, particularly if the printed output from program execution appears to be correct. It cannot be emphasized enough that discipline is required in taking this step.

## CASE STUDY: PRIME NUMBER GENERATION

This case study illustrates a structured program and the refinement process discussed in Chapter 2, as well as a number of features discussed in Chapters 2 and 3. These features include:

The Assignment statement.
Declaring coded arithmetic data.
Program switches expressed as bit-strings.
The simple IF statement.
The DO WHILE statement.
Using a built-in function.

Also, a technique to obtain the remainder after a divide operation is illustrated.

A prime number is a number that is not divisible evenly by any number other than itself and the number 1. All prime numbers other than the number 2 are odd; but all odd numbers are not prime numbers. This case study determines the numbers that are prime between 1 and 100 and prints them out.

The fact that prime numbers are odd suggests that only odd numbers should be tested for possible prime values; this cuts the computation time. Further time is saved by restricting the divisors to odd numbers because even numbers will not divide evenly into odd numbers and therefore will not be useful in determining whether or not a number is prime.

The logic of the program, then, is to devise a method for testing all the odd numbers between 1 and 100 by dividing each one by all the smaller odd numbers except the number 1. If any of the divisions result in a remainder of zero, then the number being tested is not prime. If the number divides with a remainder, then the number is a possible prime number.

Figure 3.12 shows a program flowchart for the generation of prime numbers from 1 to 100. Notice from this flowchart that the first two prime numbers, 1 and

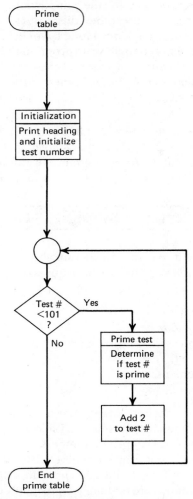

FIGURE 3.12 Flowchart of prime number generation.

2, are initially printed out. The iteration of testing for the remaining numbers begins at 3. In the program loop we see a DO-WHILE structure in which the limit value of 101 is established. Notice in this structure that a further refinement is required for the function of PRIME_TEST. This refinement is shown in Figure 3.13 where the program switches are set and the argument is tested to determine whether or not it is prime. This then provides the logic for the program, which is shown in Figure 3.14. Only the major source statements in this program are discussed.

**Source Statement 14:** A report heading is listed using PUT LIST.

**Source Statement 15:** The first prime number, 1, is printed underneath the output heading. Notice that the numeric value specified in the PUT LIST is no: 001

There was a specific reason for this constant being coded in the program with two leading zeros. Notice from Source Statement 21 that TEST# was declared as FIXED DECIMAL (3). If we wish to have all prime numbers printed in column form as shown in Figure 3.15 then program constants output must have the same arithmetic attributes as the declared identifiers. The implicit attributes of the fixed decimal constant 1 are

FIXED DECIMAL (1)

The implicit attributes for the decimal constant 001 are

FIXED DECIMAL (3)

Thus, it is necessary to specify the leading zeros in the constant value output so as to maintain proper column alignment of the data on output.

**Source Statement 16:** A second PUT LIST statement forcing output to start on a new line is given for the second prime number.

**Source Statement 17:** TEST# is initialized to the value 3.

**Source Statements 9 – 11:** A DO-WHILE structure is established to test for the occurrence of prime numbers up to and including 100. Within the DO the nested procedure PRIME_TEST is called. Following the call to this subroutine, TEST# is incremented by 2 so that the next *odd* (as opposed to even) number may be tested.

**Source Statement 20:** The divisor is initialized to 3 because the prime-number test begins testing with the value of 3. This identifer will be initialized to 3 each time the PRIME_TEST procedure is entered.

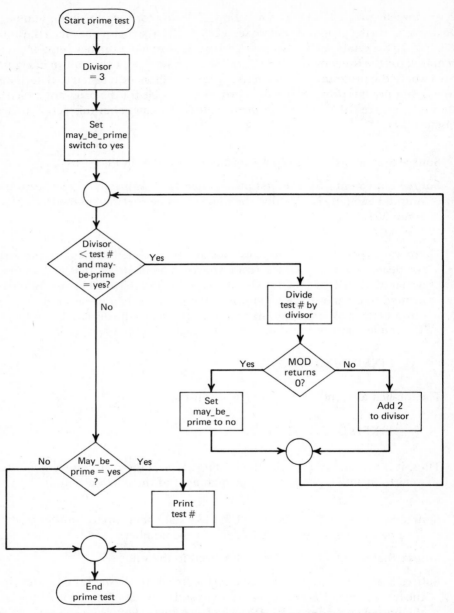

FIGURE 3.13  Expansion of PRIME TEST in prime number flowchart.

```
/* CHAPTER 3 CASE STUDY: PRIME NUMBER GENERATION                         */
/*************************************************************************/
/*                                                                       */
/*    PROGRAM NAME:   PRIMES                                             */
/*                                                                       */
/*    DESCRIPTION:    THIS PROGRAM GENERATES ALL PRIME NUMBERS BETWEEN   */
/*                    1 AND 100 AND PRINTS THEM ON A REPORT.             */
/*                    AFTER PRINTING PRIM NUMBERS 001 AND 002, ONLY      */
/*                    ODD NUMBERS ARE TESTED BY STARTING WITH 3 AND      */
/*                    AND INCREMENTING THE TEST NUMBERS BY 2.            */
/*                                                                       */
/*    INPUT:          NONE                                               */
/*                                                                       */
/*    OUTPUT:         PRIME NUMBER REPORT                                */
/*                                                                       */
/*************************************************************************/
```

| | |
|---|---|
| 1 | PRIMES: PROC OPTIONS (MAIN); |
| 2 | DCL DIVISOR               FIXED DEC(3,0); |
| 3 | DCL MAY_BE_PRIME          BIT(1); |
| 4 | DCL NO                    BIT(1)        INIT('0'B); |
| 5 | DCL TEST#                 FIXED DEC(3,0); |
| 6 | DCL YES                   BIT(1)        INIT('1'B); |
| 7 | DCL MOD                   BUILTIN; |

```
/*************************************************************************/
/*                                                                       */
/*    PROGRAM NUCLEUS                                                     */
/*                                                                       */
/*************************************************************************/
```

| | |
|---|---|
| 8 | CALL INITIALIZATION; |
| 9 | DO WHILE (TEST# < 101); |
| 10 | CALL PRIME_TEST; |
| 11 | TEST# = TEST# + 2; |
| 12 | END; |

```
/*************************************************************************/
/*                                                                       */
/*    PRINT HEADING AND INITIALIZE THE TEST NUMBER                       */
/*                                                                       */
/*************************************************************************/
```

| | |
|---|---|
| 13 | INITIALIZATION: PROC; |
| 14 | PUT LIST('PRIME NUMBERS BETWEEN 1 AND 100'); |
| 15 | PUT SKIP(2)LIST(001); |
| 16 | PUT SKIP    LIST(002); |
| 17 | TEST# = 3; |
| 18 | END INITIALIZATION; |

```
/*************************************************************************/
/*                                                                       */
/*    BEGIN BY DIVIDING THE TEST# BY PRIME NUMBER 3.  IT IS              */
/*    UNNECESSARY TO DIVIDE BY 2 SINCE NONE OF THE TEST NUMBERS ARE      */
/*    EVEN.  USE THE MOD BUILTIN FUNCTION TO DETERMINE IF THE TEST       */
/*    NUMBER CAN BE EVENLY DIVIDED BY THE DIVISOR.                       */
/*                                                                       */
/*************************************************************************/
```

| | |
|---|---|
| 19 | PRIME_TEST:  PROC; |
| 20 | DIVISOR = 3; |
| 21 | MAY_BE_PRIME = YES; |
| 22 | DO WHILE (DIVISOR < TEST# & MAY_BE_PRIME); |
| 23 | IF MOD(TEST#,DIVISOR) = 0 |
| | THEN MAY_BE_PRIME  = NO; |
| 24 | ELSE DIVISOR       = DIVISOR + 2; |
| 25 | END; |
| 26 | IF MAY_BE_PRIME |
| | THEN PUT SKIP LIST (TEST#); |
| 27 | END PRIME_TEST; |
| 28 | END PRIMES; |

FIGURE 3.14   Prime number generation source program.

PRIME NUMBERS BETWEEN 1 AND 100

```
 1
 2
 3
 5
 7
11
13
17
19
23
29
31
37
41
43
47
53
59
61
67
71
73
79
83
89
97
```

FIGURE 3.15   Sample output from prime number case study.

**Source Statement 21:** The MAY_BE_PRIME program switch is initialized to YES. This switch is also initialized each time the prime test procedure is entered.

**Source Statement 22:** The DO WHILE statement is coded to specify two conditions: 1) the divisor must be less than or equal to the test number; 2) the MAY_BE_PRIME switch must be ON (i.e., set to YES). Both conditions must be true for the statements within the range of the DO to be executed.

**Source Statements 23 and 24:** If the result of the MOD function is zero, the program switch MAY_BE_PRIME is turned OFF, (i.e., set to NO). If a remainder exists, the divisor is incremented by 2 and the MAY_BE-_PRIME switch remains unaltered.

**Source Statement 26:** If the MAY_BE_PRIME switch is still ON at this point, then TEST# contains a prime number.

**Source Statement 27:** This statement marks the end of the nested procedure. Notice the procedure name was included in the end statement for purposes of program documentation.

## SUMMARY

**Default Attributes:** These are attributes assigned to identifiers when none have been explicitly declared. Variables that begin with A through H, O through Z, @, #, or $ default to the attributes DECIMAL FLOAT (6). (The 6 is the number of digits of precision.) Identifiers that begin with the letters I through N default to FIXED BINARY (15), where the 15 is the number of bits of precision.

The I through N variables may be assigned decimal numbers even though their default attributes include BINARY. The decimal integer value that can be represented in 15 bits of precision must be within the range of $-32,768$ to $+32,767$.

**The DECLARE Statement:** This statement is used to define attributes for variables that represent data. The DECLARE statement is needed when the programmer does not wish to use the data formats assigned by the compiler by default, or when information is to be supplied to the compiler to reserve storage for a number of data items. The word used to describe the characteristics of data is *attribute*. Most attributes may appear in any sequence, and abbreviations of some words are allowed. Attributes are separated by one or more blanks in the DECLARE statement. Attributes covered include:

1. Base (DECIMAL or BINARY).
2. Scale (FIXED or FLOAT).
3. Precision (number of significant digits and decimal or binary point alignment).
4. Length (number of characters or bits for string data).
5. Mode (REAL or COMPLEX).
6. Initial value (INITIAL).

When a variable has its attributes described in a DECLARE statement, it is said to be declared *explicitly;* when variable names are simply used in a program without appearing in a DECLARE statement, they are said to be declared *implicitly.* (One of the biggest problems for the beginning PL/I programmer is failing to realize that if the base, scale, and precision of data items are not DECLAREd, the compiler will assume certain attributes by default. Often these default assumptions are not desired by the programmer.) The precision of a variable is either attributed by default or is declared along with the base and/or scale, and it is never specified alone. Figure 3.16 summarizes the allowable lengths, precisions, and ranges for each type of data we may work with in PL/I.

**The DEFINED Attribute:** This attribute allows you to equate two or more different names to the same storage area. In addition, one of the names being declared may represent either all or part of the same storage as that assigned to the other. The base identifier is the variable name to which other variable names are equated or "defined." The PL/I term for this function is *overlay-defining.* Only the base identifier may be initialized if the INITIAL attribute is specified. The base identifier must be equal to or greater than (in length) any of the other variables that are overlay-defined on it.

**The POSITION Attribute:** This attribute may be specified in overlay-defining of bit- and character-strings. It allows you to specify the beginning position within a string from which to start the overlay defining.

| Attributes | Precision/Length |
|---|---|
| FIXED DECIMAL | 1 to 15 decimal digits |
| FIXED BINARY | 1 to 31 bits<br>(mixed numbers allowed) |
| FLOAT DECIMAL | $10^{-78}$ to $10^{+75}$<br>1 to 16 decimal digits[a] |
| FLOAT BINARY | $2^{-260}$ to $2^{+252}$<br>1 to 53 bits[b] |
| CHARACTER | 1 to 32,767 for variables<br>1 to 1000 for constants |
| BIT | 1 to 32,767 bits for variables<br>1 to 8000 bits for constants |

[a] For OS PL/I Optimizing and Checkout compilers, 33 decimal digits maximum
[b] For OS PL/I Optimizing and Checkout compilers, 109 bits maximum

FIGURE 3.16  Summary of allowable precisions and lengths.

**Factored Attributes** When the same base, scale, and precision could apply to more than one variable, then the attributes may be factored; for example:

    DCL (A,B,C) FIXED;
    DCL (W FIXED, X FLOAT (6)) DECIMAL;

**The INITIAL Attribute:** In addition to declaring the base, scale, and precision of an arithmetic variable or the length of a string, it is also possible to set that variable to an initial value by adding the INITIAL attribute in the DECLARE statement; for example:

    DCL CENTER   FIXED DEC (3)   INIT (100);
    DCL NAME     CHAR(15)        INIT ('PATTI WILLIAMS');

**Partially Declared Identifiers:** We have seen that characteristics of arithmetic data are normally described with three basic attributes: base, scale, and precision. It is possible to make a partial declaration of variables by specifying one of the following:

1. Base.
2. Scale.
3. Base and precision.
4. Scale and precision.

**The Assignment Statement:** You will be using this type of statement often because it specifies which arithmetic and logical operations should take place and/or

cause data to be *moved* from one storage area to another. The assignment symbol
(=) in the arithmetic assignment statement means "replace the value of the variable on the left of the equal sign with the value of the expression on the right of the
assignment symbol (equal sign)." Expressions specify a computation and appear
to the right of the assignment symbol in an assignment statement. A variable is a
term used to indicate a quantity that is referred to by name, and a constant is an
actual number. A number of operations may be performed in expressions,
including:

**1. Arithmetic operations:** The order in which arithmetic operations are performed is (1) exponentiation (raising a number to a power, moving from right to
left in an expression); (2) multiplication or division (whichever appears first,
moving from left to right in an expression; (3) addition or subtraction (whichever
appears first, moving from left to right in the expression). When parentheses are
specified, the expression within the parentheses will be evaluated first, starting
with the innermost pair of parentheses. A prefix operator is an operator that
precedes — and is associated with — a single operand. The prefix operators in
PL/I are −, +, and ¬. Consider the following valid PL/I statement:

Y = X*−W;

In the above example, the prefix (−) does not signify a subtraction operation; it
simply means to find the negative (i.e., reverse the sign) of W. When prefix +
(positive) and prefix − (negative) symbols are indicated in an arithmetic expression, they are performed before infix + (addition) and infix − (subtraction) are
performed. Note that the prefix operators do not have to be separated from the
infix operators with parentheses, as is the restriction in other high-level languages. The expression A**B**C is evaluated by PL/I as A**(B**C), because the
exponentiation operations are performed moving from right to left in the expression. A form of the assignment statement is the statement where more than one
identifier (variable name) may appear to the left of the equal sign (e.g., A,B,C, =
0;). This statement causes A, B, and C each to be assigned a value of zero.

**2. String operation:** The concatenation operation may be specified for bit- or
character-strings. It simply means to join two strings together to form one longer
string, for example:

'J'||'.' → J.
'110'B||'11' B → 11011

See Figure 3.4 for the complete hierarchy of PL/I operations.

When you specify only the base (BINARY or DECIMAL), the scale will default
to FLOAT and the precision to 21 for BINARY or 6 for DECIMAL. When you
specify only the scale (FIXED or FLOAT), the base will default to DECIMAL and

the precision to 5 for FIXED and 6 for FLOAT. The chart in Figure 3.2 summarizes the defaults taken for partially declared identifiers.

**PL/I Data Attributes:** The data types provided in PL/I are discussed below.

**1. FIXED DECIMAL:** This is the type of data that commercial programmers most often use. It is more efficient to declare the precision of fixed decimal data as an odd number (5, 7, 9, etc.) of digits. This format can be used to represent mixed numbers (e.g., 12.98), fractions (0.035), or whole numbers (144).

**2. FIXED BINARY:** Identifiers beginning with I through N default to FIXED BINARY (15).

**3. FLOAT DECIMAL:** Because of the range of the exponent of floating-point data, scientific programmers find this data format useful for working with very large or very small numbers. Identifiers whose letters begin with anything other than I through N will default to FLOAT DECIMAL (6). Floating-point data items are not suitable for commercial programs where dollars-and-cents accuracy is required.

**4. FLOAT BINARY:** There is no difference between the internal format of FLOAT DECIMAL data and FLOAT BINARY data. The difference exists externally for the convenience of the programmer in being able to declare precision in terms of bits.

**5. CHARACTER:** Character-string data items are padded with blanks on the right if the assigned character constant is shorter than the declared length of the character-string. If the character constant is longer than the declared length of the character-string, then truncation to the right of the data occurs. A string value is not extended with blanks when it is assigned to a character-string variable that has the VARYING attribute. You may do arithmetic on data having the character attribute (although it is not recommended). In this case, the numeric characters are automatically converted to the coded arithmetic form FIXED DECIMAL.

**6. BIT:** Bit-string data items are assigned from left to right in the field, as are character-string data. Thus, if a smaller bit-string is assigned to a larger field, there is padding on the right with zeros. If a bit-string is larger than the field to which it is being assigned, then the leftmost bits only (as many as will fit) are assigned. Bit-strings are usually not used in calculations. Instead, they may be used in a program to indicate whether or not certain conditions exist (yes or no, 1 or 0, true or false).

**Arithmetic Functions:** These functions facilitate the manipulation of arithmetic data. They are summarized in Figure 3.5. The ROUND built-in function rounds a given value at a specified digit and pads spare digit positions with zeros.

**Mathematical Functions:** These functions are provided for the scientific programmer. They are listed in Figure 3.6. The functions operate on arguments in the floating-point scale. If an argument is not in floating-point, it will automatically be converted to floating-point before the function is invoked.

**Data Conversions:** The rules for conversion are:

1. If the base of the data items differs, DECIMAL is converted to BINARY.

2. If the scale of the data items differs, FIXED is converted to FLOAT.

3. If CHARACTER and BIT are specified, then BIT is converted to CHARACTER.

# CHAPTER 4

# Subroutines and Functions

A major requirement of a structured approach to programming is that a program be modular. Modularity has been illustrated in Chapter 2 through the use of nested procedures carrying out various subfunctions. Another way in which modularity is achieved is through the linking of external procedures where each external procedure may or may not contain nested procedures. An external procedure is a separate compilation. When external procedures are linked together, however, one of them must be designated as the MAIN procedure. The MAIN procedure is executed first. The remaining external procedures are called *subprograms*. In the following diagram, each box represents a separate compile.

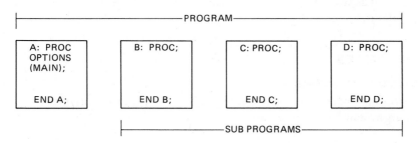

There are three types of PL/I procedures: MAIN procedures, subroutine procedures, and function procedures. MAIN procedures are always separate compilations and may or may not include nested subroutine or function procedures. Subroutines and functions may also be compiled separately. (A general term for a subroutine or function is *subprogram*.)

When subroutines or functions are compiled separately, these *subprograms* may be saved — typically on a disk.

Subprograms on a disk are catalogued by the subprogram's name. These subprograms are easily retrieved and added to a main program by a linkage editor whose function is to link together all modules at the time a main program is to be readied for execution.

There are several advantages to separately compiled procedures:

**1. Saves coding effort:** A subprogram stored in a library on a disk, for example, may be easily used by more than one program.

**2. Reduces total programming time:** Programming tasks can be divided among several programmers, thus shortening the total programming elapsed time.

**3. Improves program reliability:** A subprogram, once checked out, can be used with a reasonable degree of certainty that the correct answer will be given. This allows the programmer to concentrate on checking out the main sequence of program statements.

**4. Facilitates program maintenance:** Subprograms that are well insulated from each other are easier to maintain (i.e., modify) after the program is put into production. This is because a change to one subprogram is less likely to have a "ricocheting" effect on the rest of the program.

An **argument** is a value passed to a procedure or built-in function. Nested procedures have been illustrated, so far, without arguments because the procedures were a part of the MAIN procedure. Because these procedures usually use data items declared in the main portion of the program, arguments are not explicitly passed to the nested procedure. With a structured approach to programming, however, there is a greater need for arguments to nested procedures. These arguments typically take the form of program switches used to indicate such things as successful completion of a nested procedure or perhaps a condition noted in the nested procedure that the calling procedure should know about. Of course, with separately compiled procedures, passing arguments that represent data as well as switches is essential because *arguments* are the data the subroutine manipulates.

## PROCEDURES

### Subroutine Procedures

A subroutine procedure is invoked by a CALL. Arguments are passed by means of an **argument list.** For example:

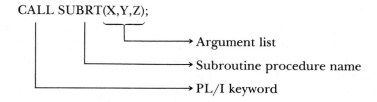

Subroutine procedures that are separately compiled from the invoking procedure are called **external procedures.** The length of these procedures' names is limited to seven or eight characters.

A STOP or an EXIT statement abnormally terminates execution of that subroutine and of the entire program associated with the procedure that invoked it. This applies to separately compiled subroutines as well as nested subroutine procedures. From a structured programming point of view, external subroutines should not terminate the entire program through either a STOP or an EXIT. The subroutine (or function) should return an error indicator to the calling program indicating whether or not an error has been detected during the execution of the subroutine. It is the MAIN program's function to decide what action is taken, terminating the program prematurely if necessary.

## Arguments and Parameters

Arguments passed to a called (invoked) procedure must be accepted by that procedure. This is done by the explicit declaration of one or more **parameters** in a parenthesized list in the PROCEDURE statement of the **invoked** procedure. Figure 4.1 shows the relationship between arguments and parameters.

The attributes of a parameter and its corresponding argument must be the same. If the attributes of an argument are not consistent with those of its corresponding parameter, an error will probably result, as no conversion is automatically performed. Here is an example of the coding steps necessary to provide consistent attributes for arguments and their corresponding parameters:

|                     | MAINPR:   PROCEDURE OPTIONS(MAIN);       |
|                     | DECLARE  X   FIXED DEC (7,2);            |
| Invoking procedure  | DECLARE  Y   FIXED DEC (7,2);            |
|                     | DECLARE  Z   FIXED DEC (8,2);            |
|                     | DECLARE SUBRT ENTRY;                     |
|                     | GET LIST (X,Y);                          |
|                     | CALL SUBRT(X,Y,Z);                       |
|                     | PUT LIST ('THE SUM IS ',Z);             |
|                     | END MAINPR;                              |

|                     | SUBRT: PROC (A,B,C)                      |
|                     | DCL A   FIXED DEC(7,2);                  |
| Invoked procedure   | DCL B   FIXED DEC(7,2);                  |
|                     | DCL C   FIXED DEC(8,2);                  |
|                     | C = A + B;                               |
|                     | END SUBRT;                               |

In the invoking procedure, the arguments X and Y are declared to have the FIXED DEC (7,2) attributes. In the invoked procedure, the corresponding parameters A and B are also declared to have the FIXED DEC (7,2) attributes. The

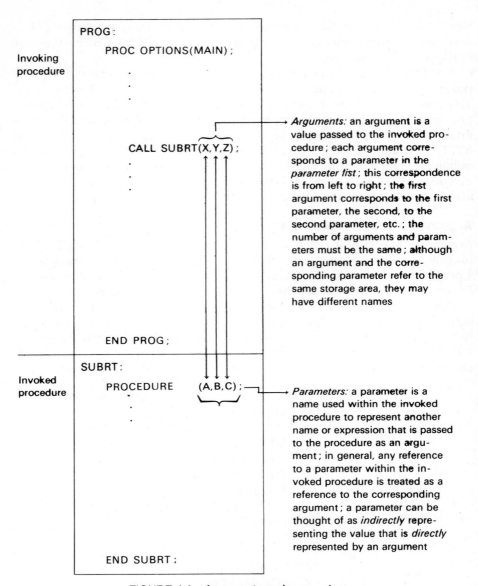

FIGURE 4.1   Arguments and parameters.

argument Z and the parameter C are given the FIXED DEC (8,2) attributes.   The preceding example illustrates a very simple, but complete, subroutine procedure.   The subroutine adds two values together and returns the sum through one of the subroutine's parameters, C.   Any change of value specified for a parameter in the invoked procedure actually is a change in the value of the argument in the invoking procedure. Such changes remain in effect when control is returned to the invoking procedure. Thus, in the preceding example, when the invoking procedure prints the value of Z, it is the sum of X and Y that is output.

In general, an argument and its corresponding parameter may be any data type. Arguments include:

Variable
Constant
Expression
Array name
Array expression
Major structure name
Minor structure name
Structure expression
Built-in function name
Entry name
File name
Label (not recommended for structured programming)

For arguments that are bit- or character-strings, the corresponding parameters may be expressed as asterisks. For example, in the calling program the statement

CALL CENTER_HEADING ('WEEKLY ACTIVITY REPORT',
    PRINT_LINE);

is coded. CENTER_HEADING is a subroutine procedure written as a generalized program to accept any heading in the form of a character-string and center it in the provided character-string variable. The subroutine procedure could be coded as follows:

```
/******************************************************************/
/*                                                                */
/*   THIS SUBROUTINE CENTERS A CHARACTER STRING IN A 133 CHARACTER */
/*   PRINT LINE USING THE FIRST POSITION FOR CARRIAGE CONTROL.    */
/*                                                                */
/******************************************************************/

CENTER_HEADING:  PROCEDURE(HEADING,OUTPUT_AREA);
    DECLARE   HEADING             CHAR(*);
    DECLARE   LENGTH_OF_STRING    FIXED BIN(15,0);
    DECLARE   OUTPUT_AREA         CHAR(133);
    DECLARE   START               FIXED BIN(15,0);

    DECLARE   LENGTH              BUILTIN;
    DECLARE   SUBSTR              BUILTIN;

    LENGTH_OF_STRING = LENGTH(HEADING);
    START            = (132 - LENGTH_OF_STRING)/2 + 1;
    OUTPUT_AREA      = '1';
    SUBSTR(OUTPUT_AREA,START,LENGTH_OF_STRING) = HEADING;

END CENTER_HEADING;
```

The identifier HEADING is a parameter; its length attribute is not declared because it is more convenient to determine the length of the argument *dynamically* (i.e., at execution time). Thus, the asterisk is specified in parentheses following the CHARACTER attribute.

The LENGTH built-in function is invoked to determine the length of the argument. This function is also useful in the manipulation of character- or bit-strings that have the VARYING attribute. Its general form is as follows:

I = LENGTH (string data item);

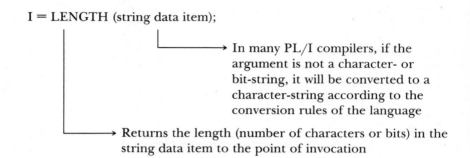

In many PL/I compilers, if the argument is not a character- or bit-string, it will be converted to a character-string according to the conversion rules of the language

Returns the length (number of characters or bits) in the string data item to the point of invocation

It is invalid to use the INITIAL attribute on parameters. For example, in the previous CENTER_HEADING subroutine, the following would be invalid:

DECLARE OUTPUT_AREA    CHAR (133) INIT (' ');

Because arguments come from the calling program, only executable statements (such as the assignment statement) may be used to manipulate arguments that correspond to parameters in the subprogram. The INITIAL attribute is not an executable statement.

## CHECKPOINT QUESTIONS

**1.** What is the difference between an argument and a parameter?

**2.** Assuming default attributes apply for I,J,K,A,B,C, is the following valid? Why or why not?

CALL SUBRT (I,J,K);
:
:
SUBRT: PROCEDURE (A,B,C);
.

**3.** In the declaration of parameters, what two types of identifiers may utilize asterisks? Of what value is the asterisk notation?

**4.** When a subroutine or function procedure encounters an unrecoverable error, what programming technique should be used in handling the error?

## A Sample Subroutine Procedure

Let us now examine a subroutine whose function is to prorate rent due from a tenant who moves into an apartment on a day other than the first. This is a typical property management requirement because it is easier for management to collect rent from all tenants on the first of every month. The function of this subroutine may be diagramed as follows:

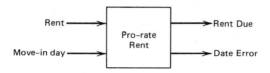

There are two arguments—rent amount and day of the month the tenant moves in. The computations for prorating rent assume an average of 30 days in a month to determine the rent per day. The subroutine returns two values—rent amount due and/or an error indication if the move-in day is out of normal range (i.e., more than 30). We can assume, for the purposes of this problem, that if the actual move-in day is the 31st of the month, it is the same rent as if the tenant moved in on the first day of the month. Here is the calling sequence for this subroutine. Notice how the statement immediately following the CALL tests the DATE_ERROR indicator:

```
CALL PRORATE(MONTHLY_RENT,DAY_IN,RENT_DUE,
    DATE_ERROR);
IF DATE_ERROR THEN
    PUT SKIP LIST ('INPUT DATE IS INVALID');
```

The arguments, whose names may or may not match those of the actual subroutine, have the following attributes:

```
DECLARE DATE_ERROR       BIT (1);
DECLARE DAY_IN           FIXED DECIMAL(2);
DECLARE MONTHLY_RENT     FIXED DECIMAL(5,2);
DECLARE RENT_DUE         FIXED DECIMAL(5,2);
```

Here is the subroutine that prorates monthly rent and tests for a valid move-in day:

```
/**********************************************************************/
/*                                                                    */
/*   PRORATE THE FIRST MONTHS RENT BASED ON THE MOVE IN DATE          */
/*                                                                    */
/**********************************************************************/

PRORATE:   PROCEDURE(RENT,MOVE_IN_DAY,RENT_DUE,DATE_ERROR);

     DECLARE   DATE_ERROR          BIT(1);
     DECLARE   DAYS_REMAINING      FIXED DECIMAL(2);
     DECLARE   MOVE_IN_DAY         FIXED DECIMAL(2);
     DECLARE   NO                  BIT(1)              INIT ('0'B);
     DECLARE   RENT                FIXED DECIMAL(5,2);
     DECLARE   RENT_DUE            FIXED DECIMAL(5,2);
     DECLARE   RENT_PER_DAY        FIXED DECIMAL(5,2);
     DECLARE   YES                 BIT(1)              INIT ('1'B);

     IF MOVE_IN_DAY > 31 THEN
        DATE_ERROR = YES;
     ELSE DO;
             DATE_ERROR     = NO;
             DAYS_REMAINING = 31 - MOVE_IN_DAY;
             RENT_PER_DAY   = RENT/30;
             IF MOVE_IN_DAY = 1 | MOVE_IN_DAY = 31 THEN
                RENT_DUE = RENT;
             ELSE
                RENT_DUE = DAYS_REMAINING * RENT_PER_DAY;
          END;

END PRORATE;
```

A number of important programming techniques are illustrated in the preceding example. First notice that the DAYS_REMAINING calculation involves subtracting MOVE_IN_DAY from 31 (not 30) even though the problem statement says to assume 30 days in every month. Do you see why? Apply some test data (e.g., MOVE_IN_DAY = 25) to the statement that calculates DAYS_REMAINING to test the algorithm.

Also observe the IF statement in which the OR operation is used. Because of the logical operators in PL/I, alternatives for testing can be methodically specified in a statement such as the IF. Notice how the variable names selected are descriptive of their functions.

### Built-in Function Arguments

Built-in functions may be specified as arguments to other subprograms. Built-in functions that are passed as arguments to a subroutine or a function procedure are handled differently depending on whether the functions themselves have arguments.

Built-in functions *with* arguments are invoked before the subroutine is called, so that it is the value from the function that is being passed. For example:

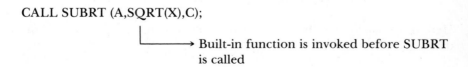

CALL SUBRT (A,SQRT(X),C);

→ Built-in function is invoked before SUBRT
  is called

Built-in functions *without* arguments will not be invoked before the subroutine is called. For example:

DCL DATE BUILTIN;
CALL SUBRT(A,DATE,C);

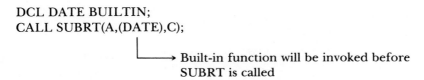
→ Function name will be passed to SUBRT

If you wish to have built-in functions without arguments invoked *before* the subprogram is invoked, specify an extra set of parentheses around the function name. For example:

DCL DATE BUILTIN;
CALL SUBRT(A,(DATE),C);

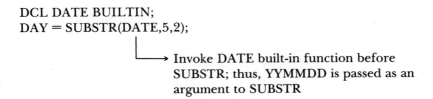
→ Built-in function will be invoked before
   SUBRT is called

Note, however, if the built-in function without arguments is part of the argument list to another built-in function, an extra set of parentheses is not needed. For example:

DCL DATE BUILTIN;
DAY = SUBSTR(DATE,5,2);

→ Invoke DATE built-in function before
   SUBSTR; thus, YYMMDD is passed as an
   argument to SUBSTR

## Dummy Arguments

In this discussion of arguments and parameters, it is important to understand that the name of an argument, not its value, is passed to a subroutine or function. However, there are times when an argument has no name. A constant, for example, has no name; nor does an operational expression or the results from a built-in function. As an illustration, the following arguments might be specified when invoking SUBRT:

CALL SUBRT (7.5,X−Y,Z);

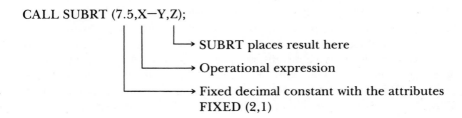
→ SUBRT places result here

→ Operational expression

→ Fixed decimal constant with the attributes
   FIXED (2,1)

Because the first two arguments to SUBRT do not have names, the compiler must select a name for the constant 7.5 and a name for the results of the arithmetic operation X—Y. For example:

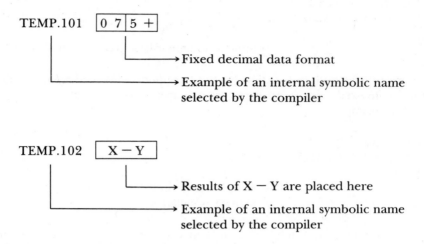

TEMP.101 | 0 7 | 5 + |

→ Fixed decimal data format

→ Example of an internal symbolic name selected by the compiler

TEMP.102 | X — Y |

→ Results of X — Y are placed here

→ Example of an internal symbolic name selected by the compiler

**Internal names** are called **dummy arguments.** They are not accessible to the PL/I programmer, but the programmer should be aware of their existence. If we substitute the internal names for the constant and the expression in the preceding CALL, we have, in effect, the following statement:

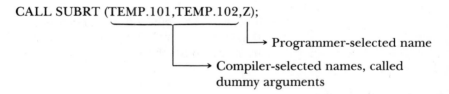

CALL SUBRT (TEMP.101,TEMP.102,Z);

→ Programmer-selected name

→ Compiler-selected names, called dummy arguments

Of course, you could not code the preceding statement, because internal names are not available to the PL/I programmer.

Recall the statement:

CALL SUBRT (7.5,X—Y,Z);

Recall, also, that in SUBRT, the first and second parameters had the attributes FIXED (7,2). We know that an argument must agree precisely with its corresponding parameter in terms of attributes. Previously, we saw that a dummy argument was created for the constant 7.5. When a dummy argument is created for an argument that is a constant, the attributes of the dummy argument will be those indicated by the constant. Thus, 7.5 will have the attributes FIXED (2,1). These attributes do not correspond to the attributes of the first parameter of SUBRT. This is an error, and incorrect results will be produced by SUBRT. One way to avoid the error is to declare an identifier to have the proper attributes and assign the constant to that identifier. For example:

```
DCL ARG1    FIXED DEC(7,2);
ARG1 = 7.5;
CALL SUBRT(ARG1,X—Y,Z);
```

Note, also, that argument expressions could cause the same kind of inconsistent attributes problem raised by specifying argument constants. This is because of the PL/I language rules governing arithmetic operations and conversion of data types.

When in doubt about the attributes of results from an expression, it would be wise to assign the results to an identifier having the desired attributes. For example:

```
DCL ARG1    FIXED DEC(7,2);
DCL ARG2    FIXED DEC(7,2);
ARG1 = 7.5;
ARG2 = X — Y
CALL SUBRT(ARG1,ARG2,Z);
```

Another method for ensuring consistent attributes and parameters is to use the ENTRY attribute. The general form is:

```
DCL identifier ENTRY (parameter attribute, parameter attribute . . . );
```

The ENTRY attribute allows you to direct the compiler to generate coding to convert one or more arguments to conform to the attribute of the corresponding parameters, should arguments and their corresponding parameters have different attributes.

As an example of how the ENTRY attribute is used to cause the conversion of arguments to match the attributes of their corresponding parameters, assume we are still working with the procedure called SUBRT, where its first two parameters must be FIXED (7,2) and the third parameter must be FIXED (8,2); that is:

```
SUBRT: PROCEDURE(A,B,C);
    DCL A               FIXED DECIMAL(7,2);
    DCL B               FIXED DECIMAL(7,2);
    DCL C               FIXED DECIMAL(8,2);
    C = A + B;
END SUBRT;
```

In the program that invokes SUBRT, assume that the first two arguments appear in floating-point format; the third argument has the same attribute as the third parameter. Here is a segment of coding from the invoking procedure:

```
DCL X   FLOAT DEC(6);
DCL Y   FLOAT DEC(6);
DCL Z   FIXED DEC(8,2);
GET LIST (X,Y);
CALL SUBRT (X,Y,Z);
```

The previous example will cause an error, because X and Y do not have the same attributes as their corresponding parameters. However, explicit declaration of SUBRT as an ENTRY solves this problem:

```
DCL SUBRT ENTRY
   (FIXED(7,2),FIXED(7,2),FIXED(8,2));
```

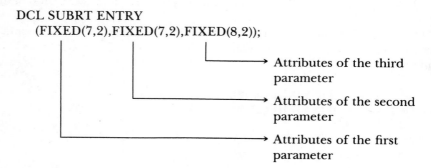

→ Attributes of the third parameter

→ Attributes of the second parameter

→ Attributes of the first parameter

The declaration tells the compiler that SUBRT is an **entry** name that has three parameters, as indicated by the attribute list in parentheses. This declaration causes the arguments specified in a CALL to SUBRT to be converted to the declared attributes that presumably match the parameter list of SUBRT. The conversion is done at the time the CALL is executed. If the attributes of a particular argument and parameter already match, then do not specify attributes for that argument in the ENTRY attribute. Rather, keep the parameter's place by a comma. For example, the third argument in the calling sequence matches the attributes of the third parameter. Thus, the following DECLARE should be specified:

```
DCL SUBRT ENTRY
   (FIXED DEC(7,2),FIXED DEC(7,2),);
```

└→ Because the attributes of the third parameter are not stated, no assumptions are made and no conversions are performed

Specifying a comma is particularly important if the argument is actually a result field. This is because the field has no value initially; hence, no conversion is to take place before the subroutine is called.

Another subtle problem with dummy arguments is illustrated by a simple subroutine procedure. A subroutine called ADD3 is designed to compute the total of three arguments and place the sum into the third argument (thereby destroying the original contents of the third argument). You have seen this subroutine before:

```
ADD3: PROCEDURE(A,B,C);
        DCL A          FIXED DEC(7,2);
        DCL B          FIXED DEC(7,2);
        DCL C          FIXED DEC(8,2);
        C = A + B + C;
END ADD3;
```

Assume that the invoking procedure has arguments in floating-point format. This means that the ENTRY attribute will be specified to direct the compiler to generate statements affecting the conversion of arguments to match the parameters of ADD3. The calling program's code would include the following:

```
DCL ADD3 ENTRY (FIXED DEC(7,2),FIXED DEC(7,2),
    FIXED DEC(8,2));
DCL X                  FLOAT DEC(6);
DCL Y                  FLOAT DEC(6);
DCL Z                  FLOAT DEC(6);
    .
    .
GET LIST (X,Y,Z);
CALL ADD3 (X,Y,Z);
```

Assume the GET statement causes the values 1.2, 3.45, and 67.89 to be assigned to the identifiers X,Y, and Z, respectively. The program's storage locations would contain the following:

X   `.12E+01`

Y   `.345E+01`

Z   `.6789E+02`

⟶ Floating-point data

⟶ Identifiers selected by the programmer

When the subroutine ADD3 is invoked, compiler-generated coding causes X and Y to be converted to FIXED(7,2) and Z to be converted to FIXED(8,2). The converted values (i.e., the FIXED DECIMAL equivalents of the DECIMAL FLOAT data) are not placed into the identifiers X, Y, or Z, but rather into new locations selected by the compiler. Internal symbolic names will be assigned to represent the new locations. For example:

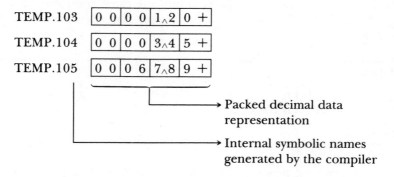

As previously stated, internal names are dummy arguments. To illustrate:

| *Original arguments* *(converted to →)* | | *Dummy arguments* | |
|---|---|---|---|
| X | .12E+01 | TEMP. 103 | 00 00 12 0+ |
| Y | .345E+01 | TEMP. 104 | 00 00 34 5+ |
| Z | .6789E+02 | TEMP. 105 | 00 07 25 4+ |

Recall that ADD3 specifies the statement:

$C = A + B + C;$

In the original example of arguments being associated with parameters, we saw that A indirectly represented X, B indirectly represented Y, and C indirectly represented Z. However, in the case of dummy arguments, A (in the preceding example) indirectly represents dummy argument TEMP.103, B indirectly represents dummy argument TEMP.104, and C indirectly represents dummy argument TEMP.105. In the subroutine, A, B, and C are added together. Using the data illustrated, the sum would be 72.54. The sum is assigned to C, which is associated with the dummy argument TEMP.105. Thus, it is the dummy argument that is modified to contain the result, rather than the original argument's location. When the invoking procedure executes the statement

PUT LIST ('THE SUM IS' , SUM);

the original floating-point value of Z (that is, 67.89) will be output, not the result (72.54) contained in the dummy argument. To avoid this error, if a subroutine is to modify a parameter, make sure an actual argument (*not* a dummy argument) of the identical attributes is passed to the subprogram. In other words, the type of function depicted for ADD3 is not really possible. Rather, the results should be placed in a fourth argument field by the subroutine procedure. In this way, the fourth parameter need not be a dummy argument. A dummy argument is always created in the following cases:

1. If an argument is a constant.
2. If an argument is an expression involving operators.
3. If an argument is an expression in parentheses.
4. If an argument is a variable whose data attributes are different from the data attributes declared for the parameter in an entry name attribute specification appearing in the invoking block.
5. If an argument is itself a function reference containing arguments.

In all other cases, the argument name is passed directly. The parameter becomes identical with the passed argument; thus, changes to the value of a parameter will be reflected in the value of the original argument only if a dummy argument is not passed.

## CHECKPOINT QUESTIONS

**5.** A subroutine requires the time of day as the first of three arguments. Write the CALL statement where the first argument is the TIME built-in function and the second and third arguments are called A and B. The subroutine procedure's name is COMPUTE.

**6.** In the following statement, which arguments will be dummy arguments?

CALL CALC ((DATE),100,SIN(X),A*B,C);

**7.** Given the following DECLARE for the preceding CALL, which of the arguments could be modified by the subroutine procedure for the purpose of passing results back to the calling program?

DCL CALC ENTRY (,FIXED (5),,FIXED (7),FIXED (9));

## A Subroutine Procedure Example

Figure 4.2 illustrates a subroutine procedure that calculates the Julian date, if given an argument in the form YYMMDD. To CALL this subroutine, the following statements could be coded:

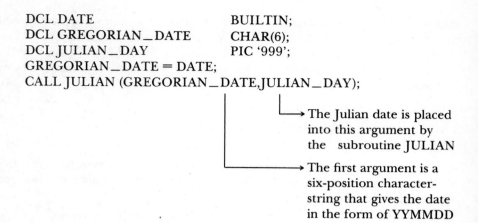

```
DCL DATE                  BUILTIN;
DCL GREGORIAN_DATE        CHAR(6);
DCL JULIAN_DAY            PIC '999';
GREGORIAN_DATE = DATE;
CALL JULIAN (GREGORIAN_DATE,JULIAN_DAY);
```

The Julian date is placed into this argument by the subroutine JULIAN

The first argument is a six-position character-string that gives the date in the form of YYMMDD

Following is a description of the statements in the subroutine in Figure 4.2.

**Statement 1:** Following the keyword PROCEDURE, the parameters are specified within parentheses. These parameters will be associated with the arguments passed from the calling program. Notice that the parameter DATE refers to a six-position character-string, not the built-in function. This is because the DATE function will actually be invoked before JULIAN is called. What is stored in the first parameter of JULIAN is the result returned from the DATE built-in function.

**Statements 2–7:** The attributes of data items are defined. DAYS_TABLE is a data aggregate called an **array.** It is a one-dimensional list of the number of days in each month of the year and may be pictured as follows:

```
 1 | 31 | (Jan.)
 2 | 28 | (Feb.)
 3 | 31 | (Mar.)
 4 | 30 | (etc.)
 5 | 31 |
 6 | 30 |
 7 | 31 |
 8 | 31 |
 9 | 30 |
10 | 31 |
11 | 30 |
12 | 31 |
```

Arrays are discussed in Chapter 6.

```
/**********************************************************************/
/*                                                                    */
/*      THIS PROCEDURE ACCEPTS A GREGORIAN DATE AND CALCULATES THE     */
/*      JULIAN DATE.   THE JULIAN DAY IS THEN RETURNED.                */
/*                                                                    */
/**********************************************************************/
 1   JULIAN:   PROCEDURE (DATE,DAY_IN_YEAR);

 2       DECLARE DATE                    CHAR (6);
 3       DECLARE DAY_IN_YEAR             PIC '999';
 4       DECLARE DAYS_TABLE(12)          FIXED DEC (3)
             INIT (31,28,31,30,31,30,31,31,30,31,30,31);
 5       DECLARE INDEX                   FIXED BIN(15,0);
 6       DECLARE MONTH                   PIC '99';
 7       DECLARE YEAR                    PIC '99';

 8       DECLARE MOD                     BUILTIN;

 9       YEAR        = SUBSTR(DATE,1,2);
10       MONTH       = SUBSTR(DATE,3,2);
11       DAY_IN_YEAR = SUBSTR(DATE,5,2);
12       IF MOD(YEAR,4) = 0 & YEAR ¬= 2000 THEN
             DAYS_TABLE(2) = 29;
13       IF MONTH ¬= 1 THEN
             DO INDEX = 1 TO MONTH - 1;
14               DAY_IN_YEAR = DAY_IN_YEAR + DAYS_TABLE(INDEX);
15           END;

16   END JULIAN;
```

FIGURE 4.2   A subroutine procedure.

**Statements 9 – 11:** The substring built-in function is used to retrieve the year, month, and day from the longer string called DATE.

**Statement 12:** February is set equal to 29 days for those years that are leap years. (A leap year is a year that is evenly divisible by 4 or 400.)

**Statements 13 – 15:** DAY_IN_YEAR is modified to contain the results of the calculation that gives the Julian date.

**Statement 16:** Return to the calling program.

## Function Procedures

A function is a procedure that returns a single value to the invoking procedure. A function is invoked in the same manner that PL/I built-in functions are referenced. For example, to invoke a function procedure whose name is CALC and has two arguments, the following could be coded:

Z=CALC(X,Y);

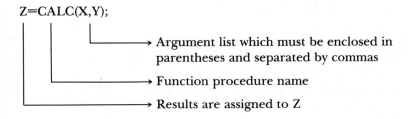

→ Argument list which must be enclosed in parentheses and separated by commas

→ Function procedure name

→ Results are assigned to Z

Here, CALC was invoked by reference in an assignment statement. It could appear in other types of PL/I statements such as a PUT LIST or an IF statement. For example:

    IF CALC (X,Y) < 0 THEN
        CALL NEGATIVE_RT;

Functions should not be invoked by a CALL, nor should subroutines be invoked by a function reference.

When a function is invoked, the arguments of the invoking statement are associated with the parameters of the entry point, and control is then passed to that entry point. The function is thus activated and execution begins.

The RETURN statement is used to terminate a function. Its use in a function differs somewhat from its use in a subroutine; in a function, not only does it return control, but it also returns the value to the point of invocation. For example:

    RETURN (element-expression);
           └──────────────→ The value returned to the invoking
                            procedure; it must be a single value

The RETURN statement, then, is always needed in a function subprogram.

We have seen how the programmer must be concerned with the attributes of arguments and those of the matching parameters. When writing a function, an additional consideration is that of the attributes of the value returned by the function. If the attributes of the value returned by the function are different from those expected by the invoking procedure, errors will result. As an example, consider the following function procedure:

    CALC: PROCEDURE(A,B,C);
        RETURN(A + B + C);
    END CALC;

When the previous function is invoked, for example,

    W = CALC (X,Y,Z);

the sum of the three arguments is calculated by CALC, and the result is returned to the point of invocation. The compiler must know the attributes of the result returned by a function so that the proper conversion instructions may be generated for the purpose of converting the result to the data format of the variable on the left of the assignment symbol (=). The attributes of returned values may be declared in two ways:

**1.** They may be declared by default according to the first letter of the function name. For example, if the function name begins with the letters A through H or O through Z, then the result will be DECIMAL FLOAT (6), because that is the default attribute of identifiers beginning with those letters. Function names beginning with the letters I through N return a result with the attributes FIXED BINARY (15). Thus, in invoking a function such as CALC, the following rules apply:

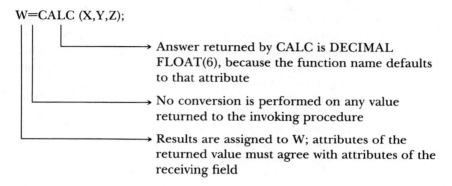

W=CALC (X,Y,Z);

→ Answer returned by CALC is DECIMAL FLOAT(6), because the function name defaults to that attribute

→ No conversion is performed on any value returned to the invoking procedure

→ Results are assigned to W; attributes of the returned value must agree with attributes of the receiving field

**2.** Because the default attributes for function names do not allow us to return a result that is FIXED DECIMAL or FLOAT DECIMAL (16), for example, we must have another method of specifying the attributes of a returned value. This is accomplished through the RETURNS keyword. The general form is:

RETURNS (attribute list)

This keyword will appear in both the invoking procedure and the invoked procedure. To illustrate, assume that CALC is to return a FIXED DECIMAL (7) result. The function procedure would be written as follows:

```
CALC: PROC(A,B,C) RETURNS(FIXED DECIMAL (7));
      RETURN(A + B + C);
END CALC;
```

The RETURNS keyword, when specified in a PROCEDURE or ENTRY statement, is referred to as *the RETURNS option.* In the example, the value returned by CALC will have the attributes FIXED and DECIMAL. The invoking procedure must also specify that CALC is returning a FIXED DECIMAL value of the same precision because these attributes differ from the attributes determined from the first letter of the function name. The *RETURNS attribute,* specified in a DECLARE statement for an entry name, indicates the attributes of the value returned by that function. For example, the following procedure invokes the CALC function:

```
MAINPR: PROCEDURE OPTIONS (MAIN);
    DCL CALC ENTRY RETURNS (FIXED DEC(7));
    DCL SUM                    FIXED DEC(7);
    GET LIST (A,B,C);
    SUM = CALC(A,B,C);
    .
    .
    .
END MAINPR:
```

In summary, then, it is important to understand that a function is written to compute a single value that is returned to the point of invocation. The value returned may not be an array or a structure. A subroutine, on the other hand, may return none, one, or many results to the invoking procedure through the modification of arguments in the subroutine CALL. A subroutine can alter an argument and thereby "return" an array or structure value. Thus, you would code a function when your program needs a single value to replace the function reference. Use a subroutine when no results are to be returned to the invoking procedure. Or, code a subroutine when results are to be placed in arrays or structures, or when more than one value is to be returned to the invoking procedure.

### Recursive Procedures

When a procedure invokes *itself*, it is said to be *recursive*. For an example of when this facility is useful, consider the computation of n factorial (n!) where

$$n! = 1 \times 2 \times 3 \times 4 \times \ldots \times n$$

One method for computing n! is to write a function procedure where the value of n is passed as an argument to the function. Here is the function reference:

```
I = 4;
RESULT = N_FACTORIAL(I);
```
$\llcorner\!\rightarrow$ Function reference with an argument
value of 4

The function procedure could be coded as follows:

```
N_FACTORIAL: PROCEDURE(N);
    K = 1;
    DO I = 1 TO N;
        K = K * I;
    END;
    RETURN(K);
END N_FACTORIAL;
```

Another method for coding this same function is to specify a *recursive* procedure. By affixing the RECURSIVE option to a PROCEDURE statement, you are specifying that this procedure should be capable of invoking or calling itself. Here is N_FACTORIAL coded as a recursive function procedure:

```
N_FACTORIAL: PROCEDURE (N) RECURSIVE;
    K = N − 1;
    IF K = 1 THEN
        I = N;
    ELSE
        I = N * N_FACTORIAL(K);
    RETURN(I);
END N_FACTORIAL;
```

└────→ Function reference to N_FACTORIAL within N_FACTORIAL

It is often difficult for the student of PL/I (and even experienced programmers) to understand initially the iterative process that is taking place in RECURSIVE procedures. One method is to visualize each step by drawing boxes representing the contents of variables in the procedure *for each invocation.* Figure 4.3 shows a visualization of the process in which it was desired to compute 4! where:

$$1 * 2 * 3 * 4 = 24$$

In this example, it is easier to compute n! by the nonrecursive method. Recursive

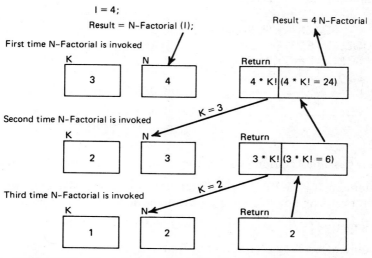

FIGURE 4.3   Steps to calculating 4! using recursion.

procedures can require considerable computer memory and program overhead. There are some cases, however, where recursion simplifies the programming task. This is the case with printing the *binary tree* illustrated in Chapter 10.

## CHECKPOINT QUESTIONS

**8.** How many values may be returned by the following?

(a) A function.
(b) A subroutine.

**9.** What is the difference between the RETURNS *attribute* and the RETURNS *option?*

**10.** Look up the keyword REENTRANT in the glossary of this text. Explain the difference between REENTRANT and RECURSIVE.

### A Function Procedure Example

Figure 4.4 illustrates a function procedure that converts 24-hour clock time (e.g., 1740 hours) to A.M. or P.M. time (e.g., 5:40 P.M.). No arguments are passed to this function procedure. The result from this function, which is called TIMEX, is a 14-position character-string,

> HH:MM AM    or    HH:MM PM or
> HH:MM Noon    or    HH:MM MIDNIGHT

where HH stands for hours and MM stands for minutes. To invoke this function, the following statements could be coded:

DCL TIMEX RETURNS(CHAR(14));
DCL TIMEOUT                 CHAR(14);
TIMEOUT = TIMEX;

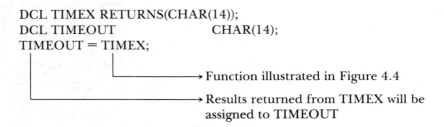

→ Function illustrated in Figure 4.4

→ Results returned from TIMEX will be assigned to TIMEOUT

Following is a description of the statements in the function procedure.

**Statement 1:** The PROCEDURE statement specifies the attributes of the result returned by this function through the RETURNS option.

**Statements 2 – 7:** Identifiers are declared.

**Statement 8:** TIME, as a built-in function, is invoked. Result is hours and minutes. The seconds and thousandths of seconds also returned by TIME are ignored by this subprogram.

```
/*   TRANSLATE MILITARY TIME TO A.M AND P.M                               */
/************************************************************************/
/*                                                                      */
/*    PROGRAM NAME:    TIMEX                                            */
/*                                                                      */
/*    DESCRIPTION:     THIS PROCEDURE TRANSLATES THE CURRENT TIME ON     */
/*                     THE COMPUTER CLOCK INTO A.M. AND P.M.             */
/*                                                                      */
/*    INPUT:           NONE                                             */
/*                                                                      */
/*    OUTPUT:          PRINTER                                          */
/*                                                                      */
/************************************************************************/
     1    TIMEX:  PROC RETURNS(CHAR(14));
     2        DCL CONVERTED_TIME                CHAR(14) INIT('   :');
     3        DCL CURRENT_TIME                  PIC'(9)9';
     4        DCL HOURS                         PIC'Z9';
     5        DCL MINUTES                       PIC'99';
     6        DCL SUBSTR                        BUILTIN;
     7        DCL TIME                          BUILTIN;

     8        CURRENT_TIME = TIME;
     9        HOURS       = SUBSTR(CURRENT_TIME,1,2);
    10        MINUTES     = SUBSTR(CURRENT_TIME,3,2);

    11        IF HOURS > 0 & HOURS < 12 THEN
                  SUBSTR(CONVERTED_TIME,7,2) = 'AM';
    12        ELSE
                  IF HOURS > 12 & HOURS < 24 THEN
                      DO;
    13                    SUBSTR(CONVERTED_TIME,7,2) = 'PM';
    14                    HOURS = HOURS - 12;
    15                END;
    16            ELSE
                      IF HOURS = 0 | HOURS = 24 THEN
                          DO;
    17                        IF MINUTES = 0 THEN
                                  SUBSTR(CONVERTED_TIME,7,8) = 'MIDNIGHT';
    18                        ELSE
                                  SUBSTR(CONVERTED_TIME,7,2) = 'AM';
    19                        HOURS = 12;

    20                    END;
    21                ELSE
                          IF HOURS = 12 THEN
                              IF MINUTES = 0 THEN
                                  SUBSTR(CONVERTED_TIME,7,4) = 'NOON';
    22                        ELSE
                                  SUBSTR(CONVERTED_TIME,7,2) = 'PM';

    23        SUBSTR(CONVERTED_TIME,1,2) = HOURS;
    24        SUBSTR(CONVERTED_TIME,4,2) = MINUTES;

    25        RETURN(CONVERTED_TIME);

    26    END TIMEX;
```

**FIGURE 4.4**

**Statements 9 – 10:** Hours and minutes are extracted from CURRENT_
TIME.

**Statements 11 – 22:** These statements test the hours value so that the 24-hour
time format returned by the TIME built-in function may be converted to the
morning and afternoon time designation.

**Statements 23–24:** Hours and minutes are moved to the output area containing the results.

**Statement 25:** This statement causes a return to the invoking procedure, with the results specified in parentheses following the keyword RETURN.

## SCOPE OF IDENTIFIERS

In PL/I, an identifier may have only one meaning at any point in time. For example, the same name cannot be used for both a file and a floating-point variable. It is not necessary, however, for a name to have the same meaning throughout a program. Because it is possible for a name to have more than one meaning, it is important to define to which part of the program a particular meaning applies. In PL/I, a name is given attributes and a meaning by a declaration that is not necessarily explicit. The part of the program for which the meaning applies is called the **scope of the declaration** of that name. Generally, the scope of a name is determined entirely by the position at which the name is declared within the program (or assumed to be declared if the declaration is not explicit).

Consider the following nested blocks:

```
P1: PROCEDURE;
    DECLARE X    CHAR(2);
    DECLARE Y    CHAR(2);
    DECLARE Z    CHAR(2);
    .
    .
    .
    CALL P2;
P2: PROCEDURE;
    DECLARE A    FIXED DEC(6);
    DECLARE B    FIXED DEC(6);
    DECLARE C    FIXED DEC(6);
    .
    .
    .
    END P2;
    END P1;
```

Because of the way in which storage is allocated, a name declared within a block has a meaning only within that block or blocks nested within it. In the above example, here is how the scope of identifiers is affected:

Activate P1:          Storage is allocated for X, Y, and Z. At this point, the variables A, B, and C are not known to P1 because storage has not yet been allocated.

Activate P2:          Storage is allocated for A, B, and C. P2 can manipulate not only A, B, and C but also X, Y, and Z, because the P1 procedure is still active.

Deactivate P2:     When there is an exit from P2, the storage for A, B, and C is released.  Do you see how A, B, and C can be known only within the P2 block?

Here is an example of how the scope of an identifier may be limited to a given block.  Had the nested blocks been specified, A, B, and C in the outer block would refer to different data items than do A, B, or C in the inner block.  In some instances, the use of nested blocks to limit or redefine the scope of a variable provides an ease of programming not usually available in other computer languages.  For example, assume a programmer has coded a problem in which the variable name DATE is used to represent a FIXED DECIMAL value. This data name is used a number of times in the program.  Later, it is decided to have the date printed with the output from this program.  The appropriate coding that invokes the DATE built-in function and prints the date edited with slashes can be easily inserted.  However, there is one problem: the programmer has already used the identifier DATE to mean something else, so it cannot be used to refer to the DATE built-in function at the same time.  One solution to this problem is to create a nested block that *limits the scope* of a variable.  For example:

```
P1: PROCEDURE OPTIONS (MAIN);
    DECLARE DATE      FIXED DEC(3);
    DECLARE TODAY     CHAR(6);
    DATE = 302;
    CALL P2;
    .
    .
    .
P2: PROCEDURE;
    DECLARE DATE BUILTIN;
    TODAY = DATE;
    END P2;
    END P1;
```

In this example, DATE is declared in the outer block to be FIXED DECIMAL (3) and is initialized to the value 302.  Also, TODAY is declared to be a character-string of length six.  When it is desired to invoke the DATE function, a nested block is created.  Within this block, DATE is declared to have the BUILTIN attribute; thus, the scope of the identifier, DATE is being redefined — actually, its scope is being *limited* to the internal block.  The value returned from the DATE function is a character-string that is assigned to TODAY.  Notice that TODAY is declared outside the nested block, but may be referenced by statements within the nested block.  An analogy that might be drawn regarding the scope of identifiers is to think of the declaration as a "one-way looking glass."  Inner blocks can "see out," but the outer blocks cannot "see in."  In other words, within the block, any variable declared inside of it is known only to that block or any other block nested within it.  However, identifiers declared outside the block are known to the inner block, providing that a "redefinition" of the variable name is not specified in the nested block.  This, of course, is the case with the identifier DATE.

## Scope of an Explicit Declaration

The scope of an explicit declaration of a name is that block to which the declaration is internal. This includes all nested blocks *except* those blocks (and any blocks contained within them) to which another explicit declaration of the same identifier is internal. For example:

```
P1: PROC;
      DCL A        FIXED DEC(6);
      DCL B        FIXED DEC(6);
      .
      .
  P2: PROC;
      DCL B        CHAR(8);
      DCL C        CHAR(8);
      .
      .
  P3: PROC:
      DCL C        FIXED BIN(15);
      DCL D        FIXED BIN(15);
      X = C * D;
      .
      .
      END P3;
      END P2;
      END P1;
```

The lines to the right indicate the scope of the names: B and B′ indicate the two distinct uses of the name B; C and C′ indicate the two uses of the name C.

The scope of a contextual declaration is determined as if the declaration were made in a DECLARE statement immediately following the PROCEDURE statement of the **external** procedure in which the name appears.

It is important to understand that contextual declaration has the same effect as if the name were declared in the *external* procedure. This is the case even if the statement that causes the contextual declaration is internal to a block (called P3, for example) that is contained in the external procedure. Consequently, the name is known throughout the entire external procedure, except for any blocks in which the name is explicitly declared. It is as if block P3 has inherited the declaration from the containing external procedure.

## CHECKPOINT QUESTIONS

**11.** True or false? In the following example, P refers to two different variables:

```
A: PROC;
   DCL P    FIXED DEC(6);
   .
   .
```

```
B: PROC;
DCL P    CHAR(20);
.
.
END B;
END A;
```

**12.** In the following nested procedures, is Y an *implicit* or *explicit* declaration? Name the procedures in which Y is known.

```
P1: PROC;
     DCL A      FIXED DEC(6);
     DCL B      FIXED DEC(6);
     .
     .
  P2: PROC;
       .
       .
  P3: PROC;
       DCL A      FLOAT DEC(6);
       DCL B      FLOAT DEC(6);
       Y = A * B;
       .
       .
     END P3;
   END P2;
 END P1;
```

## MODULE DESIGN

Now that subroutine and function procedures have been presented, we must take another look at module design. Subprograms make up the modules in a program or system of programs.

Simplicity is the primary measurement of good modules. And, it is the relationship of data between modules that affects simplicity. For example, the fewer the number of arguments passed to a subroutine, the better. Rather than pass an entire record as an argument to another procedure, pass only the needed fields. In this way, should it be necessary to change the record layout later, there is a chance that only the invoking module will have to be changed and not the module receiving a few selected fields. To state it in the reverse, if two modules both worked with the same record, a change to the record's layout would require modification in both modules. Each module should have its own set of variables and be as independent from other modules as possible.

A technique in widespread use is establishing **common** data areas called **global** variables. Variables common to a number of modules are placed in a *data pool*.

This approach has been observed as complicating modules and could result in disastrous "rippling" effects, where changes in one part give rise to new errors in another part, which necessitate changes elsewhere, etc. Consider, for example, three modules that are interrelated:

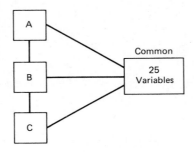

Module A calls module B, which calls module C. Because there are three modules, increased complexity results due to the number of possible paths along which errors can propagate. The formula may be expressed as N elements shared by M modules times (M − 1):

$$N*M \ (M-1) = 25 * 3 * 2 = 150$$

Thus, for three modules sharing a common pool of 25 variables, there are 150 possible relationships in which something could go wrong!

PL/I does offer the common data pool facility just described. By giving identifiers the EXTERNAL attribute, data items are then placed in a common data area *external* to the module in which the identifier was declared and is known *by name*. EXTERNAL as an attribute tells the compiler that this variable is known outside this procedure and will be referenced by the same name. It is the responsibility of the other procedures using the same external data item to declare it with the identical name and attributes. The preciseness with which these EXTERNAL variables must be declared makes the language feature less than desirable — simply because of implementation and program maintenance problems.

When arguments such as switches are passed, it is best if the switch can be a bit. Thus, only two alternatives are possible for the state of this switch, thereby reducing the number of test data sets required to test the module fully. A called module should never tell the invoking module what to do. It can pass an indicator back, but then let the higher level module make the decision and take the action. Thus, passing the name of a subroutine or function as an argument to another procedure is to be avoided. For example:

        DECLARE ERROR ENTRY;
        CALL SUBRT (A,B,C,ERROR); /* POOR DESIGN */

Here the implication is that SUBRT will invoke the ERROR routine should it need to. This is a form of telling another module what to do.

A proper program may only have one entry point. It is better to code near duplicate modules than to define a module with multiple entries. In other words, eliminate duplicate functions but not duplicate codes.

Subroutine or function procedure size can be a means of limiting module complexity. Modules that contain five or fewer statements are probably too small, just as procedures that contain more than 100 statements are probably too large. Small procedures can be eliminated by placing their statements in the invoking procedures. Large modules probably have more than one function and should be divided. A problem with the large module is not only maintainability but also readability. About 30 to 50 executable statements can be comfortably mastered in the first reading of a procedure listing.

## CASE STUDY

This chapter introduced you to subroutines and functions as a means of achieving modularity in your structured programs. The procedures, in which arguments are passed to them, are typically kept in libraries on a disk and linked to a PL/I program when needed. In addition, procedures may also be coded within a PL/I program that represent subfunctions of the program's main function. The case study for this chapter illustrates both types of requirements.

Assume a program is to calculate a loan payment given the loan amount, number of years of amortization, interest rate, and loan payback period. After the monthly loan payment is determined, produce an amortization schedule showing the reduction of principal on the loan amount as well as the interest paid by month and by year. The program logic takes into consideration that the loan could begin in any month of the first year. Note that the loan amortization period (the number of years required to pay the loan in full) and the loan payback period may be different. Figure 4.5 shows sample output for this problem. Figure 4.6 shows a hierarchy chart for the program solution and Figures 4.7 through 4.11 show the PL/I solution. Here are some comments about the program statements:

**Statement 2:** Declares the external procedure as well as the attributes of the sending and receiving arguments.

**Statements 3 – 26:** All declare statements are specified.

**Statements 27 – 33:** The program nucleus is always the first module.

**Statement 27:** Reads the data that is used to create the amortization schedule.

**Statements 28 – 29:** The validate input module is called. The validate input procedure sets the error indicator ON if there are any errors. This indicator is tested in *Statement 29* and either an error message is printed or CALLS to other modules that produce the loan amortization schedule are invoked. The procedures are listed in alphabetic order in this program, which is not necessarily their logical order.

**Statements 34 – 40:** CALCULATE_NEXT-PAYMENT_DATE procedure. This procedure calculates the next payment date. It is assumed that

| NO | PAYMENT DATE | INTEREST | PRINCIPAL | PRINCIPAL BALANCE AFTER PAYMENT |
|----|----|----|----|----|
| 0 | 01-01-88 | 0.00 | 0.00 | 3000.00 |
| 1 | 02-01-88 | 31.25 | 36.24 | 2963.76 |
| 2 | 03-01-88 | 30.87 | 36.62 | 2927.14 |
| 3 | 04-01-88 | 30.49 | 37.00 | 2890.14 |
| 4 | 05-01-88 | 30.10 | 37.39 | 2852.75 |
| 5 | 06-01-88 | 29.71 | 37.78 | 2814.97 |
| 6 | 07-01-88 | 29.32 | 38.17 | 2776.80 |
| 7 | 08-01-88 | 28.92 | 38.57 | 2738.23 |
| 8 | 09-01-88 | 28.52 | 38.97 | 2699.26 |
| 9 | 10-01-88 | 28.12 | 39.37 | 2659.89 |
| 10 | 11-01-88 | 27.71 | 39.78 | 2620.11 |
| 11 | 12-01-88 | 27.29 | 40.20 | 2579.91 |
| | TOTALS FOR THIS YEAR: | 322.30 | 420.09 | |
| 12 | 01-01-89 | 26.87 | 40.62 | 2539.29 |
| 13 | 02-01-89 | 26.45 | 41.04 | 2498.25 |
| 14 | 03-01-89 | 26.02 | 41.47 | 2456.78 |
| 15 | 04-01-89 | 25.59 | 41.90 | 2414.88 |
| 16 | 05-01-89 | 25.15 | 42.34 | 2372.54 |
| 17 | 06-01-89 | 24.71 | 42.78 | 2329.76 |
| 18 | 07-01-89 | 24.27 | 43.22 | 2286.54 |
| 19 | 08-01-89 | 23.82 | 43.67 | 2242.87 |
| 20 | 09-01-89 | 23.36 | 44.13 | 2198.74 |
| 21 | 10-01-89 | 22.90 | 44.59 | 2154.15 |
| 22 | 11-01-89 | 22.44 | 45.05 | 2109.10 |
| 23 | 12-01-89 | 21.97 | 45.52 | 2063.58 |
| | TOTALS FOR THIS YEAR: | 293.55 | 516.33 | |
| 24 | 01-01-90 | 21.49 | 46.00 | 2017.58 |
| 25 | 02-01-90 | 21.02 | 46.47 | 1971.11 |
| 26 | 03-01-90 | 20.53 | 46.96 | 1924.15 |
| 27 | 04-01-90 | 20.04 | 47.45 | 1876.70 |
| 28 | 05-01-90 | 19.55 | 47.94 | 1828.76 |
| 29 | 06-01-90 | 19.05 | 48.44 | 1780.32 |
| 30 | 07-01-90 | 18.54 | 48.95 | 1731.37 |
| 31 | 08-01-90 | 18.03 | 49.46 | 1681.91 |
| 32 | 09-01-90 | 17.52 | 49.97 | 1631.94 |
| 33 | 10-01-90 | 17.00 | 50.49 | 1581.45 |
| 34 | 11-01-90 | 16.47 | 51.02 | 1530.43 |
| 35 | 12-01-90 | 15.94 | 51.55 | 1478.88 |
| | TOTALS FOR THIS YEAR: | 225.18 | 584.70 | |

FIGURE 4.5   Sample output—Loan amortization schedule.

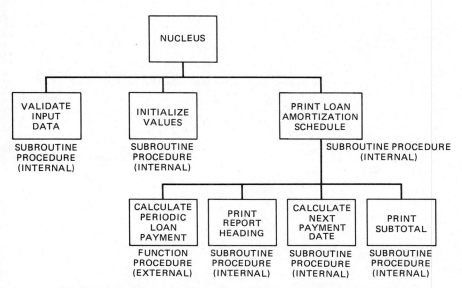

FIGURE 4.6   Hierarchy chart of modules in amortization program.

the payments are due on the first of the month.   The month number is incremented.   If the month is greater than 12 *(Statement 36)* the month is reset to 1 and the year is incremented.

**Statements 41 – 55:** The initialization procedure sets the necessary numeric variables such as total and subtotal amounts to zero.   Other variables such as MONTH, YEAR, and BALANCE are initialized to the validated input data.

**Statements 56 – 63:** PRINT_HEADING procedure.

**Statement 57:** Increments page number so that the first page printed is 1.

**Statement 62:** YEARS_PRINTED is set to 0.   The YEARS_PRINTED variable is a counter that keeps track of the number of years printed on each page of the loan schedule.   Only three years can be fully reported on one page.   When the YEARS_PRINTED variable is 3, a new page is started and a new heading is printed.

**Statements 64 – 95:** PRINT_LOAN_SCHEDULE procedure.

**Statement 66:** Prints first line for payment 0.

**Statement 67:** Invokes the function REMIT, which returns the monthly payment.

**Statement 68:** Divides the annual interest rate by 12 to obtain the monthly interest rate.

```
/* CHAPTER 4 CASE STUDY: LOAN AMORTIZATION SCHEDULE                         */
/***************************************************************************/
/*    PROGRAM NAME:    PAYLOAN                                             */
/*    DESCRIPTION:     THIS PROGRAM CALCULATES A LOAN AMORTIZATION TABLE  */
/*                     AND PAYMENT SCHEDULE BASED ON THE TERM IN YEARS    */
/*                     OF THE LOAN, THE ANNUAL INTEREST RATE, THE LOAN    */
/*                     AMOUNT AND THE STARTING MONTH AND YEAR.  TWELVE    */
/*                     PAYMENTS ARE MADE PER YEAR.  EACH PAYMENT IS DUE   */
/*                     ON THE FIRST DAY OF EVERY MONTH.                   */
/*                     A SUBTOTAL LINE IS PRINTED AT THE END OF EACH      */
/*                     YEAR SHOWING THE YEAR-TO-DATE AMOUNTS PAID FOR     */
/*                     INTEREST AND TOWARDS THE PRINCIPAL.  A SUMMARY IS  */
/*                     PRINTED AFTER THE PAYMENT SCHEDULE.                */
/*    INPUT:           SYSTEM INPUT                                       */
/*    OUTPUT:          LOAN AMORTIZATION SCHEDULE ON THE PRINTER          */
/***************************************************************************/
1  PAYLOAN:  PROC OPTIONS (MAIN);
2     DCL REMIT ENTRY (FIXED DEC(5,2),FIXED DEC(9,2),FIXED DEC(3),
                       FIXED DEC(3)) RETURNS(FIXED DEC(7,2));
3     DCL ANNUAL_INTEREST_RATE        FIXED DEC (5,2);
4     DCL BALANCE                     FIXED DEC (9,2);
5     DCL ERROR                       BIT(1)           INIT ('0'B);
6     DCL INTEREST_PAYMENT            FIXED DEC (7,2);
7     DCL INTEREST_SUBTOTAL           FIXED DEC (7,2);
8     DCL INTEREST_TOTAL              FIXED DEC (7,2);
9     DCL LAST_PAYMENT                FIXED DEC (7,2);
10    DCL MONTH                       PIC '99';
11    DCL MONTHLY_INTEREST_RATE       FIXED DEC (7,4);
12    DCL MONTHLY_PAYMENT             FIXED DEC (7,2);
13    DCL PAGE#                       FIXED DEC (2)    INIT (0);
14    DCL PAYMENT_NO                  FIXED DEC (3);
15    DCL PAYMENTS_PER_YEAR           FIXED DEC (3);
16    DCL PRINCIPAL                   FIXED DEC (9,2);
17    DCL PRINCIPAL_PAYMENT           FIXED DEC (7,2);
18    DCL PRINCIPAL_PAYMENT_SUBTOTAL  FIXED DEC (7,2);
19    DCL PRINCIPAL_PAYMENT_TOTAL     FIXED DEC (7,2);
20    DCL RUN_DATE                    CHAR (8);
21    DCL START_DATE                  PIC '9999';
22    DCL TERM_IN_YEARS               FIXED DEC (3);
23    DCL YEAR                        PIC '99';
24    DCL YEARS_PRINTED               FIXED DEC (1);
25    DCL YES                         BIT(1)           INIT ('1'B);
26    DCL (DATE,SUBSTR,TRANSLATE)  BUILTIN:

   /***************************************************************************/
   /*   PROGRAM NUCLEUS                                                       */
   /***************************************************************************/
27 GET (TERM_IN_YEARS, PRINCIPAL, ANNUAL_INTEREST_RATE, START_DATE);
28 CALL VALIDATE_INPUT;
29 IF ERROR THEN
      PUT SKIP LIST ('INPUT ERRORS ------- PROGRAM TERMINATED');
30 ELSE
      DO;
31       CALL INITIALIZATION;
32       CALL PRINT_LOAN_SCHEDULE;
33    END;
   /***************************************************************************/
   /*   CALCULATE NEXT PAYMENT DATE MONTH AND YEAR                           */
   /***************************************************************************/
34    CALCULATE_NEXT_PAYMENT_DATE:  PROC;
35       MONTH = MONTH + 1;
36       IF MONTH > 12 THEN
            DO;
37             MONTH = 1;
38             YEAR  = YEAR + 1;
39          END;
40    END CALCULATE_NEXT_PAYMENT_DATE;
```

FIGURE 4.7

```
/***********************************************************************/
/*    INITIALIZE PROGRAM VALUES                                        */
/***********************************************************************/
41   INITIALIZATION: PROC;
42      RUN_DATE = TRANSLATE('MO/DA/YR',DATE,'YRMODA');
43      INTEREST_SUBTOTAL          = 0;
44      INTEREST_TOTAL             = 0;
45      PRINCIPAL_PAYMENT_SUBTOTAL = 0;
46      PRINCIPAL_PAYMENT_TOTAL    = 0;
47      MONTH                      = SUBSTR(START_DATE,1,2);
48      YEAR                       = SUBSTR(START_DATE,3,2);
49      PAYMENT_NO                 = 0;
50      PAYMENTS_PER_YEAR          = 12;
51      YEARS_PRINTED              = 0;
52      INTEREST_PAYMENT           = 0;
53      PRINCIPAL_PAYMENT          = 0;
54      BALANCE                    = PRINCIPAL;
55   END INITIALIZATION;
     /***********************************************************************/
     /*    PRINT HEADING                                                    */
     /***********************************************************************/
56   PRINT_HEADING:  PROC;
57      PAGE# = PAGE# + 1;
58      PUT PAGE       LIST (RUN_DATE,
                               'LOAN AMORTIZATION SCHEDULE',' ',
                       PAGE '|| PAGE#);
59      PUT SKIP (2) LIST(' ',' PAYMENT',' ',' ','PRINCIPAL BALANCE');
60      PUT SKIP      LIST('     NO',' DATE ','   INTEREST','   PRINCIPAL',
                       ' AFTER PAYMENT');
61      PUT SKIP      LIST(' ');
62      YEARS_PRINTED = 0;
63   END PRINT_HEADING;
```

FIGURE 4.8

**Statements 69–79:** DO-LOOP to print the load schedule is provided where each iteration of the do-loop prints one payment line on the report.

**Statement 72:** Tests if PAYMENT MONTH = 1 and calls the PRINT_SUBTOTAL procedure. Subtotals at the end of a calendar year are printed on each page.

**Statements 73–77:** Calculates the amounts to be placed in the fields on the report line and adds the calculated interest and principal to the subtotal amounts.

**Statements 80–89:** Calculates and prints the last payment.

**Statements 91–94:** Prints the final totals and summary.

**Statements 96–105:** PRINT_SUBTOTAL procedure.

**Statements 97–98:** Adds subtotal amounts to TOTAL.

**Statements 101–102:** Sets subtotals back to zero.

**Statements 103–104:** Increments YEARS_PRINTED tests. If three years have been printed, then a call is made to the PRINT_HEADING subroutine to start a new page.

```
/**************************************************************************/
/*   PRINT LOAN SCHEDULE                                                  */
/*   THIS PROCEDURE FIRST CALLS AN EXTERNAL FUNCTION TO OBTAIN THE        */
/*   MONTHLY PAYMENTS FOR THE PRINCIPAL LOAN AMOUNT, ANNUAL INTEREST      */
/*   RATE AND TERM IN YEARS OF THE LOAN, AND NUMBER OF PAYMENT PER        */
/*   YEAR.  THE AMOUNT OF THE MONTHLY PAYMENT PAID TOWARD THE             */
/*   INTEREST IS CALCULATED BY MULTIPLYING THE MONTHLY INTEREST RATE      */
/*   TIMES THE UNPAID BALANCE OF THE LOAN.  THE MONTHLY PAYMENT MINUS     */
/*   THE INTEREST PAYMENT IS APPLIED TOWARD THE PRINCIPAL.                */
/*   THIS PROCESS IS REPEATED UNTIL THE BALANCE LEFT ON THE LOAN IS       */
/*   LESS THAN THE MONTHLY PAYMENT.  AT THIS POINT, THE LAST PAYMENT      */
/*   IS CALCULATED.                                                       */
/**************************************************************************/
64    PRINT_LOAN_SCHEDULE:  PROC;
65       CALL PRINT_HEADING;
66       PUT SKIP LIST (PAYMENT_NO,MONTH || '-01-' || YEAR.
                  INTEREST_PAYMENT,PRINCIPAL_PAYMENT,BALANCE);
67       MONTHLY_PAYMENT = REMIT(ANNUAL_INTEREST_RATE,PRINCIPAL,
                           PAYMENTS_PER_YEAR,TERM_IN_YEARS);
68       MONTHLY_INTEREST_RATE = ANNUAL_INTEREST_RATE / 12;

69       DO WHILE (BALANCE > MONTHLY_PAYMENT);
70          PAYMENT_NO     = PAYMENT_NO + 1;
71          CALL CALCULATE_NEXT_PAYMENT_DATE;
72          IF MONTH = 1 THEN
                  CALL PRINT_SUBTOTAL;
73          INTEREST_PAYMENT   = BALANCE * MONTHLY_INTEREST_RATE /100 + .005;
74          INTEREST_SUBTOTAL = INTEREST_SUBTOTAL + INTEREST_PAYMENT;
75          PRINCIPAL_PAYMENT = MONTHLY_PAYMENT - INTEREST_PAYMENT;
76          PRINCIPAL_PAYMENT_SUBTOTAL
                     = PRINCIPAL_PAYMENT_SUBTOTAL + PRINCIPAL_PAYMENT;
77          BALANCE           = BALANCE - PRINCIPAL_PAYMENT;
78          PUT SKIP LIST (PAYMENT_NO,MONTH || '-01-' || YEAR,
                  INTEREST_PAYMENT,PRINCIPAL_PAYMENT,BALANCE);
79       END;

80       PAYMENT_NO = PAYMENT_NO + 1;
81       CALL CALCULATE_NEXT_PAYMENT_DATE;
82       IF MONTH = 1 THEN
                  CALL PRINT_SUBTOTAL;
83       INTEREST_PAYMENT   = BALANCE * MONTHLY_INTEREST_RATE / 100 + .005;
84       INTEREST_SUBTOTAL = INTEREST_SUBTOTAL + INTEREST_PAYMENT;
85       PRINCIPAL_PAYMENT = BALANCE;
86       PRINCIPAL_PAYMENT_SUBTOTAL = PRINCIPAL_PAYMENT_SUBTOTAL +
                  PRINCIPAL_PAYMENT;
87       LAST_PAYMENT       = INTEREST_PAYMENT + PRINCIPAL_PAYMENT;
88       BALANCE            = 0;
89       PUT SKIP     LIST (PAYMENT_NO,MONTH || '-01-' || YEAR,
                  INTEREST_PAYMENT,PRINCIPAL_PAYMENT,BALANCE);
90       CALL PRINT_SUBTOTAL;
91       PUT SKIP (2) LIST (' ','SUMMARY:  ');
92       PUT SKIP (2) LIST (' ','    TOTAL INTEREST PAID',INTEREST_TOTAL);
93       PUT SKIP (2) LIST (' ','    MONTHLY PAYMENTS ARE',MONTHLY_PAYMENT);
94       PUT SKIP (2) LIST (' ','    THE LAST PAYMENT SHOULD BE',
                  LAST_PAYMENT);
95    END PRINT_LOAN_SCHEDULE;
```

**FIGURE 4.9**

```
/***************************************************************************/
/*   PRINT SUBTOTAL                                                        */
/*   A SUBTOTAL OF THE YEAR-TO-DATE INTEREST AND PRINCIPAL PAYMENTS        */
/*   IS PRINTED.   THE SUBTOTAL AMOUNTS ARE THEN SET TO 0.   AFTER         */
/*   PAYMENTS FOR THREE YEARS ARE DISPLAYED ON A PAGE, A CALL IS MADE      */
/*   TO THE PRINT_HEADING PROCEDURE.                                       */
/***************************************************************************/
96   PRINT_SUBTOTAL:   PROC;
97      INTEREST_TOTAL            = INTEREST_TOTAL + INTEREST_SUBTOTAL;
98      PRINCIPAL_PAYMENT_TOTAL   = PRINCIPAL_PAYMENT_TOTAL +
            PRINCIPAL_PAYMENT_SUBTOTAL;
99      PUT SKIP(2) LIST (' ','TOTALS FOR THIS YEAR:',
            INTEREST_SUBTOTAL,PRINCIPAL_PAYMENT_SUBTOTAL);
100     PUT SKIP LIST (' ');
101     INTEREST_SUBTOTAL         = 0;
102     PRINCIPAL_PAYMENT_SUBTOTAL = 0;
103     YEARS_PRINTED   = YEARS_PRINTED + 1;
104     IF YEARS_PRINTED = 3 THEN
            CALL PRINT_HEADING;
105  END PRINT_SUBTOTAL;


/***************************************************************************/
/*   VALIDATE INPUT                                                        */
/***************************************************************************/
106  VALIDATE_INPUT:   PROC;
107     IF TERM_IN_YEARS < 0 | TERM_IN_YEARS > 30 THEN
            DO;
108            ERROR = YES;
109            PUT SKIP LIST ('TERM IN YEARS FIELD IS OUT OF RANGE');
110            END;
111     IF ANNUAL_INTEREST_RATE < 0 | ANNUAL_INTEREST_RATE > 100 THEN
            DO;
112            ERROR = YES;
113            PUT SKIP LIST ('ANNUAL INTEREST RATE IS OUT OF RANGE');
114            END;
115     IF SUBSTR(START_DATE,1,2) < 01 | SUBSTR(START_DATE,1,2) > 12 THEN
            DO;
116            ERROR = YES;
117            PUT SKIP LIST ('STARTING DATE MONTH IS INVALID');
118            END;
119     IF SUBSTR(START_DATE,3,2) < SUBSTR(DATE,1,2) THEN
            DO;
120            ERROR = YES;
121            PUT SKIP LIST ('STARTING DATE YEAR IS BEFORE CURRENT YEAR');
122            END;
123  END VALIDATE_INPUT;
124  END PAYLOAN;
```

**FIGURE 4.10**

**Statements 106 – 123:** VALIDATE_INPUT procedure.

**Statements 107 – 110:** Validates the TERM_IN_YEARS input value. Loans are amortized for a maximum of 30 years. (In this program, however, the formula can be applied to more years.)

**Statements 111 – 114:** Validates interest rate for range from 0 to 100%. (This range is arbitrary to the program because interest could exceed 100%.)

**Statements 115 – 118:** Validates month.

**Statements 119 – 122:** Validates day.

```
/*   FUNCTION TO CALCULATE PAYMENTS FOR LOAN                            */
/***********************************************************************/
/*   PROGRAM NAME: REMIT                                                */
/*   DECRIPTION:    THIS PROGRAM CALCULATES THE MONTHLY PAYMENT FOR A    */
/*                  LOAN GIVEN THE TERM IN YEARS OF THE LOAN, THE        */
/*                  ANNUAL INTEREST RATE, THE LOAN AMOUNT AND THE        */
/*                  NUMBER OF PAYMENTS PER YEAR.                         */
/*   INPUT:         PARAMETERS FROM THE CALLING PROGRAM                  */
/*   OUTPUT:        RETURNS THE MONTHLY PAYMENT AMOUNT                   */
/***********************************************************************/
1   REMIT:    PROC (ANNUAL_INTEREST_RATE,PRINCIPAL,PAYMENTS_PER_YEAR,
                    TERM_IN_YEARS) RETURNS (FIXED DEC (7,2));
2         DCL ANNUAL_INTEREST_RATE    FIXED DEC(5,2);
3         DCL MONTHLY_PAYMENT         FIXED DEC(7,2);
4         DCL PRINCIPAL               FIXED DEC(9,2);
5         DCL PAYMENTS_PER_YEAR       FIXED DEC (3);
6         DCL TERM_IN_YEARS           FIXED DEC (3);
7         DCL FLOAT                   BUILTIN;

8         MONTHLY_PAYMENT =
              (FLOAT(ANNUAL_INTEREST_RATE/100) *
              FLOAT(PRINCIPAL / PAYMENTS_PER_YEAR)) /
              (1 - (1/FLOAT((ANNUAL_INTEREST_RATE/100)/
                  PAYMENTS_PER_YEAR + 1)) **(PAYMENTS_PER_YEAR *
                  TERM_IN_YEARS));

9         RETURN(MONTHLY_PAYMENT);
10  END REMIT;
```

**FIGURE 4.11**

## SUMMARY

**Functions versus Subroutines:** A function is a procedure that returns a single value to the invoking procedure.  By contrast, a subroutine cannot return a value to the point of invocation.  The value of arguments, in certain cases, may be modified by the subroutine, and in this way results are effectively returned to the invoking program.  A subroutine may return none, one, or many results to the invoking procedure through the modification of arguments in the subroutine call.  The RETURN statement is used to terminate a function.  Its use in a function differs somewhat from its use in a subroutine; in a function, it not only returns control, but it also returns the value to the point of invocation; for example:

RETURN (element-expression);

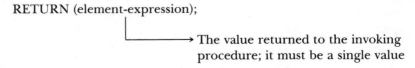

→ The value returned to the invoking
procedure; it must be a single value

**Arguments and Parameters:** Arguments passed to an invoked procedure must be accepted by that procedure.  This is done by the explicit declaration of one or more parameters in a parenthesized list in the PROCEDURE statement of the invoked procedure.  The attributes of a parameter and its corresponding argument must be the same. If the attributes of an argument are not consistent with those of its corresponding parameter, an error will probably result. The maximum number of arguments allowed in one subroutine CALL or function reference is 64 and may be less in some compilers.

**Dummy Arguments:** It is important to understand that the name of an argument, not its value, is passed to a subroutine or function. There are times when an argument has no name. A constant, for example, has no name; nor does an operational expression. *Internal names* are given to constants or expressions and are called *dummy arguments*.

**ENTRY Attribute:** It is necessary to declare a subprogram with the ENTRY attribute:

    DCL SUB2 ENTRY;
    CALL SUB1 (SUB2,A,B);

Allowable forms of the ENTRY attribute include:

    DCL name ENTRY;
    DCL name ENTRY (parameter attribute, parameter attribute . . .);

The ENTRY attribute also allows you to direct the compiler to generate coding to convert one or more arguments to conform to the attributes of the corresponding parameters, should arguments and their corresponding parameters have different attributes.

**RETURNS Attribute:** The attributes of returned values are declared in two ways:

**1.** They may be declared by default according to the first letter of the function name. If the function name begins with the letters A through H or O through Z, then the result will be DECIMAL FLOAT (6). Function names beginning with the letters I through N return a result with the attributes FIXED BINARY (15).

**2.** They may be defined through the use of the RETURNS keyword, which specifies the attributes of a returned value.

The RETURNS attribute also specifies, by implication, the ENTRY attribute for the name. The RETURNS attribute is specified in the *invoking* procedure.

**RETURNS Option:** This keyword is specified in a PROCEDURE statement of function procedures when it is desired to override the default attributes of the entry name. The RETURNS option is specified in the *invoked* procedure.

**RECURSIVE Option:** This keyword is specified in a PROCEDURE statement of a subroutine or function if the procedure might be reactivated while it is still active. This attribute may be used with the RETURNS option.

# CHAPTER 5

# Logical
# Testing

This chapter deals with those aspects of the PL/I language that are related to the elements of logical testing in your program.

## THE IF STATEMENT

The IF statement is used in a PL/I program when a test or decision is to be made between alternatives.   Comparison operators are used to specify the test to be made.   These operators include:

| Symbols | Operation |
|---------|-----------|
| GE or >= | Greater than or equal to |
| GT or > | Greater than |
| NE or ¬= | Not equal to |
| = | Equal to |
| LT or < | Less than |
| LE or <= | Less than or equal to |
| NL or ¬< | Not less than |
| NG or ¬> | Not greater than |

These operators are used to compare two data items to determine the relationship that exists between them.

## The Simple IF

You have already seen the use of the *simple* IF statement, but it will be reviewed here in a more formal way.  In this statement type, a single statement will appear as the action to be taken if the expression (condition) tested is true.  The following diagram represents this type of IF (where *exp* stands for expression):

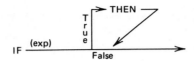

If the condition tested is true, the statement following the THEN keyword is executed before the program proceeds to the next sequential statement in your program.  If the condition tested is false, the THEN keyword is ignored, and the program continues immediately with the next sequential statement.

## The Compound IF

This IF statement is called **compound** because it contains two PL/I statements. Its form includes the use of the keyword ELSE.  Here is a logical diagram:

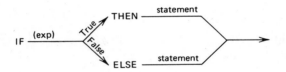

If the condition tested is true, the statement following the THEN clause is executed; if the condition tested is false, the statement following the ELSE clause is executed.  For example:

```
IF A = B THEN
    X = 1; ──────────────────────→ First statement in the
ELSE                                compound IF
    X = 2; ──────────────────────→ Second statement in the
                                   compound IF
```

If A is equal to B (in which case X is set to 1), the ELSE clause is ignored.  If A is not equal to B, the THEN clause is ignored and X is set equal to 2.

## The Do-Group in an IF Statement

The IF statement is designed to execute *one* statement following the THEN or ELSE clause.  Sometimes, however, it is logically necessary to execute more than one statement following the THEN or ELSE.  This can be accomplished through the use of a do-group.  The do-group is simply a series of PL/I statements headed by the word DO and terminated by the keyword END.  For example:

```
DO;
    X = 1;
    Y = 2;
    Z = 3;
END;
```

Placing the do-group in an IF statement gives us the necessary flexibility of being able to execute more than a single statement following a THEN or ELSE. The following example utilizes multiple do-groups.

```
IF A = B THEN
    DO;
        X = 1;
        Y = 2;
        Z = 3;
    END;
ELSE
    DO;
        X = 4;
        Y = 5;
        Z = 6;
    END;
```

There are several uses of the END statement. You already know that END must be the very last statement in your PL/I source program. It also terminates a nested PROCEDURE statement. Terminating a do-group is another use. Yet, as you can see from the previous example, the END may appear to be embedded in your PL/I program. However, the PL/I compiler can always tell by the context which END represents the *true* end of your program because each DO in the program has its own END.

## Formatting the IF

At this point you may be thinking about formatting the IF statement. Actually, there are no rules about how an IF statement should be coded in your program. The guideline to follow is to select a format that provides *program readability* and shows *logical structuring*.

The format most often used in this text shows the keyword ELSE in vertical alignment with its matching IF statement. For example:

```
Vertically ⎫         ┌──→ IF MORE_RECORDS THEN
align these ⎬              CALL PROCESS_DATA;
keywords   ⎭         └──→ ELSE
                          CALL END_OF_JOB_ROUTINE;
```

Some programmers prefer to write the keywords THEN and ELSE on separate lines indented under the IF.  For example:

```
IF MORE_RECORDS
    THEN CALL PROCESS_DATA;
    ELSE CALL END_OF_JOB_ROUTINE;
```

Either format is clear and readable.

## Nested IF Statements

A logical diagram of the nested IF statement looks like this:

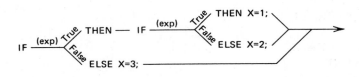

In a series of nested IF statements, each ELSE clause is paired with the closest IF that is not already paired, starting at the innermost level.  The conditions in the IF are tested in the order in which they are written.  As soon as a condition tested is false, testing subsequent conditions is stopped and the matching ELSE clause is executed.  Control is then transferred out of the entire series of nested IF statements.  Study the following example.  The comment statements indicate the conditions under which X is set to a 1, 2, or 3.

```
IF A = B THEN
    IF A = C THEN
        X = 1; /* A=B AND A=C  */
    ELSE
        X = 2; /* A=B BUT A¬=C */
ELSE
    X = 3;      /* A¬=B          */
```

In the nest of IF statements, an associated ELSE clause may or may not appear for the outermost IF.  But every nested IF must have an associated ELSE clause whenever any IF statement at the next outermost level requires an associated ELSE.

The use of nested IFs at this point may seem a bit complicated.  However, let us look at an example where the use of nested IF statements actually simplifies our programming task.  Assume an insurance company plans to base the premiums charged for life insurance on a number of characteristics about the potential insured person.  To illustrate the nested IF, let us consider only two conditions: smoking and weight.  There are four possibilities or categories into which people could be classified according to these two conditions:

| Doesn't smoke, normal weight | Doesn't smoke, overweight | Smokes, normal weight | Smokes, overweight |
|---|---|---|---|
| Insure using regular rates | Hold for further analysis | Insure using higher rates | Do not insure |

As can be seen, a person who does not smoke and is of normal weight qualifies for being insured using standard rates. For the other sets of conditions, the person may be insured with a higher rate schedule or perhaps may not be insured at all.

To test for this set of conditions, a nested IF meets our needs:

```
IF SMOKE = NO THEN
    IF WEIGHT = OK THEN
        PUT LIST ('INSURE USING REGULAR RATES');
    ELSE
        PUT LIST ('HOLD FOR FURTHER ANALYSIS');
ELSE
    IF WEIGHT = OK THEN
        PUT LIST ('INSURE USING HIGHER RATES');
    ELSE
        PUT LIST ('DO NOT INSURE');
```

The alternative to using nested IF statements is to code four successive IF statements where each statement tests for one of the conditions listed in the previous chart.

## A Null ELSE in Nested IF Statements

Earlier, a nested IF statement was shown that set X equal to 1, 2, or 3, depending on the condition tested. The statement was:

```
IF A = B THEN
    IF  A = C THEN
        X = 1;        /* A = B AND A = C  */
    ELSE
        X = 2;        /* A = B BUT A ¬= C */
ELSE
    X = 3;            /* A ¬= B            */
```

In other words:

```
Set X = 1 when A = B and A = C.
Set X = 2 when A = B but A ¬= C.
Set X = 3 when A ¬= B.
```

Now, let us assume that we would like to do the following:

Set X = 1 when A = B and A = C.
Set X = 3 when A ¬= B.

For the condition of A = B but A ¬= C, we do not want to alter X. This situation builds the case for the use of the *null* ELSE. The null ELSE is an ELSE with a null statement as its clause. The null statement is simply a semicolon:

;

Or it may be a semicolon with a label attached to it:

POINT:;

The null ELSE is, as its name implies, a nonoperative statement. It gives no direction to the computer. Instead, its effect here is to supply the necessary ELSE clause to be associated with the innermost IF. The example could be written as follows to illustrate the null ELSE:

```
IF A = B THEN
   IF A = C THEN
      X = 1;
   ELSE;            /* NULL ELSE */
ELSE
   X = 3;
```

Consider what would have happened had you omitted the null ELSE. The statement would have been written:

```
IF A = B THEN
    IF A = C THEN
       X = 1;
ELSE ─────────────────→ This ELSE, regardless of its
    X = 3;                position in the code, is
                         paired with the closest IF
                         (i.e., the IF A = C . . .)
```

Thus, for the condition under which we did not want to change X, X was erroneously set equal to 3.

Always express IFs in their positive form. Avoid null ELSEs through an alternate choice of logic. The preceding set of conditions could be handled with two simple IF statements:

```
IF A = B & A = C THEN
   X = 1;
IF A ¬ = B THEN
   X = 3;
```

These examples have illustrated the nesting of IF statements only to the second level. Deeper nesting is allowed and follows the same reasoning and rules. However, a nested depth of more than three is difficult to follow.

In formatting on the source listing, do not let an IF statement be separated across page boundaries. Initially, you may not know if the IF statement you are coding can be completely contained on a given source-listing page. But after the first compiled run, you will be able to determine if the IF statement can fit on one page. If the compiler, in printing out the source listing, has skipped to a new page in the middle of an IF statement, you need to provide the necessary spacing (e.g., % PAGE preceding the IF) to keep the entire IF on one page of printed output.

## Program Switches in the IF Statement

Program switches may be tested in an IF statement simply by using the indicator name. For example:

```
DECLARE MORE_RECORDS BIT(1);
        ·
        ·
IF MORE_RECORDS THEN
    CALL PROCESS_DATA;
ELSE
    CALL END_OF_JOB;
```

Testing the identifier name alone is testing, whether or not there is a value present in the identifier. If MORE_RECORDS = '1'B, the test is said to have yielded a true condition. Because the MORE_RECORDS indicator can only be a 1 or a 0 (i.e., true or false), the implied test by the presence of its name following the IF is simply for a true or false condition (or whether MORE_RECORDS contains the contents of YES or NO).

It is possible to have coded,

```
IF MORE_RECORDS ¬= '0'B
```

in which the comparison operator (¬=) is specified. The effects of this statement and the immediately preceding example are the same. However, in light of the goal of *readability* in structured programming, the second example is not recommended.

1. (True or False) The null statement is executable.

2. What is the purpose of the do-group?

3. Write the IF statement to test an indicator for a 1, 2, or 3. CALL the appropriate subroutine as follows:

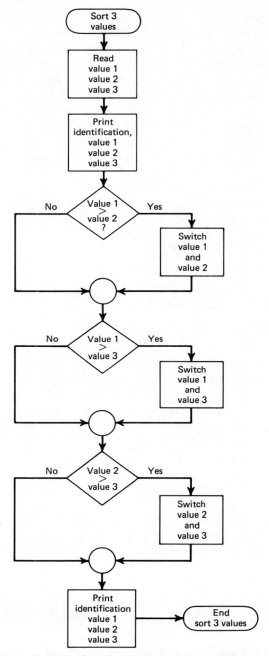

FIGURE 5.1   Program flowchart using bubble sort technique.

1 = STRAIGHT_LINE_DEPRECIATION
2 = SUM_OF_DIGITS_DEPRECIATION
3 = DOUBLE_DECLINING_DEPRECIATION

## A Programming Example

Now let us look at an application using IF statements and do-groups. Assume it is desired to input three values at random and sort these values into ascending sequence. The input data should be printed as entered (unsorted), tested and rearranged using IF and assignment statements, and then printed in their sorted form as follows:

| ORDER OF INPUT VALUES | 4376 |
|---|---|
| | 752 |
| | 2040 |
| SORTED VALUES ARE | 752 |
| | 2040 |
| | 4376 |

Figure 5.1 shows a flowchart for the solution to this problem and Figure 5.2 shows the program. The program begins by reading the three input values via a GET LIST. The first column of printed output consists of either a description ('ORDER OF INPUT VALUES') or a blank. Notice how the second and third PUT LIST statements output a character constant of a "blank" to the first tab position:

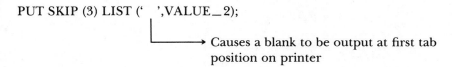

PUT SKIP (3) LIST (' ',VALUE_2);

        → Causes a blank to be output at first tab position on printer

The first IF statement tests for the relationship between VALUE_1 and VALUE_2. If VALUE_1 is greater than VALUE_2, the contents of the variables are exchanged. To do this, a temporary variable (VALUE_SAVE) must hold one of the items during the exchange. Following the THEN clause, multiple statements must be performed, necessitating the use of the do-group. Subsequent relationship tests are made and the results printed.

## THE CASE STRUCTURE

Three basic structures (sequence, IF-THEN-ELSE, and DO-WHILE) are all that are needed to express the solution of any program problem. A fourth structure, not required but useful, is introduced here because it is a variation of the IF-THEN-ELSE. This structure is called CASE.

One typical application of the CASE structure is testing a special field in an input record and processing that record based on its unique code. For example, a department store's credit customers may be assigned different codes depending on the type of charge account they have. Assume that

```
/*   SORT THREE VALUES                                                      */
/************************************************************************/
/*   PROGRAM NAME: SORT3                                                 */
/*                                                                       */
/*   DECRIPTION:     THIS PROGRAM SORTS THREE INPUT VALUES INTO          */
/*                   ASCENDING ORDER.  TWO VALUES ARE COMPARED AT A      */
/*                   TIME AND SWITCHED IF THE FIRST VALUE IS GREATER     */
/*                   THAN THE SECOND.                                    */
/*                                                                       */
/*   INPUT:          SYSTEM INPUT                                        */
/*                                                                       */
/*   OUTPUT:         PRINTER                                             */
/************************************************************************/
SORT3:  PROCEDURE OPTIONS(MAIN);
    DECLARE   VALUE_SAVE          FIXED BINARY(15,0);
    DECLARE   VALUE_1             FIXED BINARY(15,0);
    DECLARE   VALUE_2             FIXED BINARY(15,0);
    DECLARE   VALUE_3             FIXED BINARY(15,0);

    GET LIST (VALUE_1,VALUE_2,VALUE_3);
    PUT LIST ('ORDER OF INPUT VALUES',VALUE_1);
    PUT SKIP (3) LIST (' ',VALUE_2);
    PUT SKIP (3) LIST (' ',VALUE_3);

    IF VALUE_1 > VALUE_2 THEN
       DO;
           VALUE_SAVE = VALUE_1;
           VALUE_1    = VALUE_2;
           VALUE_2    = VALUE_SAVE;
       END;
    IF VALUE_1 > VALUE_3 THEN
       DO;
           VALUE_SAVE = VALUE_1;
           VALUE_1    = VALUE_3;
           VALUE_3    = VALUE_SAVE;
       END;
    IF VALUE_2 > VALUE_3 THEN
       DO;
           VALUE_SAVE = VALUE_2;
           VALUE_2    = VALUE_3;
           VALUE_3    = VALUE_SAVE;
       END;
    PUT SKIP (3) LIST ('SORTED VALUES ARE:',VALUE_1);
    PUT SKIP (3) LIST (' ',VALUE_2);
    PUT SKIP (3) LIST (' ',VALUE_3);
END SORT3;
```

FIGURE 5.2   Program to sort 3 values using IFs and do-groups.

| CODE = 1 | 30-DAY ACCOUNT |
| 2 | 60-DAY ACCOUNT |
| 3 | 90-DAY ACCOUNT |
| 4 | 12-MONTH ACCOUNT |
| OTHER | SPECIAL |

Figure 5.3 shows a series of nested IF statements in which the code is tested and the appropriate subfunction (e.g., 30-day, 60-day, etc.) is performed. Actually, this nested IF is one way of expressing the CASE structure.

As can be seen, the CASE structure is an extension of the IF-THEN-ELSE structure. The need for it arises when a test is performed and many alternatives are subsequently executed. The structure may be drawn as follows:

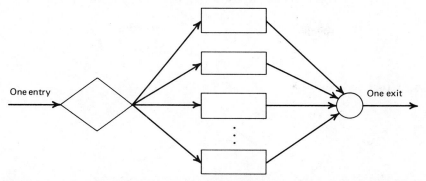

Here, as with the IF-THEN-ELSE, the paths from the various process programs merge at the same point and then continue in a forward direction. The flow is always from the entry point to the exit point with the exact path to be determined by the test. The justification for using the *decision* symbol to begin the

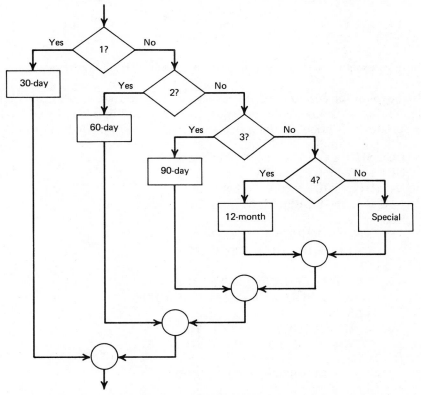

FIGURE 5.3 CASE structure implemented using nested IFs.

CASE structure is that CASE is a variation of the IF-THEN-ELSE structure. As an alternative, some people prefer using a unique symbol to start and end the CASE structure. You may wish to use these symbols instead:

Entry                                    Exit

The structure then may be drawn as follows:

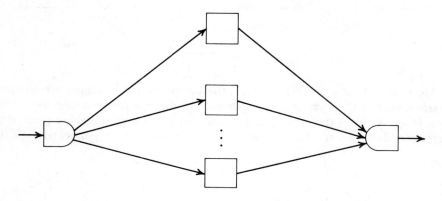

If these symbols are used, they should be standard for the data processing installation.

In the following nested IF (CASE structure), five alternatives are evaluated. A code indicating the method by which goods are to be shipped is tested, and the appropriate subroutine handling that shipping method is coded. For example:

```
DCL SHIP_CODE          FIXED DEC(3);
GET LIST (SHIP_CODE);
IF SHIP_CODE = 110 THEN
   CALL SHIP_BEST_WAY_COD;
ELSE
   IF SHIP_CODE = 120 THEN
      CALL SHIP_UPS_REGULAR;
   ELSE
      IF SHIP_CODE = 130 THEN
         CALL SHIP_UPS_BLUE_LABEL;
      ELSE
         IF SHIP_CODE = 140 THEN
            CALL SHIP_UPS_RED_LABEL;
         ELSE
            CALL SHIP_CODE_ERROR;
```

When there are more than three alternatives to be evaluated, nested IFs can be difficult to code as well as to read.  The SELECT statement provides a practical alternative to coding the CASE structure in which a large number of alternatives must be evaluated.

## The SELECT Statement

The SELECT statement takes the general form:

```
SELECT (optional expression here);
    WHEN (expression) action 1;
    WHEN (expression) action 2;
    OTHERWISE action 3;
END;
```

This is called a *select-group* (similar to a do-group) because it begins with the keyword SELECT and ends with the keyword END.  Notice that following the keyword SELECT, an expression may be specified.  Optionally, that expression could be eliminated.

One or more WHEN clauses may be specified.  Following each WHEN clause is an expression in parentheses and a *program action*.  The program action could be a single statement such as a CALL or an assignment statement.  Or it could be a do-group, another select-group, or a begin block.  (Begin blocks are explained later in this chapter.)

Here is an example of a select-group in which an expression follows the SELECT:

```
SELECT (SHIP_CODE);
    WHEN (110) CALL SHIP_BEST_WAY_CODE;
    WHEN (120) CALL SHIP_UPS_REGULAR;
    WHEN (130) CALL SHIP_UPS_BLUE_LABEL;
    WHEN (140) CALL SHIP_UPS_RED_LABEL;
    OTHERWISE CALL SHIP_CODE_ERROR;
END;
```

When program control reaches the SELECT statement, the identifier SHIP_CODE is saved.  The expressions in the WHEN clauses are then evaluated in the order in which they appear, and each value is compared with the value in SHIP_CODE.  If a value is found that is equal to the value of SHIP_CODE, the action following the current WHEN clause is performed.  No further WHEN clause expressions are evaluated.  After the specified action has been completed, transfer of control is to the next sequential statement immediately following the END statement that terminates the select-group.  If none of the expressions in the WHEN clauses are equal to the value in the SELECT statement, the action specified following the OTHERWISE clause is automatically executed.  If the

OTHERWISE clause is omitted and the execution of the select-group does not result in the selection of a specified action following one of the WHEN clauses, the ERROR condition is raised. (The ERROR condition is discussed later in this chapter.)

Here is an example of a select-group *without* an expression following the SELECT:

```
SELECT;
    WHEN (BALANCE < 0)  CALL NEGATIVE_BAL_RT;
    WHEN (BALANCE = 0)  CALL ZERO_BAL_RT;
    OTHERWISE           CALL POSITIVE_BAL_RT;
END;
```

In this case a logical expression must be specified in parentheses following the WHEN clause.

As mentioned earlier, do-groups and begin blocks may follow the WHEN or OTHERWISE clauses. Here is an example:

```
SELECT;
    WHEN (BALANCE < 0)
        DO;
                /* EXECUTABLE CODE HANDLING     */
                /* NEGATIVE BALANCE CONDITION */
        END;
    WHEN (BALANCE = 0)
        DO;
                /* PROGRAM LOGIC FOR HANDLING   */
                /* ZERO BALANCE CONDITION        */
        END;
    OTHERWISE
        DO;
                /* POSITIVE BALANCE CONDITION    */
        END;
END;
```

It is also possible to nest select-groups within other select-groups. For example:

```
DCL HOW_TO_SHIP_CODE        FIXED DEC(3);
DCL TYPE                     CHAR (1);
SELECT (HOW_TO_SHIP_CODE);
    WHEN (110)
        SELECT (TYPE);
            WHEN ('A') CALL AIRMAIL;
            WHEN ('P') CALL PRIORITY_MAIL;
```

```
            WHEN ('S') CALL SPECIAL_DELIVERY;
            OTHERWISE CALL FIRST_CLASS;
        END;
    WHEN (120) CALL SHIP_UPS_REGULAR;
        .
        .
        .
END;
```

When the HOW_TO_SHIP_CODE is equal to 110, then another SELECT is specified causing an evaluation of the identifier called TYPE. TYPE in the previous example should be set to some value before the select-group is entered. Within the nested select-group various codes are tested to determine the type of prepaid shipping. The maximum permissible depth of nesting of select-groups is more than you'll ever need—49. Note, however, that there is no limit to the number of WHEN clauses that may be specified within any select-group.

In the previous chapter, Figure 4.4 depicted a function procedure in which a number of nested IFs were used. Compare the readability of that program (page 163) with the following solution which uses the CASE structure.

```
TIMEX:   PROC RETURNS(CHAR(14));
    DCL CONVERTED_TIME            CHAR(14) INIT('    :');
    DCL CURRENT_TIME              PIC'(9)9';
    DCL HOURS                     PIC'Z9';
    DCL MINUTES                   PIC'99';
    DCL SUBSTR                    BUILTIN;
    DCL TIME                      BUILTIN;
    CURRENT_TIME = TIME;
    HOURS       = SUBSTR(CURRENT_TIME,1,2);
    MINUTES     = SUBSTR(CURRENT_TIME,3,2);
    SELECT;
        WHEN(HOURS > 0 & HOURS < 12) SUBSTR(CONVERTED_TIME,7,2) = 'AM';
        WHEN(HOURS >12 & HOURS < 24)
            DO;
                SUBSTR(CONVERTED_TIME,7,2) = 'PM';
                HOURS = HOURS - 12;
            END;
        WHEN(HOURS = 0 | HOURS = 24)
            DO;
                IF MINUTES = 0
                    THEN SUBSTR(CONVERTED_TIME,7,8) = 'MIDNIGHT';
                    ELSE SUBSTR(CONVERTED_TIME,7,2) = 'AM';
                HOURS = 12;

            END;
        WHEN(HOURS = 12)
            DO;
                IF MINUTES = 0
                    THEN SUBSTR(CONVERTED_TIME,7,4) = 'NOON';
                    ELSE SUBSTR(CONVERTED_TIME,7,2) = 'PM';
            END;
        OTHERWISE PUT SKIP LIST('ERROR IN DATE ===>',CURRENT_TIME);
    END;
    SUBSTR(CONVERTED_TIME,1,2) = HOURS;
    SUBSTR(CONVERTED_TIME,4,2) = MINUTES;
    RETURN(CONVERTED_TIME);
END TIMEX;
```

## LOGICAL OPERATORS

Three logical operations are provided in PL/I.  These are

| Symbol | Operation |
|--------|-----------|
| ($\neg$) | NOT |
| (&) | AND |
| (\|) | OR |

These operators are useful in several programming circumstances.

**1.** They are used in the IF statement.

**2.** They are used occasionally in the assignment statement.

**3.** They are used to manipulate bit-string data.

## LOGICAL OPERATORS IN THE IF STATEMENT

The logical operators can be used in the IF statement to eliminate nested IF statements.  For example, the nested IF statement,

```
IF A = B THEN
    IF C = D THEN
        X = 1;
```

could also be written using the AND operation.  For example:

```
IF A = B & C = D THEN
    X = 1;
```

When the AND symbol (&) is specified, the expressions to the left and right of the symbol must both be true for the statement following the THEN to be executed. If either expression is not true, the statement following the THEN is bypassed.

For a comparison expression containing the OR (\|) operator, consider the following example:

```
IF A = B | C = D THEN
    X = 0;
```

In this case, if either the expression to the left or the expression to the right of the OR symbol is true, the statement following the THEN is executed.  If both expressions are true, X is still set to 0.  The only condition that would keep the program from setting X to 0 is if A is not equal to B and C is not equal to D.

Here is an example using the NOT operation ($\neg$):

```
IF ¬ MORE_RECORDS THEN
    CALL END_OF_JOB_ROUTINE;
ELSE
    CALL PROCESS_RECORD;
```

There are four possible combinations of true/false conditions when two conditions are evaluated:

| *First Expression* | *Second Expression* |
|---|---|
| True | True |
| True | False |
| False | True |
| False | False |

Substituting a 1 for true and a 0 for false, the following tables define the result (either a 0 or a 1) for the AND and OR operations:

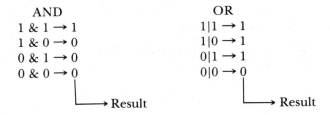

The NOT operation simply yields a result of the opposite condition: if a bit is a 1, result is 0; if a bit is a 0, result is a 1. For example:

$$\neg 1 \to 0$$
$$\neg 0 \to 1$$

Notice there is only one operand with the NOT operation.

## LOGICAL OPERATORS IN THE ASSIGNMENT STATEMENT

*Comparison* operators, as mentioned earlier, may be used in an assignment statement. Note the results assigned to the variable on the left of the assignment symbol in the following examples:

$$A = \underbrace{B = C};$$

     &rarr; If B = C, then A will be assigned a value of 1

       If B is not equal to C, then A will be assigned a value of 0

$$A = B > C;$$

      &rarr; A = 1 if B > C

        A = 0 if B is not greater than C

Additionally, *comparison* operators and *logical* operators may be combined in one assignment statement expression. For example:

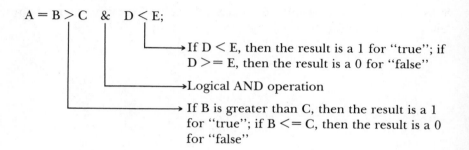

$$A = B > C \quad \& \quad D < E;$$

      &rarr; If D < E, then the result is a 1 for "true"; if D >= E, then the result is a 0 for "false"

     &rarr; Logical AND operation

    &rarr; If B is greater than C, then the result is a 1 for "true"; if B <= C, then the result is a 0 for "false"

Because the logical operation is AND, the identifier A will be set to a 1 if *both* expressions have a 1 generated as a result of a *comparison operation*. In all other cases, A in the previous example will be set to 0.

  If the example were an OR operation:

$$A = B > C \,|\, D < E;$$

then A would be set to 1 if *either* expression has a 1 generated.

## CHECKPOINT QUESTIONS

**4.** How may the CASE structure be implemented in PL/I?

**5.** Write a select-group for the test specified in Checkpoint Question 3 of this chapter.

**6.** Given the following set of conditions for which X is to be set write the required IF statement(s):

| Conditions | $A = B$ $C = D$ | $A = B$ $C \neg = D$ | $A \neg = B$ $C = D$ | $A \neg = B$ $C \neg = D$ |
|---|---|---|---|---|
| Action | $X = 1$ | $X = 2$ | $X = 3$ | $X = 4$ |

(a)  First, using four simple IF statements with logical operators.
(b)  Then, using a series of nested IF statements.

## CONDITIONS AND ON-UNITS

During the execution of a PL/I program, a number of **conditions** could arise. A condition is an occurrence within a PL/I program that causes a program interrupt. It may be the detection of an unexpected error or of an occurrence that is expected but at an unpredictable time. An unexpected error that might occur is OVERFLOW. It results from an arithmetic expression generating an answer that is too large for the specified data format (e.g., a fixed-point binary answer is larger than 31 bits). The ENDFILE condition is an example of an occurrence that is expected, but at an unpredictable time.

The title of this chapter is *Logical Testing*—the IF statement is one of the primary ways in which logical tests are specified. The occurrence of conditions and subsequent program response to these conditions may be thought of as another form of logical testing. In a sense, an implied IF is related to the response to these conditions. This is because, when the various conditions occur, the question must be asked, "What action—if any—should be taken?" The question could be diagramed as follows:

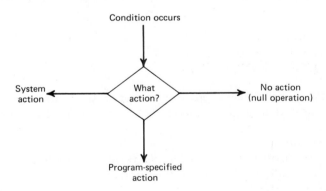

As can be seen, there are three basic alternatives, or responses, to the occurrence of a condition.

You are already familiar with the ENDFILE condition and were briefly introduced to the OVERFLOW condition.

Keep these types of conditions in mind as the various options to any condition are described.

## Responses to Occurrence of Conditions

**System Action.** For all of the conditions, a standard system action exists as part of PL/I. In the absence of your program specifying an action to be taken when conditions are detected, a standard system action will take place. *For most conditions, the standard system action is to print a message and then raise the ERROR condition.* The ERROR condition is raised as a result of the standard system *action.* Unless otherwise specified, when the ERROR condition is raised, the standard system action for the ERROR condition is to terminate the PL/I program and return control to the operating system.

**Program-specified Action.** In some cases, you would not want the system to take its standard action in response to a given condition. For example, when the ENDFILE condition occurs, rather than a standard system action of terminating the job, an end-of-job processing routine is more appropriate. Thus, your program specifies the action taken for a given condition. This is done through the use of the ON statement.

The ON statement is used to specify action to be taken when any subsequent occurrence of a specified condition causes a program interrupt. The ON statement takes the form:

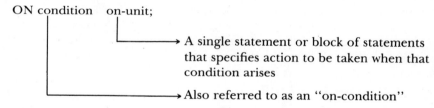

ON condition    on-unit;

→ A single statement or block of statements that specifies action to be taken when that condition arises

→ Also referred to as an "on-condition"

For example:

```
ON ENDFILE (SYSIN)
    MORE_RECORDS = NO;
```

This statement specifies that when an interrupt occurs as the result of trying to read beyond the end of the file named SYSIN, the specified program switch is to be turned off.

When execution of an on-unit is successfully completed, control will normally return to the point of the interrupt or to a point immediately following it, depending on the condition that caused the interrupt.

Another form of the ON statement is:

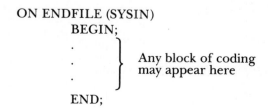

```
ON ENDFILE (SYSIN)
        BEGIN;
          .
          .
          .
        END;
```

Any block of coding may appear here

The begin block, as shown, starts with the word BEGIN and ends with the word END, as does a do-group. This block of coding is similar to a **subroutine.** The begin block is entered when the ENDFILE condition is detected for the SYSIN file. When the END statement is encountered, there is an automatic return to the statement following the READ or GET that caused the ENDFILE condition to be raised.

Begin blocks may be specified as the on-unit for any condition. Note that a do-group may not be specified as the object of the ON statement.

Here is an example of how a complete begin block might be coded:

```
ON ENDFILE (SYSIN)
    BEGIN;
        PUT SKIP (3) LIST (TOTAL);
        PUT PAGE LIST ('NUMBER OF RECORDS PROCESSED',COUNT);
        END_OF_FILE = YES;
    END;
```

The begin block sets END_OF_FILE to YES to terminate the DO-WHILE and prints the number of records processed. The input processing loop could be coded as follows:

```
    END_OF_FILE = NO;
    GET FILE (SYSIN) LIST (INPUT);
    DO WHILE (¬END_OF_FILE);
        COUNT = COUNT + 1;
        GET FILE (SYSIN) LIST (INPUT);
    END;
```

In summary, the ON statement is used to specify action taken when any subsequent occurrence of a specified condition causes a program interrupt. The ON statement must be logically placed in your program. For example, the ON statement for the ENDFILE condition is logically placed *before* all GET statements.

## TYPES OF CONDITIONS

A number of conditions may be specified in the ON statement. Some of the conditions that may be raised during I/O operations include:

    ENDFILE(file name)
    ENDPAGE(file name)
    RECORD(file name)
    TRANSMIT(file name)
    CONVERSION
    SIZE

**The ENDFILE Condition.** This condition is raised during a GET or READ operation. It is caused by an attempt to read past the last record for the file named in the GET or READ statement. After ENDFILE has been raised, no further GETs or READs should be executed for that file.

The most common form of the ON statement for this condition involves the setting of an indicator or switch in the on-unit:

```
ON ENDFILE (TRANS)
    MORE_RECORDS = NO;
```

**The ENDPAGE Condition.** The ENDPAGE condition is raised when a PUT statement results in an attempt to start a new line beyond the limit specified for PAGESIZE. This limit can be specified by the PAGESIZE option in an OPEN statement, which is described in detail in Chapter 7. If PAGESIZE has not been specified, an installation-defined system limit applies. The attempt to exceed the limit may be made during data transmission, by the LINE option, or by the SKIP option. ENDPAGE is raised only once per page. When the ENDPAGE condition is raised, the standard system action is to skip to a new page and continue execution with the PUT statement, which caused the ENDPAGE condition to occur.

PL/I maintains a *current line counter* that is incremented by one each time a new line is printed. When this line counter exceeds the maximum number specified by the PAGESIZE option (or the default) the ENDPAGE condition is raised. Thus, at this point, the current line counter is one greater than the maximum page size value.

After ENDPAGE has been raised, a new page may be started in either of the following ways:

**1.** Execution of a PAGE option or a PAGE format item (Chapter 7).

**2.** Execution of a LINE option or a LINE format item specifying a line number less than the current line number.

If a new page is not started, the current line number may increase indefinitely. When ENDPAGE is raised, it is possible to continue writing on the same page. Any time execution of the PAGE, SKIP, or LINE option causes a new page to be started, the current line counter will be reset, but the ENDPAGE condition will *not* be raised.

A begin block may follow the ENDPAGE keyword. For example:

```
ON ENDPAGE (PRINTR)
    BEGIN;
       .
       .
       .
    END;
```

This begin block is treated like a subroutine in that the block is entered when the ENDPAGE condition is raised and returns to the place in the program immediately following the point of interruption.   Here is an example of how the begin block could be used for the purpose of printing headings:

```
ON ENDFILE (SYSIN)
    MORE_DATA = NO;
ON ENDPAGE (PRINTR)
    BEGIN;
        PUT PAGE LIST (' ', 'WEEKLY STATUS REPORT',
            SUBSTR(TODAY,3,2) || '/' || SUBSTR(TODAY,5,2)
            || '/' || SUBSTR(TODAY,1,2), 'PAGE' || PAGE_NUMBER);
        PAGE_NUMBER = PAGE_NUMBER + 1;
    END;
TODAY          = DATE;
PAGE_NUMBER = 1;
OPEN FILE(PRINTR) PAGESIZE (45);
SIGNAL ENDPAGE (PRINTR);
MORE_DATA     = YES;
GET LIST (DATA);
DO WHILE (MORE_DATA);
    CALL PROCESS_DATA;
    CALL PRINT_DATA;
    GET LIST(DATA);
END;
```

Notice how the statement,

SIGNAL ENDPAGE (PRINTR);

is used to cause a heading to be printed on the *first* page of output.   (The SIGNAL statement has the same effect as if the condition had actually occurred.)   The loop operation consists of reading records and printing on the printer.   In this program, the ENDPAGE condition will be detected *before* the PUT statement is executed for the forty-sixth time.

The ENDPAGE condition is raised when the maximum number of specified lines has been printed on a page.   The ENDPAGE condition may not be disabled.

**Null Action.** It is possible to specify a *null* action for some (but not all) conditions.   The null form says simply, "No action is to be taken for this on-unit."   For example, an I/O condition called ENDPAGE occurs for stream output files to the printer.   When the ENDPAGE condition occurs, the standard system action is simply to cause the printer to skip to a new page.   If you have had occasion to output more than 60 lines to a line printer using a PUT LIST, or other stream output statement, and did not specify page skipping, you probably noticed that this function was automatically handled.

Perhaps you have had the opportunity of seeing some "computer art." This art takes the form of "Snoopy" calendars, "Happy Birthday" signs, etc., that span a number of line printer pages in which the picture or image prints across the perforation. In writing a program to generate these pictures, if the "computer art" output is to span more than one page to make one continuous picture and stream output (PUT) is used, then it is important to specify a null action for the ENDPAGE condition.

When the ENDPAGE condition is detected, we do not want the system to skip to a new page. Hence, the program must specify null action. A semicolon following the condition name indicates a null action. For example:

    ON ENDPAGE (PRINTR);

Some conditions may be raised during arithmetic operations. These include:

    CONVERSION
    FIXEDOVERFLOW
    OVERFLOW
    UNDERFLOW
    ZERODIVIDE
    SIZE

If you compare the names in the previous list with the conditions that may occur during I/O operations, you will see that CONVERSION and SIZE are common to both lists. The arithmetic conditions will be discussed here, the I/O conditions in Chapter 7. Two "debugging" conditions, STRINGRANGE and STRINGSIZE, will be presented in the debugging section of this chapter.

**The CONVERSION Condition.** The CONVERSION condition occurs whenever a conversion is attempted on character data containing characters that are invalid for the conversion being performed. This attempted conversion may be made internally or during a stream I/O operation.

Here is an example of when the CONVERSION condition would be raised during an internal operation:

    DCL X        BIT (4);
    X = '10A1';               /* CONVERSION CONDITION RAISED */

The CONVERSION condition is raised because the character-string assigned to X contains a character other than a 0 or 1.

All conversions of character-string data are carried out character-by-character in a left-to-right sequence, and the condition occurs for the first illegal character. When such a character is encountered, an interrupt occurs and the current action specification for the condition is executed. When CONVERSION occurs, the contents of the entire result field are undefined. The CONVERSION condition may also occur during stream I/O for the same reason. For example, a data input item could be identified as BIT but contain an illegal character ('101A').

**The FIXEDOVERFLOW Condition.** The FIXEDOVERFLOW condition occurs when the precision of the result of a fixed-point arithmetic operation exceeds N digits. For most PL/I implementations, N is 15 for decimal fixed-point values and 31 for binary fixed-point values.

```
DCL A          FIXED DEC (15);
DCL B          FIXED DEC (15);
DCL C          FIXED DEC (15);
A = 40000000;
B = 80000000;
C = A * B;      /* FIXEDOVERFLOW CONDITION BECAUSE */
                /* RESULT IS LARGER THAN 15 DIGITS    */
```

**The OVERFLOW Condition.** The OVERFLOW condition occurs when the magnitude of a floating-point number exceeds the permitted maximum. (For most PL/I implementations, the magnitude of a floating-point number or intermediate result must not be greater than approximately $10^{75}$ or $2^{252}$. Compare this with UNDERFLOW.)

```
A = 55E71;
B = 23E11;
C = A * B;  /* OVERFLOW CONDITION BECAUSE RESULTING */
            /* EXPONENT IS GREATER THAN 10**75          */
```

**The UNDERFLOW Condition.** The UNDERFLOW condition occurs when the magnitude of a floating-point number is smaller than the permitted minimum. (For most PL/I implementations, the magnitude of a floating-point value may not be less than approximately $10^{-78}$ or $2^{-260}$.)

```
A = 23E−71;
B = 3E−9;
C = A * B;  /* UNDERFLOW CONDITION BECAUSE */
            /* RESULTING EXPONENT IS LESS    */
            /* THAN 10**−78                  */
```

**The ZERODIVIDE Condition.** The ZERODIVIDE condition occurs when an attempt is made to divide by zero. This condition is raised for both fixed-point and floating-point division.

```
A = 15;
B = 0;
C = A/B; /* ZERODIVIDE CONDITION */
```

**The SIZE Condition.** The SIZE condition occurs when high-order (i.e., leftmost) nonzero binary or decimal digits (also known as significant digits) are lost in an assignment operation (i.e., assignment to a variable or to an intermediate result) or in a stream input operation. This loss may result from a conversion involving different data types, bases, scales, or precisions. The SIZE condition differs from the FIXEDOVERFLOW condition in an important sense. We noted that FIXEDOVERFLOW occurs when the length of a calculated fixed-point value exceeds the maximum precision allowed. The SIZE condition, however, occurs when the value being assigned to a data item exceeds the declared (or default) size of the data item. The SIZE condition can occur on the assignment of a value whether or not the FIXEDOVERFLOW condition arose in the calculation of that value. For example:

```
DCL V1   FIXED DEC (4);
DCL V2   FIXED DEC (5)   INIT (12345);
V1 = V2; /* SIZE CONDITION */
```

The identifiers V1 and V2 both require three bytes of storage even though their precisions differ. However, V1 must always have a 0 in its leftmost position of the leftmost byte:

| 0 | 9 | 9 | 9 | 9 | ± |   FIXED (4) field

Physically, the space is there to contain an additional digit; logically, however, the space is not available. Hence, the SIZE condition is raised. The same situation also occurs in this example:

```
DCL V3   FIXED BIN (5);
DCL V4   FIXED BIN (15) INIT (3000);
V3 = V4;   /* SIZE CONDITION */
```

V3 will require a half word (two bytes) of storage, but the program contains instructions to ensure that all binary digit positions beyond five in the preceding example will be zero. Note that both examples require that extra code be generated within PL/I so that proper precisions are maintained. For efficiency in IBM compilers, an odd number of decimal digits and either 15 or 31 binary digits should be declared when the SIZE tests are not really needed by the program. The SIZE condition could also occur during stream input for the same reason.

### The Status of Conditions

Some conditions are always **enabled** unless explicitly **disabled;** others are *disabled* unless explicitly *enabled.* When a condition is enabled, it means that if the condition occurs, either programmer-defined action or system action takes place. Thus, when conditions are disabled, errors may go undetected. The I/O conditions are always enabled and may not be disabled. The following computational conditions are enabled unless the programmer specifies that they should be disabled:

CONVERSION
FIXEDOVERFLOW
OVERFLOW
UNDERFLOW
ZERODIVIDE

The SIZE condition, conversely, is disabled unless enabled by the programmer.

Conditions are enabled or disabled through a **condition prefix,** which is the name of one or more conditions separated by commas, enclosed in parentheses, and prefixed to a statement by a colon.  The word NO preceding the condition name indicates that the condition is to be disabled.  For example:

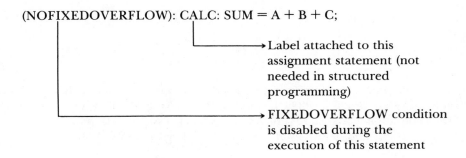

(NOFIXEDOVERFLOW): CALC: SUM = A + B + C;

Label attached to this assignment statement (not needed in structured programming)

FIXEDOVERFLOW condition is disabled during the execution of this statement

Notice how the condition name precedes the statement's label.  Of course, the label is optional.  If it is desired to disable or enable a condition for the entire execution of a procedure, specify the condition prefix on a PROCEDURE statement.  For example:

(SIZE, NOFIXEDOVERFLOW):
PROG1: PROC OPTIONS (MAIN);

In the example, the SIZE condition is enabled and the FIXEDOVERFLOW condition is disabled during the execution of the procedure labeled PROG1. Continuing with this example, assume it is later desired to disable the SIZE condition during the execution of a single statement.  The following could be coded:

(NOSIZE): Y = A*B/C;

Even though some conditions may never be disabled, it does not mean that some action must take place for those conditions.  It is possible to specify a *null* action for conditions that cannot be disabled.  For example:

ON ENDPAGE;

## Changing the Action Taken

You have seen how to enable and disable the recognition of conditions as well as how to specify what action should be taken if and when a condition does arise. It is possible to specify more than one ON statement for the same condition in a program. For example, during the first phase of a program, a table needs to be initialized with data. If an end-of-file occurs during this time, it is an error because other data records are expected to follow. During the second phase of that program, the end-of-file condition is not an error because it is expected. In this example, two ON statements would be specified to indicate different program actions at different points in time. For example:

```
ON ENDFILE (SYSIN)
    CALL ERROR_RT;
.
.
.
ON ENDFILE (SYSIN)
    CALL NORMAL_END_OF_JOB;
.
.
.
```

In the absence of a program-supplied ON statement for an enabled condition, standard system action will be taken. If, after having supplied your own on-unit for a condition, you wish to return to the standard system action for that on-unit, simply specify another ON statement with the keyword SYSTEM. For example:

```
ON FIXEDOVERFLOW
    TOO_MUCH = YES;
A = B + C;
IF TOO_MUCH THEN
    CALL OVERFLOW_ROUTINE;
.
.
.
ON FIXEDOVERFLOW
    SYSTEM;
```

## Simulating Conditions

The programmer can simulate the occurrence of a condition through the use of the SIGNAL statement. Execution of the SIGNAL statement has the same effect as if the condition had actually occurred. If the signaled condition is not enabled, the SIGNAL statement is treated as a null statement. The general form is

SIGNAL condition;
   └──────────→ Any condition name may appear here

One of the uses of this statement is in program checkout to test the action of an on-unit and to determine that the correct program action is associated with the condition.

Figure 5.4 summarizes the conditions covered in this section and includes the CHECK condition covered in Chapter 1. It provides the status of each condition, probable cause, and gives you some idea about what you can do to correct the error.

7. What is the ON statement used for?

8. Under what conditions is the ERROR condition raised?

9. What does the *condition prefix* accomplish?

10. What does the *null* form of the ON statement indicate?

11. How can the programmer simulate the occurrence of an ON condition?

12. Distinguish between FIXEDOVERFLOW and SIZE.

## DEBUGGING

In this section, we will look at additional tools that will help you in the checkout of any PL/I program, as well as in the checkout of those programs responding to the various conditions described in this chapter. The first tool is the PUT DATA statement.

## PUT DATA

Data-directed I/O will be fully discussed in Chapter 7. But you could start using one simple form of this type of I/O now. It consists of the statement:

    PUT DATA;

This statement causes *all* variables known to the program at the point of the PUT statement to be output in the form of assignment statements. (The output resembles the format that comes from using the CHECK feature.)

PUT DATA can be a powerful debugging tool; however, it is at the expense of considerable program overhead. Thus, it should only be used in debugging. In fact, to see just how expensive it is, try running your program without the PUT DATA statement and note the main storage requirements. Then insert the desired PUT DATA statement or statements and note the difference in storage requirements.

One of the most useful places to use the PUT DATA statement is in the ERROR on-unit. Recall that the ERROR condition is raised as a standard system action

| Type of condition | ON-condition | Normally enabled/disabled | Cause | What the programmer should do—or—what the result is | Normal return to (if null on-unit is used) | Standard system action |
|---|---|---|---|---|---|---|
| Program checkout | CHECK (optional name list) | Disabled (can be enabled) | (1) Procedure invoked (2) Assignment statement executed | Programmer should study output to determine cause of program error | | Current statement number and data are printed. |
| Standard system action | ERROR | Enabled (cannot be disabled) | (1) Another ON-condition for which it is the standard system action (2) An error for which there is no ON-condition | Programmer action depends on requirements of installation | Control returned to the operating system control program | Message printed and control returned to operating system control program (execution terminated) |
| Computational conditions | CONVERSION | Enabled | Illegal conversion attempt on character-string data internally or on input/output operation | Results are undefined | Null on-unit cannot be specified | ERROR condition |
| | FIXEDOVERFLOW | Enabled | Result of arithmetic fixed-point operation that exceeds maximum precision allowed (15 for decimal, 31 for binary) | Results are undefined | The point logically following the point of the interrupt | ERROR condition |
| | OVERFLOW | Enabled | Magnitude of a floating-point number greater than permitted maximum | Results are undefined | The point logically following the point of the interrupt | ERROR condition |
| | SIZE | Disabled | Nonzero high-order binary or decimal digits are lost in an assignment operation (i.e., assignment to a variable or an intermediate result) or in an input/output operation | Results are undefined | The point logically following the point of the interrupt | ERROR condition |
| | UNDERFLOW | Enabled (can be disabled) | Magnitude of a floating-point number smaller than allowable minimum | Invalid floating-point value set to 0 | The point logically following the point of the interrupt | Message printed and execution continues |
| | ZERODIVIDE | Enabled (can be) disabled) | Attempt to divide by zero | Results are undefined | The point logically following the point of the interrupt | ERROR condition |

for other conditions. When the ERROR condition is raised, your program is about to be terminated. Before termination, it might be useful to capture the contents of program variables so that you may better understand what has gone wrong in your program. Thus, the following might be erroneously coded:

```
ON ERROR
     PUT DATA;
```

This, however, is potentially dangerous because there is the possibility that the ERROR condition could be raised during the stream output operation, PUT DATA. An interminable loop can result because the second time the ERROR condition is raised, the PUT DATA statement attempts to output all program variables until it encounters the ERROR condition again. The process is repeated again and again until your program is canceled by the operator or operating system. To avoid this iteration, the following approach is needed:

```
ON ERROR
     BEGIN;
          ON ERROR SYSTEM;
          PUT DATA;
     END;
```

Within the begin block, the ON ERROR SYSTEM statement tells the system that if an ERROR condition is raised during the execution of statements within the begin block, take *system action* (i.e., terminate the program). Now the PUT DATA statement causes the contents of all program variables to be printed *until* an ERROR condition is detected. If no ERROR condition occurs during the printout, then all program variables will be printed.

## BUILT-IN FUNCTIONS FOR ON-UNITS

This section will discuss four built-in functions that are useful to you in handling on-units for some specific conditions. By the proper use of aids provided by PL/I, almost all debugging can be done at the source level. You need not resort to listings of the generated object code or hexadecimal storage dumps. Moreover, after encountering an error that might normally require abnormal termination, you may wish to continue with the execution of your program following the point of interruption. In doing this, several different errors might be detected in a single test run, thus improving the profitability of each run and helping to shorten program debugging time. This is especially important in installations where program test turnaround time is long.

The four built-in functions discussed here are ONCODE, ONLOC, ON-CHAR, and ONSOURCE. Do not confuse these built-in function names with the ON statement. These names start with the word ON because these functions were designed to be invoked in on-units responding to various conditions in the ON statement.

**ONCODE.** This function may be used in any on-unit to determine the type of interrupt that caused the on-unit to become active. This code defines the type of interrupt that caused the entry into the active on-unit. These codes are listed in the PL/I reference manual for the compiler you are using. For example:

```
ON ERROR
    PUT LIST (ONCODE);
```

The ONCODE function is invoked as a list item in the PUT LIST statement. The result returned from this function is a binary integer of default precision. Assume the value printed from the previous statement is 70. Checking with the table in the reference manual would indicate the cause of the condition as being ENDFILE. If the ONCODE built-in function is used out of context (that is, it appears in something other than an ON statement), a value of 0 is returned.

**ONLOC.** This built-in function may also be used in any on-unit to determine the entry point of the procedure in which that condition was raised. For example:

```
MAIN: PROC OPTIONS (MAIN);
    .
    .
    SUBRT: PROC;
    .
    .
    END SUBRT;
END MAIN;
```

If an ON condition is raised as a result of a condition occurring in the main procedure, then ONLOC returns the name of that procedure; in this case, 'MAIN'. If the ON condition is raised in the nested procedure in the previous example, then ONLOC would return the value 'SUBRT'. As can be seen, this built-in function will help you to pinpoint the location of the error more closely.

**ONCHAR and ONSOURCE.** ONCHAR and ONSOURCE are pseudovariables as well as built-in functions. As built-in functions, ONCHAR and ONSOURCE return the character and source fields, respectively, containing the character that caused the CONVERSION condition to be raised. As pseudovariables, ON-CHAR and ONSOURCE may be used to modify the data in the source field that caused the CONVERSION condition.

CHAR = ONCHAR;

└──────→ Extracts the character that caused the
CONVERSION condition to be raised; it can
be used in an on-unit for the CONVERSION
condition or in an ERROR on-unit as a result
of a conversion error.  If it is used out of
context, it returns a blank.  The value returned
by this function is a character-string of length
1, containing the character that caused the
CONVERSION condition to be raised.

SOURCE = ONSOURCE;

└──────→ Extracts the contents of the field that was
being processed when a CONVERSION
condition was raised.  This function can
be used in the on-unit for a
CONVERSION condition or in an
on-unit for an ERROR condition.  When
used out of context, a null string is
returned.  The value returned by this
function is a varying-length character-
string giving the contents of the field
being processed when CONVERSION
was raised.

## PROGRAM-CHECKOUT CONDITIONS

You may wish to enable two on-units—normally disabled—for the purpose of
debugging your program.  The conditions are STRINGRANGE and STRING-
SIZE.

**The STRINGRANGE Condition.**  This condition is raised whenever the lengths of
the arguments to the SUBSTR built-in function reference a nonexistent part of
string data.  For example:

```
DECLARE NAME   CHAR (20);
DECLARE LAST   CHAR (16);
LAST = SUBSTR(NAME,5,20); /* STRINGRANGE ERROR */
```

Recall that the second argument to SUBSTR indicates the starting string position,
and the third argument indicates the number of characters to be retrieved from

the specified string. In the previous example, if the starting position is 5, then the maximum number of characters remaining in the 20-character string is 16. The example indicated a value of 20 — four more positions beyond the end of the string. The standard system action, providing that STRINGRANGE has been enabled, is to print an appropriate message; then program execution continues from the point of interruption. In addition, the arguments to SUBSTR are revised to force them to be within limits. In the previous example, the third argument, 20, would be changed to 16, because that is the maximum length that may be specified if the starting position is 5. If the starting position is outside the limits of the string data, a null string is returned.

STRINGRANGE is disabled by default. To enable it, specify a condition prefix. For example:

```
(STRINGRANGE):
PERSONL: PROCEDURE OPTIONS (MAIN);
   .
   .
   .
END PERSONL;
```

After your program has been debugged, you should remove this condition prefix because checking for STRINGRANGE errors can add considerable overhead to your program.

**The STRINGSIZE Condition.** This condition is raised when a string is about to be assigned to a shorter string. The standard system action, providing that STRINGSIZE has been enabled, is to print a message; then execution continues from the point of interruption. The right-hand characters or bits of the *source string* are truncated to accommodate the size of the *target string*. For example:

```
DCL RECEIVE    CHAR (5);
DCL SEND       CHAR (12);

RECEIVE = SEND; /* STRINGSIZE ERROR */
```
                              └──────→ Source string
         └──────────────────────→ Target string

Only the first five characters of SEND will be assigned to RECEIVE. The seven rightmost characters of SEND are ignored for this move operation. This condition is disabled by default. It may be enabled by a condition prefix. For example:

```
(STRINGSIZE):
RECEIVE = SUBSTR (SEND,J,K);
```

Figure 5.5 shows a sample of the type of programming that might be done in handling two conditions: CONVERSION and ERROR. Statements twenty-seven through thirty-eight contain "driver code" designed to test the logic expressed in the on-units for CONVERSION and ERROR. This code was designed to force CONVERSION errors, as well as ERROR errors. Following is a discussion of some of the statements in Figure 5.5.

**Statements 11–14:** The four built-in functions were declared to have the BUILTIN attribute. Recall that built-in functions for which there are no arguments should be explicitly declared to have the attribute BUILTIN. This avoids an error message from the compiler on your source listing.

**Statement 15:** The on-unit specified for the CONVERSION is a begin block.

**Statement 16:** This statement causes a skip to the next line and an ERROR message is printed, indicating that a CONVERSION error has occurred. Note in the first line following this PUT that the ONLOC built-in function has been invoked and the result returned is concatenated to the output message. In the next line, the ONCODE built-in function is invoked and its returned results are concatenated to the output message:

'ONCODE = ' ‖ ONCODE

Following that, the source field causing the error is displayed along with the message that the entire field has been changed to zeros to enable processing to continue.

**Statement 19:** The condition prefix NOSTRINGSIZE is affixed to the statement that causes the source field to be changed. Notice that the word ONSOURCE, a built-in function, is being used here as a pseudovariable. Using it as a pseudovariable means that the receiving field (i.e., the field causing the error in the first place) will be set to a maximum of 16 zeros. Why 16 zeros? Recall that the CONVERSION condition is caused when there is an attempt to convert a character-string to an arithmetic value where the character-string contains characters other than numbers. Arithmetic data on a System/360 or 370 using PL/I can be a maximum of 16 digits long. This on-unit code is written in generalized form; we do not know the size of the data field that caused the error. Specifying a receiving field as receiving the maximum number of zeros possible allows us to handle a field of any precision length from 1 to 16. The NOSTRINGSIZE condition prefix was necessary because the STRINGSIZE condition could be raised if the receiving field is shorter than the sending field. In this case, we disabled the STRINGSIZE condition by prefixing the word NO to the name

```
/*   CHAPTER 5  -- DEBUGGING EXAMPLE          FIG. 5.5              */
/*****************************************************************/
/*   PROGRAM NAME: DEBUG                                         */
/*   DECRIPTION:    THIS PROGRAM DEMONSTRATES THE USE OF PL/I     */
/*                  DEBUGGING TOOLS IN YOUR PROGRAM.             */
/*   INPUT:         NONE                                         */
/*   OUTPUT:        PRINTER                                      */
/*****************************************************************/
 1  DEBUG:  PROCEDURE OPTIONS(MAIN);
 2     DCL A                      FIXED BINARY(15,0);
 3     DCL B                      CHARACTER (4);
 4     DCL C                      FIXED BINARY(15,0);
 5     DCL D                      FIXED BINARY(15,0);
 6     DCL E                      FIXED BINARY(15,0);
 7     DCL F                      FIXED BINARY(15,0);
 8     DCL G                      FIXED BINARY(15,0);
 9     DCL H                      FIXED BINARY(15,0);
10     DCL I                      FIXED BINARY(15,0);

11     DCL ONCHAR                     BUILTIN;
12     DCL ONCODE                     BUILTIN;
13     DCL ONLOC                      BUILTIN;
14     DCL ONSOURCE                   BUILTIN;

15     ON CONVERSION BEGIN;
16        PUT SKIP LIST('CONVERSION ERROR IN PROCEDURE ' || ONLOC);
17        PUT SKIP LIST('ONCODE = ' || ONCODE);
18        PUT SKIP LIST('SOURCE FIELD CAUSING ERROR IS ''' || ONSOURCE ||
                '''.  THIS FIELD CHANGED TO ZERO TO CONTINUE PROCESSING.');
19        (NOSTRINGSIZE):
          ONSOURCE = (16)'0';
20     END;


21     ON ERROR BEGIN;
22        ON ERROR SYSTEM;                /* SAFETY VALVE  */
23        PUT SKIP (3) LIST
             ((54)'*' || ' DEBUG AID ' || (54)'*');
24        PUT SKIP DATA;
25        PUT SKIP (3) LIST
             ((54)'*' || ' DEBUG END ' || (54)'*');
26     END;

27     A = 100;
28     B = 'A100';
29     C = 76;
30     D = 42;
31     E = 53;
32     F = 175;
33     G = 82;
34     H = -505;
35     I = 4500;

36     A = B;
37     A = (A + 2) * 42;
38     SIGNAL ERROR;

39  END DEBUG;
```

FIGURE 5.5



STRINGSIZE.   In this way, we are disabling the recognition of the condition should the STRINGSIZE condition be raised.

Statement 21: The on-unit is specified for the ERROR condition in the form
of a begin block.   Recall that the ERROR condition causes the automatic
termination of your program.   What is left for us to do in this on-unit is to

```
CONVERSION ERROR IN PROCEDURE DEBUG
ONCODE = 612
SOURCE FIELD CAUSING ERROR IS 'A100'.  THIS FIELD CHANGED TO ZERO TO CONTINUE PROCESSING.

******************************************* DEBUG AID *********************************************
I=    4500       H=    -505       G=    82       F=    175       E=    53
D=    42         C=    76         B='0000'       A=    84;
********************************************* DEBUG END *******************************************

**************************************************************************************************
```

FIGURE 5.6

try and get a snapshot of the data errors in our program so as to give us some sort of picture of what went wrong.

**Statement 22:** This statement is essential for it provides a safety feature that will keep your program from looping interminably, should an ERROR condition occur in the output statements that follow. What this statement does is tell the system that if the ERROR condition is now raised, the standard system action should be taken.

**Statements 23 – 25:** A line of asterisks is printed on the line printer followed by the contents of data areas in your program. The data statement causes all data areas to be printed in the form of assignment statements.

Figure 5.6 shows the sample output from this program. The volume of output, of course, is considerably less than you would have in a regular program.

## CONCLUSION

The coding shown in Statements 15 through 26 of Figure 5.5 could be used as standard routines handling the CONVERSION and ERROR conditions. Of course, they could be modified to fit your individual program needs.

One technique to facilitate the use of these generalized on-units is to store the source code in a source statement library at your computer installation. The code, when it is stored in the library, is given a *book name*. This code can then be included in any PL/I program through the use of the PL/I preprocessor statement:

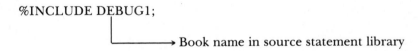

%INCLUDE DEBUG1;

⟶ Book name in source statement library

Check with personnel in your installation for assistance on the JCL required to accomplish this job.

## CASE STUDY

An important aspect of programming is *data validation*. Before a program can manipulate data to produce meaningful output, it must be established that the data items to be processed are valid. Some application programs include tests for data reliability. For example, if an employee number is supposed to be an all-numeric field, then the program could test that field to be sure that all characters within that field are in fact numeric. Should an alphabetic or special character be inadvertently keyed in, then we know a data-entry error has occurred. This error must be corrected; otherwise, we would not have accuracy in the processing and/or output data.

Other types of data validation include checking a field for *reasonableness*. For example, it is not usually reasonable that an hourly rate of more than $40 an hour is ever paid to an employee in company XYZ. Thus, anything over $40 that might be inadvertently entered into the system is not reasonable. A computer program can make this determination.

As another example, a specific field in an input record might contain a code indicating one of several alternatives. For example, in a cost-accounting application, a number of job codes may be defined indicating the type of work completed. Any code inadvertently entered that is not known to the computer program, then, could be assumed to be an error. Again, the application program is to test for this possibility.

Many types of data validation may be performed. They include historic comparisons, logical checking (e.g., it is not logical to have a "negative" value input for quantity purchased), or limit checks. Because the number of tests could be extensive, it is possible to perform data validation in a separate job run particularly in a batch processing environment. This case study provides a programming example centered around the validation of data.

Assume that the Picture Perfect Company wholesales a variety of art goods, prints, and craft supplies. The minimum order accepted by Picture Perfect is $25. Each item ordered by a customer is recorded on a separate input record. Each record contains information about the customer (e.g., the customer's assigned computer number, the purchase order number, the department that stocks the item, etc.). The input record layout is shown in Figure 5.7. Because there is one record for each item purchased, typically there will be a number of item records for each customer, pictured as follows:

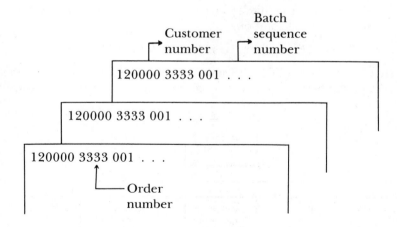

The sequence number field must contain numbers in ascending sequence within each customer group of records. Notice also that a department code

| CUSTOMER NUMBER | ORDER NUMBER | SEQUENCE NUMBER | DEPT | DISCOUNT CODE | ITEM NUMBER | QUANTITY PURCHASED | SALES PRICE | UNUSED |
|---|---|---|---|---|---|---|---|---|
| 6 | 4 | 3 | 1 | 1 | 8 | 5 | 5,2 | 47 |

FIGURE 5.7   Picture Perfect customer input record layout.

appears in the input record.   The validation program is to test for valid department codes.   These codes include:

A F P W Z 5 *

For Department P the *discount code* in the input record must be some value between 1 and 6.   If the department code is other than P, the discount code field must contain a 0.   If either of these conditions does not exist, then the data value is not valid.

Because the minimum order that Picture Perfect will accept is $25, the QUANTITY field must be multiplied by the PRICE and accumulated into a total field to determine that the minimum order requirement for a given customer has been met.   In addition, the program is to test for the possibility of the SIZE condition occurring when QUANTITY is multiplied by PRICE.   Notice from the record layout in Figure 5.7 that the QUANTITY field is a five-digit field and that the PRICE field is also a five-digit field.   If we multiply QUANTITY by PRICE, then the possible resulting field could be 10 positions.   However, a 10-position answer will never result.   This is because, typically, expensive items such as picture frames will be purchased in small lots.   Inexpensive items such as erasers are typically purchased in larger quantities.   Thus, the resulting precision will never be more than six digits.   A receiving field whose precision is 6,2 must be tested to determine that a SIZE error does not occur.

Figure 5.8 shows a program hierarchy chart for the case study.   Figures 5.9 through 5.11 show the PL/I solution.

**Statement 1:** The SIZE condition is enabled with the SIZE prefix.

**Statements 2 – 21:** ALL DECLARE statement variables are listed in alphabetical order at the beginning of the program.   Notice that it is necessary to

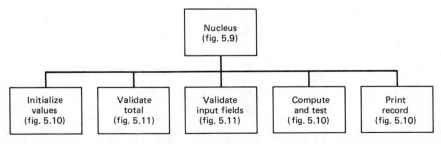

FIGURE 5.8   Segment hierarchy chart for the Validate Data case study.

```
       /* CASE STUDY -- CHAPTER FIVE                        CH5CSTDY         */
       /***********************************************************************/
       /*                                                                     */
       /*    PROGRAM NAME:  VALIDTE                                           */
       /*                                                                     */
       /*    DESCRIPTION:   THIS PROGRAM READS THE CUSTOMER ORDER INPUT FILE   */
       /*                   AND VALIDATES EACH RECORD.  ALL DATA THAT IS IN    */
       /*                   ERROR IS LISTED ON THE REPORT.  THERE IS ONE       */
       /*                   RECORD FOR EACH ITEM ORDER SO SEVERAL RECORDS      */
       /*                   CAN MAKE UP ONE ORDER.                             */
       /*                                                                     */
       /*    INPUT:         CUSTOMER ORDER FILE                                */
       /*                                                                     */
       /*    OUTPUT:        PRINTER                                            */
       /*                                                                     */
       /***********************************************************************/
  1    (SIZE):
       VALIDTE: PROCEDURE OPTIONS(MAIN);
  2       DCL AMOUNT                    FIXED DEC(6,2);
  3       DCL CUSTOMER#                 CHAR(6);
  4       DCL DEPT                      CHAR(1);
  5       DCL DISCOUNT_CODE             FIXED DEC(1);
  6       DCL ERROR_RECORD              BIT(1);
  7       DCL ITEM#                     FIXED DEC(8);
  8       DCL LEGAL_DEPARTMENTS         CHAR(7)      INIT('AFPWZ5*');
  9       DCL MORE_RECORDS              BIT(1)       INIT('1'B);
 10       DCL NO                        BIT(1)       INIT('0'B);
 11       DCL ORDER#                    CHAR(4);
 12       DCL PRICE                     FIXED DEC(5,2);
 13       DCL QUANTITY                  FIXED DEC(5);
 14       DCL SAVE_CUSTOMER#            CHAR(6);
 15       DCL SAVE_ORDER#               CHAR(4);
 16       DCL SAVE_SEQUENCE#            FIXED DEC(3);
 17       DCL SEQUENCE#                 FIXED DEC(3);
 18       DCL SIZE_ERROR                BIT(1);
 19       DCL TOTAL                     FIXED DEC(9,2);
 20       DCL YES                       BIT(1)       INIT('1'B);
 21       DCL (ONCHAR,ONSOURCE,VERIFY)  BUILTIN;

 22       ON ENDFILE(SYSIN)
             MORE_RECORDS = NO;
 23       ON SIZE
             SIZE_ERROR = YES;
 24       ON CONVERSION
             BEGIN;
 25             PUT SKIP LIST('INVALID NUMERIC FIELD = ',ONSOURCE);
 26             ONCHAR = '0';
 27             ERROR_RECORD = YES;
 28          END;

       /***********************************************************************/
       /*    PROGRAM NUCLEUS                                                  */
       /***********************************************************************/
 29    CALL INITIALIZATION;
 30    GET FILE(SYSIN)LIST (CUSTOMER#,ORDER#,SEQUENCE#,DEPT,DISCOUNT_CODE,
          ITEM#,QUANTITY,PRICE);
 31    SAVE_CUSTOMER# = CUSTOMER#;
 32    SAVE_ORDER#    = ORDER#;
 33    SAVE_SEQUENCE# = 0;
 34    DO WHILE(MORE_RECORDS);
 35       IF CUSTOMER# = SAVE_CUSTOMER# & ORDER# = SAVE_ORDER# THEN
             SAVE_SEQUENCE# = SAVE_SEQUENCE# + 1;
 36       ELSE DO;
 37             CALL VALIDATE_TOTAL;
 38             SAVE_CUSTOMER# = CUSTOMER#;
 39             SAVE_ORDER# = ORDER#;
 40             SAVE_SEQUENCE# = 1;
 41          END;
 42       CALL VALIDATE_INPUT_FIELDS;
 43       CALL COMPUTE_AND_TEST_AMOUNT;
 44       IF ERROR_RECORD THEN
             DO;
 45             CALL PRINT_RECORD;
 46             ERROR_RECORD = NO;
 47          END;
 48       GET FILE(SYSIN)LIST (CUSTOMER#,ORDER#,SEQUENCE#,DEPT,DISCOUNT_CODE,
             ITEM#,QUANTITY,PRICE);
 49    END;
 50    CALL VALIDATE_TOTAL;
 51    PUT SKIP(3) LIST('ALL DATA HAS BEEN PROCESSED');
```

FIGURE 5.9

```
/***************************************************************************/
/*   COMPUTE AND TEST AMOUNT                                               */
/*                                                                         */
/*   CALCULATE THE TOTAL PRICE FOR ALL THE ITEMS ORDERED AND ADD THE       */
/*   ITEM TOTAL TO THE ORDER TOTAL.  AN ITEM TOTAL OF $10,000 OR           */
/*   MORE IS FLAGGED AS AN ERROR.                                          */
/***************************************************************************/
52  COMPUTE_AND_TEST_AMOUNT: PROCEDURE;

53     AMOUNT = PRICE * QUANTITY;
54     IF SIZE_ERROR THEN
          DO;
55            PUT SKIP LIST('PRICE * QUANTITY EXCEEDS MAXIMUM AMOUNT',
                            PRICE,QUANTITY);
56            AMOUNT        = 0;
57            SIZE_ERROR    = NO;
58            ERROR_RECORD  = YES;
59        END;
60     TOTAL = TOTAL + AMOUNT;

61  END COMPUTE_AND_TEST_AMOUNT;

/***************************************************************************/
/*   INITIALIZATION                                                        */
/***************************************************************************/
62  INITIALIZATION:   PROCEDURE;

63     ERROR_RECORD = NO;
64     SIZE_ERROR   = NO;
65     TOTAL        = 0;

66  END INITIALIZATION;

/***************************************************************************/
/*   PRINT THE RECORD                                                      */
/***************************************************************************/
67  PRINT_RECORD:   PROCEDURE;
68     PUT SKIP    LIST(CUSTOMER# || '   ' || ORDER# || '   ' ||
                        SEQUENCE# || '   ' || DEPT || '   ' || DISCOUNT_CODE
                        || '   ' || ITEM# || '   ' || QUANTITY || PRICE);
69     PUT SKIP(2)LIST((120)'*');
70     PUT SKIP(3);

71  END PRINT_RECORD;
```

**FIGURE 5.10**

specify the built-in functions ONCHAR and ONSOURCE as having the
BUILTIN attribute because these functions do not have arguments.   Had
the attribute BUILTIN been omitted, an error message from the compiler is
generated.

Statement 23: When the SIZE condition occurs, the on-unit specified sets an
   indicator called SIZE_ERROR to the ON or YES position.   This indicator
   is tested later in the program.

Statements 24 – 28: The on-unit specified for the CONVERSION condition is
   in the form of a begin block.   In this block an error message is printed,
   followed by the contents of the field causing the error.   The ONSOURCE
   built-in function, as a list item in the PUT LIST statement, causes the
   contents of the field in error to print.   In Statement 26, ONCHAR is used as
   a pseudovariable.   The character causing the CONVERSION error is set to

```
/**************************************************************************/
/*    VALIDATE INPUT FIELDS                                             */
/*                                                                      */
/*    VALIDATE DEPARTMENT CODE AND DISCOUNT CODE FOR THE DEPARTMENT.    */
/*    VERIFY THAT THE INPUT RECORDS ARE IN SEQUENCE.                    */
/**************************************************************************/
72   VALIDATE_INPUT_FIELDS:  PROCEDURE;

73      IF VERIFY(DEPT,LEGAL_DEPARTMENTS) ¬= 0 THEN
            DO;
74              PUT SKIP LIST('INVALID DEPARTMENT CODE = ' || DEPT);
75              ERROR_RECORD = YES;
76          END;
77      IF (DEPT = 'P' & (DISCOUNT_CODE < 1 | DISCOUNT_CODE > 6)) |
            (DEPT ¬= 'P' & DISCOUNT_CODE ¬= 0) THEN
            DO;
78              PUT SKIP LIST ('INVALID DISCOUNT CODE (' || DISCOUNT_CODE ||
                    ') FOR DEPARTMENT ' || DEPT);
79              ERROR_RECORD = YES;
80          END;
81      IF SEQUENCE# ¬= SAVE_SEQUENCE# THEN
            DO;
82              PUT SKIP LIST('SEQUENCE NUMBER ERROR','PREVIOUS SEQUENCE # = '
                    || SAVE_SEQUENCE#,'NEW SEQUENCE # = ' || SEQUENCE#);
83              SAVE_SEQUENCE# = SEQUENCE#;
84              ERROR_RECORD = YES;
85          END;

86   END VALIDATE_INPUT_FIELDS;

/**************************************************************************/
/*    VALIDATE THE TOTAL ORDER AMOUNT                                   */
/*                                                                      */
/*    TEST FOR A MINIMUM $25.00 PER CUSTOMER ORDER AND RESET TOTAL TO   */
/*    ZERO FOR THE NEXT CUSTOMER ORDER.                                 */
/**************************************************************************/
87   VALIDATE_TOTAL:  PROCEDURE;

88      IF TOTAL < 25 THEN
            PUT SKIP LIST('TOTAL IS BELOW MINIMUM',TOTAL,
                    'CUSTOMER # = ' || SAVE_CUSTOMER#,
                    'ORDER # = ' || SAVE_ORDER#);
89      TOTAL = 0;

90   END VALIDATE_TOTAL;

91   END VALIDTE;
```

**FIGURE 5.11**


0 so that the program processing may continue. Statement 27 causes the
indicator ERROR_RECORD to be turned ON.

**Statement 29:** The INITIALIZATION subroutine is called.

**Statements 30–33:** The first input record is read; CUSTOMER# and
ORDER# are save in appropriately named fields for comparison in the
program later. The SAVE_SEQUENCE# field is initialized to 0. Later,
this field is incremented for each record read and compared with the sequence number keyed into the input record.

**Statements 34–49:** These statements provide the basic program loop. Statement 35 tests the customer number to determine the control break. If
the record just read is related to the customer number currently being

processed, then the SAVE_SEQUENCE# counter is incremented by 1. Otherwise, as indicated in Statements 36 through 41, the initialization for the new customer record coming in must be specified. The VALIDATE_TOTAL subroutine is invoked to test if the total amount of the previous customer's purchase is less than $25. Statements 42 and 43 call the lower-level segments related to the data validation that must be performed for each of the specified fields in the input record. Statement 44 tests the ERROR_RECORD indicator. If an error has occurred, then the PRINT_RECORD procedure is called. This program prints only records that are in error. A record that passes all validation tests is not listed. Statement 48 causes the next input record to be read; the program loop repeats itself until the end-of-file is encountered.

**Statement 50:** We reach this point when the end-of-file is encountered. One final test, however, must be specified for the last group of records read. That test involves validating that the customer's total is $25 or more. The VALIDATE_TOTAL subroutine is called again.

**Statement 51:** An end-of-job message is printed. If all input data items are valid (i.e., customer's totals are $25 or more), the only output message is the one shown in Statement 51. Had an end-of-job message not been included and all data passed the validation tests, you would have no real way of knowing that the program ran to successful completion.

**Statements 72–86:** Validates input fields and verifies sequential input. In Statement 73, the VERIFY built-in function is invoked to determine that DEPT contains only valid characters (AFPWZ5*). This function examines two strings to verify that each character or bit in the first string is represented in the second string, returning a fixed binary value of 0 if this is the case; otherwise the value returned is the position of the first character in the first string that is not represented in the second string. For example:

```
DCL STR        CHAR (5);
DCL DIGITS     CHAR (1) INIT ('0123456789');
STR = '01232';
I     = VERIFY(STR,DIGITS); /* I = 0 */
STR = '123.2';
I     = VERIFY(STR,DIGITS); /* I = 4 */
```

**Statements 87–90:** The total order amount for a minimum of $25 is tested and an exception message printed.

**Statement 89:** The TOTAL field is re-initialized to 0. This is the field into which the amount of purchase is accumulated to determine that a customer order meets the minimum requirement of $25.

**Statements 52–61:** The total price for all items ordered is calculated. If a SIZE error is raised, it means that the item total exceeds $9,999.99.

**The Null Statement:** The null statement is simply a semicolon, or a semicolon with a label attached to it. It is an executable statement, but nothing happens.

**The IF Statement:** The IF statement is used in a PL/I program when a test or decision is to be made between alternatives.

**1. Simple IF:** In this statement, a single statement will appear as the action to be taken if the condition is true (e.g., IF X < 0 THEN X = 1;).

**2. The compound IF:** This IF statement is called compound because it contains two PL/I statements. Its form includes the use of the keyword ELSE. If the condition tested is true, the statement following the THEN is performed; if the condition tested is not true, the statement following the ELSE is performed (e.g., IF A = B THEN X = 1; ELSE X = 2;).

**3. Nested IF statements:** There may be IF statements contained in either the THEN or ELSE clause of another IF statement.

**4. A null ELSE in nested IF statements:** The null ELSE is an ELSE with a null statement (recall the semicolon) as its clause. It is, as its name implies, a nonoperative statement. It gives no direction to the computer. Rather, its effect is to supply the necessary ELSE clause to be associated with the innermost IF.

**5. The do-group in an IF statement:** The IF statement is designed to execute one statement following the THEN or ELSE clause. If it is desired to execute more than one statement following the THEN or the ELSE, a do-group may be specified.

**6. Bit-string operators in the IF statement:** The operators AND (&) and OR (|) can be used in the IF statement to eliminate nested IF statements.

**Logical Operations:**

| AND | OR | NOT |
|-----|-----|-----|
| 1 & 1 → 1 | 1\|1 → 1 | ¬0 → 1 |
| 1 & 0 → 0 | 1\|0 → 1 | ¬1 → 0 |
| 0 & 1 → 0 | 0\|1 → 1 | |
| 0 & 0 → 0 | 0\|0 → 0 | |

These operations, when applied to bit-strings, are also referred to as *Boolean operations*.

**CASE Structure:** This structure is an extension of the IF-THEN-ELSE structure. The need for it arises when a test is performed and one of many alternatives is subsequently executed. The CASE structure may be drawn in flowchart form as a series of nested IFs in which the shaped decision symbol is used. Another way in which the CASE structure may be drawn is:

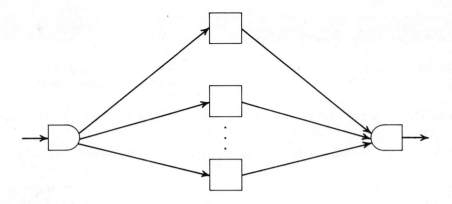

Two methods in which the CASE structure may be implemented are nested IF-THEN-ELSE and the select-group. The select-group begins with the keyword SELECT and ends with the word END. An expression may or may not follow the SELECT. Indented within the select-group are one or more WHEN clauses and optionally an OTHERWISE clause. Following each of these clauses a single statement, a do-group or a begin block, may be specified.

**Conditions:** The ON statement is used to specify the action to be taken when an exceptional condition arises. An exceptional condition is the occurrence of an unexpected event at an unpredictable time. In the absence of your program specifying an action to be taken, when these exceptional conditions are detected, a standard system action will take place. For most conditions, the standard system action is to print a message and then raise the ERROR condition, which usually results in termination of your PL/I program. Some conditions are always enabled unless explicitly disabled. When a condition is enabled, it means that if the condition occurs, either programmer-defined action or system action will take place. Thus, when conditions are disabled, errors may go undetected. The I/O conditions are always enabled and may not be disabled. Conditions are enabled through a condition prefix, which is the name of one or more conditions separated by commas, enclosed in parentheses, and prefixed to a statement by a colon. The word NO preceding the condition name indicates that the condition is to be disabled. Through the use of the SIGNAL statement, the programmer may simulate the occurrence of any of the exceptional conditions. Execution of the SIGNAL statement has the same effect as if the condition had actually occurred. Figure 5.12 depicts the PL/I logic path when a condition occurs. An earlier chart, Figure 5.4, summarizes conditions presented in this chapter.

**Built-in Functions:** The following built-in functions facilitate program debugging:

**1. ONCODE:** This built-in function may be specified in any on-unit. It returns a

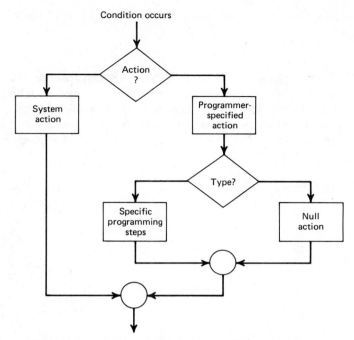

Condition occurs

Action ?

System action

Programmer-specified action

Type?

Specific programming steps

Null action

FIGURE 5.12 PL/I logic path when a condition occurs.

FIXED BINARY (15) integer that defines the type of interrupt that caused the unit to become active. These are called **on-codes** and are defined in Appendix E.

**2. ONLOC:** This built-in function may also be specified in any on-unit. It returns a character-string indicating the name of the procedure in which the condition was raised. This is particularly useful when your program contains nested procedures. A typical way in which this built-in function and the ONCODE function are used is simply to print the values returned using a PUT LIST. For example:

    PUT LIST (ONLOC, ONCODE);

**3. ONSOURCE:** This built-in function returns a character-string whose value is the contents of the field that was being processed when the CONVERSION condition was raised. ONSOURCE may be specified in an on-unit for the CONVERSION or ERROR conditions. ONSOURCE may also be specified as a pseudovariable. This means that ONSOURCE will appear on the left-hand side of an equal sign. It causes the current value of the field that caused the CONVERSION error to be reset to the specified value. For example:

    ONSOURCE = ' ';

In the case of resetting an arithmetic field, the following could be coded:

ONSOURCE = 0;

**4. ONCHAR:** As a built-in function, ONCHAR returns the character that caused the CONVERSION condition to be raised. It may only be used in an on-unit for the CONVERSION or ERROR conditions. ONCHAR may also be used as a pseudovariable. As a pseudovariable, it causes the current value of the character causing the CONVERSION error to be changed to the specified value. For example:

ONCHAR = '0';

# CHAPTER 6

# DOs and Arrays

Repetition is one of the primary tasks for which the computer is designed. One method for achieving repetition is through the use of the DO-WHILE. Two other PL/I statements that facilitate program looping are the DO-UNTIL and the iterative DO. These statements are used to control the repeated processing of data stored as records in files on tapes or disks or the processing of data in **arrays.** An array is a collection of data in main memory.

Collections of data, called **data aggregates** in PL/I, are referred to by a single name. There are two types of *data aggregates* in PL/I: *arrays* and **structures.** In this chapter, we will look at arrays in detail and examine the PL/I statements that are used to manipulate them.

## DO-UNTIL Structure

The DO-UNTIL structure provides essentially the same loop capability as the DO-WHILE. It differs from the DO-WHILE in two respects:

**1.** The test for loop control is done *after* the execution of statements within the range of the DO. Thus, the contained statements will always be executed at least once.

**2.** The DO-UNTIL is terminated when the condition tested is true (DO-WHILE terminates when the condition tested is false). Here is the structure:

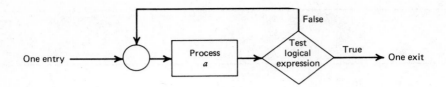

The DO UNTIL PL/I statement, which may or may not be available in the compiler you are using, is coded as follows:

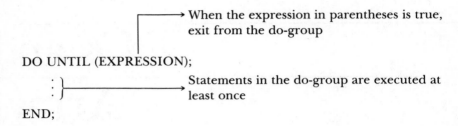

Here are the steps performed in the DO-UNTIL structure:

**1.** Execute statements in the do-group.

**2.** When the END statement is encountered, test the expression specified in parentheses following the DO UNTIL STATEMENT.

**3.** If the expression is false, repeat execution of the do-group; otherwise, transfer program control to the statement following the END terminating the DO.

The DO-UNTIL structure is an alternative method for handling the repetitive reading of records until the end-of-file is encountered. Notice in the following coding,

```
ON ENDFILE(SYSIN)
    EOF = YES;
EOF = NO;
GET FILE(SYSIN) LIST (DATA);
IF EOF THEN
    CALL NO_RECORDS_IN_FILE;
ELSE
    DO UNTIL (EOF);
        CALL PROCESS_DATA;
        GET FILE(SYSIN) LIST (DATA);
    END;
```

that the end-of-file indicator, EOF, is to be turned on (i.e., set equal to YES) when the end-of-file condition is encountered. The EOF indicator is then initialized to NO.

The DO-UNTIL structure is equivalent to the following sequence and DO-WHILE structures:

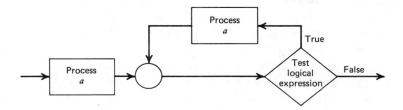

This concatenates a duplicate of box *a* with a DO-WHILE structure. Thus, a DO-UNTIL structure can be transformed into an equivalent structure containing simple sequence and a DO-WHILE.

## CHECKPOINT QUESTIONS

**1.** Into which two basic structures may the DO-UNTIL be reduced?

**2.** In a DO-UNTIL, when is the testing of the expression performed?

**3.** True or false? Statements contained within the DO-UNTIL may never be executed if the expression in parentheses is true when the structure is entered.

### The Iterative DO

The iterative DO statement, introduced earlier, is described in more detail here because it is a widely used form of the DO. Note the terminology used to describe the various parts of this iterative form of the DO.

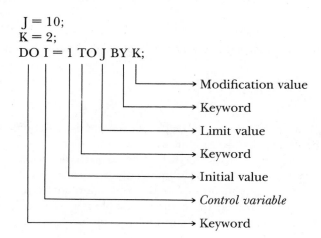

$$J = 10;$$
$$K = 2;$$
$$DO\ I = 1\ TO\ J\ BY\ K;$$

→ Modification value

→ Keyword

→ Limit value

→ Keyword

→ Initial value

→ *Control variable*

→ Keyword

The iterative DO is a DO-WHILE structure; it performs the following steps in the sequence listed:

**1. Initialize the control variable:** This variable (I, in the previous example) is set equal to the initial value (1, as specified in the example). Greater program efficiency results if you select a FIXED BINARY identifier for your variable. You may modify this variable inside the do-loop.

**2. Test control variable:** If the control variable is less than or equal to the limit value (10 in the example), execute the sequence of statements that follow the DO; otherwise, transfer to the statement following the END statement that terminates the DO. Upon entering a DO, the limit value is copied into a "temporary storage area" that is not accessible by your program. Thus, even if your program modified the limit value within the range of the DO, the change in value has no effect on the number of times through the loop. This is because the "copied" value is used for comparison in the program loop.

**3. Execute statements following the DO:** The statements headed by the DO and terminated by the END are executed.

**4. Modify control variable:** The modification value is added to the control variable. Using the previous example, the value 2 is added to the contents of I.

**5. Return to step 2:** This form of the DO is a DO-WHILE structure because the comparison of the control variable with the limit value is performed *before* any statements in the do-group are executed. Thus, it is possible (as is characteristic of the DO-WHILE) that the do-group may never be executed as shown in the following example:

```
J = 10;
K = 5;
L = 2;
DO I = J TO K BY L;
    :
    :
END;
```

Consider the value of the **control variable** each time through a loop controlled by the statement

```
DO K = 1 TO 100 BY 5;
```

The first time through the loop, K will be equal to 1. The second time through the loop, K will be equal to 6. Recall that the modification value, in this case 5, is to be added to the control variable (5 + 1 = 6). The third time through the loop, K will be equal to 11. The last time the statements within the do-group are executed, K will be equal to 96. When the modification value of 5 is again added to K, K becomes 101. Then, when the test on the control variable is performed, the do-loop is terminated, because K is greater than the limit value.

The preceding explanation of the steps performed in a do-loop applies when the modification value is positive. It is also possible to specify a negative modification value, in which case a "countdown" operation is in effect. For example, in the loop

DO K = 60 TO 1 BY − 1;
.
.
.
END;

the steps performed would be the following:

**1.** Initialize K to 60.

**2.** Test K: If the control variable is *greater than* or *equal to* the limit value, execute statements that follow the DO; otherwise, transfer to the statement following the END. The negative modification value causes the DO group to be executed on the *greater* than rather than the *less* than condition. (In the previous example, when the loop is terminated, K will be equal to 0.)

**3.** Execute statements following the DO.

**4.** When END is encountered, modify K by − 1.

**5.** Return to step 2.

So far, you have been introduced to this form of the DO:

DO I = 1 TO 100 BY 1;

Notice in the following variation of the previous DO statement that the BY 1 and the TO 100 have been reversed:

DO I = 1 BY 1 TO 100;

Reversing the position of the limit and modification values in the DO does not alter the way in which the steps will be executed.

Also, if the modification value is a 1, it is not necessary to specify it. For example, the statement

DO I = 1 TO 100;

accomplishes the same number of iterations as if

DO I = 1 TO 100 BY 1;

had been coded. Or the limit value may be omitted from the DO. For example:

DO I = 1 BY 1;

Here, the termination of the do-group must be accomplished by other coding within the DO, because there is no comparison made with a limit value. However, if there is no other coding to terminate the DO, the control variable will eventually be increased to the point where an overflow (FIXEDOVERFLOW or OVER-FLOW) condition is raised.

In a DO, the initial value, the limit value, and the modification value may be specified in the form of constants, variables, or expressions. In addition, these values may be whole numbers, fractions, or mixed numbers, and they may be positive or negative. Here are some examples:

```
DO I = K*2 TO K*5 by J — 4;
DO A = 0.1 TO 1 BY 0.1;
DO B = 1.5 TO 10 BY 0.025;
DO J = 5 TO −5 BY −1;
```

Here is another variation of the DO — it makes use of *multiple specifications:*

```
DO M = 1 TO 10, 21 TO 30, 41 TO 50;
```
└─────────→ Implied DO M = 21 to 30;

```
    ·
    ·
    ·
END;
```

In this example, the loop would be executed 30 times. The index M goes from 1 to 10; then M is initialized to 21 and goes to 30; finally, M is set to 41 and goes to 50 in the loop. Upon exit from the loop, M would contain the value of 51. Note that it is not necessary to specify any numeric sequence or pattern in this form of the DO. For example:

```
DO K = 1 TO 5, 8 TO 18 BY 2, 50 TO 55, 40 TO 44;
    ·
    ·
    ·
END;
```

Here is another form of the DO:

```
DO J = 1,8,9,11,6,13;
    ·
    ·
    ·
END;
```

The statements are executed a total of six times. The first time through the loop, J is a 1; the second time J is an 8; the third time J is a 9; etc. Upon exit from the loop, J is a 13. It is also possible to include the WHILE option with the iterative DO we have been examining. For example:

```
DO K = 1 TO 10 WHILE(X>100);
    .
    .
END;
```

The control variable (K in this case) is tested against the limit value (10). If it is within the limits established ($<$ or $=$ 10), then the expression following the WHILE is tested. Both tests must be met *before* statements following the DO are performed. If the expression (X $>$ 100) is true, the do-loop is executed. If X remains greater than 100, the loop is performed a maximum of 10 times. However, if the expression is false (in this example, when X $<=$ 100), then there is a transfer to the statement following the END statement.

In the following example, the DO specifies that the group is to be executed at least 10 times, and then (providing that A is equal to B) once more:

```
DO I = 1 TO 10, 11 WHILE(A = B);
    .
    .
END;
```

If "BY 0" were inserted after the 11,

```
DO I = 1 TO 10, 11 BY 0 WHILE(A = B);
    .
    .
END;
```

then execution continues with I set to 11 as long as A remained equal to B. Note that a comma separates the two specifications. A succeeding specification is considered only after the preceding specification is satisfied.

The control variables may also be character-string constants:

```
DO OUTCOME = 'WIN', 'LOSE', 'DRAW';
    .
    .
END;
```

The UNTIL option may also be specified with the iterative DO in the same manner that the WHILE option may be specified. For example:

```
DO I = 1 TO 8 UNTIL (A = B);
```

As long as A is not equal to B, the do-group is executed up to a maximum of eight times. The test of the index specification

```
DO I = 1 TO 8;
```

is performed at the *beginning* of the do-group; the test of the expression following the UNTIL is performed at the *end* of the do-group. Thus, in the following example, the loop is executed only once assuming that the first pair of values input is 5 and 5:

```
A    = 0;
B    = 0;
SUM = 0;
DO I = 1 TO 8 UNTIL (A = B);
    GET LIST (A,B);
    SUM = A + B + SUM;
END;
```

## Nested Do-Groups

Do-groups may be nested within other do-groups. For example:

```
DO I = 1 TO 99;
    DO J = 1 TO 100;
    .
    .
    END;
.
.
END;
```

The statements within the inner DO are executed 100 times for each execution of the outer DO.

All statements in the range of the inner DO must be within the range of the outer DO. This arrangement of do-groups is referred to as *nested do-groups* and takes the following form (brackets are used to indicate the range of the do-groups):

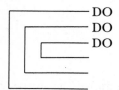

```
DO
DO
DO
```

The following configuration is not valid:

```
DO
DO
```

It is possible to transfer out of a do-group before the maximum number of iterations has been performed. However, it is not permitted to transfer to a statement in an iterative do-group.

### Leaving a Do-Loop

The logic of a problem expressed using a program loop sometimes requires a transfer out of the loop *before* the established limits have been reached. Historically, a GO TO statement was used—an approach not accepted in the structured programming discipline. Another technique is to set the index variable to the maximum value, thereby terminating the loop earlier than the maximum specified. For example:

```
DO I = 1 TO 50;
     GET LIST (A,DATA);
     IF A < 0 THEN
          I = 50;
     ELSE CALL PROCESS_DATA;
END;
```

**4.** What are the three steps performed *automatically* in an iterative DO?

**5.** Is the iterative DO a DO-WHILE or DO-UNTIL structure?

**6.** What value does K contain after execution of each of the following?

(a)
```
J = 3;
K = 4;
DO M = 1 TO J;
  K = K + M;
END;
```
(b)
```
J = 3;
L = 10;
K = 2;
DO M=J to L WHILE (K < 5);
  K = K + M;
END;
```
(c)
```
SUM = 0;
DO K = 1 TO 50 BY 2;
  GET LIST (DATA);
  SUM = SUM + DATA;
END;
```

**7.** Of the following methods, which ones are acceptable in structured programming for causing control to transfer out of a do-group while maintaining program logic in a forward "flow?"

(a) CALL
(b) GO TO
(c) LEAVE
(d) Reset limit value to less than index value
(e) Set index variable greater than limit value

## An Example Using Iterative DOs

Figure 6.1 shows a program in which a file of names is processed. To illustrate character-string manipulation using iterative DOs, assume that the file consists of first names followed by last names. For example:

MADELINE WARBURG
JIM FRIEDL

```
/*   SWITCH FIRST AND LAST NAME                                            */
/*************************************************************************/
/*   PROGRAM NAME: SURNAME                                                */
/*                                                                        */
/*   DECRIPTION:    THIS PROGRAM READS A NAME FILE CONTAINING NAMES       */
/*                  IN FIRST NAME FIRST AND LAST NAME LAST ORDER AND       */
/*                  SWITCHES THEM SO THAT LAST NAME IS FIRST AND FIRST     */
/*                  NAME IS LAST.  THE LAST NAME IS FOLLOWED BY A          */
/*                  COMMA AND A BLANK.                                     */
/*                                                                        */
/*   INPUT:         SYSTEM INPUT                                          */
/*                                                                        */
/*   OUTPUT:        PRINTER                                               */
/*************************************************************************/
SURNAME:   PROCEDURE OPTIONS(MAIN);
    DCL FIRST_CHAR          FIXED BINARY(15,0);
    DCL FULL_NAME           CHAR (40);
    DCL LAST_CHAR           FIXED BINARY(15,0);
    DCL LENGTH_OF_NAME      FIXED BINARY(15,0);
    DCL MORE_RECORDS        BIT(1)            INIT ('1'B);
    DCL NO                  BIT(1)            INIT ('0'B);

    DCL SUBSTR              BUILTIN;

    ON ENDFILE (SYSIN)
       MORE_RECORDS = NO;

    PUT PAGE LIST('FIRST NAME FIRST',' ','LAST NAME FIRST');
    PUT SKIP (2);
    GET LIST(FULL_NAME);
    PUT SKIP LIST(FULL_NAME);

    DO WHILE(MORE_RECORDS);
       DO LAST_CHAR     = 40 TO 1 BY -1
                    WHILE(SUBSTR(FULL_NAME,LAST_CHAR,1) = ' ');
       END;
       DO FIRST_CHAR    = LAST_CHAR TO 1 BY -1
                    UNTIL(SUBSTR(FULL_NAME,FIRST_CHAR,1) = ' ');
       END;
       LENGTH_OF_NAME = LAST_CHAR - FIRST_CHAR;
       FIRST_CHAR     = FIRST_CHAR + 1;
       IF FIRST_CHAR   > 1 THEN
          FULL_NAME    = SUBSTR(FULL_NAME,FIRST_CHAR,LENGTH_OF_NAME) ||
                    ', ' || SUBSTR(FULL_NAME,1,FIRST_CHAR - 1);
       PUT LIST (FULL_NAME);
       GET LIST(FULL_NAME);
       PUT SKIP LIST(FULL_NAME);
    END;
END SURNAME;
```

FIGURE 6.1   Character-string manipulation using iterative DOs.

The string manipulation involves exchanging first and last names and placing a comma immediately following the last name. For example:

WARBURG, MADELINE
FRIEDL, JIM

Within the DO-WHILE, the first do-group searches from the end of the string to the beginning to determine the first non-blank character which is the end of the name. The next do-group searches for the blank separating the first name from the last name. At this point, the lengths of the individual names can be calculated as well as the length of the entire name. The variable FULL_NAME is reset to the last name concatenated with a comma and a blank and then concatenated with the first name. The results are printed.

## ARRAYS

An **array** is a table of data items in which each item has the same attribute as every other item in the array. An array has storage reserved for it by means of a DECLARE statement. For example:

DECLARE TEMPERATURES (365)   FIXED DEC (4,1);

In the DECLARE statement, TEMPERATURES is the name of the array. It is declared with four attributes:

1. (365) is the number of elements in the array — *its* **extent.**
2. DECIMAL is the base attribute of all its elements.
3. FIXED is the scale attribute of all its elements.
4. (4,1) is the precision attribute of all its elements.

As you can see, the attribute defining the number of elements in an *array* is placed immediately after the name of the array in the DECLARE statement. A precision attribute, if written, must always follow a base or scale attribute; thus, you can tell by its position in the DECLARE statement whether an attribute is a precision attribute or whether it defines the number of elements in an array.

### Bounds
In declaring the size of an array, a **bound** is specified. In the example,

DCL TEMPERATURES (365)   FIXED DEC (4,1);

the number 365 specifies the **upper** bound of the array. The **lower** bound in this example is assumed to be 1.

It is possible to specify both a lower and an upper bound. For example:

DCL TABLE (0 : 11)   FIXED DEC (5);

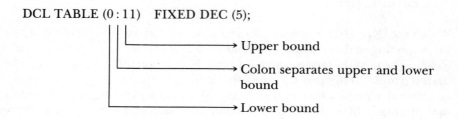

→ Upper bound

→ Colon separates upper and lower bound

→ Lower bound

The *extent* is 12 because there are 12 elements between 0 and 11. It is also possible to specify a negative value for bounds. For example:

DCL GRAPH (−5 : +5);   FLOAT DEC (6);

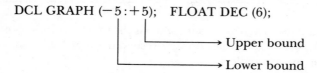

→ Upper bound

→ Lower bound

Thus, the array GRAPH might be thought of as follows:

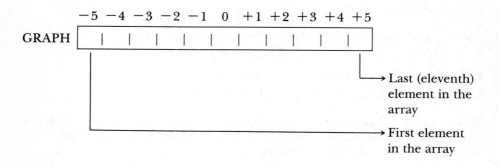

Here is another example of specifying upper and lower bounds with the array pictured in a vertical manner (note the use of the INITIAL attribute):

DCL LIST (−2 : 6)   FIXED BIN (15,0)   INIT
    (91,20,82,11,73,48,19,16,70);

```
LIST(−2)  [91]
   (−1)  [20]
    (0)  [82]
    (1)  [11]
    (2)  [73]
    (3)  [48]
    (4)  [19]
    (5)  [16]
    (6)  [70]
```

Bounds may be constants, variables, expressions, or asterisks. Bounds that are variables or expressions are determined when storage is allocated for the array. An asterisk means that the actual bounds are defined later either in an ALLOCATE statement (Chapter 9) or via an argument to a subroutine or function procedure.

## Dimensions

The number of sets of upper and lower bounds specifies the number of dimensions in an array. For example, 12 data items could be arranged in two groups of six items each. The array could be declared,

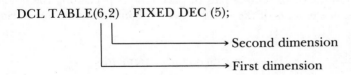

and could be thought of as a two-dimensional table. For example,

```
              Column 1    Column 2
Row 1   ┌──────────────┬──────────────┐
        │              ┊              │
Row 2   ├──────────────┼──────────────┤
        │              ┊              │
Row 3   ├──────────────┼──────────────┤
        │              ┊              │
Row 4   ├──────────────┼──────────────┤
        │              ┊              │
Row 5   ├──────────────┼──────────────┤
        │              ┊              │
Row 6   └──────────────┴──────────────┘
```

In referring to two-dimensional arrays, sometimes the terms *rows* and *columns* are used. These terms, however, are not used to describe parts of arrays that have more than two dimensions.

Here is an example of declaring a two-dimensional array in which the upper and lower bounds are explicitly declared:

DCL AXIS(−3:3,−4:4)   FLOAT DEC (6)   INIT ((63)0);

| AXIS | −4 | −3 | −2 | −1 | 0 | 1 | 2 | 3 | 4 |
|---|---|---|---|---|---|---|---|---|---|
| −3 | 0 | 0 | 0 | 0 | 0 | 0 | 0 | 0 | 0 |
| −2 | 0 | 0 | 0 | 0 | 0 | 0 | 0 | 0 | 0 |
| −1 | 0 | 0 | 0 | 0 | 0 | 0 | 0 | 0 | 0 |
| 0 | 0 | 0 | 0 | 0 | 0 | 0 | 0 | 0 | 0 |
| 1 | 0 | 0 | 0 | 0 | 0 | 0 | 0 | 0 | 0 |
| 2 | 0 | 0 | 0 | 0 | 0 | 0 | 0 | 0 | 0 |
| 3 | 0 | 0 | 0 | 0 | 0 | 0 | 0 | 0 | 0 |

There are 63 elements in the AXIS array. Notice how the INITIAL attribute specified an iteration factor of 63 in a pair of parentheses preceding the 0 constant. This causes all elements of the AXIS array to be initialized to zero. Had the statement

DCL AXIS (−3:3,−4:4)   FLOAT DEC (6)   INIT (0);

been declared, only the first element (upper leftmost corner of the array) would be initialized to zero.

A three-dimensional array could also be declared. For example, assume it is desired to store statistical data on the urban and rural population of each state in the United States for 10 decades. The statement declaring such an array could be written

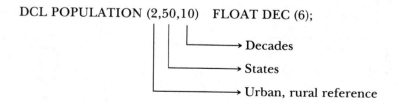

In most PL/I implementations, more than three dimensions may be specified. Generally, the number of dimensions allowed is 15.

## Subscripts

Only the array itself is given a name. We reference an element of an array by means of a **subscript**. For example:

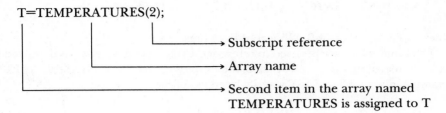

T=TEMPERATURES(2);

→ Subscript reference

→ Array name

→ Second item in the array named TEMPERATURES is assigned to T

Assume that a two-dimensional table of a salesperson's commission rates is to be defined for three products a company sells. A commission rate depends on the quantity the salesperson sells. For example:

| | Commission rate for item | | |
|---|---|---|---|
| Quantity sold | #1 | #2 | #3 |
| 1–50 | 0.010 | 0.010 | 0.020 |
| 51–100 | 0.020 | 0.015 | 0.025 |
| 101–500 | 0.025 | 0.022 | 0.030 |
| 501–999 | 0.030 | 0.031 | 0.035 |
| 1000 or more | 0.032 | 0.035 | 0.040 |

To declare this table we would write

DCL COMMISSION (5,3)   FIXED DEC (4,3);

where the table could be pictured as follows:

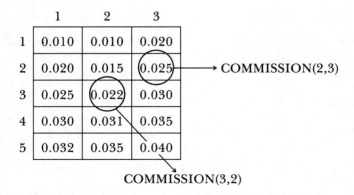

In the previous example, row 1 contains the commission rates for 1 to 50 units sold; row 2 contains rates for 51 to 100 units sold; row 3 for 101 to 500 units sold, etc. Column 1 corresponds to item 1, column 2 to item 2, and column 3 to item 3. To retrieve the commission amount if the salesperson sold 450 units of item 1, we could code

    AMOUNT = PRICE * QUANTITY * COMMISSION(3,1);

where a commission of 0.025 would have been used.

The range of subscripts used to reference an element in an array is determined by the dimension attribute — that is, the bounds of the array. In the array LIST example given earlier, LIST was declared as follows:

    DCL LIST (−2:6)   FIXED BIN (15,0)
        INIT (91,20,82,11,73,48,19,16,70);

To access the element containing the value 20, the subscript is (−1). To reference the last element, a subscript of (6) is used.

## CHECKPOINT QUESTIONS

**8.** In a DECLARE statement, how can you tell whether an attribute is a precision attribute or whether it defines the number of elements in an array?

**9.** In reference to an array, what are *bounds*?

**10.** When a *lower bound* is not specified in an array declaration, what is it assumed to be?

**11.** True or false? A *one-dimensional* array would appear differently in main storage from the way a *two-dimensional* array of the same number of elements would appear.

**12.** How do you reference individual elements of an array?

**Variable Subscripts.** Subscripts may be constants, variables, or expressions. Here is an example of a variable subscript:

    K = 3;
    T = TEMPERATURE (K);

                └────→ Because K was assigned a value of 3, it
                       is element number 3 of
                       TEMPERATURES that is assigned to T

Here are some other examples of retrieving values from the COMMISSION array (note the use of variable subscripts):

```
J = 3;
RATE = PRICE * QUANTITY * COMMISSION(J,1);
/ * COMMISSION (3,1) IS REFERENCED */

K = 2;
RATE = PRICE * QUANTITY * COMMISSION(J,K);
/* COMMISSION (3,2) IS REFERENCED */
```

The following example is invalid because the value assigned to K is outside the declared range of the COMMISSION array:

```
K = 7;
RATE = PRICE * QUANTITY * COMMISSION(1,K); /* IN ERROR */
```

Care must be taken to guard against referencing a position outside of the declared array. This is particularly true if you are specifying the array as a receiving field. For example:

```
DCL TABLE(5)   FLOAT DEC (6);
K = 50;
TABLE(K) = 0;
```

In this case, zero will be assigned TABLE(50), which is not part of the declared array. Typically, any position outside of an array could still be part of your program; hence, the value assigned might destroy part of an instruction or another data item. Often, this kind of destruction causes a program to "hang up." The computer may simply "stop," and you have no clues as to "what went wrong."

If the subscript is input during program execution, then check the data read to ensure that a reference is not made to an element outside the bounds of the array. For example, rates for various job codes could be stored in an array:

```
DCL RATES (7)   FIXED DEC (4,2)
        INIT (7.25, 3.50, 18.75, 9.25, 4.00, 5.50, 10.00);
```

The job code and hours are read from an input record:

```
GET LIST (EMPLOYEE#, JOB_CODE, #_OF_HOURS);
```

Amount to be paid could be calculated:

```
AMOUNT_TO_PAY = RATES(JOB_CODE) * #_OF_HOURS;
```

However, the program should first check that JOB_CODE $>=1$ *and* JOB_CODE $<=7$.

Referencing a location outside the bounds of the array will cause the SUB-SCRIPTRANGE condition to be raised if the condition has been enabled. Because this condition involves a substantial overhead, it is normally used only in program testing. SUBSCRIPTRANGE will be discussed in the debugging section of this chapter.

**Subscript Expressions.** In addition to constants and variables, *any* valid PL/I arithmetic expression may be specified as a subscript. For example:

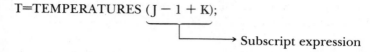

$$T = TEMPERATURES \ (J - 1 + K);$$

⟶ Subscript expression

**Subscripted Subscripts.** Subscript expressions may include subscripted items resulting in nested subscripts. For example:

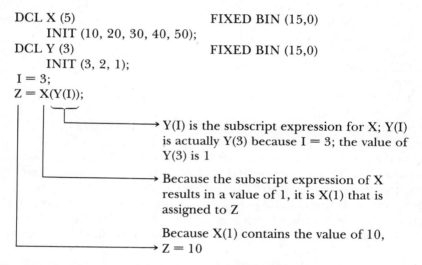

```
DCL X (5)                    FIXED BIN (15,0)
    INIT (10, 20, 30, 40, 50);
DCL Y (3)                    FIXED BIN (15,0)
    INIT (3, 2, 1);
I = 3;
Z = X(Y(I));
```

⟶ Y(I) is the subscript expression for X; Y(I) is actually Y(3) because I = 3; the value of Y(3) is 1

⟶ Because the subscript expression of X results in a value of 1, it is X(1) that is assigned to Z

⟶ Because X(1) contains the value of 10, Z = 10

## ARRAY MANIPULATION BUILT-IN FUNCTIONS

A number of built-in functions facilitate the manipulation of array data. These functions are presented in Appendix B in detail but are briefly summarized below.

All of these functions require array-name arguments, and they return, as a result, a single value. Because only a single value is returned from these functions, a function reference to any array function is considered an element expression, as contrasted with an array expression. The array manipulation built-in functions include:

**1. The DIM built-in function:** This function provides the current extent (i.e., number of elements) for a specified dimension in a given array.

**2. The LBOUND built-in function:** This function finds the current lower boundary for a specified dimension of a given array.

**3. The HBOUND built-in function:** This function finds the current upper boundary for a specified dimension of a given array.

**4. The SUM built-in function:** This function finds the sum of all elements in an array.

**5. The PROD built-in function:** This function finds the product of all the elements of an array.

**6. The POLY built-in function:** This function is used to form a polynomial expansion from two arguments.

**7. The ANY built-in function:** This function is used to test the bits of a given bit-string array. If any in the same position of the elements of an array is a '1'B, then the result is a '1'B; otherwise, the result is '0'B.

**8. The ALL built-in function:** This function is used to test all bits of a given bit-string array. If all bits in the same position within each element are '1'Bs, then the result is a '1'B; otherwise, the result is a '0'B.

### An Example Illustrating Variable Array Bounds

Subroutines and functions were covered in Chapter 4. Let's look at an example in which a subroutine is written to compute the sum of the odd-numbered elements of any size array passed to it. The calling sequence could be:

```
DCL SAMPLE_ARRAY(500)   FIXED BIN(31) INIT ((500)7);
DCL DATA_SUM            FIXED BIN(31);
CALL ODDSUM (SAMPLE_ARRAY,DATA_SUM);
/* ODDSUM IS THE NAME OF THE SUBROUTINE */
/* ANSWER IS PLACED IN DATA_SUM         */
```

Here is the subroutine procedure:

```
ODDSUM: PROC (ARRAY,SUM);
     DCL ARRAY (*)              FIXED BIN (31);
     DCL HIGH                   FIXED BIN (15);
     DCL INDEX                  FIXED BIN (15);
     DCL LOW                    FIXED BIN (15);
     DCL SUM                    FIXED BIN (31);
     DCL (HBOUND,LBOUND,MOD)    BUILTIN;
     LOW  = LBOUND(ARRAY,1);
     HIGH = HBOUND(ARRAY,1);
     IF MOD(LOW,2) = 0 THEN
         LOW = LOW + 1;
     SUM = 0;
     DO INDEX = LOW TO HIGH BY 2;
         SUM = SUM + ARRAY(INDEX);
     END;
END ODDSUM;
```

The asterisk notation for the array declaration indicates the number of dimensions. For a two-dimensional array, two asterisks are specified. For example:

DECLARE TABLE(*,*);

Not only does the asterisk indicate the number of dimensions, but also that the actual boundaries of the array will be defined later. In this case, "later" is when the actual array argument is passed to the subroutine procedure.

In the summation subroutine, the LBOUND and HBOUND built-in functions are invoked to determine the lower boundary, respectively, of ARRAY. These functions are described in Appendix B. The MOD built-in function, described in Chapter 3, is invoked to determine whether or not the lower boundary is an even or odd number. The do-loop totals the odd-numbered elements of the array with the statement:

DO INDEX = LOW TO HIGH BY 2;

The variable INDEX in the iterative DO is used as a *pointer* to the appropriate element of the array called ARRAY. The answer is passed back to the calling program through the second parameter, DATA_SUM.

## I/O Operations and Arrays

In the absence of explicit element specifications, data items are read into arrays starting with the lowest numbered subscripted element and finishing with the highest subscripted element. For example:

DCL AMOUNT (20)     FIXED DEC (3);
GET LIST (AMOUNT);

If each data item in the input stream is recorded in three positions with one trailing blank, then positions 1 through 3 will be read into AMT (1), positions 5 through 7 into AMT (2) and so on, to positions 77 through 79, which are placed in AMT (20).

If a multidimensional array is specified, then the *right-hand subscript varies most rapidly.* For example:

DCL AMOUNT (5,4)     FIXED DEC (3);
GET LIST (AMOUNT);

Data items are read into the AMT array elements in this order.

AMOUNT(1,1)
AMOUNT(1,2)
AMOUNT(1,3)
AMOUNT(1,4)

AMOUNT(2,1)
AMOUNT(2,2)
AMOUNT(2,3)
AMOUNT(2,4)
AMOUNT(3,1)

$\vdots$

AMOUNT(5,3)
AMOUNT(5,4)

Assigning data items to an array with the rightmost subscript varying most rapidly is called *row major order*.   Here is an example for a three-dimensional array:

DCL TABLE (2,3,4)    FLOAT DEC (6);
GET LIST (TABLE);

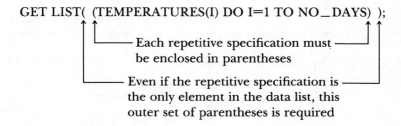

As many data items are read as necessary to fill the entire array

To determine the number of elements in the previous array, simply multiply each extent by the next: 2*3*4=24 elements.

### The Repetitive Specification of a Data Item

In stream I/O, data list elements may contain a repetitive specification that is similar to the iterative DO.   For example:

GET LIST(  (TEMPERATURES(I) DO I=1 TO NO_DAYS) );

Each repetitive specification must be enclosed in parentheses

Even if the repetitive specification is the only element in the data list, this outer set of parentheses is required

In the case of the repetitive specification of a data item, an END statement is not used to terminate the DO in the data list.

Repetitive specifications may be nested; that is, an element of a repetitive specification can itself be a repetitive specification.   Each DO portion must be delimited on the right with a right parenthesis, with its matching parenthesis added to the beginning of the entire repetitive specification.   For example:

GET LIST (((A(I,J)DO I = 1 TO 5) DO J = 3 TO 7));

When DO portions are nested, the rightmost DO is at the outer level.   Thus, the previous GET statement is equivalent to:

```
DO J = 3 TO 7;
    DO I = 1 TO 5;
        GET LIST(A(I,J));
    END;
END;
```

Here is an example of several data list items containing repetitive specifications:

GET LIST((A(I)DO I = 1 TO 50),(B(J),C(J)DO J = 1 TO 12));

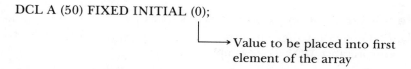

First, 50 data items are read into element numbers 1 to 50 of array A. Then data items are read into element number 1 of arrays B and C, then element number 2 of B and C and into each successive element until element number 12 is filled in both arrays.

### The INITIAL Attribute for Arrays

How to initialize arrays using the INITIAL attribute has been illustrated in previous examples of array declarations. Here are some more details about the INITIAL attribute and arrays:

DCL A (50) FIXED INITIAL (0);

└──→ Value to be placed into first
element of the array

Only the first element, A(1), will be initialized to a value of zero. If it is desired to initialize the entire array to zeros, then an iteration factor must be specified.

DCL A (50) FIXED INITIAL ((50)0);

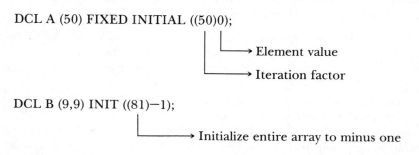

└──→ Element value
└──→ Iteration factor

DCL B (9,9) INIT ((81)−1);

└──→ Initialize entire array to minus one

Here are some general rules for using the INITIAL attribute to initialize arrays:

**1.** More than one value may be given for an array, whereas only one initial value may be specified for an element variable.

**2.** Initial values specified for an array are assigned to successive elements of the array in the order where the right-hand subscript varies most rapidly. The example,

DECLARE A (2,2) INITIAL (1,2,3,4);

results in the following:

A(1,1) = 1

A(1,2) = 2             or

A(2,1) = 3

A(2,2) = 4

A    (1)(2)

(1) | 1 | 2 |

(2) | 3 | 4 |

If too many initial values are specified for an array, excess values are ignored; if not enough are specified, the remainder of the array is not initialized.

**3.** Each item in the initial value list may be a constant, an iteration specification, or — in the case of string initial values — a repetition factor.  The iteration specification has one of the following general forms:

((iteration factor) constant)          DCL A (25) INIT ((25)0);

((iteration factor) item, item . . . )   DCL B (10) INIT ((7)0,1,2,3);

The iteration factor must be a decimal integer constant equal to or greater than one.

**4.** If only one parenthesized decimal integer constant precedes a *string* initial value, it is interpreted as a repetition factor for the string.  If two appear, the first is taken to be an initialization iteration factor, and the second a string repetition factor.  For example,

DCL TABLE (10) CHAR (2) INIT ((2)'A');

causes the *first* element of the array TABLE to be initialized to the character-string value AA because (2)'A' is equivalent to 'AA'.  Should it be desired to initialize the first *two* elements of TABLE, then the following statement would be specified:

DCL TABLE(10) CHAR(2)
    INIT((2) (2)'A');

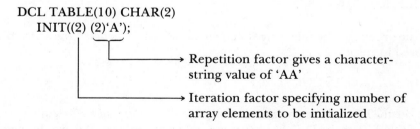

→ Repetition factor gives a character-string value of 'AA'

→ Iteration factor specifying number of array elements to be initialized

To indicate an iteration factor specifying the number of array elements to be initialized *without* a repetition factor for a character-string, indicate a repetition factor of 1.

DCL TABLE (10)               CHAR (5)
    INIT ((10) (1) 'EMPTY');

**5.** If it is desired to skip certain elements of an array during initialization, an asterisk may be specified to indicate the skip.   For example:

```
DCL A(3)              FLOAT DEC (6)
     INIT (10, *, 30);
```

Here, A (1) will be initialized to 10, A (3) will be initialized to 30, and A (2) will not be initialized.

## CHECKPOINT QUESTIONS

**13.** What will C contain when the following assignment statements are executed:

```
DCL A (3)              FIXED BIN (15)
     INIT (55, 56, 57);
DCL B (5)              FIXED BIN (15)
     INIT (3, 3, 2, 2, 1);
K = 2;
C = A(B(K));
```

**14.** Given the declaration and input statement,

```
DECLARE TIC (3,3)   FLOAT DEC (6);
GET LIST (TIC);
```

what will TIC (2,3) contain if the input stream consists of these values (in the order shown, reading from left to right):

```
1, 2, 3, 4, 5, 6, 7, 8, 9
```

**15.** True or false?  The following statement causes all elements of the array to be initialized to zero:

```
DCL A (100) INIT (0);
```

**16.** Write the DECLARE statement to initialize all elements of a 20-element array called CODE.  Use the INITIAL attribute.  Each element is to be five characters long and contain the alphameric characters

'99999'

**17.** Write the DECLARE statement to initialize to zero the first and last elements of a five-element, one-dimensional array.  Use the INITIAL attribute.

## An Example Illustrating DOs and Arrays

As a means of tieing together the use of PL/I repetition statements to manipulate data in an array, assume that the temperature for each day of a given year has been entered into a file. It is desired to input these values and find the average temperature for the year.

First, we begin by declaring an array containing the year's daily temperatures as well as two single variables containing the sum of the temperatures and the average temperature.

```
DCL TEMPERATURES (365)   FIXED DEC (4,1);
DCL TOTAL_YEAR           FIXED DEC (7,1);
DCL YEARLY_AVERAGE       FIXED DEC (4,1);
```

Next, it is necessary to read the values into the array. This can be accomplished with the following statement:

```
GET LIST (TEMPERATURES);
```

Notice that only the array name is specified in parentheses following the keywords GET LIST. In this case, data items are read from the input stream until the entire array is filled with data or an end-of-file condition is detected. TEMPERATURES(1) through TEMPERATURES(31) contain the daily temperatures for the month of January; TEMPERATURES(32) through TEMPERATURES(59) (assuming a non-leap year) contain the daily values for the month of February; and so on. Assume it is desired not only to find the average yearly temperature but also to calculate the average monthly temperature. The number of days in each month is placed in a 12-element array called DAYS_IN_MONTH. Figure 6.2 shows the complete program consisting of two modules: the nucleus and calculate monthly average. Here are a few comments about key statements in the program:

**Statement 15:** The temperatures are read using the GET statement. It is expected that either 365 or 366 temperatures will be read. The GET is terminated when the end-of-file indicator is sensed or when 366 temperatures are read, whichever comes first.

**Statement 16:** After all temperatures have been read, the built-in function COUNT is invoked and returns the number of values read in the GET statement.

Note that if 366 temperatures are read, the GET is terminated by reaching the limit of the table.

**Statement 24:** The program invokes the COUNT built-in function again to determine whether 365 temperatures (non-leap year) or 366 temperatures (leap year) have been read. The number of days in February is set to 29 if 366 temperatures have been read. Note that the second element of the array DAYS_IN_MONTH represents the number of days in February,

```
/*        PROGRAM TO COMPUTE TEMPERATURE AVERAGES FOR YEAR AND MONTH  */
/**************************************************************************/
/*                                                                      */
/*   PROGRAM NAME:    AVGTEMP                                            */
/*                                                                      */
/*   DESCRIPTION:     THIS PROGRAM READS THE DAILY TEMPERATURES FOR ONE */
/*                    YEAR INTO AN ARRAY.  THEN THE AVERAGE DAILY        */
/*                    TEMPERATURE FOR THE YEAR AND THE AVERAGE DAILY     */
/*                    TEMPERATURE FOR EACH MONTH ARE CALCULATED.  THE    */
/*                    TEMPERATURE AVERAGES ARE PRINTED ON A REPORT.      */
/*                                                                      */
/*   INPUT:           SYSIN                                             */
/*                                                                      */
/*   OUTPUT:          PRINTER                                           */
/*                                                                      */
/**************************************************************************/
1    AVGTEMP:  PROC OPTIONS (MAIN);

2       DCL DAY_OF_YEAR             FIXED BIN(15)  INIT (1);
3       DCL DAYS_IN_MONTH (12)      FIXED DEC (3)  INIT
            (31,28,31,30,31,30,31,30,31,30,31);
4       DCL I                       FIXED BIN(15);
5       DCL MONTH                   FIXED BIN(15);
6       DCL MONTH_NAME (12)         CHAR(9)        INIT
            ('JANUARY  ','FEBRUARY ','MARCH    ',
             'APRIL    ','MAY      ','JUNE     ',
             'JULY     ','AUGUST   ','SEPTEMBER',
             'OCTOBER  ','NOVEMBER ','DECEMBER ');
7       DCL MONTHLY_AVERAGE         FIXED DEC(4,1);
8       DCL TEMPERATURES (366)      FIXED DEC(4,1) INIT ((366)0);
9       DCL TOTAL_MONTH             FIXED DEC(7,1);
10      DCL TOTAL_YEAR              FIXED DEC(7,1);
11      DCL YEARLY_AVERAGE          FIXED DEC(4,1);

12      DCL (COUNT,MOD,SUM)         BUILTIN;

13      ON ENDFILE (SYSIN);
    /**************************************************************************/
    /*                                                                      */
    /*   PROGRAM NUCLEUS                                                     */
    /*                                                                      */
    /**************************************************************************/
14      TEMPERATURES = 0;
15      GET LIST(TEMPERATURES);
16      IF COUNT(SYSIN) < 365 THEN
            PUT SKIP LIST
                ('LESS THAN 365 TEMPERATURES INPUT --- PROGRAM TERMINATED');
17      ELSE DO;
18          CALL AVERAGE_EACH_MONTH;
19          TOTAL_YEAR = SUM(TEMPERATURES);
20          YEARLY_AVERAGE = TOTAL_YEAR / COUNT(SYSIN);
21          PUT SKIP(3) LIST ('AVERAGE DAILY TEMPERATURE FOR YEAR IS',
                YEARLY_AVERAGE);
22          END;
```

**FIGURE 6.2   (page 1)**

having initialized to 28 by the DECLARE statement. DAYS_IN_MONTH(2) is left at 28 or replaced by the value 29.

**Statements 25–34:** All the temperatures for a given month are accumulated into the variable TOTAL_MONTH. Upon exit from the inner DO, TOTAL_MONTH is divided by one of the elements in the array DAYS_IN_MONTH, the number of days in a given month. In statement 3, DAYS_IN_MONTH has the attributes FIXED DECIMAL. Had

```
/**********************************************************************/
/*                                                                    */
/*    CALCULATE THE AVERAGE DAILY TEMPERATURE EACH MONTH AND PRINT     */
/*    FOUR MONTHS PER LINE.                                            */
/*                                                                    */
/**********************************************************************/
23  AVERAGE_EACH_MONTH:   PROC;

24      IF COUNT(SYSIN) = 366 THEN
            DAYS_IN_MONTH(2) = 29;
25      DO MONTH = 1 TO 12;
26          TOTAL_MONTH = 0;
27          IF MOD(MONTH,4) = 1 THEN
                PUT SKIP(2)LIST (MONTH_NAME(MONTH),MONTH_NAME(MONTH + 1),
                    MONTH_NAME(MONTH + 2),MONTH_NAME(MONTH + 3),' ');
28          DO I = DAY_OF_YEAR TO (DAY_OF_YEAR + DAYS_IN_MONTH(MONTH) - 1);
29              TOTAL_MONTH = TOTAL_MONTH + TEMPERATURES(I);
30          END;
31          MONTHLY_AVERAGE = TOTAL_MONTH / DAYS_IN_MONTH(MONTH);
32          PUT LIST (MONTHLY_AVERAGE);
33          DAY_OF_YEAR = DAY_OF_YEAR + DAYS_IN_MONTH(MONTH);
34      END;
35  END AVERAGE_EACH_MONTH;

36  END AVGTEMP;
```

**FIGURE 6.2   (page 2)**

DAYS_IN_MONTH been declared with attributes other than FIXED
DECIMAL and then divided into TOTAL, which has the attributes FIXED
DECIMAL, the accuracy of the average monthly temperature could have
been affected.   This error in accuracy can occur in arithmetic operations on
data items that have decimal positions (i.e., fractions) when the PL/I attributes differ (e.g., FIXED DECIMAL versus FIXED BINARY).

Avoid mixed data types in the same arithmetic expression!   Hence,
TOTAL_MONTH and DAYS_IN_MONTH are declared as FIXED
DECIMAL.   We will obtain the accurate answer when the statement

MONTHLY_AVERAGE = TOTAL_MONTH / DAYS_IN_MONTH
(MONTH);

is executed.

The subscripted identifier (MONTH) is used in the DO statement:

DO I = DAY_OF_YEAR TO (DAY_OF_YEAR
+ DAYS_IN_MONTH(MONTH) − 1);

It does generate a comparison between FIXED BINARY 'I' and FIXED
DECIMAL DAY_OF_YEAR.   In this case, however, no fractions are involved, and the conversion occurs only when the DO is executed the first
time—not on each repetitive test.

**Statement 27:** The PUT LIST in the IF statement illustrates the use of an
arithmetic expression in a subscript.

Four months' average temperatures are printed on one line.   When the

| JANUARY | FEBRUARY | MARCH | APRIL |
|---------|----------|-------|-------|
| 60.9 | 57.4 | 55.0 | 63.3 |
| MAY | JUNE | JULY | AUGUST |
| 72.9 | 80.0 | 90.5 | 91.2 |
| SEPTEMBER | OCTOBER | NOVEMBER | DECEMBER |
| 85.6 | 75.3 | 65.8 | 66.0 |

```
AVERAGE DAILY TEMPERATURE FOR YEAR IS          72.0
```

FIGURE 6.3   Sample output from temperature average program.

month is "1," print the headings "January," "February," "March," and "April." Adding another blank in quotes in the PUT LIST statement causes all the tabs to be used. The average temperatures will now line up under their respective months when they are printed. The next time the month headings are printed is when month is 5 and month is 9. To accomplish this without specifically testing for month = 1, month = 5, or month = 9, the MOD built-in function is used.

Figure 6.3 shows the sample output from the temperature-calculation program. On closer inspection of this output, you may wonder why the numeric values are not lined up or left justified under the month's name. The output is:

```
J A N U A R Y
     6 0 . 9
```

not:

```
J A N U A R Y
6 0 . 9
```

The reason for the indentation of the temperatures under their respective headings has to do with the rules for **data conversion** on output. The temperatures have the attributes FIXED DECIMAL (4, 1). The rule for converting FIXED DECIMAL data to a character-string designated for list-directed or data-directed output is:

Character-string length = Precision of decimal value + 3

The constant of 3 was selected to allow room for the following:

**1.** A leading blank.

**2.** A minus sign, if value is negative; otherwise, a blank for a positive value.

**3.** A decimal point, if the value is a mixed number.

Thus, in Figure 6.3 we see the numeric data printed as character-strings of length 7. To illustrate:

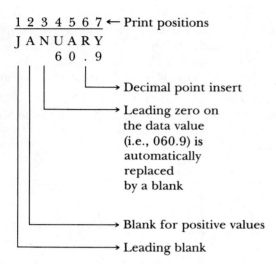

$\underline{1\ 2\ 3\ 4\ 5\ 6\ 7}$ ← Print positions

J A N U A R Y

6 0 . 9

→ Decimal point insert

→ Leading zero on
the data value
(i.e., 060.9) is
automatically
replaced
by a blank

→ Blank for positive values

→ Leading blank

### Array Assignment

Two types of move operations may be specified for arrays: scalar-to-array and array-to-array.

**Scalar-to-Array.** In this type of array assignment, an entire array is assigned a single (scalar) value. For example:

```
DCL MONTHS (12)   FIXED DEC (4,1);
MONTHS = 0;
```

An array name without a subscript as used here refers to all elements in the array. Each element in the MONTHS array will be set to zero. To assign a value to a single element of the array, a subscript must be specified. For example,

```
MONTHS (5) = 72.6;
```

assigns 72.6 to the fifth element of the array MONTHS.

**Array-to-Array.** In this case, one array may be moved (assigned) to another array, providing the arrays have identical dimensions and bounds. For example,

```
DCL A (5,5)   FLOAT DEC (6);
DCL B (5,5)   FLOAT DEC (6);
A = B;        /* ARRAY-TO-ARRAY ASSIGNMENT */
```

each element of the B array assigned to the corresponding element of the A array.

### Array Expressions

An array expression is an expression whose evaluation yields an array result. All operations performed on arrays are performed on an element-by-element basis. All arrays referred to in an array expression must have identical dimensions and bounds. Following are discussions and examples of different types of array expressions.

**Prefix Operators and Arrays.** When a prefix operator is specified for an array, the result is an array of identical bounds in which each element is the result of the operation having been performed. Consider:

If A is the array

| 1 | 3 | $-5$ |
|---|---|---|
| 4 | $-2$ | $-7$ |
| 6 | 12 | 13 |

then A $= -$ A would cause the array to be changed to this $\longrightarrow$

| $-1$ | $-3$ | 5 |
|---|---|---|
| $-4$ | 2 | 7 |
| $-6$ | $-12$ | $-13$ |

**Infix Operators and Arrays.** When an infix operator is specified for an array and a scalar variable, the result is an array of identical bounds in which each element is the result of the infix operation having been performed. For example:

If A is the array

| 5 | 10 | 15 |
|---|---|---|
| 20 | 25 | 30 |

then A*5 is this array $\rightarrow$

| 25 | 50 | 75 |
|---|---|---|
| 100 | 125 | 150 |

If, for example,

        B = A * 5;

is coded, the resulting array (A * 5) is stored in array B, which must have the same dimensions and bounds as array A. Array A is unchanged.

All operations on the array are performed on an element-by-element basis in an order in which the rightmost subscript varies most rapidly. To illustrate the effect of this order of operations, assume

A is
| 1 | 2 | 3 |
|---|---|---|
| 4 | 5 | 6 |

If the statement

A = A * A(1,2);

is specified, the result is the following array:

A is
| 2 | 4 | 12 |
|----|----|----|
| 16 | 20 | 24 |

Note that the original value for A (1,2), which is 2, is used in evaluation for only the first two elements of A. Since the result of the expression is assigned to A, changing the value of A, the new value of A (1,2) is used for all subsequent operations. The first two elements are multiplied by 2, the original value of A; all other elements are multiplied by 4, the new value of A (1,2).

When an infix operator is specified for two arrays, both arrays must have the same number of dimensions and identical bounds. The result is an array with dimensions and bounds identical to those of the original arrays; the operation is performed on the corresponding elements of the two original arrays.

If A is the array
| 2 | 4 | 3 |
|---|---|---|
| 6 | 1 | 7 |
| 4 | 8 | 2 |

and if B is the array
| 1 | 5 | 7 |
|---|---|---|
| 8 | 3 | 4 |
| 6 | 3 | 1 |

then A + B is the array
| 3 | 9 | 10 |
|----|----|----|
| 14 | 4 | 11 |
| 10 | 11 | 3 |

When an assignment or infix operation involves more than one array, the arrays may have different bases, scales, or precisions.

The examples in this discussion of array expressions have shown only single arithmetic operations. The rules for combining operations and for data conversion of operands are the same as those for element operations.

## Cross Sections of Arrays

So far we have seen that a subscript is an element expression specifying a location within a dimension of an array. A subscript may also be an asterisk, in which case it specifies the entire extent of the dimension. This extent is referred to as a **cross section** of an array.

A subscripted name containing asterisk subscripts represents not a single data element, but a larger part of the array. For example, assume PERCENT has been declared as follows:

      DCL PERCENT (3,4)  FIXED DEC (3,2);

PERCENT (*,1) refers to all of the elements in the first column of the array. It specifies the cross section consisting of PERCENT (1,1), PERCENT (2,1), and PERCENT (3,1). PERCENT (2,*) refers to all of the data items in the second row of the array (i.e., PERCENT (2,1), PERCENT (2,2), PERCENT (2,3), and PERCENT (2,4)).

As an illustration of how cross sections of arrays may be useful in manipulating data, the following arrays are declared:

      DCL PERCENT (3,4)   FIXED DEC (3,2);
      DCL PRICE     (3)     FIXED DEC (3,2);
      DCL TOTALS  (3)     FIXED DEC (3,2);

Assume the following arrays have been assigned the values shown in the various elements:

| PERCENT | (1) | (2) | (3) | (4) | PRICE | | TOTALS |
|---------|-----|-----|-----|-----|-------|---|--------|
| (1) | 0.04 | 0.02 | 0.04 | 0.03 | (1) | 4.00 | |
| (2) | 0.06 | 0.03 | 0.05 | 0.04 | (2) | 2.50 | |
| (3) | 0.05 | 0.03 | 0.06 | 0.05 | (3) | 3.60 | |

Item ↓ (vertical label on left); ← Salesperson → (horizontal label below)

The PERCENT array represents commission rates various salespeople receive for three different items they sell. To find the commission paid to salesperson 4 for selling a single unit of each of the three items, the following could be coded:

      TOTALS=PERCENT (*,4) * PRICE;

Each element in the fourth column of the PERCENT array is multiplied by the corresponding element of the PRICE array, and the product is assigned to the corresponding element of the TOTALs array. Note that a cross section of an array is an **array expression;** thus, any other array appearing in an arithmetic operation with the cross section must have the same bounds and dimensions as the cross section.

## An Exchange Sort Example

In computing there is a frequent requirement to sort data into different sequences. The different sequences give us insight into the nature of the data and facilitate our use of the information in various business activities. Take a company's customer list for example. One sort sequence is alphabetical so that a given customer (and related data) can be easily located on a report. Another sequence might be by sales rep for the customer and then alphabetical order within sales rep. In this sequence, each sales rep can obtain a printout of his or her customers. Another sequence might be to list customers by total dollar volume of purchases during the past 12 months as an aid to marketing and servicing a firm's top customers. Or, customers could be sorted by balance due, from largest to smallest amount owed. As you can see, the sequences could almost be endless.

There are many algorithms for sorting. One popular technique is presented here because it is efficient yet simple.

The sorting technique is called an exchange sort. Pairs of values in an array are compared and "flip-flopped" whenever any two adjacent values are not in ascending sequence. The algorithm calls for searching through the array until a complete pass can be made without making a single exchange (hence, the need for a program switch). When there are no more exchanges, the values are in ascending sequence. This technique works on either numeric or alphabetic data and is flowcharted in Figure 6.4.

The exchange-sorting technique could involve a great deal of *data movement* because we physically change the location of all data in the array we are sorting. This is particularly time-consuming for alphabetic data. And of course, the longer the strings to be sorted, the greater that cost.

Another method of sorting, called tag sorting, will help us eliminate much of the data movement. In this approach, we declare two arrays. The first array will contain the data (character-strings) to be sorted. For example:

DCL NAMES (10)   CHAR (35);

The second array will contain the subscripts of the first array:

DCL TAGS (10)   FIXED BIN (15);

The second array should be initialized at the beginning of the program to contain the numbers 1 through 10 in the first ten elements. A picture of the arrays before sorting might help:

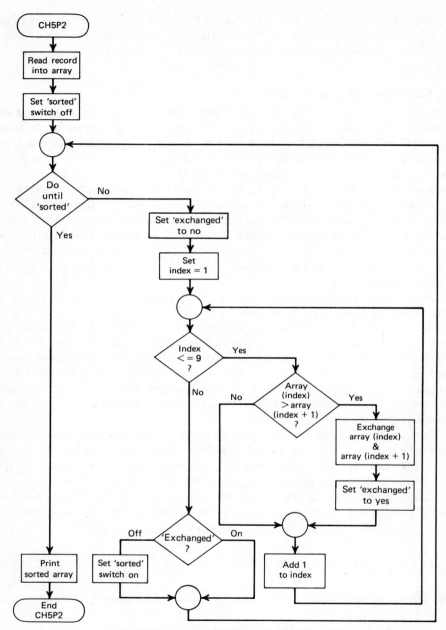

FIGURE 6.4  Flowchart for an exchange sort.

|  | Array containing data to be sorted |  | Array containing subscripts |  |
|---|---|---|---|---|
| NAMES (1) | WINEGARDEN, R | ← | 1 | TAGS (1) |
| NAMES (2) | LYNCH, F | ← | 2 | TAGS (2) |
| NAMES (3) | CLAUS, L | ← | 3 | TAGS (3) |
| NAMES (4) | GEROME, M | ← | 4 | TAGS (4) |
| NAMES (5) | DEMPSEY, D | ← | 5 | TAGS (5) |
| NAMES (6) | ARDIGO, J | ← | 6 | TAGS (6) |
| NAMES (7) | GALLIEN, G | ← | 7 | TAGS (7) |
| NAMES (8) | FOX, A | ← | 8 | TAGS (8) |
| NAMES (9) | CHAMBERS, M | ← | 9 | TAGS (9) |
| NAMES (10) | Mc CALLICK, F | ← | 10 | TAGS (10) |

Now we are ready to begin sorting. Notice that the subscript array acts as a list of pointers into the data array. In tag sorting, we use the subscript array TAGS to reference the NAMES data array elements. We do this by nesting subscripts. Nested subscripts are called *subscripted subscripts*. Here is an example:

NAMES(TAGS (N))

The element of NAMES referenced is that element whose subscript is found in the Nth element of TAGS.

Tag sorting now merely becomes an exchange sort where we compare the elements in the data array; but when an exchange is required, we exchange not the data but the subscripts. The coding

```
IF NAMES(TAGS(N)) > NAMES(TAGS(N + 1)) THEN
    DO;
        TEMP            = TAGS(N);
        TAGS(N)         = TAGS(N + 1);
        TAGS(N + 1)     = TEMP;
        EXCHANGED       = YES;
    END;
```

Notice that the data items in the array NAMES are never moved; only the subscripts are moved.

After one comparison pass through the data array, the two arrays look like this:

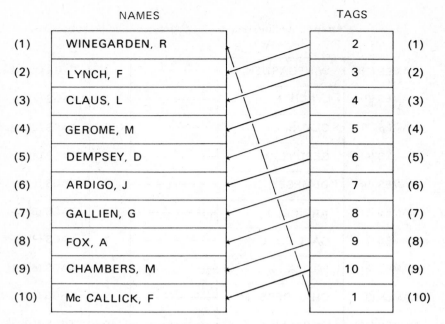

|     | NAMES | TAGS |      |
|-----|-------|------|------|
| (1) | WINEGARDEN, R | 2 | (1) |
| (2) | LYNCH, F | 3 | (2) |
| (3) | CLAUS, L | 4 | (3) |
| (4) | GEROME, M | 5 | (4) |
| (5) | DEMPSEY, D | 6 | (5) |
| (6) | ARDIGO, J | 7 | (6) |
| (7) | GALLIEN, G | 8 | (7) |
| (8) | FOX, A | 9 | (8) |
| (9) | CHAMBERS, M | 10 | (9) |
| (10) | Mc CALLICK, F | 1 | (10) |

Just as in exchange sorting, you must keep making passes through the data array (always referenced through the subscript array) until no exchanges are required. At that point, the data items are still not in sequence (because we did not move the data). However, the subscript array contains the subscripts of the data in ascending sequence. The two arrays, after sorting, look like this:

|     | NAMES | TAGS |      |
|-----|-------|------|------|
| (1) | WINEGARDEN, R | 6 | (1) |
| (2) | LYNCH, F | 9 | (2) |
| (3) | CLAUS, L | 3 | (3) |
| (4) | GEROME, M | 5 | (4) |
| (5) | DEMPSEY, D | 8 | (5) |
| (6) | ARDIGO, J | 7 | (6) |
| (7) | GALLIEN, G | 4 | (7) |
| (8) | FOX, A | 2 | (8) |
| (9) | CHAMBERS, M | 10 | (9) |
| (10) | Mc CALLICK, F | 1 | (10) |

The data can now be printed in sequence using *nested subscripts*. The program in Figure 6.5 shows the solution to the tag sort problem just described. Although an array of just 10 items, 35 characters each, is defined, the technique would work on an array of 100, 1000, or 10,000 items with the same few lines of code.

A DO UNTIL defines the outer loop; as long as the array is not sorted, we loop through this loop. An inner do-loop (the iterative DO) defines the limits for one pass through the array and the do-group within the IF-THEN clause causes the exchange or "flip-flop" of the subscript references.

Upon leaving the DO UNTIL, another iterative DO causes the contents of the NAMES array to be printed.

```
/* TAG SORTING OF CHARACTER STRINGS USING AN EXCHANGE SORT TECHNIQUE */
/*******************************************************************/
/*                                                                 */
/*  PROGRAM NAME:    TAGSORT                                        */
/*                                                                 */
/*  DESCRIPTION:     THIS PROGRAM USES AN ARRAY NAMED TAGS TO CONTAIN */
/*                   THE SUBSCRIPTS OF THE SECOND ARRAY NAMED NAMES. */
/*                   THE SUBSCRIPTS IN TAGS REFERENCE THE ELEMENTS  */
/*                   IN NAMES IN ALPHABETICAL ORDER.  THE SUBSCRIPTS */
/*                   IN THE TAGS ARRAY ARE SORTED USING THE EXCHANGE */
/*                   SORT TECHNIQUE.  THE NAMES ARRAY IS THEN PRINTED */
/*                   IN ALPHABETICAL ORDER.                         */
/*                                                                 */
/*  INPUT:           SYSIN                                          */
/*                                                                 */
/*  OUTPUT:          PRINTER                                        */
/*                                                                 */
/*******************************************************************/
TAGSORT:  PROC OPTIONS (MAIN);

    DCL N                     FIXED BIN(15);
    DCL NAMES (10)            CHAR (35);
    DCL NO                    BIT(1)      INIT ('0'B);
    DCL EXCHANGED             BIT(1);
    DCL SORTED                BIT(1);
    DCL TAGS  (10)            FIXED BIN(15) INIT (1,2,3,4,5,6,7,8,9,10);
    DCL TEMP                  FIXED BIN(15);
    DCL YES                   BIT(1)      INIT ('1'B);

    GET LIST (NAMES);
    SORTED = NO;
    DO UNTIL (SORTED);
       EXCHANGED = NO;
       DO N = 1 TO 9;
          IF NAMES(TAGS(N)) > NAMES(TAGS(N + 1)) THEN
             DO;
                TEMP          = TAGS(N);
                TAGS(N)       = TAGS(N + 1);
                TAGS(N + 1)   = TEMP;
                EXCHANGED     = YES;
             END;
       END;
       IF ▫ EXCHANGED THEN
          SORTED = YES;
    END;

    PUT LIST ('SORTED STRINGS');
    DO N = 1 TO 10;
       PUT SKIP (2) LIST (NAMES(TAGS(N)));
    END;
END TAGSORT;
```

FIGURE 6.5  Program to tag sort string data using exchange sort technique.

In debugging PL/I programs that contain arrays, there are several features of the compiler you may find useful.

### The AGGREGATE Option

The first feature is the AGGREGATE option in the *PROCESS statement:

    *PROCESS AGGREGATE;

The AGGREGATE option may be specified with any other desired option in the *PROCESS statement. The AGGREGATE option specifies that the compiler is to include in the compiler source listing an *aggregate length table*. This table will supply the length — that is, the amount of storage required — for all arrays. This feature is most useful during the checkout phase of your program if you inspect the aggregate length printout to determine that the array sizes (i.e., number of elements) are, in fact, the number required. In addition, this table provides useful documentation to the programmer doing program maintenance and/or modifications from the source listing.

### The SUBSCRIPTRANGE Condition

The SUBSCRIPTRANGE condition is used for program checkout. It can be raised whenever there is a reference to an element outside the boundaries of an array. Inadvertent references to boundaries outside the declared array size can be disastrous if the reference is specified in a receiving field. Consider the following code:

    DCL ARRAY (10)   FLOAT DEC (6);
    GET LIST (K);
    ARRAY(K) = J;
       .
       .

If the input value K is greater than 10, some location nearby but *outside* the array will be altered by the assignment statement shown. This "destroyed" location might be another data array or it could even be some instructions in your program.

The previous coding example is not a standard approach to the programming of arrays. In that example, the subscript reference K should have been tested in an IF statement to determine that K was within the declared array boundaries. However, during debugging, situations do arise in which there is an inadvertent subscript reference to an element outside array boundaries. For this reason, you should enable the SUBSCRIPTRANGE condition during program checkout. This condition is usually in a disabled state. To enable it, simply prefix the keyword to the main procedure in your program. For example:

(SUBSCRIPTRANGE):
MATRIX: PROC OPTIONS(MAIN);

Then, when the PL/I compiler code detects a SUBSCRIPTRANGE error, **standard system action** will be taken notifying you of the error.   The standard system action causes a message to be printed that includes an error code and appropriate message indicating that SUBSCRIPTRANGE occurred at source statement *nnn* in your program.   Standard system action causes your program to terminate.   At this point, you should correct the situation causing the SUBSCRIPTRANGE error and rerun your program.

Because SUBSCRIPTRANGE checking involves a substantial overhead in both main storage required and execution time, you should remove the SUBSCRIPTRANGE prefix from your program after it has been debugged and tested.   SUBSCRIPTRANGE is a normally disabled condition.

It is possible to specify an on-unit for SUBSCRIPTRANGE.   For example:

ON SUBSCRIPTRANGE
    K = 1;

However, it is not really practical to specify an on-unit for SUBSCRIPTRANGE that in any way attempts to correct the error.   This is because the *normal* return from a SUBSCRIPTRANGE on-unit raises the ERROR condition, which causes the termination of your program.

One type of coding you might attempt in the on-unit of a SUBSCRIPTRANGE would be printing or "dumping" data areas in your program.   This could be done with a PUT DATA statement.   For example:

ON SUBSCRIPTRANGE
    PUT DATA (ARRAY1, ARRAY2);

## CASE STUDY

"Now," said Rabbit, "this is a Search and I've organized it —"
"Done what to it?" said Pooh.
"Organized it.   Which means — well, it's what you do to a Search when you don't all look in the same place at once."

**from *The House at Pooh Corner***
**by A. A. Milne**

The *binary search technique* is a method that may be used for locating data in a table.   As an illustration, assume that two tables are stored on a direct access device.   These tables consist of codes and corresponding premiums.   For example:

| Codes | | Premiums | |
|---|---|---|---|
| (1) | 107 | (1) | 25.90 |
| (2) | 137 | (2) | 35.16 |
| (3) | 243 | (3) | 14.75 |
| (4) | 375 | (4) | 47.35 |
| (5) | 491 | (5) | 5.23 |
| (6) | 503 | (6) | 15.34 |
| (7) | 620 | (7) | 4.10 |
| (8) | 745 | (8) | 5.95 |
| (9) | 847 | (9) | 13.46 |
| (10) | 960 | (10) | 10.57 |
| Codes (11) | 988 | Premiums (11) | 39.22 |

In an insurance application, each code in the table identifies a specific type of coverage offered by the insurer. The corresponding premium is the cost that the insured must pay for that coverage. Typically, the tables in which the codes and premiums are stored are fairly large, although only 11 items are shown here for purposes of simplicity.

Assume that both tables (CODES and PREMIUMS) are read into main storage from the direct access device in the initialization phase of the program. The values in the table called CODES are referred to as the *table arguments*. These codes are in ascending sequence.

Assume that it has been determined that several coverages are to be included in a given insurance policy for a customer. Codes indicating the types of coverage desired, along with the customer name and the number of codes in the record, are in a disk file.

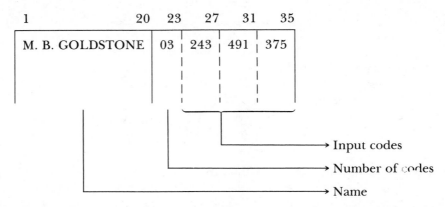

These input codes (a maximum of 14 per customer) are referred to as the *search arguments*. The program reads each search argument from the record and "searches" the codes table for a matching value. When an equal code is found, the corresponding premium should be added to a total. When all premiums have been summed up for a given customer, the customer's name and total premiums due are printed. If a record contains an invalid code (one not in the table), an error message is printed and the record is bypassed. The term *table function* is often associated with table look-up techniques. The table functions in this case are the corresponding premiums. Each table function must be in the same relative position in the function table as its code is in the argument table. , Because the purpose of this case study is to illustrate the binary search technique, the program processing and formatting of output is kept to a minimum.

One method for locating a code in the CODES table is to take the search argument and compare it with each table argument, beginning at the top of the table and sequentially continuing down the table until either an equal compare occurs or the end of the table is reached. Because the search arguments (input codes) are in random order, each new search through the CODES table must begin at the top of the table. If the CODES table contains 500 table arguments, the sequential method of comparing is time-consuming. If the table arguments are sequentially organized, as they are in the CODES table, another way to locate the desired code is to use the *binary search* method. In a binary search, the technique is to take the search argument and compare it with the middle table argument. For example, if there are 500 table arguments, the search argument is to be compared with the 250th table argument. If the search argument is less than the table argument, we know that the corresponding code for the search argument must lie within the first half of the table. This method allows us to eliminate searching half of the table with just *one* compare. Of course, for this method to work, the table arguments must be sorted into ascending sequence. The binary search method is so named because the technique is to divide each remaining portion of the table in half (by two), and compare the search argument with the table argument until an equal compare occurs or the last compare has

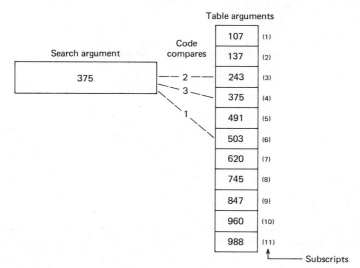

been made.  What is so striking about this method is that after two compares, three-fourths of the table have been eliminated from the search.

Once the matching table argument has been located, the location of the table function is known.  For example, if the matching coverage code is located by a subscript (4), then the correct premium amount will also be found by using the subscript reference (4).

The case study program is divided into two segments with the following subfunctions:

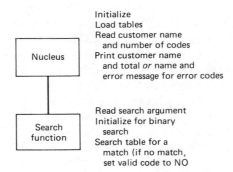

Figure 6.6 shows the pseudocode for the top segment, the nucleus.  The pseudocode for the SEARCH segment is not shown; rather, a program flowchart (Figure 6.7) is provided.  Actually, this flowchart is general enough in nature that you may find it useful in the programming of any binary search application.  To see the logic of the search algorithm, it is suggested that you select a search argument and

```
PREMIUM ON ENDFILE turn MORE_RECORDS switch off
        read CODES and AMOUNT, and load into tables
        read customer NAME and the field containing the number of
        codes that are on the record (NUMBER_OF_CODES)
        DO WHILE MORE_RECORDS switch is on
          set TOTAL = 0
          turn on a switch to indicate that all the codes tested so far are valid
            (VALID_CODES)
          DO INDEX = 1 TO the number of elements in the table
            CALL SEARCH
          END DO
          IF VALID_CODE switch is on
            print NAME & TOTAL_PREMIUM
          ELSE
            print NAME and error message
          read customer NAME and NUMBER_OF_CODES
          END DO
```

FIGURE 6.6   Top segment or nucleus pseudocode solution for insurance premium calculation case study.

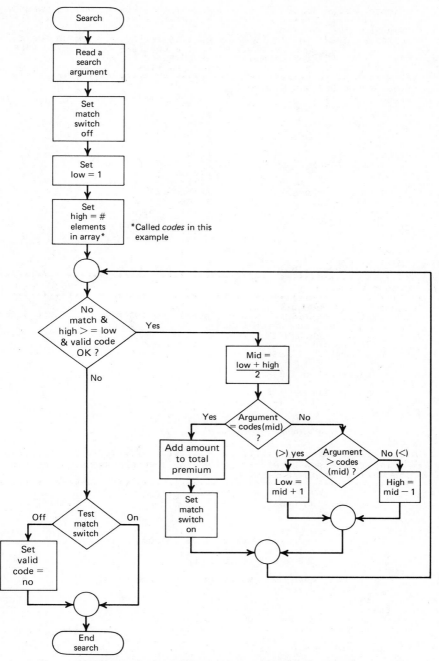

FIGURE 6.7    Generalized solution for a binary search.

```
/* CHAPTER 6 CASE STUDY ---    BINARY SEARCH FOR INSURANCE PREMIUM */
/*******************************************************************/
/*   PROGRAM NAME:   PREMIUM                                       */
/*   DESCRIPTION:    THIS PROGRAM CALCULATES THE TOTAL PREMIUM FOR A */
/*                   POLICY BY LOCATING THE COVERAGE CODES IN A TABLE */
/*                   AND ADDING ALL THE COVERAGE AMOUNTS.          */
/*   INPUT:     SYSIN          OUTPUT:   PRINTER                   */
/*******************************************************************/
1    PREMIUM:  PROC OPTIONS(MAIN);
2        DCL AMOUNT(11)              FIXED DEC (5,2);
3        DCL CODES (11)              FIXED DEC (3);
4        DCL HIGH                    FIXED DEC (3);
5        DCL INDEX                   FIXED BIN (15);
6        DCL LOW                     FIXED DEC (3);
7        DCL MATCH                   BIT (1);
8        DCL MID                     FIXED DEC (3);
9        DCL MORE_RECORDS            BIT (1) INIT ('1'B);
10       DCL NAME                    CHAR(20);
11       DCL NO                      BIT (1)          INIT ('0'B);
12       DCL NUMBER_OF_CODES         FIXED DEC (3);
13       DCL PREMIUM_CODE            FIXED DEC (3);
14       DCL TABLE_SIZE              FIXED BIN (15);
15       DCL TOTAL_PREMIUM           FIXED DEC (7,2);
16       DCL VALID_CODE              BIT (1);
17       DCL YES                     BIT (1)          INIT ('1'B);
18       DCL HBOUND                  BUILTIN;
19       ON ENDFILE (SYSIN)
              MORE_RECORDS = NO;
/*******************************************************************/
/*   PROGRAM NUCLEUS                                               */
/*******************************************************************/
20       TABLE_SIZE = HBOUND(CODES,1);
21       GET LIST ((CODES(INDEX),AMOUNT(INDEX)  DO INDEX = 1 TO TABLE_SIZE));
22       GET LIST (NAME, NUMBER_OF_CODES);
23       DO WHILE(MORE_RECORDS);
24           TOTAL_PREMIUM = 0;
25           VALID_CODE   = YES;
26           DO INDEX = 1 TO NUMBER_OF_CODES;
27               CALL SEARCH;
28           END;
29           IF VALID_CODE THEN
                   PUT SKIP LIST (NAME, TOTAL_PREMIUM);
30           ELSE
                   PUT SKIP LIST (NAME,  ERROR CODE');
31           GET LIST(NAME,NUMBER_OF_CODES);
32       END;

/*******************************************************************/
/*   SEARCH TABLE FOR PREMIUM CODE AND ADD THE CORRESPONDING PREMIUM */
/*   AMOUNT TO THE TOTAL PREMIUM.                                  */
/*******************************************************************/
33   SEARCH:   PROCEDURE;
34       GET LIST (PREMIUM_CODE);
35       MATCH     = NO;
36       LOW       = 1;
37       HIGH      = TABLE_SIZE;
38       DO WHILE (HIGH >= LOW &  ¬MATCH & VALID_CODE);
39           MID = (LOW + HIGH) / 2;
40           IF PREMIUM_CODE = CODES(MID) THEN
                   DO;
41                     TOTAL_PREMIUM = TOTAL_PREMIUM + AMOUNT(MID);
42                     MATCH = YES;
43                 END;
44           ELSE
                   IF PREMIUM_CODE > CODES(MID) THEN
                       LOW = MID + 1;
45                 ELSE
                       HIGH = MID - 1;
46           END;
47           IF ¬MATCH THEN
                   VALID_CODE = NO;
48       END SEARCH;
49   END PREMIUM;
```

FIGURE 6.8

work through the flowchart using the 11-element CODES table illustrated in the introduction of this case study.

Figure 6.8 illustrates the program solution to the insurance premium calculation problem. Following is a discussion of key statements:

**Statement 20:** This statement uses the HBOUND built-in function to establish the upper boundary of the CODES table. Should it be necessary to modify the program's array sizes later, it will not be necessary to modify the PL/I code related to array manipulation. This is because array sizes are determined *dynamically*—that is, at execution time—through the HBOUND function.

**Statement 21:** The arrays CODES and AMOUNT are initialized with data read in.

**Statements 26–28:** An iterative DO is established in which the SEARCH subroutine is called as many times as there are insurance premium codes for a given customer.

**Statements 29–31:** The VALID-CODE indicator is tested for a true condition, in which case the customer's name and total premium due are printed. If an invalid code is found in a given customer record, then the customer's name and an error message are printed.

**Statements 33–37:** These statements are centered around the initialization portion of the subroutine. The search argument is read using a GET LIST. The MATCH indicator is turned off and the table boundaries are established.

**Statements 38–46:** These statements provide the basic binary search technique. Notice that in statement 41 the *table function* is that of accumulating the preliminary amount into the variable called TOTAL_PREMIUM.

**Statement 47:** The MATCH indicator is tested for a false condition. If this indicator is turned off, then there was no matching argument found during the binary search. In this case, then, we know that there must have been an invalid search argument. Thus, the VALID_CODE indicator is turned off. Recall that the top segment tested this indicator to determine whether standard printout or an error message should be displayed.

## CHECKPOINT QUESTIONS

18. Is the following array assignment statement valid? Why or why not?

```
DCL A(6)       FLOAT DEC (6);
DCL B(2,3)     FLOAT DEC (6);
GET LIST (A);
B = A;
```

**19.** Given the statement

    DCL X (10)   FLOAT DEC (6);

which of the following statements are equivalent?

(a)   GET LIST (X);
(b)   GET LIST ((X(K) DO K = 1 to 10));
(c)   DO K = 1 TO 10;
          GET LIST (X(K));
      END;

**20.** In which of the following PL/I statements may a *repetitive specification* appear?

(a)   Assignment statement          (c)   GET and PUT
(b)   DECLARE                       (d)   Iterative DO

## SUMMARY

**Arrays:** An array is a table of data items in which each item has the same attribute as every other item in the array.   An array has storage reserved for it by means of a DECLARE statement.

**Bounds:** In declaring the size of an array, a bound is specified.   All arrays have upper and lower bounds.   When a single bound is specified, it is the upper bound, in which case the lower bound is assumed to be 1.

**Dimensions:** The number of sets of upper and lower bounds specifies the number of dimensions in an array.   In referring to two-dimensional arrays, the terms *rows* and *columns* are sometimes used.   Maximum number of dimensions generally allowed is 15.

**Subscripts:** To reference an element of an array, specify a subscript in parentheses following an array name in an expression; for example, TABLE(7) refers to the seventh element in the array called TABLE.   Subscripts may be constants, variables, expressions, or subscripted subscripts; for example, TABLE(J(K)).

**SUBSCRIPTRANGE Condition:** Referencing a location outside the bounds of the array will cause the SUBSCRIPTRANGE condition to be raised if the condition is enabled.   Because this condition is initially disabled, it will be necessary to enable the condition in your program.   The SUBSCRIPTRANGE condition is a useful debugging tool, for it is during the program checkout phase that you are most likely to specify inadvertently a subscript that references a nonexistent position of an array.

**Cross Sections of Arrays:** A subscript may also be an asterisk, in which case it specifies the entire extent of the dimension.   This extent is referred to as a cross

| | Examples | Comments |
|---|---|---|
| Type 1 | DO; | • Noniterative<br>• Used in the IF statement<br>• Used in the SELECT statement |
| Type 2 | DO WHILE (expression);<br>DO WHILE (expression) UNTIL (expression);<br>DO UNTIL (expression);<br>DO UNTIL (expression) WHILE (expression); | • Iterative<br>• Loop terminated by the WHILE<br>  or UNTIL clause or LEAVE<br>  If WHILE is omitted, do-group<br>  will be executed at least once |
| Type 3 | DO INDEX = J;<br>DO INDEX = J TO K BY L;<br>DO INDEX = J BY L TO K;<br>DO INDEX = J TO K;<br>DO INDEX = J BY L;<br>DO INDEX = I,J,K,L;<br>DO INDEX = J TO K, L TO M, X TO Y; | • Iterative<br>• WHILE or UNTIL option may be<br>  added to any of the type 3<br>  examples<br>• WHILE *and* UNTIL may be<br>  included *together* with any of<br>  the type 3 examples in either<br>  order |

FIGURE 6.9  Various forms of the DO statement.

section of an array. A subscripted name containing asterisk subscripts represents not a single data element, but rather a larger part of the array; e.g., PERCENT (*,1) refers to all of the elements in the first column of the array called PERCENT.

**I/O Operations and Arrays:** In the absence of explicit element addressing, data items are read into arrays starting with the lowest numbered subscripted element and finishing with the highest subscripted element. If a multidimensional array is specified in an I/O statement, the right-hand subscript varies most rapidly.

**Array Assignments:** Two types of move operations may be specified for arrays:

**1. Scalar-to-array:** In this type of array assignment, an entire array is assigned a single value.

**2. Array-to-array:** In this case, one array may be assigned to another array, providing the arrays have identical dimensions and bounds.

**Array Expressions:** An array expression is a single-array variable or an expression that includes at least one array operand. Array expressions may also include operators (both prefix and infix), element variables, and constants. Evaluation of an array expression yields an array result. All operations performed on arrays are performed on an element-by-element basis. All arrays referred to in an array expression must have identical dimensions and bounds.

**The DO Statement:** See Figure 6.9 for a summary of the various formats of the DO statement. There are four general forms of the DO statement:

**1. The do-group — noniterative:** Specifies that the do-group is to be treated logically as a single statement. It is used in an IF statement to specify a group of statements to be executed in the THEN or ELSE clause and in the SELECT statement following the WHEN clause.

**2. The DO-WHILE:** Specifies that the instructions contained between the DO and its corresponding END are to be executed repetitively as long as the expression following the WHILE is true. If the condition tested is not true initially, statements within the DO will not be executed.

**3. The DO-UNTIL:** Specifies that the instructions contained between the DO and its corresponding END are to be executed repetitively until the expression following the UNTIL is true. If the condition tested is not true, the statements within the DO will be executed. Statements within the DO will be executed at least once because the test for the condition is made at the end of the loop.

**4. The do-group — iterative:** Specifies that instructions contained between the DO and its corresponding END are to be executed repetitively until the index variable is greater than the limit value; for example, DO K = 1 to 100; when K = 101, loop is terminated. The WHILE and/or UNTIL option may be specified with the iterative form of the DO.

**Nested Do-Groups:** Do-groups may be nested within other do-groups. All statements in the range of the inner DO must be within the range of the outer DO. It is possible to transfer out of a do-group before the maximum number of iterations have been performed. However, it is not permitted to transfer to a statement in an iterative do-group.

**The Repetitive Specification of a Data Item:** In stream I/O, data list elements may contain a repetitive specification similar to the iterative DO — for example:

GET LIST ((TABLE(K) DO K = 5 TO 10));

# CHAPTER 7

# File Declarations and Stream I/O

This chapter covers two important aspects of PL/I programming—the declaration of files and the various forms of stream I/O. A *file* is a collection of records. In some systems (such as IBM's mainframes) the term **data set,** rather than **file,** is used. The records in a file or data set are *logically related.* All employee payroll information, for example, is kept in records in the *payroll file,* and names and addresses of all vendors supplying parts to a company are kept in an accounts payable *vendor name and address file.* A file or data set is located on an external storage medium such as a floppy diskette, a reel of magnetic tape, or a hard disk. The contents of a file can even be located on a "piece of paper" (e.g., a printed report output to a line printer).

Several programming steps must take place when input or output operations are specified. These steps, shown in Figure 7.1, may or may not be explicitly coded in your PL/I program. The first step is to define the file via a DECLARE. We have not been declaring files for GET or PUT LIST because default file definitions have been used. The method in which you specify file attributes depends on which implementation of PL/I you are using.

The next step is to open the file. Before we can communicate with a file, that file must be *opened.* We have not been explicitly opening files because files are automatically opened with the first GET or PUT to that file. One purpose of the OPEN statement is to specify additional file attributes at *open* time. The first

| | PL/I Statement | Purpose |
|---|---|---|
| 1. Define the file | DECLARE PAYROLL FILE . . . | Specifies attributes to be associated with the file name |
| 2. Open the file | OPEN FILE (PAYROLL); | Completes the file declaration, if necessary; associates the file name with the physical device on which the file is located |
| 3. Process information in the file | READ or WRITE or REWRITE GET or PUT | I/O statements for RECORD files; I/O statements for STREAM files |
| 4. Close the file | CLOSE FILE (PAYROLL); | Files are automatically closed when your program terminates normally; disassociates the file name with the physical device where file was located |

FIGURE 7.1   I/O programming steps.

section of this chapter addresses the declaration of files and the OPEN statement that is typically used to complete the file declaration.

The third step in Figure 7.1 is processing information in files using READ or WRITE statements (record I/O) or GET or PUT statements (stream I/O). In the initial design of PL/I, stream I/O was intended for scientific applications because it resembled the type of I/O used in FORTRAN (FORmula TRANslation), a mathematician's programming language and forerunner of PL/I. Today, however, stream I/O is used in both scientific and commercial programming applications, although the majority of commercial applications use record I/O. Stream I/O is most often used for a terminal or for printer files, although it could also be used for tape or disk unblocked records in consecutive files.

## FILE DECLARATIONS

The set of records in the file or data set is referred to in a PL/I program by a **file name.** The file name may be from one to seven characters long and may be explicitly declared in a DECLARE statement. For example:

DECLARE PAYROLL FILE (other attributes);

Select a file name that is descriptive of the application or type of records stored in the data set. Attributes associated with a file include the type of transmission (STREAM or RECORD), the direction of transmission (INPUT, OUTPUT, or UPDATE in the case of disk files), and the physical environment of the file. For example:

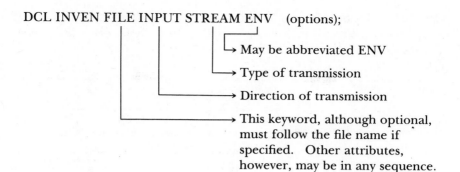

DCL INVEN FILE INPUT STREAM ENV   (options);

→ May be abbreviated ENV

→ Type of transmission

→ Direction of transmission

→ This keyword, although optional, must follow the file name if specified.  Other attributes, however, may be in any sequence.

The options specified in the ENVIRONMENT attribute are related to such physical characteristics of the file as the record size (BLKSIZE and/or RECSIZE) or device type.

Options in the ENVIRONMENT attribute may be specified in any sequence, as may be the other file attributes.  For example:

DCL ACCTS FILE ENV (F BLKSIZE (80)) INPUT STREAM;

## File Attributes

The file declarations in this chapter use the STREAM attribute because stream I/O programming is being discussed.  Note, however, that most of the attributes also apply to files with the RECORD attribute.  Following is a discussion of the attributes that may be specified for files.

**FILE Attribute.**  This attribute specifies that the identifier being declared is a file name.  FILE can be implied if other file attributes are present in the DECLARE that enable the compiler to deduce the FILE attribute.  In the following example, while FILE is not explicitly coded,

DCL BILLING INPUT STREAM ENV (F BLKSIZE (150));

the FILE attribute is, nevertheless, implicitly declared because of other file attributes (INPUT, etc.) in the DECLARE statement.  For program readability, it is recommended that FILE always be specified.

**INPUT/OUTPUT Attributes.**  One of these attributes must be specified either in the DECLARE statement or in the OPEN statement.  Both attributes could not be specified or "in effect" at the same time.  If neither is explicitly specified, INPUT is the default attribute unless the file has the PRINT attribute (then OUTPUT is default).  For program readability and maintainability, code either attribute in the DECLARE or the OPEN statement if allowed.

**STREAM Attribute.** This attribute specifies that data items are accessed by GET or PUT statements and that they are a continuous stream. There are three forms of stream I/O:

| | |
|---|---|
| List-directed | GET LIST (A,B,C); <br> PUT LIST (A,B,C); |
| Edit-directed | GET EDIT (A,B,C) (F(5), F (7,2), A (20)); <br> PUT EDIT (A,B,C) (PAGE, COL (5), F (5), E (15,2), <br> X(10), A); |
| Data-directed* | GET DATA (A,B,C); <br> PUT DATA (A,B,C); |

* NOT available in all implementations of PL/I.

The opposite of STREAM is RECORD. If neither is specified, STREAM is assumed.

**ENVIRONMENT Attribute.** This attribute is coded when one or more options is declared. The ENVIRONMENT attribute could be omitted if the equivalent information is provided in JCL. The options that apply to STREAM files are the record form and record size option. The F in the ENVIRONMENT section of the file declaration specifies the record type as fixed length. For some of the examples in this text, the record type is fixed and each record is 80 bytes long [e.g., F BLKSIZE (80)]. Eighty is the number of characters on one line on a video display terminal; it is also the number of characters in a punched card—the forerunner of today's terminal-oriented computers. For line printer output, the record type can be variable (V instead of F).

The record length of a printer file—that is, the number of printed positions on a line—may be any value as long as that value does not exceed the maximum number of print positions plus 1 position for a carriage control character for the line printer you are using. Typically, a printer is either 120, 132, 144, 150, or 230 print positions wide. Thus, F BLKSIZE (133) might be the specification you would write in the ENVIRONMENT section of the file declaration statement for a printer.

**PRINT Attribute.** This attribute is added to the file declaration for stream files associated with a line printer so that the carriage control options such as PAGE and LINE may be specified in the PUT statement. The PRINT attribute applies only to files with the STREAM and OUTPUT attributes. It indicates that the file is to be printed on a line printer. The PRINT attribute causes the initial byte of each record of the associated data set to be reserved for a printer control character. The printer control character, initialized through the use of such keywords as PAGE, SKIP, or LINE in your PUT statement, does not appear on the printed output. Here is an example of a file declaration for a line printer in which a 60-position message is printed:

DCL PRINTR FILE OUTPUT STREAM PRINT ENV (F BLKSIZE (61));

Required if PAGE or LINE is ←⎤
used in a PUT statement

Record size is equal to desired print line size plus one ←⎤
position for carriage control character

Here is an example of the DECLARE and PUT LIST statements for a STREAM
file having the PRINT attribute:

DCL PRINTR FILE OUTPUT STREAM PRINT ENV (F BLKSIZE(133));
DCL AREA CHAR (133);
PUT FILE (PRINTR) PAGE LIST (AREA);

Without the PRINT attribute, we have the following DECLARE and PUT:

DCL PRINTR FILE OUTPUT STREAM ENV (F BLKSIZE (132));
DCL AREA                          CHAR (130);
PUT FILE (PRINTR) LIST (AREA);  .

Notice that the record size (132) is one less than that in the first example, because
the first position of the output area will not be used for a carriage control character.   Quote marks are supplied by list-directed output routines around character-
strings output to *non-PRINT files*.   AREA (130 characters long) and two single
quote marks add up to a record length of 132.   This means that there will be a
space of one line before print because the data output occupies an entire print
line.

A built-in function called LINENO finds the current line number for a file
having the PRINT attribute and returns that number to the point of invocation.
For example:

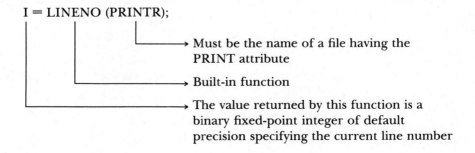

I = LINENO (PRINTR);

→ Must be the name of a file having the
  PRINT attribute

→ Built-in function

→ The value returned by this function is a
  binary fixed-point integer of default
  precision specifying the current line number

## Default or Predefined Files

When file names are omitted from a GET or PUT, default file names are assumed: SYSIN for the standard input file and SYSPRINT for the output file. Thus, the statements

        GET LIST (A,B,C);
        PUT LIST (A,B,C);

are equivalent to

        GET FILE (SYSIN) LIST (A,B,C);
        PUT FILE (SYSPRINT) LIST (A,B,C);

List-directed I/O statements, where a file name is explicitly coded, take this general form:

        GET FILE (file name) LIST (data names);
        PUT FILE (file name) LIST (data names);

The SYSIN and SYSPRINT file names and their attributes do not have to be explicitly declared.

The SYSIN file is referenced in the ENDFILE statement. For example:

        ON ENDFILE (SYSIN)
            MORE_RECORDS = NO;

Thus, we may take program-specified action on the end-of-file condition without having to declare explicitly the SYSIN file. Here are the file attributes and options that apply to SYSIN and SYSPRINT for IBM implementations of PL/I.[1]

|          | *Attributes and Options* |
|----------|--------------------------|
| SYSIN    | FILE STREAM INPUT ENV (F BLKSIZE (80)) |
| SYSPRINT | FILE STREAM OUTPUT PRINT ENV (V BLKSIZE (129)) |

[1] For microcomputer implementations such as the PL/I from Digital Research, SYSIN and SYSPRINT have the following attributes:

        SYSIN     STREAM INPUT ENV(LOCKED,BUFF(128))TITLE('$CON')
                      LINESIZE(80) PAGESIZE(0)
        SYSPRINT  STREAM PRINT ENV(LOCKED,BUFF(128))TITLE('$CON')
                      LINESIZE(80) PAGESIZE(0)

The TITLE option $CON refers to the console keyboard and video display. If you reference SYSIN in an ENDFILE statement then the file must be explicitly declared.

The V record specification stands for variable-length record as contrasted with F for fixed-length record. With V-type records, each record size may vary in length; however, in this example, no record may be larger than 120 print positions. A blocksize of 129 is used because 8 extra bytes are required for the variable-length record specification and 1 byte is required for the carriage control character. The following options are also in effect for the SYSPRINT file:

LINESIZE = 120 positions per line
PAGESIZE = 60 lines per page

## CHECKPOINT QUESTIONS

**1.** True or false? File names may be the same length as any other PL/I identifier, 1 to 31 characters long.

**2.** Give examples of Keywords that may be specified in the ENVIRONMENT attribute.

**3.** What does the PRINT attribute accomplish in a file declaration statement?

**4.** What are the default attributes for SYSIN? SYSPRINT?

**5.** Assume variable-length records are output to a printer. The longest record is 100 bytes. Write the file declaration.

### The OPEN Statement

Before a PL/I program can communicate with a file, that file must be opened. The opening of files is automatic; therefore, it would not be necessary for you to include an explicit OPEN statement in your program to accomplish this function. The reason for using the open statement is so that additional file attributes and/or options may be specified at open times. Several files may be opened with *one* OPEN statement. For example:

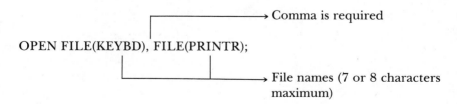

Another way in which the statement may be formatted is

```
OPEN
     FILE(KEYBD),
     FILE(PRINTR),
     FILE(TAPE);
```

where each file name appears on a separate line and the file names appear in alphabetical order.

The opening of files is necessary because it is at that time that device readiness is checked (e.g., is the power on and is the device in a ready state?) and all attributes for the file are merged. In other words, some attributes may be specified in job control statements, others (but not conflicting ones) may be in the DECLARE statement, and still other attributes may be in the OPEN statement. It is at *open* time that attributes from these three sources are combined to form the description of the file with which the program is going to communicate.

STREAM files are automatically opened when the first GET or PUT to that file is issued. In the case of a file with the PRINT attribute, there is an automatic advance to a new page for the first PUT to that file. A number of attributes and options may be specified in the OPEN statement. Of the keywords presented so far, these include:

        STREAM or RECORD
        INPUT or OUTPUT
        PRINT

For stream files that have the PRINT attribute, PAGESIZE and/or LINESIZE may be specified as follows:

        OPEN FILE(PRINTR)PAGESIZE(50);
                        └──→ Specifies number of lines to be output
                             per page of print; if PAGESIZE is not
                             specified, the default is 60

        OPEN FILE (PRINTR) LINESIZE (121);
                         └──→ Specifies number of print positions
                              per printed line (plus space for
                              carriage control character); if this
                              option is used; it is not necessary to
                              specify a record size [e.g., F BLKSIZE
                              (121)] file declaration

If output is to SYSPRINT, LINESIZE may be used to override the default size of 120. For example:

OPEN FILE (SYSPRINT) LINESIZE (133);

PAGESIZE and LINESIZE may only appear in an OPEN statement — never in a file DECLARE statement.

Another option of the OPEN statement is the TITLE option:

OPEN FILE (DATAIN)TITLE(FILENAME);

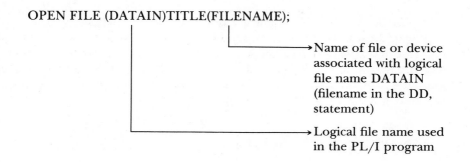

→ Name of file or device associated with logical file name DATAIN (filename in the DD, statement)

→ Logical file name used in the PL/I program

OPEN FILE (EMPLOYEE_ROSTER) TITLE ('SYSIN');
GET FILE (EMPLOYEE_ROSTER) LIST (NAME_ADDR);

Several steps are taken when files are opened:

**1. Attributes are merged:** When a file is opened, the attributes from three sources (JCL, DECLARE, OPEN) are located and combined to form the description that applies to the file being opened.

**2. Device readiness is checked:** An I/O device may not be in a *ready* state for several reasons. Perhaps the operator failed to press the START button that readies a device or perhaps there is no power supplied to the device. Typically, an error message is displayed on the operator's console when device failure is noted at OPEN time.

**3. Labels are checked:** If you are communicating with disk or tape data sets, *data set labels* are also checked at OPEN time. (Labels are provided to guard against inadvertent destruction of the file.) When a tape or disk data set is created, a label is defined through job control statements. This label contains the name by which the data set is identified to the operating system and is not to be confused with the file name you specify in your file declaration statement. On subsequent programs communicating with established files, the **label** information must be specified again through JCL. If the subsequent label information does not exactly match the label information recorded for the data set, your program is not allowed access to that file. An error message is printed and your program terminated.

## The CLOSE Statement

Only the file name is specified in the CLOSE statement (no options or attributes). For example:

CLOSE FILE (PAYROLL);

When files are closed, the file name is dissociated from the data set. The CLOSE is optional, because when a PL/I program ends, all files are automatically closed. In the case of output files to magnetic tape or disk, an end-of-file mark is written to the device, signaling the physical end of the file or data set. If a file is open and an attribute is to be changed, the file must first be closed. Then it may be reopened with the new attribute(s). For example:

```
OPEN FILE (WORK) OUTPUT;
        .
        .
        /* WRITE RECORDS */
        .
        .
CLOSE FILE (WORK);
OPEN FILE (WORK) INPUT;
        .
        .
        /* READ RECORDS  */
```

Should your program abnormally terminate (e.g., through an error such as the CONVERSION condition raised), files will not be closed. This presents a problem if a tape or disk file is being *created* because no end-of-file mark is written unless the file is closed. Thus, if a program is creating a tape or disk file and the program is abnormally terminated, you will have to correct the error in the program and create the file again.

## CHECKPOINT QUESTIONS

**6.** What is the primary reason for explicitly opening files?

**7.** What happens when a file is opened? closed?

**8.** Where may the options PAGESIZE and LINESIZE be specified and what do they accomplish?

## A Sample Program Using File Declarations and OPEN Statements

Figure 7.2 shows a program in which names and addresses are input from a terminal via prompts from the program. The names and addresses are written into a stream-oriented disk file named by the user. The names and addresses are also printed on the printer as address labels:

The program in Figure 7.2 begins by declaring all variables needed by the program. There are four files: SYSPRINT (terminal display), SYSIN (keyboard input), DISKFILE (logical file to be named later by data entry operator), and LABEL (printer file). The ENDFILE condition action is specified. When the operator is prompted for a NAME and there are no more names to enter, the operator signals the end of data by responding with an 'EOF.' Notice in the IF statement how the test for EOF is made and how the ENDFILE condition is

```
/*  CREATE A NAME AND ADDRESS FILE AT THE TERMINAL              */
/*****************************************************************/
/*                                                              */
/*  PROGRAM NAME:   CREATE                                      */
/*                                                              */
/*  DESCRIPTION:    THIS PROGRAM CREATES A NAME AND ADDRESS FILE */
/*                  IN A DISK FILE WHOSE NAME IS SELECTED BY THE */
/*                  DATA ENTRY OPERATOR.  DATA IS INPUT FROM THE */
/*                  TERMINAL AND WRITTEN TO THE DISK FILE AS WELL*/
/*                  AS THE PRINTER IN THE FORM OF AN "ADDRESS    */
/*                  LABEL"  SUITABLE FOR MAILING.               */
/*                                                              */
/*  INPUT:          SYSIN  -  ENTERED BY OPERATOR AT THE TERMINAL*/
/*                                                              */
/*  OUTPUT:         SYSPRINT - MESSAGES DISPLAYED AT THE TERMINAL*/
/*                  LABEL    - MAILING ADDRESS LABELS           */
/*                  DISKFILE - MAILING NAME AND ADDRESS DISK FILE*/
/*                                                              */
/*****************************************************************/
```

FIGURE 7.2   (page 1)

```
 1   CREATE: PROC OPTIONS(MAIN);

 2   DCL    SYSPRINT            FILE OUTPUT STREAM;
 3   DCL    SYSIN               FILE INPUT  STREAM;
 4   DCL    DISKFILE            FILE OUTPUT STREAM;
 5   DCL    LABEL               FILE OUTPUT STREAM PRINT;
 6   DCL    DATA_OK             BIT(1);
 7   DCL    MORE_RECORDS        BIT(1)        INIT('1'B);
 8   DCL    NO                  BIT(1)        INIT('0'B);
 9   DCL    YES                 BIT(1)        INIT('1'B);
10   DCL    FILENAME            CHAR(14) VAR;
11   DCL    NAME                CHAR(30) VAR;
12   DCL    ADDR                CHAR(30) VAR;
13   DCL    CITY_ST_ZIP         CHAR(30) VAR;
14   DCL    RESPONSE            CHAR(1);

15   ON ENDFILE(SYSIN)
        MORE_RECORDS = NO;

16   PUT SKIP FILE (SYSPRINT) LIST('ENTER THE DD NAME OF THE OUTPUT FILE:');
17   GET FILE (SYSIN) LIST  (FILENAME);
18   OPEN FILE (DISKFILE) TITLE (FILENAME);

19   OPEN FILE (LABEL)   PAGESIZE(7)   LINESIZE(39);

20   DO WHILE(MORE_RECORDS);
21      PUT SKIP FILE (SYSPRINT) LIST ('                NAME:');
22      GET FILE (SYSIN) LIST (NAME);
23      IF NAME = 'EOF' THEN
           SIGNAL ENDFILE(SYSIN);
24      ELSE DO;
25            DATA_OK = NO;
26            DO UNTIL(DATA_OK);
27               PUT SKIP FILE (SYSPRINT) LIST('             ADDRESS:');
28               GET FILE (SYSIN) LIST(ADDR);
29               PUT SKIP FILE (SYSPRINT) LIST('  CITY/STATE/ZIP:');
30               GET FILE (SYSIN) LIST(CITY_ST_ZIP);
31               PUT SKIP FILE (SYSPRINT) LIST('IS DATA OK?(Y/N):');
32               GET FILE (SYSIN) LIST(RESPONSE);
33               IF RESPONSE = 'Y' THEN
                     DATA_OK = YES;
34            END;

35            PUT FILE (DISKFILE) LIST(NAME,ADDR,CITY_ST_ZIP);
36            PUT PAGE FILE(LABEL)LIST(NAME);
37            PUT SKIP FILE(LABEL)LIST(ADDR);
38            PUT SKIP FILE(LABEL)LIST(CITY_ST_ZIP);
39         END;
40      END;

41      CLOSE FILE(DISKFILE);

42   END CREATE;
```

**FIGURE 7.2** (page 2)

triggered via a SIGNAL *condition* statement. The body of the program (statements 20–40) loops while there are more data to input. The DATA_OK switch is turned off so that the inner DO-WHILE structure may loop as long as the data entered by the operator is not correct. In this way, the operator has the ability to reenter data that is not correct as initially keyed. In the do-group following the ELSE, prompts are sent to the console display and responses obtained via GET LIST. After the entire name and address is entered, it is written as a record onto the disk file and printed as a label on the printer. When there are no more records to enter, the program terminates.

## STREAM I/O

In stream I/O, all input and output data items are in the form of a continuous stream of characters. In stream input, characters from the input stream are converted to the internal attributes of the identifiers specified in the GET statement. On output, coded arithmetic data items are automatically converted back to character form before the output takes place.

## EDIT-DIRECTED I/O

### Introduction

Each form of stream I/O offers the PL/I programmer certain advantages and disadvantages. Advantages of list-directed I/O are that it is easy to code and it is a useful debugging tool. A disadvantage of GET LIST is that the data items must be PL/I constants separated by blanks or commas; therefore, more space is usually required to represent the data on the input medium than in other types of stream input.

A disadvantage of PUT LIST for printed output is that data may be printed beginning only at predetermined "tab positions" on the printer. There is therefore little flexibility in the formatting of data to provide a meaningful and esthetically pleasing report.

Edit-directed I/O eliminates some disadvantages of list-directed I/O. Edit-directed I/O is not as easy to code, but you will find that it provides for considerable efficiency in the representation of input data and offers a great deal of flexibility in the formatting of output data for printed reports.

Note that we are still discussing input and output of character data. Data in arithmetic coded form—i.e., packed decimal or binary—on an external device such as disk or magnetic tape may not be read or written by stream I/O, but must be accessed by record I/O—to be covered in the next chapter.

Assume that the following record is read using list-directed input. The data would have to be entered as follows:[2]

| EMPLOYEE NUMBER | NAME | RATE OF PAY | HRS WKD | DEDUC- TIONS |
|---|---|---|---|---|
|   |   1 | 2 3 3 | 3 4 4 | 4 4 |
| 1           8 | 9 0 | 9 0 1 5 6 | 7 0 1 | 2 7 |
| '435928' | 'DAVID P. GOLDSMITH' | 10.55 | 41.3 | 103.21 |

[2] Recall that data items for list-directed input must be PL/I constants. Hence, the character-strings must be surrounded by single quotation marks.

In this example, a minimum of 47 positions are needed to represent the data that are read using the following GET LIST statement:

GET LIST (EMP#, NAME, RATE, HOURS, DEDUCTIONS);

Using edit-directed input, the number of positions needed to represent the preceding record can be reduced because no blanks are needed to separate the data items in the input stream, and no punctuation marks are needed to indicate the type of input data (e.g., single quotation marks surrounding character data or a decimal point indicating the true decimal value). The data input using GET EDIT could be entered as follows:

| 1 | 6 | 7 | | 2 4 | 2 5 | 2 8 | 2 9 | 3 1 | 3 2 | 3 6 |
|---|---|---|---|---|---|---|---|---|---|---|
| 435928 | | DAVID P. GOLDSMITH | | 1055 | | 413 | | 10321 | | |

Implied decimal point

As can be seen, only 36 positions are needed to represent the payroll information for edit-directed input, as compared to 47 positions for list-directed input. However, with no punctuation marks or delimiters in the input stream to indicate the characteristics of the various data fields, it is necessary for the GET EDIT statement to provide this information through a **format list.** Edit I/O statements take this general form:

GET EDIT (data list)(format list);
PUT EDIT (data list)(format list);

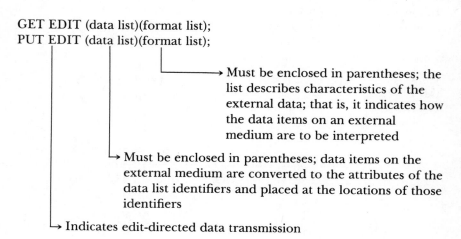

→ Must be enclosed in parentheses; the list describes characteristics of the external data; that is, it indicates how the data items on an external medium are to be interpreted

→ Must be enclosed in parentheses; data items on the external medium are converted to the attributes of the data list identifiers and placed at the locations of those identifiers

→ Indicates edit-directed data transmission

A file name could also be specified:

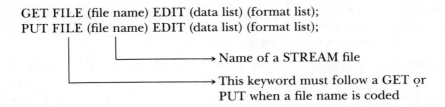

GET FILE (file name) EDIT (data list) (format list);
PUT FILE (file name) EDIT (data list) (format list);

→ Name of a STREAM file

→ This keyword must follow a GET or
PUT when a file name is coded

To input the data previously illustrated, the following statement could be coded:

GET EDIT (EMP#,NAME,RATE,HOURS,DEDUCTIONS)
(COLUMN (1),A(6),A(20),F(4,2),F(3,1),F(5,2));

The **data list** consists of EMP#, NAME, RATE, HOURS, DEDUCTIONS. The **format list** consists of the items COLUMN (1), A (6), A (20), etc. The arrows in the previous example point to the format item corresponding to each data item. These format items describe the appearance of data on an external medium. The COLUMN (1) format item indicates that input begins at column one or position one of the external storage medium. The A format item describes alphameric data, and the F format item describes fixed-point numeric data. The numbers in parentheses following the A and F specifications describe the width of the input field. Thus, six characters are taken from the input stream and assigned to EMP# 3, 20 characters are assigned to NAME; four digits, of which two are fractions, are assigned to RATE; and so on. Notice that we have not yet declared the attributes of EMP#, NAME, RATE, etc. It is important to understand that external data formats do not have to match the data declarations that describe the way data appears in main storage. A sample DECLARE statement for these data items could be as follows:

```
DCL EMP#         CHAR (6);
DCL NAME         CHAR (25);
DCL RATE         FIXED DEC (4,2);
DCL HOURS        FIXED DEC (3,1);
DCL DEDUCTIONS   FIXED DEC (7,3);
```

Notice that NAME is declared to be a character-string of length 25 in main storage, whereas only 20 characters were taken from the input stream and assigned to NAME. Because NAME has a length attribute of 25, there will be padding on the right of the field with blanks. The RATE and HOURS field in the DECLARE have precision attributes that match the width specifications of their corresponding format items. The DEDUCTIONS field has a precision (7,3); the

---

[3] EMP#, in this case, is being treated as an alphanumeric field rather than a fixed-point numeric field, because fixed numeric fields are generally used to identify data that will be used in calculations.

input deductions, which has a precision (5,2) will be stored with one zero to the left of the high-order integers and one zero to the right of the fraction.

Format items may be divided into three categories:

**1. Data format items:** These are items describing the format of the external data. These items describe whether data in the stream are characters or arithmetic values in character form and how long they are. In the preceding format list, the A specifies *alphameric* data (i.e., CHARACTER data), and the F indicates arithmetic values in the *fixed-point* notation (as contrasted with floating-point notation, which is an E format item).

**2. Control format items:** These are items describing page control, line control, and spacing operations. In the format list example, COLUMN (1) is a control format item.

**3. Remote format item:** This item indicates that one or more data format items and/or control format items are located *remotely* from the GET or PUT EDIT statement in a FORMAT statement. Here is an illustration of this type, which will be discussed in greater detail later:

GET EDIT(EMP#,NAME,RATE,HOURS,DEDUCTIONS)(R(RFMT));

RFMT: FORMAT(COLUMN(1),A(6),A(20),F(4,2),F(3,1),F(5,2));

The remote format item, R(label), is useful when the same format list or parts of a list apply to more than one GET or PUT EDIT statement. Using the R format item would eliminate redundant coding in the specification of identical format items.

## CHECKPOINT QUESTIONS

**9.** Under what circumstances is the remote format item useful?

**10.** Give the primary advantage of using edit-directed I/O over list-directed I/O.

### How Edit I/O Works

The following paragraphs explain the principles of edit-directed I/O. The examples show the GET statement; however, the principles explained also apply to PUT.

**All Data List Items Have Corresponding Format Items.** In the statement

GET EDIT (A,B) (F(5), F(6,2));

the format item F(5) specifies that five positions in the input stream are to be interpreted as a fixed-decimal constant, its value assigned to the variable A. The value of the fixed decimal constant in the next six positions in the input stream is assigned to B. The item F(6,2) further specifies that, of the six positions, two represent the fractional part of the value. If the characters in the input stream is 123456, then the value 1234.56 is assigned to B. With this specification, it is also permissible to have the decimal point appear with the data in the input stream. For example, the specification for 123.4 would be F(5,1), where the width (5) includes the decimal point. If the data value in the input stream has a decimal point specified that does not match the format description, the decimal point in the stream overrides the GET EDIT format item. For example, if

```
DCL A              FIXED DEC (7,3);
GET EDIT (A) (F(7));
```

is coded and the input value is 12.34, then A will be given the value of 12.340.

**If There Are More Format Items than Data Items, the Extra Format Items Are Ignored.** For example:

GET EDIT(A, B)(F(4), F(5), F(6));

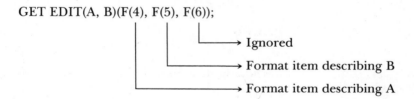

→ Ignored

→ Format item describing B

→ Format item describing A

**If There Are Less Format Items than Data Items, There Is a Return to the Beginning of the Format List.** For example:

GET EDIT(A, B, C) (F(4), F(5));

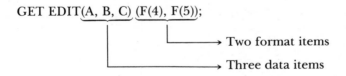

→ Two format items

→ Three data items

Here, the first format item will be used again to describe a remaining data list item. Thus,

F (4) describes A's external data
F (5) describes B's external data
F (4) describes C's external data

**The Data List Item Need Not Have the Same Width Specification as the Corresponding Format Item.** In the example,

```
DCL NAME              CHAR (15);
GET EDIT (NAME) (A(20));
```

20 characters are taken from the input stream and assigned to NAME. Because NAME has a length attribute of 15, there will be truncation on the right before assigning the value to NAME. Here is an example in which an arithmetic data item does not have the same "width" as its format item:

```
DCL RATE                  FIXED DEC (5,2);
GET EDIT (RATE) (F(4,2));
```

Four characters are taken from the input stream, *converted* to the internal attributes of FIXED DECIMAL (5,2), and assigned to RATE.

**I/O Continues Until the Data List Is Exhausted.** Because stream I/O continues until all data items have been read or written, it is possible to handle more than one record with just one GET or PUT statement. For example:

```
DCL A                     CHAR (70);
DCL B                     CHAR (40);
GET EDIT (A,B) (A(70), A(40));
```

The following picture illustrates how the data from two records are assigned to the variables A and B:

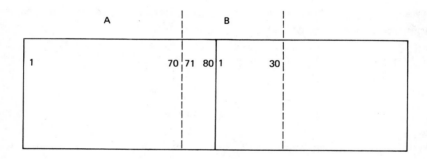

Suppose it is desired to take the first 70 positions of the first record and assign them to A, as above, but to take positions 1 through 40 of the second record and assign them to B. To accomplish this, the COLUMN control format item could be specified. For example:

```
DCL A   CHAR (70);
DCL B   CHAR (40);
GET EDIT (A,B) (COLUMN(1),A(70),COLUMN(1),A(40));
```

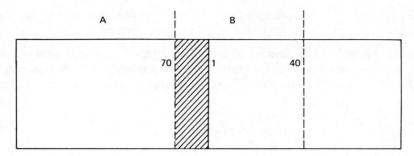

In some implementations of PL/I, the COLUMN control format item is not available.  To accomplish the above *spacing* between records, however, the X control format item, which is available in all implementations of PL/I, could be specified.   Here is an example:

```
DCL A   CHAR (70);
DCL B   CHAR (40);
GET EDIT (A,B) (A(70),X(10),A(40));
```

→ On input, 10 positions are to be spaced over and ignored

→ Control format item to signify horizontal spacing

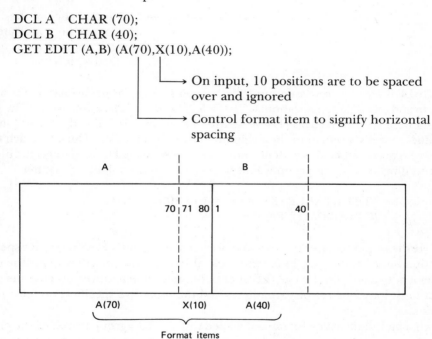

Format items

Assume it is desired to read the first 40 positions of 10 records and list the records on the printer.   How is this accomplished using GET and PUT EDIT?   Here is a solution:

```
DCL INPUT_DATA   CHAR (40);
DO I = 1 TO 10;
    GET EDIT (INPUT_DATA) (COLUMN (1),A(40));
    PUT EDIT (INPUT_DATA) (COLUMN (1),A(40));
END;
```

Notice that COLUMN is used for both an input and output control format item. On output to a printer, COLUMN refers to print position.

**Data List Items May Be Names of Data Aggregates.** The edit-directed examples you have seen so far have shown only single data elements in the data list. It is possible, however, to specify the name of an array as a list item. For example:

DCL TABLE(100)   FLOAT DEC(6);
GET EDIT(TABLE) (COLUMN(1), F(6, 2));

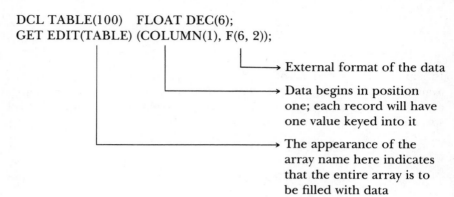

External format of the data

Data begins in position one; each record will have one value keyed into it

The appearance of the array name here indicates that the entire array is to be filled with data

TABLE is an array representing 100 data items. The format list has one control item and one data specification: COLUMN (1) and F (6,2), respectively. The first data item read—TABLE (1)—exhausts the format list. For the second input value, there is a return to the beginning of the format list. Thus, for each new value read, input begins with position one. If we wished to read only part of the preceding array, a do-group would be included in the following manner:

GET EDIT ((TABLE (K) DO K = 1 to 50))
    (COLUMN (1), F(6,2));

Note the required parentheses in the previous statement. Each repetitive specification must be enclosed in parentheses. If a repetitive specification is the only element in a data list, two sets of outer parentheses are required because the data list must have one set of parentheses and the repetitive specification must have another.

If a multidimensional array is specified without a do-group to qualify the order and/or number of items to be processed, then the rightmost subscript varies most rapidly. This is called row-major order. For example, the PUT statement for the TT array

DCL TT (81,9)   FLOAT DEC (6);
PUT EDIT (TT) (F(10));

causes data output in the following order:

TT (1,1), TT (1,2), TT (1,3), TT (1,4), . . . , TT (81,8), TT (81,9)

Nested DOs may be specified in a GET or PUT statement. When DO portions are nested, the rightmost DO is at the outer level of nesting. For example:

```
DCL TT (81,9)  FLOAT DEC (6);
GET EDIT (((TT(I, J) DO J = 1 TO 9) DO I = 1 TO 81)) (F(10));
```

Note the three sets of parentheses, in addition to the set used to delimit the subscript. The outermost set is the set required by the data list; the next is that required by the outer repetitive specification. The third set of parentheses is that required by the inner repetitive specification. This statement is equivalent to the following nested DOs:

```
DO I = 1 TO 81;
    DO J = 1 TO 9;
        GET EDIT (TT(I, J)) (F(10));
    END;
END;
```

Values are given to the elements of the array TT in the following order:

TT (1, 1), TT (1, 2), TT (1, 3), TT (1, 4), . . . , TT (81, 8), TT (81, 9)

If, within the data list of a GET statement, a variable is assigned a value, this *new* value is used if the variable appears in a later reference in the data list. For example:

GET EDIT (N, (X(I) DO I = 1 TO N)) (COLUMN (1), F (4,2));

When this statement is executed, a new value is assigned to N. Next, elements in the X array are assigned values in the order of X (1), X (2), . . . , X (N).

All elements of an array have the same attributes. However, data read into an array may have varying external data formats. For example, assume that half of an array is filled with data in the external form of F (3) and the other half in the form of F (4). Here are the statements to accomplish this:

```
DCL TABLE(50)  FLOAT DEC(6);
GET EDIT(TABLE) (25 F(3),25 F(4));
```

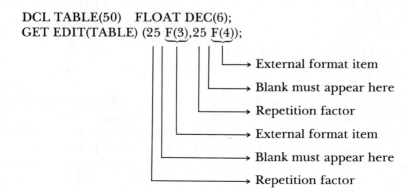

→ External format item

→ Blank must appear here

→ Repetition factor

→ External format item

→ Blank must appear here

→ Repetition factor

**Input Data Items May Be Pseudovariables.** The SUBSTR built-in function is used to manipulate smaller parts of string data (i.e., SUB STRings). For example, to extract the last five characters of a 20-position character-string called TITLE, the following is coded:

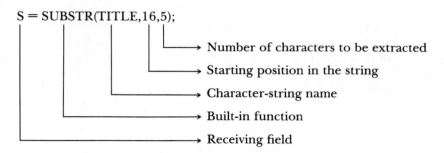

S = SUBSTR(TITLE,16,5);

→ Number of characters to be extracted
→ Starting position in the string
→ Character-string name
→ Built-in function
→ Receiving field

SUBSTR may also be a pseudovariable (i.e., it may be designated as a receiving field). For example:

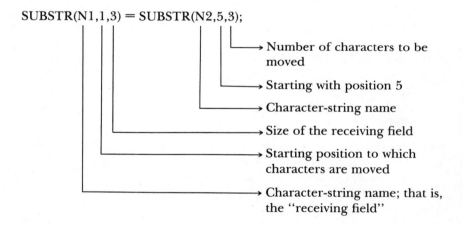

SUBSTR(N1,1,3) = SUBSTR(N2,5,3);

→ Number of characters to be moved
→ Starting with position 5
→ Character-string name
→ Size of the receiving field
→ Starting position to which characters are moved
→ Character-string name; that is, the "receiving field"

Pseudovariables may appear on the left side of an assignment symbol or in a GET statement. For example:

```
DCL NAME_FIELD   CHAR (35);
GET EDIT (SUBSTR(NAME_FIELD,5,20)) (A(20));
```

Twenty characters from the input stream are assigned to the identifier NAME_FIELD, beginning with position five of the character-string.

Care must be taken to guard against referencing a position outside the string length. Typically, any position outside the string data could still be part of your program; hence, the value assigned to that outside position destroys, perhaps, part of an instruction or another data item. Often, this kind of destruction causes a program to "hang up" and you have no clues as to what went wrong.[4]

**Output Data Items May Be Built-in Functions.** When included as a data item in a PUT statement, the specified built-in function is invoked and the value it returns is output. For example:

PUT EDIT(SUBSTR(NAME_FIELD,5,8))   (A(8));

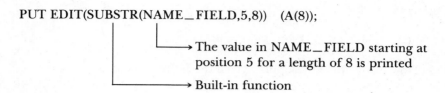

→ The value in NAME_FIELD starting at position 5 for a length of 8 is printed

→ Built-in function

**Output Data Items May Be PL/I Constants.** This capability is particularly useful for printing literal data; that is, character-string constants.

PUT EDIT ('WEEKLY ACTIVITY REPORT')(COLUMN (40), A(22));

**Data Items May Consist of Element Expressions.** Operational expressions may be specified in the data list of a PUT statement. For example:

PUT EDIT (A*3, B+C/D) (F(10), F (8,2));

**More than One Data List and Corresponding Format List May Be Specified.** Here is another variation of edit-directed I/O:

GET EDIT (data list) (format list) (data list) (format list) . . . ;

You may specify as many pairs of data lists and format lists as you wish. This format is useful when there are a lot of data items specified and it is desired to keep the format item *closer* to the specified data item. This improves readability of the program by clarifying which format items belong to which data items. For example:

PUT EDIT (A,B,C)   (F (12), F (15,3), A (5))
         (D,E,F)   (B (10), F (5,2), COLUMN (60), A (7))
         (G,H)     (F (8), A (22));

---

[4] If STRINGRANGE condition is available and *enabled,* then there is notification on a reference to a position outside the string.

**11.** Given the following statement, what format item applies to C?

GET EDIT (A,B,C) (F(4), F(5));

**12.** Is this valid?

GET EDIT (A,B) (F (2), F (3), F (4));

**13.** How many lines are skipped, given the following statement:

PUT EDIT (A,B,C) (SKIP (1), 3 F (5,2), SKIP (2));

**14.** What control format items may be specified to affect printed output so as to begin on a new line?

**15.** Which of the following may be specified for files that do not have the PRINT attribute?

(a) PAGE
(b) SKIP
(c) COLUMN
(d) LINE

**16.** Given the input value 12.34 and the statements,

```
DCL VALUE               FIXED DEC (4);
GET EDIT (VALUE) (F(5,2));
```

what will VALUE contain?

**17.** Given the following statements, what value will be output?

```
DCL VALUE               FIXED DEC (5,3);
VALUE = 12.347;
PUT EDIT (VALUE) (F(5,2));
```

## The STRING Option

The STRING option may appear in a GET or PUT statement in place of the file option. For example, instead of

GET FILE (INPUT) EDIT (A,B,C) (F(5),F(6),F(7));

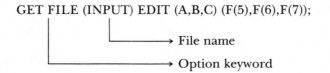

→ File name

→ Option keyword

the statement

GET STRING (DATA) EDIT (A,B,C) (F(5), F(6), F(7));

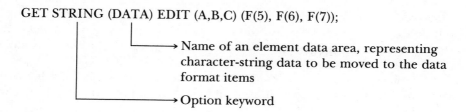

Name of an element data area, representing character-string data to be moved to the data format items

Option keyword

may be specified. The STRING option causes internal data movement; it does not cause an I/O operation. Instead of getting data from an external device (a file), the data is "read" from a character-string. It offers another method for effecting data movement, the assignment statement being the most common. In addition, this feature provides another method for converting character type of data to a coded arithmetic form.

The following example illustrates a character-string-to-character-string data movement. Assume that NAME is a string of 36 characters and that FIRST, MIDDLE, and LAST are string variables:

GET STRING (NAME) EDIT (FIRST,MIDDLE,LAST) (A(15),A(1),A(20));

This statement specifies that the first 15 characters of NAME are to be assigned to FIRST, the next character to MIDDLE, and the remaining 20 characters to LAST.

The PUT statement with the STRING option in the following example specifies the reverse operation:

PUT STRING (NAME) EDIT (FIRST,MIDDLE,LAST) (A(15),A(1),A(20));

Instead of putting to a file, the data is put into the character-string. This statement specifies that the values of FIRST, MIDDLE, and LAST are to be concatenated (in that order) and assigned to the string variable NAME.

In addition, the STRING option may be used to effect character-string-to-arithmetic or arithmetic-to-character-string conversion. For example:

```
DCL EMP#      CHAR (7);
DCL HOURS     FIXED DEC (3,1);
DCL NAME      CHAR (20);
DCL RATE      FIXED DEC (4,2);
DCL RECORD    CHAR (80);
PUT STRING (RECORD) EDIT (NAME, EMP#, HOURS * RATE)
     (A(20),A(7),F(7,2));
```

This statement specifies that the character-string value of NAME is to be assigned to the first (leftmost) 20 character positions of the string named RECORD, and that the character-string value of EMP# is to be assigned to the next seven character positions of RECORD. The value of HOURS is then multiplied by the value of RATE, and the product is to be handled like F format output consisting of four integers, one decimal point, and two fraction positions, and assigned to the next seven character positions of RECORD. In addition, the product is rounded to the second decimal position before it is placed into RECORD.

Sometimes records of different formats appear in the same file. Each record, then, would carry with it an indication of its format in the form of a code. For example:

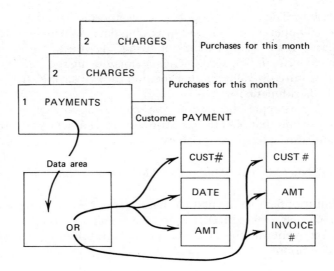

The STRING option facilitates manipulation of these different record formats in the same file. For example:

```
GET EDIT (INFO) (A(80));
SELECT (SUBSTR(INFO,1,1));
    WHEN ('1') GET STRING (INFO) EDIT (CUST#, DATE, AMT)
                (X(1), A(6), X(3), A(6), X(1), F(7,2));
    WHEN ('2') GET STRING (INFO) EDIT (CUST#, AMT, INVOICE#)
                (X(1), A(6), X(1), F(7,2), X(1), A(8));
    OTHERWISE CALL ERROR_IN_INPUT;
END;
```

The print option format items (e.g., COLUMN, SKIP, etc.) may not be specified in the STRING option of a GET or PUT.

### Writing Headings

To see the flexibility that edit-directed output provides in writing headings on printed output, assume the following data is to be printed:

Assume that the date in the previous heading has been read into the following character-strings:

DCL MM   CHAR (2);
DCL DD   CHAR (2);
DCL YY   CHAR (2);

Our program may manipulate the month, day, and year through the names MM, DD, and YY, respectively. To output the PAYROLL REGISTER heading, we may begin by coding the following statement:

PUT EDIT('PAYROLL REGISTER--WEEK ENDING')(PAGE, COLUMN (21), A(32));

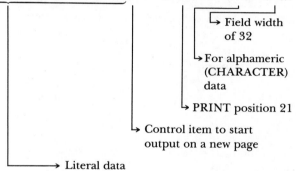

→ Field width of 32

→ For alphameric (CHARACTER) data

→ PRINT position 21

→ Control item to start output on a new page

→ Literal data

On output, however, it is not necessary to specify the field width following the A format item if the field width is to be the same length as the data item. Thus, the statement could be shortened by coding:

PUT EDIT('PAYROLL REGISTER--WEEK ENDING') (PAGE, COLUMN (21), A);

Width is automatically ← calculated as being equal to the length of the data item — in this case, 32

Next, the date is output:

PUT EDIT (MM, '/', DD, '/', YY) (A,A,A,A,A);

→ Because width is automatically calculated, only the A need be specified

Notice that there are *five fields* of the A format item. When the same format item is to be repeated a number of times, a repetition factor may be specified. Thus, the previous statement could be coded

    PUT EDIT (MM, '/', DD, '/', YY) (5  A);
                                         └──────→ Must have a blank here
                                      └────────→ Repetition factor

A repetition factor may be specified in parentheses; for example:

    PUT EDIT (...) (COLUMN (5), (10)A (12));
                                 └────────→ Repetition factor in
                                            parentheses

and it may be an expression as well, for example:

    K = 10;
    PUT EDIT (...) (SKIP, (K) A (10));
                          └────────→ Repetition factor may be an
                                     expression

Returning to the payroll register headings, we see that the next line of output could be coded:

    PUT EDIT ('EMPLOYEE NO.   NAME')(SKIP(2),A)
            ('RATE   HOURS   DEDUCTIONS   NET PAY')(COL(40),A);

A SKIP (2) causes one blank line of output. The first literal is output, automatically beginning in print position one, because of the SKIP to a new line. The second literal ('RATE   HOURS   DEDUCTIONS   NET PAY') is output beginning in print position 40 as indicated by the COLUMN (40) format item.

The preceding explanation separated parts of the output into several PUT EDIT statements so that various points could be illustrated more simply. However, to code the output of these two heading lines in a PL/I program, only one statement need be written:

    PUT EDIT('PAYROLL REGISTER--WEEK ENDING',
            MM,'/',DD,'/',YY,'EMPLOYEE NO.   NAME',
            'RATE   HOURS   DEDUCTIONS   NET PAY')
            (PAGE, 6 A, SKIP(2),A,COLUMN(40),A);

Or, here is another way in which the statement may be coded:

PUT EDIT('PAYROLL REGISTER--WEEK ENDING',
    MM,'/',DD,'/',YY,'EMPLOYEE NO.  NAME',
    'RATE   HOURS   DEDUCTIONS   NET PAY')
    (PAGE, 6 A, SKIP(2),A,X(21),A);

> In effect, the spacing of 21 positions causes the next data item to be output beginning at print position 40 [i.e., COLUMN (40)]

Note that commas are always used to separate the data list items and the format items. Thus, blanks separating these items are used only if it is desired to improve readability of the GET or PUT. Remember that a blank is required between the repetition factor and the format item to which it applies. A blank is not required following the repetition factor in the format list if there is another punctuation mark separating the repetition factor from the format items to which it applies. For example, assume data items are to be output where the format consists of F (5), F (3, 1), F (5), F (3, 1), F (5), F (3, 1). As you can see, there are three pairs of (F(5), F (3, 1)) format items. The following statement accomplishes the output of data items according to this pattern of format items:

PUT EDIT(A,B,C,D,E,F)(PAGE, 3(F(5),F(3, 1)));

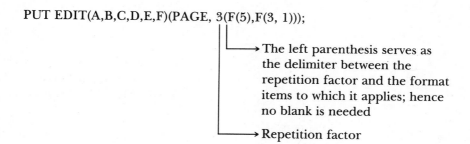

> The left parenthesis serves as the delimiter between the repetition factor and the format items to which it applies; hence no blank is needed

> Repetition factor

## Data Format Items

**A (w).** On input, a string of length $w$ characters is read into a variable. If the variable's declared length attribute is greater than $w$ characters, blanks are padded on the right; if the length is less than $w$ characters, input data will be truncated on the right. On output, the data item is left-justified in the field and, if necessary, padded on the right with blanks.

**A.** Allowed for output only; the length of the character-string variable is the value of the declared character-string length. Character-strings enclosed in apostrophes may also be included as data list items. They are handled in the same manner as character-string variables.

| Internal data | Format specification | Output result |
|---|---|---|
| ABC12 | A | ABC12 |
| ABC12 | A(3) | ABC |
| ABC12 | A(7) | ABC12*bb* |

**B (w).** On input, a string of length $w$ characters is read into a variable having the BIT attribute. Only characters 0 or 1 should appear in the input stream or the CONVERSION condition is raised. If the variable's declared length attribute is greater than $w$ characters, 0s are padded on the right; if the length is less than $w$ characters, input data will be truncated on the right. On output, a bit-string is converted to a character-string of 0s and 1s and left-justified in the output field. The bit-string data is padded with blanks on the right if the bit-string is shorter than $w$ for output.

**B.** Allowed for output only; the length of the bit-string variable is the value of the declared bit-string length.

| Internal value | Format specification | Output result |
|---|---|---|
| 1101 | B | 1101 |
| 1101 | B(4) | 1101 |
| 1101 | B(3) | 110 |
| 1101 | B(6) | 1101*bb* |

**C.** Complex variables are specified in one of two forms:

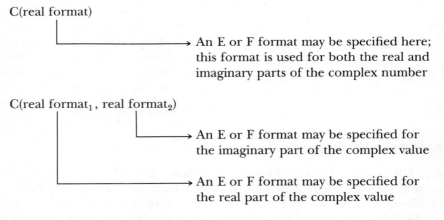

C(real format)

→ An E or F format may be specified here; this format is used for both the real and imaginary parts of the complex number

C(real format$_1$, real format$_2$)

→ An E or F format may be specified for the imaginary part of the complex value

→ An E or F format may be specified for the real part of the complex value

**E (w,d).** The input stream contains data in floating-point notation (e.g., 57E+13). On input, if no decimal point is present, the format specification $d$ represents the number of fractional decimal places. The letter $w$ represents the total number of characters including the decimal point (if present), signs, and the designation E. If a blank field is input under the E specification, the CONVERSION condition is raised.

On output, the exponent always requires four characters (E ± xx). The number is printed with $d$ fractional decimal places. The sign, blank or minus, of the value precedes the value. The value is right-justified in the field of $w$ characters. It is not necessary to include a space for the sign if the value is positive.

The number of significant digits($s$) is equal to 1 plus $d$. For example, if 175.36E+05 is the internal value and the output format specification is E(10,2), then the output result is bb1.75E+07. This is because out of a field width ($w$) of ten, two positions (d) will be fractional digits. The number of significant digits is three (d+1). Thus, only the leftmost three digits of the value (175.36E+05) appear in the output stream. To illustrate:

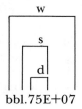

bbl.75E+07

If the value 175.36E+05 is output according to the specification E(15,5), the result is

bbbb0.17536E+08

If it is desired to print five digits of significance where more than *one* integer digit is to appear in the output value, the E (w,d,s) format may be specified.

**E (w,d,s).** On input, the $s$ is ignored. The decimal point is assumed to be $d$ digits from the right of the fraction; if a decimal point is present, the actual decimal point overrides the $d$ specification.

On output, $s$ indicates the number of significant digits output.

| Internal value | Format specification | Output result |
|---|---|---|
| 175.36E+05 | E(12, 2, 5) | bb175.36E+05 |
| 175.36E+05 | E(11, 0, 5) | bb17536E+03 |
| 175.36E+05 | E(12, 5, 5) | bb.17536E+08 |

**F (w).** The input or output field consists of $w$ characters containing a fixed-point decimal value. On input, if no decimal point is present, the number is an integer. A minus sign precedes a negative number. For positive values, a plus sign is optional.

On output, the data item is printed as an integer and no decimal point appears. For negative values, a minus sign appears to the left of the value; for positive values, a blank appears. There is automatic zero suppression to the left of the number.

| Internal value | Format specification | Output result |
|---|---|---|
| 123 | F(3) | 123 |
| −123 | F(3) | SIZE error |
| −123 | F(4) | −123 |
| 123 | F(5) | bb123 |

If $w$ is not large enough to contain the output value, the SIZE error condition is raised; the results of the output field are undefined.

**F (w,d).** On input, if no decimal point is specified, it is assumed that there are $d$ decimal places in the field. For example, if the input stream contains the digit characters 1234 and the format item F (4,2) is specified, input value becomes 12.34. If a decimal is actually present, its position overrides the $d$ specification.

On output, a decimal point is written or printed if the $d$ specification is greater than zero. If $w$ is not large enough to contain the output value, then asterisks appear in the output field and the SIZE condition is raised. Notice in the fourth and fifth examples in the table that if fewer fractional digits are output than the data item contains, the fraction is rounded off.

| Internal value | Format specification | Output |
|---|---|---|
| 123.45 | F (4,0) | b123 |
| 123.45 | F (6,2) | 123.45 |
| 123.45 | F (7,3) | 123.450 |
| 123.45 | F (6,1) | b123.5 |
| 123.45 | F (5,2) | SIZE error |
| 123.65 | F (4,0) | b124 |

**F (w,d,p).** The designation $p$ is a scaling factor; normally it is written with a sign. It effectively multiplies the value of the data item in the stream by 10 raised to the power of the value of $p$. Thus, if $p$ is positive, the number is treated as though the decimal point appeared $p$ positions to the right of its given position. If $p$ is negative, the number is treated as though the decimal point appeared $p$ positions to the left of its given position. The given position of the decimal point is that indicated either by an actual point, if it appears, or $d$, in the absence of an actual point.

| Value in the stream | Format specification | Resulting value |
|---|---|---|
| 12345.67 | F(10, 2, −2) | bb123.4567 |
| 12345.67 | F(10, 2, +2) | bbb1234567 |
| 1234567. | F(10, 2, +1) | bb12345670 |

**X (w).** On input, $w$ characters are ignored. On output, $w$ blanks are inserted into the stream.

**P 'picture specification'.** The picture (P) format item is used to edit numeric data in fixed-point decimal form. The result is a character-string whose form is determined by the picture specification as shown in the following table:

| Character | Purpose |
|---|---|
| $ + − S | static or drifting characters inserted where specified |
| Z | digit character or zero suppress (insert blanks) |
| 9 | digit character (0 – 9) |
| V | decimal point alignment |
| / , . B | insertion characters (B = insert blank) |

There are many options provided in the P format specification that correspond to the PICTURE attribute discussed at length in the next chapter. You may wish to consult that section of the chapter for an in-depth view of this specification.

## Conversion of External Data to Internal Data Formats

Arithmetic data items normally have only the format items F (fixed-point) or E (floating-point) specified. The following data types may be input or output using the F, E, or P format item specifications:

```
FIXED BINARY
FIXED DECIMAL
FLOAT BINARY
FLOAT DECIMAL
```

Remember, E and F describe external data formats. It is possible, for example, to read a value according to an E format item and have that value converted to the internal form of FIXED DECIMAL. The reverse is true for the F format item; data may be input according to the F format item and converted to FLOAT BINARY or FIXED BINARY or FLOAT DECIMAL. Similarly, it is possible to code

```
DCL HOURS           FIXED DEC (3);
GET EDIT (HOURS) (A(3));
```

providing HOURS contains only the digits 0 through 9 on the external medium. In

```
DCL VALUE           FIXED BIN (31);
GET EDIT (VALUE) (B(31));
```

the GET EDIT is valid, even though VALUE is an arithmetic data item, and is usually only described with the F or E format item.

## Control Items

When control items appear inside the format list, they are called **control format items;** if they appear outside the format list, they are called **control options.** For example:

PUT SKIP EDIT(A,B) (SKIP(3),F(7,2));

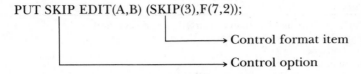

→ Control format item

→ Control option

Control format items and control options are performed in the order in which they appear in a GET or PUT statement. For example:

PUT PAGE EDIT (A,B) (F(5), PAGE, F (7,2));

The control option PAGE causes the printer to advance to a new page before any data items are printed. The data format item F (5) causes A to print on a new page. The PAGE control format item causes the form to advance to another new page. B is then printed on the following new page. This example,

PUT PAGE EDIT (A,B) (F(5), F (7,2));

is equivalent to

PUT EDIT (A,B) (PAGE, F (5), F (7,2));

A control format item has no effect unless it is encountered before the data list is exhausted. For example:

PUT EDIT(A) (F(8),SKIP);

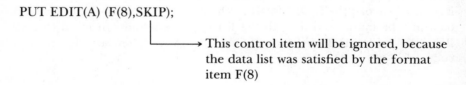

→ This control item will be ignored, because the data list was satisfied by the format item F(8)

**COLUMN (n).** On input, this format item positions the input stream to the nth byte or position of the record. On output, it positions the output stream to the nth byte in the record or the nth print position on the line printer. The abbreviation COL may be used in place of COLUMN.

**LINE (n).** Used for printed output only, this format item specifies that the next data item is to be printed on the nth line on a page of a PRINT file. LINE may be specified only for stream files that have the PRINT attribute. If the printer is on the specified line and there has been no printing on that line, then output to that line occurs. If the specified line has already been passed on the current page, the ENDPAGE condition is raised. Programmer-specified code in response to the ENDPAGE condition determines the action taken.

It would not be logical to specify a line number that is negative or zero [i.e., LINE (− 3) or LINE (0)]; however, if a negative or zero value is specified, PL/I will substitute LINE (1).

**PAGE.** According to the rules of the PL/I language, PAGE may only be specified for stream files that have the PRINT attribute. PAGE causes a skip to the first print line of the next page.

**SKIP.** On input, SKIP means to start or continue reading at the beginning of the next logical record. For input, this means to the beginning of the next physical record. For printer output, its meaning is summarized as follows:

| Format item | Action taken |
|---|---|
| SKIP (0) | Suppresses line feed |
| SKIP or SKIP (1) | Starts printing on the next line |
| SKIP (expression) | Causes "expression minus 1" lines to be left blank before printing on the next line |

**18.** Write the PUT EDIT statement to print the following heading, centered on a 120-print position line; be sure to include the underline:

WEEKLY ACTIVITY REPORT

**19.** Distinguish between *control format item* and *control option* in the following statement:

PUT PAGE EDIT (A,B,C) (SKIP (3), F(5));

**20.** What does the LINENO built-in function do?

# DATA-DIRECTED I/O

Data-directed I/O gives the programmer the flexibility of transmitting self-identifying data.

## Data-Directed Input[5]

Each item in the input stream is in the form of an assignment statement that specifies both the value and the variable to which it is to be assigned. For example, the input stream could contain the following assignment statements:

---

[5] Not available in subset D and G implementations of PL/I.

A = 12.3, B = 57, C = 'ABCDEF', D = '1110'B;

Notice that the values are in the form of valid PL/I constants. Statements are separated by a comma and/or one or more blanks; a semicolon ends each group of items to be accessed by a single GET statement. Here is an example of a data-directed statement that accomplishes the input of the previous assignment statement items:

GET DATA (A, B, C, D);

The GET will read all data items until a semicolon is detected. The maximum number of elements permitted in a list for data-directed input is 320.

All names in the stream should appear in the data list; however, the order of the names need not be the same. Thus, the GET statement could have been written:

GET DATA (C, B, A, D);

Also, the data list may include names that do not appear in the stream; for example:

GET DATA (A, B, C, D, E);

In this case, E is not altered by the input operation. However, it is an error if there is an identifier in the input stream but not in the data list. For example, C and D are in the input stream but not in the data list:

GET DATA (A, B); /* ERROR */

This error raises the NAME condition, which may be handled in your program in the same manner as with other on-units; for example:

ON NAME (SYSIN)
  BEGIN;
    .
    .
  END;

It is possible (and not contradictory) to omit entirely data list names in the GET statement. The GET may be simply specified as:

GET DATA;

In this case, the names in the stream may be any names known at the point of the GET statement. A data list in the GET statement is optional, because the semicolon determines the number of items to be obtained from the stream.

If the data list includes the name of an array, subscripted references to that array may appear in the stream, although subscripted names cannot appear in the data list. The entire array need not appear in the stream; only those elements that actually appear in the stream will be assigned. For example, the following could be coded:

```
DCL TABLE (50)        FIXED DEC (5,2);
GET DATA (TABLE);
```

where the input stream consists of the following assignment statements:

```
TABLE(3) = 7.95, TABLE(4) = 8.43, TABLE(7) = 50;
```

Although the data list has only the name of the array, the associated input stream may contain values for individual elements of the array. In this case, three elements are assigned; the remainder of the array is unchanged.

### Data-Directed Output

On output, each data item is placed in the stream in the form of assignment statements separated by blanks. The last item output by each PUT statement is followed by a semicolon. Leading zeros of arithmetic data are suppressed. The character representation of each value reflects the attributes of the variable, except for fixed-point binary and floating-point binary data, which appear as values expressed in fixed-point decimal notation.

For PRINT files, data items are automatically aligned on preset tab positions described for list-directed I/O. For example, given the statements,

```
DCL A          FIXED DEC (5)    INIT (0);
DCL B          FIXED DEC (5)    INIT (0);
DCL C          FIXED BIN (15)   INIT (175);
PUT DATA (A,B,C);
```

output to the default file SYSPRINT would be in the format:

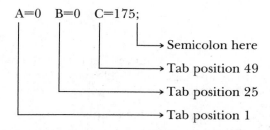

If output is to other than a PRINT file, one blank is placed between each assignment statement. The data list may be an element, array, a subscripted name, structure variable or a repetitive specification involving any of these elements or further repetitive specifications.

In addition, any of the printer spacing options described for list-directed I/O may be specified for data-directed I/O; for example:

PUT PAGE DATA (A, B, C);
PUT SKIP (3) DATA (A, B, C);
PUT LINE (5) DATA (A, B, C);

It is also possible to specify,

PUT DATA;

in which case all variables known to the program at the point of the PUT statement will be output. This feature is a powerful debugging tool.

Only data names may be output. Constants would have to be assigned to a data name and the name output. For example,

PUT PAGE DATA ('OUTPUT FROM TEST #1'); /* INVALID */

is an error because a character-string constant is specified—a violation of the rule just stated.

There is considerable program overhead for data-directed I/O. Thus, it is not suitable for production-type jobs. It is most useful as a debugging tool (PUT DATA). It is also practical in special-purpose scientific or heavy computational programs that are typically run only once or have limited use.

## COUNT Built-in Function

One built-in function may be particularly useful to you when using the form of GET DATA where no data list is specified. The function is called COUNT; it determines the number of data items that were transmitted during the last GET or PUT operation on a given file, and it then returns the result to the point of invocation. For example:

DCL INFILE FILE INPUT STREAM;
GET FILE (INFILE) DATA;
I = COUNT (INFILE);

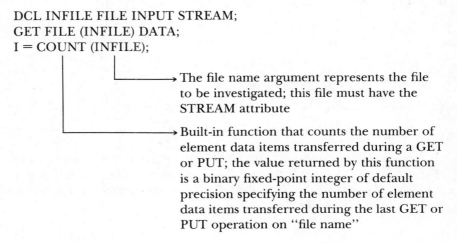

The file name argument represents the file to be investigated; this file must have the STREAM attribute

Built-in function that counts the number of element data items transferred during a GET or PUT; the value returned by this function is a binary fixed-point integer of default precision specifying the number of element data items transferred during the last GET or PUT operation on "file name"

If a begin block or another procedure is entered during a GET or PUT operation, and within that begin block or procedure a GET or PUT is executed for the same file, the value of COUNT is reset for the new operation and is not restored when the original GET or PUT is continued. For example, if the ENDPAGE condition were raised and it is desired to print page headings, the COUNT field will be reset by the PUT of the heading information. If the COUNT function is to be used, one solution would be to set a switch on in the ON ENDPAGE statement and test the switch at an appropriate point in the program.

### CHECKPOINT QUESTIONS

**21.** For data-directed input, how must the values in the input stream be represented?

**22.** For data-directed input, input continues until what punctuation mark is encountered?

**23.** What is the purpose of the COUNT built-in function?

**24.** What are the advantages/disadvantages of data-directed I/O?

### STREAM FILE CONDITIONS

Conditions that could arise during the computation phase of a program were introduced in Chapter 5. These conditions included FIXEDOVERFLOW, OVERFLOW, UNDERFLOW, etc. This section introduces the conditions that could occur during input or output operations, particularly those that apply to files with the STREAM attribute. These include:

| | |
|---|---|
| ENDFILE | A condition indicating that the end of a given file has been reached (stream or record files). |
| ENDPAGE | A condition indicating that the end of a page of printed output has been completed (stream files only). |
| TRANSMIT | A condition indicating that an input or output device did not transmit data correctly (stream or record files). |
| RECORD | A condition indicating that the size of a record in a given file does not match the record size declared in the PL/I program (stream or record files). |
| SIZE | A condition indicating that the number of significant digits in a coded arithmetic data item exceeds the declared or default size of the identifier (stream files only). |

CONVERSION   A condition indicating that the data includes illegal characters for the type of data item declared (stream files only).

The ENDFILE, ENDPAGE, CONVERSION, and SIZE conditions were covered in detail in Chapter 5. Following is a description of each of the other conditions that may be raised during communication with a STREAM file:

## The TRANSMIT Condition

The TRANSMIT condition indicates that an input or output device did not transmit data correctly. Thus, data transmitted is potentially incorrect. Usually, a hardware malfunction causes this condition to occur. If this condition occurs consistently, the on-unit specified almost has to be:

        "ON TRANSMIT (DISKRDR)
            CALL SERVICE_ENGINEER;"

(with tongue in cheek).

## The RECORD Condition

The RECORD condition is raised when there is a conflict in the specification of the size of a record in a file. For example, the RECORD condition would be raised if you indicated that the number of positions in a record is 80 when the record actually contains 100 characters. Generally speaking, you would not need to code an on-unit to this condition. Rather, let standard system action be taken and then correct your program so that the RECORD condition will not occur.

## The CONVERSION Condition

This on-unit is raised if any alphameric characters appear within a field of data that is to be a numeric field. For example, a blank is an alphameric character that will cause the CONVERSION condition to be raised if it is embedded within a numeric field. Thus, the data,

input by the statement,

        GET EDIT (VALUE) (COLUMN (1),F(5));

causes the CONVERSION condition to be raised. However, a blank (but *not* any other alphameric character) may appear before a numeric value, in which case the leading blank is interpreted as a leading zero on input. For example, given the data field,

the edit-directed statement,

GET EDIT (VALUE) (COLUMN (1),F(5));

causes the identifier VALUE to be set to 05798. If a blank follows a numeric field, for example,

it is ignored. Thus, if the previous data field were input with the statement,

GET EDIT (VALUE) (COLUMN(1),F(5));

then VALUE would contain 05798. If the entire field is blank, it is interpreted as zero. See page 219 for an example of coding for the CONVERSION on-unit.

## The SIZE Condition

This on-unit is raised during output if the width specification for a FIXED BINARY or a FIXED DECIMAL number is not large enough to contain the total value. For example, if,

VALUE = $-123$;

and it is output using the specification,

PUT EDIT (VALUE) (F(3));

the SIZE condition will be raised, providing it is enabled. To print the above negative value, a minimum field width of four must be specified. According to the rules of the PL/I language, the results of the output field are *undefined*. In some compilers, the output field is filled with asterisks; in other compilers, high-order truncation occurs, and that value will be output; in still other compilers, blanks may appear.

## Null Action

The null form of the ON statement simply indicates "no action should be taken for this on-unit." A null action may be specified for any of the exceptional conditions except CONVERSION, ENDFILE, TRANSMIT, RECORD, and KEY. (The KEY condition is covered in Chapter 10.)

## CHECKPOINT QUESTIONS

**25.** When are BEGIN blocks needed in an on-unit?

**26.** Upon exit from a begin block, where is control returned to?

**27.** Name two ways in which an on-unit may be "triggered."

## CASE STUDY: SALES HISTORY BAR CHARTS

This case study illustrates a number of facilities of edit-directed I/O — repetitive specifications, SKIP, COLUMN, remote format items (R), nested format lists, and the STRING option of the GET statement. The program is designed to produce a series of bar charts graphically depicting the net sales of each item produced by the Acme Tool Company in the last three years. The net sales figure for each item is to be displayed by month as a horizontal bar across the page, with each print position representing 1000 units sold. Figure 7.3 illustrates this bar chart.

Data for this graph is keyed into two types of records as shown in Figure 7.4.

**1. Order records:** These contain the gross orders for a particular item for each month of a given year. The letter O keyed into position 79 identifies this record type.

**2. Cancellation records:** These contain cancellations for the corresponding item. The letter C keyed into position 79 identifies this record type.

(It is more common to use digits 1 and 2 to represent record types, and it is more common to enter these values in position 1 — rather than position 79; however, the formats described above were selected to illustrate some edit-directed I/O coding techniques.)

Notice that an item number is keyed into positions one through four of each record; however, five positions are then used to represent quantity ordered for each of 12 months, whereas, only four positions are used for quantity canceled for each of 12 months. Typically, identical field widths (five positions, in this case) for quantity ordered and quantity canceled would be selected in the design of these record layouts. However, having two different formats in the input stream will illustrate the need for using the GET STRING option of edit-directed I/O. The net sales figures per month are determined by subtracting quantity canceled from quantity ordered.

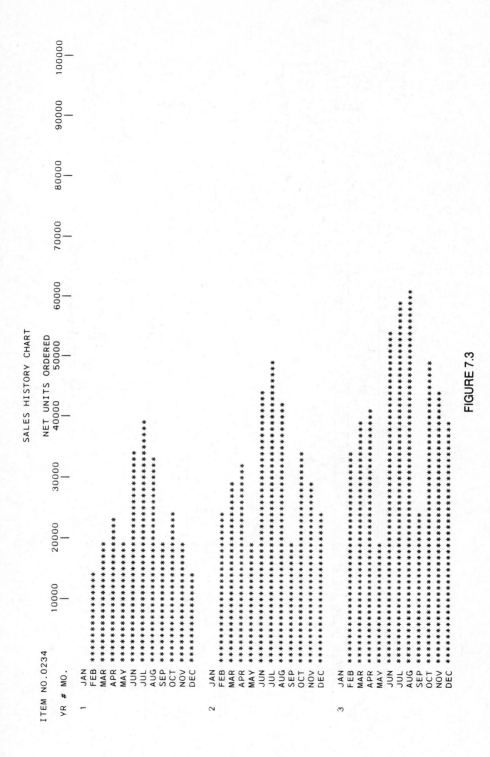

FIGURE 7.3

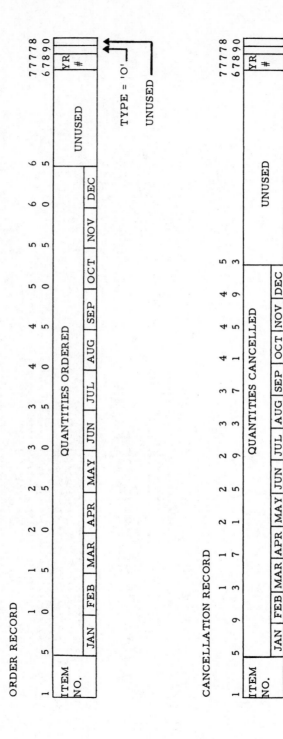

FIGURE 7.4 Layout of order and cancellation records.

Because it is desired to compare sales history for the past three years, there will be up to six records per item—one order record and one cancellation record for each of three years. Assume the records are arranged in ascending sequence by item number; thus, all six records for a given item will be together in the file. However, the six records may be in any order. The records could also have been sorted into sequence by year within item number. This has been intentionally avoided for this case study to illustrate how the same thing may be accomplished by program logic. For this reason, positions 77 and 78 of the input have been used to designate the year to which the order or cancellation record applies (e.g., year 1 or year 2 or year 3). A pseudocode solution is given in Figure 7.5. The source program is shown in Figure 7.6.

```
Start Case Study 7
Specify ENDFILE on-unit
GET first record
Save ITEM#
DO WHILE MORE_RECORDS
  IF not same ITEM#
      CALL PRINT_GRAPH routine
      Move current ITEM# to ITEM# save area
      SELECT TYPE
      CASE1: TYPE is O
          GET string for orders
      CASE2: TYPE is C
          GET string for cancels
      CASE3: TYPE is neither O nor C
          PUT error message
      GET next record
ENDDO
CALL PRINT_GRAPH routine
RETURN
Start PRINT_GRAPH
Orders = orders − cancels
Print heading
DO year = 1 to 3
  Print year
  DO month = 1 to 12
    Print this month's bar
  ENDDO
ENDDO
END PRINT_GRAPH
END Case Study 7
```

FIGURE 7.5   Pseudocode solution for sales history bar charts.

```
      /* CHAPTER 7 CASE STUDY - BAR CHART FOR ACME SALES HISTORY              */
      /**********************************************************************/
      /*                                                                    */
      /*    PROGRAM NAME:    BARCHART                                        */
      /*                                                                    */
      /*    DESCRIPTION:     THIS PROGRAM READS THE ACME SALES HISTORY FILE  */
      /*                     WHICH CONTAINS THE ORDER AND CANCELLATION FIGURES */
      /*                     FOR EACH ITEM PRODUCED IN THE LAST THREE YEARS. */
      /*                     EACH RECORD CONTAINS 12 MONTHS WORTH OF SALES   */
      /*                     FIGURES.  THE INPUT RECORDS FOR EACH ITEM ARE   */
      /*                     READ INTO EITHER THE ORDER TABLE OR THE CANCEL- */
      /*                     LATION TABLE.  THE CANCELLATIONS ARE SUBTRACTED */
      /*                     FROM THE ORDERS.  A BAR CHART IS PRINTED FOR EACH */
      /*                     ITEM BASED ON THE ADJUSTED ORDER AMOUNT.        */
      /*                                                                    */
      /*    INPUT:           SALEHIST    -    ACME SALES HISTORY FILE        */
      /*                                                                    */
      /*    OUTPUT:          SYSPRINT    -    SALES HISTORY BAR CHART        */
      /*                                                                    */
      /**********************************************************************/
1     BARCHART:   PROC OPTIONS(MAIN);

2     DCL SALEHIST FILE INPUT STREAM ENV (F BLKSIZE(80));

3     DCL AMOUNT_FIELDS            CHAR(60);
4     DCL BAR                      FIXED BIN(15);
5     DCL CANCELS(3,12)            FIXED DEC(5)        INIT((36)0);
6     DCL I                        FIXED BIN(15);
7     DCL ITEM#                    CHAR(4);
8     DCL LIMIT                    FIXED BIN(15);
9     DCL MONTH                    FIXED BIN(15);
10    DCL MONTH_NAME(12)           CHAR(3)             INIT
          ('JAN','FEB','MAR','APR','MAY','JUN',
           'JUL','AUG','SEP','OCT','NOV','DEC');
11    DCL MORE_RECORDS             BIT(1)              INIT('1'B);
12    DCL NO                       BIT(1)              INIT('0'B);
13    DCL ORDERS(3,12)             FIXED DEC(5)        INIT((36)0);
14    DCL SAVE_ITEM#               CHAR(4);
15    DCL THOUSANDS                FIXED BIN(15);
16    DCL TYPE                     CHAR(1);
17    DCL YEAR                     FIXED BIN(15);
18    DCL YEAR_CODE                FIXED BIN(15);
19    DCL YES                      BIT(1)              INIT('1'B);

20    ON ENDFILE(SALEHIST)
          MORE_RECORDS = NO;

21    GET FILE(SALEHIST)EDIT (ITEM#,AMOUNT_FIELDS,YEAR_CODE,TYPE)
                              (A(4),A(60),X(12),F(2),A(1));
22    SAVE_ITEM# = ITEM#;

23    DO WHILE(MORE_RECORDS);
24       IF SAVE_ITEM# ¬= ITEM# THEN
             DO;
25               CALL PRINT_GRAPH;
26               SAVE_ITEM# = ITEM#;
27           END;
28       SELECT (TYPE);
29           WHEN('O') GET STRING(AMOUNT_FIELDS) EDIT
                       ((ORDERS(YEAR_CODE,MONTH)  DO MONTH=1 TO 12)) (F(5));
30           WHEN('C') GET STRING(AMOUNT_FIELDS) EDIT
                       ((CANCELS(YEAR_CODE,MONTH) DO MONTH = 1 TO 12)) (F(5));
31           OTHERWISE PUT PAGE EDIT ('TYPE FIELD INVALID FOR ITEM ',ITEM#)
                       (A,A);
32       END;
33       GET FILE(SALEHIST)EDIT (ITEM#,AMOUNT_FIELDS,YEAR_CODE,TYPE)
                               (SKIP,A(4),A(60),X(12),F(2),A(1));
34    END;

35    CALL PRINT_GRAPH;
```

FIGURE 7.6   (page 1)

```
/******************************************************************************/
/*                                                                          */
/*    THE BAR CHART IS FORMATTED SO THAT EACH ITEM'S SALES HISTORY FOR       */
/*    THREE YEARS IS PRINTED ON ONE PAGE.  EACH MONTH'S BAR APPEARS ON       */
/*    A NEW LINE.  SALES ARE REPORTED IN THE THOUSANDS.                      */
/*                                                                          */
/******************************************************************************/
36    PRINT_GRAPH: PROC;

37        ORDERS = ORDERS - CANCELS;
38        PUT EDIT
              ('SALES HISTORY CHART')                    (PAGE,COL(47),A)
              ('ITEM NO.',SAVE_ITEM#)                    (SKIP(2),2 A)
              ('NET UNITS ORDERED')                      (COL(48),A)
              ((THOUSANDS,'0000' DO THOUSANDS=1 TO 10))
                                                         (SKIP,COL(18),10(F(2),
                                                         A,X(4)))
              ('YR # MO.',('|' DO I = 1 TO 10))          (SKIP,COL(2),A,
                                                         COL(21),10 A (10));
39        DO YEAR = 1 TO 3;
40          PUT EDIT(YEAR)                               (SKIP(2),F(3));
41          DO MONTH = 1 TO 12;
42            PUT EDIT(MONTH_NAME(MONTH))                (COL(7),A(4));
43            LIMIT = ORDERS(YEAR,MONTH)/1000 + .5;
44            DO BAR = 1 TO LIMIT;
45              PUT EDIT('*')                            (A);
46            END;
47          END;
48        END;

49    END PRINT_GRAPH;

50    END BARCHART;
```

FIGURE 7.6   (page 2)

Here is an explanation of the PL/I source statements in the program.

**Statements 2–19:** All DECLARE statements are provided here with initialization for the identifiers that require it.

**Statements 20–21:** These statements provide the initialization necessary for this program.  The ENDFILE on-unit is established, and the first input record is read using a GET EDIT statement.

**Statement 22:** ITEM# is saved for future comparison when subsequent input records are read.

**Statements 23 and 34:** These statements mark the range of the do loop for the reading and processing of input records.

**Statements 24 and 25:** When a new item number is read (e.g., SAVE_ITEM# ¬1 ITEM#), then it is time to print the graph for the sales figures for the past three years for a given item.

**Statements 28–32:** The input record type is tested for an 'O' (orders) in position 79.  Then, one of two GET STRING EDIT statements will be executed.  Here the STRING option facilitates the interpretation of the input record when different record formats exist in the input file.  Note also the use of the repetitive specification in the two GET STRING EDIT statements.

**Statement 33:** This statement causes the reading of subsequent records from the input file. Here it was necessary to provide, as a format item, SKIP. The SKIP control item is required because only 79 columns are read from the first input record. The SKIP indicates that input is to begin with position 1 of the next record in the file. Had the SKIP been omitted, input would have started with position 80 of the first record read. (Recall the STREAM concept.)

**Statement 35:** This statement is executed when the end-of-file is encountered. It causes the printing of the bar chart for the last item in the input file.

**Statements 36 – 49:** These statements are centered around the subfunction of actually printing the bar chart. Net orders are computed in statement 37 and column headings are printed via statement 38. Note the formatting of the alphabetic headings and their corresponding format items. Statements 39 to 48 make use of three nested do-loops to print each line with a variable number of asterisks.

## SUMMARY

**File Declarations:** A PL/I file is represented in the program by a file name with the FILE attribute. It is through the use of this name that we access data records stored on an external device such as a disk or tape. The collection of records is called a *data set* or *file*.

Here is a summary list of the attributes and options that may appear in your DECLARE statement for stream files:

| Attributes/Options | Comment |
|---|---|
| FILE | Optional |
| STREAM | Default if not specified |
| INPUT/OUTPUT | OUTPUT is default if file has PRINT attribute; otherwise, INPUT is default |
| PRINT | |
| ENVIRONMENT | ENV is the abbreviation |
| F BLKSIZE (n) | Fixed-length record |
| V BLKSIZE (n) | Variable-length record |

**The OPEN Statement:** This statement associates a file name with a data set. It can also be used to specify additional attributes for a file if a complete set has not been previously declared.

**Standard PL/I File Names:** The identifiers SYSIN and SYSPRINT are the file names for the standard input and output files, respectively. The statements

```
GET LIST (A, B, C);
PUT LIST (A, B, C);
```

are equivalent to:

```
GET FILE (SYSIN) LIST (A, B, C);
PUT FILE (SYSPRINT) LIST (A, B, C);
```

These files need not be declared, because a standard set of attributes is applied automatically.  These include:

```
SYSIN INPUT STREAM ENV (F BLKSIZE (80))
SYSPRINT OUTPUT STREAM PRINT ENV (V BLKSIZE (129))
```

**Edit-Directed I/O:** This form of stream I/O provides for considerable efficiency in the representation of input data and offers a great deal of flexibility in the formatting of output data.  The general form of edit-directed I/O statements is

```
GET EDIT (data items) (format items);
GET FILE (file name) EDIT (data items) (format items);
```

The following points should be remembered when using the GET EDIT and PUT EDIT statements:

**1.** All data list items have corresponding format items.  There are three types:
   **(a) Data format items:** These are items describing the format of the external data.
   **(b) Control format items:** These are items describing page control, line control, and spacing operations.
   **(c) Remote format item:** This item indicates that one or more data format items and/or control format items are located remotely from the GET or PUT EDIT statement in a FORMAT statement.

**2.** If there are more format items than data items, the extra format items are ignored.

**3.** The data list item need not have the same width specification as the corresponding format item.

**4.** Input continues until all data items have been read.

**5.** Data list items may be names of data aggregates.  It is possible to specify the name of an array as a list item.  If an array is specified without a do-group to qualify the order and/or number of items to be processed, the rightmost subscript varies most rapidly from the lowest to the highest value.  If a repetitive specification (DO) appears in a data list, the repetitive specification must have a separate set of parentheses.  In addition, the data list must have one set of parentheses.

**6.** Input data items may be pseudovariables. Pseudovariables are built-in functions that may be designated as receiving fields; hence, pseudovariables may appear on the left side of an equal sign or in a GET statement. Typically, the SUBSTR pseudovariable might be used.

**7.** Output data items may be built-in functions.

**8.** Output data items may be PL/I constants. This capability is particularly useful for the printing of literal data (i.e., character-string constants that constitute headings).

**9.** Data items may consist of element expressions. Operational expressions may be specified in the data list of a PUT statement.

**Format Items:** Here are the various format items [Key: [ ], optional; $w$, width; $d$, decimals (fractional digits); $s$, significant digits; $p$, decimal point scale factor; $n$, number.]: Data formats:

| | | |
|---|---|---|
| 1. | Character-string | A $(w)$ |
| 2. | Bit-string | B $(w)$ |
| 3. | Complex | C (real format item [, real format item]) |
| 4. | Floating-point | E $(w, d \, [,s])$ |
| 5. | Fixed-point | F $(w, \, [,d \, [,p]])$ |
| 6. | Editing characters for fixed point | P'picture specification' |

Control formats:

| | | |
|---|---|---|
| 1. | Stream input or printer output | COL $(n)$, SKIP $[(n)]$ |
| 2. | Printer output | LINE $(n)$, PAGE |
| 3. | Spacing for any input or output operation | X $(w)$ |

Remote format:R (label)

It is permissible to specify expressions for $w$, $d$, and $s$. If a SIZE error occurs during output controlled by an F or E format item, the results of the output field are undefined.

**The STRING Option:** This option may appear in a GET or PUT statement in place of the FILE option. For example:

GET STRING (DATA) EDIT (X,Y,Z) (B(5), 2 F(9,2));

The STRING option causes internal data movement. It may be used to convert character data to coded arithmetic data. (Of course, converting character data to coded arithmetic data may be accomplished through the assignment statement.) The STRING option also facilitates manipulation of differing record formats in the same file.

| Type of condition | ON-condition | Normally enabled/disabled | Cause | What the programmer should do or result | Action if null on-unit is used | Standard system action |
|---|---|---|---|---|---|---|
| Input/output | ENDFILE (file name) | Enabled (cannot be disabled) | An attempt to read past the end-of-file of the file named in the GET or READ statement | Not attempt to READ or GET again from file; CLOSE the file | Null on-unit cannot be specified | ERROR condition |
| | ENDPAGE (file name) | Enabled (cannot be disabled) | PUT statement resulting in an attempt to start a new line beyond the limit specified for the current page | Write a required footing (or total lines) and skip to another page | Leave printer at current line | New page started |
| | TRANSMIT (file name) | Enabled (cannot be disabled) | Hardware malfunction or damaged file | Restore or recreate the file | Null on-unit cannot be specified | ERROR condition |
| | RECORD (file name) | Enabled (cannot be disabled) | Wrong length record | Correct record size specification in JCL or program | Null on-unit cannot be specified | ERROR condition |
| Computational and I/O conditions | CONVERSION | Enabled (cannot be disabled) | Illegal conversion attempt on character-string data internally or on input/output operation | Undefined | Null on-unit cannot be specified | ERROR condition |
| | SIZE | Disabled (can be enabled) | Nonzero high-order binary or decimal digits are lost in an assignment operation (i.e., assignment to a variable or an intermediate result) or in an input/output operation | Undefined | The point logically following the point of the interrupt | ERROR condition |

FIGURE 7.7 Summary of conditions that may occur during stream I/O.

**Data-Directed I/O:** Data-directed I/O provides the facility for transmitting self-identifying data. Each data item in the input stream is in the form of an assignment statement that specifies both the value and the variable to which it is to be assigned. The input values are in the form of valid PL/I constants. Input items are separated by a comma and/or one or more blanks; a semicolon ends each group of items to be assessed by a single GET statement. The NAME condition will be raised if the input stream contains an identifier not in the data list unless the data list is omitted entirely.

**Conditions:** The ON statement is used to specify the action to be taken when an exceptional condition arises. In the absence of your program specifying an action to be taken, a standard system action will take place when these exceptional conditions are detected.

Figure 7.7 summarizes the information pertinent to the handling of conditions in your program.

# CHAPTER 8

# Record I/O, Structures, Pictures

Record I/O is the type of input and output that is used by business or commercial applications programmers. It is also the I/O type used by scientific programmers when their applications require tape or disk files. Thus, in a sense, "record I/O is for everyone."

## RECORD I/O

As a means of introducing the concepts of record I/O programming, an 80/80 list program will be illustrated. This basic program simply reads 80-character records that have been entered via a text editor and prints them on a line printer. The pseudocode for this program could be as follows:

```
ON ENDFILE more records = no
more records = yes
READ first record
DO WHILE more records
    WRITE record
    READ next record
ENDDO
```

The keywords READ and WRITE specify the input and output operations, whereas earlier in this text the keywords GET and PUT were used. In addition to the program logic just depicted for the record I/O program, several declarations are needed:

Define files
Declare I/O data areas

These declarations may be coded as follows:

```
DCL DATA      FILE INPUT    RECORD ENV(F RECSIZE(80));
DCL PRINTR    FILE OUTPUT   RECORD ENV(F RECSIZE(80));
DCL DATA_AREA   CHAR(80);
```

Notice that in the file declaration the keyword RECORD is specified to indicate the type of I/O operation. It indicates to the compiler that only the statements READ or WRITE are used to access records in the defined file. If RECORD is eliminated from the file definition, then the compiler usually assumes that the attribute STREAM applies; thus, for record I/O, the RECORD attribute must be explicitly declared. Because an 80-character record is being read and listed, the RECSIZE specification in both file declarations is 80 characters. The area into which records are read or written must be the same length in number of characters (or bytes) as the declared RECSIZE for fixed-length (F) records. Thus, in this example, DATA_AREA had to be declared for a character length of 80.

Here is the record I/O coding for the 80/80 list program:

```
ON ENDFILE(DATA)
    MORE_RECORDS = NO;
MORE RECORDS = YES;
READ FILE(DATA)INTO(DATA_AREA);
DO WHILE(MORE_RECORDS);
    WRITE FILE(PRINTR)FROM(DATA_AREA);
    READ FILE(DATA)INTO(DATA_AREA);
END;
```

This program accomplishes the function of listing records on the line printer, but there are some problems with the solution as shown. First, the output begins wherever the line printer stopped after the last job was run. In some operating systems, it is possible that the output appears on the same page as the output from the job run just prior to the list program. Second, if there are more than 66 lines to be listed (assuming single spacing), the data prints on the perforation of the paper. These two problems occur because the program does not make provision for printing a certain number of lines per page, nor does it give the *equivalent* record I/O command for the PUT PAGE statement that accomplishes skipping to a new page on stream files. (*Note:* PUT PAGE causes an advance to a new page for *stream* files associated with a line printer.) PUT PAGE may not be used to accomplish carriage control options for *record* files associated with a line printer.

## Carriage Control in Record I/O

The method for handling page overflow in record I/O is to count the number of lines that are being output. Each time a WRITE is issued for a printer file, a *program counter* would be incremented by one. When the program counter

| Character code | Resulting carriage control operation |
|----------------|--------------------------------------|
| (blank) | Space one line before printing |
| 0 | Space two lines before printing |
| - | Space three lines before printing |
| + | Suppress space before printing |
| 1 | Skip to channel 1 before printing |
| 2 | Skip to channel 2 before printing |
| 3 | Skip to channel 3 before printing |
| 4 | Skip to channel 4 before printing |
| 5 | Skip to channel 5 before printing |
| 6 | Skip to channel 6 before printing |
| 7 | Skip to channel 7 before printing |
| 8 | Skip to channel 8 before printing |
| 9 | Skip to channel 9 before printing |
| A | Skip to channel 10 before printing |
| B | Skip to channel 11 before printing |
| C | Skip to channel 12 before printing |
| V | Select stacker 1 |
| W | Select stacker 2 |

FIGURE 8.1  Carriage control characters that can be used with CTLASA option.

reaches the maximum number established for the desired output page size, then the program gives the "command" to the printer to skip to a new page.

To accomplish carriage control for record output, append an extra character to the beginning of each record. In that character, place a code specifying the action to be performed; for example, skip to a new page, skip two lines, etc. A keyword must be added to the ENVIRONMENT section of the file declaration to notify PL/I that these carriage control characters are being used in the program and that the I/O routines are to interpret the first character of each record accordingly. Two different sets of carriage control characters may be used in PL/I. The choice is made by specifying in the ENV attribute either the keyword CTLASA[1] or the keyword CTL360[2]. If either of these keywords is used, the first character of the output area is the carriage control character. The programmer must place a meaningful character in this position. Figure 8.1 gives the character codes that can be used with the CTLASA option.

The difference between CTLASA and CTL360 is that when CTLASA is specified, the carriage control operation will take place *before* the print operation, whereas if CTL360 is specified, the carriage control operation will take place *after* the print operation.

[1] CTL stands for *control* and ASA refers to the American Standards Association, which has now changed its name to ANSI — American National Standards Institute.

[2] CTL360 may be used on IBM computers. This code set is found in the PL/I Operators' Guide that accompanies the IBM computer you are using.

```
/*   SKIP TO A NEW PAGE                                                      */
/*****************************************************************************/
/*                                                                          */
/* PROGRAM NAME: LINECNT                                                     */
/*                                                                          */
/* DESCRIPTION:   THIS PROGRAM READS AN INPUT FILE AND LISTS THE DATA        */
/*                RECORDS ON THE PRINTER. THE LINE COUNTER IS CHECKED        */
/*                AND A SKIP TO A NEW PAGE IS FORCED WITH CARRIAGE           */
/*                CONTROL CHARACTERS IF THE LINE NUMBER EXCEEDS 55.          */
/*                                                                          */
/* INPUT:         DATAIN                                                     */
/*                                                                          */
/* OUTPUT:        PRINTR                                                     */
/*                                                                          */
/*****************************************************************************/

1    LINECNT: PROC OPTIONS(MAIN);

2       DCL DATAIN FILE INPUT RECORD        ENV(F RECSIZE(80));
3       DCL PRINTR FILE OUTPUT RECORD       ENV(F RECSIZE(81) CTLASA);

4       DCL DATA_AREA            CHAR(80);
5       DCL LINE_COUNT           FIXED(3);
6       DCL MORE_RECORDS         BIT(1)     INIT('1'B);
7       DCL NO                   BIT(1)     INIT('0'B);
8       DCL PRINT_AREA           CHAR(81);

9       ON ENDFILE(DATAIN)
           MORE_RECORDS = NO;

10      OPEN FILE(DATAIN),
           FILE(PRINTR);

11      LINE_COUNT = 55;
12      READ FILE (DATAIN) INTO (DATA_AREA);
13      DO WHILE (MORE_RECORDS);
14        LINE_COUNT = LINE_COUNT + 1;
15        IF LINE_COUNT > 55 THEN
             DO;
16               PRINT_AREA = '1' || DATA_AREA;
17               LINE_COUNT = 0;
18             END;
19        ELSE PRINT_AREA  = ' ' || DATA_AREA;
20        WRITE FILE (PRINTR) FROM (PRINT_AREA);
21        READ FILE (DATAIN) INTO (DATA_AREA);
22      END;
```

**FIGURE 8.2**

Which option, CTLASA or CTL360, should you select? Generally CTL360 carriage control is faster than CTLASA. However, programmers generally find it easier to program carriage control options that take place *before* the print operation (CTLASA).

Figure 8.2 shows a modified version of the list program to provide for printing 55 lines per page. Some comments follow:

**Statements 2 – 3:** Notice that the keyword CTLASA has been added to the ENVIRONMENT section of the PRINTR file declaration. The record size has been changed from RECSIZE (80) to RECSIZE (81). Because we are using CTLASA, an extra position must be added to the record size to allow for the placement of the carriage control character.

**Statements 4 – 8:** All scalar identifiers are declared in alphabetical order. The declaration of PRINT_AREA is necessary because the output area is a different length than the input area.

**Statement 10:** All files must be opened before a READ or WRITE can be issued to a given file. In most PL/I implementations, the first READ or WRITE statement executed will automatically open the file with the respective attribute INPUT or OUTPUT if the file has not been explicitly opened.

**Statement 11:** This statement sets LINE_COUNT to 55—the maximum number of lines to be printed on a page in this problem. Initializing LINE_COUNT to the maximum value at the start of the program causes, later on, a skip to a new page *before* the first record is printed. Had the skip to a new page for the first line of output been omitted, the printed output would have appeared wherever the line printer paper was last positioned. There is a possibility that there is already printing on that page, so the new data in our program would appear with previous printout from some other program.

**Statement 14:** The line counter is incremented here. For the first record, the line count will now equal 56.

**Statements 15–19:** The IF statement tests the line counter. If the line counter is greater than 55, it is the time to reset it to zero and put a character of 1 in the first position of the print area. The 1 specifies that we want to skip to channel 1 before printing the line. Channel 1 corresponds with the punch in the carriage tape that is lined up with the first print line on a page. Notice how the carriage control character is concatenated to DATA_AREA so that the two fields could be moved as a single string into the PRINT_AREA. If the line counter has not reached the maximum, then control is transferred to the ELSE clause in the IF statement. A blank space (' '), which is also concatenated to DATA_AREA, is a carriage control character to space one line before printing.

**Statement 20:** The data record is output using a WRITE statement.

## Record I/O Statements

Here are some more details about the READ and WRITE statements:

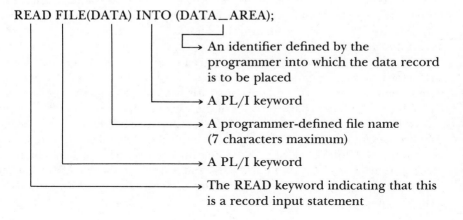

READ FILE(DATA) INTO (DATA_AREA);

→ An identifier defined by the programmer into which the data record is to be placed

→ A PL/I keyword

→ A programmer-defined file name (7 characters maximum)

→ A PL/I keyword

→ The READ keyword indicating that this is a record input statement

In the READ statement, blanks between FILE and (DATA) and INTO and (DATA_AREA) are optional, because the parentheses serve as delimiters. The same is true of the options specified in the WRITE statement.

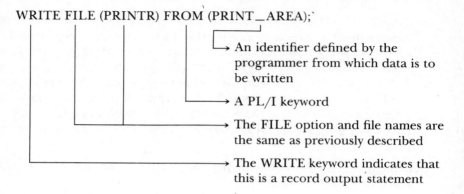

WRITE FILE (PRINTR) FROM (PRINT_AREA);

→ An identifier defined by the programmer from which data is to be written

→ A PL/I keyword

→ The FILE option and file names are the same as previously described

→ The WRITE keyword indicates that this is a record output statement

The file names DATA and PRINTR are programmer-defined identifiers. In a READ or WRITE statement, the data area may be a character-string, an array, or a structure (to be covered in the next section). Here is an example of reading data into an array:

        DCL TABLE (20) CHAR (4);
        READ FILE (DATA) INTO (TABLE);

→ May be an array name *but* must be *unsubscripted* when specified here

Positions 1 through 4 will be placed into TABLE (1), positions 5 through 8 in TABLE (2), and so on until positions 77 through 80 are placed into TABLE (20).

### Record versus Stream

In stream data transmission, input consists of a stream of **characters** representing numeric data or strings. In stream input, PL/I scans the input stream and converts the data in the stream into the data type of the matching element in the **data list** of the GET statement.

In list-directed I/O, input data items are in the form of PL/I constants (e.g., character-strings are enclosed in quotes, etc.). In data-directed I/O, input data items are in the form of PL/I constants expressed in assignment statements. In edit-directed I/O, the characteristics of the various data items are indicated by a format list. Therefore, in all forms of stream I/O, the characteristics of the input data are known to the input routine. An input data item is converted, if necessary, to the attributes declared for the identifier into which the data item is to be placed. One of the functions of the GET statement is to convert these dissimilar forms in the stream to the base, scale, and precision (or length in the case of strings) of the receiving field.

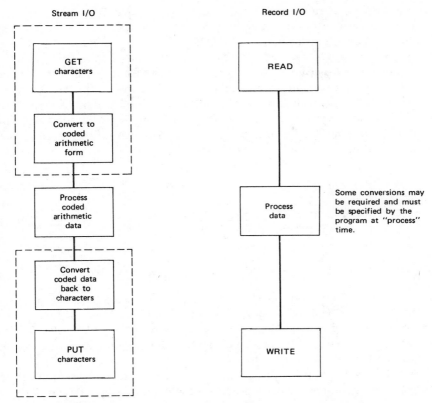

**FIGURE 8.3** Comparison of conversions to coded arithmetic form.

For stream output, the data items are converted to characters and editing (such as leading zero suppression) takes place. In fact, a major function of the PUT statement is to convert data list items to a character representation suitable for printing.

Record I/O does not perform these conversions. A READ statement simply transfers a complete record of data into a main storage location; it does not scan the data; it does not verify its validity, nor does it perform any conversions.

Figure 8.3 illustrates the difference between stream and record I/O with respect to data conversions. The broken-line box encloses the first two steps of stream input to illustrate that both steps are accomplished by the stream input operation. The same is true for stream output.

When a READ or WRITE statement is given in PL/I, an *entire record* is read or written. No more than one record can be read with one READ statement (recall that this is not the case with the GET statement). Or, when a WRITE statement is executed, if the output is to a line printer, then one line is printed. No more than one line of output (i.e., a record) may be written with one WRITE statement. Suppose a magnetic tape file contains unblocked employee payroll records that are 280 characters long. A READ or WRITE statement would accomplish input or output for 280 characters at a time — that is, one employee's payroll record of 280 bytes in length. By contrast, in stream data transmission, *less than, more than,* or *one* record may be processed with *one* GET or PUT statement.

One of the advantages of record I/O over stream I/O is that data in formats other than character may be read or written. Thus, fixed decimal or fixed binary data can be input or output using record I/O. This applies to data stored on magnetic tapes, disks, or drums. Thus, a data item requiring seven *storage* positions when in character format will use fewer positions (bytes, in this case) when that item is correspondingly converted to FIXED DECIMAL and saved on magnetic tape or disk.

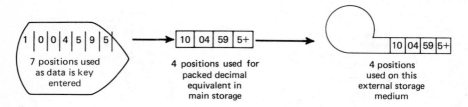

| 1 | 0 | 0 | 4 | 5 | 9 | 5 |

7 positions used
as data is key
entered

| 10 | 04 | 59 | 5+ |

4 positions used for
packed decimal
equivalent in
main storage

| 10 | 04 | 59 | 5+ |

4 positions
used on this
external storage
medium

Once a data record has been stored on an external storage medium such as tape or disk where the record contains fields in an internal coded arithmetic format, then fixed binary or fixed decimal data, for example, can be input by a READ statement. This, of course, is not possible with a GET statement because the external data must always be in character form.

Record I/O, since it has relatively little processing to perform, is usually faster; the record I/O routines usually require less main storage than stream I/O. In

| Record | Stream |
|---|---|
| 1. Respects physical record boundaries | 1. Ignores physical boundaries. I/O is considered to be a continuous stream |
| 2. Stores data in exactly the same form as input; no conversion or validity checks | 2. Converts character data in input stream to the attributes of the declared identifiers |
| 3. Outputs data in exactly the same form as internally stored | 3. Converts and edits internally stored data to character format |
| 4. Input and output may be any data type (packed decimal, fixed-point binary, etc.) | 4. Input and output are a stream of characters |
| 5. Keywords: READ, WRITE | 5. Keywords: GET, PUT |
| 6. May be used with any data set organization (sequential, indexed sequential, VSAM, direct) | 6. May only be used for sequential data sets |

FIGURE 8.4 Comparison between record and stream I/O.

some cases, record I/O is the only form that may be used to communicate with a data set. For example, direct-access devices may contain files that are organized according to the *sequential access method* (SAM), the *indexed sequential access method* (ISAM), the *virtual storage access method* (VSAM), or *direct access method* (DAM). These data set organizations (discussed in Chapter 10) may only be accessed by record I/O statements. The major distinctions between record and stream I/O are summarized in Figure 8.4.

## CHECKPOINT QUESTIONS

**1.** List as many differences as you can recall between record I/O and stream I/O characteristics.

**2.** The data area reference in a READ or WRITE may represent data aggregates or one type of scalar variable. What are they?

**3.** Is the following valid? Why or why not?

```
DCL AREA FIXED BIN(31);
READ FILE (CARD) INTO (AREA);
```

**4.** What is the difference between CTLASA and CTL360?

### Introduction to Structures

In the discussion of record I/O statements so far, the I/O area is an 80-position character-string. More frequently, we are interested in manipulating fields within a record. To illustrate, assume the input records contained names and addresses as shown in Figure 8.5. There are four data items in each record. We could declare those data items with the following declare statement:

```
DCL NAME          CHAR(20);
DCL STREET        CHAR(25);
DCL CITY_STATE    CHAR(25);
DCL ZIP           CHAR(9);
```

If you add up the total number of bytes declared in the previous statement, you will find that there are only 79 characters accounted for in the record. The missing character is in the unused area of the record. However, we must have an

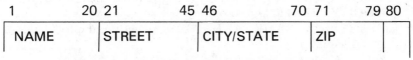

FIGURE 8.5 Sample name and address record layout.

80-byte input area because the physical record is 80 positions long. Therefore, we must append to our declaration an identifier—call it REST_OF_RECORD—with the attribute CHAR(1). Now we will have a total of 80 characters declared—the size of the record.

A couple of problems that are not so obvious are still facing us. We must provide a *contiguous area* equal in length to the record size, because a READ statement simply places the 80 bytes of the record into main storage starting at the location specified in the INTO option. The 80-byte area must encompass the identifiers NAME, STREET, CITY_STATE, ZIP, and REST_OF_RECORD. When independent variables are declared (as in the previous DECLARE statement), there is no guarantee that the identifier STREET will immediately follow, in storage, the variable NAME.

With the previous declaration, we cannot be sure that these data variables are in storage *relative to one another*. That last phrase is most important. We do not care *where* the variables are in main storage as long as they are contiguous and in the proper sequence relative to one another. To accomplish this, we must use a new type of data called a **structure.**

A **structure** is a collection of data items whose locations relative to one another are critical. Usually, the data items that appear in a structure have a logical relationship to each other. To describe the layout in Figure 8.5, the following structure could be coded:

```
DCL 1 NAME_AND_ADDR,
      2 NAME              CHAR(20),
      2 STREET            CHAR(25),
      2 CITY_STATE        CHAR(25),
      2 ZIP               CHAR(9),
      2 REST_OF_RECORD    CHAR(1);
```

In this structure, the individual items are declared with the CHARACTER attribute and preceded with the digit 2. This digit is referred to as a **level number.** All of the items are grouped together under the structure name of NAME_AND_ADDR, which has a level number of 1. Major structure names always have a level number of 1. Any number greater than 1 may be used for subdivisions of the structure. Thus, in the example, although a level number of 2 was specified for the fields within NAME_AND_ADDR, the value 3 or 5 or 66 could have been selected—just as long as it is greater than 1. All of the data items are at the same logical level and are each a part of NAME_AND_ADDR. The 80 bytes declared in this structure are made up of contiguous fields in the sequence in which they are declared. That is, the first 20 bytes of the structure make up the NAME, the next 25 bytes of the structure make up the STREET, the next 25 bytes make up the CITY_STATE, and so on.

To read data into the NAME_AND_ADDR structure, the following record input statement could be coded:

READALE FILE (RECIN) INTO (NAME\_AND\_ADDR);

READ FILE (RECIN) INTO (NAME_AND_ADDR);

In a READ or WRITE statement, only the major structure name may be specified. Note that level 1, the major structure identifier, does not contain any attributes. It is assumed to be a collection of fields, and the number of bytes reserved is equal to the sum of all the bytes required for its subdivisions. A level number that is not further subdivided is called an *elementary* item.

Structures are used not only for describing input data, but also for formatting output data. Assume it is desired to print the name and address fields where each field is separated from the other with five spaces or blanks. The structure to describe this report layout could be coded as follows:

```
DCL 1 PRINT_AREA,
        2 CARRIAGE_CONTROL   CHAR(1),
        2 PRINT_NAME          CHAR(20),
        2 UNUSED_1            CHAR(5)    INIT(' '),
        2 PRINT_STREET        CHAR(25),
        2 UNUSED_2            CHAR(5)    INIT(' '),
        2 PRINT_CITY_STATE    CHAR(25),
        2 UNUSED_3            CHAR(5)    INIT(' '),
        2 PRINT_ZIP           CHAR(9);
```

Notice that the carriage control character is provided as the first elementary item in the output structure. This position does not print; it controls the spacing of the carriage. *Print* position 1 will contain what is in the second position of the structure because of the CTLASA specification in the file declaration. CARRIAGE_CONTROL may be initialized,

CARRIAGE_CONTROL = '1';

to provide for spacing to the top of the next page.

To cause the next line to be printed after a single space,

CARRIAGE_CONTROL = ' ';

should be coded in the body of the program.

The names selected for the unused space within a given structure must be *unique*. Thus, in UNUSED_1, UNUSED_2, etc., the digits provide the uniqueness, while the word UNUSED provides the continuity of function of these fields.[3]

The remaining elementary items describe the rest of the fields in the print line. The line requires 94 print positions; therefore, the structure PRINT_AREA encompasses 95 bytes (94 plus 1 for carriage control).

---

[3] PL/I does not contain a feature comparable to FILLER in COBOL.

```
      /*    RECORD I/O AND CARRIAGE CONTROL                                    */
      /************************************************************************/
      /*                                                                      */
      /* PROGRAM NAME: LIST                                                    */
      /*                                                                      */
      /* DESCRIPTION:  THIS PROGRAM READS AN INPUT RECORD AND MOVES IT        */
      /*               TO A FORMATTED PRINT LINE.   A LINE COUNTER IS         */
      /*               INCREMENTED SO THAT A NEW PAGE IS PRINTED WHEN THE      */
      /*               LINE COUNT EXCEEDS 55.                                  */
      /*                                                                      */
      /* INPUT:        DATAIN                                                  */
      /*                                                                      */
      /* OUTPUT:       PRINTR                                                  */
      /************************************************************************/
 1  LIST: PROC OPTIONS(MAIN);
      /************************************************************************/
      /*    FILE DECLARATIONS                                                  */
      /************************************************************************/
 2      DCL DATAIN FILE INPUT RECORD          ENV(F RECSIZE(80));
 3      DCL PRINTR FILE OUTPUT RECORD         ENV(F RECSIZE(95) CTLASA);
      /************************************************************************/
      /*    RECORD LAYOUTS                                                     */
      /************************************************************************/
 4      DCL 1 NAME_AND_ADDR,
              2 NAME                CHAR(20),
              2 STREET              CHAR(25),
              2 CITY_STATE          CHAR(25),
              2 ZIP                 CHAR(9),
              2 REST_OF_RECORD      CHAR(1);

 5      DCL 1 PRINT_AREA,
              2 CARRIAGE_CONTROL    CHAR(1),
              2 PRINT_NAME          CHAR(20),
              2 UNUSED_1            CHAR(5)    INIT(' '),
              2 PRINT_STREET        CHAR(25),
              2 UNUSED_2            CHAR(5)    INIT(' '),
              2 PRINT_CITY_STATE    CHAR(25),
              2 UNUSED_3            CHAR(5)    INIT(' '),
              2 PRINT_ZIP           CHAR(9);
      /************************************************************************/
      /*    CONSTANTS AND VARIABLES                                            */
      /************************************************************************/
 6      DCL LINE_COUNT              FIXED(3);
 7      DCL MORE_RECORDS            BIT(1)     INIT('1'B);
 8      DCL NO                      BIT(1)     INIT('0'B);

      /************************************************************************/
      /*    ON CODES                                                          */
      /************************************************************************/
 9      ON ENDFILE(DATAIN)
            MORE_RECORDS = NO;
      /************************************************************************/
      /*    MAIN PROGRAM                                                       */
      /************************************************************************/
10      OPEN FILE(DATAIN),
             FILE(PRINTR);

11      LINE_COUNT = 55;
12      READ FILE (DATAIN) INTO (NAME_AND_ADDR);
13      DO WHILE(MORE_RECORDS);
14         LINE_COUNT = LINE_COUNT + 1;
15         IF LINE_COUNT > 55 THEN
              DO;
16                CARRIAGE_CONTROL = '1';
17                LINE_COUNT = 0;
18            END;
19         ELSE CARRIAGE_CONTROL = ' ';
20         PRINT_NAME        = NAME;
21         PRINT_STREET      = STREET;
22         PRINT_CITY_STATE  = CITY_STATE;
23         PRINT_ZIP         = ZIP;
24         WRITE FILE (PRINTR) FROM (PRINT_AREA);
25         READ FILE (DATAIN) INTO (NAME_AND_ADDR);
26      END;
27  END LIST;
```

**FIGURE 8.6**

The list program as modified for inclusion of blanks between the fields is illustrated in Figure 8.6. Some comments follow:

**Statements 15–19:** The carriage control character is set to effect either skipping to a new page or single spacing.

**Statements 20–23:** Input data fields are moved to the elementary items in the output structure, PRINT_AREA. Note the use of the new identifier PRINT_NAME to distinguish the field from the input record field NAME.

**Statement 24:** The carriage is controlled according to the character in position 1 of the output structure. The line is printed exactly as the data appears in the structure.

## A Built-in Function for Structures

The STRING function concatenates all the elements in an array or a structure into a single character- or bit-string element. Thus, if it is desired to concatenate a number of elementary items found in a structure or array, it would be easier to code the STRING function than to code the concatenation operation a number of times. STRING may also be used as a pseudovariable.

### Examples

```
DCL 1 STRUCTURE,
      2 ELEMENT1   CHAR(5)   INIT ('ABCDE'),
      2 ELEMENT2   CHAR(3)   INIT ('123'),
      2 ELEMENT3   CHAR(7)   INIT ('XYZXYZX');
DCL ITEM             CHAR(15);
ITEM       = STRUCTURE;           /* ILLEGAL MOVE                    */
ITEM       = STRING(STRUCTURE); /* ITEM = ABCDE123XYZXYZX           */
STRUCTURE = ITEM;                 /* STRUCTURE.ELEMENT1 = 'ABCDE'    */
                                  /* STRUCTURE.ELEMENT2 = 'ABC'      */
                                  /* STRUCTURE.ELEMENT3 = 'ABCDE12'  */
STRING(STRUCTURE) = ITEM;         /* STRUCTURE.ELEMENT1 = 'ABCDE'    */
                                  /* STRUCTURE.ELEMENT2 = '123'      */
                                  /* STRUCTURE.ELEMENT3 = 'XYZXYZX'  */
```

## PICTURES

There are a number of reasons for using PICTURE data:

**1.** To treat character-strings as arithmetic quantities (example: record input).

**2.** To treat arithmetic quantities as character-strings (example: record output).

**3.** To edit data (example: $ amount punctuation).

**4.** To validate data (example: examine specific positions for the presence of a digit 0–9).

Let us now look at the use of PICTUREs to accomplish items 3 and 4. The general form of the PICTURE attribute specification follows:

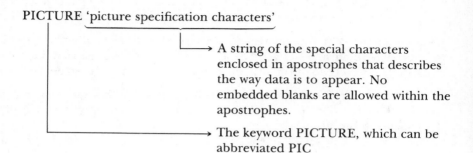

PICTURE 'picture specification characters'

    → A string of the special characters enclosed in apostrophes that describes the way data is to appear. No embedded blanks are allowed within the apostrophes.

    → The keyword PICTURE, which can be abbreviated PIC

Two types of PICTURE attributes are covered in this text: decimal pictures[4] and character-string pictures.

## DECIMAL PICTURES

The decimal picture specifies the form an arithmetic value is to assume. It allows such editing features as character insertion (e.g., the decimal point and commas in the previous example), zero suppression (Z picture character), decimal point alignment (indicated by a V, which stands for virtual point picture character), and sign insertion (+, −, and the commercial debit and credit symbols DB and CR). The decimal picture indicates the data item *already is* or *will be* stored internally in character form. Each digit, insertion character, and sign occupies one byte. Even though it has the appearance of a character-string, the data item declared with the PICTURE attribute retains the attributes necessary to qualify it as an arithmetic quantity with an associated base, scale, and precision. The base and scale are *implicitly* DECIMAL and FIXED, respectively. (Never declare a variable to have both the PICTURE attribute and either DECIMAL and/or FIXED.) The precision is determined by the number of 9s and Zs in the picture and the location of the V picture character.

Because an identifier retains the arithmetic attributes, arithmetic may be performed on the data item even though the PICTURE specifies insertion characters and zero suppression. It is not efficient for computer execution, however. Therefore, decimal pictures as they are normally used (i.e., when arithmetic needs to be performed on data input in character form) will be discussed. Then, pictures that might be used to edit data for output will be covered.

Here are some examples of simple picture declarations:

---

[4] In some PL/I reference manuals, you will see *decimal picture* referred to as *numeric character picture*. The trend is toward the use of the term *decimal picture*.

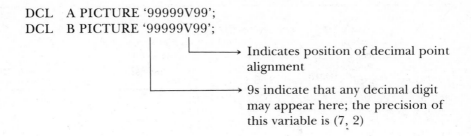

```
DCL   A PICTURE '99999V99';
DCL   B PICTURE '99999V99';
```

→ Indicates position of decimal point alignment

→ 9s indicate that any decimal digit may appear here; the precision of this variable is (7, 2)

In the preceding example, both A and B occupy seven bytes of storage. The V or decimal alignment character does not require a byte of storage. Another way in which the statement can be written is

```
DCL   A PICTURE '(5)9V99';
DCL   B PICTURE '(5)9V99';
```

→ Repetition factor must be in parentheses inside the apostrophes. It specifies that five picture character 9s are to replace the string (5)9

### Decimal Picture Specification Characters

The basic picture specification characters include:

9          Indicates any decimal digit.

V          Indicates the assumed location of a decimal point; it does not specify an actual decimal point character in the character representation of the data item; thus, no additional storage is needed if a V appears in the picture. If no V is specified, then it is assumed that the decimal point is to the right of the number; a V may not appear more than once in a picture.

The chart in Figure 8.7 shows some picture examples using the V and 9 characters. Notice the numbers referring to comments. These comments explain the corresponding example.

**Comment 1.** The decimal point alignment of the picture and its data caused the two most significant digits of the constant to be truncated as follows:

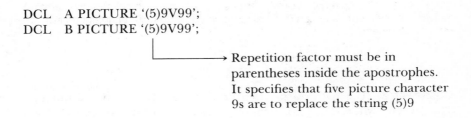

```
  |   |
  999V99
  |   |
12345 00
  |   | 
      └──────── Zeros are filled in
```

| PICTURE specification | Number of bytes of main storage used | Equivalent coded arithmetic form (conversion occurs prior to arithmetic operation) | Constant value assigned to the corresponding picture | Internal decimal picture result | Comment number |
|---|---|---|---|---|---|
| 99999 | 5 | FIXED (5) | 12345 | 12345∧ | |
| 99999V | 5 | FIXED (5) | 12345 | 12345∧ | |
| 999V99 | 5 | FIXED (5,2) | 123.45 | 123∧45 | |
| 999V99 | 5 | FIXED (5,2) | 12345 | 345∧00 | 1 |
| V99999 | 5 | FIXED (5,5) | 12345 | ∧00000 | 2 |
| 99999 | 5 | FIXED (5) | 123 | 00123∧ | |
| 999V99 | 5 | FIXED (5,2) | 123 | 123∧00 | |
| 9V9 | 2 | FIXED (2,1) | 123.45 | 3∧4 | 3 |
| 999V99 | 5 | FIXED (5,2) | −123.45 | 123∧45 | 4 |

FIGURE 8.7   Examples of decimal pictures (*note:* in the fifth column, the caret (∧) indicates position of assumed decimal point; in the sixth column, the numbers refer to comments in the text).

**Comment 2.** The picture specified here indicated a fractional number only. Thus, when a whole number is assigned to a fractional number, the whole number is lost, and the corresponding picture will be set to zero.

**Comment 3.** In this example, note that there is automatic decimal point alignment of the V in the picture with the decimal point in the constant:

**Comment 4.** A negative constant was specified, but the picture does not include provision for a sign.   The minus sign was dropped, making the value positive in main storage.

This last example points up the need for some way to indicate the presence of a sign in the PICTURE field.   Most of the PICTURE items to be used as factors for calculations are originally read from some external device.   Even though record I/O stores the bytes read exactly as they are coded on the external media, it is good programming practice to indicate the presence of a sign if there could be one. Then if program execution, other than a READ, moves information to the identifier, the sign will be properly maintained.

**5.** Declare a structure that could be used for reading a record containing the following fields in character form:

| Columns | Contents |
|---------|----------|
| 1–6 | Customer number |
| 7–31 | Customer name |
| 32 | Credit rating |
| 33–38 | Last active date |
| 39–63 | Reference (alphameric) |
| 64–80 | Unused |

**6.** Given the following PICTURE specifications, indicate the equivalent arithmetic form.

*PICTURE specification*

(a)   9
(b)   9V999
(c)   V (5)9

**7.** The record format shown in Figure 8.8 represents the general ledger for a construction company. The two balance amounts are assumed to contain dollar and cents amounts upon which calculations need to be performed. The structure shown in Figure 8.9 is to be used to read the general ledger accounts. Have any errors been made in the structure declaration? If so, what are they?

**8.** How many bytes of storage would be required by the following structure?

```
DCL 1 RENTAL_UNIT,
      2 UNIT_NO            CHAR(6),
      2 TENANT_NAME        CHAR(15),
      2 PHONE              CHAR(7),
      2 MOVE_IN_DATE       CHAR(6),
      2 MONTHLY_RENT       PIC'(5)9V99',
      2 PARKING_FEE        PIC'999V99',
      2 SECURITY_DEPOSIT   PIC'(5)9',
      2 BALANCE_DUE        PIC'(6)9V99';
```

| | CATEGORY NUMBER | CATEGORY NAME | TYPE | CURRENT BALANCE | BALANCE LAST GL | TITLE CODE |
|---|---|---|---|---|---|---|
| Record Positions | 1–6 | 7–36 | 37–38 | 39–49 | 50–60 | 61 |

FIGURE 8.8

```
DCL 1 GENERAL_LEDGER_ACCOUNT,
        2 CATEGORY_NUMBER          CHAR(6);
        2 CATEGORY_NAME            CHAR(30);
        2 TYPE                     CHAR(2);
        2 CURRENT_BALANCE          PIC (9(9)V99);
        2 BALANCE_LAST_GL          PIC (999999999V99);
        2 TITLE                    CHAR(1);
```

FIGURE 8.9

## More Decimal Picture Specification Characters

S      Indicates that the sign of the value (+ if >0 and − if <0) is to appear in a separate byte position in the variable.

+      Indicates that a plus sign (+) is to appear in the character representation of the variable if the value is greater than or equal to zero and that a blank is to appear if the value is less than zero.

−      Indicates that a minus sign (−) is to appear in the character representation of the variable if the value is less than zero and that a blank is to appear if the value is greater than or equal to zero.

The picture characters S, +, and − may appear to the left or right of all digit positions in the picture.

The chart in Figure 8.10 shows some picture examples using the S, +, and − characters. Some comments explain the corresponding example.

**Comment 1.** These two examples show ways of carrying a negative sign as a separate character.

| Picture specification | No. of bytes | Equivalent coded arithmetic form | Constant value assigned to the corresponding picture | Internal decimal picture result | Comment number |
|---|---|---|---|---|---|
| S999V99 | 6 | FIXED (5,2) | −123.45 | −123$_\wedge$45 | 1 |
| −999V99 | 6 | FIXED (5,2) | −123.45 | −123$_\wedge$45 | 1 |
| S999V99 | 6 | FIXED (5,2) | +123.45 | +123$_\wedge$45 | 2 |
| 999V99S | 6 | FIXED (5,2) | −123.45 | 123$_\wedge$45− | 2 |
| +999V99 | 6 | FIXED (5,2) | +123.45 | +123$_\wedge$45 | 3 |

FIGURE 8.10    Examples of decimal pictures (*note:* in the fifth column, the caret (∧) indicates position of assumed decimal point; in the sixth column, the numbers refer to comments in the text).

**Comment 2.** When an S appears in the picture, a sign must precede or follow the numeric value; it cannot be embedded in the numeric value.

**Comment 3.** Here, the value being placed in the picture may have a + sign or no sign.

### Arithmetic Operations on Decimal Picture Data

When an arithmetic operation is specified for decimal picture data, the data is automatically converted to the coded arithmetic form FIXED DECIMAL. For example, assume the program statements

```
DCL SUM       PIC'9999';
DCL A         PIC'999';
DCL B         PIC'999';
SUM = A + B;
```

are coded. To add A to B and assign the results to SUM, the following steps are performed automatically:

1. Convert A from decimal picture to FIXED DECIMAL data format.
2. Convert B from decimal picture to FIXED DECIMAL data format.
3. Add A and B together.
4. Convert the results to numeric character form (PICTURE).
5. Place the results in the variable called SUM.

## EDITING DATA FOR PRINTED OUTPUT

A number of characters may appear in pictures for the purpose of editing data. The data declared with pictures that contain these "editing" characters can be used in calculations, but it is very inefficient to do so and should be avoided. Editing characters are actually stored internally in the specified positions of the data item. The editing characters are considered to be part of the character-string value but not part of the variable's arithmetic value.

Data items with the PICTURE attribute to be used as output (i.e., to a printer) usually receive their values via an assignment statement. Values are normally developed during a program's execution using a coded arithmetic data type. When final results are obtained, the values are assigned to picture data variables for printing. A wide variety of output editing is required in many applications. To meet these requirements, a large number of picture specification characters can be used to create the properly edited fields for output. Let us discuss the functions of the more commonly used editing characters.

| PICTURE specification | Value to be assigned to variable | Internal character representation |
|---|---|---|
| ZZZZ9 | 100 | bb100 |
| ZZZZ9 | 0 | bbbb0 |
| ZZZZZ | 0 | bbbbb |
| ZZZV99 | 123 | 12300 |
| ZZZVZZ | 1234 | 23400 |
| ZZZVZZ | .01 | bbbb1 |
| ZZZV99 | 0 | bbb00 |
| Z9999 | 0 | b0000 |
| ZZZVZ9 | INVALID PICTURE—if a Z appears to the right of the V character, then *all* digits to the right must be specified as Z | |
| ZZ9ZZ | INVALID PICTURE—all Z characters must appear to the left of all 9's | |

FIGURE 8.11  Pictures illustrating zero suppression.

### The Z Picture Character — Zero Suppression

The Z may be used to cause the suppression of leading zeros in the data field, replacing the nonsignificant zeros with blanks.   Figure 8.11 shows some examples of how PICTURE with the Z character will cause zeros to be suppressed (that is, replaced with blanks) in the character representation of the data variable.

If a value is to have leading blanks as well as a sign, then the S PICTURE character may be used.   For example:

DCL A PIC'SZZZ9'; /* OR PIC'ZZZ9S' */

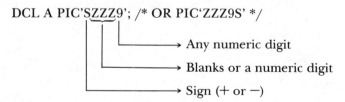

In the previous example, a sign will always appear in the leftmost or rightmost position of the character-string representation.

### The Decimal Point (.)

The decimal point is an **insertion character,** meaning that the decimal point will be inserted in the output field in the position where it appears in the picture specification.   For example:

DCL PRICE PIC'999V.99' INIT (12.34);
PUT LIST (PRICE); /* 012.34 WILL BE PRINTED */

Note that if the PICTURE is specified without the decimal point, the output will appear as follows:

    DCL UNIT_COST PIC'999V99' INIT (12.34);
    PUT LIST (UNIT_COST); /* 01234 WILL BE PRINTED */

Do not think of the decimal point as causing alignment; only the V accomplishes this function. Consider the following:

    DCL VALUE PIC'999.99' INIT (12.34);
    PUT LIST (VALUE); /* 000.12 IS PRINTED */

Because the V accomplishes the function of alignment and the decimal point the function of inserting a physical indication of this alignment, we normally specify the V and the decimal point in adjacent positions in our picture specification.

In the previous example, no V is specified; thus, the implied decimal point is to the right of the number. When the constant 12.34 is aligned with the implied V, we have this undesirable result:

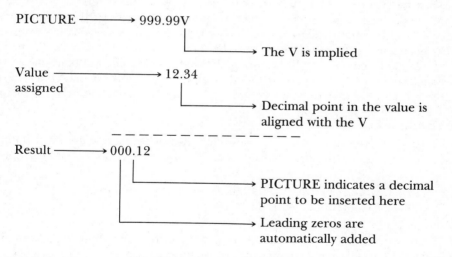

This "undesirable" result may be useful. Consider printing a discount percent field. Discount is entered as a field with three positions to the right of the decimal and therefore would be declared with a picture:

    DISCOUNT_PERCENT    PICTURE 'V999'

When the discount is printed, it is to appear as a percentage. For example, .125 is actually to print as 12.5 percent, or just as 12.5 under a heading of discount *percent*. The output identifier could be declared:

    PRINT_DISCOUNT_PERCENT    PICTURE 'VZZ.9'

The usual case is to place the V to the left of the decimal point in a picture specification, although it may appear to the right of the decimal point:

    DCL PRICE PIC'999.V99' INIT (12.34);
    PUT LIST (PRICE); /* 012.34 IS OUTPUT */

In this example, the output is the same as if the V had appeared to the left of the decimal point. However, in other cases, the position of the V in relationship to the decimal point is most significant. To illustrate, let us look at what happens when zero suppression is specified in a PICTURE containing a V and a decimal point (small b represents a blank):

    DCL A PIC'ZZZV.99' INIT (.05);
    PUT LIST (A); /* bbb.05 IS OUTPUT */
    DCL B PIC'ZZZ.V99' INIT (.05);
    PUT LIST (B); /* bbbb05 IS OUTPUT */ .

The rule to be derived from the preceding example is this: When the V is to the left of the decimal point, the V may be thought of as "guarding" the decimal point; hence, if leading zeros are to be suppressed, the decimal point will not be replaced with a blank. However, if the V is to the right of the decimal point in the picture and leading zeros are to be suppressed, the decimal point will be replaced by a blank whenever the integer portion of the number is zero. We may conclude that the V ought *normally* to be located to the left of the decimal point in the picture.

### The Comma (,)

The comma is another **insertion character.** It will be inserted in the output field in the position corresponding to its location in the PICTURE. For example:

    DCL BIG_VALUE PIC'999,999V.99' INIT (104056.98);
    PUT LIST (BIG_VALUE); /* 104,056.98 IS OUTPUT */

If zero suppression is specified, the comma is inserted only when a significant digit appears to the left of the comma; otherwise, the comma is replaced with a blank, as the following example illustrates:

    DCL AMT          PIC 'ZZZ,ZZZV.99';
    AMT = 450.75;
    PUT LIST(AMT);    /* bbbb450.75 IS OUTPUT */
    AMT = 1450.75;
    PUT LIST(AMT);    /* bbl,450.75 IS OUTPUT  */
    AMT = 0;
    PUT LIST(AMT);    /* bbbbbbb.00 IS OUTPUT */

## The Blank (B)

The blank is another **insertion character.** It is used to insert blanks to the right of a value on output. (Of course, to obtain blanks on the left of the value, the Z picture character is used.) Here are some examples:

```
DCL A   PIC'999V99BBB';
DCL B   PIC'Z,ZZZV.99(7)B';
```

The B picture character may also be embedded in a decimal picture. For example, the following DECLARE could be used to insert blanks between the month, day, and year portions of a date field.

```
DCL EDITED_DATE   PIC'99B99B99';
```

## The Slash (/)

This insertion character is used to insert slashes at the specified position in the picture. Its use is primarily for inserting slashes between the month, day, and year portions of a date field. For example:

```
DCL RUN_DATE                        CHAR(6);
DCL EDITED_RUN_DATE                 PIC 'Z9/99/99';
EDITED_RUN_DATE = RUN_DATE;
```

The leading Z in the picture causes zero suppression for months 1 to 9.
Note that the following is invalid:

```
DCL EDITED_RUN_DATE PIC'Z9/Z9/99'; /* INVALID */
```

This is because zero suppressions applies only to leading zeros — not to embedded zeros.

## The Dollar Sign ($)

The $ character specifies a currency symbol in the character representation of numeric data. This character may be used in either a *static* or *drifting* manner. The static use of the $ specifies that a currency symbol will always appear in the position fixed by its location in the picture. In the drifting form, there are multiple adjacent occurrences of the character. A drifting dollar sign specifies that leading zeros are to be suppressed and that the rightmost suppressed zero will be replaced with the $ symbol. Here are some examples:

```
DCL A        PIC'$999V.99'      INIT(12.34);
PUT LIST(A);            /* $012.34  IS OUTPUT        */
DCL B        PIC'$$$$V.99'      INIT(12.34);
PUT LIST (B);          /* b$12.34  IS OUTPUT        */
```

```
DCL C            PIC'$$,$$$V.99(5)B'   INIT(1024.76);
PUT LIST(C);             /* $1,024.7   6bbbbb IS OUTPUT */
DCL D            PIC'$Z,ZZZV.99'    INIT(12.34);
PUT LIST(D);             /* $bbb12.34  IS OUTPUT         */
```

## The Sign Characters (S, +, −)

We have seen the sign characters used in their static form. These editing characters may also be drifting. Here are some examples using the sign characters in both their static and drifting forms:

```
DCL A            PIC'S999'           INIT(12);
PUT LIST(A);             /* +012 IS OUTPUT         */
DCL B            PIC'SSS9'           INIT(12);
PUT LIST(B);             /* b+12 IS OUTPUT         */
DCL C            PIC'9999S'          INIT(1234);
PUT LIST(C);             /* 1234+ IS OUTPUT        */
DCL D            PIC'−9'             INIT(−12);
PUT LIST(D);             /* b−12 IS OUTPUT         */
D = +12;
PUT LIST(D);             /* bb12 IS OUTPUT         */
DCL E            PIC'+99' INIT(144); /* ERROR      */
PUT LIST(E);             /* +44 IS OUTPUT          */
DCL F            PIC'999V.99S'       INIT(−123.45);
PUT LIST(F);             /* 123.45− IS OUTPUT      */
```

## The Asterisk (*)

The asterisk is a fill character and is used in much the same way as the Z. The "asterisk fill" capability is useful in applications that require check protection. For example, in using a computer to print checks or statements indicating amounts paid, it is desirable to precede the dollar and cents amounts with a drifting dollar sign or leading asterisks so as to preclude any tampering with or modification of those amounts. The asterisk *cannot* appear with the picture character Z, nor can it appear to the right of a 9 or any drifting character. Here are some examples:

```
DCL PAY          PIC'*****9V.99'          INIT(104.75);
PUT LIST(PAY);         /*     ***104.75 IS OUTPUT        */
DCL AMT_PAID     PIC'*****V.**'           INIT(843.50);
PUT LIST(AMT_PAID);    /*     **843.50 IS OUTPUT         */
AMT_PAID = .75;        /* SEE PICTURE DECLARED ABOVE     */
PUT LIST(AMT_PAID);    /*     *****.75 IS OUTPUT         */
DCL PAYS         PIC'****V.99'            INIT(4.75);
PUT LIST(PAYS);        /*     ***4.75 IS OUTPUT          */
DCL QTY          PIC'***'                 INIT(123);
PUT LIST(QTY);         /*     123 IS OUTPUT              */
```

From the last example we can see that — for check protection, at least — one extra asterisk should be provided in the picture.

### Credit (CR) and Debit (DB) Characters

The paired characters CR and/or DB specify the sign of negative numeric fields. They are used most often on business report forms (e.g., billing, invoicing). Do not confuse these symbols with the general ledger accounting terms:

DR   debit(positive value)
CR   credit(negative value)

In PL/I usage

CR          Indicates that the associated positions will contain the letters CR *if* the value of the data is negative; otherwise, the positions will contain two blanks. The characters CR can only appear to the right of *all* digit positions in a PICTURE.

DB          Is used in the same fashion as the CR, except that the letters DB appear in the associated print positions if the value is negative.

CR and DB may not appear with any other sign indication.

```
DCL D       PIC'99V.99CR'        INIT(- 12.34);
PUT LIST(D);        /* 12.34CR IS OUTPUT          */
DCL E       PIC'99V.99DBBBBB'  INIT(- 12.34);
PUT LIST(E);        /* 12.34DBbbbb IS OUTPUT      */
DCL F       PIC'S999V.99CR';
/* INVALID PICTURE BECAUSE BOTH 'S' AND 'CR' ARE */
  /* SPECIFIED */
DCL G       PIC'99V.99CR'        INIT(+ 12.34);
PUT LIST(G);        /* 12.34bb IS OUTPUT          */
```

Both DB and CR will appear in the edited field of *negative* values.

## CHARACTER-STRING PICTURES

Another type of PICTURE attribute is the character-string picture specification. Its form is like decimal pictures, except that the characters that make up the picture specification are A, X, and 9. Furthermore, the data item declared with the character-string picture *does not* have the arithmetic attributes of base, scale, and precision, but does have the character-string *length* attribute.

Thus, string built-in functions such as SUBSTR, LENGTH, INDEX, or VERIFY may be used on character-string pictures.

The actions performed by the picture specification characters for character-string pictures are as follows:

A  Specifies that the associated position of the picture may contain the alphabetic characters A through Z or a blank.

X  Specifies that the associated position of the picture may contain *any* character.

9  Specifies that the associated position of the picture may contain only the digits 0 through 9.

Some examples of character-string pictures are shown in Figure 8.12 where b represents a blank.

The comma and decimal point insertion characters may not be specified in a character-string picture; also, the B insertion character may not be specified. For example,

DCL OUTPUT_FIELD   PIC 'BBBXXXXX'; /* INVALID */

is illegal. The minus sign may not be used in character-string pictures.

The character-string PICTURE attribute is used primarily in *data validation* rather than in output editing. For example, assume an inventory item is identified by a part number that consists of alphabetic and numeric characters such as

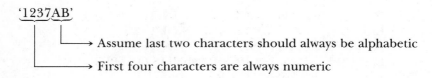

| Source attributes | Source data in constant form | PICTURE specification | Character-string value |
|---|---|---|---|
| CHAR(4) | 'ABCD' | AAAA | ABCD |
| CHAR(4) | 'ABCD' | XXXX | ABCD |
| CHAR(5) | 'ABCDb' | AAAAAA | ABCDbb |
| CHAR(5) | '12Q21' | 99A99 | 12Q21 |
| CHAR(5) | '#B123' | XA999 | #B123 |
| CHAR(5) | '12bbb' | 99XXX | 12bbb |
| CHAR(5) | '12AB9' | 99AAA | INVALID |
| CHAR(5) | 'AB123' | AAA99 | INVALID |
| CHAR(5) | 'L26.7' | A99X9 | L26.7 |

FIGURE 8.12   Examples of character-string pictures.

On input, this part number could be *validated* by assigning it to a picture that contains A and 9 picture specifications. For example:

```
DCL PART_NUM          PIC '9999AA';
DCL ITEM              CHAR(6);
PART_NUM = ITEM;
```

When ITEM is assigned to PART_NUM, data validation occurs. If the part number consists of four leading digits followed by two alphabetic characters, we know that the part number is in the correct form. Of course, we do not know if it is an actual part number in our inventory without doing further checking.

If the number is incorrectly keyed as

'123ABC'

and read into ITEM, the CONVERSION condition is raised when ITEM is assigned to PART_NUM. The raising of this condition means that an error has occurred. In this example, it would be a data validation error.

A picture containing a 9 and an X instead of the A may also be specified; or all three characters may be coded together in one picture.

## CHECKPOINT QUESTIONS

**9.** What are the uses of the PICTURE attribute?

**10.** Each time a decimal picture is to be used in a calculation, what conversion takes place?

**11.** Give the numeric results after the following identifiers are initialized:

| | | | | |
|---|---|---|---|---|
| (a) | DCL GROSS_PAY | PIC '9999V99' | INIT (550); |
| (b) | DCL REORDER_QTY | PIC '999' | INIT (1000); |
| (c) | DCL HOURS_WORKED | PIC '99' | INIT (40.75); |
| (d) | DCL INTEREST_DUE | PIC '999V99' | INIT (3.4567); |

**12.** How many bytes of storage will each of the following identifiers require?

| | | |
|---|---|---|
| (a) | DCL PRICE | PIC '999V99'; |
| (b) | DCL QUANTITY | PIC '9999'; |
| (c) | DCL BACK_ORDERED | PIC 'S999999'; |
| (d) | DCL AMT | PIC 'SSSSV99'; |
| (e) | DCL FLD | PIC '(5)X(7)9'; |

**13.** Given the following DECLARE, what would the *output* values look like?

    DCL AVALUE    PIC'ZZZ99';

(a)   AVALUE = 12345;
(b)   AVALUE = 123;
(c)   AVALUE = 0;

## Pictures in Stream I/O

Some editing of data in stream I/O is automatic. For example, in list-directed and data-directed output of arithmetic coded data, leading zeros will be suppressed, and a minus sign and decimal point inserted if necessary. Full editing capability may be achieved in list-directed output by simply assigning data items to identifiers that have the PICTURE attribute and then issuing a PUT LIST on those identifiers. For example:

```
DCL VALUE              FIXED DEC(8,2);
DCL EDIT_VALUE         PIC'$$$$,$$$V.99CR';
VALUE = A * B;
EDIT_VALUE = VALUE;
PUT FILE(SYSPRINT) LIST(EDIT_VALUE);
```

In edit-directed I/O, full editing of data may be implemented by using a format item called P-format. It is specified in the format list, may contain any characters allowed in a PICTURE, and is used to describe the characteristics of external data.

## P 'picture specification'

The **picture specification** consists of any character allowed in the PICTURE declaration. On input, the picture specification describes the form of the data item expected in the data stream and, in the case of a numeric picture item, how its arithmetic value is to be interpreted. Note that the picture specification should accurately describe the data in the input stream, including characters represented by editing characters. If the indicated character does not appear in the stream, the CONVERSION condition is raised.

| Input value | Format specification | Resulting internal value |
|---|---|---|
| bb15 | P'ZZZ9' | 0015 |
| 1234 | P'99V99' | 12$_\wedge$34 |
| AB123 | P'AA999' | AB123 |
| AB123 | P'99999' | CONVERSION error |

    GET FILE(SYSIN) EDIT(A,B,C,D)
        (COL(1), P'ZZZ9',P'99V99',P'AA999',P'(5)9');

We frequently have the need to edit data in order to improve readability. For example, instead of printing the value

    45326985.76

we might *edit* the data by inserting a dollar sign and commas so that the output would look like this:

$45,326,985.76

To accomplish this in a PUT EDIT statement, the following could be coded:

```
DCL ASSETS            FIXED DEC(11,2);
ASSETS = 45326985.76;
PUT EDIT(ASSETS)(P'$$$$,$$$,$$$V.99');
```

Specifying a dollar sign ($) in every position where a decimal character might appear causes the number to be edited with a *floating* dollar sign — that is, the $ is placed to the immediate left of the most significant digit.  ASSETS would print as follows:

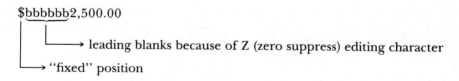

b$45,326,985.76

   → floating dollar sign

  → leading blank (determined by number of editing characters in the P 'specification')

Here is another example:

```
ASSETS = 2500.00;
PUT EDIT(ASSETS)(P'$ZZZ,ZZZ,ZZZV.99');
```

Printout would be:

$bbbbbb2,500.00

   → leading blanks because of Z (zero suppress) editing character

  → "fixed" position

The V character in the P format specification causes decimal point alignment between the internal data item and the external printed value.  For example, if you forgot to specify the V in the following

```
AMT = 123.75;
PUT EDIT(AMT)(P'999.99');
```

PL/I assumes the alignment at the right of the picture specification in the absence of a "V."  Thus, in the preceding example, the value

001.23

is erroneously printed.   This is illustrated as follows:

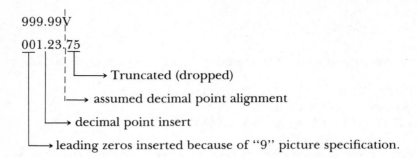

999.99V
001.23.75
→ Truncated (dropped)
→ assumed decimal point alignment
→ decimal point insert
→ leading zeros inserted because of "9" picture specification.

The correct specification is

PUT EDIT(AMT) (P'999V.99');

To edit a date, the following P specification may be specified:

DCL TODAY          CHAR(6);
TODAY = '080888';
PUT EDIT(TODAY) (P'99/99/99');

This causes the date to be printed as follows:

08/08/88

On output, the value of the associated element in the data list is edited to the form specified by the picture specification before it is written into the data stream.

| Internal value | Format specification | Resulting output |
| --- | --- | --- |
| 12.34 | P'$$$$V.99' | $12.34 |
| −12.34 | P'S999V.99' | −012.34 |
| 2112.34 | P'$$,$$$V.99CR' | $2,112.34 |
| −2112.34 | P'$$,$$$V.99CR' | $2,112.34CR |
| 15 | P'ZZZ9' | bb15 |
| 0 | P'ZZZ9' | bbb0 |
| 12.34 | P'****V.99' | **12.34 |

## CHECKPOINT QUESTION

14. Given the following statements:

DCL VALUE          FIXED DEC(7,2);
VALUE = 1024.57;

write the PUT EDIT statement to print the output in this form:

$1024.57

## STRUCTURES

A **structure** is a collection of data items requiring storage for each item to be in a particular order and having a logical relationship to one another. For example, in a payroll application, a number of data items about one employee could be logically grouped together, such as the following:

| Names used in the program | Data |
|---|---|
| LAST | DOE |
| FIRST | JOHN |
| MIDDLE | J |
| EMP_NO | 72535 |
| REGULAR | 40 |
| OVERTIME | 4 |
| REG_PAY | 4.00 |
| OT_PAY | 6.00 |

Declaring these items as a **structure** allows us to give a name to the whole collection. SALARY_RECORD, for example, could be the name given to the above list of variables.

It is often more convenient, however, to subdivide the entire structure into smaller logical groups so as to be able to refer collectively to more than one, but not all, of the variables in the structure. The preceding example might be subdivided as follows:

| Names used in the program | | | Data |
|---|---|---|---|
| | NAME | LAST | DOE |
| | | FIRST | JOHN |
| | | MIDDLE | J |
| SALARY_RECORD | EMP_NO | | 72535 |
| | HOURS | REGULAR | 40 |
| | | OVERTIME | 4 |
| | WAGES | REG_PAY | 4.00 |
| | | OT_PAY | 6.00 |

It would now be possible to refer to NAME in your PL/I program; the implication is that you are actually referring to the items LAST, FIRST, and MIDDLE. Thus, if the statement

    PUT LIST(NAME);

were specified, the items LAST, FIRST, and MIDDLE would be printed. Structuring allows you the additional flexibility of being able to reference the individual item as well as the substructure NAME. For example, in the statement

    PUT LIST(LAST);

only the last name will be printed.

The hierarchy of items just shown can be considered to have different *levels*. At the highest level is the *major structure* name, SALARY_RECORD; at an intermediate level are substructure names called *minor structures* (NAME, HOURS, WAGES); at the lowest level are *elementary* items (LAST, EMP_NO, REGULAR, etc.). EMP_NO is considered to be an elementary item because there is no further division of the item.

When a structure is declared, the level of each name is indicated by a **level number.** The major structure name (at the highest level) must be numbered 1. Each name at a deeper level is given a greater number to indicate the level depth. Note that the level number must be followed by a blank. The maximum level number that may be specified is 255. This is the sequence to follow in declaring structures:

**1.** The major structure name is declared first.

**2.** The elementary items in each minor structure are completely declared before the next minor structure is declared.

**3.** The elementary items contained in a minor structure must be declared with a greater level number than that of the minor structure.

```
DCL 1 SALARY_RECORD, /* MAJOR STRUCTURE */
      2 NAME,          /* MINOR STRUCTURE */
        3 LAST,        /* ELEMENTARY ITEM */
        3 FIRST,       /* ELEMENTARY ITEM */
        3 MIDDLE,      /* ELEMENTARY ITEM */
      2 EMP_NO,        /* ELEMENTARY ITEM */
      2 HOURS,         /* MINOR STRUCTURE */
        3 REGULAR,     /* ELEMENTARY ITEM */
        3 OVERTIME,    /* ELEMENTARY ITEM */
      2 WAGES,         /* MINOR STRUCTURE */
        3 REG_PAY,     /* ELEMENTARY ITEM */
        3 OT_PAY;      /* ELEMENTARY ITEM */
```

In references to the structure or its elements, no level numbers are used.

A single declared variable is not preceded by a level number when coded, because it is assumed to be a "level 1" identifier. For example, in the statement

    DCL 1 SINGLE_VALUE   FIXED DEC(5);

the 1 specification is redundant.

Most attributes are explicitly declared in a structure at the elementary item level.  For example:

```
DCL 1 SALARY_RECORD,
      3 NAME,
            5 LAST          CHAR(13),
            5 FIRST         CHAR(8),
            5 MIDDLE        CHAR(1),
      3 EMP_NO              PIC '99999',
      3 HOURS,
            5 REGULAR       PIC '99',
            5 OVERTIME      PIC '99',
      3 WAGES,
            5 REG_PAY       PIC '99V99',
            5 OT_PAY        PIC '99V99';
```

(Notice that the level numbers do not have to be successive; however, each item must have a higher number than that of the level it is subdividing).  Other attributes such as dimension and storage class are specified at the major level.

## Factored Attributes in Structures

**Factoring** in PL/I is grouping identifiers together for the purpose of giving them a common attribute.  The elementary names under HOURS and WAGES in the above example could have been factored as follows:

```
3 HOURS,
      5 (REGULAR,OVERTIME)   PIC '99',
3 WAGES,
      5 (REG_PAY,OT_PAY)     PIC '99V99';
```

Generally, the factoring of attributes can be confusing and not good programming style.

## The INITIAL Attribute in Structures

Elementary items in structures may be initialized using the INITIAL attribute, providing the structure is not overlay-defined on another structure, character-string, or other data item.  As long as the structure is the *base identifier* (the structure onto which other identifiers may be overlayed), it may contain the INITIAL attribute.  For example:

```
DCL 1 A,          /* BASE IDENTIFIER */
      2 B,
            3 C   CHAR(11)      INIT('ALAN KIRKBY'),
            3 D   PIC '999V99'  INIT(100.00),
      2 E         CHAR(25)      INIT(' ');
DCL AA            CHAR(39)      DEFINED A;
```

## Qualified Names

All names within a single procedure must be unique. But within structures, it is often desirable to be able to use the same identifier for related names and yet retain the uniqueness. For example, in the SALARY_RECORD structure, the last portion of the structure might have been declared:

```
3 HOURS,
     5 REGULAR    PIC '99',
     5 OVERTIME   PIC '99',
3 WAGES,
     5 REGULAR    PIC '99V99',
     5 OVERTIME   PIC '99V99';
```

Notice that we now have two REGULARs and two OVERTIMEs. Using a **qualified name** in referring to the individual data item avoids ambiguity. A qualified name is a substructure or element name that is made unique by qualifying it with one or more names of a higher level. The individual names within a qualified name are connected by a period. If, for example, you wanted to process the data items that were read into the structure declared above, the following arithmetic operations might be specified:

```
REGULAR_PAY  = HOURS.REGULAR  * WAGES.REGULAR;
OVERTIME_PAY = HOURS.OVERTIME * WAGES.OVERTIME;
```

The qualified name HOURS.REGULAR refers to REGULAR in the substructure HOURS, the qualified name WAGES.REGULAR refers to REGULAR in the substructure WAGES, etc. Qualified names are merely used for reference to avoid ambiguity; they are not declared in a structure. A qualified name may not contain commas. In some compilers, blanks may appear on either side of the period (e.g., A . B). Qualification need go only as far as necessary to make the name unique. Intermediate qualifying of names can be omitted. Consider the following structure:

```
DCL 1 A,
      2 B,
           3 C   CHAR(9),
           3 D   PIC '999V99',
      2 BB,
           3 C   CHAR(7),
           3 E   PIC '999';
```

In this example, to refer to the first C in the structure, you could write:

```
A.B.C
```

or simply:

> B.C

Do you see the ambiguity that would arise if you wrote:

> A.C

Suppose E is a name used in another structure in the same procedure; then to qualify E in this structure, you may write:

> A.E

or:

> BB.E

or:

> A.BB.E

The maximum length allowed for qualified names varies slightly in the different PL/I compilers. Generally, if you keep the maximum length under 140 characters, including the periods, you will be within the limit of the various compilers' restrictions.

## Arrays in Structures

Like a structure, an array is a collection of data. Unlike a structure, all elements in an array have identical attributes. It is possible to include an array within a structure:

```
DCL 1 INVENTORY_ITEM,
      2 PART_NO            CHAR(8),
      2 QTY_ON_HAND        PIC '9999',
      2 MINIMUM_NO         PIC '9999',
      2 SALES_HISTORY(12)  PIC '99999';
```

In the example of an inventory record, each record would contain the part number, the present quantity on hand, a minimum quantity to be kept on hand at all times, and finally a *sales history*. SALES_HISTORY is an array of 12 elements. Each element represents a month in the year. For example, SALES_HISTORY (1) contains the number of items sold in January, SALES_HISTORY (2) the number of items in February, SALES_HISTORY (3) in March, and so on. If the product is a seasonal one, this kind of historical information might be valuable in a program for determining varying reorder quantities at different times of the year.

## Arrays of Structures

An array of structures is an array whose elements are structures having identical names, levels, and elements. For example, if a structure, WEATHER, were used to process meteorological information for each month of a year, it might be declared as follows:

```
DCL 1 WEATHER(12),
        2 TEMPERATURE,
           3 HIGH              FIXED DEC(4,1),
           3 LOW               FIXED DEC(3,1),
        2 WIND_VELOCITY,
           3 HIGH              FIXED DEC(3),
           3 LOW               FIXED DEC(2),
        2 PRECIPITATION,
           3 TOTAL             FIXED DEC(3,1),
           3 AVERAGE           FIXED DEC(3,1);
```

Thus, a programmer could refer to the weather data for the month of July by specifying WEATHER(7). Portions of the July weather could be referred to by TEMPERATURE (7), WIND_VELOCITY (7), and/or PRECIPITATION (7). TOTAL (7) would refer to the total precipitation during the month of July. TEMPERATURE.HIGH (3), which would refer to the high temperature in March, is called a *subscripted qualified name*.

## A Programming Example

Let us look at a programming example in which a structure contains 35 students' names and their corresponding grade-point averages received for History 101; for example:

```
DCL 1 HISTORY_101,
        2 NAME(35)   CHAR(20),
        2 GPA(35)     FIXED DEC(4,1);
```

It is desired to identify all students who have a grade-point average of 92.5 or better. Write a program to read test data into the structure. Then search the structure for names of students who received a grade of 92.5 or better, and place those names into the following array:

```
DCL HONOR_STUDENTS(35)   CHAR(20)   INIT((35)(1)' ');
```

Results are written to a disk file called HONORS. Figure 8.13 shows the program.

```
/* SAMPLE PROGRAM TO COMPUTE ARRAYS IN A STRUCTURE                   */
/******************************************************************/
/* PROGRAM NAME: GPA                                                 */
/*                                                                   */
/* DESCRIPTION:   THIS PROGRAM READS STUDENTS NAMES AND GRADES INTO  */
/*                A STRUCTURE.  THE STRUCTURE IS SEARCHED TO IDENTIFY */
/*                THOSE STUDENTS WITH A GRADE POINT AVERAGE OF 92.5   */
/*                OR BETTER.  THE HONOR STUDENTS NAMES ARE PRINTED.   */
/*                                                                   */
/* INPUT:         GRADES                                             */
/*                                                                   */
/* OUTPUT:        HONORS                                             */
/******************************************************************/
GPA: PROC OPTIONS(MAIN);

/******************************************************************/
/* FILE DECLARATIONS                                                */
/******************************************************************/
   DCL   GRADES FILE INPUT  RECORD;
   DCL   HONORS FILE OUTPUT RECORD;

/******************************************************************/
/* RECORD DECLARATIONS                                              */
/******************************************************************/
   DCL 1 HISTORY_101,
         2 NAME(35)                  CHAR(20),
         2 GPA(35)                   FIXED(4,1);

   DCL 1 INPUT_AREA,
         2 INPUT_NAME                CHAR(20),
         2 INPUT_GPA                 PIC'999V9',
         2 UNUSED                    CHAR(56);

/******************************************************************/
/* CONSTANTS AND VARIABLES                                          */
/******************************************************************/
   DCL FILL_ARRAY                FIXED BIN(15);
   DCL HONOR_COUNT               FIXED BIN(15);
   DCL HONOR_STUDENTS(35)        CHAR(20)        INIT((35)(1)' ');
   DCL PRINT_NAME                CHAR(20);
   DCL PRINT_OUT                 FIXED BIN(15);
   DCL TEST                      FIXED BIN(15);
/******************************************************************/
/* MAIN PROGRAM                                                     */
/******************************************************************/
   OPEN FILE (GRADES),
        FILE (HONORS);

   DO FILL_ARRAY = 1 TO 35;
      READ FILE (GRADES) INTO (INPUT_AREA);
      NAME(FILL_ARRAY) = INPUT_NAME;
      GPA(FILL_ARRAY)  = INPUT_GPA;
   END;
   HONOR_COUNT = 0;
   DO TEST = 1 TO 35;
      IF GPA(TEST) >= 92.50 THEN
         DO;
            HONOR_STUDENTS(HONOR_COUNT) = NAME(TEST);
            HONOR_COUNT = HONOR_COUNT + 1;
         END;
   END;
   DO PRINT_OUT = 1 TO HONOR_COUNT;
      PRINT_NAME = HONOR_STUDENTS (PRINT_OUT);
      WRITE FILE (HONORS) FROM(PRINT_NAME);
   END;
 END GPA;
```

FIGURE 8.13   Sample program to manipulate arrays in a structure.

## The LIKE Attribute

The LIKE attribute is used to indicate that the name being declared is to be given the same structuring as the major structure or minor structure name following the attribute LIKE.   For example:

```
DCL 1 BUDGET,
        2 RENT                FIXED DEC(5,2),
        2 FOOD,
          3 MEAT              FIXED DEC(5,2),
          3 DAIRY             FIXED DEC(4,2),
          3 PRODUCE           FIXED DEC(5,2),
        2 TRANSPORTATION      FIXED DEC(7,2),
        2 ENTERTAINMENT       FIXED DEC(5,2);
DCL 1 COST_OF_LIVING          LIKE BUDGET;
```

This declaration for COST_OF_LIVING is the same as if it had been declared:

```
DCL 1 COST_OF_LIVING,
        2 RENT                FIXED DEC(5,2),
        2 FOOD,
          3 MEAT              FIXED DEC(5,2),
          3 DAIRY             FIXED DEC(4,2),
          3 PRODUCE           FIXED DEC(5,2),
        2 TRANSPORTATION      FIXED DEC(7,2),
        2 ENTERTAINMENT       FIXED DEC(5,2);
```

The LIKE attribute copies structuring, names, and attributes of the structure below the level of the specified name only.   No dimensionality of the specified name is copied.   For example, if BUDGET were declared as 1 BUDGET (12), the declaration of COST_OF_LIVING LIKE BUDGET would not give the dimension attribute to COST_OF_LIVING.   To achieve dimensionality of COST_OF_LIVING, the declaration would have to be DECLARE 1 COST_OF_LIVING (12) LIKE BUDGET.

A minor structure name can be declared LIKE a major structure or LIKE another minor structure.   A major structure name can be declared LIKE a minor structure or LIKE another major structure.   However, in a structured programming environment, it is recommended that these facilities be used sparingly in an effort to maintain program readability and ease of modification.

## Structure Assignment: Structure-to-Structure

Structures may be moved (that is, assigned) to other structures or parts of structures.   The structure name to the right of the assignment symbol must have the same relative structuring as the structure name to the left.   Relative structuring means that the structures must have the same minor structuring, the same number of elementary items within each minor and/or major structure, and, if arrays are contained in structures, the same values for bounds. You may assign major structures to major structures, minor structures to major structures, and vice versa, as long as the relative structuring is the same. For example:

```
DCL 1 INPUT_REC,
        2 KEY_FIELD      CHAR(10),
        2 OTHER          CHAR(70);
DCL 1 DISK_REC,
        2 DELETE_FLAG    CHAR(1),
        2 DISK_MASTER,
          3 KEY          CHAR(10),
          3 OTHER        CHAR(70);
DISK_MASTER = INPUT_REC; /* STRUCTURE ASSIGNMENT */
```

In the previous example, the major structure INPUT_REC is assigned to the minor structure DISK_MASTER. After the assignment, KEY will contain the value in KEY_FIELD, and DISK_MASTER.OTHER will contain the value in INPUT_REC.OTHER. As you can see from this example, the level numbers need not be identical when a structure or part of a structure is being assigned to another structure. The important thing is to have the same number of elementary items contained within each structure or minor structure name as well as the same relative structuring.

The attributes of the corresponding elementary items in the structure assignments do not have to be the same. If the elementary items have different attributes, the variables will be converted according to the arithmetic rules explained in the previous chapters. Let us look at an example in which conversions would take place when structure AA is assigned to structure A.

```
DCL 1 A,
        2 B     FIXED DEC(5),
        2 C     FIXED BIN(31),
        2 D     CHAR(20),
        2 E     FIXED BIN(15),
        2 F     FLOAT DEC(5);
DCL 1 AA,
        2 BB    FIXED BIN(15),
        2 CC    FIXED DEC(5),
        2 DD    CHAR(10),
        2 EE    FIXED DEC(4),
        2 FF    FIXED DEC(6);
A = AA;        /* STRUCTURE ASSIGNMENT */
```

There are a number of things to observe in the above example:

**1.** In a structure move, elementary items are moved to the corresponding elementary items. In other words, the first item in AA is assigned to the first item in A, the second item in AA is assigned to the second item in A, etc.

**2.** When the elementary items of one structure are moved to their corresponding variables in another structure through a structure assignment statement, arithmetic conversion occurs, if necessary. In the above example, FF is a FIXED DECIMAL value that will be converted to FLOAT DECIMAL when it is assigned to F.

**3.** The receiving field does not have to be the same length as the sending field: D in structure A is 20 characters long; DD is only 10 characters long. When DD is assigned to D, it will be placed in the 10 leftmost positions of D, and then D will be padded on the right with blanks. Of course, care must be taken not to assign a longer arithmetic field to a shorter field, for you will lose significance in your resulting value or cause the SIZE condition to be raised if it has been enabled. And you may not specify illegal combinations. For example, a variable whose attribute is CHARACTER and contains characters other than 0 or 1 may not be assigned to a variable whose attribute is BIT.

**4.** When the structure assignment statement

    A = AA;

is given, in essence, five assignment statements are generated:

    B = BB;
    C = CC;
    D = DD;
    E = EE;
    F = FF;

## Structure Assignment BY NAME

One exception to the rule that structures assigned to other structures must have the same relative structuring is the case in which the structure expression appears in an assignment statement with the BY NAME option. For example, consider the following INPUT and OUTPUT structures:

```
DCL 1 INPUT,
        2 EMP_NAME          CHAR(20),
        2 EMP_NUMBER        CHAR(6),
        2 HOURS,
            3 REGULAR       PIC '99',
            3 OVERTIME      PIC '99',
        2 GROSS_PAY         PIC '999V99';
DCL 1 OUTPUT,
        2 CARRIAGE_CNTL     CHAR(1),
        2 EMP_NUMBER        CHAR(12),
        2 EMP_NAME          CHAR(25),
        2 GROSS_PAY         PIC '$999V.99';
```

To move those elements of INPUT whose names are identical to elements of OUTPUT, simply write

    OUTPUT = INPUT, BY NAME;

The BY NAME option may only appear in an assignment statement, and it must always be preceded by a comma. If structures contain minor structure names, then these names must also be identical for the matching elementary names to be moved. For example:

    DCL 1 FIRST,
            2 MINOR_1,
              3 A,
              3 B,
            2 C,
            2 D;
    DCL 1 SECOND,
            2 MINOR_2,
              3 A,
              3 B,
            2 C,
            2 D;
    FIRST = SECOND, BY NAME;

Elementary items C and D will be moved. Elementary items A and B will not be assigned because they appear in minor structures whose names are different.

## Structure Assignment: Scalar-to-Structure

A *scalar* is simply a single data element, and it is sometimes called an elementary item. You may assign a scalar to a structure. For example:

    DCL 1 CUSTOMER,
            2 NAME          CHAR(20),
            2 ADDRESS,
              3 STREET      CHAR(25),
              3 CITY_STATE  CHAR(25),
              3 ZIP_CODE    CHAR(5),
            2 ACCOUNT#      CHAR(7);
    CUSTOMER = ' '; /* CLEAR STRUCTURE TO BLANKS */

The blank character constant is a scalar. Because we are assigning character-to-character, the assignment is valid. Five assignment statements are effectively generated from the statement

    CUSTOMER = ' ';

The five statements are

```
NAME        = ' ';
STREET      = ' ';
CITY_STATE  = ' ';
ZIP_CODE    = ' ';
ACCOUNT#    = ' ';
```

Recall that when a smaller field, in this case a single blank, is assigned to a larger character field, there is padding on the right of the larger field with blanks.

## Overlay Defining: Scalar Variable on a Structure

There is actually a more efficient way to clear the CUSTOMER structure and that is through the use of the DEFINED attribute. The DEFINED attribute allows us to refer to the same area of storage by different names, and perhaps different attributes. Assume the following statement is added to the structure example above:

```
DCL CUST CHAR(82) DEFINED CUSTOMER;
```

If you will count the character lengths of each elementary item in the CUS-TOMER structure, you will find there is a total of 82 characters. Therefore, a character-string called CUST with a length attribute of 82 was overlay defined on the CUSTOMER structure, setting aside one area of storage, but providing two ways of looking at it: first, as a structure, and second, as a *single* character-string. When the statement

```
CUST = ' ';
```

is given, only *one* assignment statement is generated: moving a blank to the first position of CUST and then padding on the right with 81 more blanks. Thus, through the technique of overlay defining a scalar variable on the structure, we were able to save four assignment statements from being generated for clearing our structure to blanks. At the same time, program readability is maintained.

## Overlay Defining: A Structure on a Structure

It is also possible to overlay define a major structure on a major structure. The need for overlay defining one structure on another arises when you are working with two or more different input data formats for records being read from the same device. For example, assume a program is to process data containing either information on items *received* into a company's inventory or items *issued* from inventory. The records are formatted as follows:

```
                          1 1 1 1 1 1 1 1 1 1 2      Record
        1 2 3 4 5 6 7 8 9 0 1 2 3 4 5 6 7 8 9 0 ←── Positions
```

| ISSUES record format | 1 | QTY | JOB NO | PART NO | DEPT | |

```
                          1 1 1 1 1 1 1 1 1 1 2
        1 2 3 4 5 6 7 8 9 0 1 2 3 4 5 6 7 8 9 0
```

| RECEIPTS record format | 2 | QTY | PART NO | SUPPLIER | |

The records have been sorted into sequence by part number. However, the program can only differentiate between issues and receipts by the "transaction code" keyed into position one of each record: a 1 represents an issue and a 2 a receipt. The structures, which are overlay defined, and the READ statement follow:

```
DCL 1 ISSUES,
        2 CODE               CHAR(1),
        2 QTY                PIC '9999',
        2 JOB_NO             CHAR(4),
        2 PART_NO            CHAR(7),
        2 DEPT               CHAR(3),
        2 REST_OF_RECORD     CHAR(61);
DCL 1 RECEIPTS             DEFINED ISSUES,
        2 CODE               CHAR(1),
        2 QTY                PIC '9999',
        2 PART_NO            CHAR(7),
        2 SUPPLIER           CHAR(6);

READ FILE (INPUT) INTO (ISSUES);
SELECT (ISSUES.CODE);
    WHEN('1') CALL PROCESS_ISSUES;
    WHEN('2') CALL PROCESS_RECEIPTS;
    OTHERWISE CALL ERROR;
END;
```

Note that the overlay defined structure (RECEIPTS) did not have to define an area as large as the base identifier. However, it must *never* define an area larger than the base identifier.

Notice how the SELECT statement tests position one of the input record for the transaction code. If the code is a 1, then a CALL is made to the routine in our program that processes the issues. If the code in position one is not a 1, we might logically assume that it must be a 2 and that the program will CALL PROCESS_RECEIPTS. It is good programming practice, however, to test for the code, because there might be a data-entry error.

You may code an overlay define at the major structure, minor structure, or elementary item level. Record I/O may be performed from either the base identifier or the overlay-defined identifier.

### Structures in Stream I/O

Names of structures may also be specified in edit-directed and list-directed I/O statements. The names may be major level or intermediate level structure names. Of course, elementary names in a structure may also be specified. Here is an example of specifying a major structure name in a GET EDIT:

```
DCL 1 INVENTORY,
        2 PART_NUMBER    CHAR(6),
        2 QTY_ON_HAND    FIXED DEC(5),
        2 PRICE          FIXED DEC(5,2);
GET EDIT(INVENTORY) (A(6),F(5),F(5,2));
```

Notice that three format items were specified. You must specify as many format items as elementary data items. Of course, if there are not as many format items as elementary items in the structure specified in the data list, then there is a return to the beginning of the format list and the format items are used again in describing the remaining elements of the structure.

Here is an example of specifying a minor structure name in a PUT EDIT statement:

```
DCL 1 INVENTORY,
        2 PART#,
          3 TYPE         CHAR(2),
          3 CODE         CHAR(3),
        2 REORDER_QTY   PIC '(4)9';
PUT EDIT(PART#,REORDER_QTY) (A(2),A(3),F(9));
```

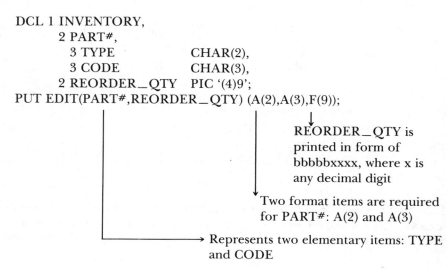

REORDER_QTY is printed in form of bbbbbxxxx, where x is any decimal digit

Two format items are required for PART#: A(2) and A(3)

Represents two elementary items: TYPE and CODE

The above PUT statement is equivalent to:

    PUT EDIT(TYPE,CODE,REORDER_QTY) (A(2),A(3),F(9));

Notice how the format specification for REORDER_QTY has a *width* larger than the internal specification. The precision of REORDER_QTY is 4. The F (9) specification will cause the four decimal digits to be printed right-justified in the output field; to the left of the value will be five blanks. Thus, spacing between the PART# and REORDER_QTY is achieved.

If a data list element is a structure variable, the elements of the structure are transmitted in the order specified in the structure declaration. For example, if a declaration is

    DCL 1 A,
          2 B(10),
          2 C(10);

then the statement

    PUT EDIT(A) (F(12));

would result in the output being ordered as follows:

    A.B(1) A.B(2) A.B(3) . . . A.B(10) A.C(1) A.C(2) A.C(3) . . . A.C(10)

In the case of data-directed input, if the data list includes the names of structure elements, then *fully* qualified names must appear in the stream, although full qualification is not required in the data list. Consider the following structures:

    DCL 1 INPUT,
          2 PARTNO        CHAR(6),
          2 DESCRIPTION   CHAR(20),
          2 PRICE,
            3 RETAIL      FIXED DEC(7,2),
            3 WHOLESALE   FIXED DEC(7,2);

If it is desired to read a value for INPUT. PRICE. RETAIL, the data specification could be

    GET DATA(INPUT.RETAIL);

but the input data stream must have the following form:

    INPUT.PRICE.RETAIL = 4.75;

The maximum number of elements permitted in a list for data-directed input is 320. Each elementary item of a structure counts as a separate list element.

**15.** What will YY, MM, and DD contain after the DATE function is invoked assuming the date is July 7, 1977? (Be careful, this is a "trick" question.)

```
DCL DATE          BUILTIN;
DCL 1 TODAY,
        2 YY      CHAR(2),
        2 MM      CHAR(2),
        2 DD      CHAR(2);
    TODAY = DATE;
```

**16.** Write the structure given in question 15 above, but *factor* the attributes.

**17.** When may elementary items in a structure not be initialized using the INITIAL attribute?

**18.** Which of the following is a valid qualified name?

(a)   HOURS_REGULAR
(b)   HOURS-REGULAR
(c)   HOURS.REGULAR
(d)   HOURS REGULAR

**19.** What is the purpose of the LIKE attribute?

**20.** Is this a valid example of a structure move? Why or why not?

```
DCL 1 CAT,
        2 A,
          3 B,
          3 C,
        2 D;
DCL 1 DOG,
        2 A,
        2 B,
        2 C,
        2 D;
    DOG = CAT;
```

**21.** Under what circumstances may a structure be assigned to another structure that does not have the same relative structuring?

**22.** Write the most efficient coding to clear the following structure to blanks (spaces).

```
DCL 1 A,
       2 B     CHAR(20),
       2 C     CHAR(10),
       2 D,
         3 E   CHAR(5),
         3 F   CHAR(7);
```

**23.** Why would one structure be overlay defined on another structure?

In record I/O, you must be particularly careful to describe data in exactly the same form that they appear on an external device. For example, assume that a magnetic tape file contains records in the following form:

```
DCL 1 RECORD,
       2 A         FIXED DEC(7,2),
       2 B         FIXED DEC(7,2);
```

Notice that the fields are stored in the internal coded form packed decimal. The numbers each occupy four bytes of external storage. When reading this record into main storage using record I/O, we merely state to PL/I where we want the record placed. For example:

READ FILE (TAPE) INTO (RECORD);

We must ensure that there is enough main storage starting at that location to contain the record and, most importantly, that the attributes of the data items located where the record is to be placed match exactly the attributes of the data in the record. In the example, both numbers are in the internal coded form of FIXED DECIMAL (7,2) and could be pictured as follows:

| First number | | | | Second number | | | |
|---|---|---|---|---|---|---|---|
| 1  3 | 4  2 | 7  3 | 3  + | 3  2 | 5  7 | 2  4 | 9  − |

Assume, now that A and B are declared (erroneously) FIXED DECIMAL (9,2);

```
DCL 1 RECORD,
       2 A         FIXED DEC(9,2),
       2 B         FIXED DEC(9,2);
```

Here an extra byte of storage would be reserved for each variable. When the record previously illustrated (items A and B with the FIXED (7,2) attributes) is read into the contiguous space provided by the second and erroneous declaration of RECORD, two problems are present:

**1.** The signs of the data will not be in the low-order positions of A and B.

**2.** The values of each field will not be as initially intended (i.e., 13427.33 and −32572.49).

When A and B are declared as FIXED (9,2), their fields may be pictured as follows where the lowercase d represents a digit position and the S the sign of the value:

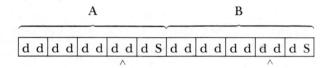

If we read the numeric values shown earlier, fields A and B would contain the following information:

A                    B
| 1 | 3 | 4 | 2 | 7 | 3 | 3 | + | 3 | 2 | 5 | 7 | 2 | 4 | 9 | − | G | G | G | G |

The capital G in the picture represents *garbage* — unusable data. But that is not the only problem we face due to our mistake. Notice the value in the sign position of the variable A. It is a digit 2, the second digit of the second number we had stored in our file. The 2 is an invalid sign. Should we ever attempt to use this data item in our program, we will encounter an error condition. Record I/O did not check the values it was placing in the variables A and B for validity, nor did it convert any data from one type to another. It simply placed the record in main storage as is.

The problem just described is a very difficult one to debug. The CONVERSION error will be raised if field A or B is used in a computation. You may be tempted to think that the problem lies with the data in the file rather than with your own program. Being aware of this type of problem brings you one step closer to avoiding its occurrence. A feature of the PL/I compiler that will assist you in checking your structures for accurateness is the *aggregate length table*.

The information printed includes a list of all elementary item names in your structures along with the length of each of those items. The total length of each structure is also computed and printed out. Computing structure length for the purpose of selecting the proper record size (for the RECSIZE option of the

DECLARE) is often a place where a programmer can easily "miscount." The aggregate length table is an easy way to verify that you have, in fact, calculated the record length as you intended. This table printout from the compiler may be obtained by the PROCESS statement option, AGGREGATE. For example, the statement requests three of the most useful compiler output options — an attribute listing combined with a cross-reference listing and an aggregate length table listing. Note that the aggregate length list also includes number of dimensions and total length of arrays (See Figure 8.17).

## CASE STUDY

This case study implements a great deal of the technical information presented in this chapter. Record I/O is used to generate a printed report. Structures containing the PICTURE attribute are used to format this report. In commercial applications, the techniques depicted here are those typically used.

Assume that a college bookstore has ordered a number of books for the coming school year. In some instances, however, some, or all, of the books ordered are not currently on hand in the publisher's warehouse. In this situation, if the order can be partially filled, it will be, leaving a smaller number of books in a back-order situation. Otherwise, the publisher notifies the bookstore that the entire order is now back-ordered. The bookstore keeps a record of orders by entering a record for each title ordered noting any back-order situations.

This case study centers around writing a program that generates a book-status report showing, among other things, the amount due for books delivered and the number of books that are back ordered. The layout of the report is

| | BOOK STATUS REPORT | | PAGE XXX |
|---|---|---|---|
| RUN DATE = XX/XX/XX | WEEK ENDING XX/XX/XX | | |
| CATALOG NO. | TITLE | BACK ORD | AMT DUE FOR BOOKS DELV'D |
| XXXXX | XXXXXXXXXXXXXXXXXXXX | XXXX | $  XX,XXX.XX |
| | FINAL TOTAL | | $XXX,XXX.XX |
| END OF JOB | | | |

Notice that each page in the printout is to contain a page number. From an inspection of the headings, you can see that there are two dates: the week-ending

| Positions | Description |
|-----------|-------------|
| 1–5 | Catalog number: a five-digit field |
| 6–9 | Author number: a four–character field |
| 10–13 | Quantity ordered: a four-digit field |
| 14–17 | Quantity delivered: a four-digit field |
| 18–23 | Unused at this time |
| 24–27 | Unit price: a four-digit field with an assumed decimal point between the second and third digits |
| 28–47 | Title: an alphameric description |
| 48–58 | Author: an alphameric description |
| 59–68 | Publisher: an alphameric description |
| 69–80 | Unused at this time |

FIGURE 8.14   Case study input format.

and the run date.   In status reports of this type, the report is typically run on a day of the week that is different from the ending period for which the printed results apply.   The run date for this report will be obtained by invoking the DATE built-in function.   The week-ending date is obtained by keying the appropriate date into a record that precedes the book order information.   This report concludes with a final total and the message END OF JOB.

The input data records are described in Figure 8.14.   There are eight items of data in each record, as well as the two unused fields (Positions 18–23 and 69–80).   The data items are described with the following DECLARE statement:

```
DCL 1 BOOK_STATUS_REC,
        2 CATALOG_NO        PIC '(5)9',
        2 AUTHOR_NO         CHAR(4),
        2 QTY_ORDERED       PIC '9999',
        2 QTY_DELIVERED     PIC '9999',
        2 UNUSED            CHAR(6),
        2 PRICE             PIC '99V99',
        2 TITLE             CHAR(20),
        2 AUTHOR_NAME       CHAR(11),
        2 PUBLISHER         CHAR(10),
        2 REST_OF_RECORD    CHAR(10);
```

Figure 8.15 shows the hierarchy chart for this program.   It consists of six segments.   The nucleus includes program looping in the reading of records.

There are four segments on the second level in the hierarchy chart that include the INITIALIZATION, HEADING_ROUTINE, PROCESS_DETAIL and TOTAL_ROUTINE.   These segments comprise the subfunctions of the pro-

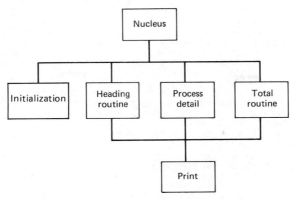

FIGURE 8.15   Book status report program hierarchy chart.

gram.  The INITIALIZATION procedure processes the date record that must be read to indicate the *week-ending* date and also invokes the DATE built-in function.

The HEADING_ROUTINE generates page headings and increments the PAGE_NO counter.  In this report, 45 detail lines will be printed per page.  In HEADING_ROUTINE, the LINE_COUNT identifier is set to 45.  Later in the program you will see that a *countdown* technique is being used.  In this text, counters have typically started at 1 and been incremented to the maximum.  The countdown technique is illustrated here simply to show you an alternative method.

The PROCESS_DETAIL segment, as its name implies, performs the required calculations, accumulates the final total, and calls the segment that handles the printing of a line.  This segment also calls the HEADING_ROUTINE every time 45 detail lines have been printed.  The TOTAL_ROUTINE causes the total line to be printed along with the end-of-job message.

Figure 8.16 shows the book-status report program.  Key program statements are explained as follows:

Statements 2–18: Figure 8.17 (page 1) provides all DECLARE statements needed for this program.  This program is larger than other case studies previously shown in this text.  As programs grow in size, comments may be needed to improve readability.  Notice how comment statements were used to identify logical groups of DECLARE statements.  Thus, we see the file declarations identified, as well as the record definitions, variables, etc.

In examining these statements, be sure to notice the attributes of the output areas as shown in Statement 7.  For example, the BACK identifier has the attribute:

PIC'(3)Z9(5)B'

This field is 9 positions in length: 3 Zs, a 9, and 5 Bs.  As you can see, this field has

```
      /* CHAPTER 8 CASE STUDY ---- CREATE A BOOK STATUS REPORT            */
      /*******************************************************************/
      /*    PROGRAM NAME:   BOOKSTAT                                       */
      /*    DESCRIPTION:    THIS PROGRAM READS THE BOOK STATUS INPUT FILE  */
      /*                    AND CALCULATES THE AMOUNT DUE FOR DELIVERED    */
      /*                    BOOKS, THE NUMBER OF BOOKS BACKORDERED AND THE */
      /*                    TOTAL AMOUNT DUE FOR ALL DELIVERED BOOKS.  EACH*/
      /*                    STATUS INPUT RECORD IS PRINTED ON THE REPORT.  */
      /*    INPUT:          BOOK  - BOOK STATUS RECORDS                    */
      /*    OUTPUT:         PRINTR - BOOK STATUS REPORT                    */
      /*******************************************************************/
   1  BOOKSTAT: PROC OPTIONS(MAIN);
      /*******************************************************************/
      /*   FILE DECLARATIONS                                              */
      /*******************************************************************/
   2  DCL BOOK   FILE INPUT  RECORD ENV( F BLKSIZE(80));
   3  DCL PRINTR FILE OUTPUT RECORD ENV(CTLASA F BLKSIZE(66));
      /*******************************************************************/
      /*   RECORD DEFINITIONS                                             */
      /*******************************************************************/
   4  DCL 1 BOOK_STATUS_REC,
            2 CATALOG_NO            PIC'(5)9',
            2 AUTHOR_NO             CHAR(4),
            2 QTY_ORDERED           PIC'9999',
            2 QTY_DELIVERED         PIC'9999',
            2 UNUSED                CHAR(6),
            2 PRICE                 PIC'99V99',
            2 TITLE                 CHAR(20),
            2 AUTHOR_NAME           CHAR(11),
            2 PUBLISHER             CHAR(10),
            2 REST_OF_RECORD        CHAR(12);
   5  DCL 1 DATE_REC                DEF BOOK_STATUS_REC,
            2 FIRST_6_POS           CHAR(6),
            2 REST_OF_DATE          CHAR(74);
   6  DCL PRINT_AREA                CHAR(66);
   7  DCL 1 DETAIL_AREA             DEF PRINT_AREA,
            2 CARRIAGE_CONTROL      CHAR(5),
            2 CATALOG_NO            PIC'(5)9(9)B',
            2 TITLE                 CHAR(27),
            2 BACK                  PIC'(3)Z9(5)B',
            2 PRINT_AMT             PIC'$$,$$$V.99BB';
   8  DCL 1 TOTAL_OUTPUT_AREA       DEF PRINT_AREA,
            2 CLEAR_AREA            CHAR(55),
            2 PRINT_TOTAL_AMT       PIC'$$,$$$V.99BB';

      /*******************************************************************/
      /*   CONSTANTS AND VARIABLES                                        */
      /*******************************************************************/
   9  DCL AMT                       FIXED(7,2);
  10  DCL DIGITS                    CHAR(10)            INIT('0123456789');
  11  DCL INPUT_DATE                PIC'Z9/99/99';
  12  DCL LINE_COUNT                FIXED(3);
  13  DCL MORE_BOOKS                BIT(1)              INIT ('1'B);
  14  DCL NO                        BIT(1)              INIT ('0'B);
  15  DCL PAGE_NO                   PIC'ZZ9';
  16  DCL RUN_DATE                  CHAR(8);
  17  DCL TOTAL_AMT                 FIXED(9,2);
  18  DCL (DATE,TRANSLATE,VERIFY)   BUILTIN;

  19  ON ENDFILE(BOOK)
         MORE_BOOKS = NO;
      /*******************************************************************/
      /*   NUCLEUS                                                        */
      /*******************************************************************/
  20  READ FILE(BOOK)INTO(BOOK_STATUS_REC);
  21  CALL INITIALIZATION;
  22  CALL HEADING_ROUTINE;
  23  READ FILE(BOOK)INTO(BOOK_STATUS_REC);
  24  DO WHILE(MORE_BOOKS);
  25     CALL PROCESS_DETAIL;
  26     READ FILE(BOOK)INTO(BOOK_STATUS_REC);
  27  END;
  28  CALL TOTAL_ROUTINE;
```

FIGURE 8.16   (page 1)

```
     /******************************************************************/
     /* HEADING ROUTINE                                                */
     /******************************************************************/
29   HEADING_ROUTINE:   PROC;
30      LINE_COUNT         = 45;
31      PRINT_AREA = '1' || (24)' ' || 'BOOK STATUS REPORT' || (15) ' '
               || 'PAGE ' || PAGE_NO;
32      CALL PRINT;
33      PRINT_AREA = 'O' || (23)' ' || 'WEEK ENDING ' || INPUT_DATE;
34      CALL PRINT;
35      PRINT_AREA = ' RUN DATE = ' || RUN_DATE;
36      CALL PRINT;
37      PRINT_AREA = '- CATALOG NO.' || (10)' ' || 'TITLE' ||(16)' '
               || 'BACK ORD   AMT DUE FOR';
38      CALL PRINT;
39      PRINT_AREA = (54)' '|| 'BOOKS DELV''D';
40      CALL PRINT;
41      PRINT_AREA = ' ';
42      CALL PRINT;
43      PAGE_NO            = PAGE_NO + 1;
44      CARRIAGE_CONTROL = ' ';
45   END HEADING_ROUTINE;
     /******************************************************************/
     /* INITIALIZATION                                                 */
     /******************************************************************/
46   INITIALIZATION: PROC;
47      PAGE_NO     = 1;
48      TOTAL_AMT   = O;
49      LINE_COUNT = 55;
50      IF VERIFY(FIRST_6_POS,DIGITS) = O & REST_OF_DATE = ' ' THEN
            DO;
51              INPUT_DATE = FIRST_6_POS;
52              RUN_DATE   = TRANSLATE('MO/DA/YR',DATE,'YRMODA');
53          END;
54      ELSE
            DO;
55              PRINT_AREA = 'FIRST RECORD IS NOT A PROPER DATE RECORD';
56              CALL PRINT;
57              EXIT;
58          END;
59   END INITIALIZATION;
     /******************************************************************/
     /* PRINT ROUTINE                                                  */
     /******************************************************************/
60   PRINT:   PROC;
61      WRITE FILE(PRINTR)FROM(PRINT_AREA);
62      LINE_COUNT = LINE_COUNT - 1;
63   END PRINT;

     /******************************************************************/
     /* THIS ROUTINE CALCULATES THE BACK ORDERED QUANTITY, THE AMOUNT DUE */
     /* FOR BOOKS DELIVERED AND KEEPS A RUNNING BALANCE OF THE TOTAL    */
     /* AMOUNT DUE FOR BOOKS DELIVERED.                                */
     /******************************************************************/
64   PROCESS_DETAIL:   PROC;
65      BACK        = QTY_ORDERED - QTY_DELIVERED;
66      AMT         = PRICE * QTY_DELIVERED;
67      PRINT_AMT   = AMT;
68      TOTAL_AMT   = TOTAL_AMT + AMT;
69      DETAIL_AREA = BOOK_STATUS_REC, BY NAME;
70      IF LINE_COUNT <= O THEN
            CALL HEADING_ROUTINE;
71      CALL PRINT;
72   END PROCESS_DETAIL;
     /******************************************************************/
     /* TOTAL ROUTINE                                                  */
     /******************************************************************/
73   TOTAL_ROUTINE:   PROC;
74      CLEAR_AREA = '-' || (21)' ' || 'FINAL TOTAL';
75      PRINT_TOTAL_AMT = TOTAL_AMT;
76      CALL PRINT;
77      PRINT_AREA = 'OEND OF JOB';
78      CALL PRINT;
79   END TOTAL_ROUTINE;
80   END BOOKSTAT;
```

FIGURE 8.16    (page 2)

AGGREGATE LENGTH TABLE

| DCL NO. | IDENTIFIER | LVL | DIMS | OFFSET | ELEMENT LENGTH. | TOTAL LENGTH. |
|---------|-----------|-----|------|--------|-----------------|---------------|
| 4 | BOOK_STATUS_REC | 1 | | | 80 | 80 |
| | CATALOG_NO | 2 | | | 5 | |
| | AUTHOR_NO | 2 | | 5 | 4 | |
| | QTY_ORDERED | 2 | | 9 | 4 | |
| | QTY_DELIVERED | 2 | | 13 | 4 | |
| | UNUSED | 2 | | 17 | 6 | |
| | PRICE | 2 | | 23 | 4 | |
| | TITLE | 2 | | 27 | 20 | |
| | AUTHOR_NAME | 2 | | 47 | 11 | |
| | PUBLISHER | 2 | | 58 | 10 | |
| | REST_OF_RECORD | 2 | | 68 | 12 | |
| 5 | DATE_REC | 1 | | | DEF | DEF |
| | FIRST_6_POS | 2 | | | DEF | |
| | REST_OF_DATE | 2 | | 6 | DEF | |
| 7 | DETAIL_AREA | 1 | | | DEF | DEF |
| | CARRIAGE_CONTROL | 2 | | | DEF | |
| | CATALOG_NO | 2 | | 5 | DEF | |
| | TITLE | 2 | | 19 | DEF | |
| | BACK | 2 | | 46 | DEF | |
| | PRINT_AMT | 2 | | 55 | DEF | |
| 8 | TOTAL_OUTPUT_AREA | 1 | | | DEF | DEF |
| | CLEAR_AREA | 2 | | | DEF | |
| | PRINT_TOTAL_AMT | 2 | | 55 | DEF | |

SUM OF CONSTANT LENGTHS     80

FIGURE 8.17

zero suppression and trailing blanks specified.  If a value of 23, for example, is assigned to this picture, the resulting character-string would be

bb23bbbbb

where b indicates a blank.

**Statement 20:** The first record in the file should be the *week-ending* date record.  This statement reads that record.

**Statements 21–22:** INITIALIZATION is invoked followed by the HEADING_ROUTINE for the first page of output.

**Statements 24–27:** The basic loop operation of reading and processing records is specified.

**Statement 28:**  The TOTAL_ROUTINE is invoked to print totals and end-of-job message.

**Statements 29–45:** This HEADING_ROUTINE is fairly straightforward in that it simply assigns character-string constants to PRINT_AREA.  These character-string constants include the concatenation of blanks and carriage control characters where necessary.  Look at Statement 37.  Another way in which this heading line could be declared and initialized is to use a structure:

```
DCL 1 HEADING _ 1,
      2 CARRIAGE _ CONTROL  CHAR(2)    INIT('-'),
      2 COL _ 1              CHAR(21)   INIT('CATALOG NO.'),
      2 COL _ 2              CHAR(21)   INIT('TITLE'),
      2 COL _ 3              CHAR(11)   INIT('BACK ORD'),
      2 COL _ 4              CHAR(11)   INIT('AMT DUE FOR');
```

Notice how fields larger than the character-string constants were defined. Assigning a smaller character-string to a larger character-string field causes padding of blanks on the right. In this way, spacing between the character constants is achieved. In Statement 30, the LINE _ COUNT variable is initialized to 45 because this is the number of detail lines we wish to print on each page. The PAGE _ NO counter is incremented by 1 for the next time the HEADING _ ROUTINE will be invoked.

**Statements 47 – 49:** The initialization steps of setting the page number reference to 1, and clearing the TOTAL _ AMT identifier to zero are specified.

**Statement 50:** The VERIFY built-in function is invoked to test for the presence of the week-ending date. It is assumed that a week-ending date is present if the first six positions of the input record contain digits and the rest of the record contains blanks.

**Statement 51:** If the first six positions of the record are digits, they are edited into the field called INPUT _ DATE. The PICTURE attribute associated with the INPUT _ DATE identifier is

PIC'Z9/99/99'

This causes slashes to be inserted between the month, day, and year specification. (Input record was in the form of MMDDYY.)

**Statements 54 – 57:** These statements will be executed if the first record in the input deck is not a date. Note that an error message is generated and an EXIT statement is provided. The EXIT statement differs from the RETURN statement in that EXIT is considered to be abnormal termination of the program, whereas RETURN results in a normal termination of the program. If a program terminates abnormally, some operating systems automatically terminate other job steps (if any) in a given run. If this is the case with the operating system you are using, then your programs must make the distinction between a normal and an abnormal end.

**Statements 60 – 63:** This is the print segment that consists of two executable statements. Although small, this segment is called from a number of points in the program.

**Statements 65 – 68:** The BACK _ ORDER _ AMOUNT is calculated as well as the amount due for books delivered. AMT is accumulated into TOTAL _ AMT.

**Statement 69:** The BOOK_STATUS_REC fields, whose elementary items may match those in the DETAIL_AREA structure, are correspondingly moved.

**Statement 70:** The line counter is tested for zero. If it is zero, it is time to start a new page of output.

**Statement 71:** The PRINT segment is called.

**Statements 73–80:** Inspect Statement 8 in this program. Notice how the TOTAL_OUTPUT_AREA is *overlay-defined* on the PRINT_AREA. Within the TOTAL_OUTPUT_AREA structure, we see two elementary items. Notice, then, in Statement 74 how the CLEAR_AREA item is initialized to the carriage control character '-' followed by blanks and the literal FINAL TOTAL. TOTAL_AMT is assigned to PRINT_TOTAL_AMT, causing editing to take place. This line is printed, followed by the END OF JOB message. Notice the 0 carriage control character preceding this message.

## SUMMARY

**Record I/O File Declaration:** A PL/I file is represented in the program by the file name that is declared to have the FILE and RECORD attributes. Through the use of this name data records stored on an external device such as a disk or tape are accessed. The ENVIRONMENT attribute of the DECLARE statement describes the physical environment of the file. To accomplish carriage control for record I/O, the keyword CTLASA (or CTL360) must be added to the ENVIRONMENT section of the file declaration to notify PL/I that these carriage control characters are being used in the program and that the I/O routines are to interpret the first character of each record to indicate the action we want performed.

**Record I/O Areas:** For text editor and printer record I/O operations, declare character-strings, major structures, or arrays. In record I/O, there is no conversion of the external characters to an internal format, or vice versa. Thus, when you issue a READ statement for character data or a WRITE statement for the line printer, the structures on which you are doing input or output would normally have either CHARACTER or PICTURE attributes. The I/O area must be equal to the length of the record declared in the ENVIRONMENT options list; for example,

    ENV (F BLKSIZE (80))
                  └─────────────────────→ I/O area must also be length 80

**Opening Record I/O Files:** Files must be opened before a READ or WRITE to these files is executed. A file is automatically opened the first time a READ or

WRITE to that file is issued. Opening files causes attributes to be merged, labels to be checked, and device readiness to be established.

**READ/WRITE Statements:** General syntax is:

WRITE FILE (file name) FROM (variable);
READ FILE (file name) INTO (variable);

> Must be an array or a structure name or an unsubscripted variable not contained in a structure; it cannot be a label variable

Following each READ, the system checks for an end-of-file condition and takes the action specified in the ON ENDFILE statement if the last record has been read.

When a WRITE statement is executed, a carriage control operation will take place first, if the CTLASA option is specified; then the data will be printed. The rules and syntax for the WRITE statement are the same as for the READ statement.

**Structures:** A structure is a collection of data items whose locations relative to each other are critical. Usually, the data items that appear in a structure have a logical relationship to each other. Structure names always have a level number of 1. Any number greater than 1 may be used for subdivisions of the structure. At the highest level is the major structure name, at an intermediate level are substructure names called minor structures, and at the lowest level are elementary items. The major structure name must be numbered 1. Each name at a deeper level is given a greater number to indicate the level depth. Level numbers must be followed by a blank.

**The INITIAL Attribute in Structures:** Elementary items in structures may be initialized using the INITIAL attribute, providing the structure is not overlay defined on another data item.

**Qualified Names:** A qualified name is a substructure or element name that is made unique by qualifying it with one or more names of a higher level. The individual names within a qualified name are connected by a period; for example, the qualified name HOURS.REGULAR refers to REGULAR in the substructure HOURS. Qualification need go only as far as necessary to make the name unique. Intermediate qualifying of names can be omitted (except in the case of data-directed input where the identifier names in the input stream must be fully qualified).

**Arrays in Structures:** An array may be thought of as a table of data elements. Structures may contain arrays; for example,

```
DCL 1 A,
      2 B(5),
      2 C(10);
```

Here, the A structure contains two arrays: the B array of five elements and the C array of ten elements.

**Arrays of Structures:** An array of structures is an array whose elements are structures having identical names, levels, and elements; for example:

```
DCL 1 A(10),
      2 B,
      2 C,
      2 D;
```

Here, there are ten A structures consisting of three elementary items: B, C, and D.

**The LIKE Attribute:** The LIKE attribute is used to indicate that the name being declared is to be given the same structuring as the major structure or minor structure name following the attribute LIKE.

**Structure Assignment:** There are several types of structure assignments:

**1. Structure-to-structure:** Structures may be moved (i.e., assigned) to other structures or parts of structures. The structure name to the right of the assignment symbol must have the same relative structuring as the structure name to the left. You may assign major structures to major structures, minor structures to major structures, and vice versa, as long as the relative structuring is the same.

**2. BY NAME:** One exception to the rule that structures assigned to other structures must have the same relative structuring is the case in which the structure expression appears in an assignment statement with the BY NAME option; for example:

```
OUTPUT = INPUT, BY NAME;
```

**3. Scalar-to-structure:** A scalar is simply a single data element. When a scalar is assigned to a structure, it results in being assigned to each elementary item of the structure.

**Overlay-Defining:** The DEFINED attribute is often useful in manipulating data in a structure. Two types of define overlays are possible:

**1. Scalar variable on a structure:** The DEFINED attribute allows us to refer to the same area of storage by different names.

**2. Structure on a structure:** Example:

```
DCL 1 A,
        2 B          CHAR(20),
        2 C          CHAR(40),
        2 D          CHAR(20);
DCL 1 AA     DEFINED A,
        2 B          CHAR(40),
        2 C          CHAR(40);
```

**The PICTURE Attribute:** This attribute provides a picture of the form we want the data in the variable with the PICTURE attribute to assume. There are a number of reasons for using PICTURE:

Character-String
- X     Position may contain any character
- A     Position may contain any alphabetic character or blank
- 9     Position may contain any decimal digit

Digit and point specifiers
- 9     Any decimal digit
- V     Assumed decimal point

Zero suppression characters
- Z     Digit or blank if leading zeros
- *     Digit or * if leading zeros

Static or drifting characters
(These are also zero suppression characters.)
- $     Digit, $, or blank
- S     Digit, ± sign, or blank
- +     Digit, +, or blank
- −     Digit, −, or blank

Insertion characters
- ,     If zero suppression and no preceding digit, a blank, an asterisk, or a drifting character appears; otherwise the character (in this case, comma) appears.
- .     Decimal point (same criteria as comma)
- /     Slash (same criteria as comma)
- B     Blank

Credit and debit
- CR     CR if field < 0
- DB     DB if field < 0

FIGURE 8.18   Picture specification characters.

1. To edit data.
2. To validate data.
3. To treat arithmetic quantities as character-strings.
4. To treat character-strings as arithmetic quantities.

The table on page 385 shows the picture specification characters covered in this chapter.

**Decimal Picture:** This type of picture specifies the form that an arithmetic value is to assume. The base and scale are implicitly DECIMAL and FIXED, respectively. The precision is determined by the number of 9s and Zs in the picture and the location of the V picture character.

**Decimal Picture Specification Characters:** The basic picture specification characters include 9, V, S, $+$, $-$.

**Arithmetic Operations on Decimal Picture Data:** In order for an arithmetic operation on decimal picture data to take place, the data must be converted to the coded arithmetic form FIXED DECIMAL.

**Editing Data for Printed Output:** Output data items use the PICTURE attribute and usually receive their values via an assignment statement. Values developed during a program's execution use the coded arithmetic data type. When final results are obtained, the values are assigned to PICTURE data variables for printing.

**Character-String Picture:** The characters that make up this type of picture are A, X, and 9. The data item declared with the character-string picture does not have the arithmetic attributes of base, scale, and precision, but does have the character-string length attribute.

## CHAPTER 9

# Storage Classes and List Processing

This chapter covers a somewhat advanced but most interesting part of programming: **list processing.** First, the four PL/I storage classes (AUTOMATIC, STATIC, BASED, and CONTROLLED) that facilitate the processing of various types of *lists* are presented followed by list processing concepts and programming techniques.

## STORAGE CLASSES

Data names (i.e., variables) actually represent locations in main storage where the data items are recorded. When a location in main storage has been associated with a data name, the storage is said to be *allocated.* In PL/I, we have the facility to allocate main storage at different times. The time at which storage is to be allocated depends on the *storage class* of the data.

### Automatic Storage

Unless declared to have another storage class, most variables will have the AUTO-MATIC attribute. As an illustration of what this attribute means in a PL/I program, three procedures are shown in Figure 9.1.

P1 and P2 are internal procedures; that is, they are nested within the MAIN procedure.

Data names, such as STRUCTURE, TABLE, and LIST in the example, actually represent locations in main storage where the data items are recorded. When a

```
MAIN:        PROC OPTIONS (MAIN);
             DCL 1 STRUCTURE,
                 2 (A, B, C)   FIXED (5,2),
                 2 D   FIXED (5);
             •
             •
             •
             DO WHILE (MORE_DATA);
                 CALL P1;
                 CALL P2;
             END;
             •
             •
             •

P1:          PROC;
             DCL TABLE (100)   CHAR (10);
             •
             •
             •
             END P1;

P2:          PROC;
             DCL LIST (500)   FIXED;
             •
             •
             •
             END P2;

             END MAIN;
```

FIGURE 9.1    A main program with two internal procedures.

location in main storage has been associated with a data name, the storage is said to be **allocated.** The fact that certain variables, such as TABLE, are used in one procedure of a program and not in others makes it possible to allocate the same storage space at different times to different variables.

For example, P1 manipulates the data in TABLE. When P1 is finished and P2 begins execution, it is possible (and desirable from a main storage utilization standpoint) to allocate LIST to the storage area previously occupied by TABLE. If the value of TABLE is not needed when the procedure is invoked again, there is no need to keep the space reserved after execution of the procedure is completed. The storage area can be freed and then used for other purposes. Such use of main storage is called **dynamic storage** *allocation.*

When storage is allocated dynamically, it is allocated during the execution of a procedure. Storage remains allocated as long as the procedure in which it was allocated remains active. To illustrate this concept, when the MAIN procedure in Figure 9.1 is activated (i.e., "called by the operating system"), the storage for

STRUCTURE will be allocated, giving the following main storage conceptual configuration:

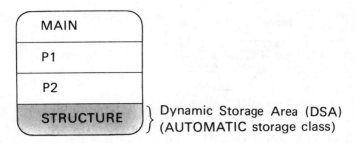

Even though P1 and P2 are nested within MAIN, these blocks of coding will be extracted by the compiler and placed below the coding for the MAIN procedure. Following the PL/I procedure blocks will be the dynamic storage area, often referred to as the DSA.

To see how more dynamic storage (that is, AUTOMATIC storage in this example) is allocated, assume the MAIN procedure calls P1. MAIN remains an active procedure; hence, storage for STRUCTURE stays allocated. The only way in which MAIN may be deactivated is to terminate this procedure with a STOP, END, EXIT, or RETURN.

When P1 is activated (e.g., by a CALL), storage is allocated for the data area called TABLE. The program in main storage now has this configuration:

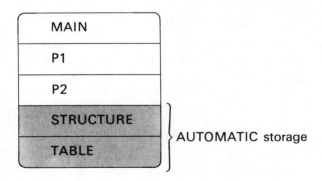

In some operating systems, AUTOMATIC storage may not be contiguous to the program area. What is being illustrated here is a *concept* of the dynamic allocation of storage. Its actual position in main storage is not usually important to the programmer.

When P1 is terminated, it is "deactivated"; hence, storage for TABLE is released to give the following configuration:

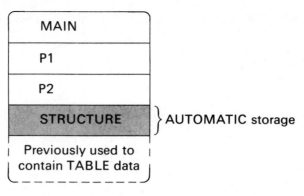

AUTOMATIC storage

Next, the MAIN procedure calls P2. The activation of P2 causes storage to be allocated for the data area called LIST shown previously in Figure 9.1. Main storage would now look like this:

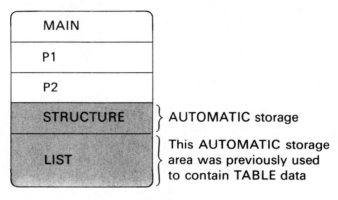

AUTOMATIC storage

This AUTOMATIC storage area was previously used to contain TABLE data

This example illustrates an important point: When a procedure (such as P1) is activated and deactivated, the contents of its data areas may be lost. Thus, if P1 is called a second time from MAIN, data recorded in TABLE the first time P1 was executed will not be there the second time. As illustrated before, this is because an intervening procedure, P2, was executed, and its data area (LIST) was allocated to the area where TABLE once resided. The dynamic allocation of storage applies to *begin* blocks as well as procedure blocks.

This dynamic allocation of main storage is one of the outstanding features of PL/I, because it provides for efficient use of main storage. Total storage requirements of a program may be reduced because of this automatic data overlay feature. The programmer does not have to code extra instructions or steps to cause this allocation to take place. It is done *automatically*. All the programmer needs to do is be aware of how and when storage is allocated. Most variables that have not been explicitly declared with a storage class attribute usually have the AUTOMATIC attribute. The attribute listing provided by the PL/I compiler following the source listing includes the storage class attribute for each identifier. (See Chapter 3, page 127 for an example.)

**Prologue.** The allocation of dynamic storage — that is, for variables that have the AUTOMATIC attribute — is performed by a routine called a **prologue.** This routine is set up by the compiler and attached to the beginning of each block. It is always executed as the first step of a block. One of the prologue's functions is to allocate dynamic storage for AUTOMATIC variables declared within the block to which it is attached.

**Epilogue.** The release of main storage that has been allocated to AUTOMATIC variables is handled by a routine called an **epilogue.** In addition, it reestablishes the on-units to the status that existed before the block was activated. The epilogue routine is logically appended to the end of each block and is executed as the final step before the termination of the block. Prologues and epilogues are set up by the compiler, not the programmer.

### Static Storage

We saw earlier that if MAIN calls P1 and then P2, P1's data area (TABLE) was overlayed by P2's data area (LIST). In some cases, we may not want LIST to overlay TABLE. Whenever the value of a variable must be saved between different invocations of the same procedure, storage for that variable has to be allocated statically. In this case, storage is allocated before execution of the program and remains allocated throughout the entire execution of the program.

Data areas have the AUTOMATIC attribute by default. However, had the procedures declared STRUCTURE, TABLE, and LIST to have the STATIC attribute; for example,

```
DCL 1 STRUCTURE    STATIC,
        2 A        FIXED DEC (5,2),
        2 B        FIXED DEC (5,2),
        2 C        FIXED DEC (5,2),
        2 D        FIXED DEC (5);
    DCL TABLE (100)    CHAR(10) STATIC;
    DCL LIST (500)     STATIC FIXED DEC(5);
```

Then main storage would conceptually appear like this:

```
 _____
/  MAIN procedure                       |
|--------------------------------------|
|  P1 procedure                        |
|--------------------------------------|
|  P2 procedure                        |
|--------------------------------------|
|  STATIC storage                      |
|--------------------------------------|
|  AUTOMATIC storage                   |
\  (for miscellaneous variables)       |
 _____/
```

Thus, STATIC storage follows the procedures MAIN, P1 and P2, and is then followed by AUTOMATIC storage. Had MAIN, P1, and P2 each been a separately compiled procedure such as,

```
MAIN: PROC OPTIONS(MAIN);
      .
      .
      .
END MAIN;
P1: PROC;
      .
      .
      .
END P1;
P2: PROC;
      .
      .
      .
END P2;
```

then main storage would typically appear like this:

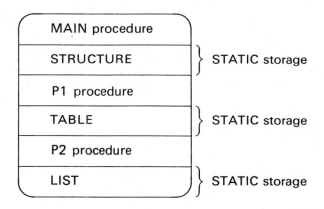

In this example, there is no AUTOMATIC storage. Typically, however, a program will have both STATIC and AUTOMATIC storage areas. Program constants and variables implicitly or explicitly declared with the EXTERNAL attribute have the STATIC storage class attribute. For example, file names default to the EXTERNAL storage class attribute. Thus, information related to the definition of a file will be placed in the STATIC storage area.

**Initializing STATIC versus AUTOMATIC Variables.** Variables, whether main storage space is allocated to them dynamically or statically, may be given **initial values** at the time of storage allocation. You can save program overhead by declaring main procedure variables that are to be initialized as having the STATIC attribute. For example:

```
DCL MORE_RECS   BIT(1) STATIC;
DCL NO          BIT(1) INIT ('0'B) STATIC;
DCL YES         BIT(1) INIT ('1'B) STATIC;
```

STATIC variables are initialized only once—before execution of a program begins. STATIC variables are established with their respective values at compile-time. AUTOMATIC variables are reinitialized at each activation of the block in which they are declared.

**1.** Distinguish between dynamic storage and static storage.

**2.** How is a *main* procedure block activated and deactivated? How is an internal or external (but not *main*) procedure block activated and deactivated?

**3.** What are the advantages of allocating storage dynamically? Any disadvantages?

**4.** What kinds of identifiers should be declared to have the STATIC attribute?

## Based Storage

The storage class of a variable determines the way in which the address of that variable is obtained. In STATIC storage, we saw that the address of an identifier is determined when the program is loaded into main storage for execution. For a variable of the AUTOMATIC storage class, the address is determined upon entry to a block. With BASED storage, the address is contained in a **pointer variable.** For example:

```
DCL P          POINTER;
DCL A (100)    FIXED DEC (5) BASED (P);
```
                              ↓
                       Indicates that the address of the A array is
                       determined by the contents of P (that is, the
                       storage address found in P); the contents of
                       P have not been established yet

The identifier P has been given the POINTER attribute.

A **pointer variable** is a special type of variable you can use to locate data—that is, to "point" to data in main storage. Consequently, a pointer variable can be thought of as an **address.** Before a reference can be made to a **based variable** (the A array in the previous example), a value must be given to the pointer (P, in this case) associated with it. This can be done in one of the following ways:

**1.** By assignment of the value returned by the ADDR built-in function.

**2.** By assignment of the value of another pointer.

**3.** With the SET option of a READ or LOCATE statement.

**4.** By an ALLOCATE statement.

| How an address is placed in a POINTER variable | Facilitates | Example |
|---|---|---|
| By assignment of the value returned by the ADDR built-in function | Overlay-defining of identifiers that do not have same base, scale, and precision | DCL VALUE1 BIT (32) BASED (P);<br>DCL VALUE2 FLOAT (6);<br>P = ADDR (VALUE2); |
| By the assignment statement | Saving POINTER values for subsequent use by the program | DCL (P,Q) POINTER;<br>P = ADDR (AREA);<br>Q = P; |
| By the SET option of a READ or LOCATE statement | Processing of data records in their buffers rather than in storage work areas | READ FILE (INPUT) SET (P);<br>LOCATE FILE (OUTPUT) SET (Q); |
| By the ALLOCATE statement | List processing | DCL (P,Q) POINTER;<br>DCL AREA CHAR (100)<br>　　BASED (P);<br>ALLOCATE (AREA);<br>ALLOCATE (AREA) SET (Q); |

FIGURE 9.2  POINTER variables: how to initialize and use.

Figure 9.2 summarizes these methods, states their function or programming purpose, and shows a PL/I coding example. Each of the functions is described in the following paragraphs.

## Simulating Overlay Defining

The DEFINED attribute allows you to overlay one storage area on another. For example:

```
DCL A (100)   FIXED BIN (15);
DCL B (50)    FIXED BIN (15) DEFINED A;
```

Both A and B reference the same storage area; thus, two different identifier names may be used to refer to the same space in main storage. A restriction of the DEFINED attribute is that only identifiers of the same base, scale, and precision may be overlay defined. For example, if we would like to have a storage area contain a FIXED BINARY array at one time during the execution of our program and then contain a structure of various attributes at another time, this may not be accomplished through overlay defining. However, BASED storage will provide this facility. A **based variable** is a *description of data* — that is, a pattern for which no storage space is reserved but that will be overlaid on data in storage *pointed* to by an associated pointer variable. For example, let us declare a 100-element array with the following attributes:

```
DCL A (100)   FIXED BIN (31);
```

Next, assume it is desired to overlay define on A an array of a different base, scale, and precision. The array is declared:

DCL B (50)   FLOAT DEC (6) BASED (P);

The address for the B array will be established by the pointer variable P. P is assumed to have the attribute POINTER because of its *contextual* use. If you wish, however, P could be explicitly declared as follows:

DCL P   POINTER;

If B is to be, in effect, overlay defined on A, we must set P equal to the address of the A array. This is done by a built-in function called ADDR.

P = ADDR(A);

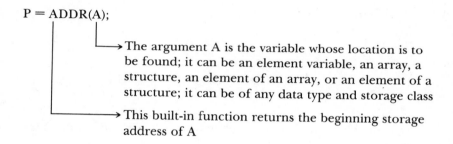

The argument A is the variable whose location is to be found; it can be an element variable, an array, a structure, an element of an array, or an element of a structure; it can be of any data type and storage class

This built-in function returns the beginning storage address of A

If A is itself a based variable, the returned value is determined from the pointer variable declared within A. (If this pointer variable contains no value — i.e., the storage for the variable has not been allocated — the value returned by ADDR is undefined.)

The program in Figure 9.3 illustrates how a based variable may be used to simulate overlay defining. The purpose of this program is simply to find the sums of two arrays; one array has the attributes FIXED BINARY (31) and the other array has the attributes FLOAT DECIMAL (6). All identifiers are declared in Statements 2 through 6. TABLE_1 has the AUTOMATIC storage class by default. TABLE_2 has the BASED storage class. Both arrays will require the same amount of storage. The data for TABLE_1 is input using list-directed input and the sum of the input data is found using the SUM built-in function. In Statement 10, the address of TABLE_1 is assigned to the pointer variable TABLE_POINTER. Now that the pointer address has been established, it is possible to read data into the B array. TABLE_2 occupies the same area of storage as TABLE_1 did. Thus, as data is being input to TABLE_2, the previous contents of TABLE_1 are being destroyed. Statement 12 finds the sum of the fixed-point data in TABLE_2 and Statement 13 prints the results.

```
/*     USE BASED VARIABLES TO SIMULATE OVERLAY DEFINING              */
/**********************************************************************/
/*                                                                    */
/*   PROGRAM NAME: BASED                                              */
/*                                                                    */
/*   DESCRIPTION:   THIS PROGRAM FINDS THE SUM OF 2 ARRAYS.  THE       */
/*                  ARRAYS USE THE SAME STORAGE BUT HAVE DIFFERENT    */
/*                  ATTRIBUTES.                                        */
/*                                                                    */
/*   INPUT:         NONE                                              */
/*                                                                    */
/*   OUTPUT:        PRINTER                                           */
/*                                                                    */
/**********************************************************************/
 1  BASED: PROC OPTIONS(MAIN);
 2     DCL SUM1             FLOAT DEC(6);
 3     DCL SUM2             FIXED BIN(31);
 4     DCL TABLE_1(10)      FLOAT DEC(6);
 5     DCL TABLE_2(20)      FIXED BIN(15) BASED(TABLE_POINTER);
 6     DCL TABLE_POINTER    POINTER;

 7     GET LIST(TABLE_1);
 8     SUM1 = SUM(TABLE_1);
 9     PUT DATA(SUM1);

10     TABLE_POINTER = ADDR(TABLE_1);
11     GET LIST(TABLE_2);
12     SUM2 = SUM(TABLE_2);
13     PUT DATA(SUM2);

14  END BASED;
```

FIGURE 9.3   Using based variables to simulate overlay defining.

It is also possible to have more than one variable based on the contents of the same pointer.   For example:

```
DCL PTR            POINTER;
DCL 1 A,
      2 B          PIC '9999',
      2 C          FIXED DEC (13,2),
      2 D          CHAR (21);
DCL 1 J   BASED(PTR),
      2 X          FIXED BIN (15),
      2 Y          FLOAT DEC (6),
      2 Z          BIT (7);
DCL 1 W   BASED(PTR),
      2 K          FIXED BIN (15),
      2 L          FIXED BIN (15);
PTR = ADDR(A);
```

Any reference to the W structure or the J structure elements points to the storage area occupied by A.   Note that a based variable should not describe *more* storage than the identifier on which it is based uses.

One other example of *overlay defining* using based storage involves a special consideration that must be given to character-strings with the VARYING attribute:

```
DCL FIELD          CHAR(100) VARYING;
DCL 1 STRUCTURE    BASED(ADDR(FIELD)),
      2 LENGTH     FIXED BIN(15,0),
      2 DATA       CHAR(100);
```

The LENGTH field must be specified in the structure to accommodate the two-byte field that always precedes a variable-length character-string.

**5.** Name four ways a pointer variable may be assigned an address.

**6.** When would based variables be used instead of the DEFINED attribute to accomplish the function of overlay defining?

**7.** Assuming the following declaration:

```
DCL FIELD_1   CHAR(5)                 INIT ('12345');
DCL FIELD_2   PIC '999V99'  BASED(X);
DCL FIELD_3   PIC '9V99'    BASED(Y);
```

write the statement(s) that must be executed before FIELD_2 and FIELD_3 may be used to reference the data stored in FIELD_1.

### Saving Pointer Variables for Subsequent Use

The contents of a pointer variable may be saved by assigning the pointer to another pointer variable.  For example:

```
DCL ARRAY (25)    FLOAT DEC (6);
DCL P             POINTER;
DCL Q             POINTER;
P = ADDR(ARRAY);      /* P = ADDRESS OF 'ARRAY'        */
Q = P;                /* Q ALSO = ADDRESS OF 'ARRAY'   */
```

### Using BASED Variables to Process Data in Buffers

When data values are input, the general flow is this:

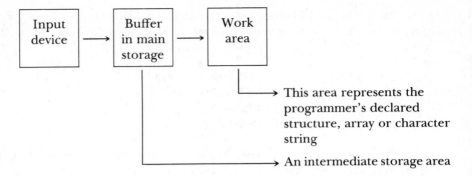

This area represents the programmer's declared structure, array or character string

An intermediate storage area

This flow of data is termed *move mode,* because the data record is moved into or from program storage via a buffer. In move mode, a READ statement causes a record to be transferred from external storage to the variable named in the INTO option (via an input buffer); a WRITE or REWRITE statement causes a record to be transferred from the variable named in the FROM option to external storage (usually via an output buffer). The variables named in the INTO and FROM options can be of any storage class.

Figure 9.4 illustrates data flow for blocked records. Assume the following statements cause the reading and writing of these blocked records:

```
READ FILE (DKIN) INTO (AREA);
DO WHILE (MORE_RECS);
   :
   :
   WRITE FILE (DKOUT) FROM (AREA);
   READ FILE (DKIN) INTO (AREA);
END;
```

The first time the READ statement is executed, a block is transmitted from the data set DKIN to an input buffer, and the first record in the block is assigned to the variable AREA; further executions of the READ statement assign successive records from the buffer to AREA. When the buffer is empty, the next READ statement causes a new block to be transmitted from the data set. The WRITE statement is executed in a similar manner, building physical records in an output buffer and transmitting them to the data set associated with the file DKOUT each time the buffer is filled.

Another processing mode allows the programmer to process data directly in a buffer (that is, without moving the data into a work storage area allocated in the program); this is termed the *locate mode,* because executing a data transmission statement merely identifies the *location* of the storage allocated to a record in the buffer. Locate mode is applicable only to BUFFERED SEQUENTIAL files. Which mode is used (locate or move) is determined by the data transmission statements and options coded by the programmer.

Processing data in buffers can reduce execution time by avoiding an additional

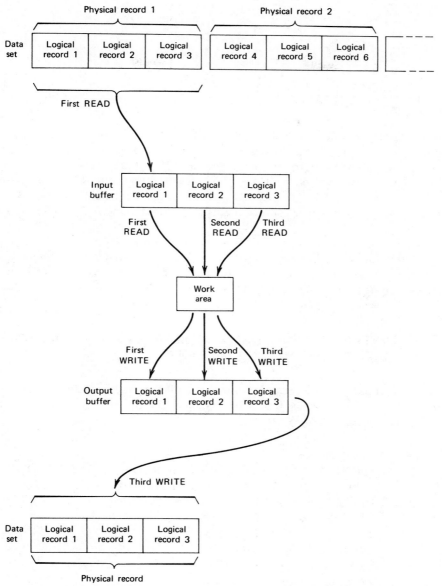

**FIGURE 9.4** Input and output; move mode.

move of the record to another place in main storage (referred to above as *work area*), and save the allocation of an additional storage area the size of the logical record.

Here is an example of how to declare a **based variable** and set the corresponding pointer to process data directly in the input buffer:

```
DCL P                        POINTER;
DCL 1 IN_REC                 BASED(P),
    2 A                      PIC '99',
    2 B                      CHAR (8),
    2 C                      FIXED DEC (7,2),
    2 REST_OF_RECORD   CHAR(66);
READ FILE (TAPEIN) SET (P);
```

The READ statement causes a block of data to be read from the file named TAPEIN to an input buffer, if necessary, and then sets the pointer variable named in the SET option to point to the location in the buffer of the next record; the data in the record can then be processed by reference to the based variable (the structure called IN_REC) associated with the pointer variable. The record is available only until the execution of the next READ statement that refers to the same file.

Thus, the SET option of the READ statement causes the pointer variable P to be *set* to the starting address of the next record in the internal buffer. When data is to be processed in an input buffer, improved throughput of data results if at least two input buffers are reserved. This is done in the file declaration statement. For example:

```
DCL TAPEIN FILE INPUT RECORD BUFFERED ENVIRONMENT(F
    BLKSIZE (800) RECSIZE (80) BUFFERS (2));
```

The use of based variables and pointers also allows you to read more than one type of record into the same buffer by using a different based variable to define each record format. For example:

```
DCL P   POINTER;
DCL TAPE FILE INPUT RECORD BUFFERED ENVIRONMENT (F
    BLKSIZE (240) RECSIZE (24) BUFFERS (2));
DCL 1 ISSUES       BASED (P),
    2 CODE         CHAR (1),
    2 QTY          PIC '(4)9',
    2 JOB_#        PIC '(4)9',
    2 PART_#       PIC '(7)9',
    2 DEPT         PIC '99',
    2 UNUSED       CHAR (6);
DCL 1 RECEIPTS     BASED (P),
    2 CODE         CHAR (1),
    2 QTY          PIC '(4)9',
    2 UNUSED       CHAR (6),
    2 PART_#       PIC '(7)9',
    2 SUPPLIER     PIC '(6)9';
```

```
READ FILE (TAPE) SET (P);
SELECT (ISSUES.CODE);
    WHEN ('1') CALL PROCESS_ISSUES;
    WHEN ('2') CALL PROCESS_RECEIPTS;
END;
```

The PROCESS_ISSUES routine will reference variables ISSUES.xxx while the PROCESS_RECEIPTS routine will reference RECEIPTS.xxx variables. Figure 9.5 illustrates locate mode input and move mode output for blocked records.

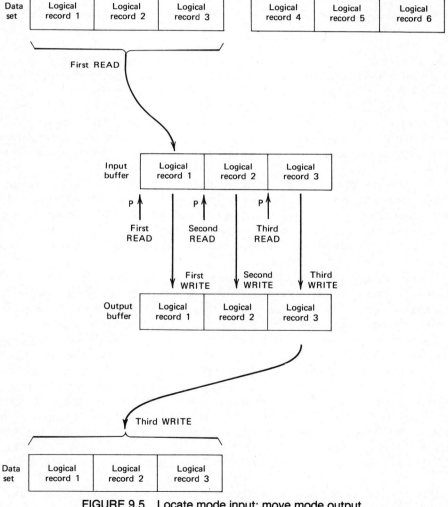

FIGURE 9.5   Locate mode input; move mode output.

Locate mode may be specified for output operations as well as input operations. Locate mode for output requires the use of based variables, the same as it does for input. When writing from based variables in buffers, the WRITE statement is replaced with the LOCATE statement. In the following example, the pointer variable Q is set by the LOCATE statement:

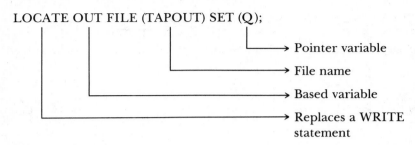

LOCATE OUT FILE (TAPOUT) SET (Q);

→ Pointer variable
→ File name
→ Based variable
→ Replaces a WRITE statement

By means of the LOCATE statement, the structure of the based variable is superimposed on the data in the output buffer so that any reference to that allocation of the based variable is a reference to the data. The pointer variable associated with the based variable will be set to point to the buffer if the SET option is omitted. The output record area, once *located,* is now available; data may be moved to it via assignment statements. The next LOCATE statement causes the pointer to be set to the next buffer area. As soon as a buffer is filled or a file closed, the buffer will be written.

As pointed out earlier, processing data in the buffers has the advantage of saving time and computer instructions spent in moving data from a buffer to a work area or vice versa. Typically, locate mode is used for either input or output when there are a minimum number of references to data elements in the buffer.[1] Rarely, if ever, would locate mode be used for both input and output of the same data records in a given program.

Even though the LOCATE statement replaces a WRITE statement, the LOCATE statement will not appear in the same place as a WRITE statement might appear in a program. Figure 9.6 illustrates the placement of the LOCATE statement with respect to the READ statement and processing steps.

Locate mode can provide faster execution than move mode, because there is less movement of data. Less storage may be required because work areas are eliminated. But locate mode must be used carefully; in particular, the programmer must be aware of how the data will be aligned in the buffer and how the structure will be mapped. (You may wish to consult the appropriate PL/I programmer's guide for a discussion of *structure mapping.*) You should be aware that boundary alignment problems could arise (hence, your program "blows up") with blocked records that contain FIXED BINARY, FLOAT BINARY, or FLOAT DECIMAL data where the record size is not divisible by 4 (or 8 if long-form

---

[1] Because of the way in which based variables' addresses are resolved, many references to data in a buffer can be more costly in time and computer instructions than that spent in moving data from the buffer to a work area.

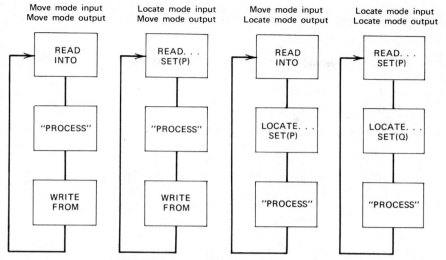

| Move mode input<br>Move mode output | Locate mode input<br>Move mode output | Move mode input<br>Locate mode output | Locate mode input<br>Locate mode output |
|---|---|---|---|
| READ<br>INTO | READ. . .<br>SET(P) | READ<br>INTO | READ. . .<br>SET(P) |
| "PROCESS" | "PROCESS" | LOCATE. . .<br>SET(P) | LOCATE. . .<br>SET(Q) |
| WRITE<br>FROM | WRITE<br>FROM | "PROCESS" | "PROCESS" |

FIGURE 9.6    Move versus locate mode.

floating-point is being used). Move mode may be simpler to use than locate mode, because there are no buffer alignment problems in move mode. Furthermore, move mode can result in faster execution where there are numerous references to the contents of the same record, because of the overhead incurred by the indirect addressing technique used in locate mode.

BASED storage is the most powerful of the PL/I storage classes, but it must be used carefully; many of the safeguards against error that are provided for other storage classes cannot be provided for in BASED storage.

Figure 9.7 shows a file copy program using locate mode I/O output. Notice that it is optional to specify explicitly the SET option. For example, the statement,

LOCATE OUT FILE (TAPOUT);

when executed, causes the pointer associated with the data area called OUT to be set. In other words, because a pointer variable appears in a DECLARE statement, that is,

DCL 1 OUTPUT_REC BASED (Q),

the pointer Q will be automatically set when the LOCATE statement without the SET option is executed. Also, it is not necessary to declare pointer variables explicitly to have the POINTER attribute. This is because they will be recognized contextually by the compiler. For example:

DCL OUT BASED (Q);

    └──→ By context, Q could only be a pointer variable

```
/*   COPY INPUT FILE TO OUTPUT FILE USING LOCATE MODE                    */
/***********************************************************************/
/*                                                                     */
/* PROGRAM NAME: COPY                                                   */
/*                                                                     */
/* DESCRIPTION:   THIS PROGRAM READS A RECORD IN THE INPUT BUFFER       */
/*                AND MOVES IT TO THE OUTPUT BUFFER USING LOCATE MODE   */
/*                                                                     */
/* INPUT:         INPUT                                                 */
/*                                                                     */
/* OUTPUT:        OUTPUT                                                */
/*                                                                     */
/***********************************************************************/
COPY: PROC OPTIONS(MAIN);
    DCL INPUT FILE INPUT RECORD SEQUENTIAL BUFFERED
           ENV(F BLKSIZE(800) RECSIZE(80) BUFFERS(2));
    DCL OUTPUT FILE OUTPUT RECORD SEQL BUFFERED
           ENV(F BLKSIZE(400) RECSIZE(80) BUFFERS(2));

    DCL 1 INPUT_REC BASED(P),
          2 FIELD1            CHAR(20),
          2 FIELD2            CHAR(60);
    DCL 1 OUTPUT_REC BASED(Q),
          2 FIELD1            CHAR(20),
          2 FIELD2            CHAR(60);
    DCL MORE_RECS,            BIT(1) INIT('1'B);
    DCL NO                    BIT(1) INIT('0'B);
    DCL P                     POINTER;
    DCL Q                     POINTER;

    ON ENDFILE(INPUT)
       MORE_RECS = NO;

    READ FILE(INPUT)SET(P);
    DO WHILE(MORE_RECS);
       LOCATE OUTPUT_REC FILE(OUTPUT)SET(Q);
       OUTPUT_REC = INPUT_REC;
       READ FILE(INPUT)SET(P);
    END;

END COPY;
```

FIGURE 9.7   File copy program using locate mode I/O.

## CHECKPOINT QUESTIONS

**8.** What are the advantages of using the locate mode for handling input/output? the disadvantages?

**9.** How many times will a logical record be moved within storage if it is to be read and copied to an output file using the move mode for both input and output files?

**10.** What file attributes are required for the locate mode?

**11.** What option is required in the READ statement to enable processing in the input buffer? What option is required for processing in a work area?

**12.** Is the following a proper sequence of steps for processing in an output buffer? If not, why not?

```
DCL OUT_AREA   CHAR (80) BASED (ANY_PTR);
READ FILE (INDATA) INTO (WORK_AREA);
DO WHILE (MORE_DATA);
    OUT_AREA = WORK_AREA;
    LOCATE OUT_AREA FILE (OUTDATA);
    READ FILE (INDATA) INTO (WORK_AREA);
END;
```

## CONTROLLED STORAGE

CONTROLLED storage is used to create a *stack*. It is similar to BASED storage in that the programmer has a greater degree of control in the allocation of storage than for AUTOMATIC or STATIC storage.

### The Stack Concept

You may think of a stack as a table of items in much the same way you would picture an array. Items may be added to the stack and they may be deleted from the stack. However, unlike an array list, only the most current generation of the stack is referenced. In the following diagram,

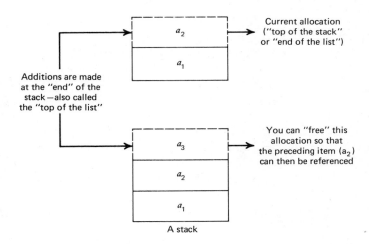

A stack

two elements are shown in the first stack: $a_1$ and $a_2$. The element $a_1$ was placed into the stack (using the ALLOCATE statement) followed by $a_2$. Because $a_2$ is the most recent allocation, it becomes the current and only element that may be referenced. The element $a_1$ exists; however, it has been "pushed down" and is not currently available to the program. The second stack in the previous diagram shows $a_3$ as having been added to the stack. The *top of the stack* ($a_3$) is also referred to as the *end of the list*. (How's that for confusing?) The items in the stack can be released by the FREE statement so that the preceding item in the stack can then be referenced. This capability is referred to as a "last in, first out" (LIFO) technique.

Stacks are useful in several types of applications. They may be useful in computer language translations such as the translation process that must be programmed when converting PL/I syntax to machine language (binary language). Another place where they are useful is in handling errors in your program and/or by the operating system. For example, we know that a number of errors could occur during the running of programs in the computer system. At one point in time it may be desirable, when a given error occurs, for the operating system to take one type of corrective action and at another point in time take a different type of action for the same error. The stack provides the vehicle to let the operating system know which error routine is to be currently invoked for a given error that might occur. The most current allocation consists of the name of an error routine to which the operating system should transfer. Later on, your program may decide an alternative action is to be taken. It would remove (free) the current error routine name from the stack, thereby allowing the previously entered error routine to take control should an error occur.

### The CONTROLLED Attribute

Arrays, structures, or scalar variables may be declared to have the CONTROLLED attribute:

```
DCL MSSG    CHAR(100)        CONTROLLED;
DCL A (100) FIXED DEC (5)    CONTROLLED;
DCL 1 S                      CONTROLLED,
      2 T   FLOAT BIN (16),
      2 U   FIXED DEC (7);
```

The storage for **controlled variables** is allocated in your program by the ALLOCATE statement and released by the FREE statement. For example:

```
DCL A (100)         FIXED DEC (5) CONTROLLED;
ALLOCATE A;
GET LIST (A);
TOTAL = SUM(A);
FREE A;
```

A variable that has the CONTROLLED attribute is allocated upon the execution of an ALLOCATE statement specifying that identifier name. This allocation remains in effect even after the termination of the block in which it is allocated. Storage remains allocated until the execution of a FREE statement in which the identifier name is specified.

The ALLOCATE statement may also be used to specify the amount of storage required for arrays if the array size is to be established during program execution rather than at compile-time. For example:

```
DCL ARRAY (*,*)   FIXED DEC (5)   CONTROLLED;
GET LIST (I,J);              /* ARRAY BOUNDARY LIMITS */
ALLOCATE ARRAY (I,J);
```

> A two-dimensional array whose upper boundaries are specified by I and J, respectively, is allocated

Note the use of asterisks to indicate number of dimensions. CONTROLLED storage provides the vehicle for implementing *stacks*. For example, assume that during the execution of a program, exceptional conditions, irregularities, or errors in input data are to be noted. Rather than printing out error messages as the errors occur, the messages are to be *queued* in a stack. Then, at a convenient time, these messages will be printed. The messages could be entered into the stack in the following manner:

```
DCL MSSG   CHAR (100)   CONTROLLED;
    :
    :
IF ERROR THEN
    DO;
        ALLOCATE MSSG;
        MSSG = 'APPROPRIATE ERROR MESSAGE HERE';
    END;
```

Thus, a stack could be created as follows:

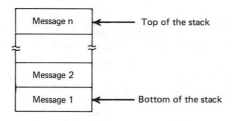

A nested procedure to print the contents of the stack could be written. This procedure will need to use a built-in function designed for *controlled storage* applications. It is the ALLOCATION built-in function; it determines whether or not storage is allocated for a controlled variable and returns an appropriate indication to the point of invocation. For example:

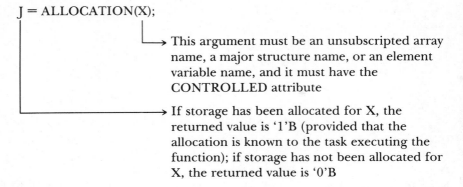

J = ALLOCATION(X);

→ This argument must be an unsubscripted array name, a major structure name, or an element variable name, and it must have the CONTROLLED attribute

→ If storage has been allocated for X, the returned value is '1'B (provided that the allocation is known to the task executing the function); if storage has not been allocated for X, the returned value is '0'B

This built-in function is needed by the procedure that will print the contents of the stack because ALLOCATION will control the print loop operation. For example:

```
PRINT_STACK: PROC;
    /*  INVOKE ALLOCATION BUILT-IN FUNCTION */
    DO WHILE(ALLOCATION(MSSG) > 0);
        PUT SKIP LIST (MSSG);
        FREE MSSG;
    END;
END PRINT_STACK;
```

The ALLOCATION built-in function is specified in parentheses following the DO WHILE. It is invoked each time through the loop. When the last message in the stack has been released by the FREE statement, the value returned by ALLO-CATION will be zero. Of course, had there been no error messages in the stack, the DO WHILE would never have been executed.

## CHECKPOINT QUESTIONS

**13.** What does LIFO stand for?

**14.** How and when is CONTROLLED storage allocated?

**15.** What is an advantage of CONTROLLED storage?

**16.** How can you tell if storage has been allocated for a CONTROLLED variable?

## LIST PROCESSING

**List processing** is the method of processing data without altering the physical location of items within the list. Five types of lists will be discussed here:

Sequential list (review)
Linear list
Circular list
Bidirectional list
Binary tree

A sixth type of list — the stack — was covered when CONTROLLED storage was explained.

## The Sequential List

A list, in its most basic form, is an array:

| |
|---|
| Apples |
| Bananas |
| Cantaloupe |
| Dates |
| Honeydew |
| Oranges |
| String Beans |
| Watermelon |
| Zucchini |

To locate items in the array, the search argument (the item being sought) is sequentially compared with each item in the array, starting at the top of the list and moving down until a *match* is found.

The *binary search* technique provides an efficient alternative method for locating random items in the array. For this technique, it is necessary to arrange the array elements into either ascending or descending sequence. Then the search argument can be compared with the midpoint of the array for an *equal, less than,* or *greater than* condition. With the very first compare, half of the table is eliminated from further comparisons for an item; thus, the binary search reduces the number of comparisons needed to locate a given item in the table. (See Chapter 6 Case Study for a full discussion of *binary search*.) A disadvantage of sequenced arrays subject to possible additions or deletions is that there must be a reshuffling or re-sorting of the array elements to keep them in sequence.

## The Linear List

An alternative that provides for greater programming flexibility is the *linear list*. A *linear list* is a collection of elements in which each element is a **structure** (also called **data structure**). Included in the structure is a **pointer variable** containing the storage address of the next item in the list. For example, assume we would like to describe an element with the following structure:

```
DCL 1 PRODUCT,
        2 DESCRIPTION          CHAR(20),
        2 NEXT_PRODUCT_PTR   POINTER;
```

The identifier NEXT_PRODUCT_PTR has the attribute POINTER. This attribute tells the compiler that a storage address will appear in this identifier name. Your program will use the pointer variable to locate the next item in the list. Assume the sequential array list is stored as a linear list. It would have this configuration:

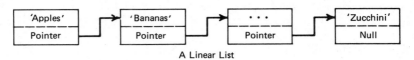

A Linear List

Each element in this list is a structure, typically with more elementary items in the structure than the "scaled-down" example being depicted. Each element structure contains a pointer address to the next element in the list.

The elements of the list do not have to be contiguous in main storage. This is an advantage because it allows more efficient utilization of available main storage. Main storage need only be **allocated** for those items that are currently in the list and subsequently *freed* when specific items no longer need to remain in the list. Here is an example of how the structures in the list might appear in storage with actual main storage addresses contained in the pointer variables:

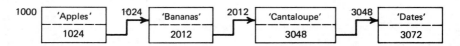

Because the number of items in a list may vary, we must have a way of indicating the end of the linear list. For example:

The asterisk (*) symbol does not actually appear in the pointer variable for the last item in the list. Rather, it is a value provided by a built-in function called NULL. This built-in function has no arguments; it simply returns a unique value that is recognized, when used in the proper context, as indicating the end of a list. To invoke the built-in function for the purpose of assigning a *null value* to the last pointer in the list, simply specify its name in an assignment statement:

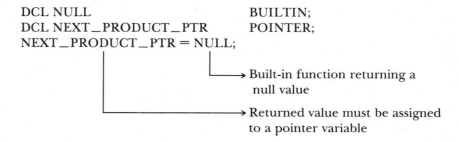

To avoid a compiler diagnostic, NULL needs to be explicitly declared as having the BUILTIN attribute. (This is the case for all built-in functions that do not have arguments.)

Another advantage of the linear list over a sequential list is that inserts and deletes can be made without re-sorting the list. You simply add an item "in sequence" by changing the appropriate pointers. For example:

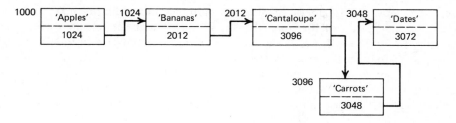

Notice that the addition 'CARROTS' appears in the highest physical storage location but is logically connected in the proper sequence through the use of these pointer variables. Pointers are also generally referred to as *links*. As can be seen from the previous example, each structure in the list is *linked* or *chained* together through the use of these pointer variables.

## The Circular List

The *circular list* is a linear list in which the last element contains the address of the first element in the list rather than an end-of-list indicator (null value). For example:

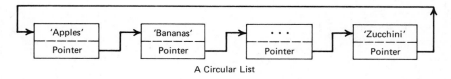

A Circular List

This type of list is useful when you wish to enter the list at any point and access all items.

## The Bidirectional List

The Bidirectional list contains two pointers per element. One pointer points to the preceding element in the list and the other pointer to the succeeding element. For example:

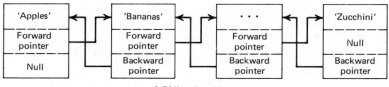

A Bidirectional List

The bidirectional list is useful for those applications requiring processing in either a forward or backward direction. It also facilitates the ease with which new elements may be added to the list or existing elements deleted from the list.

In the lists that we have been working with, the elements have been arranged in ascending sequence. This is not necessary, although structures in the list usually are arranged into alphabetic or numeric sequence (according to a key field) to facilitate processing of the linear list later. If a linear list is always processed serially, although not *logically* sequentially, then an alternative to the ascending sequence is to place the most "active items" at the beginning of the list to reduce the probable number of compares required for each search argument. Of course, when lists are arranged in sequence, then the binary search technique described in Chapter 6 may be used to reduce the number of comparisons required to locate a given item.

### The Binary Tree

An alternative to the linear list is the *binary tree*. It has the advantage of not requiring items to be prearranged into ascending or descending sequence. As will be seen, the binary tree can reduce the maximum number of comparisons required when locating a given item in the list. For example, consider the following unalphabetized list:

Honeydew
Watermelon
Cantaloupe
Zucchini
Bananas
Oranges
Apples
Dates
String Beans

These items can be placed into a binary tree structure without first sorting the items. By setting appropriate pointers associated with each item, they still can be retrieved in sequence. The search time required to locate one item randomly can be less than that required for a serial search through a linear list in which searching begins at the top and sequentially searches to the bottom.

A *binary tree,* like a list, is a collection of structures that are linked together so that every item can be reached by a sequence of pointers. Each element in the binary tree is called a *node*. The first element or node placed in the binary tree is referred to as the *top of the tree*. Each node has two pointers associated with it: a *left* pointer and a *right* pointer:

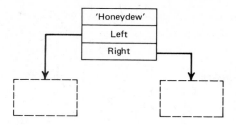

These pointers link to the other elements in a way that reflects a logical relationship between each element.

Recall the unalphabetized list of fruits and vegetables. Assume these items are input and a binary tree created. The data structure for each item (node) has the BASED storage class and is declared as follows:

```
DCL 1 PRODUCT        BASED,
      2 ITEM_NAME    CHAR(20),
      2 LEFT         POINTER,
      2 RIGHT        POINTER;
```

The first item input is 'HONEYDEW'. Because it is the first item, it becomes the top of the list. Associated with 'HONEYDEW' are LEFT and RIGHT pointers. These pointers will link to subsequent items in the input stream based on the relationship of those items to the first item. 'WATERMELON' is the second input value. Because the name has a collating sequence value *greater than* 'HONEYDEW', the RIGHT pointer will be set to the location of the data structure containing information about 'WATERMELON'. For example:

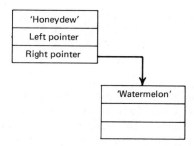

'CANTALOUPE' is the third item input from the unsorted list. Because 'CANTALOUPE' has a collating sequence value *less than* 'HONEYDEW' the

LEFT pointer associated with 'HONEYDEW' will be set to the location of the 'CANTALOUPE' node:

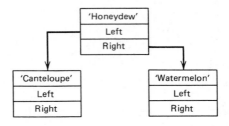

The fourth item in the unalphabetized input list is 'ZUCCHINI'. It is placed into the tree structure by taking that name and comparing it with the top of the tree ('HONEYDEW'). Because it is greater than 'HONEYDEW' it will be chained off of the right-hand side of the tree structure. The RIGHT pointer in 'HONEYDEW' links up to 'WATERMELON', so a comparison between 'ZUC-CHINI' and 'WATERMELON' is made. Because 'ZUCCHINI' has a collating sequence value greater than 'WATERMELON', the RIGHT pointer associated with 'WATERMELON' will be set to link to 'ZUCCHINI'. For example:

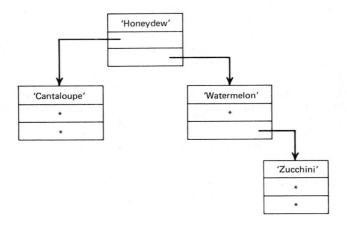

In the preceding figure notice that asterisks indicate a null value for those pointers (LEFT or RIGHT) that do not link to any other nodes in the binary tree.

The fifth item from the unalphabetized input list is 'BANANAS'. Again, starting at the top of the list, 'BANANAS' is compared with 'HONEYDEW'. Again, because 'BANANAS' has a lower collating sequence than 'HONEYDEW' and CANTALOUPE', it is chained off of the 'CANTALOUPE' node's LEFT pointer. For example:

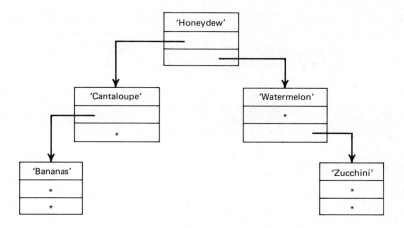

There are nine elements in the unalphabetized list of items. These elements are linked together in the following binary tree:

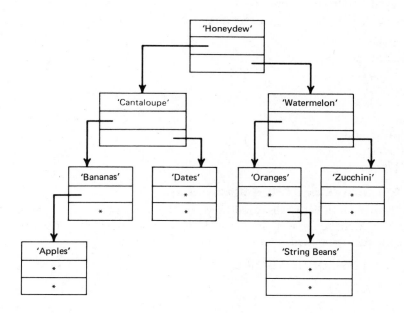

The advantage of creating this type of list structure is that the items entered into the binary tree did not have to be sorted.

Search time (i.e., number of comparisons required) to locate an item is reduced—a primary advantage of the binary tree. Notice, for example, that to locate 'DATES' only three comparisons through the chained list are needed before a match is found. 'DATES' was the eighth element in the unalphabetized list thereby requiring eight comparisons when using a serial search.

Of course, only a few list items are used here. The real "pay off" occurs when a more realistic and larger number of items are in the list.

## CHECKPOINT QUESTIONS

**17.** What is the name of the PL/I data aggregate in which the *elements of a list* must be expressed?

**18.** What is the PL/I term used to indicate the end of a list?

**19.** What is an advantage of a bidirectional list over a linear list?

**20.** The configuration of a binary tree depends on the relationship of the unsorted items that are input. Each tree will be different to each unique sequence of the input data.

Given the following sequence of input items, draw the binary tree with appropriate LEFT and RIGHT pointers linking to the various nodes within the tree:

Oranges
Cantaloupe
String Beans
Zucchini
Honeydew
Dates
Watermelon
Bananas
Apples

### The ALLOCATE and FREE Statements

Each element in a list is allocated by your PL/I program at the time storage is needed for that item. One method for allocating storage is to declare a based structure and associated pointer variable. For example:

```
DCL 1 PRODUCT   BASED(P),
       2
          :
          :
```

Then, storage may be allocated with this form of the ALLOCATE statement:

```
ALLOCATE PRODUCT;
```

Another way in which the previous structure could have been declared is to specify the BASED attribute but without a specific associated pointer variable. For example:

```
DCL 1 PRODUCT   BASED,
      2
        .
        .
        .
```

To allocate this structure it will be necessary to include the SET option with the ALLOCATE statement.   For example:

```
ALLOCATE PRODUCT SET (P);
```

In other words, if a pointer variable has not been declared with the BASED variable, then the ALLOCATE statement must indicate the name of the pointer to be set.   In this case, however, PRODUCT must always be referenced by a *locator qualifier.*   For example:

```
P —> PRODUCT
```

Assuming that P was just set by the ALLOCATE statement, the reference is to the *current generation* of PRODUCT.

It is also possible to declare a based variable and associated pointer but then specify a different pointer variable in the ALLOCATE statement.   For example:

```
DCL 1 PRODUCT   BASED (START),
      2 DATA
        .
        .
        .
ALLOCATE PRODUCT SET (CURRENT);
```

The pointer variable CURRENT will contain the starting storage address of the PRODUCT structure.   The pointer variable START will not be affected or altered in any way when the preceding ALLOCATE statement is executed.

To release storage of an allocated based variable, the FREE statement is used. For example, if the based variable has been declared with a pointer variable [DCL 1 PRODUCT BASED (P) . . . ], the *current* generation of a list may be freed by the following statement:

```
FREE PRODUCT;
```

To release a *previous generation* of a list, a locator qualifier is needed:

```
FREE HELP —> PRODUCT;
```

Once main storage has been released, that space becomes available for reuse.

**21.** Are the following statements correct?  If not, why not?

```
DCL 1 LIST_AREA          BASED,
        2 DATA_PART      CHAR(25),
        2 PTR            POINTER;
     ALLOCATE LIST_AREA;
     LIST_AREA = INAREA;
```

**22.** What is returned by the NULL built-in function?

**23.** What is required to enable accessing of a previous generation of a based variable?

**24.** State two ways a pointer may be associated with a based variable.

### A Linear List Program

In developing items for a linear list, the following structure could be declared:

```
DCL 1 PRODUCT                   BASED (P),
        2 DATA,
           3 ITEM#              PIC '9999',
           3 DESCRIPTION        CHAR(20) VARYING,
           3 PRICE              FIXED DEC (5,2),
        2 NEXT_PRODUCT_PTR   POINTER;
```

The linear list is made up of multiple generations of this structure.  Notice that the *level-1* structure name has the attribute BASED followed by the pointer variable (P) that will be associated with the structure.  This variable will be set to the storage address given to the structure when the structure is allocated by the ALLOCATE statement.  For example,

```
ALLOCATE PRODUCT;
```

causes storage for the PRODUCT array to be allocated, and the pointer P will be set equal to the starting main storage address where this generation of the structure resides.

Once storage has been allocated for an element in a list, then data may be read into that data structure.  For example:

```
ALLOCATE PRODUCT;
GET LIST (DATA);
```

For purposes of simplicity, let us scale down the previous structure and work only with the product description and associated pointer that must be manipulated in

the creation of the linear list. We begin, then, with the following DECLARE
statements:

```
DCL HELP                      POINTER;
DCL INPUT                     CHAR(20);
DCL MORE_DATA                 BIT(1)     INIT ('1'B);
DCL NO                        BIT(1)     INIT ('0'B);
DCL NULL                      BUILTIN;
DCL 1 PRODUCT   BASED (CURRENT_PRODUCT_PTR),
      2 DESCRIPTION           CHAR(20),
      2 NEXT_PRODUCT_PTR      POINTER;
DCL START                     POINTER;
```

Two pointers are declared: START and HELP. The START pointer will be used
to hold the starting address of the first element in the linear list. HELP is a
pointer variable that will, as its name suggests, aid in setting the pointer variable
within each generation of the PRODUCT structure.

The program that processes the linear list reads input records and builds a list.
After the list has been built (i.e., no more input records), a function called
PRINT_LIST is invoked to output the list just created. Here is the coding to
accomplish these steps:

```
ON ENDFILE(SYSIN)
    MORE_DATA = NO;
START = NULL;
GET LIST (INPUT) COPY;
DO WHILE (MORE_DATA);
    CALL BUILD_LIST;
    GET LIST (INPUT) COPY;
END;
CALL PRINT_LIST;
```

The COPY option in a GET LIST causes the input values to be listed on the
SYSPRINT file. Notice that the START pointer variable is initialized to a *null*
value by invoking the NULL built-in function. Each time an input record is read,
the BUILD_LIST procedure is called. The complete program is shown in Figure 9.8. Now let us look at the BUILD_LIST procedure in detail.

We begin by allocating the PRODUCT structure. The CURRENT_
PRODUCT_PTR is the pointer variable associated with the PRODUCT structure. It is automatically set to the starting address of the structure that has just
been allocated. Now that storage has been allocated, the input data is moved to
the based structure element DESCRIPTION. The IF in Statement 21 tests the
pointer variable START for a null value. START will contain a null value the first
time through the program because it was initialized to a null at the beginning of
the program *(Statement 11)*. START will be set to the address of the first element
of the list, as indicated by the assignment statement

```
       /*   CREATE A LINEAR LIST                                              */
       /*******************************************************************/
       /*                                                                 */
       /*   PROGRAM NAME: LINEAR                                          */
       /*                                                                 */
       /*   DESCRIPTION:   THIS PROGRAM BUILDS A LINEAR LIST USING CONTROLLED */
       /*                  STORAGE.  THE LIST IS THEN PRINTED OUT.        */
       /*                                                                 */
       /*   INPUT:         SYSIN                                          */
       /*                                                                 */
       /*   OUTPUT:        SYSPRINT                                       */
       /*                                                                 */
       /*******************************************************************/
 1     LINEAR: PROC OPTIONS(MAIN);
 2        DCL CURRENT_PRODUCT_PTR      POINTER;
 3        DCL HELP                     POINTER;
 4        DCL INPUT                    CHAR(20);
 5        DCL MORE_DATA                BIT(1) INIT('1'B);
 6        DCL NO                       BIT(1) INIT('0'B);
 7        DCL NULL                     BUILTIN;
 8        DCL 1 PRODUCT BASED(CURRENT_PRODUCT_PTR),
                2 DESCRIPTION          CHAR(20),
                2 NEXT_PRODUCT_PTR     POINTER;
 9        DCL START                    POINTER;

10        ON ENDFILE(SYSIN)
              MORE_DATA = NO;

11        START = NULL;
12        GET LIST (INPUT) COPY;
13        DO WHILE(MORE_DATA);
14           CALL BUILD_LIST;
15           GET LIST (INPUT) COPY;
16        END;
17        CALL PRINT_LIST;

       /*******************************************************************/
       /*                                                                 */
       /*   STORAGE IS ALLOCATED FOR PRODUCT AND ITS ADDRESS IS PLACED IN */
       /*   THE 'NEXT_PRODUCT_PTR' FIELD OF THE PREVIOUS ALLOCATED PRODUCT. */
       /*                                                                 */
       /*******************************************************************/
18     BUILD_LIST: PROC;
19        ALLOCATE PRODUCT;
20        DESCRIPTION = INPUT;
21        IF START = NULL THEN
              START = CURRENT_PRODUCT_PTR;
22        ELSE
              HELP -> NEXT_PRODUCT_PTR = CURRENT_PRODUCT_PTR;
23        NEXT_PRODUCT_PTR = NULL;
24        HELP = CURRENT_PRODUCT_PTR;
25     END BUILD_LIST;

       /*******************************************************************/
       /*                                                                 */
       /*   THE LIST IS PRINTED BY STARTING WITH THE ADDRESS OF THE FIRST */
       /*   STORAGE AREA ALLOCATED.  THE 'NEXT_PRODUCT_PTR' CONTAINS THE  */
       /*   ADDRESS OF THE NEXT STORAGE AREA ALLOCATED IN THE LIST.       */
       /*                                                                 */
       /*******************************************************************/
26     PRINT_LIST: PROC;
27        HELP = START;
28        DO WHILE(HELP ¬= NULL);
29           PUT SKIP LIST(HELP -> DESCRIPTION);
30           HELP = HELP -> NEXT_PRODUCT_PTR;
31        END;
32     END PRINT_LIST;

33     END LINEAR;
```

**FIGURE 9.8**

START = CURRENT_PRODUCT_PTR;

The pointer variable within the PRODUCT structure is then set in Statement 23 to a null value by the statement

NEXT_PRODUCT_PTR = NULL: /* INVOKE BUILT-IN */
　　　　　　　　　　　　/* FUNCTION　　　*/

In Statement 24, HELP is set equal to the starting address of the current generation of the PRODUCT structure:

HELP = CURRENT_PRODUCT_PTR;

Picture, if you will, the following configuration with the START and HELP pointers both pointing to the first element of the list:

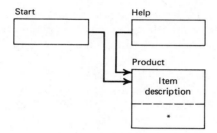

Now let us add the second element to the list by going back to Statement 15, etc., in Figure 9.8. The next generation of the PRODUCT structure is allocated (Statement 19). The ELSE clause of the IF statement (Statement 22) will be executed because the START pointer no longer contains a null value. Here is the statement in the ELSE clause:

HELP −> NEXT_PRODUCT_PTR = CURRENT_PRODUCT_PTR;

This statement causes the pointer in the previous generation to be set to the value of the current structure that has just been allocated. In referring to the NEXT_PRODUCT_PTR field of the most recent generation, the identifier

NEXT_PRODUCT_PTR

may be used. To refer to a generation other than the current one, a pointer variable must be used to *qualify* or *locate* a generation other than the most recent one. The HELP pointer accomplishes this function. Recall that HELP was set to the *start* of the list in the earlier example. It "points to" the appropriate generation by the use of a new symbol designed explicitly for this type of processing. The symbol is called a *locater qualified reference*. It is a composite symbol comprised of the minus sign immediately followed by the "greater-than" symbol.  For example:

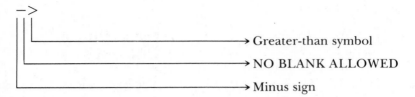

This composite symbol means "points to" or "is qualified by."  For example:

PTR —> AN_AREA

→ Must be a BASED variable

The pointer variable HELP is used to point to the previous generation of PROD-UCT for the purpose of establishing the link between it and the current genera-tion of PRODUCT.  In Figure 9.8 notice that Statement 23 causes the current-generation pointer to be set to a null value.  If this is the last item in the list, then it will be appropriately marked.  Otherwise, on a subsequent execution of this procedure, the pointer will be modified so as to link to the next item in the list. Statement 24 in Figure 9.8 causes the CURRENT_PRODUCT_PTR to be cop-ied into the HELP pointer, giving us the following configuration after the genera-tion of the second list item:

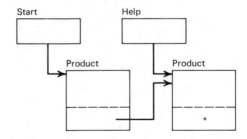

The concepts of adding successive elements will follow the same logic as illus-trated for the second item in the list.  Let us now examine the PRINT procedure that will output the contents of each element in the linear list:

```
PRINT_LIST:   PROC;
    HELP = START;
    DO WHILE(HELP ¬= NULL);
        PUT SKIP LIST (HELP —> DESCRIPTION);
        HELP = HELP —> NEXT_PRODUCT_PTR;
    END;
END PRINT_LIST;
```

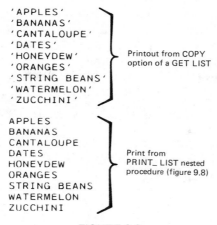

```
'APPLES'
'BANANAS'
'CANTALOUPE'
'DATES'
'HONEYDEW'                Printout from COPY
'ORANGES'                 option of a GET LIST
'STRING BEANS'
'WATERMELON'
'ZUCCHINI'

APPLES
BANANAS
CANTALOUPE
DATES                     Print from
HONEYDEW                  PRINT_ LIST nested
ORANGES                   procedure (figure 9.8)
STRING BEANS
WATERMELON
ZUCCHINI
```

**FIGURE 9.9**

The pointer variable HELP is set to the address of the first element in the list. Recall that this address was saved in the START pointer variable as a "first-time" step in Statement 21 (Figure 9.8). The DO-WHILE loops until HELP contains a null value. The PUT statement causes the output of DESCRIPTION with HELP pointing to the appropriate generation in the list. The NEXT_ PRODUCT_PTR contained in the current PRODUCT structure is then moved into HELP with the following statement:

HELP = HELP —> NEXT_PRODUCT_PTR;

NEXT_PRODUCT_PTR contains the link to the next element in the list. This address or link is assigned to HELP. When the last item in the list is encountered, a null value will be assigned to HELP. This, of course, forces us out of the DO-WHILE structure. Figure 9.9 shows the output from the execution of the program in Figure 9.8.

The programming of BASED variables for the circular and bidirectional lists is similar to the techniques just described for the linear list. The differences are only related to the setting of pointers as they pertain to a circular list or a bidirectional list. For example, note that more than one pointer may need to be declared for the purpose of "holding" pointer addresses related to a given list. For example, in the following *multidirectional list*

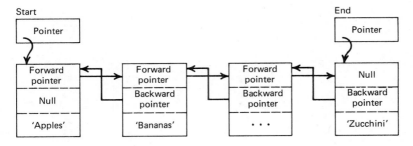

a START pointer and an END pointer may be needed. The START pointer (once initialized) would be used to locate the *head* of the list for forward processing and the END pointer (again, after initialization) would be used to locate the *tail* of the list if backward processing is to be performed.

## CASE STUDY

This case study shows how to create a binary tree and print the contents of that type of list where the printout is to be in alphabetical order. Recall the binary tree developed earlier in this chapter.

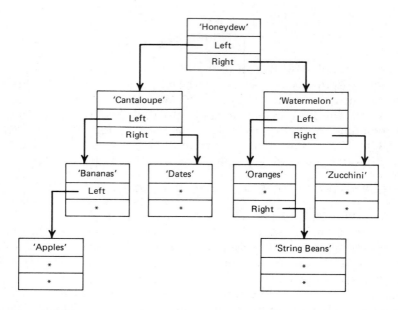

The LEFT and RIGHT pointers link to the next logical element in the tree. The asterisks (*) indicate *null* values in some of the LEFT and RIGHT pointers. It is this tree that will be created and printed.

The binary tree program is divided into three segments:

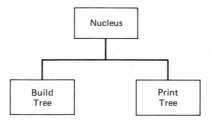

```
/*      BUILD A BINARY TREE AND PRINT THE RESULTS                          */
/****************************************************************************/
/*                                                                        */
/*   PROGRAM NAME: TREE                                                    */
/*                                                                        */
/*   DESCRIPTION:   THIS PROGRAM READS INPUT RECORDS AND STORES            */
/*                  THEM SO THAT THEY CAN BE RETRIEVED IN ALPHABETICAL     */
/*                  ORDER.                                                 */
/*                                                                        */
/*   INPUT:         SYSIN                                                  */
/*                                                                        */
/*   OUTPUT:        SYSPRINT                                               */
/*                                                                        */
/****************************************************************************/
1    TREE: PROC OPTIONS(MAIN);
2        DCL CURRENT                 POINTER;
3        DCL DESCRIPTION             CHAR(20);
4        DCL MORE_DATA               BIT(1) INIT('1'B);
5        DCL NO                      BIT(1) INIT('0'B);
6        DCL NULL                    BUILTIN;
7        DCL P                       POINTER;
8        DCL 1 PRODUCT               BASED(CURRENT),
                 2 DESC              CHAR(20),
                 2 LEFT              POINTER,
                 2 RIGHT             POINTER;
9        DCL START                   POINTER;

10       ON ENDFILE(SYSIN)
             MORE_DATA = NO;

11       START = NULL;
12       GET LIST (DESCRIPTION) COPY;
13       DO WHILE(MORE_DATA);
14           ALLOCATE PRODUCT;
15           DESC     = DESCRIPTION;
16           LEFT     = NULL;
17           RIGHT    = NULL;
18           IF START = NULL THEN
                 START = CURRENT;
19           ELSE
                 CALL BUILD_TREE;
20           GET LIST (DESCRIPTION) COPY;
21       END;
22       PUT PAGE;
23       CALL PRINT_TREE(START);
```

**FIGURE 9.10** Binary tree program — part I.

The nucleus provides the basic loop control for the program. Except for the first item, each input data item causes the BUILD_TREE segment to be called. The PRINT_TREE segment is called, once, at the end of the program to print all data placed in the tree structure.

Figures 9.10 and 9.11 show the compiler listing for this program. The DE-CLARE statements are in Statements 2-9. Notice the PRODUCT structure with its associated LEFT and RIGHT pointers. Keep in mind the various pointers and their contents (i.e., where they point to) as you study the program. Other pointers include:

START

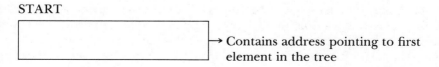

→ Contains address pointing to first
element in the tree

**CURRENT**

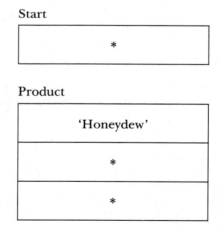

→ Associated with the PRODUCT structure, this pointer is changed by the ALLOCATE statement each time a new generation is allocated

**P**

→ This pointer is used to help in the retrieving of items linked off of the LEFT and RIGHT pointers in each PRODUCT structure

The program will be described by segments.

**The Nucleus.** This is contained in Statements 11 through 23. START is initialized to a null value. For each data item read, storage is allocated. Then the input data item is moved from the input area to the area within the based variable (Statement 15). The LEFT and RIGHT pointers of the current generation are set to null values through the NULL built-in function. Assuming that 'HONEY-DEW' is the first item read, we now have the following storage configuration following the execution of Statement 17:

Start

|       |
| :---: |
|   *   |

Product

|             |
| :---------: |
| 'Honeydew'  |
|      *      |
|      *      |

Statement 18 tests the value of START. If it is a null value (which it is the first time through the program), it is set to the address of the first item in the tree (the *top* of the list). The pointer variable START is never changed again for the duration of the program. On subsequent executions of the IF (Statement 18), the ELSE clause is executed, causing the BUILD_TREE procedure to be invoked (Statement 19). Statement 20 obtains the input of subsequent data items for the binary tree. Statement 21 terminates the DO-WHILE. At the logical end of the program, the PRINT_TREE procedure is invoked (Statement 23).

```
23  /************************************************************************/
    /*                                                                      */
    /*    START AT THE TOP OF THE TREE AND COMPARE DESCRIPTIONS.  IF THE     */
    /*    DESCRIPTION IS LESS THEN THE CURRENT DESCRIPTION BEING LOOKED AT   */
    /*    FOLLOW THE LEFT POINTER.  IF THE DESCRIPTION IS GREATER THEN THE   */
    /*    CURRENT DESCRIPTION FOLLOW THE RIGHT POINTER.  REPEAT THIS         */
    /*    PROCEDURE UNTIL THE POINTER YOU WANT TO FOLLOW IS NULL.  ASSIGN    */
    /*    TO THE NULL POINTER THE ADDRESS OF THE NEW DESCRIPTION.            */
    /*                                                                      */
    /************************************************************************/
24  BUILD_TREE: PROC;
25      P = START;
26      DO WHILE(P ¬=NULL);
27          SELECT;
28              WHEN(DESC < P ->DESC)
                    IF P -> LEFT = NULL THEN
                        DO;
29                          P -> LEFT = CURRENT;
30                          P = NULL;
31                      END;
32                  ELSE
                        P = P -> LEFT;
33              WHEN(DESC > P -> DESC)
                    IF P -> RIGHT = NULL THEN
                        DO;
34                          P -> RIGHT = CURRENT;
35                          P = NULL;
36                      END;
37                  ELSE
                        P = P -> RIGHT;
38              OTHERWISE
                    DO;
39                      P = NULL;
40                      PUT LIST
                            ('DUPLICATE NAME ON INPUT IS IGNORED.');
41                  END;
42          END;
43      END;
44  END BUILD_TREE;

    /************************************************************************/
    /*                                                                      */
    /*    TO PRINT THE TREE IN ORDER, PRINT THE LEFT SIDE OF THE TREE,       */
    /*    AND THEN THE RIGHT SIDE OF THE TREE STARTING AT THE TOP.           */
    /*                                                                      */
    /************************************************************************/
45  (CHECK):
    PRINT_TREE: PROC(Q) RECURSIVE;
46      DCL Q POINTER;

47      IF Q ¬= NULL THEN
            DO;
48              CALL PRINT_TREE(Q -> LEFT);
49              PUT SKIP LIST(Q -> DESC);
50              CALL PRINT_TREE(Q -> RIGHT);
51          END;
52  END PRINT_TREE;

53  END TREE;
```

FIGURE 9.11   Binary tree program—part II.

**BUILD_TREE Segment.** The source listing for the nested procedure is shown in Figure 9.11. Before examining the actual coding, study the logic depicted in the program flowchart in Figure 9.12. This logic shows how the current input item in the tree is compared with previous generations of input items. The comparison is based on the alphabetic (collating) sequence of data in DESC. The LEFT and RIGHT pointers of each generation, starting at the top of the tree and working

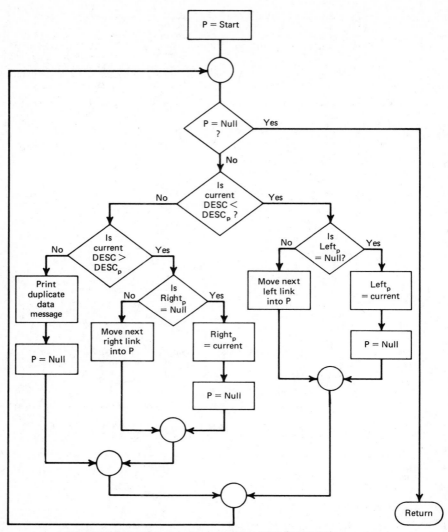

FIGURE 9.12 Program flowchart for BUILD TREE procedure.

down, are examined. As soon as a null value is found in the appropriate LEFT or RIGHT pointer, that pointer is set to link to the current input item. Assume that 'CANTALOUPE' is the second input item and 'WATERMELON' is the third. Take each of these values and work your way through the program flowchart to see the logic of setting the appropriate pointers as a means of linking the based variables together in the binary tree.

The pointer variable P in the BUILD_TREE segment is used to point to various generations of the PRODUCT structure. It must be set to the starting value of the tree structure upon entry to the procedure. It is changed in Statements 32 or 37 through the assignment of LEFT or RIGHT pointer values as subsequent items in the tree are examined. Statements 30, 35 and 39 in Figure 9.11,

$$P = NULL;$$

set P to a null value to force the exit from the DO-WHILE after the current item has been connected to the chain of other items in the tree.

**PRINT_TREE Segment.** The segment is shown in Statements 45 through 52 of the source listing in Figure 9.11. The argument to this subroutine is a pointer variable. The parameter Q has been declared to have the POINTER attribute to assure compatibility with the argument being passed. The logic, in essence, is to print the left side of the tree and then the right side of the tree starting at the top. For example:

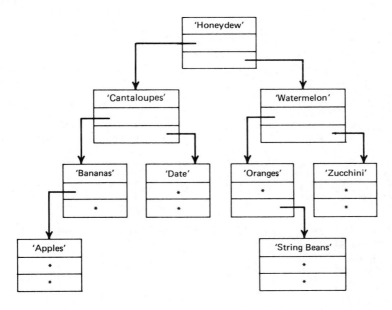

Moving "down" the left side of the tree, the first element that contains a null value in the LEFT pointer should be printed first. Then, the RIGHT pointer of this element is checked. If it contains a value other than null, the item it points to will be retrieved and printed. The logic of this problem requires that each preceding element's LEFT and RIGHT pointers be checked for null values. If a value other than null is present, the "pointed to" element will be retrieved. For example, 'CANTALOUPE' has addresses in both its LEFT and RIGHT pointers. The contents of the element linked to by the LEFT pointer is printed first followed by the contents of the element linked to by the RIGHT pointer. Thus, Statements

```
PRINT_TREE;
    AT 48 IN PRINT_TREE
    FROM 23 IN TREE
PRINT_TREE;
    AT 48 IN PRINT_TREE
    FROM 48 IN PRINT_TREE
PRINT_TREE;
    AT 48 IN PRINT_TREE
    FROM 48 IN PRINT_TREE
PRINT_TREE;
    AT 48 IN PRINT_TREE
    FROM 48 IN PRINT_TREE
PRODUCT.LEFT=NULL;
    AT 48 IN PRINT_TREE
APPLES
PRINT_TREE;
    AT 50 IN PRINT_TREE
PRODUCT.RIGHT=NULL;
    AT 50 IN PRINT_TREE
PRODUCT.LEFT=ADDR(PRODUCT);
    AT 48 IN PRINT_TREE
    FROM 48 IN PRINT_TREE
    FROM 48 IN PRINT_TREE
    FROM 23 IN TREE
BANANAS
PRINT_TREE;
    AT 50 IN PRINT_TREE
PRODUCT.RIGHT=NULL;
    AT 50 IN PRINT_TREE
PRODUCT.LEFT=ADDR(PRODUCT);
    AT 48 IN PRINT_TREE
    FROM 48 IN PRINT_TREE
    FROM 23 IN TREE
CANTELOUPE
PRINT_TREE;
    AT 50 IN PRINT_TREE
PRINT_TREE;
    AT 48 IN PRINT_TREE
    FROM 50 IN PRINT_TREE
PRODUCT.LEFT=NULL;
    AT 48 IN PRINT_TREE
DATES
PRINT_TREE;
    AT 50 IN PRINT_TREE
PRODUCT.RIGHT=NULL;
    AT 50 IN PRINT_TREE
PRODUCT.RIGHT=ADDR(PRODUCT);
    AT 50 IN PRINT_TREE
    FROM 48 IN PRINT_TREE
    FROM 23 IN TREE
PRODUCT.LEFT=ADDR(PRODUCT);
    AT 48 IN PRINT_TREE
    FROM 23 IN TREE
HONEYDEW
PRINT_TREE;
    AT 50 IN PRINT_TREE
PRINT_TREE;
    AT 48 IN PRINT_TREE
    FROM 50 IN PRINT_TREE

PRINT_TREE;
    AT 48 IN PRINT_TREE
    FROM 48 IN PRINT_TREE
PRODUCT.LEFT=NULL;
    AT 48 IN PRINT_TREE
ORANGES
PRINT_TREE;
    AT 50 IN PRINT_TREE
PRINT_TREE;
    AT 48 IN PRINT_TREE
    FROM 50 IN PRINT_TREE
PRODUCT.LEFT=NULL;
    AT 48 IN PRINT_TREE
STRING BEANS
PRINT_TREE;
    AT 50 IN PRINT_TREE
PRODUCT.RIGHT=NULL;
    AT 50 IN PRINT_TREE
PRODUCT.RIGHT=ADDR(PRODUCT);
    AT 50 IN PRINT_TREE
    FROM 48 IN PRINT_TREE
    FROM 50 IN PRINT_TREE
    FROM 23 IN TREE
PRODUCT.LEFT=ADDR(PRODUCT);
    AT 48 IN PRINT_TREE
    FROM 50 IN PRINT_TREE
    FROM 23 IN TREE
WATERMELON
PRINT_TREE;
    AT 50 IN PRINT_TREE
PRINT_TREE;
    AT 48 IN PRINT_TREE
    FROM 50 IN PRINT_TREE
PRODUCT.LEFT=NULL;
    AT 48 IN PRINT_TREE
ZUCCHINI
PRINT_TREE;
    AT 50 IN PRINT_TREE
PRODUCT.RIGHT=NULL;
    AT 50 IN PRINT_TREE
PRODUCT.RIGHT=ADDR(PRODUCT);
    AT 50 IN PRINT_TREE
    FROM 50 IN PRINT_TREE
    FROM 23 IN TREE
PRODUCT.RIGHT=ADDR(PRODUCT);
    AT 50 IN PRINT_TREE
    FROM 23 IN TREE
```

FIGURE 9.13   Output from CHECK in the execution of PRINT TREE.

```
'HONEY DEW'
'WATERMELON'
'CANTALOUPE'
'ZUCCHINI'                    Output from
'BANANAS'                     COPY option
'ORANGES'                     of GET
'APPLES'
'DATES'
'STRING BEANS'


APPLES
BANANAS
CANTALOUPE
DATES                         Output from
HONEY DEW                     RECURSIVE
ORANGES                       procedure
STRING BEANS
WATERMELON
ZUCCHINI
```

FIGURE 9.14  Sample output from binary tree program.

47 through 51 are successively executed until the last logical element in the list is processed.

As a means of helping you to understand the steps taken in the RECURSIVE procedure, the output from CHECK is shown in Figure 9.13 using the OS PL/I checkout compiler. Figure 9.14 shows the output from the binary tree program when it was run without the CHECK condition prefix.

## SUMMARY

**Storage Classes:** When a location in main storage has been associated with a data name, the storage is said to be allocated. In PL/I, we have the facility to allocate main storage at different times. The time at which storage is to be allocated depends on the storage class of the data. There are four storage classes:

> **AUTOMATIC storage:** Unless declared to have another storage class, all variables will have the AUTOMATIC attribute. The fact that certain variables are used in one procedure of a program and not in others makes it possible to allocate the same storage space at different times to different variables. When storage is allocated dynamically, it is allocated during the execution of a procedure. Storage remains allocated as long as the block in which it was allocated remains active. When a block is activated and deactivated, the contents of its data areas may be lost. This is because an intervening block may be executed and its data area will be allocated to the area where the first

block's data once resided. The dynamic allocation of storage applies to begin blocks as well as procedure blocks. This dynamic allocation of main storage is one of the outstanding features of PL/I, because it provides for efficient use of main storage. Total storage requirements of a program may be reduced because of this automatic data overlay feature. The programmer does not have to code extra instructions or steps to cause this allocation to take place. It is done automatically. All the programmer needs to do is to be aware of how and when storage is allocated.

**1. Prologue:** Allocation of dynamic storage is performed by a routine called a prologue. This routine is set up by the compiler and attached to the beginning of each block. It is always executed as the first step of a block.

**2. Epilogue:** Release of main storage that has been allocated to AUTOMATIC variables is handled by a routine called an epilogue. The epilogue routine is logically appended to the end of each block and is executed as the final step before the termination of the block.

**STATIC storage:** Whenever the value of a variable must be saved between different invocations of the same procedure, storage for that variable has to be allocated statically. In this case, storage is allocated before execution of the program and remains allocated throughout the entire duration of the program. Typically, a program will have both STATIC and AUTOMATIC storage areas. Program constants and variables declared with the EXTERNAL attribute have the STATIC storage class attribute. Variables, whether main storage space is allocated to them dynamically or statically, may be given initial values at the time of storage allocation. You can save program overhead by declaring variables that are to be initialized to have the STATIC attribute. STATIC variables are initialized only once before execution of a program begins. AUTOMATIC variables are reinitialized at each activation of the declaring block.

**BASED storage:** The storage class of a variable determines the way in which the address of that variable is obtained. With BASED storage, the address is contained in a pointer variable. A pointer variable can be thought of as an address. Before a reference can be made to a based variable, a value must be given to the pointer associated with it. This can be done in any of four ways:

**1.** By assignment of the value returned by the ADDR or NULL built-in functions.

**2.** By assignment of the value of another pointer.

**3.** With the SET option of a READ or LOCATE statement.

**4.** By an ALLOCATE statement.

A based variable is a description of data—that is, a pattern for which no storage is reserved but which will be overlaid on data in storage pointed to by an associated pointer variable. Thus, based storage may be used to simulate overlay defining. Based variables may also be used to process data in buffers. Processing data while it remains in a buffer is termed the locate mode. Processing data in buffers slightly reduces execution time by avoiding an additional move of the record to a work area. The SET option of the READ statement causes the pointer variable to be set to the starting address of the next record in the internal buffer. When data items are to be processed in an input buffer, improved throughput of data results if two input buffers are reserved. The use of based variables and pointers allows you to read more than one type of record into the same buffer by using a different based variable to define each record format.

**CONTROLLED storage:** A variable that has the CONTROLLED attribute is allocated upon the execution of an ALLOCATE statement specifying that variable. Storage remains allocated for that variable until the execution of a FREE statement in which the variable is specified. This storage class facilitates the creation and processing of stacks.

**ALLOCATION Built-in Function:** This function determines whether or not storage is allocated for a given controlled variable and returns an appropriate indication to the point of invocation.

**Lists:** The following types of lists have been presented in this chapter:

**1.** A Linear List:

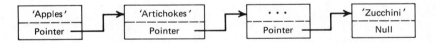

**2.** A Circular List

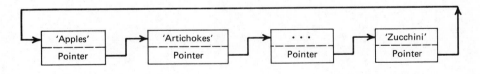

**3.** A Bidirectional List

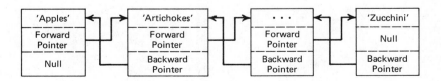

**4.** A Binary Tree

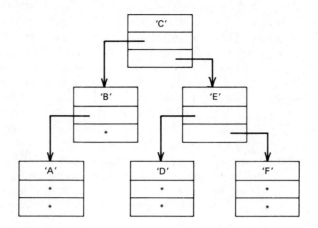

**5.** A Stack

| Error RT1 |
|-----------|
| Error RT 7 |
| Error RT4 |

# CHAPTER 10

# File
# Processing

This chapter introduces you to some basic file programming terminology and concepts.  Data records must be arranged in a file according to an organization that facilitates ease of processing.  The file organizations available in PL/I will be discussed followed by a description of the various I/O statements, file attributes and options, and file on-units that support the programming of tape and disk files.

## TERMS AND CONCEPTS

**File.**  A **file** is a collection of logically related records stored on a medium that is separate from the internal storage of the computer.  You are already familiar with a **file** of sequential records, but most computing applications will access several files stored on magnetic tapes, magnetic disks, or diskettes.  The term **data set** is also used to refer to a file as just defined.

**Record and Key.**  A **record** is a collection of elements or fields treated as a unit, such as all the information that refers to one customer or one account.  For example, the following INVENTORY record describes information about *one* product in an inventory.  The PAYROLL record contains information about *one* employee.  For example:

INVENTORY Record

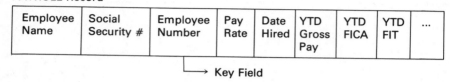

| Part Number | Unit Cost | Supplier | Quantity On-hand | Reorder Quantity | Minimum Quantity | YTD Sold | ... |

└───────→ Key field

PAYROLL Record

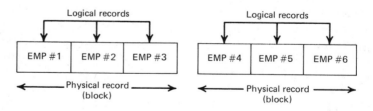

| Employee Name | Social Security # | Employee Number | Pay Rate | Date Hired | YTD Gross Pay | YTD FICA | YTD FIT | ... |

└───────→ Key Field

A **key** is a unique data item that identifies and distinguishes each record in a file. Usually, the key is a character-string. Notice in the previous INVENTORY record that *part number* is designated as the key field. Each record in the INVENTORY file has a character-string part number that must be unique. No other record will have the exact same part number. The key field does not have to be the first field in a record. Notice, for example, in the PAYROLL record that *employee number* is the third field in the record. Although it is possible to have alphabetic key fields, note in this example that it would not be advisable to specify the *employee name* field as the key field because there may not be complete uniqueness. If there are two employees both with the name Tom Jones, the keys would not be unique. Looking at the PAYROLL record description, however, it would have been possible to name the *Social Security* number as the key field.

In some file organizations, the key is not a field within the record but the location where the record is stored in the data set. However, the key still serves to distinguish the record from the others in the data set.

**Logical versus Physical Records.** The INVENTORY and PAYROLL records are examples of *logical* records because the data items are logically related. Records may be grouped together to form a **physical record** or **block.** A physical record refers to the manner in which data items are stored. For example:

Records are grouped together in blocks for the purpose of efficiency on external storage media. Efficiency is achieved because between each **physical** record on tape or disk is an interblock gap (IBG). One of the goals in applications design is to minimize the number of IBGs in a given file because they are essentially "wasted" space on the external device. The size of the gap differs depending on the manufacturer and the model of the physical device.

An advantage to blocking records is conserving space on the external storage medium. It might seem desirable to make blocks as large as possible, like 100,000 bytes. However, the physical record represents the amount of data read or written in one I/O operation. When data records are input or output, the records pass through a **buffer** that is actually a reserved area of main storage. For example:

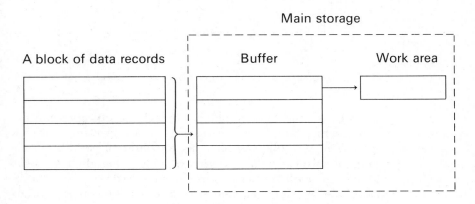

The size of the buffer must be big enough to hold the entire physical record. Therefore, the amount of storage available must be considered in determining the *blocking factor* (the number of logical records in the block). Also, it must be remembered that other programs may need to access this same file, so that the amount of storage available in this program or *any other* program that must process this file must be considered. Larger physical records require larger buffers. Thus, it is not desirable to make blocks as large as possible, because a corresponding amount of main storage must be reserved for the buffer. On input, records are moved one at a time to a work area that is the size of the logical record. This is called *unblocking* or **deblocking** records. On output, records are moved, one at a time, from the work area to the buffer. This is called **blocking** records.

For a direct access device, the physical record may not be larger than the number of bytes in one track of that device (see Figure 10.3).

**Record Formats.** Logical records can exist in one of three general formats: fixed-length (F), variable-length (V), and undefined-length (U).

*Fixed-length records* are records whose size is exactly the same for every record in a given file. Fixed-length records may be either blocked or unblocked, but blocked records may only reside on a magnetic tape or direct-access storage device (DASD). Figure 10.1 shows an example of fixed-length records.

**Variable-length records** are those whose lengths may vary from record to record in a given file. There are a number of applications in which variable-length records are used. For example, in a banking application most customers

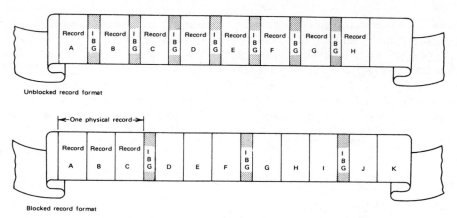

Unblocked record format

|←One physical record→|

Blocked record format

FIGURE 10.1   Example of fixed-length records on magnetic tape.

write a different number of checks each month.   If each record represents one customer's set of transactions, then the records' lengths will vary, not only from customer to customer, but also for each customer for different periods of time. If the variable-length record capability were not provided, then the bank's customer files would have to be established in which each record was fixed at a size large enough to hold the largest anticipated number of transactions of any customer.   In other words, every record in the file would require as much space as the single largest customer's record requires.   This approach would result in large amounts of external storage being wasted.   Variable-length records may be blocked or unblocked for tape or disk files.   For variable-length records to the line printer, unblocked records are typically specified.   When defining the size of variable-length records, the maximum block length must be specified.   The maximum record length may also be given.

Each logical record in a variable-length record file carries a four-byte field called the record length (RL) that indicates the number of bytes in that record. Because variable-length records may be blocked, each **block** contains an extra four-byte field called the block length (BL).   It indicates the length of the block.

The format of variable-length, unblocked records is:

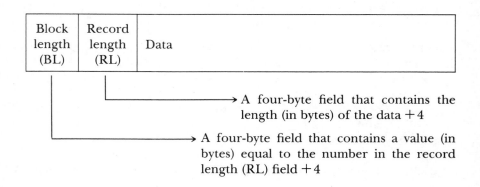

There is one block-length field for each physical record (block) and one record-length field for *each* logical record within the physical record.

To apply these formulas, let us assume that we have a data record for output to a 132-position line printer. To represent this data record in the variable format, we would establish the following values for block length and record length:

---

BL = 141     RL = 137     DATA = 133[1]

---

In variable-length **blocked** records, record length is still computed as being equal to the size of the data area plus 4 bytes. The block length, however, is computed as being equal to the sum of the values in each record length field in the block plus 4 bytes. Inserting the block length (BL) and record length (RL) values is done automatically by the system when the file is created.

The format of variable-length blocked records is:

| I B G | BL | RL | DATA RECORD 1 | RL | DATA RECORD 2 | RL | DATA RECORD 3 |
|---|---|---|---|---|---|---|---|

Variable-length records are automatically blocked if their lengths are such that two or more records can be placed into a block. In writing a PL/I file declaration for this type of data set, the programmer simply specifies the *maximum* number of bytes for a block. In selecting a maximum block size, one must take into account the bytes required for block and record lengths. For example, assume that the largest record in a variable-length file will *not* exceed 250 bytes and that we wish to assign up to three maximum-sized records to a block. The maximum block size we would specify is 766 bytes, which is computed as follows:

        750   (3 × 250-byte records)
         12   (3 × 4-byte record length fields)
          4   (1 × 4-byte block length field)
        766   bytes

When variable-length records are processed, neither the block-length nor the record-length values are transferred to any declared structures, arrays, or scalar variables.

Figure 10.2 shows two examples of variable-length records, one unblocked and the other blocked.

*Undefined-length records* also provide the capability of handling records whose lengths vary. However, undefined-length records are seldom used because each physical record (block) may consist of only one logical record and the determination of record lengths must be handled by the programmer. The maximum length of the largest record in the file, which would also be the maximum length of

---

[1] Includes one byte for carriage control character.

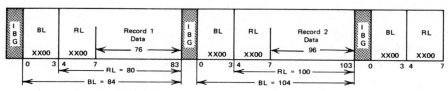

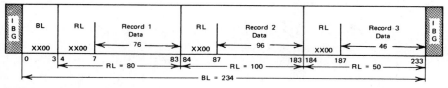

Variable–length blocked record format

FIGURE 10.2    Example of variable-length records on magnetic tape (KEY: BL, blocklength; RL, record length).

the block, is specified.   There are no record-length or block-length fields automatically maintained by the I/O routines, as is done in variable-length records. When the record is written, only the data specified is written.   When the records are read, you must determine yourself, through programming, the size of the records to ensure processing only valid data.   This could be accomplished through a length specification you insert as a data field in the record, or you may read into a VARYING character-string.   The actual length of the character-string read may be determined by the LENGTH built-in function.

An advantage of undefined records over the unblocked variable-length format is that the extra eight bytes required for the block-length and record-length fields in variable-length records are not needed.

## CHECKPOINT QUESTIONS

**1.** What is the difference between a logical record and a physical record?

**2.** On which storage devices is blocking permitted?

**3.** What are the major factors in determining whether a file should be blocked?

**4.** If a file is to be blocked, what is the major factor in determining the blocking factor?

**5.** When would a variable-length record format be used?

**6.** What are the essential differences between the variable-length record format and undefined?

**DASD.** A disk is referred to as a direct access storage device (DASD). The term *direct* is used because these devices provide a facility not available with printer or magnetic tape files. The facility is **direct access.** As an analogy, consider the "direct access capability" of a long-playing record versus stereo tape. If you wish to listen to the fourth selection of a long-playing record, all you have to do is lift the tone arm and move it to the band that marks the beginning of the fourth selection on the record. This is **direct access.** On the other hand, consider the *sequential* approach required if you wish to listen to the fourth selection recorded on stereo tape. What you must do is "run through" the first three selections before the fourth number is positioned at the "playback head." Thus, the fourth selection could only be *sequentially* accessed on stereo tape.

In this analogy, direct access to the fourth selection on the long-playing record provides a faster response time than the time required to get to the fourth selection on the stereo tape. The same parallel is present when we consider the "trade-offs" in the time required to locate specific records in files stored on magnetic tapes versus files stored on a direct access device.

Sometimes the question is asked, "How are records recorded on a disk?" Figure 10.3 shows a sketch of how records might be stored sequentially in 20 tracks of a cylinder. The records have been numbered from 1 to 13 in track 0 (the first track in the cylinder). Then in track 1, the next group of 13 records appear. If these are fixed-length unblocked records and 13 records per track are being stored, then one cylinder (i.e., 20 tracks) holds a maximum of 260 records. Actually, the number of bytes per track varies from disk pack to disk pack and from computer manufacturer to computer manufacturer. This figure and those that follow do not illustrate the IBG that is present between each physical record. The IBG must be taken into consideration in determining the number of records that fit on a given track.

Records are stored in a location relative to the beginning of that track. (An *index marker* indicates the physical beginning of each track so that the read/write

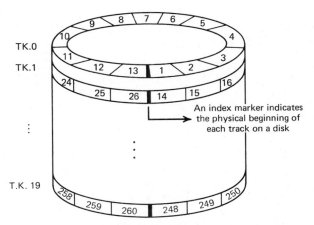

**FIGURE 10.3**   Physical records in 20 tracks of a cylinder.

heads will be able to sense when the first record on the track is being read.) The system maintains on each track an indication of the number of records written there. In the case of variable-length records, the number of bytes left available on the track is maintained.

**Volume.** This term refers to a reel of magnetic tape or a disk pack. It is possible for a file to occupy part or all of a **volume.** Optionally, a file may be stored across several volumes. For example, a large file may require several volumes (reels) of magnetic tape.

**Access Techniques.** Records in a file may be accessed by one of two general techniques: sequential or direct.

Because of the physical characteristics of magnetic tape as a storage medium, it is impossible to think of *directly* accessing a record—say, in the middle of a tape file, because the record preceding the desired record must first be processed. With a file stored on a disk, however, we have the hardware capability of being able to access information in the middle of a file without reading or processing the records that precede the desired record.

It is possible for records in some DASD files to be accessed *sequentially* at one point in time and *directly* at another point in time. A payroll application is one example where this could be the case. At the end of a payroll period, selected information from *all* records in the payroll file would be summarized and printed in various reports (e.g., payroll register, deductions summary, union dues reports). The *sequential* access technique is used to read all records in a file. At another point in time, however, only selected payroll records may be needed. If, for example, a manager wanted to know when John Jones received his last merit increase and for how much, then Jones' payroll record needs to be retrieved. In this situation, the payroll file is *directly* accessed.

To access a record *directly* is to call for that record by means of a **key.** A **key** is a combination of characters that makes a record unique from all other records in a given file. Keys may be numeric, alphabetic, or a combination of alphabetic and numeric characters from 1 to 255 characters in length.

With respect to PL/I programming, there are two kinds of keys: recorded keys and source keys. A **recorded key** is a character-string that actually appears with each record in the file to identify that record. The recorded key may be composed of one or more contiguous fields in a record. A **source key** is the character-string value specified in a record I/O statement and indicates which record is to be accessed. For example:

```
READ FILE(INVEN)INTO(INVENTORY_REC)KEY(PART#);
```

Source key:
character-string indicating desired
record to be read

**7.** What is the difference between a *file* and a *volume?*

**8.** Indicate for the following devices whether files may be accessed sequentially, directly, or both:

(a)   Magnetic tape.
(b)   Disk drive.
(c)   Line printer.

**9.** What is a key?   Explain the difference between a SOURCE key and a RE-CORDED key.

## FILE ORGANIZATIONS

The PL/I terms for the *access techniques* are

    SEQUENTIAL
    DIRECT

The *file organizations,* as specified in PL/I, are

    CONSECUTIVE (sequential)
    INDEXED (indexed sequential)
    REGIONAL (direct or random)
    VSAM
        1.  Entry-Sequenced Data Set (ESDS)
        2.  Key-Sequenced Data Set (KSDS)
        3.  Relative-Record Data Set (RRDS)

Following is a brief description of each file organization.   The concepts presented are designed as an overview as space in this text does not permit a full treatment of these topics.

## CONSECUTIVE

In CONSECUTIVE file organization, records are placed in physical sequence. This organization is used for all magnetic tape devices and printers; it may be selected for direct access devices.   If CONSECUTIVE is specified for a file on a direct access device, then the record layout in that file may be visualized as shown in Figure 10.3.   The records in a CONSECUTIVE file are arranged sequentially in the order in which they are written.   They are retrieved in the same order. After the file is created, new records may only be added at the end of the file.

Inserting new records *within* the file is accomplished by creating a new version of that file in which the "old" file and a file with the "new" records are read, and a "new" merged file is written.

If the file is stored on a disk, it is possible to update that file by specifying that the file has the UPDATE attribute. **Updating** records involves changing a field or fields within an existing record without changing the size of the record. In this case, existing records are READ and then optionally *rewritten* (REWRITE) in place.

## INDEXED

INDEXED file organization gets its name because records are organized in much the same way we might file letters, documents, or memos according to an index. As an illustration, Figure 10.4 shows three file drawers, each labeled with alphabetical letters that indicate something about the contents of the drawers. We know, from looking at the drawers, that the document related to Jones & Co. goes into the drawer labeled "I – L." In the future it will be possible to retrieve the Jones & Co. file folder by going directly to that drawer.

Records in an *indexed sequential* file are arranged in sequence according to a key that accompanies every record on the track of a disk. An index (or set of indexes)

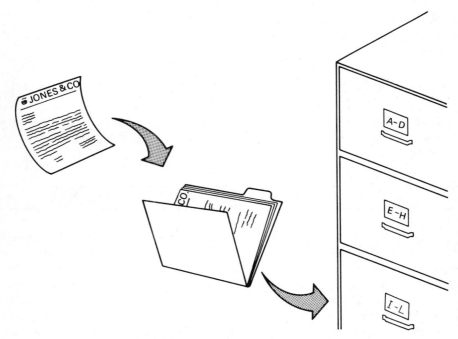

FIGURE 10.4   An indexed filing system.

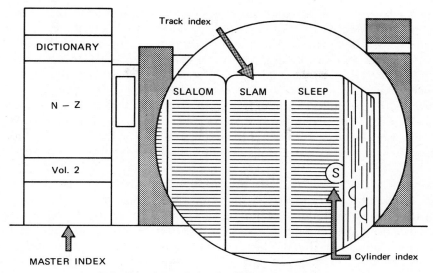

FIGURE 10.5 Indexed organization concept.

is maintained by the system and gives the location of certain principal records. Several levels of indexes may be provided. To explain these levels, consider the analogy depicted in Figure 10.5 in which we see a two-volume dictionary. The *master index* tells us which volume to turn to, depending on whether we are looking for a word beginning with letters A through M or N through Z. The next level of index is the *cylinder index*. It corresponds to the alphabetical marking on the dictionary pages. After turning to the appropriate section, the pair of words printed at the top of the dictionary page serves as the lowest-level index, the *track index*. Figure 10.6 translates this general analogy into specifics as related to indexed sequential files.

Unlike CONSECUTIVE organization, INDEXED organization does not require every record to be accessed in sequential fashion. An INDEXED file must

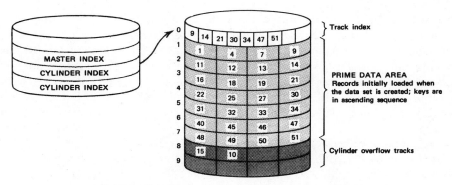

FIGURE 10.6 Indexed sequential file organization.

be created sequentially; but once it has been created, the records in the file may be retrieved by either the DIRECT or SEQUENTIAL access technique.

The track index contains the values of the highest key on each track. The cylinder index contains the highest key of each cylinder (i.e., the highest key of each track index), and the master index contains the highest key of each track of cylinder index. To access a record directly, the system will use the source key and access the master index, if there is one, to determine the appropriate track of cylinder index that encompasses the desired key. From the cylinder index it can be determined which track index contains the source key. From the track index it can be determined where the desired record should be recorded. The record is then accessed.

Unlike the CONSECUTIVE file organization, records may be inserted into the file. One method is to reserve one or more tracks in each cylinder to accommodate the subsequent addition of new records to the file. These are called *overflow tracks* and are shown in Figure 10.7 as empty, as they would be after file creation. Figure 10.7 illustrates the file after the addition of a record whose key is 5. The addition is placed in its appropriate place in sequence on the track. The record on the end is "bumped off" into the overflow area. Additional entries in the index, not illustrated, make it possible to locate these overflow records when they are accessed either directly from a SOURCE key or sequentially in the proper keyed sequence. Note that SEQUENTIAL access for an INDEXED file means in *key sequence* regardless of where the records are physically written (i.e., prime data areas or overflow areas).

The I/O routines written to handle the addition and retrieval of records from an INDEXED file are able to *read* the records in logical sequence; that is, the record whose key is 9 would be logically presented to your PL/I program after the record whose key is 7 has been processed, even though record 9 is not in physical sequence. This occurs because *pointers* indicating the next logical record in sequence have been inserted in the index by the I/O routines provided by the computer manufacturer. The keys in this example ranged from 1 to 51. But not all the numbers in that sequence are actual records. Any key falling within the range of 1 to 51 would be placed on these tracks.

The time required to locate all but the first overflow record of each track in the overflow area is more than for records in the prime data area. Therefore, as the number of additions increases, the efficiency of the access method decreases. Thus, it is usually necessary, in an INDEXED file, to re-create the file periodically, placing all records in sequence in the prime data area. This may be done by reading INDEXED records sequentially; then create a new INDEXED file on another area of the disk. Another method is to read INDEXED records and create a CONSECUTIVE file; then read that file to re-create the INDEXED file in its original space. This activity is called **file maintenance.** In some installations, this re-creation of INDEXED files could take place as often as once a week.

It is also possible to delete records from an INDEXED file. This deletion is a form of **updating** and is accomplished by the DELETE statement. When you specify a delete operation, the record in the file is "flagged" as being deleted.

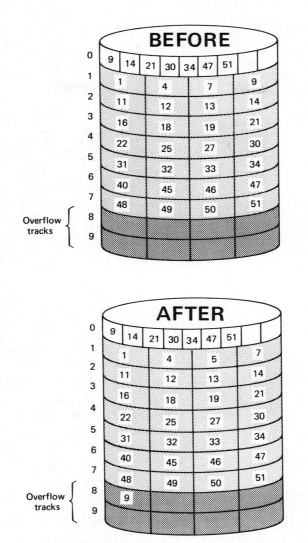

FIGURE 10.7  Shifting of records in an indexed data set.

Actually, the record is not physically removed from the file, but rather the first byte is flagged with a bit-string of

(8)'1'B

This bit-string indicates that the record is a *dummy record* — that is, a null or void record.  On a *sequential* access, the delete byte signals the I/O routine that this is a deleted record and should be ignored.  If a program *directly* accesses a previously

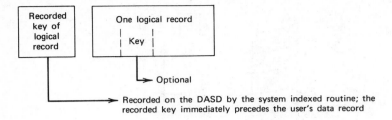

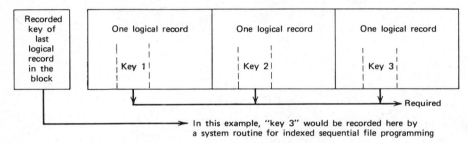

FIGURE 10.8   Unblocked and blocked records in an indexed data set.

deleted INDEXED file record, the record is returned.   The program must be prepared to recognize these dummy or deleted records.

Typically, the first byte of a record declaration (i.e., a structure declaration) for an INDEXED file is set aside as a "flag" byte; the remaining bytes contain the key and other data.   For example:

```
DCL 1 EMP_REC,
      2 FLAG                  CHAR(1)            INIT (' '),
      2 EMP_#                 CHAR(8),
      2 HOURLY_RATE           FIXED DEC(4,2),
      2 NO_OF_DEDUCTIONS      FIXED DEC(2),
      2 REST_OF_RECORD        CHAR(50);
```

If there are a large number of deletions from a file, then there is a large amount of unused space within that file.   Because deleted records are bypassed in a sequential access when file maintenance is performed, only valid records and not the deleted records are placed into the new file.   Therefore, file maintenance performs two functions: 1) it increases the efficiency of future access to the file by placing all records in sequence in the prime data area and 2) it increases available space because deleted records are eliminated from the new file.

Logical records may be blocked or unblocked in an INDEXED data set. Figure 10.8 illustrates the format of the physical records in an INDEXED data set. To access a record from a blocked data set, the I/O routines read the correct physical record by comparing the source key to the recorded key preceding the physical records. The source key is compared to the key within each logical record. When the matching logical record is found, it is moved to the work area specified in the I/O statement.

## CHECKPOINT QUESTIONS

**10.** How are insertions and deletions made to a CONSECUTIVE file?

**11.** When would file maintenance be required on an INDEXED file?

**12.** Would the indexes need to be consulted by the I/O routines to access an INDEXED file sequentially?

**13.** Why would a MASTER INDEX be created?

**14.** What is a dummy record?

## REGIONAL

There are three variations of the REGIONAL file organization: REGIONAL (1), REGIONAL (2), and REGIONAL (3). The records within these types of data sets must be on a hard disk. No space is required for indexes. You specify the keys by which records are stored and retrieved *directly*. The REGIONAL organization permits you to control the physical placement of records in the data set and enables you to optimize the access time for a particular application. Such optimization is not available with CONSECUTIVE, INDEXED, VSAM-KSDS, or VSAM-ESDS organizations.

The term *regional* was selected to describe the types of data sets that are divided into regions rather than records. One or more records may be stored in each region depending on the type of REGIONAL organization used. Each region is identified by a region number where the regions are numbered in succession beginning with zero. A record is accessed by specifying its region number in a record-oriented I/O statement.

In the INDEXED organization for direct access you provide a key, and the I/O routine determines where the record is to be placed. In the REGIONAL organization you essentially tell the I/O routine *where* the record is to be stored (for example, in Region 73).

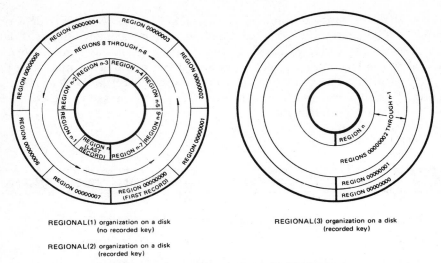

REGIONAL(1) organization on a disk
(no recorded key)

REGIONAL(3) organization on a disk
(recorded key)

REGIONAL(2) organization on a disk
(recorded key)

FIGURE 10.9    Conceptual layout of REGIONAL files.

### Relative Record versus Relative Track

Two kinds of regional specifications are used: relative record and relative track. A *relative record* is a block (i.e., physical record) called a region in the data set; it is referenced by a number relative to the first record in the **data set,** which is number zero.    If it were desired to access the 25th record in the data set, the region number (i.e., relative record number) of 24 would be used.    The disk on the left in Figure 10.9 illustrates the relative record specification.    The concentric circles in this figure represent the tracks into which a disk is divided — one circle represents one track.    As can be seen, a number of regions may appear in one track.

A *relative track* specification refers to a region of the data set by specifying the number of a particular track relative to the first track of the data set, which is track zero.    The disk on the right in Figure 10.9 illustrates this type of disk arrangement, which is used in REGIONAL (3) data sets.    As can be seen, each region is a track.    REGIONAL (3) organization allows *more than one* record to be stored in each region.    By contrast, REGIONAL (1) and REGIONAL (2) allow only *one* record per region.    A relative track or relative record specification always refers uniquely to one region in a data set.

### Record Types and Region Layouts

Only unblocked records are allowed in REGIONAL data sets.    Fixed-length records are allowed in all three REGIONAL data sets.    In addition, variable-length (V) and undefined-length (U) records may be specified for REGIONAL (3) data sets.

**REGIONAL (1).**    Each region contains one unblocked F format record that does not have a recorded key:

| Region 0 | Region 1 | Region 2 |
|---|---|---|
| Logical record 1 | Logical record 2 | Logical record 3 ... |

Each region number represents one logical record within a data set. The largest region number that may be specified for REGIONAL (1) is $16777215$ $(2^{24} - 1)$.

**REGIONAL (2).** Each region contains one unblocked F format record that is identified by a recorded key preceding each record:

| Region 0 | | Region 1 | | Region 2 | | |
|---|---|---|---|---|---|---|
| Recorded key | Logical record | Recorded key | Logical record | Recorded key | Logical record | ... |

Each region number represents one logical record within a data set. The largest region number that may be specified for REGIONAL (2) is $32767$ $(2^{15} - 1)$. The actual position of a record in the data set relative to other records is determined not by its recorded key, but by the *region number* supplied in the source key of the WRITE statement that adds a record to the data set. For example, assume we have a data set containing four records and two of those four records have meaningful data, while the other two contain dummy records. To illustrate:

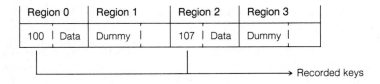

Recall the layout of regions in the physical tracks of a direct-access storage device as shown in Figure 10.9. When a record is added to a REGIONAL (2) data set, it is written with its recorded key in the first available space after the beginning of the track that contains the region specified. Given the file declaration and assignment statement,

```
DCL REGION#   CHAR(8);
DCL REG2 FILE RECORD UPDATE DIRECT KEYED
     ENV (REGIONAL(2) F BLKSIZE(100) KEYLENGTH(3));
KEY = '109';
REGION# = '00000000';
```

and the WRITE statement,

WRITE FILE(REG2)FROM(AREA)KEYFROM(KEY ‖ REGION#);

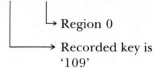

→ Region 0

→ Recorded key is
'109'

the added record will be placed into region 1, which is the first available space after the beginning of the track that contains the region specified. Now, with the added record, we have the following configuration:

| Region 0 | | Region 1 | | Region 2 | | Region 3 | |
|---|---|---|---|---|---|---|---|
| 100 | Data | 109 | Data | 107 | Data | Dummy | ... |

Thus, in the above example, region 0 was specified in the WRITE statement, but the record and its recorded key were actually written in region 1.

When a record is read, the search for a record with the appropriate recorded key begins at the start of the track that contains the region specified. Unless it is limited by the LIMCT subparameter of the DD statement that defines the data set in OS, the search for a record or for space to add a record continues right through to the end of the data set. The closer a record is to the specified region, the more quickly it can be accessed.

Note that it is possible to place records with identical keys in a REGIONAL (2) data set. If there are records with duplicate keys, the record farthest from the region specified will never be retrieved during a direct access if they were written with the same region number.

**REGIONAL (3).** Each region is a track that may contain one or more unblocked records. Typically F format records are used but V format or U format may also be specified. Here is a sample layout of F format records in a REGIONAL (3) data set:

Region 0

| Recorded key | Logical record | Recorded key | Logical record | Recorded key | Logical record |
|---|---|---|---|---|---|

Region 1

| Recorded key | Logical record | Recorded key | Logical record | ... |
|---|---|---|---|---|

Each region will typically contain a number of logical records. The largest region number that may be specified is $32767$ ($2^{15} - 1$). The addition of records to a REGIONAL (3) data set is the same as described for REGIONAL (2) (including the duplicate key considerations).

## When to Use Which Type of REGIONAL File

An application in which REGIONAL (1) might be useful is that of *text preparation and maintenance*. Assume, for example, that the entire contents of a book are to be kept in computer storage in a REGIONAL (1) file. Each region number contains all the words that appear on one page of a book. If it is desired to recall a specific page of that stored book, simply code the specific page as the *region number* (i.e., relative record number) in the appropriate READ statement. For example:

```
DCL PAGE_NO    PIC '999';
PAGE_NO = 50;
READ FILE(TEXT) INTO (PAGE_REC) KEY (PAGE_NO);
```

> Region number (i.e., "relative record numbers") for the REGIONAL (1) file called TEXT

The region number consists of an eight position character-string containing the digits 0 through 9; if more than eight characters appear in the key, only the rightmost eight are used as a region number. If fewer than eight appear, it will be interpreted as being preceded by blanks (effectively treated as zeros).

REGIONAL (2) could be used instead of REGIONAL (1) to store pages of a textbook. The difference is simply that records in REGIONAL (2) have a recorded key. In this case, the recorded key would most logically be the page number. (Thus, the recorded key and the region number would always be the same.) This, however, is not required for REGIONAL (2). Usually, the recorded key is *not* the same as the region number.

To illustrate how REGIONAL (3) might be used in storing textbook pages, assume that individual paragraphs need to be selectively referenced. If each paragraph on a page is numbered successively and each paragraph is a record, the REGIONAL (3) organization could best suit our needs in storing and retrieving paragraphs on a page within a book. In REGIONAL (3), each region will still correspond to a page number in the text. Additionally, the **recorded key** becomes the paragraph number reference. To retrieve text by paragraph, rather than by the entire page, the following statement might be coded:

```
DCL PAGE_NO        PIC '999';
DCL PARAGRAPH_NO  PIC '99';
PAGE_NO       = 50;
PARAGRAPH NO = 2;
READ FILE(TEXT) INTO (PARAGRAPH_REC) KEY
   (PARAGRAPH_NO || PAGE_NO);
```

Here the page number is concatenated to the paragraph number to form the **source key.** The page number corresponds to the region number, and the paragraph number corresponds to the **recorded key** recorded with each paragraph record. Note that the region number follows the actual key when forming the source key in an I/O statement for REGIONAL (3).

Using the key of a record as its address is called *direct addressing* (as opposed to *indirect addressing*). In the examples just cited, direct addressing was suggested as the means for identifying records. The method of direct addressing not only allows minimum disk time when processing at random, but is also ideal for sequential processing, because the records are written in key sequence. A disadvantage of this approach is that there may be a large amount of unused storage. For example, in an inventory file, assume the part numbers are used as the keys and that the numbers range from 10000 to 99999. Out of this range, however, there are only 3000 inventory items. Thus, if the part number is the key, there will be a large amount of *unused* direct-access storage, because a location must be reserved for every key in the file's range even though many of them are not used.

## Addressing Techniques for REGIONAL Files

There are a number of techniques that may be used to relate the key of a record to a region number while minimizing the amount of unused direct access storage space. Several of the often-used techniques will be discussed here.

**Direct Addressing.** In this type of addressing, every possible key in the data set corresponds to a unique storage address on the disk. In this case, the key could only be numeric. A location must be reserved in the data set for every key in the range. As an example other than storing pages in a book, assume a company markets its products in various sales territories. Each territory is given a number (i.e., 1, 2, 3, etc.). Then information regarding sales in each of the territories could be stored, where each logical record corresponds to a sales territory. Thus, region 1 contains sales information on territory 1, region 2 on territory 2, etc. In the area of scientific computation, tables of data to be reduced could be stored — one table per region. Or historical maintenance information on power plant equipment could be stored where, perhaps, region 1 contains the performance record of generator number 1, region 2 of generator number 2, etc.

**Index Searching.** In this method, an index is maintained consisting of keys and assigned hardware (e.g., region number) addresses. For example, when a REGIONAL file is created, the programmer also constructs an index table, which is typically another file.

Notice that the keys are not in sequence. They are simply assigned a region number within the file. The index table is saved on a DASD along with the REGIONAL data set. When a stored record is retrieved from the REGIONAL data set, the index table is first read by your program into main storage and then searched to locate the required key value. When the corresponding region number is obtained, that number is used to access the given stored record. The *index search* method allows files to be allocated space based only on the actual space requirements of the stored records and not on all possible key values within a range. Thus, in the previous inventory example in which the key values ranged

| Key | Region number |
|-----|--------|
| 012 | 001 |
| 035 | 002 |
| 020 | 003 |
| 435 | 004 |
| 250 | 005 |
| 176 | 006 |
| 551 | 007 |
| 043 | 008 |

from 10000 to 99999 but there were only 3000 actual inventory items, a considerable saving of DASD space can be effected by using the index search technique. Also, keys do not have to be numeric values, as in direct addressing. Unique addresses are assured and any record can be accessed with only one seek to the DASD once the address is obtained from the index. However, time is required to look up the address in the index — which may be a serious disadvantage when it contains many entries. The index also requires additional storage in excess of that required by the stored records in the REGIONAL file. For sequential retrieval, the index can be sorted into key sequence.

**Indirect Addressing.** This method may be used for nonnumeric keys (i.e., alphabetic) or when the range of keys for a file contains so many unused values that direct addressing is impractical, or when the number of records is so large that using an index table is cumbersome. The purpose of indirect addressing is to manipulate keys in a data set by some algorithm to compress the range of key values to a smaller range of stored addresses (region numbers). This manipulation of the key is referred to as *randomizing*. There are different techniques of transforming a record key into the corresponding record address. One technique is the *division/remainder* method. The bytes in the key are treated as a binary value. The key is divided by a prime number that is closest to the number of records in the data set or the number of tracks in a file. The *number of records* value is used for REGIONAL (1) or REGIONAL (2). The *number of tracks* value is used for REGIONAL (3).

As an illustration, assume we have a file of 1000 records and that there is enough room on each track of the direct-access storage device to store 15 records. Thus, if we divide the number of records by the number of records per track, we see that this file will require 67 tracks:

$$\overset{66.6}{15\overline{)1000}} \longleftarrow \text{Number of tracks needed for file}$$

$\uparrow$ ————— Records per track

(To determine the number of records per track, you will have to reference the hardware specifications for the particular disk you are using.)

To determine a relative record region number for a given key in this 1000-record data set, divide any key in the file by the prime number closest to 1000 — in this case 997. For example, assume the key is 1898:

$$\begin{array}{r} 1 \\ \hline 997\overline{)1898} \end{array} \quad \text{Remainder} = 901$$

The remainder, 901, could be the relative region number in REGIONAL (1) or REGIONAL (2) data sets. Recall that in REGIONAL (2), the key — 1898 in the above example — would be recorded with the record. The key would not be recorded in the REGIONAL (1) data set record. (It could be embedded in your record, however.)

In REGIONAL (3), the region number is a relative track number. To determine a relative track address, divide the key by the prime number closest to the number of tracks (61 in this example) required for the file:

$$\begin{array}{r} 31 \\ \hline 61\overline{)1898} \end{array} \quad \text{Remainder} = 7$$

Relative track 7 is a valid reference that could be used in REGIONAL (3).

### Recorded and Source Keys

A *recorded key* is a character-string that immediately precedes each record in the data set to identify that record. Here is a REGIONAL (2) example:

| Region 0 | | Region 1 | | Region 2 | | |
|---|---|---|---|---|---|---|
| Recorded key | Logical record | Recorded key | Logical record | Recorded key | Logical record | ... |

The recorded key may be from 1 to 255 characters long. This length is specified either through job control statements or through the KEYLENGTH option of the ENVIRONMENT attribute in a file declaration statement.

A *source key* is the character-string value specified in the record-oriented I/O statements following the KEY or KEYFROM options.

REGIONAL (1), the source key is a region number that served as the sole identification of a particular record. For example:

```
READ FILE(REG1)INTO(AREA)KEY(REGION#);
```

→ The region number consisting of up to an eight-position character-string containing the digits 0 to 9; if more than eight characters appear in the key, only the rightmost eight are used as the region number

The character-string value of the source key for REGIONAL (2) and REGIONAL (3) files can be thought of as having two logical parts: the *region number* and the *comparison key*. For example:

```
WRITE FILE(REG2)FROM(AREA)KEYFROM(PART# ‖ REGION#);
```

Region number ⎯⎦

Comparison key ⎯⎯⎯⎯⎦

The source key need not be specified as an expression with concatenation as shown above, but may be written as one character-string. For example:

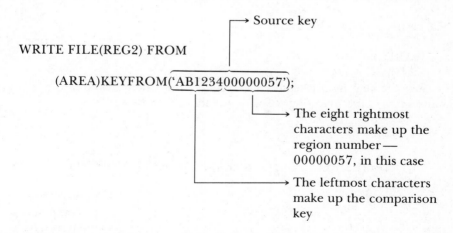

→ Source key

```
WRITE FILE(REG2) FROM

    (AREA)KEYFROM('AB123400000057');
```

→ The eight rightmost characters make up the region number — 00000057, in this case

→ The leftmost characters make up the comparison key

The KEYLENGTH option (or KEYLEN in the DD statement) specifies the number of characters in the comparison key. *On output, the comparison key is written as the recorded key.* For example, assume the ENVIRONMENT attribute specifies KEYLENGTH (6). Then, in the statement,

WRITE FILE(REG2) FROM (AREA) KEYFROM ('AB123400000057');

the recorded key would be the character-string value:

'AB1234'

If KEYLENGTH (14) were specified, then the recorded key would be the character-string value:

'AB123400000057'

As can be seen, then, the comparison key can actually include the region number, in which case, the source key and the comparison key are identical; alternatively, part of the source key may be unused. For example, if KEYLENGTH (4) is specified, the comparison key consists of the leftmost four characters:

'AB12'

The characters between the comparison key and the region number ('34' in this case) are ignored.

*On input, the comparison key is compared with the recorded key.* For example, assume KEYLENGTH (8) is specified, and the following WRITE statement creates a record:

WRITE FILE(REG2) FROM (AREA) KEYFROM ('AB123400000057');

The recorded key in this case is

'AB123400'

because the keylength is eight characters. Thus, when it is desired to read the above record, the following READ statement might be coded:

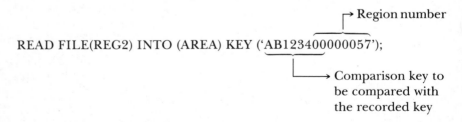

## Preformatting REGIONAL Files

Preformatting consists of writing *dummy records* into a data set. A dummy record does not contain meaningful data, but rather some constant that is unlikely to appear in meaningful data records. This constant then identifies the record as being a dummy record—one that is available in which to store new and meaningful information.

If a REGIONAL file has the OUTPUT attribute, the data set will automatically be written with dummy records, when the file is opened; the nature of dummy records depends on the type of REGIONAL organization.

In REGIONAL files containing fixed-length records, dummy records are identified by the constant (8)'1'B. In REGIONAL (1) files, the (8)'1'Bs are in the first byte of each record. In REGIONAL (2) and REGIONAL (3), the '1' bits are in the first byte of the key. A dummy record is also written when a record is deleted from a REGIONAL file. In a REGIONAL (1) file, dummy records are presented to the program even though the specified region contains the (8)'1'B configuration. Thus, your PL/I program must include logic to handle them. In reading records from a REGIONAL (2) or REGIONAL (3) file, however, dummy records will be bypassed. In any REGIONAL organization, dummy records can be replaced by valid records.

REGIONAL (3) allows variable-length (V) and undefined-length (U) records as well as fixed-length. Dummy records cannot be inserted when a file is created with V format or U format records, because their lengths cannot be known before they are written; however, the operating system maintains a *capacity record* at the beginning of each track, in which it records the amount of space available on that track.

V format and U format dummy records are identified by (8)'1'B in the first byte. The four control bytes in each V format dummy record are retained, but otherwise the contents of V format and U format dummy records are undefined. V format and U format dummy records are inserted in a data set only when a record is deleted; the space they occupied cannot be used again.

## VSAM

The data set organization called VSAM stands for Virtual Storage Access Method. It is a file organization unique to IBM. In this section discussing VSAM, the term **data set** will be used rather than the term **file** simply because IBM uses that term. Remember, however, that in the context of this chapter **file** and **data set** are synonymous.

There are three basic data organizations in VSAM:

1. Entry-Sequenced Data Set (ESDS).
2. Key-Sequenced Data Set (KSDS).
3. Relative-Record Data Set (RRDS).

**Entry-Sequenced Data Set (ESDS).** This data set, which must always be on a direct-access device, generally corresponds to the CONSECUTIVE organization. Records are loaded into the data set in physical sequence without respect to their contents. Records may be retrieved in the sequence in which they were initially stored. New records are added at the end of the data set. (To add new records to the middle of the file, the "old" ESDS must be merged with "new" records to form a new ESDS.)

**Key-Sequenced Data Set (KSDS).** This organization generally corresponds to the INDEXED organization. Records are loaded into the data set in ascending key sequence and controlled by an index or indexes, as in the INDEXED file organization. Records are stored and retrieved by means of a key. New records are inserted in the data set in key sequence. However, as we shall see, there are no *separate* tracks to handle overflow as in the INDEXED organization. Unlike the INDEXED file organization, when records are deleted from a KSDS they are actually removed from that data set, thereby "freeing up" the disk space for subsequent records that may be added later to the data set.

Figure 10.10 shows a conceptual layout of VSAM data sets. VSAM-KSDS has two levels of indexes corresponding roughly to the cylinder index and track index in the INDEXED file organization. Notice in Figure 10.10 that the second-level index points to the location of records in the actual data set. The indexed sequential term *prime data area* is not used in VSAM. The reason there is no need for separate overflow areas in VSAM-KSDS is because "free space" is inserted throughout the data set when it is created. This free space could either grow in size as records are deleted from the file or diminish in size as records are added to the file. The manipulation of this free space is automatically provided by the VSAM I/O routines.

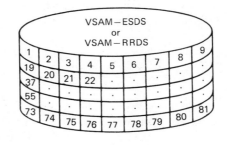

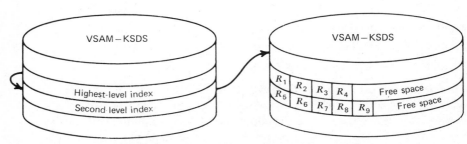

FIGURE 10.10   Conceptual layout of VSAM data sets.

**Relative-Record Data Set (RRDS).** This organization generally corresponds to a REGIONAL (1) data set. Records in an RRDS are located by a relative record number used as a key to access the data set. The relative record numbers start at 1 and are incremented by 1 for each record written on the data set. The records may be accessed sequentially or directly.

Why did IBM provide the VSAM file organization, which closely approximates the features provided in CONSECUTIVE, INDEXED, and REGIONAL (1) files? There are several advantages. One major advantage in VSAM-KSDS, for example, is that you would never have to perform **file maintenance** as you would for INDEXED files that have had substantial additions or deletions made to them. This is because of the "free space" approach in VSAM-KSDS.

Additionally, VSAM provides improved data security techniques. For example, a PASSWORD procedure is implemented in which the problem program must provide one or a series of passwords that, if correct, allow access to the file. This improved approach to data security helps to guard against inadvertent destruction of a file, as well as keeps unauthorized persons from gaining access to that file's information.

Another feature is that of *data portability*. VSAM is the only organization in which a disk containing VSAM data sets may be carried from one computer to another to allow processing of those data sets by the second computer.

## CHECKPOINT QUESTIONS

**15.** In what file organizations might dummy records be used? How are dummy records indicated in these files?

**16.** What are the major differences between an INDEXED data set and a VSAM-KSDS data set?

**17.** Which file organizations allow direct accessing of a specific record in the data set?

## DECLARING RECORD FILES

There are a number of attributes and options that you may specify in the declaration of files. Many of these were introduced in Chapter 7. Some of those will be reviewed here. New attributes and options that apply to the concepts discussed in this chapter will also be discussed. The attributes and/or options may be specified in any order. Thus,

    DCL INVEN FILE INPUT RECORD;

is the same as

    DCL INVEN FILE RECORD INPUT;

where the keywords INPUT and RECORD have been reversed in the sequence in which they appear. Here is a description of various file attributes:

## FILE Attribute

The FILE attribute, when used, denotes the identifier preceding FILE as a file name. For example, MASTER is declared to be a file name in the following statement:

DECLARE MASTER FILE . . .

However, the word FILE does not have to be specified if the compiler can determine from the other attributes (INPUT, OUTPUT, etc.) that the name declared could only be referring to a file. For documentation purposes, the FILE attribute should be declared.

## EXTERNAL/INTERNAL Attributes

EXTERNAL means that a declared file may be known in other PL/I procedures, providing those blocks also contain an external declaration of the same file name. The INTERNAL attribute specifies that the file name be known only in the procedure block in which it was declared. EXTERNAL is the default attribute. INTERNAL would be used when you want to ensure that the file you are declaring is *not* to be assumed to be the same as a file that might be named the same in another procedure that is part of the same program.

## STREAM/RECORD Attributes

STREAM/RECORD attributes describe the characteristics of the data to be used in input and output file operations. The STREAM attribute causes the file associated with the file name to be treated as a continuous stream of data in character format. The STREAM attribute can be specified only for files of CONSECUTIVE organization.

The RECORD attribute causes the file associated with the file name to be treated as a sequence of logical records, each record consisting of one or more data items recorded in any internal data format. RECORD may be used for any file organization and *must* be used for organizations other than CONSECUTIVE. STREAM is the default attribute.

## INPUT/OUTPUT/UPDATE Attributes

INPUT/OUTPUT/UPDATE attributes determine the direction of data transfer. The INPUT attribute applied to files that are to be read only. The OUTPUT attribute applies to files that are to be created or extended, and hence are to be written only. The UPDATE attribute describes a file that can be used for both input and output; it allows records in an existing DASD file to be altered. Tape records may not be rewritten because even rewriting a physical record of the same number of bytes may cause the following physical record to be adversely affected by the resulting interblock gap.

## BUFFERED/UNBUFFERED Attributes

A **buffer** is an area of main storage that is automatically reserved by PL/I for files having the BUFFERED attribute.

A buffer is an intermediate storage area through which data records pass in an input or output operation. Buffers are provided so that data can be read concurrently with the processing of a previously read record or written concurrently with the processing of the next record that is to be output. For blocked records, buffers provide the means for reading or writing a physical record while allowing the I/O routines to access one logical record in the buffer for each READ or WRITE. The buffer must be large enough to hold a physical record. The work area must be large enough to hold a logical record. For F BLKSIZE (800) RECSIZE (80) the associated buffer will be 800 bytes in size.

When an input file is "buffered," input data items are first read into the buffer and then transferred to your named structure or other data area.

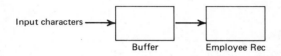

While a program is processing data in the EMPLOYEE_REC, it is possible for the system input routines to be reading the next record into another buffer. (Reading another record while concurrently processing the previous record is referred to as *overlapping*.) It would be necessary to have at least two buffers reserved to overlap input and processing from the same file, or processing and output to the same file. For blocked records, at least one buffer would have to be provided, even if no overlap is desired.

BUFFERED or UNBUFFERED only apply to files with the RECORD attribute. The UNBUFFERED attribute indicates that a physical record in a file *need* not pass through a buffer, but can be transferred directly to and from the internal storage area associated with the variable name in the READ or WRITE statement. In OS or OS/VS "hidden buffers," which may be needed by the I/O routines for processing the data, will be provided by PL/I and will in fact be used if INDEXED, REGIONAL (2), or REGIONAL (3) is specified or if the record is variable length. Records may not be blocked in a data set having the UNBUFFERED attribute. UNBUFFERED is the default for files accessed using the DIRECT access technique. Generally, there are no performance advantages to specifying the UNBUFFERED attribute.

The BUFFERED attribute normally applies to a file that has the SEQUENTIAL as well as the RECORD attributes. The BUFFERED attribute indicates that physical records transferred to and from a file *must* pass through an intermediate storage area. The use of buffers may help speed up processing by allowing overlap of I/O and compute time and is required for blocked files. To indicate the number of buffers, use the BUFFERS option in the ENVIRONMENT section of a file declaration. A tape file with ten 80-character records per block might be declared as follows:

> DCL TAPE FILE INPUT RECORD SEQUENTIAL BUFFERED
> ENV (F BLKSIZE(800) RECSIZE(80) BUFFERS(2));

There are two 800-character buffers provided, enabling two physical records (1600 bytes, total) to be held in storage. A READ statement,

> READ FILE (INPUT) INTO (DATA_AREA);

requires DATA_AREA to be 80 bytes, the size of one logical record.

## BACKWARDS Attribute

The BACKWARDS attribute applies to files stored on magnetic tape when reverse processing (i.e., from last record to first) is desired.

## KEYED Attribute

The KEYED attribute indicates that records in the file can be accessed by means of a key. KEYED applies to INDEXED, VSAM/KSDS, and REGIONAL files and therefore only to files with the RECORD attribute.

## SEQUENTIAL/DIRECT Attributes

SEQUENTIAL/DIRECT attributes are *access* attributes and apply only to files with the RECORD attribute. These attributes describe how the records are created or retrieved — the access technique.

The SEQUENTIAL attribute specifies that records are accessed in physical sequence — that is, from the first record of the file to the last for CONSECUTIVE, REGIONAL, and VSAM data sets. INDEXED data sets are accessed in key sequence.

The DIRECT attribute specifies that records are accessed in random order. The location of the record in the file is determined by its key or by its relative region number. For example:

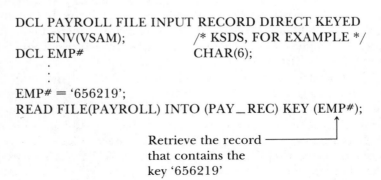

> DCL PAYROLL FILE INPUT RECORD DIRECT KEYED
>    ENV(VSAM);         /* KSDS, FOR EXAMPLE */
> DCL EMP#            CHAR(6);
>    :
>    :
> EMP# = '656219';
> READ FILE(PAYROLL) INTO (PAY_REC) KEY (EMP#);
>
>               Retrieve the record
>               that contains the
>               key '656219'

## ENVIRONMENT Attribute

The ENVIRONMENT attribute specifies the physical characteristics of the file. The characteristics are indicated in a parenthesized list of **options** following the attribute specification. For example:

ENVIRONMENT (option list);

⎣————→ Options specified must be separated by
a blank if there is no punctuation mark
associated with a given option

The options are not part of the *standard* PL/I language; they are keywords related to the capabilities or limitations of specific PL/I implementations on a given computer under its operating system. In this text, IBM's mainframe computers are referenced.

Figure 10.11 shows a partial list of options that may be specified in the ENVIRONMENT attribute for OS/VS type of operating systems. Note that some

| Purpose | ENVIRONMENT attribute options |
|---|---|
| Record format | F \| FB \| V \| VB \| U<br>RECSIZE (record-size)<br>BLKSIZE (block-size) |
|  | BUFFERS (n) |
| Type of file organization | CONSECUTIVE<br>INDEXED<br>VSAM<br>REGIONAL ( 1 \| 2 \| 3) |
| Magnetic tape options | LEAVE<br>REREAD |
| Indexed sequential file options | KEYLENGTH (n)<br>KEYLOC (n)<br>INDEXAREA (index-area-size)<br>ADDBUFF (n) |
| REGIONAL (2) or REGIONAL (3) file options | KEYLOCK (n)<br>KEYLENGTH (n) |
| Printer options | CTLASA<br>CTL360 |
| VSAM file options | PASSWORD<br>BUFND (n)<br>BUFNI (n)<br>BUFSP (n) |

FIGURE 10.11   Partial list of options for the ENVIRONMENT attribute in OS/VS PL/I implementations.

options are in conflict with other file attributes. For example, the INDEXED option is in conflict with the STREAM attribute. The number of "conflicts" that could arise could be considerable if you do not understand the principles of each type of file organization. For example, CONSECUTIVE files do not have recorded keys associated with them. If you specify KEYLOC for a CONSECUTIVE file, there is a conflict with the options specified. If such conflicts are noted on the output source listing of your PL/I program, consult a PL/I reference manual for the compiler you are using. Following is a description of some of the options listed in Figure 10.11.

**Record Format Options.** Record types may be specified in one of the following formats:

| | |
|---|---|
| F | Fixed-length, unblocked |
| FB | Fixed-length, blocked |
| V | Variable-length, unblocked |
| VB | Variable-length, blocked |
| U | Undefined-length (cannot be blocked) |

Following the record format designation (i.e., F, FB, etc.) the keyword BLKSIZE (n) and/or RECSIZE (n) is to be specified, where n may be a decimal integer constant or a variable with the attributes FIXED BINARY (31) STATIC. Here are some examples:

```
F BLKSIZE (80)   or   F RECSIZE (80)
FB BLKSIZE (800) RECSIZE (80)
V BLKSIZE (400)   or   V RECSIZE (400)
VB BLKSIZE (256) RECSIZE (126)
U BLKSIZE (1000)
```

Here is an example in which the record length specified is a variable whose value is determined when the program is executed:

```
DCL SIZE   FIXED BIN(31) STATIC;
DCL ALPHA FILE RECORD OUTPUT ENV(F BLKSIZE(SIZE));
GET LIST (SIZE); /* ESTABLISH BLOCKSIZE */
```

**BUFFERS (n) Option.** The BUFFERS (n) option specifies the number of buffers for files having the BUFFERED attribute. OS/VS VSAM files use the BUFND, BUFNI, and BUFSP options instead of the BUFFERS option.

**BUFND (n), BUFNI (n), BUFSP (n) Options.** These options supply information about the buffers for OS/VS VSAM data sets. The BUFND (n) option specifies the number of data buffers required. The BUFNI (n) specifies the number of index buffers required. The total buffer space, in bytes, required by the VSAM data set is specified in the BUFSP (n) option.

**CONSECUTIVE Option.** This is the type of data set organization in which records are organized on the basis of their successive physical positions in the data set. Records can only be processed in sequential order. Input/output devices permitted for CONSECUTIVE files include magnetic tape drives, line printers, disks, and drums.

**INDEXED Option.** In this type of organization, records are organized sequentially in a file stored on a direct access device. When the file is created, several levels of indexes are created. The indexes are subsequently used to locate specific records in INPUT and UPDATE operations.

**VSAM Option.** Before a VSAM data set is used for the first time, the data set structure, such as the record and key length, is defined to the system by commands that are provided in a program package called Access Method Services (AMS). Consequently, many of the ENVIRONMENT options required for INDEXED or REGIONAL are not needed for VSAM. All you need to specify in the ENVIRONMENT attribute is simply the keyword VSAM.

**REGIONAL (1|2|3) Option.** If any of these file organizations is desired, simply specify the appropriate designation in the ENVIRONMENT attribute. REGIONAL (2) is not available in DOS operating systems.

**LEAVE Option.** The LEAVE option positions the current volume at its logical end. It specifies that no rewind operation is to be performed on a tape file at the end of a tape volume or at close time. When used for files having the BACKWARDS attribute, the positioning of the file is at the physical beginning of the data set.

**REREAD Option.** This volume disposition option allows you to specify the action to be taken when the end of a magnetic tape volume is reached, or when a file on a magnetic tape volume is closed. This option rewinds the tape to permit reprocessing of the tape volume or data set. Repositioning of a BACKWARDS file will be at the physical end of the data set.

**KEYLENGTH (n) Option.** This option is used to specify the length of the key in INDEXED, REGIONAL (2), or REGIONAL (3) files.

**KEYLOC (n) Option.** This option is used to specify the high-order position (leftmost position) of the **keyfield** within the data record of an INDEXED file. For unblocked records, this keyword is optional; for blocked records, KEYLOC must be specified. The first position is numbered 0.

**INDEXAREA (n) Option.** This option is used for INDEXED DIRECT files. It specifies that the highest level of index is to be held in main storage.

For OS the index area size (n) allows you to limit the amount of main storage you are willing to provide. The highest-level index will be held in storage completely if the index area size is sufficient to hold it or if the index area size is omitted.

**ADDBUFF (n) Option.** This option is used when records are being added to an INDEXED file. The ADDBUFF option specifies the amount of main storage to be reserved for the shifting of records within a track when new records are being added to a DIRECT UPDATE INDEXED file. The value of n is generally the number of bytes on a track of a given DASD.

**CTLASA|CTL360 Options.** The CLTASA and the CTL360 options are two mutually exclusive options of the ENVIRONMENT attribute. They are used for record printer files; they specify whether the first character of the record to these files is to be interpreted as an ASA or SYSTEM/360 control character. It is the programmer's responsibility to provide a correct control character as the first character of the record. CTLASA is a before-print operation and CTL360 is an after-print operation.

The character codes that can be used with CTLASA are listed with their interpretations in Chapter 8, Figure 8.1.

**PASSWORD (Password-Specification).** When a VSAM data set is defined, passwords that control authorization of reading or updating the file may be specified. Declarations of PL/I files that access the VSAM data set must then provide the password. This is done in the PASSWORD option of the ENVIRONMENT attribute. The password is a maximum of eight characters. For example:

```
DCL MARINE FILE RECORD INPUT KEYED EXTERNAL DIRECT
    BUFFERED ENV (VSAM BUFND(2) BUFNI(2)
        PASSWORD ('NAUTILUS'));
```

Figure 10.12 contains some sample file declarations. Following are some comments on the declarations:

FILE1 An output file is written on magnetic tape or disk. The records are blocked variable length with a maximum record size of 100 bytes plus 4 bytes for the record-length field. A block size of 1252 bytes is specified to allow up to 12 maximum-sized records in a block.

FILE2 An INDEXED file is accessed directly with the possibility of updating (rewriting) selected records. The records are blocked, so both the KEYLENGTH and KEYLOC are specified. The key is in the sixth byte (OS/VS numbers from zero) and is seven bytes long. An INDEX AREA is provided, which is large enough to hold the highest level of index. The ADDBUFF option causes a storage area large enough to hold an entire track of data to speed up the addition of records to the file.

FILE3 A REGIONAL (1) data set is to be read directly. The data set is unblocked. The KEY provided will contain the region number of the desired record. This file name

```
DCL FILE1 FILE RECORD OUTPUT SEQUENTIAL BUFFERED EXTERNAL
    ENV(CONSECUTIVE VB BLKSIZE(1252) RECSIZE(104) BUFFERS(2));

DCL FILE2 FILE RECORD UPDATE DIRECT UNBUFFERED EXTERNAL KEYED
    ENV(INDEXED FB BLKSIZE(900) RECSIZE(150) KEYLOC(5) KEYLENGTH(7)
    INDEXAREA ADDBUFF);

DCL FILE3 FILE RECORD INPUT DIRECT UNBUFFERED INTERNAL KEYED
    ENV(REGIONAL(1) F BLKSIZE(267) RECSIZE(267));

DCL FILE4 FILE RECORD OUTPUT SEQUENTIAL BUFFERED EXTERNAL KEYED
    ENV(REGIONAL(3) U BLKSIZE(600) RECSIZE(600) KEYLENGTH(6));

DCL FILE5 FILE RECORD UPDATE DIRECT BUFFERED EXTERNAL KEYED ENV(VSAM);

DCL FILE6 FILE RECORD OUTPUT SEQUENTIAL BUFFERED EXTERNAL KEYED
    ENV(INDEXED FB BLKSIZE(800) RECSIZE(200) BUFFERS(2) KEYLENGTH(10)
    KEYLOC(2) INDEXAREA MEDIUM(SYS005,2314));
```

FIGURE 10.12   Sample file declarations.

|       | (FILE3) is known only to this procedure and any procedures nested within it. |
|-------|---|
| FILE4 | A REGIONAL (3) data set is to be created sequentially with records in the UNDEFINED format. The KEY specifies the relative track and control field which identifies the record. A capacity record on each track will indicate the amount of space left to hold records. |
| FILE5 | A VSAM file is to be accessed directly with the possibility of rewriting selected records. Most of the options required by VSAM are provided in the access method services program. |
| FILE6 | This is a declaration for the creation of a DOS/VS IN-DEXED file containing blocked fixed length records. The KEY is in the second byte of the record (DOS/VS numbers starting with position 1) and is 10 bytes long. The file will be on a 2314 disk drive. An index area large enough to hold the track is to be allocated. |

## Open Statement Attributes

The OPEN statement for a stream or record file associates a file name declared in the PL/I program with a physical data set on an external storage device. It can also be used to specify additional attributes for a file if a complete set of attributes has not been previously declared. The general format is

OPEN FILE (file name) additional attributes;

If attributes are specified in the OPEN statement (see Figure 10.13), then those attributes must not be specified in the file declaration statement. The options LINESIZE and PAGESIZE were described in Chapter 7, which covered stream I/O, as these options may only be specified for stream files. The TITLE option

| Attributes that may be specified in OPEN statement | |
|---|---|
| DOS or DOS/VS | PAGESIZE<br>INPUT and OUTPUT if file has UNBUFFERED attribute<br>TITLE |
| OS or OS/VS | BUFFERED or UNBUFFERED<br>STREAM or RECORD<br>INPUT, OUTPUT, or UPDATE<br>PRINT, LINESIZE, PAGESIZE<br>DIRECT or SEQUENTIAL<br>BACKWARDS<br>KEYED<br>TITLE |

FIGURE 10.13  File attributes allowed in the OPEN statement.

allows you to choose dynamically — at open time — one among several data sets to be associated with a particular file name.  For example:

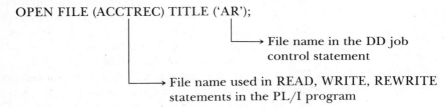

OPEN FILE (ACCTREC) TITLE ('AR');

File name in the DD job control statement

File name used in READ, WRITE, REWRITE statements in the PL/I program

The file name (ACCTREC) is not used outside the program.  The title name (AR) is assumed to identify the appropriate data set.  In OS, the title name relates to the DD job control statement.  For example:

```
// GO.AR   DD   DSN = ACCOUNTS.RECEIVABLE,
//                 etc.
```

## I/O STATEMENTS

The record I/O statements that are used to communicate with files include READ, WRITE, REWRITE, and DELETE.  The READ and WRITE statements cause the transfer of data into main storage (READ) or from main storage (WRITE).  The REWRITE statement is an output statement that transfers a record from an area in main storage to a file that has the UPDATE attribute.  The REWRITE statement is used when modifying an *existing* record in a file.  A WRITE statement is issued when *creating* a file or adding a new record to an existing file.  The DELETE statement physically removes a record from the file (as in the case of VSAM-KSDS files) or "flags" the record as a null record (INDEXED files).  Note that DELETE does not apply to CONSECUTIVE or VSAM-ESDS files.

Figure 10.14 shows a number of forms that I/O statements may take for each file organization. To use this chart, first determine the type of processing you wish to accomplish from the *file attributes* column on the left. Following that column are the *corresponding valid statements* that may be used to communicate with a file that has the specified attributes. The *comments* column tells you when to use each type of I/O statement.

## ON-UNITS AND BUILT-IN FUNCTIONS

### On-Units

The on-units for record I/O files are as follows:

**KEY Condition.** The KEY condition is raised during operations on keyed records in any of the following cases:

**1.** The keyed record cannot be found for a READ or REWRITE statement. In this case, the contents of the variable are unpredictable.

**2.** An attempt is made to add a duplicate key by a WRITE statement.

**3.** The key has not been correctly specified (this typically shows up during the debugging phases of programming).

**4.** No space is available to add the keyed record.

In the absence of an on-unit, the system prints a message and raises the ERROR condition. KEY is always enabled; it cannot be disabled and a null on-unit cannot be specified. Here is a sample statement:

```
ON KEY(FILE1)
    BEGIN;
        KEY_ERROR_SWITCH = YES;
        CODE = ONCODE;
        PUT SKIP EDIT('KEY ERROR FOR FILE1, ONCODE IS',
            CODE) (A);
    END;
```

Your program would then test KEY_ERROR_SWITCH following the I/O operation that could have raised the key condition. For example:

```
READ FILE (INDEXED) INTO (INVENTORY_RECORD_AREA)
    KEY (PART_NUMBER);
IF KEY_ERROR_SWITCH THEN
    CALL NO_MATCHING_PART_NUMBER;
ELSE
    CALL UPDATE_PART_IN_INVENTORY;
```

**UNDEFINEDFILE Condition.** The UNDEFINEDFILE condition is raised whenever an attempt to open a file is unsuccessful. Some causes for the condition occurring include:

**1.** A conflict in attributes exists (e.g., opening a CONSECUTIVE data set with DIRECT or KEYED attributes).

**2.** Attributes are incomplete (e.g., no block size specified, no keylength specified for creation of indexed data sets).

In the absence of an on-unit, the system prints a message and raises the ERROR condition. The UNDEFINEDFILE condition is always enabled and cannot be disabled. Upon normal completion of the on-unit, control is given to the statement immediately following the statement that caused the condition to be raised.

**RECORD Condition.** The RECORD condition can be raised during a READ, WRITE, or REWRITE operation. On input operations it is raised by either of the following:

**1.** The size of the record on the data set is greater than the size of the variable into which the record is to be read (for F, V, U formats).

**2.** The size of the record is less than the size of the variable (for F format).

If the size of the record is greater than the size of the variable, the excess data in the record is lost. If the size of the record is less than the size of the variable, the excess data area in the variable is unaltered. For a WRITE or REWRITE operation, the RECORD condition can be raised:

**1.** When the size of the variable from which the record is to be written is greater than the maximum size specified for the record (F, V, U formats).

**2.** When the size of the variable is less than the size specified for the record (F format).

If the size of the variable is greater than the maximum record size, then the excess data in the variable is not transmitted. If the size of the variable is less than the stated record size for fixed length record, then the contents of the excess data position in the record are unpredictable. (In the case of fixed blocked records, the RECORD condition is raised as many times as there are records in the block.) In the absence of an on-unit, the system prints a message and raises the ERROR condition. RECORD is always enabled; it cannot be disabled.

### Built-In Functions

The following built-in functions are useful in responding to errors detected by the system during the execution of PL/I statements that communicate with files typically located on direct access devices.

**ONKEY Built-In Function.** ONKEY extracts the value of the key for the record that caused an I/O condition to be raised. This function can be used in the on-unit for an I/O condition or a CONVERSION condition; it can also be used in an on-unit for an ERROR condition. The value returned by this function is a varying length character-string giving the value of the key for the record that caused an I/O condition to be raised. For example:

```
DCL KEY_IN_ERROR   CHAR(9) VARYING;
DCL ONKEY          BUILTIN;
ON KEY(FILE1)
    BEGIN;
        KEY_IN_ERROR = ONKEY;
        .
        .
        .
    END;
```

If the interrupt is not associated with a keyed record, the returned value is the null string.

**ONFILE Built-In Function.** ONFILE determines the name of the file for which an I/O or CONVERSION condition was raised and returns that name to the point of invocation. This function can be used in the on-unit for any I/O or CONVERSION condition. The value returned by this function is a varying-length character-string, of 31-character maximum length, consisting of the name of the file for which an I/O or CONVERSION condition was raised. For example, this built-in function is needed in the KEY on-unit if there is more than one keyed data set for which the KEY condition could be raised:

```
DCL NAME       CHAR(31) VARYING;
DCL ONFILE     BUILTIN;
ON KEY(FILE2)
    BEGIN;
        NAME = ONFILE;
        .
        .
        .
    END;
```

In the case of a CONVERSION condition, if that condition is not associated with a file, the returned value is the null string.

## CHECKPOINT QUESTIONS

**18.** If records in a DASD file are modified, is it necessary to create a new file as it is with tape files?

**19.** What are the advantages of a BUFFERED file?

**20.** In the following DECLARE statement, which omitted attribute is mandatory?

DCL FILE FILE RECORD OUTPUT SEQUENTIAL ENV(INDEXED F
BLKSIZE(400) RECSIZE(80) EXTENTNUMBER(2)
KEYLENGTH(16) OFLTRACKS(2));

(a) EXTERNAL
(b) DIRECT
(c) KEYED
(d) BACKWARDS

**21.** In the following DECLARE statement, which attribute must also be declared?

DCL KEYED FILE RECORD INPUT DIRECT ENV(F BLKSIZE(1024)
REGIONAL(1));

(a) EXTERNAL
(b) BUFFERED
(c) UNBUFFERED
(d) KEYED

**22.** Which of the following combinations of attributes and options are in conflict
with each other?

(a) STREAM UPDATE
(b) ENV (U BLKSIZE(800) RECSIZE(80) CONSECUTIVE)
(c) SEQUENTIAL ENV (REGIONAL (1))
(d) KEYED ENV (CONSECUTIVE)
(e) SEQL KEYED ENV (INDEXED)

**23.** Write the PL/I output statement to transmit a record from the variable
AREA_1 to XFILE, a REGIONAL (1) output file. The file has been declared

DCL XFILE FILE RECORD OUTPUT DIRECT KEYED
ENV (F BLKSIZE(100) REGIONAL(1));

The record is to be written to region number 293.

**24.** Which types of organization use recorded keys on the external medium?

(a) CONSECUTIVE
(b) INDEXED
(c) VSAM-ESDS
(d) VSAM-KSDS
(e) REGIONAL (1)
(f) REGIONAL (2)
(g) REGIONAL (3)

**25.** What would happen if you issue a READ to an indexed data set supplying a key, processing DIRECT, and there is no record with the specified key in the data set?

## CASE STUDY: FILE CREATE AND FILE UPDATE

This case study illustrates two major steps in disk file programming: file create and file update. Before a disk file can be **updated** it must be *created*. File creation typically involves reading records from a medium such as disk (diskette) or mini-magnetic tapes, and storing that information in the disk file. Once created, the file can be updated with subsequent transactions. These transactions take the form of "updates" to the file. Updating involves changing the contents of existing records (e.g., "adding" or "subtracting" from the quantity on hand in an inventory file). Updating could also involve adding new records to a file or deleting records from that file. This case study illustrates all of these file programming activities through two separate programs: file create and file update.

This case study has been selected because it incorporates as many file organization types as might be realistic for a program application. The file organizations include a CONSECUTIVE file, two INDEXED sequential files, and one REGIONAL (1) file. Before examining the actual PL/I coding, let us consider a situation where the disk file processing approach is feasible. Figure 10.14 shows some sample data related to plant materials that could be used in landscaping. The information could be stored in a record as follows:

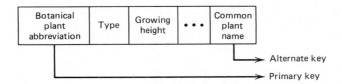

This record is stored in a disk file based on the record's key. In this particular case, the abbreviation for the botanical plant name is the *primary key*. Records will be stored in ascending sequence according to this key. On occasion, however, it will be necessary to generate reports based on the common plant name in ascending sequence. The common plant name then becomes an *alternate key* because it represents another way to view the contents of the file.

If a file is stored in a given sequence, it is necessary to sort the input records into ascending sequence based on that sequence before creating the permanent file. If it is necessary to process records based on sequence, then it is necessary to re-sort a copy of the file, this time arranging the records into ascending sequence based on an alternate sequence.

An alternative method to sorting records each time an alternate sequence of

| BOTANICAL ABBREVIA- TION | TYPE | GROWING HEIGHT | ORIGIN | SEASON | CLIMATE | SOIL | COMMON NAME |
|---|---|---|---|---|---|---|---|
| AJUGA | PERENNIAL | 4 INCHES | EUROPE | SUMMER | GRND COVER | REG WATER | BLUE BUGLE |
| ALOE | SUCCULENT | 15 FEET | SO AFRICA | SPRING | ORNAMENTAL | DRY AREAS | TREE ALOE |
| ARUM | PERENNIAL | 15 INCHES | ISRAEL | SPRING | FULL SHADE | HVY WATER | BLACKCALLA |
| ASTER | PERENNIAL | 3 FEET | NO. AMER. | AUTUMN | FULL SUN | RICH SOIL | HEATHASTER |
| BIXA | SHRUB | 20 FEET | W. INDIES | SUMMER | TROPICAL | HVY WATER | LIPSTICK P |
| BUTEA | TREE | 50 FEET | E. INDIES | SUMMER | SUBTROPIC | WARM | DHAK TREE |
| CANNA | PERENNIAL | 6 FEET | W. INDIES | SUMMER | TROPICAL | CUT STEMS | IND. SHOT |
| CYCAS | TREE | 7 FEET | CHINA | ALL YEAR | MILD CLIM | SLOW GROW | SAGO PALM |
| ERICA | SHRUB | 5 FEET | EUROPE | WINTER | FULL SUN | SANDY SOIL | SPAN HEATH |
| FAGUS | TREE | 30 FEET | EUROPE | SPRING-AUT | SHADE | LIME SOIL | COPPER BCH |
| FICUS | SHRUB | 10 FEET | AFRICA | ALL YEAR | TROPICAL | | BANJO FIG |
| HAKEA | TREE | 20 FEET | W. AUSTRAL | WINTER | FULL SUN | ACID SOIL | SEA URCHIN |
| HEBE | SHRUB | 5 FEET | NEW ZEAL | WINTER | MILD | GOOD DRAIN | VERONICA |
| HOYA | CLIMBER | 30 FEET | S. CHINA | SPRING | SUBTROPIC | POTBOUND | WAXFLOWER |
| HUMEA | BIENNIAL | 6 FEET | AUSTRALIA | SUMMER | SUBTROPIC | NO WIND | INCENSE PL |
| IBOZA | SHRUB | 5 FEET | S. AFRICA | WINTER | MILD | SANDY SOIL | NUTMEG BSH |
| IRIS | RHIZOME | 3 FEET | HYBRID | SPRING | | | FLAG IRIS |
| IXIA | BULB | 3 FEET | S. AFRICA | SPRING | NO COLD | IN LAWNS | BLUE IXIA |
| LOTUS | SHRUB | 6 INCHES | CANARY ILE | SPRING | SUBTROPIC | ROCK POCK | CORAL GEM |
| MALUS | TREE | 8 FEET | U S A | L. SPRING | SHADE | WELL-DRAIN | FLOR APPLE |
| MALVA | PERENNIAL | 2 FEET | EUROPE | SUMMER | HARDY | AVG SOIL | MUSK MALLO |
| MELIA | TREE | 20 FEET | WORLD-WIDE | SUMMER | DRY-MOIST | | WH. CEDAR |
| OCHNA | SHRUB | 5 FEET | S. AFRICA | SPRING | SUBTROPIC | HARDY | MICK MOUSE |
| PHLOX | ANNUAL | 10 INCHES | HYBRID | SUMMER | HOT | ANY SOIL | STAR PHLOX |
| PICEA | TREE | 20 FEET | W. USA | ALL YEAR | COLD | ANY SOIL | BLUE SPRUC |
| PILEA | PERENNIAL | 18 INCHES | VIETNAM | SUMMER | TROPICAL | LEAFY SOIL | ALUMINUM |
| RHOEO | PERENNIAL | 15 INCHES | MEXICO | ALL YEAR | TROP-SUBTR | LT WATER | ADAM & EVE |
| SALIX | TREE | 20 FEET | N. ASIA | WINTER | BOGGY | HVY WATER | PUSSY WILL |
| SASA | PERENNIAL | 15 INCHES | JAPAN | ALL YEAR | SHADY | DAMP | DWF BAMBOO |
| SEDUM | SUCCULENT | 6 INCHES | MEXICO | SPRING | ROCKY | ANY SOIL | JELLY BEAN |
| ULEX | SHRUB | 6 FEET | EUROPE | SPRING | HARDY | USED SOIL | GORSE |
| VINCA | PERENNIAL | TRAILING | EUROPE | SPRING | SHADY | HVY WATER | PERIWINKLE |
| VITIS | CLIMBER | 90 FEET | JAPAN | AUTUMN | S. HEMISPH | QUICK GROW | GLORY VINE |
| YUCCA | PERENNIAL | 6 FEET | SE EUROPE | SPRING | ADAPTABLE | DESERT-DRY | SP BAYONET |
| ZEA | ANNUAL | 6 FEET | U S A | AUTUMN | SPRNG SOW | | IND. CORN |

FIGURE 10.14

records is needed is to create multiple indexes. For the plant example, this could be handled by placing the records into a REGIONAL (1) file. Recall that in a REGIONAL (1) file, records are referenced by *region number;* thus the plant 'AJUGA' might be placed in region 1, 'VINCA' placed in region 2, 'ALOE' in region 3, etc. To locate specific records in the regional file, it is necessary to keep the plant abbreviations and their region location in another file — an indexed sequential file. For example:

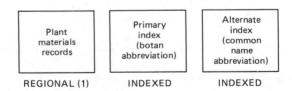

The alternate index approach has the advantage that records in a file will not have to be sorted when records in that sequence are desired. This simply saves computer time spent in the repetitive task of rearranging records every time it is desired to generate reports based on alternative sequences.

## THE FILE CREATE PROGRAM

The File Create program creates a REGIONAL (1) data set from a CONSECU-TIVE data set called INPUT.

## Index and Master File

Records that contain an 'L' in the first position of records in the INPUT file are to be placed into the REGIONAL (1) file, called REG1 in these programs. At the same time records are being stored into the REG1 file, an INDEXED data set called ISAM is also created. ISAM will be the primary index. Here are the record descriptions for each of these files:

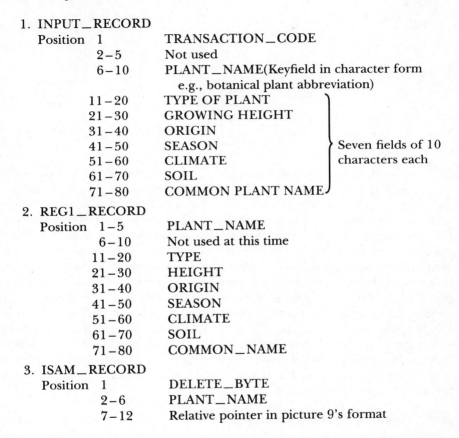

1. INPUT_RECORD

   Position 1            TRANSACTION_CODE
   
          2–5        Not used
   
         6–10      PLANT_NAME(Keyfield in character form
   
                                   e.g., botanical plant abbreviation)
   
       11–20      TYPE OF PLANT ⎫
   
       21–30      GROWING HEIGHT ⎪
   
       31–40      ORIGIN ⎪
   
       41–50      SEASON ⎬ Seven fields of 10
   
       51–60      CLIMATE ⎪ characters each
   
       61–70      SOIL ⎪
   
       71–80      COMMON PLANT NAME ⎭

2. REG1_RECORD

   Position 1–5      PLANT_NAME
   
        6–10      Not used at this time
   
       11–20      TYPE
   
       21–30      HEIGHT
   
       31–40      ORIGIN
   
       41–50      SEASON
   
       51–60      CLIMATE
   
       61–70      SOIL
   
       71–80      COMMON_NAME

3. ISAM_RECORD

   Position 1          DELETE_BYTE
   
        2–6      PLANT_NAME
   
       7–12      Relative pointer in picture 9's format

As an example of how records in the ISAM data set would actually look on the disk, consider the following diagram:

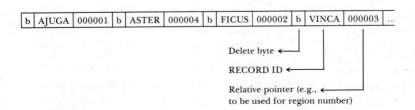

The lowercase b represents the delete byte required for ISAM records under IBM's operating systems. The keys are in ascending sequence.

The term RECORD_ID is used to indicate that any primary key may be specified. Following the key specification is the *relative pointer*. This is the region number in which the corresponding record is stored in the REG1 data set. As will be seen, the *file create program* generates this ISAM file of keys and relative pointers.

As further illustrations, records in the REG1 file would look like this:

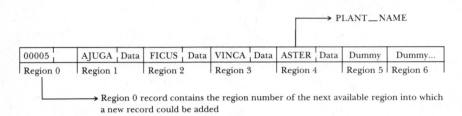

Notice from this illustration that the first record is placed in region 1, the second record in region 2, etc. One of the considerations in the design of the plant materials file is to provide for changes to the size of the file.

Thus, it is necessary to define a file space large enough to contain new records. Notice then from the preceding example that *dummy* records are shown to handle the subsequent addition of records. (In this case study, the addition of records is made at the end of the REG1 file rather than inserted in any available space that may develop due to subsequent deletions within the file.) Because the entire file space is not filled with records, we must have a way of keeping track of the next available region into which a new record could be placed. Region 0 is used for this purpose. It contains the region number of the next available region into which a new record could be added. Thus, as will be seen, the *file create program* keeps track of the successive region numbers into which records are written and then writes the next available region number into region 0 as one of the last processing steps in the program.

### Building the Alternate Index

In this case study, an alternative index is created based on the field called COMMON_NAME. Here is a description of the alternate index record for this case study:

| Position | 1 | Delete byte |
| | 2–11 | Key (COMMON_NAME, a character-string of length 10) |
| | 12–17 | Relative pointer in picture 9s |

The *file create program* writes these records in a CONSECUTIVE work file because the indexed sequential file cannot be created for the alternative index at this time. This is because records initially written into an indexed sequential file must

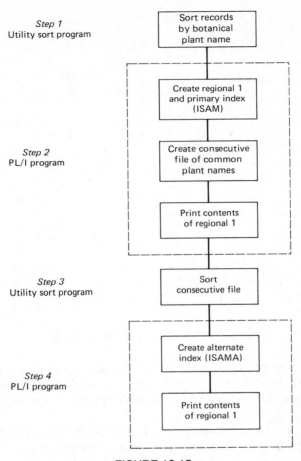

Step 1
Utility sort program

Sort records
by botanical
plant name

Step 2
PL/I program

Create regional 1
and primary index
(ISAM)

Create consecutive
file of common
plant names

Print contents
of regional 1

Step 3
Utility sort program

Sort
consecutive file

Step 4
PL/I program

Create alternate
index (ISAMA)

Print contents
of regional 1

FIGURE 10.15

be in ascending sequence based on the key field. In this example, the key field COMMON_NAME will not be in ascending sequence because the input records have been sorted in botanical plant name sequence for the creation of the primary index. To create the alternate index, a sort program used to arrange the alternate sequence index records into ascending sequenced based on the COMMON_ NAME field. This sorting of records, however, is a one-time operation because creating a file is "in theory" a one-time operation.

Figure 10.15 illustrates the four-step job required to create the master file. Step 1 involves using a *sort program* to arrange records by botanical plant name. Step 2 involves execution of the PL/I *file create program*. This program will be illustrated in the case study. Notice in this step that the INDEXED file created is the primary index. A CONSECUTIVE file of common plant names is also created and the contents of the REGIONAL (1) file are listed on the line printer. This printing of file contents is a typical program step, executed so that file

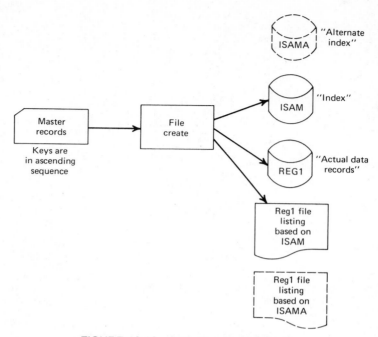

FIGURE 10.16 Data flow for file create.

contents may be visually inspected to ensure that the file contains the information it was intended to hold. (This visual inspection of printed output of file contents is of greater value in achieving data reliability if done by someone other than the programmer.)

Step 3 in Figure 10.15 shows the sorting of the CONSECUTIVE file output from Step 2. Again, a *sort program* is used. Step 4 again involves a PL/I program which takes the output from the *sort program* and creates the alternate index file called ISAMA. The program for Step 4 will not be illustrated in this case study. It would require reading the sorted CONSECUTIVE file which was created in Step 2 and creating the INDEXED data set. Figure 10.16 provides another view of the data just described.

Now let us examine the PL/I program that creates the master file and primary index. Here is the hierarchy chart for the file create program.

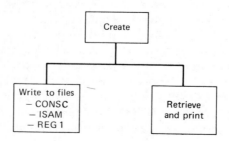

```
                                                                        */
/**********************************************************************/
/*   PROGRAM NAME:  CREATE                                            */
/*                                                                    */
/*   DESCRIPTION:   THIS PROGRAM READS AN INPUT FILE AND CREATES AN   */
/*                  ISAM DATASET USING PLANT NAME AS KEY.  EACH ISAM  */
/*                  RECORD HAS A FIELD CALLED RELATIVE POINTER WHICH  */
/*                  CONTAINS THE KEY INTO THE REGIONAL DATASET WHERE  */
/*                  THE DATA IS STORED.  A CONSECUTIVE FILE IS ALSO   */
/*                  WRITTEN.  IT IS THE SAME AS THE ABOVE FILE, BUT   */
/*                  INSTEAD OF PLANT NAME, THE COMMON NAME IS IN ITS  */
/*                  PLACE.  THE CONSECUTIVE FILE IS LATER SORTED BY   */
/*                  THIS COMMON NAME AND AN ISAM FILE IS CREATED.     */
/*                  LASTLY, THE REGIONAL FILE IS PRINTED TO VERIFY    */
/*                  INPUT.                                            */
/*                                                                    */
/*   INPUT:         INPUT - INPUT RECORDS FOR CREATION OF FILES.      */
/*                  ISAM, REG1 - AFTER THESE FILES ARE CREATED THEY   */
/*                      ARE CLOSED AND REOPENED AS INPUT TO PRINT     */
/*                      CONTENTS OF THE REGIONAL FILE ON THE REPORT.  */
/*                                                                    */
/*   OUTPUT:        CONSC - CONSECUTIVE FILE                          */
/*                  ISAM  - KEYED BY PLANT NAME                       */
/*                  REG1  - REGIONAL FILE CONTAINING PLANT DATA       */
/*                                                                    */
/**********************************************************************/
CREATE:  PROC OPTIONS(MAIN);
/**********************************************************************/
/*   FILE DECLARATIONS                                               */
/**********************************************************************/
DCL CONSC FILE RECORD ENV(CONSECUTIVE);
DCL INPUT FILE RECORD INPUT ENV(CONSECUTIVE F BLKSIZE(80));
DCL ISAM  FILE RECORD KEYED ENV(INDEXED);
DCL REG1  FILE RECORD KEYED ENV(REGIONAL(1));
```

FIGURE 10.17   (page 1)   File create program.

Figure 10.17 shows the PL/I coding.  Rather than call your attention to specific statements in the program, the logical subfunctions (i.e., segments) will be discussed as a whole.

**CREATE Segment.** Statements 14 through 27 provide the nucleus of the program.  Three files are explicitly opened (CONSC, ISAM, and REG1) because file attributes must be added to complete the file definition.  As will be seen in the next segment, two of these files are closed and then reopened with different file attributes.  The ability to specify file attributes at open time gives an increased flexibility to the PL/I program.  (Recall that attributes specified in the DE-CLARE statement remain in effect for the entire duration of the program and therefore would not give the program the flexibility of being able to **read** the file records just written.)  Notice in this segment that there is no on-unit for the KEY condition.  It is not necessary to specify such an on-unit if standard system action is acceptable should a key error occur.  Actually a key error could occur if the input records are not properly sorted because indexed sequential requires that keys be in ascending sequence.  A key error could also occur for duplicate keys. The standard system action for a key error is to print an error message and terminate the job.  This segment initializes the relative pointer for the ISAM record to 1.  This is the *region number* specification for subsequent references to

```
/*******************************************************************/
/*   RECORD DEFINITIONS                                            */
/*******************************************************************/
DCL 1 CONSECUTIVE_REC,
        2 DELETE_BYTE           CHAR(1)         INIT(' '),
        2 COMMON_NAME           CHAR(10),
        2 CR_RELATIVE_PTR       PIC'(6)9';

DCL 1 PLANT_REC1,
        2 TRANSACTION_CODE      CHAR(1),
        2 FILL_IN               CHAR(4),
        2 PLANT_NAME            PIC'(5)X',
        2 TYPE                  CHAR(10),
        2 HEIGHT                CHAR(10),
        2 ORIGIN                CHAR(10),
        2 SEASON                CHAR(10),
        2 CLIMATE               CHAR(10),
        2 SOIL                  CHAR(10),
        2 COMMON_NAME           CHAR(10);

DCL 1 PLANT_REC2,
        2 PLANT_NAME            PIC'(5)X',
        2 FILLER                CHAR(5),
        2 TYPE                  CHAR(10),
        2 HEIGHT                CHAR(10),
        2 ORIGIN                CHAR(10),
        2 SEASON                CHAR(10),
        2 CLIMATE               CHAR(10),
        2 SOIL                  CHAR(10),
        2 COMMON_NAME           CHAR(10);

DCL 1 ISAM_REC,
        2 DELETE_BYTE           CHAR(1)         INIT(' '),
        2 PLANT_NAME            PIC'(5)X',
        2 IR_RELATIVE_PTR       PIC'(6)9';

/*******************************************************************/
/*   CONSTANTS AND VARIABLES                                       */
/*******************************************************************/
DCL MORE_RECORDS                BIT(1);
DCL NO                          BIT(1)          INIT('0'B);
DCL YES                         BIT(1)          INIT('1'B);

DCL SUBSTR                      BUILTIN;

/*******************************************************************/
/*   ON CODES                                                      */
/*******************************************************************/
ON ENDFILE(INPUT)
   MORE_RECORDS = NO;

ON ENDFILE(ISAM)
   MORE_RECORDS = NO;
```

FIGURE 10.17   (page 2)   File create program.

the REG1 file. Statement 25 shows the WRITE statement to region 0. (Recall that region 0 is to contain the region number of the next available region into which a new record could be added.)

Segments are subfunctions in a hierarchy chart. Typically, these subfunctions translate into nested procedures within your program. However, they do not have to. Statement 27 for example, could represent the subfunction of retrieving REG1 file contents and listing each record on the line printer, according to the sequence indicated by the primary index.

**WRITE _ TO _ FILES Segment.** This segment is called by the nucleus. It handles the moving of data records from the input file record area to the specified output records. It shows three WRITE statements, one for each output file. Finally, it increments the relative pointer.

**PRINT _ FILE _ DATA Segment.** This segment is invoked by the *retrieve segment*. It encompasses Statements 28 – 37. Although the segment is small, actual reading of the REG1 file record and printing using a PUT EDIT were designed as a

```
/*****************************************************************/
/*                                                             */
/*   PROGRAM NUCLEUS                                           */
/*                                                             */
/*****************************************************************/
OPEN FILE(CONSC)  SEQUENTIAL OUTPUT,
     FILE(ISAM)   SEQUENTIAL OUTPUT,
     FILE(REG1)   DIRECT OUTPUT;
MORE_RECORDS     = YES;
IR_RELATIVE_PTR = 1;
READ FILE(INPUT) INTO(PLANT_REC1);
DO WHILE(MORE_RECORDS);
    IF TRANSACTION_CODE = 'L' THEN
        CALL WRITE_TO_FILES;
    READ FILE(INPUT) INTO(PLANT_REC1);
END;
PLANT_REC2.PLANT_NAME = SUBSTR(IR_RELATIVE_PTR,2,5);
WRITE FILE(REG1) FROM(PLANT_REC2) KEYFROM('0');
CLOSE FILE(ISAM),
      FILE(REG1);
CALL PRINT_FILE_DATA;
/*****************************************************************/
/*                                                             */
/*   PRINT FILE DATA                                           */
/*                                                             */
/*****************************************************************/
PRINT_FILE_DATA:  PROC;
    OPEN FILE(ISAM) SEQUENTIAL INPUT,
         FILE(REG1) DIRECT INPUT;
    MORE_RECORDS = YES;
    READ FILE(ISAM) INTO(ISAM_REC);
    DO WHILE(MORE_RECORDS);
        READ FILE(REG1) INTO(PLANT_REC2) KEY(IR_RELATIVE_PTR);
        PUT EDIT(PLANT_REC2.PLANT_NAME,PLANT_REC2.TYPE,PLANT_REC2.HEIGHT,
            PLANT_REC2.ORIGIN,PLANT_REC2.SEASON,PLANT_REC2.CLIMATE,
            PLANT_REC2.SOIL,PLANT_REC2.COMMON_NAME)
            (SKIP,A,COL(10),(7)(A(10),X(1)));
        READ FILE(ISAM)INTO(ISAM_REC);
    END;
END PRINT_FILE_DATA;
```

FIGURE 10.17   (page 3)   File create program.

```
/******************************************************************/
/*                                                                */
/*   WRITE TO FILES                                               */
/*                                                                */
/*   MOVE INPUT DATA FIELDS TO APPROPRIATE OUTPUT DATA FIELDS UNTIL */
/*   THE CONSECUTIVE, ISAM, AND REGIONAL FILES INCREMENT THE RELATIVE */
/*   POINTER.                                                     */
/*                                                                */
/******************************************************************/
WRITE_TO_FILES:  PROC;
     CONSECUTIVE_REC.COMMON_NAME = PLANT_REC1.COMMON_NAME;
     CR_RELATIVE_PTR      = IR_RELATIVE_PTR;
     ISAM_REC.PLANT_NAME = PLANT_REC1.PLANT_NAME;
     PLANT_REC2           = PLANT_REC1, BY NAME;
     WRITE FILE(CONSC) FROM(CONSECUTIVE_REC);
     WRITE FILE(ISAM)  FROM(ISAM_REC) KEYFROM(ISAM_REC.PLANT_NAME);
     WRITE FILE(REG1)  FROM(PLANT_REC2) KEYFROM(IR_RELATIVE_PTR);
     IR_RELATIVE_PTR = IR_RELATIVE_PTR + 1;
END WRITE_TO_FILES;

END CREATE;
//GO.CONSC DD UNIT=3350,DSN=EXDATA.CASE1.CONSC,
//            DISP=(NEW,CATLG),SPACE=(TRK,(1,1)),VOL=SER=TSO503,
//            DCB=(RECFM=FB,LRECL=17,BLKSIZE=170)
//GO.REG1  DD UNIT=3350,DSN=EXDATA.CASE1.REG1,
//            DISP=(NEW,CATLG),SPACE=(TRK,(1,1)),VOL=SER=TSO503,
//            DCB=(RECFM=F,LRECL=80,DSORG=DA)
//GO.ISAM DD DSN=EXDATA.CASE1.ISAM,UNIT=3350,VOL=SER=TSO503,
//            DISP=(NEW,CATLG),SPACE=(CYL,(1),,CONTIG),
//            DCB=(RECFM=F,BLKSIZE=12,
//            RKP=1,DSORG=IS,KEYLEN=5,OPTCD=L)
//GO.INPUT     DD    *
```

FIGURE 10.17   (page 4)   File create program.

separate segment because it will be useful in the *file update program*. It is always a good structured programming approach to design as separate procedures segments that may have more than one use or application. This approach can save redundant coding effort, as well as reduce program debug time.

## THE FILE UPDATE PROGRAM

Figure 10.18 shows the data flow for the update of the file that was created in the first part of this case study. The transactions that are input are in random order. This creates the need, then, for a *direct*-access method of retrieving records. The transactions are one of three types: The transaction could contain an A in column 1, in which case that record is to be *added* to the REG1 file. If the input transaction record contains a U in column 1, then an existing record in the REG1 file is to be replaced (**updated**) by the contents of the input record. Finally, if the input transaction record contains a D in column 1, then the corresponding record in the REG1 file is to be *deleted*. Of course when records are to be added to or deleted from the REG1 file, the corresponding indexes (that is, the primary index and the alternate index) must also be correspondingly updated.

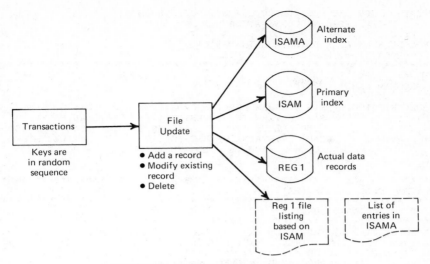

FIGURE 10.18    Data flow for file update.

Notice also from Figure 10.18 that after updating files, an output listing or listings might typically be generated.   Again, this is done as a means of being able to inspect visually the contents of the altered files, as well as for a *current* version of the file's contents.

Figure 10.19 shows the *file update program* hierarchy chart.   Four segments are shown, each representing a subfunction of the update program.   The MODIFY segment involves changing an existing RECORD, while ADD and DELETE segments cause records to either be added to or be removed from the REG1 master file and corresponding indexes.   Figure 10.20 shows the PL/I coding for the *file update program* in four parts.   Again, the program code will be discussed by segment rather than individual statements.

### UPDATE Segment (Nucleus)

This segment is shown in Part II of Figure 10.20.   The initialization steps include establishing the on-units for the KEY condition that could be raised for either ISAM or ISAMA.   The KEY condition could occur for one of several reasons.   It

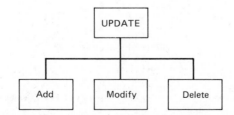

FIGURE 10.19    File update program hierarchy chart.

```
//EXDATA0   JOB (HUGHES,284300,C37,37),'JOAN HUGHES',
//       NOTIFY=SEAN,MSGCLASS=X,CLASS=X
//     EXEC    PLIXCLG
* PROCESS XREF,ATTRIBUTES,AGGREGATE;
/* CHAPTER 10 - UPDATE AN ISAM FILE                                         */
/**************************************************************************/
/*                                                                        */
/* PROGRAM NAME: UPDATE                                                    */
/*                                                                        */
/* DESCRIPTION:  THIS PROGRAM APPLIES UPDATE TRANSACTIONS TO THE           */
/*               ISAM, ALTERNATE SEQUENTIAL, AND REGIONAL FILES.           */
/*               AFTER ALL UPDATES ARE PROCESSED, THE ISAM FILE IS         */
/*               READ TO OBTAIN THE KEY TO THE REGIONAL FILE.  THE         */
/*               REGIONAL FILE IS READ AND THE CONTENTS PRINTED            */
/*               ON THE REPORT.                                           */
/*                                                                        */
/**************************************************************************/
UPDATE: PROC OPTIONS(MAIN);
/**************************************************************************/
/*    FILE DECLARATIONS                                                   */
/**************************************************************************/
DCL INPUT FILE RECORD INPUT ENV(CONSECUTIVE F BLKSIZE(80));
DCL ISAM  FILE RECORD KEYED ENV(INDEXED);
DCL ISAMA FILE RECORD KEYED ENV(INDEXED);
DCL REG1  FILE RECORD KEYED ENV(REGIONAL(1));

/**************************************************************************/
/*    RECORD DEFINITIONS                                                  */
/**************************************************************************/
DCL 1 ALTERNATE_SEQ_REC,
        2 DELETE_BYTE         CHAR(1)        INIT(' '),
        2 COMMON_NAME         CHAR(10),
        2 AS_RELATIVE_PTR     PIC'(6)9';

DCL 1 ISAM_REC,
        2 DELETE_BYTE         CHAR(1),
        2 PLANT_NAME          PIC'(5)X',
        2 IR_RELATIVE_PTR     PIC'(6)9';

DCL 1 PLANT_REC1,
        2 TRANSACTION_CODE    CHAR(1),
        2 FILL_IN1            CHAR(3),
        2 PLANT_NAME          PIC'(5)X',     /* KEY                        */
        2 FILL_IN2            CHAR(1),
        2 TYPE                CHAR(10),
        2 HEIGHT              CHAR(10),
        2 ORIGIN              CHAR(10),
        2 SEASON              CHAR(10),
        2 CLIMATE             CHAR(10),
        2 SOIL                CHAR(10),
        2 COMMON_NAME         CHAR(10);      /*  ALTERNATE KEY             */

DCL 1 PLANT_REC2,
        2 PLANT_NAME          PIC'(5)X',
        2 FILLER              CHAR(5)        INIT(' '),
        2 TYPE                CHAR(10),
        2 HEIGHT              CHAR(10),
        2 ORIGIN              CHAR(10),
        2 SEASON              CHAR(10),
        2 CLIMATE             CHAR(10),
        2 SOIL                CHAR(10),
        2 COMMON_NAME         CHAR(10);
/**************************************************************************/
/*    CONSTANTS AND VARIABLES                                             */
/**************************************************************************/
DCL KEY_ERROR_ISAM           BIT(1);
DCL KEY_ERROR_ISAMA          BIT(1);
DCL MORE_RECORDS             BIT(1);
DCL NEXT_AVAILABLE           PIC'(5)9';
DCL NO                       BIT(1)         INIT('0'B);
DCL YES                      BIT(1)         INIT('1'B);
```

FIGURE 10.20   (part I, page 1)

```
/****************************************************************/
/*   ON CODES                                                 */
/****************************************************************/
ON ENDFILE(INPUT)
   MORE_RECORDS = NO;

ON ENDFILE(ISAM)
   MORE_RECORDS = NO;

ON KEY(ISAM)
   KEY_ERROR_ISAM = YES;

ON KEY(ISAMA)
   KEY_ERROR_ISAMA = YES;

/****************************************************************/
/*                                                            */
/*   NUCLEUS                                                   */
/*                                                            */
/****************************************************************/
OPEN FILE(ISAM) UPDATE DIRECT,
     FILE(ISAMA)UPDATE DIRECT,
     FILE(REG1) UPDATE DIRECT;
MORE_RECORDS = YES;
READ FILE(REG1) INTO(PLANT_REC2) KEY('0');
NEXT_AVAILABLE = PLANT_REC2.PLANT_NAME;
READ FILE(INPUT) INTO(PLANT_REC1);
DO WHILE(MORE_RECORDS);
   SELECT(TRANSACTION_CODE);
       WHEN('A') CALL ADD_ROUTINE;
       WHEN('D') CALL DELETE_ROUTINE;
       WHEN('U') CALL UPDATE_ROUTINE;
       OTHERWISE PUT SKIP EDIT('INVALID INPUT CODE ',TRANSACTION_CODE,
                   'FOR INPUT KEY ',PLANT_REC1.PLANT_NAME) (A);
   END;
   READ FILE(INPUT) INTO(PLANT_REC1);
END;
PLANT_REC2.PLANT_NAME = NEXT_AVAILABLE;
WRITE FILE(REG1) FROM(PLANT_REC2) KEYFROM('0');
CLOSE FILE(ISAM),
      FILE(REG1);
CALL PRINT_FILE_DATA;
```

FIGURE 10.20   (part II, page 1)

could be raised if there were a transaction requesting an "add" operation but there was already a record in the ISAM or ISAMA file by that key. It could also be raised if there is a request to read a record for a specified key but that key does not exist in the file. As will be seen in a later segment, the program needs to know whether or not the KEY condition was raised for a given transaction. Notice in this segment that when files are opened, they are opened with the attributes UPDATE and DIRECT. The UPDATE attribute indicates that records in the file may be read, written, or rewritten. Statements 22 and 23 in this figure represent an initialization step in which the relative pointer is read from region 0 and placed into an identifier called NEXT_AVAILABLE. In this segment, the input transactions are read; the transaction code in column 1 is tested, and the appropriate routine is invoked. An unrecognizable code results in an error message being printed.

```
/*********************************************************************/
/*                                                                 */
/*    ADD_ROUTINE                                                  */
/*                                                                 */
/*    WHEN A RECORD IS ADDED, THE POINTER RECORDS MUST BE ADDED TO THE */
/*    ISAM FILE, AND THE ALTERNATE SEQUENTIAL ISAM FILE(ISAMA).  THEN */
/*    THE RECORD DATA IS ADDED TO THE REGIONAL FILE.               */
/*                                                                 */
/*********************************************************************/
ADD_ROUTINE:  PROC;
   ALTERNATE_SEQ_REC.COMMON_NAME = PLANT_REC1.COMMON_NAME;
   ISAM_REC         = PLANT_REC1, BY NAME;
   PLANT_REC2       = PLANT_REC1, BY NAME;
   IR_RELATIVE_PTR = NEXT_AVAILABLE;
   AS_RELATIVE_PTR = NEXT_AVAILABLE;
   KEY_ERROR_ISAM = NO;
   KEY_ERROR_ISAMA = NO;
   WRITE FILE (ISAM) FROM (ISAM_REC) KEYFROM (ISAM_REC.PLANT_NAME);
   IF KEY_ERROR_ISAM THEN
      PUT SKIP EDIT('INPUT RECORD ',PLANT_REC1.PLANT_NAME,
         ' CANNOT BE ADDED TO PRIMARY INDEX') (A);
   ELSE DO;
           WRITE FILE (ISAMA) FROM (ALTERNATE_SEQ_REC)
              KEYFROM (ALTERNATE_SEQ_REC.COMMON_NAME);
           IF KEY_ERROR_ISAMA THEN
              DO;
                 PUT SKIP EDIT('INPUT RECORD ', PLANT_REC1.COMMON_NAME,
                    ' CANNOT BE ADDED TO ALTERNATE INDEX') (A);
                 DELETE FILE (ISAM) KEY (ISAM_REC.PLANT_NAME);
              END;
           ELSE DO;
                 WRITE FILE (REG1) FROM (PLANT_REC2)
                    KEYFROM (IR_RELATIVE_PTR);
                 NEXT_AVAILABLE = NEXT_AVAILABLE + 1;
              END;
        END;
END ADD_ROUTINE;
/*********************************************************************/
/*                                                                 */
/*    DELETE_ROUTINE                                               */
/*                                                                 */
/*********************************************************************/
DELETE_ROUTINE:  PROC;
   KEY_ERROR_ISAM  = NO;
   KEY_ERROR_ISAMA = NO;
   READ FILE (ISAM) INTO (ISAM_REC) KEY (PLANT_REC1.PLANT_NAME);
   READ FILE(ISAMA) INTO(ALTERNATE_SEQ_REC) KEY(PLANT_REC1.COMMON_NAME);
   IF KEY_ERROR_ISAM | KEY_ERROR_ISAMA THEN
      PUT SKIP EDIT('INPUT RECORD ',PLANT_REC1.PLANT_NAME,
         ' CANNOT BE FOUND') (A);
   ELSE DO;
           DELETE FILE(ISAM)  KEY(ISAM_REC.PLANT_NAME);
           DELETE FILE(ISAMA) KEY(ALTERNATE_SEQ_REC.COMMON_NAME);
           DELETE FILE(REG1)  KEY(IR_RELATIVE_PTR);
        END;
END DELETE_ROUTINE;
```

FIGURE 10.20   (part II, page 2)

## ADD Segment

This segment, Statements 38–59; (Figure 10.20–part II), handles the addition of records. The first step, after moving the input record information to the output record areas, is to add the record's key to the primary index (ISAM). If the KEY condition is raised, then a record cannot be added to the file. An appropriate message is printed and the exit from the IF statement is to the end of the ADD routine. If writing a record into the primary index is successful, then an attempt is made to write the appropriate information into the alternate index. Again, if the KEY condition is raised, then an appropriate error message is printed and the previously added primary index entry deleted.

If a record is successfully added to both ISAM and ISAMA, then the REG1 record is written and the NEXT_AVAILABLE identifier is incremented by 1 to point to the next record area (region).

```
/************************************************************************/
/*                                                                    */
/*   PRINT_FILE_DATA                                                  */
/*                                                                    */
/************************************************************************/
PRINT_FILE_DATA:  PROC;
   OPEN FILE(ISAM) SEQUENTIAL INPUT,
        FILE(REG1) DIRECT INPUT;
   MORE_RECORDS = YES;
      READ FILE(ISAM)INTO(ISAM_REC);
   DO WHILE(MORE_RECORDS);
      READ FILE(REG1) INTO(PLANT_REC2) KEY(IR_RELATIVE_PTR);
      PUT EDIT(PLANT_REC2.PLANT_NAME,PLANT_REC2.TYPE,
         PLANT_REC2.HEIGHT,PLANT_REC2.ORIGIN,PLANT_REC2.SEASON,
         PLANT_REC2.CLIMATE,PLANT_REC2.SOIL,
         PLANT_REC2.COMMON_NAME) (SKIP,A,COL(10),(7)(A(10),X(1)));
      READ FILE(ISAM)INTO(ISAM_REC);
   END;
END PRINT_FILE_DATA;
/************************************************************************/
/*                                                                    */
/*   UPDATE_ROUTINE                                                   */
/*                                                                    */
/************************************************************************/
UPDATE_ROUTINE:  PROC;
   KEY_ERROR_ISAM = NO;
   READ FILE(ISAM) INTO(ISAM_REC) KEY(PLANT_REC1.PLANT_NAME);
   IF KEY_ERROR_ISAM THEN
      PUT SKIP EDIT('INPUT RECORD ',PLANT_REC1.PLANT_NAME,
         ' CANNOT BE FOUND.') (A);
   ELSE DO;
            READ FILE (REG1) INTO (PLANT_REC2) KEY (IR_RELATIVE_PTR);
            PLANT_REC2 = PLANT_REC1,BY NAME;
            REWRITE FILE(REG1) FROM(PLANT_REC2) KEY(IR_RELATIVE_PTR);
         END;
END UPDATE_ROUTINE;
END UPDATE;
//GO.SYSPRINT   DD SYSOUT=*
//GO.ISAM       DD DSN=EXDATA.CASE1.ISAM,DISP=SHR
//GO.REG1       DD DSN=EXDATA.CASE1.REG1,DISP=SHR
//GO.ISAMA      DD DSN=EXDATA.CASE1.ISAMA,DISP=SHR
//GO.INPUT      DD *
```

FIGURE 10.20   (part III)

## MODIFY Segment

This segment, shown in Figure 10.20 — part III, handles the updating of existing records in the REG1 file. It is assumed that the key in the input record is the primary key (i.e., botanical plant name). Thus, the segment reads the primary index for the region location of the master disk record to be modified. If the record cannot be found, an appropriate error message is printed and the segment terminated. Otherwise, the appropriate REG1 record is read (based on the *relative pointer*) and the appropriate REWRITE operation executed.

Only minimal updating is shown in this segment since the illustration of file-handling techniques is the objective of this case study. Note, however, that any change to the secondary key field would require deleting the entry in the ISAMA file and adding a new entry for the new secondary key. This program allowed updating the REG1 file randomly by botanical plant name. An alternative approach would be to have the input record contain an additional code to indicate whether the primary or secondary key is being used. The update segment would test the code to determine whether ISAM or ISAMA should be accessed to locate the desired REG1 record.

## DELETE Segment

The program steps specified here are essentially the same as those for the ADD subfunction. First, the entry to be deleted is read from the primary index; if successful, the entry to be deleted from the alternate index is read. If entries from both indexes can be successfully read, they are then actually deleted. The record in the REG1 file is also deleted.

## SUMMARY

**Physical and Logical Records:** A physical record is the unit of data that is physically transferred to and from an external storage medium. Each physical record consists of one or more logical records. Grouping logical records is commonly referred to as "blocking records."

### Logical Record Formats

**1. Fixed-length records:** Fixed-length records may be either blocked or un-blocked and may reside on any device.

**2. Variable-length records:** Magnetic tapes, disks, drums, etc., because of their physical features, have the flexibility for storing data sets having variable-length records. In a data set having variable-length records, each record may be of a different length, and records may be blocked or unblocked. In writing a PL/I file declaration for this type of file, the programmer simply specifies the maximum number of bytes for a block. For example, the variable-length specification for a 132-position line printer, including a carriage control character, is V BLKSIZE (141).

**3. Undefined-length records:** In this format, each block consists of only one record, although the blocks may be of varying lengths. Only the maximum length of the largest record in the file is specified.

**DASD:** A disk or a drum is referred to as a direct access storage device (DASD). The term *direct* is used because these devices provide the facility for retrieving a given record in a file without having to retrieve records that precede the desired record.

**DISK:** The most widely used DASD is a disk. A *disk pack* consists of one or more disks (platters). The number of recording surfaces in a disk pack depends on the number of disks in that pack. For example, if there are six disks, there are typically ten recording surfaces. This is because the topmost and the bottommost surfaces are not used for recording data. Thus, in an 11-platter disk pack there are 20 recording surfaces.

**Track:** A disk recording surface is further divided into tracks where one track is one concentric circle on one surface of a disk. Records are stored in a track relative to the beginning of that track. (An *index marker* indicates the physical beginning of each track so that read/write heads on the *access mechanism* will be able to sense the physical beginning of each track.)

**Volume:** A reel of magnetic tape or a disk pack.

**Access Techniques:** Records in a file may be accessed by one of two methods: SEQUENTIAL or DIRECT. It is possible for records in some files to be accessed *sequentially* at one point in time and *directly* at another point in time. To access a record *directly* is to call for that record by means of a key.

**Key:** A key makes a record unique from all other records in a given file. With respect to programming in PL/I there are two kinds of keys: recorded keys and source keys. A *recorded key* is a character-string that actually appears with each record or is embedded in each record in the file to identify that record. A *source key* is the character-string value that is specified in a record I/O statement. Keys may be from 1 to 255 characters in length.

**File Organizations:** With respect to IBM computers and batch-oriented programs, there are four major file organizations provided: CONSECUTIVE, INDEXED, VSAM, and REGIONAL.

**CONSECUTIVE:** Records are placed in physical sequence and can only be retrieved in the same order. Once the file has been created, new records may be added at the end of the file. New records may be inserted in place within the file only by creating a new version of that file. This type of organization is used for all magnetic tape devices and printers and may be selected for direct-access devices. In the case of a magnetic tape or direct-access CONSECUTIVE file, records are typically sorted prior to their being loaded into the file.

**INDEXED:** Records in this type of file are arranged in sequence according to a *key field* that is a part of every record. An index, or set of indexes, is maintained by the system and gives the location of records in the file. An INDEXED file must be created sequentially. Once it has been created, the records may be retrieved by either the DIRECT or SEQUENTIAL access technique. Unlike the CONSECUTIVE organization, records may be added in the middle of the file if overflow areas have been provided. One method is to reserve one or more tracks in each cylinder. These tracks are then filled with records as subsequent additions to the file are made. Deleting records is accomplished by the DELETE statement, which causes the first byte in the indexed sequential record to be "flagged" with a bit-string of (8) '1'B. (This bit-string indicates that the *record* is a *dummy* — that is, a null or void record.) Under OS, the first byte of an indexed sequential record should always be reserved as the *delete byte*. One disadvantage to INDEXED files is that the space from deleted records is not reusable. Another disadvantage is that most records in the overflow area require more access time than records in the prime data area.

**VSAM:** This data set organization, Virtual Storage Access Method is provided by IBM as an enhancement over the earlier file organizations CONSECUTIVE, INDEXED, and REGIONAL (1). The advantages of VSAM are improved *file maintenance* facilities for key-sequenced files (i.e., you do not have to re-create files in which there have been a number of added or deleted records), improved data security measures, and data portability in which VSAM files on a disk pack may be carried from one computer to another for use by the second computer system. There are three types of VSAM files:

**1. Entry-sequenced data set (ESDS):** This data set generally corresponds to the CONSECUTIVE organization. Records are written in physical sequence and retrieved in the same sequence in which they were stored. New records may be added only at the end of the data set.

**2. Key-sequenced data set (KSDS):** This organization generally corresponds to the INDEXED organization. Records are loaded into the data set in ascending key sequence. An index (or indexes) is created, as in the case of the INDEXED file organization. Records are stored and retrieved by means of a key and new records are inserted in key sequence. Unlike the INDEXED file organization, when records are deleted from the file they are actually removed from the data set, thereby "freeing up" the disk space for subsequent additions. There is no need for separate overflow areas in VSAM-KSDS because "free space" is inserted throughout the file when it is created.

**3. Relative-record data set (RRDS):** This organization generally corresponds to a REGIONAL (1) data set. Records in an RRDS are located by a relative record number that is used as a key to access the data set.

**REGIONAL:** Records in this type of file organization must be on a direct-access volume. No space is required for indexes. You specify the keys by which records are stored and retrieved *directly*. A REGIONAL organization permits you to control the physical placement of records in the data set and enables you to optimize the access time for a particular application. (Such optimization is not available with the other file organizations, except VSAM-RRDS organization.) The term *regional* was selected because a regional file is divided into regions rather than records. One or more records may be stored in each region depending on the type of regional file used. There are three types of REGIONAL file organizations: REGIONAL(1), REGIONAL(2), and REGIONAL(3).

## Attributes for File Declarations

**FILE attribute:** Denotes that the identifier preceding FILE is a file name.

**EXTERNAL/INTERNAL attributes:** EXTERNAL means that a declared file may be known in other PL/I procedures. The INTERNAL attribute specifies that the file name be known only in the PROCEDURE block in which it was declared.

**STREAM and RECORD attribute:** The STREAM attribute causes the file associated with the file name to be treated as a continuous stream of data items recorded in character format. The STREAM attribute can be specified only for files of consecutive organization. The RECORD attribute causes the file associated with the file name to be treated as a sequence of logical records, each record consisting of one or more data items recorded in any format.

**INPUT, OUTPUT, and UPDATE attributes:** These attributes determine the direction of data transfer. The INPUT attribute applies to files that are to be read only. The OUTPUT attribute applies to files that are to be created or extended. The UPDATE attribute describes a file that can be used for both input and output; it allows records in an existing file to be altered or added, and it applies only to files located on a direct access device.

**BUFFERED/UNBUFFERED attributes:** The BUFFERED attribute indicates that physical records transferred to and from a file must pass through an intermediate storage area called a *buffer*. The size of the buffer corresponds to the size of the physical records in the file. The BUFFERED attribute may be specified for either input or output operations and is generally most useful for sequential processing. The UNBUFFERED attribute indicates that a physical record need not pass through a buffer but can be transferred directly to and from the internal storage associated with a variable name. Records may not be blocked in a data set having the UNBUFFERED attribute. Generally, there are no performance advantages to specifying the UNBUFFERED attribute.

**BACKWARDS attribute:** This attribute applies to magnetic tape files when reverse processing (i.e., from last record to first) is desired.

**KEYED attribute:** This attribute indicates that records in the file can be accessed by means of a key.

**SEQUENTIAL, DIRECT, and TRANSIENT attributes:** These attributes may be used only for record files. They describe how records in a file are to be created or retrieved. In SEQUENTIAL files, records are accessed in physical sequence (or logical sequence for INDEXED files). In DIRECT files, records may be accessed in random order according to a *key*, which is a unique character-string identifying each record. TRANSIENT applies to teleprocessing files.

**ENVIRONMENT attribute:** This attribute specifies the physical characteristics of the file. The characteristics are indicated in a parenthesized list of options following the attribute specification. The options are not part of the standard PL/I language; they are keywords related to the capabilities of specific PL/I implementations on a given computer. Here are some ENVIRONMENT options:

**1. Record types:** Record formats may be specified in one of the following:

| | |
|---|---|
| F | Fixed-length, unblocked |
| FB | Fixed-length, blocked |
| V | Variable-length, unblocked |
| VB | Variable-length, blocked |
| U | Undefined-length, cannot be blocked |

The options RECSIZE and/or BLKSIZE must be specified with one of the previous record types.

**2. BUFFERS (n), BUFND (n), BUFNI (n), BUFSP (n) options:** These options specify the number of buffers to be used in files having the BUFFERED attribute.

**3. CONSECUTIVE, INDEXED, VSAM, REGIONAL (1|2|3) options:** Select one of these options depending on the desired file organization you are using.

**4. LEAVE option:** This option specifies that no rewind operation is to be performed at the time a tape file is opened or closed. It should be used for files having the BACKWARDS attribute.

**5. REREAD option:** This option rewinds the tape to permit reprocessing of a tape volume or data set.

**6. KEYLENGTH (n) option:** Specifies the length of the key in INDEXED, REGIONAL (2), or REGIONAL (3) files.

**7. KEYLOC (n) option:** Specifies the leftmost position of the key field within the data record. For DOS/VS the leftmost position in the *record* is 1; in OS/VS this position is numbered 0.

**8. INDEX/VS AREA (n) option:** Specifies that the highest level index be placed in main storage for indexed sequential files.

**9. ADDBUFF (n) option:** This option is used when it is desired to add new records faster to an INDEXED file. It specifies the amount of main storage to be reserved for the shifting of records when new records are being added to a DIRECT UPDATE and INDEXED file.

**10. CTLASA CTL360 options:** These options specify whether the first character of a record to a line printer is to be interpreted as an ASA or System/360 control character. CTLASA is a before-print operation and CTL360 is an after-print operation.

**11. PASSWORD option:** Available for VSAM files, it specifies the data set protection password for VSAM read and update operations.

**Record I/O Statements:** Includes READ, WRITE, REWRITE (for modifying existing records in a disk file), and DELETE (for removing records from a disk file). Refer to Figure 10.21 for the various forms of I/O statements that may be used with each file organization.

**On-Units:** The following on-units apply to record I/O transmission for DASD files:

**KEY Condition:** Raised during operations on keyed records. It is raised if a keyed record cannot be found for a READ or REWRITE. It may also be raised when a duplicate record is written during a WRITE operation for a REGIONAL (1) or INDEXED file. Also, the KEY condition could be raised if there is no space available to add a keyed record to a file.

**UNDEFINEDFILE Condition:** Raised whenever the opening of a file is unsuccessful. Some causes include a conflict in attributes for a given data set or incomplete attributes (e.g., no block size specified).

**RECORD Condition:** Raised during a READ, WRITE, or REWRITE operation. Indicates a wrong length record.

**Built-in Functions:** The following built-in functions would be used in the on-unit responding to various conditions associated with files typically located on a DASD:

**ONKEY Built-in Function:** Returns the value of the KEY that caused an I/O condition (KEY, RECORD, UNDEFINEDFILE, etc.) to be raised.

**ONFILE Built-in Function:** Returns the name of the file for which an I/O or CONVERSION condition was raised.

| File attributes | Corresponding valid statements | Comments | Consecutive | Indexed | VSAM ESDS | VSAM KSDS | Regional | VSAM RRDS |
|---|---|---|:-:|:-:|:-:|:-:|:-:|:-:|
| SEQUENTIAL OUTPUT | WRITE FILE (filename) FROM (area); | | X | | X | | | X |
| | WRITE FILE (filename) FROM (area) KEYFROM (identifier); | Records must be presented with keys in ascending sequence | | X | | X | X | X |
| SEQUENTIAL INPUT | READ FILE (filename) INTO (area); | Most commonly used sequential *read* | X | X | X | X | X | X |
| | READ FILE (filename) INTO (area) KEY (identifier *or* character-string); | Usually used to position the data set to a location other than the beginning; then a sequential READ without the KEY option is used | | X | | X | X | X |
| | READ FILE (filename) INTO (area) KEYTO (identifier); | Only needed for unblocked records that do not have key as part of the record | | X | | X | X | |
| SEQUENTIAL UPDATE | READ FILE (filename) INTO (area); | Sequential *read* possible for the purpose of a subsequent update | X | X | X | X | X | X |
| | READ FILE (filename) INTO (area) KEY (identifier *or* character-string); | Used to position the data set to a location other than the beginning; then a sequential READ without the KEY option is used | | X | | X | X | X |
| | READ FILE (filename) INTO (area) KEYTO (identifier); | Only needed for unblocked records that do not have key as part of the record | | X | | X | X | |
| | REWRITE FILE (filename) FROM (area); | Causes record just *read* and probably modified by your program to be rewritten | X | X | X | X | X | X |

| | Statement | Description | | | | | | |
|---|---|---|---|---|---|---|---|---|
| | REWRITE FILE (filename); | Causes record just read into your I/O area to be rewritten onto the file from that area | X | X | X | X | X | X |
| DIRECT INPUT | DELETE FILE (filename) KEY (identifier *or* character-string); | Causes record specified by KEY option to be deleted from file | | X | X | X | | X |
| | DELETE FILE (filename); | Causes record just *read* to be deleted | X | X | X | X | | X |
| | READ FILE (filename) INTO (area) KEY (identifier *or* character-string); | Causes record specified by the KEY option to be read into main storage | | X | X | X | X | X |
| DIRECT UPDATE | READ FILE (filename) INTO (area) KEY (identifier *or* character-string); | Causes record specified by the KEY option to be read into main storage | | X | X | X | X | X |
| | REWRITE FILE (filename) FROM (area) KEY (identifier *or* character-string); | Causes I/O area to be written over the record specified by KEY option | | X | X | X | X | X |
| | WRITE FILE (filename) FROM (area) KEYFROM (identifier *or* character-string); | Causes a record to be *added to* an existing file | | X | X | X | X | X |
| | DELETE FILE (filename) KEY (identifier *or* character-string); | Deletes specified record from the file | | X | X | X | X | X |
| DIRECT OUTPUT | WRITE FILE (filename) FROM (area) KEYFROM (identifier *or* character-string); | Used to create REGIONAL files or VSAM-RRDS | | | X | X | X | X |

FIGURE 10.21  I/O statements most commonly used for record files (*note:* if KEYFROM, KEYTO, or KEY is used in the I/O statement, then the file declaration must also include the KEYED attribute).

# APPENDIX A

# Answers to Checkpoint Questions

## Chapter 1

**1.** False.

**2.** A constant is an arithmetic data item or string data item that does not have a name and whose value does not change during the execution of the program. Examples: 'ROBERT FROST', 175.50.

**3.** Comments begin with a /* and end with */. They may appear anywhere a blank is permitted in a program. One or two paragraphs of comments should precede or immediately follow a PROCEDURE statement.

**4.** When naming a PROCEDURE, select a name that describes the procedure's primary function.

**5.** A **source program** is input to the compiler, written following the rules of the programming language. An **object program** is output from the compiler, in machine language form.

**6. Compilation** is the process of translating a source language program into an object program. **Execution** is the performance of the instructions in the object program.

**7.** *JCL*, job control language, is the group of instructions available to control the computer's operating system.

**8. Debugging** is the procedure of removing all known errors from a computer program. *Testing* involves proving the program's correctness by using a variety of test data.

**9.** A *program stub* is a skeleton of a program or subprogram.

**10.** # @ $.

**11.** An **identifier** is a programmer-selected name of data, procedures, files and labels. PL/I keywords are also identifiers. For example:

| | |
|---|---|
| CUSTOMER_NUMBER | data name |
| STOCK | procedure name |
| HEADING_ROUTINE: | label of PL/I statement |
| SYSIN | file name |
| GET | keyword |

**12.** A **keyword** is part of the vocabulary that makes up the PL/I language and has a specific meaning to the PL/I compiler when used in proper context. When the 48-character set is used, certain keywords are reserved; that is, they must not be used for any purpose except to serve as special operators.

**13.** 2–72.

**14.** (b) and (e) are valid.
    (a)   does not have an alphabetic first character.
    (c)   contains embedded blanks.
    (d)   contains a dash (or minus sign), which is an invalid character in an identifier name.

**15.** (a)   Fixed-point decimal.
    (b)   Character-string.
    (c)   Floating-point decimal.
    (d)   Bit-string.

**16.** The input must take the form of valid constants. Input data items may be separated by blanks, commas, or both.

**17.** No.

**18.** The values read will be printed on the system line printer at the predetermined tab positions.

**19.** Print Position   1:   5
                   25:  10
                   49:  15
                   73:  THIS IS SOME FUN AND MARKS THE END OF JOB
(new line)      1:  08/08/88

## Chapter 2

**1.** (a)   It must solve the problem it was intended to solve.
    (b)   It must be reliable.
    (c)   It must be easy to read and easy to maintain.

**2.** Program maintenance is the alteration of program code to correct errors detected and to reflect changes to the problem definition.

**3.** They are difficult to follow and therefore difficult to maintain.

**4.** The flowchart shows logic, the sequence in which operations will be carried out. It is a pictorial representation of program logic using graphic symbols.

**5.** A hierarchy chart shows *flow of control, function* rather than procedure, and *what needs to be done,* rather than how it is to be done. A hierarchy chart is a representation of organization similar to functions depicted in an organization chart.

**6.** A function is the change that takes place from the time a section of code is entered until it completes its action. *One module, one function* is the guideline to a well-structured program.

**7.**

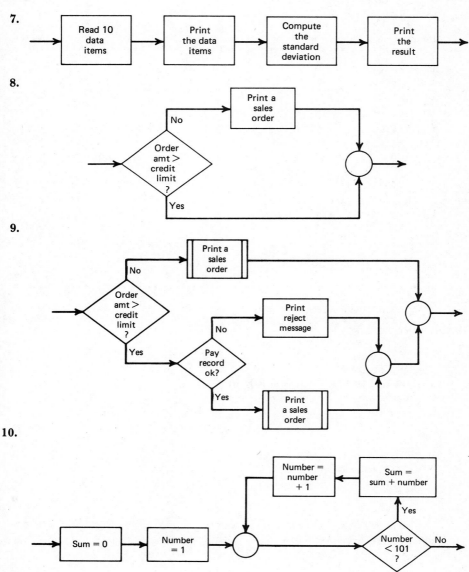

**8.**

**9.**

**10.**

**11.** A proper program has:

(a) One entry point.

(b) One exit point.

(c) No dead code.

(d) No infinite loops.

**12.** Nothing will be printed because the DO WHILE implies a test *before* statements within the DO are ever executed.

**13.** A switch is a program indicator (data name) that will affect the flow of logic when it is tested at some other point in the program execution.

**14.**

```
/*    CHAPTER 2 -- CHECKPOINT QUESTION 14                                  */
/************************************************************************/
/*                                                                      */
/*    PROGRAM NAME:    LIST                                             */
/*    DESCRIPTION:     THIS PROGRAM IS AN EXAMPLE OF USING STUBS TO     */
/*                     VERIFY THAT A PROCEDURE HAS BEEN CALLED.         */
/*    INPUT:           NONE                                             */
/*    OUTPUT:          PRINTER                                          */
/*                                                                      */
/************************************************************************/
/************************************************************************/
/*                                                                      */
/*    PROGRAM NUCLEUS                                                    */
/*                                                                      */
/************************************************************************/

 LIST: PROCEDURE OPTIONS(MAIN);
    PUT LIST ('LIST EXECUTED');
    CALL PRINT_HEADING;

/************************************************************************/
/*                                                                      */
/*    PRINT REPORT HEADING                                               */
/*                                                                      */
/************************************************************************/

 PRINT_HEADING: PROCEDURE;
    PUT LIST ('PRINT_HEADING EXECUTED');
 END PRINT_HEADING;

 END LIST;
```

**15.**    VALIDATE DATA

    set VALIDATE ERROR switch off

    perform test of specified fields

    IF error

        set VALIDATE ERROR switch on

        write exception message

    end of VALIDATE DATA

WRITE MASTER DATA

    write DISK MASTER record

    IF I/O error

        write error message

    write MASTER RECORD on printer

    end of WRITE MASTER DATA

**16.**

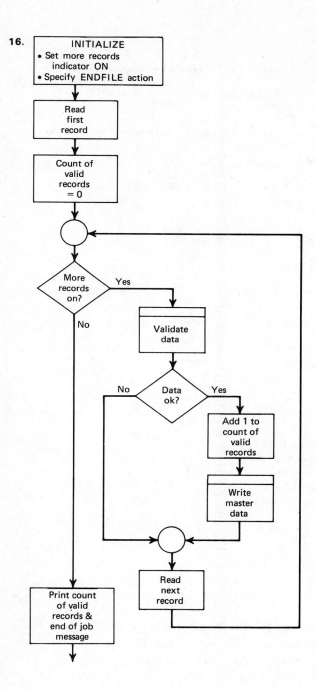

**17.** *80/80 list program:*

```
/* READ RECORDS AND LIST THEM                                              */
/**************************************************************************/
/* PROGRAM NAME:    LIST                                                   */
/* DESCRIPTION:     THIS PROGRAM READS RECORDS AND LISTS THEM              */
/*                  ON THE PRINTER.                                        */
/* INPUT:           SYSTEM INPUT                                           */
/* OUTPUT:          PRINTER                                                */
/**************************************************************************/
LIST: PROCEDURE OPTIONS (MAIN);

    DECLARE DATA            CHARACTER(75);
    DECLARE MORE_RECS       BIT(1)        INITIAL('1');
    DECLARE NO              BIT(1)        INITIAL('0'B);

    ON ENDFILE(SYSIN)
       MORE_RECS = NO;

    GET FILE(SYSIN)LIST(DATA);
    DO WHILE(MORE_RECS);
       PUT SKIP LIST(DATA);
       GET FILE(SYSIN)LIST(DATA);
    END;

END LIST;
```

## Chapter 3

**1.** Binary term.

**2.** A word uses four bytes; a halfword uses two bytes.

**3.** Three bytes.

**4.** Fixed-point binary.
Packed decimal.
Floating-point.

**5.** MEAN        fixed-point binary.
SUM          floating-point.
ALPHA       floating-point.
PAGE         floating-point.
LINE__COUNT  fixed-point binary.

**6.** Zoned decimal.
Packed decimal.
Fixed-point binary.
Floating-point.

**7.** I = 10.
J = 2.
K = 123.

**8.** Assumes attributes of a specified base, scale, and precision called *default attributes*.

**9.** Anywhere, but usually together at the beginning or end of the program.

**10.** (a)   To specify attributes other than those assumed by default.
    (b)   To specify data aggregates (structures or arrays).
    (c)   To explicitly declare input or output files.

**11.** No.   They both require four bytes.

12. (a) DECIMAL FLOAT (6).
    (b) DECIMAL FIXED (7,2).
    (c) DECIMAL FLOAT (6).
    (d) BINARY FIXED (15).
    (e) DECIMAL FLOAT (6).
    (f) BINARY FIXED (15).
    (g) BINARY FLOAT (21). Note: "21" refers to number of bits of precision. BINARY FLOAT values have the same internal format as DECIMAL FLOAT numbers.
    (h) DECIMAL FIXED (5,0).

13. (a) 345.00: decimal point alignment is maintained.  12345 is assumed to be 12345. The high-order digits are truncated and the fractional portion is set to zero.
    (b) 0: 32768 is converted to binary 1000000000000000.  Since the precision of B is (15), the high-order position is truncated; therefore, B contains 0.
    (c) 00043: precision is (5,0); the fraction is truncated.
    (d) 23.45: precision is (4,2); most significant digit is truncated.
    (e) '11000000'B: unused bit positions are padded with zero bits on the right.
    (f) '110'B extra bit positions on the right are truncated.
    (g) 'MISSISSIPPI ': extra characters on the right are truncated.

14. (a) 9.
    (b) 2.
    (c) 6.
    (d) 7.
    (e) 3.
    (f) 1.
    (g) 8.
    (h) 4.
    (i) 10.

15. Assign the variable to the left of the assignment symbol the value of the expression to the right of the assignment symbol.

16. (a) + /.
    (b) A + B / C   B/C.
    (c) Y = A + B / C.

17. To clarify or affect the order of execution of arithmetic operations.

18. (a) A * X
        B * X
        (A*X) + (B*X)
    (b) A * X
        (A*X) + B
        ((A*X) + B) * X
    (c) Y ** 2
        X ** 2
        (X ** 2) / (Y ** 2)
    (d) −Y
        (−Y) * B

**19.**

| | A | B | C |
|---|---|---|---|
| Original | 0 | 0 | 0 |
| A = 5 | 5 | 0 | 0 |
| B = −A | 5 | −5 | 0 |
| C = A/B | 5 | −5 | −1 |
| C = C + 2 | 5 | −5 | 1 |
| B = B * B + C | 5 | 26 | 1 |
| A = A ** 2 − B | −1 | 26 | 1 |
| B = B − C + A | −1 | 24 | 1 |
| C = B *C | −1 | 24 | 24 |
| B = B / 2 | −1 | 12 | 24 |
| A = C/B + 12 | 14 | 12 | 24 |

**20.** (a) and (c) are examples of arguments.

**21.** False.   Built-in functions return only *one* result.

**22.** False.   DATE and TIME are examples of functions for which there are no arguments.

**23.** When the built-in function has no arguments.

**24.** (b) and (c).

**25.** (c).   Fixed-point data may be specified as arguments, but these will be converted to floating-point before they are actually manipulated by the mathematical built-in functions.

**26.** (a)   True, but they can cause errors in computed results.
    (b)   True.
    (c)   False (BIT is converted to CHARACTER).

**27.** SIGN returns one of three values:
    −1   for a negative argument
     0   for a zero-value argument
    +1   for a positive argument

**28.** ABS returns the absolute value of an argument; for example, I = ABS (−345) causes I to be set to 345.

**29.** False.   They are allowed, but should be avoided because of possible data conversion problems.

## Chapter 4

**1.** An argument is passed to a subroutine procedure from a *calling* procedure.   A parameter is a name used within the *called* procedure to represent the value that is being passed to it.

**2.** No.   The attributes of the parameters do not match the attributes of the arguments.

**3.** The length attribute of character or bit-strings, and the boundary attribute of arrays may be declared with asterisks.   For example:

```
DCL NAME         CHAR(*);
DCL TABLE(*,*,*)  FIXED DEC(5);
```

The advantage is that generalized subroutines or functions may be written without having to know exactly the length of string data or boundaries of arrays — thereby giving greater program flexibility.

**4.** Errors detected by subroutine or function procedures should be indicated to the calling program by means of a switch passed through the argument list. In structured programming, STOP or EXIT should not be used in subprograms.

**5.** CALL COMPUTE ((TIME),A,B);

**6.** All the arguments except C will be dummy arguments.

**7.** None of the arguments could be modified because the ENTRY attribute specified attribute options for the only possibility of an argument not being a dummy argument, the identifier C. Thus, the DECLARE specified in conjunction with the arguments from the CALL in question 6 resulted in all arguments being dummy arguments. Dummy arguments, of course, should not be modified by subprograms.

**8.** (a)  One value is returned to the point of invocation.
  (b)  None, one, or more through the modification of arguments.

**9.** The RETURNS attribute is specified in a DECLARE statement in the procedure which invokes the function. The RETURNS option is in the PROCEDURE or ENTRY statement of the invoked function.

**10.** RECURSIVE specifies that a procedure may call itself. REENTRANT specifies that a procedure may be called or used by other procedures asynchronously. This facility is necessary for those computing systems where it is possible that a procedure may be interrupted for a higher-priority task and that task requires the use of the procedure that was interrupted. For example; assume *task B* invokes the SQRT function. While this function is in the process of computing square root, task A (which has a higher execution priority than task B) needs to gain control of the system and use SQRT. The SQRT function is interrupted and intermediate results for task B saved; then task A uses the SQRT function. When task A completes its execution, control is returned to task B at the point *where it was interrupted.* Then, task B completes its use of the SQRT function.

**11.** True.

**12.** Implicit; Procedures P1, P2, and P3.


## Chapter 5

**1.** False; it gives no direction to the compiler.

**2.** The do-group allows execution of more than one statement following the THEN or ELSE.

**3.**  IF DEPRECIATION_TYPE = 1 THEN
    CALL STRAIGHT_LINE_DEPRECIATION;
   ELSE
    IF DEPRECIATION_TYPE = 2 THEN
     CALL SUM_OF_DIGITS_DEPRECIATION;
    ELSE
     IF DEPRECIATION_TYPE = 3 THEN
      CALL DOUBLE_DECLINING_DEPRECIATION;
     ELSE
      CALL DEPRECIATION_TYPE_ERROR;

**4.** The CASE structure may be implemented by a series of nested IF statements or by the SELECT group.

**5.** SELECT(DEPR_CODE);
   WHEN(1) CALL STRAIGHT_LINE_DEPRECIATION;
   WHEN(2) CALL SUM_OF_DIGITS_DEPRECIATION;
   WHEN(3) CALL DOUBLE_DECLINING_DEPRECIATION;
   OTHERWISE CALL DEPRECIATION_TYPE_ERROR;
   END;

**6.** (a)   IF A = B & C = D THEN
         X = 1;
      IF A = B & C ¬= D THEN
         X = 2;
      IF A ¬= B & C = D THEN
         X = 3;
      IF A ¬= B & C ¬= D THEN
         X = 4;
   (b)   IF A = B THEN
         IF C = D THEN
            X = 1;
         ELSE
            X = 2;
      ELSE
         IF C = D THEN
            X = 3;
         ELSE
            X = 4;

**7.** The ON statement is used to specify action to be taken when any subsequent occurrence of a specified condition causes a program interrupt. This overrides the standard system action.

**8.** The ERROR condition is raised when a condition is enabled and no programmer specified action (with the exception of SUBSCRIPTRANGE) is indicated (i.e., no ON unit has been executed up to this point in the program for the condition that is raised and enabled). The ERROR condition is raised as part of the standard system action.

**9.** The condition prefix enables or disables a condition.

**10.** The null form of the ON statement indicates that if the specified condition occurs, no action should be taken and execution should continue as if the condition had not been raised.

**11.** By executing the SIGNAL statement.

**12.** FIXEDOVERFLOW occurs when the precision of a fixed-point arithmetic operation exceeds the permitted maximum of the PL/I implementation. SIZE occurs when the declared or default precision of a given identifier is exceeded.

## Chapter 6

**1.** A sequence structure and the DO-WHILE.

**2.** After one execution of the statements within the DO.

**3.** False.

**4.** (a)   Initialization of the control variable.
   (b)   Testing of the control variable against the limit.
   (c)   Modification of the control variable.

**5.** DO-WHILE.

**6.** (a) 10.
   (b) 5.
   (c) 51.

**7.** (a) Acceptable (although there is a transfer of control to the called subroutine, the subroutine returns to the statement immediately following the CALL; hence control is returned to the inner range of the DO).
   (b) Not acceptable in structured programming environment.
   (c) Acceptable, but not recommended.
   (d) Won't work because the *limit value,* established at the beginning of the do-group, is copied over to a temporary working storage area within PL/I; hence, it is unavailable to the program code within the range of the DO.
   (e) Acceptable, but not recommended.

**8.** It is determined by the position of the attribute in the DECLARE statement. The precision attribute must follow either the base or scale attribute. The dimension attribute immediately follows the array name.

**9.** The array bounds are the lowest and highest element number (i.e., subscript) that may be used to access an element in an array. The bounds determine the range of an array.

**10.** 1.

**11.** False.

**12.** By subscripts.

**13.** 57   C = A (B (K))
         C = A (B (2))
         C = A (3)
         C = 57

**14.** 6.

**15.** False. Only the first element will be initialized to zero. To initialize all elements to zero, an iteration factor of 100 would be required; for example,

   DCL A (100) INIT ((100)0);

**16.**   DCL CODE (20) CHAR (5) INIT ((20) (5) '9');
         /* OR */
         DCL CODE (20) CHAR (5) INIT ((20) (1) '99999');

Note that

   DCL CODE (20) CHAR (5) INIT ((20) '99999');

would be incorrect because the (20) would be interpreted as a repetition factor and only the first element would be initialized.

**17.**   DCL ARRAY(5)   FLOAT DEC (6)   INIT (0,*,*,*,0);

**18.** Invalid. The arrays A and B must have the same dimensions and bounds, not just the same number of elements.

**19.** All three are equivalent.

**20.** (c).

## Chapter 7

**1.** False; file names may be 1 to 7 characters long.

**2.** F,V, BLKSIZE (133).

**3.** The PRINT attribute enables stream files associated with a line printer to use carriage control options such as PAGE and LINE.

**4.** SYSIN: FILE STREAM INPUT ENV (F BLKSIZE (80))
SYSPRINT: FILE STREAM OUTPUT PRINT ENV (V BLKSIZE (129))

**5.** DCL VAROUT FILE STREAM OUTPUT PRINT ENV (V BLKSIZE (109));

**6.** (a)   To specify additional attributes and options for the file—allowing the attributes or options to be dynamically specified during the program run.
   (b)   To provide greater program readability and documentation.

**7.** When a file is opened:

   (a)   File attributes are merged from the DECLARE, OPEN statement, and JCL.
   (b)   The file name is associated with a data set.
   (c)   Device readiness is checked.
   (d)   Data set labels are checked and/or written.

When a file is closed:

   (a)   If appropriate, an end-of-file mark is written to the device.
   (b)   The file name is dissociated from the data set.

**8.** PAGESIZE and LINESIZE may be specified in an OPEN statement for stream files with the PRINT attribute. PAGESIZE specifies the number of lines to be output per page of print. LINESIZE specifies the number of characters to be output on each line.

**9.** The remote format item, R (label), is useful when the same format list or parts of a list apply to more than one GET or PUT EDIT statement. Using the R format item would eliminate redundant coding in the specification of identical format items.

**10.** Edit I/O offers flexibility in the formattting of printed output.

**11.** F (4).

**12.** It is valid; however, the format item F (4) would not be used since the data list is exhausted after the F (2), F (3).

**13.** One; only SKIP (1) will be executed since the data list is exhausted by the three F (5,2)s, which would apply to A, B, and C.

**14.** SKIP: next line if SKIP or SKIP (1), otherwise SKIP (n−1) blank lines will appear.
   LINE: the form will advance to the specified line.
   COLUMN: if COLUMN (1), the form will skip to the first position of the next line.
   PAGE: new line *and* new page.

**15.** (b) SKIP and (c) COLUMN.

**16.** 0012.   (DCL did not specify fractional digits.)

**17.** 12.35 (rounding occurs just before output).

**18.**   PUT PAGE EDIT ('WEEKLY ACTIVITY REPORT') (COLUMN (50), A)
         (22 '_') (SKIP (0), COLUMN (50), A);

**19.** When control items (PAGE, SKIP, LINE) appear inside the format list, they are called **control format items;** if they appear outside the format list, they are called **control options.** In the example, SKIP is a control format item and PAGE is a control option.

**20.** LINENO returns the current line number for a file having the PRINT attribute.

**21.** Data items in the input stream are represented in the form of assignment statements. The variable into which the data items are to be read is on the left side of the equal sign, and the value, in the form of a valid PL/I constant, is on the right.

**22.** Semicolon (;).

**23.** COUNT returns the number of data items that were transmitted during the last GET or PUT operation on a given file.

**24.** *Advantages:* easy to learn and use, a good debugging tool, provides unique program flexibility.

*Disadvantage:* large program overhead.

**25.** BEGIN blocks are needed when more than one PL/I statement needs to be executed in an on-unit.

**26.** Control returns to the place in the program immediately following the point of interruption. For example, if a conversion error occurs while reading the second of four data items to be input with this GET, control will return to the I/O statement to read the remaining items. But if the I/O operation is complete, for example, an ENDFILE has occurred, control passes to the statement following the I/O statement.

**27.** An on-unit may be activated by:

    (a)    The occurrence of the particular circumstances associated with the condition.

    (b)    The execution of the SIGNAL statement specifying the condition name.


## Chapter 8

**1.** Record I/O has the following characteristics:

    (a)    Use of the keywords READ and WRITE rather than GET and PUT.

    (b)    An entire record is read rather than one or more items in a stream.

    (c)    Data input or output may be in any format rather than just character form.

    (d)    No conversion of data formats take place. Therefore, identifiers must be declared to have the same attributes as the data items have when they are stored on the external medium.

**2.** Data aggregates: arrays and structures
Scalar variable: character-string

**3.** It is *not* valid because input for card data can only be to identifiers that have the CHARACTER or PICTURE attribute. This is because no **data conversion** takes place in record I/O.

**4.** CTLASA: the carriage control character indicates forms control to take place *before* the printing of the current line.

CTL360: carriage control indicates what is to occur *after* the current line is printed.

**5.**    DCL 1 CREDIT_RECORD,

| | | |
|---|---|---|
| 2 CUSTOMER_# | CHAR(6), | /* OR PIC '(6)9' */ |
| 2 CUSTOMER_NAME | CHAR(25), | |
| 2 CREDIT_RATING | CHAR(1), | /* OR PIC '9' */ |
| 2 LAST_ACTIVE_DATE | CHAR(6), | |
| 2 REFERENCE | CHAR(25), | |
| 2 UNUSED_COLUMNS | CHAR(17); | |

**6.** (a) FIXED DECIMAL (1)

(b) FIXED DECIMAL (4,3)

(c) FIXED DECIMAL (5,5)

**7.** The structure has the following errors:

(a) Commas should replace the semicolons following each element declaration except the last.

(b) The repetition factor should precede the picture specification character to which it refers.

(c) Picture specifications must be enclosed in single quote marks.

**8.** 59.

**9.** (a) To describe data in character form in a manner suitable for arithmetic operations.

(b) To describe arithmetic data in a format suitable for printing.

(c) To edit data for printing; for example: check protection, $, commas.

(d) To validate character data.

**10.** The data item is converted to FIXED DECIMAL; therefore, for program efficiency, if an item is to be referenced more than once, assign it to a FIXED DECIMAL identifier and use the FIXED DECIMAL identifier in calculations.

**11.** (a) $0550_\wedge00$. Note: $_\wedge$ indicates assumed decimal point

(b) $000_\wedge$.

(c) $40_\wedge$.

(d) $003_\wedge45$.

**12.** (a) 5. (c) 7. (e) 12.

(b) 4. (d) 6.

**13.** (a) 12345.

(b) bb123.

(c) bbb00.

**14.** PUT FILE (SYSPRINT) EDIT (VALUE) (P'$$,$$$V.99');[1]

**15.** TODAY = DATE; is interpreted as

    YY  = DATE;
    MM = DATE;
    DD  = DATE;

thus,

    YY  = 77
    MM = 77
    DD  = 77

To accomplish the retrieval of the date in the form YYMMDD, overlay defining is needed. For example,

    DCL DATE              BUILTIN;
    DCL DATE_TODAY        CHAR(6) DEFINED TODAY;

[1] To provide a check protection floating $ for the case of a maximum value, an extra $ must be specified.

```
DCL 1 TODAY,
      2 YY              CHAR(2),
      2 MM              CHAR(2),
      2 DD              CHAR(2);
   DATE_TODAY = DATE;
```

Now, because of the overlay define and the assignment of results returned by the DATE function to a character-string (rather than a structure), the fields YY, MM, DD will contain the year, month, and day, respectively.

**16.** DECLARE
      1 TODAY,
        2 (YY,
          MM,
          DD)   CHAR (2);

**17.** An elementary item may not be initialized when it or any structure of which it is a part is overlay defined on another data item.

**18.** (c). (a) is a non-qualified identifier; (b) contains an invalid character (−); (d) specifies two different identifiers: HOURS and REGULAR.

**19.** It saves coding effort by avoiding the **explicit** declaration of minor and elementary identifiers and attributes that are identical to another structure already declared.

**20.** No. The relative structuring is not the same. CAT has an elementary item and a minor structure containing two elementary items. DOG has four elementary items.

**21.** When the BY NAME option of the assignment statement is used.

**22.** DCL CLEAR_AREA   CHAR (42)   DEFINED A;
     CLEAR_AREA = ' ';

**23.** To allow the same area of storage to be assumed to have different formats. Most commonly, this would be used to redefine an input area when different types of records are expected.


## Chapter 9

**1.** Static storage is allocated at compile time and remains allocated during the entire execution of the external procedure. Dynamic storage is allocated during the execution of the program when storage is needed and may be subsequently released for other use, thereby reducing overall MAIN storage requirements.

**2.** A main procedure block is activated by a call from the operating system and deactivated by a return to the operating system (a STOP or EXIT is executed from any currently active procedure or an END or RETURN is executed from the main procedure). A procedure block that is not the main procedure is activated by a CALL from the main or other currently executing procedure. It is deactivated by a STOP, EXIT, END, or RETURN. STOP and EXIT will terminate all calling procedures and return to the operating system (abnormal ending).

**3.** Only storage areas actually required, not the maximum possibly required, will be allocated. Storage may be reused, thereby reducing overall storage requirements. A disadvantage is that once dynamic storage is freed, it may be reused and therefore data once available is lost.

**4.** Identifiers that will require allocation during the entire program run, where their values must be saved between invocations of the same procedures. Program constants which may be initialized during compile, should be declared STATIC. Identifiers declared and initialized in the MAIN procedure should be declared STATIC.

**5.** (a) Assignment of the value returned by the ADDR or the NULL built-in functions.
   (b) Assignment of the value contained in another pointer variable.
   (c) The LOCATE statement or the SET option of the READ statement.
   (d) The ALLOCATE statement.

**6.** Based variables would be used when the identifiers do not have the same base, scale or precision.

**7.** (a)  X = ADDR (FIELD__1);
        Y = ADDR (FIELD__1);   or   Y = X;
   (b)  X,Y = ADDR (FIELD__1);

**8.** Advantages:
   (a) Data will require fewer moves within storage.
   (b) Less storage will be required (no extra work area the size of a logical record is required).
   (c) Faster execution time in the sequential processing of records in a file.

   Disadvantages:

   (a) Accessing data as based variables (indirect addressing) requires extra execution steps in the resulting machine language program.
   (b) Boundary alignment problems may arise for blocked records with BINARY or FLOAT data items.

**9.** Three times: (1) input buffer to input work area, (2) input work area to output work area, and (3) output work area to output buffer.

**10.** BUFFERED SEQUENTIAL RECORD.

**11.** SET for input buffer processing; INTO for work-area processing.

**12.** No. A LOCATE statement must be executed prior to moving any data into OUT__AREA. Adding an initial LOCATE statement prior to the DO-WHILE would result in the writing of an extra record containing undefined data at the end of file. Instead the positions of the OUT__AREA = WORKAREA and LOCATE statements must be exchanged.

**13.** LAST IN, FIRST OUT means that the last allocation is the one that will be freed when the FREE statement is executed.

**14.** It is allocated by the ALLOCATE statement when program logic determines that storage is needed.

**15.** Storage need only be allocated for a data item if and when the storage is needed.

**16.** By the built-in function ALLOCATION.

**17.** Structure.

**18.** NULL.

**19.** (a) Lists may be processed either forward or backward.
   (b) Insertions and deletions are facilitated.

**20.**

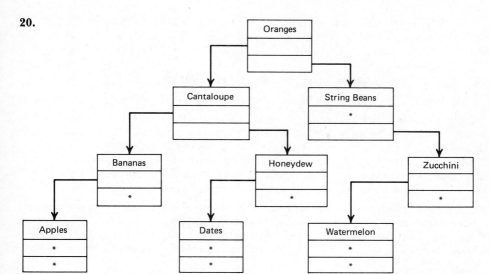

**21.** No. A pointer must be associated with the based structure LIST—AREA. This may be accomplished by specifying a pointer in the DECLARE; for example, 1 LIST—AREA BASED (LIST—PT), or by specifying a pointer in the ALLOCATE statement, for example:

ALLOCATE LIST—AREA   SET (LIST—PT);

The pointer must then be specified in the assignment statement:

LIST—PT —> LIST—AREA = INAREA;

**22.** A unique value that when used in the correct context indicates the end of the list. It is not zero.

**23.** A pointer that contains the address of the desired generation must be associated with the based variable.

**24.** (a)   The pointer may be specified in the DECLARE following the attribute BASED.
  (b)   The pointer followed by the symbol —> preceding the based variable name will associate the pointer for that program access.


## Chapter 10

**1.** A logical record is a collection of related items of data referred to as a unit, such as all the data relating to one part number or one employee. A physical record is delineated by the manner in which it is recorded. A physical record would be written or read in one I/O operation and may contain several logical records. For magnetic tape or disk, a physical record would be all the data between IBGs.

**2.** Magnetic tape, disk, drum.

**3.** To determine whether a file may be blocked consider:

  (a)   Whether blocked files are allowed on the device.

(b) Whether the record format allows blocking. For example, UNDEFINED record format may only be used for unblocked files.

(c) Whether sufficient storage is available to hold the resulting physical record (e.g., buffer size).

**4.** The amount of storage available to hold the resulting physical record.

**5.** When the amount of data to be recorded in the logical records differs significantly.

**6.** The **variable-length** record format may be blocked or unblocked. The **undefined** record format may be unblocked only. The variable-length format carries a four-byte record-length field maintained by the system for each logical record in the block and a four-byte block-length field, also maintained by the system, for each physical block. The undefined record format carries no automatically maintained length fields. The programmer must develop his or her own method for determining record lengths.

**7.** A **file** is a collection of related records. A **volume** is a recording medium that may be mounted or demounted as a unit, such as a magnetic tape reel, or the portion of a unit of storage that is accessible to a single read/write mechanism, such as a disk pack. A file may be recorded on one or more physical volumes. A volume may contain more than one file.

**8.** (a) Sequentially.
(b) Both.
(c) Sequentially.

**9.** A key is a data item that identifies a record and distinguishes it from the other records in a file. A field in a record I/O statement that identifies the record to be accessed is a SOURCE key. A key that is recorded on the direct access volume is a RECORDED key.

**10.** A program must be written to read the CONSECUTIVE file as well as a file that contains the insertions and the indication of the deletions to be made. Assuming that the original CONSECUTIVE file was arranged in sequence by a control field, the insertion/ deletion file must also be sorted by the same control field. A new file is written with the insertions and without the deletion record.

**11.** File maintenance would be required when there have been a sufficient number of additions to have reduced program performance or a sufficient number of deletions that it is desired to recover the wasted space on the storage medium.

**12.** Yes. In order to access the data in logical key sequence.

**13.** To locate the desired record more quickly, by going to the appropriate track of cylinder index instead of having to search the cylinder index from the beginning. (Generally, when more than three cylinders are required for the cylinder index, a master index is implemented by the designer responsible for the files in a system.)

**14.** A dummy record is a null or void record that consumes space on the external medium but contains no significant data.

**15.** Dummy records might normally be used for INDEXED, REGIONAL, and VSAM-RRDS files.

(a) INDEXED and REGIONAL (1): a flag of all 1 bits appears in the first byte of the data record.

(b) REGIONAL (2) and (3): a flag of all 1 bits appears in the KEY field.

**16.** (a) VSAM-KSDS has two levels of index; INDEXED may have three.

(b) VSAM-KSDS inserts "free space" throughout the data set; INDEXED handles insertions through specially allocated overflow areas.

(c)   VSAM-KSDS physically deletes records, creating more "free space"; INDEXED flags deleted records which still consume space in the data set.

(d)   VSAM-KSDS does not require the periodic file maintenance that INDEXED normally requires.

(e)   VSAM-KSDS provides improved data security through the use of a password and allows a disk pack containing VSAM data to be carried from one IBM S/370 computer to another.

17.   INDEXED
      REGIONAL (1)
      REGIONAL (2)
      REGIONAL (3)
      VSAM-KSDS
      VSAM-RRDS

**18.** No.

**19.** Buffers allow logical records to be blocked—providing an area to hold the physical block while logical records are accessed one at a time. By providing two buffers, data may be processed from one buffer while the other buffer is being used for an input/output operation.

**20.** (c).

**21.** (d).

**22.** (a), (b), (d).

**23.**   WRITE FILE (XFILE) FROM (AREA__1) KEYFROM ('293');

**24.** (b).
      (d).
      (f).
      (g).

**25.** The KEY condition would be raised.

# APPENDIX B

# Built-in
# Functions

Built-in functions were introduced in Chapter 3, page 104. Throughout this text, these functions, which are really an extension of PL/I, were presented as the need for them arose. A number of additional functions not covered elsewhere are presented here. The various built-in functions offered in PL/I are extensive. You may also wish to consult the reference manual for the compiler you are using for additional functions.

## ARRAY MANIPULATION BUILT-IN FUNCTIONS

The built-in functions examined here are those that facilitate the manipulation of array data. These functions will require array name arguments. They return results in the form of a single value. Because a single value is returned from these functions, a function reference to any array is considered an **element expression,** as contrasted with **array expression,** which was discussed in Chapter 6.

### Functions Giving Array Sizes

The following array built-in functions are provided to give boundary and extent information: (1) To facilitate ease of program modification later, and (2) to facilitate storage control manipulation.

The three functions are called DIM (for dimension), LBOUND (for lower boundary), and HBOUND (for high boundary).

**The DIM Function.** This function provides the current extent of an array. For example:

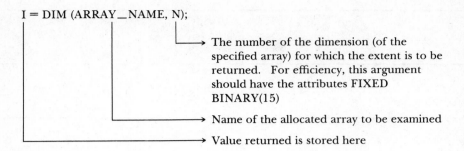

I = DIM (ARRAY_NAME, N);

→ The number of the dimension (of the specified array) for which the extent is to be returned. For efficiency, this argument should have the attributes FIXED BINARY(15)

→ Name of the allocated array to be examined

→ Value returned is stored here

As an example of the value returned by the DIM function, assume that an array has been declared as follows:

DCL ARRAY (−3: +3);

The boundary range from −3 goes through element 0 to an upper boundary of +3. Thus, there are seven elements in ARRAY. The DIM built-in function, in this case, would return a value of 7. In the case of an array whose lower boundary starts at 1, DIM returns the value equal to the current upper boundary of that declared array.

**The LBOUND Function.** This function finds the current lower bound for a specified dimension of a given array and returns it to the point of invocation. For example:

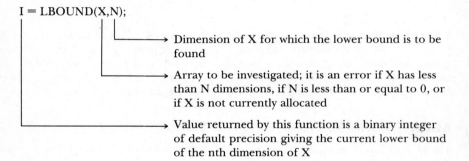

I = LBOUND(X,N);

→ Dimension of X for which the lower bound is to be found

→ Array to be investigated; it is an error if X has less than N dimensions, if N is less than or equal to 0, or if X is not currently allocated

→ Value returned by this function is a binary integer of default precision giving the current lower bound of the nth dimension of X

**The HBOUND Function.** This function finds the current upper bound for a specified dimension of a given array and returns it to the point of invocation. For example:

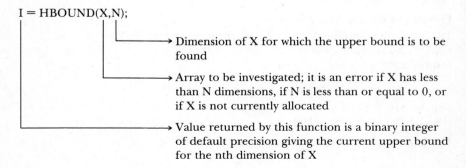

I = HBOUND(X,N);

→ Dimension of X for which the upper bound is to be found

→ Array to be investigated; it is an error if X has less than N dimensions, if N is less than or equal to 0, or if X is not currently allocated

→ Value returned by this function is a binary integer of default precision giving the current upper bound for the nth dimension of X

**An Application of These Built-in Functions.** Any one of the three previous built-in functions could be used to improve the ease with which future modifications may be made to a program. For example, assume you are coding a program in which it has been estimated that a 100-element array is needed for the present application. Later, however, the program specifications are changed and it is determined that a 150-element array is needed. If your program manipulating the array includes the iterative DO, then a do-group such as

        DO I = 1 TO 100;
          .
          .
          .
        END;

might be present. When subsequent modification to this program takes place, the declared array size must be changed from 100 to 150 as well as any other statements specifically using the upper or lower boundaries of the array. In the example we are working with, the iterative DO *limit value* must be changed from 100 to 150. If the iterative DO had invoked either the DIM or the HBOUND function, then that statement need not have been modified as long as its intent was to remain the same. For example:

        DO I = 1 TO HBOUND (ARRAY_NAME,1);

In the case of DIM and HBOUND, both functions return the same value for an array whose lower boundary starts at 1. Note that if the lower boundary of an array is to be anything other than 1, then the LBOUND function should be used in place of a *constant* reference to the first position of the array.

**The SUM Function**

The following function would be used when it is desired to total all values in an arithmetic array. Of course, the contents of arrays may be summed using the iterative DO in which an assignment statement (with subscript references) is nested. For example:

        TOTAL = 0;
        DO I = 1 TO 100;
            TOTAL = TOTAL + ARRAY (I);
        END;

The built-in function SUM accomplishes the previous coding in just one PL/I statement. For example:

        DCL AVERAGE FIXED (3);
        DCL GRADE (5) FIXED (3) INIT (90,85,76,93,81);
        AVERAGE = SUM (GRADE)/5;

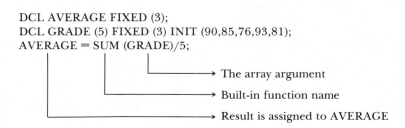

The array argument

Built-in function name

Result is assigned to AVERAGE

There are differences in the way PL/I compilers implement the SUM built-in function.

**1. IBM PL/I-F languages:** The array argument will be converted to floating-point if it is not in that form. Summation is done in floating-point and result returned is in floating-point.

A word of caution is given to the commercial programmer. The results of calculations performed on floating-point data may not be accurate to the degree that you would like. For example, assume the following values are to be summed:

```
 43.10
 57.38
  9.10
109.58
```

Assume the following had been coded:

```
DCL TABLE (3)      FIXED DEC (5,2);
DCL TOTAL          FIXED DEC (7,2);
GET LIST (TABLE);
    /* ASSUME TABLE(1) = 43.10, TABLE(2) = 57.38, TABLE(3) = 9.10 */
TOTAL = SUM(TABLE);
```

The above set of values will be converted to floating-point for the SUM function, TOTAL would contain the value 109.57. This result is not correct — it is a penny off. The problem, of course, is in decimal-binary conversion and back and has nothing to do with the adequacy of the programming or the conversion routines. To obtain the correct answer, it would be necessary to code the following:

```
TOTAL = SUM (TABLE)+.005;
```

The .005 rounds off the intermediate floating-point result to give the correct answer — in this case, 109.58. The best solution to this type of problem is to avoid the SUM function in PL/I-F.

**2. Optimizers, checkout compiler, PL/C:** Fixed-point arrays are summed using fixed-point; there is no conversion to floating-point as in IBM's PL/I-F. (Of course, floating-point arguments cause summation to be done in floating-point.) The result returned is in the scale of the argument.

### Functions Useful for Statistical Programming

The following functions may be useful to you if you are doing basic statistical applications.

**The PROD Built-in Function.** This function finds the product of all the elements of an array. For example:

```
DCL ALIST (5)              FLOAT DEC(6)   INIT (1,2,3,4,5);
PRODUCT = PROD(ALIST);
```

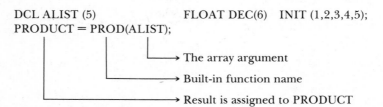

The array argument

Built-in function name

Result is assigned to PRODUCT

The statement invoking the PROD function is equivalent to the following arithmetic operation:

PRODUCT=ALIST(1)*ALIST(2)*ALIST(3)*ALIST(4)*ALIST(5);

The computation is carried out in floating-point arithmetic.

**The POLY Built-in Function.** This function is used to form a polynomial expansion in floating-point from two arguments. For example, assume the GRADE array has been declared and initialized to the following values:

GRADE  (1) | 90 |
       (2) | 85 |
       (3) | 76 |
       (4) | 93 |
       (5) | 81 |

Then, if the statements

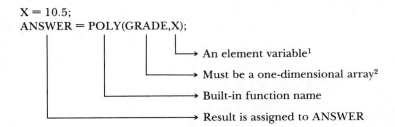

X = 10.5;
ANSWER = POLY(GRADE,X);

→ An element variable[1]

→ Must be a one-dimensional array[2]

→ Built-in function name

→ Result is assigned to ANSWER

are coded, the following arithmetic operations are performed:

$$90 + 85X + 76X^2 + 93X^3 + 81X^4$$

The values, 90, 85, etc., are the values contained in the GRADE array, and X is a constant value defined in the second argument of the POLY function. The result, then, may be expressed as:

$$\sum_{j=0}^{n-m} a(m + j) * x ** j$$

where a is the first argument (a one-dimensional array), x is the second argument, m is the lower bound of the a array, and n is the upper bound of the a array.

It is also permissible to specify the second argument, x, as a one-dimensional array. In that case, the value returned by the POLY function is defined as:

$$a(m) + \sum_{j=1}^{n-m} \left[ a(m + j) * \prod_{i=0}^{j-1} x(p + i) \right]$$

where a, x, m, and n are the same as defined above and p represents the lower bound of the second argument.

[1,2] This will be converted to floating-point if it is not in that form.

### Functions Facilitating Bit Manipulating in Arrays

Two built-in functions are useful in the manipulation of bit-strings grouped together in arrays. One application might be in the area of *pattern recognition*. Another application is *status monitoring*. As an illustration, assume that a burglar alarm system has been installed for 25 customers of the Ace Guard System. When an intruder trespasses on a customer's property, a signal is sent to the computer. The computer program's function is to note the change in status and print alarm messages informing necessary parties. Assume the status of the alarm indicators is automatically entered into successive elements of bit-string arrays once every second. Then, once every 15 seconds, a program is scheduled to scan these arrays to determine any change in status. Testing of individual bits within the array elements can be handled in a very concise manner — through the use of the ANY and/or ALL built-in functions.

**The ANY Built-in Function.** This function is used to test the bits of a given bit-string array. If *any* bit in the same position of the elements of an array is a '1'B, then the result is a '1'B; otherwise, the result is '0'B. You may recognize this operation as being the same in logic as the Boolean OR operation. Here is an example:

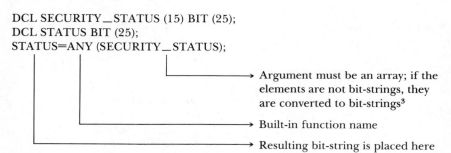

Assume that the following array elements have been initialized to the following bit-string configurations:

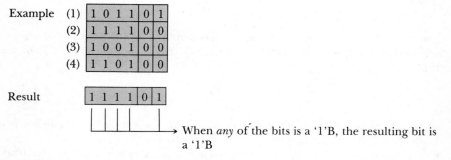

**The ALL Built-in Function.** This function is used to test all bits of a given bit-string array. If *all* bits in the same position within each element are '1'B, then the result is a '1'B;

---

[3] If the data item is CHARACTER, the character-string should contain only the characters 1 and 0. The character 1 becomes a bit 1; the character 0 becomes the bit 0. If the data item is arithmetic, the absolute value is converted, if necessary, to a fixed-point binary integer. Ignoring the plus sign, the integer is then interpreted as a bit-string.

otherwise, the result is a '0'B. You may recognize this operation as being the same in logic as the rules of the Boolean AND operation. Here is an example:

```
DCL SECURITY_STATUS (15)          BIT(25);
DCL STATUS                        BIT(25);
STATUS = ALL(SECURITY_STATUS);
```

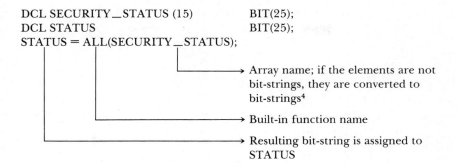

→ Array name; if the elements are not bit-strings, they are converted to bit-strings[4]

→ Built-in function name

→ Resulting bit-string is assigned to STATUS

Assume that the following array elements have been initialized to the following bit-string configurations.

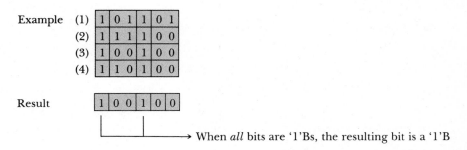

Example  (1)  1 0 1 1 0 1
         (2)  1 1 1 1 0 0
         (3)  1 0 0 1 0 0
         (4)  1 1 0 1 0 0

Result        1 0 0 1 0 0

→ When *all* bits are '1'Bs, the resulting bit is a '1'B

---

[4] See description of conversion given for the ANY built-in function.

# PL/I Language
# Comparison Charts

The majority of language features available in a number of widely used PL/I compilers are compared in charts on the following pages.[1]  The compilers include the following:

## PL/C

PL/C is a PL/I processor that was developed by a systems programming group of the Department of Computer Science at Cornell University (hence, the *C* in PL/C).  The compiler is designed to run on IBM's mainframes.  The users of PL/C are primarily educational institutions where PL/C characteristics are particularly advantageous for large numbers of relatively short programs produced by typically inexperienced programmers. PL/C provides diagnostic assistance and also attempts to repair errors.  An error message is produced, and PL/C displays the source statement that results from the repair.  A significant fraction of trivial errors of punctuation, spelling, and syntax are correctly repaired.  Repairs of substantive and semantic errors rarely reconstruct what the programmer intended, but they do prolong the life of a faulty program and greatly increase the amount of diagnostic information that can be obtained from each run.  PL/C exercises a degree of control over execution usually found only in interpretive systems, but it does so without suffering the slow execution of interpretation.  PL/C also includes several diagnostic statements that provide a convenient trace and dump capability and enhance the utility of the CHECK condition.  Figure C.1 summarizes a number of debugging tools available in PL/C.

[1] Appreciation is extended to Scott Miller for his assistance in preparing the comparison of Digital Research's PL/I-G for microcomputers.

# SERIES/1

Series/1 is a relatively new computer produced by IBM. It is designed for both real-time and batch applications in a multitasking, event-driven environment. The Series/1 PL/I is a subset of ANS PL/I plus a number of extensions that support the sensor-based and other real-time applications the computer is designed to handle.

# PL/I-D

PL/I-D is an IBM compiler designed to run on IBM computers using the Disk Operating System (DOS). The compiler is offered without a rental fee but has limited use in installations today because the compiler has had no recent enhancements made to it by IBM as have other PL/I compilers that are offered for a monthly rental fee. PL/I-D is a subset language. Following are comments and notes about the language's restrictions.

There is no standard definition of a subset PL/I language; thus, the restrictions listed in the following paragraphs may not apply if you are using a subset PL/I on a different computer running under an operating system other than DOS.

## General Restrictions

|  | Number of characters allowed for main procedure names or file names |
|---|---|
| Subset language | 1 to 6 |
| Full language | 1 to 7 |

## Data Attributes

1. Maximum character-string length for constants or variables is 255.
2. No POSITION or VARYING attribute for character-strings.
3. No arithmetic operations allowed on CHARACTER data.
4. Maximum bit-string length for constants or variables is 64.
5. FIXED BINARY data items always require four bytes regardless of precision.
6. Must explicitly declare pointer variables as having the POINTER attribute.
7. No CONTROLLED storage class.
8. No COMPLEX variables.
9. Permissable data conversions follow:

|  | Arithmetic[a] to CHARACTER | CHARACTER to Arithmetic | Arithmetic to BIT | BIT to Arithmetic | CHARACTER to BIT | BIT to CHARACTER |
|---|---|---|---|---|---|---|
| Subset language | No | No | Yes[b] | Yes[b] | No | Yes |
| Full language | Yes | Yes | Yes | Yes | Yes | Yes |

[a] Arithmetic refers to any coded arithmetic data item (FIXED, FLOAT, FIXED BINARY, etc.).
[b] The maximum number of bits allowed is 31.

| PL/C keyword | Use of keyword | Examples and other information |
|---|---|---|
| ALL | Diagnostic option of PUT statement | PUT ALL;<br>Debugging facility; places value of all *scalar* variables on SYS-PRINT file (note distinction from PUT ALL of the optimizer and checkout compilers) |
| ARRAY | Diagnostic option of PUT statement | PUT ARRAY;<br>Debugging facility; places value of all scalar *and array* variables on SYSPRINT file |
| CHECK[(a[,b])] | Statement | CHECK(10,20);<br>Enables printing for the next 10 changes of value for CHECKed variables in the current block, and the first 20 in any block entered from this one |
| DEPTH(exp) | Diagnostic option of PUT statement | PUT SNAP DEPTH(3);<br>Debugging facility; limits traceback to 3 levels |
| FLOW | Condition | ON FLOW BEGIN;<br>Specifies on-unit whenever sequential execution is interrupted by a GO TO, CALL, IF … THEN … ELSE, DO, END, RETURN, or other such statement |

FIGURE C.1  PL/C debugging tools.

| PL/C keyword | Use of keyword | Examples and other information |
|---|---|---|
| FLOW | Diagnostic option of PUT statement | PUT FLOW;<br>Debugging facility; places on SYSPRINT the current history of nonsequential execution (i.e., execution which raised the FLOW condition) |
| FLOW[(a[,b])] | Statement | FLOW(10,20);<br>Invokes automatic printing for the next 10 instances of non-sequential execution in the current block, and the first 20 in any block entered from this one |
| NOCHECK | Statement | NOCHECK;<br>Cancels printing of value changes of CHECKed variables |
| NOFLOW | Condition prefix | (NOFLOW): CALL SUB1(X);<br>Disables the FLOW condition for scope of statement |
| NOFLOW | Statement | NOFLOW;<br>Cancels automatic printing for instances of nonsequential execution |
| NOSOURCE | Star card option (*PL/C, etc.) | NOSOURCE;<br>Cancels source program listing from this point |
| OFF | Diagnostic option of PUT statement | PUT OFF;<br>Debugging facility; cancels subsequent output on SYSPRINT |
| ON | Diagnostic option of PUT statement | PUT ON;<br>Debugging facility; restores printing on SYSPRINT |

FIGURE C.1 *(continued)*

| ONDEST | Built-in function | I = ONDEST;<br>Returns the statement number of the statement which was the destination of the nonsequential execution causing the FLOW condition to be raised |
| --- | --- | --- |
| ONORIG | Built-in function | I = ONORIG;<br>Returns the statement number of the statement which was the origin of the nonsequential execution causing the FLOW condition to be raised |
| SNAP | Diagnostic option of PUT statement | PUT SNAP;<br>Debugging facility; causes a traceback of currently active blocks to be placed on SYSPRINT |
| SOURCE | Star Card option (*PL/C, etc.) | SOURCE;<br>Restores source program listing from this point |
| STMTNO (label) | Built-in function | I = STMTNO (L);<br>Returns the statement number of the statement labeled L |

FIGURE C.1 *(continued)*

## Pictures

**1.** No A picture character.

**2.** The B picture character may only appear to the right of a decimal picture; for example,

    DCL SALES PICTURE 'ZZZ9V.99BBB';

**3.** The X picture character and 9 picture character are not allowed in the same PICTURE; for example,

    DCL A PICTURE '999XX'; /* INVALID IN PL/I-D */

## Data Aggregates

**1.** Maximum structure level number allowed is 255.   Maximum number of nested levels is 8.

**2.** Overlay-define allowed at major structure level only (level 1 name overlay-defined on a level 1 name).

**3.** No LIKE attribute.

**4.** No BY NAME option in an assignment statement.

**5.** No arrays of structures.

**6.** Maximum number of dimensions is three.   You may not specify a lower bound; it is always assumed to be 1.   Bounds may only be expressed as decimal integer constants.

**7.** No cross sections of arrays.

**8.** No SUBSCRIPTRANGE condition.

## Stream I/O

**1.** PAGE, LINE, and SKIP may not all be specified in same PUT statement.

**2.** Maximum number of lines that may be skipped at one time is three:

    PUT SKIP (3);

**3.** No LINESIZE option.

**4.** No COPY option of a GET LIST.

**5.** No data-directed I/O.

**6.** For A and B format items, the corresponding data items must have the CHARACTER or BIT attribute, respectively.

**7.** For E and F format items, the corresponding data item must be in arithmetic code form (e.g., FIXED BINARY, FIXED DECIMAL, FLOAT BINARY, FLOAT DECIMAL).

**8.** The LINENO built-in function for PRINT files is not available.

**9.** No P-format in edit I/O.   The need for P-format most often arises when it is desired to **edit** data (i.e., insert dollar sign, comma, CR symbol, etc.).   You have seen how to accomplish editing—typically, by assigning data to identifiers that contain PICTURE editing characters.   For example:

    DCL PRICE PIC'$$$,$$$V.99';
    PRICE = 1050.78; /* PRICE = $1,050.78 */

In the subset language implementations of PL/I, we have a problem because it is not permitted to output (using edit-directed I/O) directly from a PICTURE that contains insertion characters (i.e., $, *, CR, DB, etc.). Thus, the following PUT EDIT (assuming the above DECLARE and assignment statements apply) would be invalid:

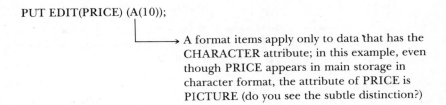

PUT EDIT(PRICE) (A(10));

A format items apply only to data that has the CHARACTER attribute; in this example, even though PRICE appears in main storage in character format, the attribute of PRICE is PICTURE (do you see the subtle distinction?)

The following examples, however, do not violate the rule in the subset language that you may not output directly from a picture that contains insertion characters:

```
DCL A   PIC '999V99'   INIT (12.34);
DCL B   PIC 'XXXX'   INIT ('ABCD');
PUT EDIT (A,B) (F(6,2),A(5));
/* ON OUTPUT, A = ' 12.34' AND B = 'ABCD   ' */
```

Two methods may be used for printing from a PICTURE identifier with editing characters. The first method is perhaps the easiest to understand. A built-in function called CHAR is provided in PL/I. This function converts its argument to a character-string. For example:

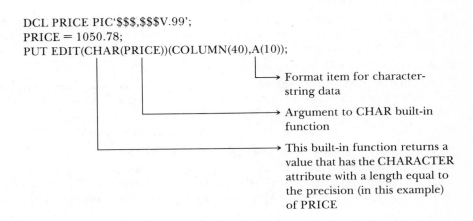

```
DCL PRICE PIC'$$$,$$$V.99';
PRICE = 1050.78;
PUT EDIT(CHAR(PRICE))(COLUMN(40),A(10));
```

Format item for character-string data

Argument to CHAR built-in function

This built-in function returns a value that has the CHARACTER attribute with a length equal to the precision (in this example) of PRICE

The other method for simulating P format is to use overlay-defining. This method is more efficient than the method of invoking the CHAR built-in function each time a PICTURE value is to be treated as a character-string. For example:

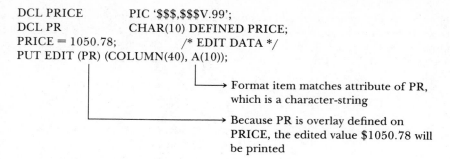

```
DCL PRICE          PIC '$$$,$$$V.99';
DCL PR             CHAR(10) DEFINED PRICE;
PRICE = 1050.78;           /* EDIT DATA */
PUT EDIT (PR) (COLUMN(40), A(10));
```

Format item matches attribute of PR, which is a character-string

Because PR is overlay defined on PRICE, the edited value $1050.78 will be printed

## Record I/O

1. May only READ or WRITE from base identifier *not* overlay defined item; for example,

```
DCL AREA CHAR (100) DEF STRUCTURE;
    .
    .
    .
READ FILE (INPUT) INTO (STRUCTURE);
```

2. Must explicitly open record I/O files.

3. Locate mode not allowed for INDEXED data sets.

4. Must use SET option in a READ or LOCATE statement for locate mode processing.

5. Variable-length records—that is, V-format records—are not allowed for the line printer.

6. The only attributes that may be specified in an OPEN statement are PAGESIZE and, for UNBUFFERED files, INPUT and OUTPUT. The TITLE option is not available.

7. The maximum number of buffers that may be specified for one file is 2.

8. REGIONAL (2) is not available in PL/I-D.

9. In REGIONAL (3), the recorded key must consist of the comparison key and the region number. This means that the KEYLENGTH specification must always be 9 or greater: 8 for the region specification plus at least 1 for the comparison key.

10. No REGIONAL file attributes may be specified in an OPEN statement.

11. REGIONAL files must be explicitly specified through job control language statements and a DOS utility program called CLRDSK (see "Preformatting REGIONAL Files" in the index of the DOS PL/I Programmers' Guide).

12. REGIONAL data sets may only be accessed by the DIRECT method.

13. Only F format records are allowed in REGIONAL data sets.

14. *The MEDIUM option:* For DOS PL/I compilers, this option must be specified. The MEDIUM option is used to specify a symbolic device name and the type of device on which the data set is stored or through which you access the data. For example:

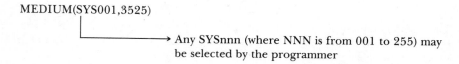

```
MEDIUM(SYS001,3525)
```

Any SYSnnn (where NNN is from 001 to 255) may be selected by the programmer

The physical device numbers you specify depend on the type of devices attached to the computer on which your PL/I program is to be run. Some of the more commonly used IBM devices are

| | |
|---|---|
| Card read/punch | 2540, 1442, 3525 |
| Card readers | 2520, 2501, 3505 |
| Line printers | 1403, 1443, 3211 |

Rather than specifying a SYSnnn symbolic device name, you may wish to use standard symbolic device names. These are

| | |
|---|---|
| SYSIPT | card reader |
| SYSPCH | card punch |
| SYSLST | line printer |

In DOS/VS, if you use a standard symbolic device name, the device type may be omitted from the MEDIUM option. For example:

    MEDIUM (SYSIPT);

### Subroutines and Functions

**1.** Arguments to subroutines and functions may not be based variables, built-in function names, array expressions, or structure expressions. Arguments may be variables, constants, expressions, array names, major structure or minor structure names, entry names, file names, and labels. (Note that the use of labels as arguments is not recommended for structured programs.)

**2.** The maximum number of arguments allowed in one subroutine CALL or function reference is 12.

### CHECK Trace Feature

Since the CHECK trace feature is not provided in the subset language, the programmer will have to *build in* a trace. This can be done through the PUT LIST facility. PUT LIST statements can be inserted at key points throughout a program. Character-string constants should also be included for identification purposes on the output listing. For example, in the grade-point average program shown in Chapter 1 of this text, a PUT LIST (A,B,C,D,E) could be inserted following the GET. PUT LIST statements could also be inserted following the calculations:

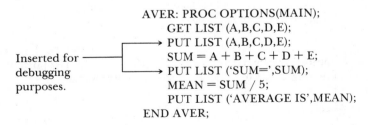

```
                    AVER: PROC OPTIONS(MAIN);
                       GET LIST (A,B,C,D,E);
                   ┌→ PUT LIST (A,B,C,D,E);
Inserted for ──────┤  SUM = A + B + C + D + E;
debugging          └→ PUT LIST ('SUM=',SUM);
purposes.             MEAN = SUM / 5;
                      PUT LIST ('AVERAGE IS',MEAN);
                    END AVER;
```

### Built-In Functions

**1.** In SUBSTR, the first argument must be a bit- or character-string. The third argument may only be a decimal constant; for example,

SUBSTR (NAME,5,4)

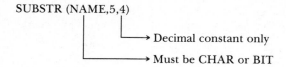
→ Decimal constant only
→ Must be CHAR or BIT

**2.** In ROUND, the second argument may only be positive (never negative); for example,

X = ROUND (Y*Z,2);
→ May only be positive

**3.** LBOUND, HBOUND, and DIM functions are not available.

### Miscellaneous

**1.** Requires specific file declaration if keyword SYSIN is used in the ENDFILE statement.

**2.** The MEDIUM option of the ENVIRONMENT attribute is always required.

**3.** A level-1 declaration for scalar variables is not allowed.   For example:

DCL 1 VALUE FIXED (7,2); /* INVALID SYNTAX */

### Conclusion

The restrictions given here are not necessarily complete.   You may wish to consult the comparison charts for keyword availability.   The reference manual for a given subset language is always the final authority.

### PL/I-F

PL/I-F is an early version of PL/I; it does provide full language capability, not a subset as in PL/I-D.   PL/I-F is no longer supported by IBM.

### PL/I-G

Digital Research PL/I is an implementation of PL/I for microcomputers that use the 8080, 8086, 8088, or similar processor.   It is formally based on American National Standard X3.74 PL/I General Purpose Subset (Subset G).   Subset G has the formal structure of the full PL/I language, but in some ways it is a new language and in many ways an improved language compared to full PL/I.

In addition to the features noted in the comparison chart at the end of this appendix the following keywords have been added to DRI's PL/I for microcomputers.

| Keyword | Use | Description |
|---------|-----|-------------|
| ASCII(x) | Built-in function | x is fixed binary.   Return a single character whose position in the ASCII collate sequence corresponds to x. |
| B | Radix indicator | For bit-string constants<br>Example: If H = '10011'B THEN; |

| Keyword | Use | Description |
|---------|-----|-------------|
| BUFF(x) \| B(x) | Option of ENVIRONMENT attribute | Directs I/O System to buffer x bytes of storage. |
| B1 | Format item | Bit-string format item equivalent to B |
| B1 | Radix (base) indicator | Equivalent to radix indicator B |
| B1(n) | Format item | Bit-string format item equivalent to B(n). |
| B2 | Format item | Bit-string format item equivalent to B, except base 4. |
| B2 | Radix (base) indicator | Equivalent to radix indicator B, except characters 0–3 represented. |
| B2(n) | Format item | Bit-string format item equivalent to B(n), except base 4. |
| B3 | Format item | Bit-string format (octal) item equivalent to B, except base 8. |
| B3(n) | Format item | Bit-string format item equivalent to B(n), except base 8. |
| B4 | Radix (base) indicator | Equivalent to base indicator B, except characters 0–8, A–F represented. |
| B4(n) | Format item | Bit-string format item equivalent to B(n), except radix 16. |
| COLLATE(x) | Built-in function | Returns CHARACTER(128) consisting of ASCII character set in collating sequence. |
| COPY(s,i) | Built-in function | s = character string, i = fixed binary
Returns i copies of s concatenated together. |
| LOCK(f,i) | Built-in function | f = file constant, i = fixed binary
Returns BIT(1), result of locking record i in file f. |
| LOCKED \| L | Option of ENVIRONMENT attribute | Opens a file in locked mode |
| PAGENO(f) | Built-in function | f is a file value. Returns page number of file specified by f. Must have PRINT attribute. |
| PARAMETER | Storage class | Not currently implemented, to be implemented in a later release. Storage class that the compiler assigns to data items that appear in a parameter list. Storage is allocated when calling procedure passes parameters to called procedure. |
| PASSWORD[(level)] \| P[(level)] | Option of ENVIRONMENT attribute | Opens a file with password protection, where the valid protection levels are R = read, W = write, D = Delete. |
| RANK(c) | Built-in function | c = character value of length 1
Returns integer representation of the ASCII character c. |

| Keyword | Use | Description |
|---|---|---|
| READONLY \| R | Option of ENVIRONMENT attribute | Opens a file in read only mode. |
| %REPLACE | Preprocessor statement | Defines global constant names. |
| REVERSE(s) | Built-in function | s is a character-string expression. Returns character-string the same length as s with the characters in reverse order. |
| SEARCH(s,c) | Built-in function | s and c are character-string expressions Returns integer indicating first character in s that matches a character in c. |
| SHARED \| S | Option of ENVIRONMENT attribute | Opens a file in shared mode. |
| STACK(n) | Option of OPTIONS attribute/option | Sets size of run-time stack to number of bytes specified by n. Default = 512. |
| TAB(n) | Format item in EDIT | Starts next field at column given by n times eight. |
| TRIM(s,[l,t]) | Built-in function | s,l,t are characters string expressions TRIM(s) returns character-string with leading and trailing blanks removed. TRIM(s,l,t) returns a character-string with all leading characters of s that appear in 1 removed, and all trailing characters of s that appear in t removed. |
| UNLOCK(f,i) | Built-in function | f = file constant, i = fixed binary Returns BIT(1), result of unlocking record i in file f. |
| VERIFY(s,c) | Built-in function | s,c are character expressions Returns 0 if each character in s appears in c, otherwise returns an integer that indicates position of leftmost character of s that does not occur in c. |

There are some additional implementation differences between DRI PL/I-86 and other PL/I compilers. They are noted as follows:

| Keyword | Notes |
|---|---|
| ALIGNED | Has no effect, but is included for compatibility with other implementations. |
| ATAN | Only one argument supported. |
| ATAND | Only one argument supported. |
| AUTO | Automatic storage is statically allocated, except for recursive procedures, so AUTO is ignored outside of recursive procedures. |

| Keyword | Notes |
|---|---|
| CONVERSION | Not implemented in DRI-PL/I, but is handled by condition ERROR(1). |
| DIM | Keyword DIMENSION also accepted. |
| ERROR | Also implemented as ERROR(x) where x is an integer-expression referring to an error code. There are four groups of subcodes: |

|  |  |  |
|---|---|---|
| 0 – 63 | Reserved for PL/I | (Nonrecoverable) |
| 64 – 127 | User-defined | (Nonrecoverable) |
| 128 – 191 | Reserved for PL/I | (Recoverable) |
| 192 – 255 | User-defined | (Recoverable) |

| Keyword | Notes |
|---|---|
| FIXEDOVERFLOW | Also implemented as FIXEDOVERFLOW(x) where x is an integer-expression referring to an error code. |
| MIN | Only supports two arguments. |
| MAX | Only supports two arguments. |
| OVERFLOW | Also implemented as OVERFLOW(x) where x is an integer-expression referring to an error code. |
| SET | Used as a keyword in 'ALLOCATE' only, not 'READ' |
| UNDERFLOW | Also implemented as UNDERFLOW(x) where x is an integer-expression referring to an error code. |
| ZERODIVIDE | Also implemented as ZERODIVIDE(x) where x is an integer-expression referring to an error code. |

## OPTIMIZERS

Two optimizing compilers are provided by IBM: DOS PL/I and OS PL/I. Each offers full language capability and is offered for a monthly rental fee. They run on IBM's S/370. The compilers offer many advantages over their "free" counterparts — PL/I-D and PL/I-F. The advantages include better object code generated and improved diagnostics and error checking.

## PL/I CHECKOUT COMPILER

The PL/I checkout compiler is used by programmers during program development time because of the extensive error checking and diagnostic facilities. In terms of language features, it is identical to IBM's OS PL/I optimizer.

## ANS PL/I

ANS stands for American National Standards. ANS PL/I is a definition by American National Standards Institute of those features that should be considered standard in a PL/I compiler. Features not identified as *standard* but offered in a particular compiler are considered as extensions of the language. The advantage to a user of the PL/I language using only the defined ANS PL/I features is that there should be uniformity among the various compilers should the user wish to run PL/I programs on different computers. Actual practice, however, indicates that most users will use a feature of the language if it is convenient to do so without regard for whether or not it is ANS PL/I.

| Keyword | Abbreviation | ANS PL/I | PL/I checkout | OS PL/I optimizer | DOS PL/I optimizer | DRI's PL/I-G | PL/I-D | Series/1 | PL/C | Use of keyword | Examples and other information |
|---|---|---|---|---|---|---|---|---|---|---|---|
| A (w) | | x | x | x | x | x | x | x | x | Format item | DCL STR CHAR (20); PUT EDIT (STR) (A(22)); Places the contents of STR in a field of length 22 in output stream |
| ABS (x) | | x | x | x | x | x | x | x | x | Built-in function | X = ABS (5 − Y/2); Calculates the absolute value of 5 − Y/2 and places it in X |
| ACOS (x) | | x | x | x | x | x | x | x | x | Built-in function | A = ACOS (Z**F); Returns the angle in radians whose cosine is Z ** F |
| % ACTIVATE | %ACT | | x | x | x | | | | | Preprocessor statement | % LOOK:ACTIVATE X,Y; Makes explicitly deactivated compile-time identifiers replaceable |
| ADD (x,y,pl,ql) | | x | x | x | x | | x | | x | Built-in function | SUM = ADD (A,B,7,3); Equivalent to A + B in a field of seven digits, three of which are fractional |
| ADDBUFF (n) | | | x | x | x | | x | x | | Option of ENVIRONMENT attribute | DCL F FILE ENV (ADDBUFF(3000)); Used to allocate additional workspace for DIRECT indexed files |
| ADDR (x) | | x | x | x | x | x | x | x | x | Built-in function | P = ADDR (A); Returns a pointer that identifies the location of the named variable |
| ALIGNED | | x | x | x | x | x | x | x | x | Attribute | DCL 1 BOY ALIGNED, . . . Specifies that each variable to start at implementation boundary |
| ALL (x) | | x | x | x | x | | | | x | Built-in function | B = ALL (TABLE); Each iterm in TABLE is converted to bit-string and logically ANDed bit-by-bit |

| Keyword | Abbrev. | | | | | | Category | Description |
|---|---|---|---|---|---|---|---|---|
| ALL |  | x |  |  | x | x | Option of PUT statement | PUT ALL;<br>Debugging facility; places values of all variables on SYSPRINT file. Ignored by optimizing compiler |
|  |  |  |  |  |  |  | Option of DEFAULT statement | DEFAULT ALL SYSTEM;<br>All variables are subject to DEFAULT specifications |
| ALLOCATE | ALLOC |  | x | x | x | x | Statement | ALLOCATE A,B,C;<br>Allocates storage for controlled or based variables |
| ALLOCATION (x) | ALLOCN (x) |  | x | x | x | x | Built-in function | IF ALLOCATION (X) THEN . . .<br>Optimizers: Returns the number of generations of CTL variables allocated; PL/1-F: Returns '1'B if CTL argument is allocated, '0'B is not |
| ANY (x) |  | x | x | x |  |  | Built-in function | D = ANY (TABLE);<br>Each item in TABLE is converted to bit-string and logically ORd bit-by-bit |
| AREA |  |  |  | x | x | x | Condition | ON AREA BEGIN;<br>Specifies on-unit when the request for allocation in an area exceeds available storage |
| AREA [(size)] |  |  |  | x | x | x | Attribute | DCL A AREA (1000);<br>Specifies that A is to be an area of storage 1000 bytes in length available for allocation of based variables |
| ARGn |  |  |  | x | x |  | Option of NOMAP, NOMAPIN, and NOMAPOUT options of the OPTIONS attribute | DCL COBA OPTIONS (COBOL NOMAP ARG1);<br>Used in interlanguage communication to specify which arguments are to be transformed |
| ASCII |  |  | x | x | x | x | Option of ENVIRONMENT attribute | DCL A FILE ENV (ASCII . . .);<br>Specifies that ASCII code is used to represent data on the data set |

*Note:* x = feature available; * = feature planned but not implemented at time of publication of this text; blank = feature not available.

| Keyword | Abbreviation | PL/C | Series/1 | PL/I-D | DRI's PL/I-G | DOS PL/I optimizer | OS PL/I optimizer | PL/I checkout | ANS PL/I | Use of keyword | Examples and other information |
|---|---|---|---|---|---|---|---|---|---|---|---|
| ASIN (x) | | × | × | × | × | × | × | × | × | Built-in function | A = ASIN (Z ** F); Returns the angle in radians whose sine is Z ** F |
| ASSEMBLER | ASM | | | | | × | × | × | | Option of OPTIONS attribute/option | DCL ASMBL ENTRY OPTIONS (ASM); Specifies that the designated entry point is in an assembler subroutine |
| ASSOCIATE | | | | | | × | | | | Option of ENVIRONMENT attribute | DCL READF FILE INPUT RECORD . . ENV (. ., ASSOCIATE (PUNCHF) . .), PUNCHF FILE OUTPUT RECORD; ENV (. ., ASSOCIATE (READF) . .); Enables multiple operations to be performed on the IBM 3525. The FUNCTION option must be specified |
| ATAN (x[,y]) | | × | × | × | × | × | × | × | × | Built-in function | A = ATAN (Z ** F); Returns the angle in radians whose tangent is Z ** F; A = ATAN (Z, F); Returns ATAN (Z/F) |
| ATAND (x[,y]) | | × | × | × | × | × | × | × | × | Built-in function | A = ATAND (Z ** F); Returns the angle in degrees whose tangent is Z ** F; A = ATAND (Z, F); Returns ATAND (Z/F) |
| ATANH (x) | | × | | × | | × | × | × | × | Built-in function | A = ATANH (Z ** Q); Returns hyperbolic arctangent of Z ** Q; if ABS (x) > 1 error will result |
| ATTENTION | ATTN | | | | | | | × | | Condition | ON ATTN CALL TERMINAL__SIGNAL; Specifies on unit when the user signals attention at the terminal during conversational processing |

| Keyword | Abbrev | | | | | | | Category | Description |
|---|---|---|---|---|---|---|---|---|---|
| AUTOMATIC | AUTO | x | x | x | x | x | x | Attribute | DCL VAR AUTOMATIC; Specifies that storage for VAR is to be allocated upon entry to the block and released upon leaving the block |
| B [(x)] | | x | x | x | x | x | x | Format item | PUT EDIT (A)(B(10)); Specifies that A is to be placed in the output stream in a field 10 characters wide as at bit value |
| BACKWARDS | | | | x | x | x | x | Attribute | DCL F FILE BACKWARDS; Specifies that file F is to be read backward; only valid for magnetic tape files with fixed-length records |
| BASED [(locator-expression)] | | x | x | x | x | x | x | Attribute | DCL A BASED, B BASED (P); Specifies that A and B are to be used in list processing or locate mode I/O; the pointer P will be associated with B |
| BEGIN ... END; | | x | x | x | x | x | x | Statement | BEGIN; . . . END; Delimits the start of a begin block; block must be terminated with an END statement |
| BINARY | BIN | x | x | x | x | x | x | Attribute | DCL A FIXED BINARY; Specifies that A is to have a binary base |
| BINARY (x[,p[,q]]) | BIN | x | x | x | x | x | x | Built-in function | A = BINARY (B,7,2); Converts B to a binary base with precision (7,2); assigns the result to A |
| BIT [(length)] | | x | x | x | x | x | x | Attribute | DCL B BIT (10); Specifies that B is to occupy 10 bit positions of main storage |
| BIT (expression [size]) | | x | x | x | x | x | x | Built-in function | A = BIT (C + D, 10); Converts the result of C + D to a bit-string length 10; assigns the result to A |
| BACKWARD | BKWD | | | x | x | | | Option of ENVIRONMENT attribute | DCL VSMSEQ FILE SEQUENTIAL . . . INPUT ENV (VSAM BKWD); Specifies VSAM UPDATE or VSAM INPUT files to be processed backward |

*Note:* x = feature available; * = feature planned but not implemented at time of publication of this text; blank = feature not available.

| Keyword | Abbreviation | PL/C | Series/1 | PL/I-D | DRI's PL/I-G | DOS PL/I optimizer | OS PL/I optimizer | PL/I checkout | ANS PL/I | Use of keyword | Examples and other information |
|---|---|---|---|---|---|---|---|---|---|---|---|
| BLKSIZE (expression) | | × | × | | | × | × | × | × | Option of ENVIRONMENT attribute | DCL F FILE ENV (BLKSIZE (K)); Specifies that size in bytes for each record in file F; K must have a valid value when file is opened and be FIXED BIN (31) STATIC |
| BOOL (x, y, z) | | × | × | × | × | × | × | × | × | Built-in function | A = BOOL (B, C, '0110'B); Performs one of 16 possible logical operations between corresponding bits of B and C; places results in A |
| BUFFERED | BUF | * | | | × | × | × | × | | Attribute | DCL F FILE BUFFERED; Records from F must pass through intermediate storage; valid only for SEQUENTIAL RECORD files |
| BUFFERS (n) | | × | × | × | × | × | × | × | × | Option of ENVIRONMENT attribute | DCL F FILE ENV (BUFFERS (5)); Specifies that F is to have 5 buffers allocated when it is opened |
| BUILTIN | | × | × | × | × | × | × | × | × | Attribute | DCL DATE BUILTIN; Specifies that appearance of the identifier DATE is to be a reference to the PL/I function |
| BUFND (n) | | | | | | × | × | × | | Option of ENVIRONMENT attribute | DCL VSAMF FILE . . ENV (VSAM BUFND (2)); Specifies the number of data buffers (n) required for a VSAM data set |
| BUFNI (n) | | | | | | × | × | × | | Option of ENVIRONMENT attribute | DCL VSAMKS FILE . . ENV (VSAM BUFND (2) BUFNI (2)); Specifies the number of index buffers (n) required for a VSAM data set |
| BUFOFF | | | | | | × | × | × | | Option of ENVIRONMENT attribute | DCL A FILE . . ENV (ASCII . . BUFOFF (25)); |

| Feature | Synonym | | | | | | | | Category | Example / Description |
|---|---|---|---|---|---|---|---|---|---|---|
| | | | | | | | | | | Indicates the length of the block prefix field that precedes each block in an ASCII data set |
| BUFSP (n) | | | | x | x | | | | Option of ENVIRONMENT attribute | DCL VS FILE .. ENV (VSAM BUFSP (4000)); Indicates in bytes (n) the total buffer space required for a VSAM data set |
| BY | | x | x | x | x | x | | | Option of DO statement | DO I = 1 BY 2; Specifies the increment amount in an iterative DO statement |
| BY NAME | BYNAME | x | x | x | x | x | x | x | Option of assignment statement | ST1 = ST2, BY NAME; Assigns to elements of structure ST1 those elements of structure ST2 whose names are identical |
| C (x[,y]) | | x | x | x | x | x | | x | Format item | PUT EDIT (CMPLX) (C(F(7,2), F(7,2))); Specifies complex number format; x and y are any two real-format items to which the two parts of the complex number CMPLX are to be transmitted |
| CALL | | x | x | x | x | x | x | x | Statement | CALL SUBRT; Specifies that control is to be passed to the entry point SUBRT |
| CALL | | x | x | x | x | x | | | Option of INITIAL attribute | DCL A INIT CALL SUB; Specifies that the subroutine SUB is to be invoked to initialize A |
| CEIL (x) | | x | x | x | x | x | x | x | Built-in function | A = CEIL (B); Returns the smallest integer not exceeded by B |
| CHAR(expression [,size]) | | x | x | x | x | x | x | x | Built-in function | A = CHAR (B, 10); Causes B to be converted to a character-string of length 10 and assigned to A |
| CHARACTER [(length)] | CHAR | x | x | x | x | x | x | x | Attribute | DCL A CHAR (10); Specifies that A is to occupy 10 bytes of storage and represent a character-string variable |

*Note:* x = feature available; * = feature planned but not implemented at time of publication of this text; blank = feature not available.

| Keyword | Abbreviation | PL/C | Series/1 | PL/I-D | DRI's PL/I-G | DOS PL/I optimizer | OS PL/I optimizer | PL/I checkout | ANS PL/I | Use of keyword | Examples and other information |
|---|---|---|---|---|---|---|---|---|---|---|---|
| CHECK [(name list)] | | x | x | x | x | x | x | x | x | Condition | ON CHECK (A, B) SYSTEM; Causes new values of A or B to be output to SYSPRINT |
| CHECK | | x | | | | x | x | x | | Statement | CHECK (A,X,AMOUNT,TOTAL_QTY); Provides dynamic enabling of the CHECK condition; information about the variables is put out whenever the variables occur in predefined situations |
| CLOSE | | x | x | x | x | x | x | x | x | Statement | CLOSE FILE (F); Closes file F and releases the resources assigned to it |
| CMDCHN | | | | | | x | | | | Option of ENVIRONMENT attribute | DCL DISKET FILE . . ENV (CMDCHN (26) . .); Allows simulation of blocked records for the 3540 diskette I/O device |
| COBOL | | | | | | x | x | x | | Option of ENVIRONMENT attribute | DCL F FILE ENV (COBOL); Specifies that records from file F are to be mapped according to the COBOL algorithm |
| COBOL | | | | | | x | x | x | | Option of OPTIONS attribute/option | DCL E ENTRY OPTIONS (COBOL); Specifies that E is a COBOL program |
| COLBIN | | | | | | x | | | | Option of ENVIRONMENT attribute | DCL CARDS FILE . . ENV (COLBIN . . . MEDIUM (SYS004,3505)); Specifies that data items in a 3505 or 3525 device are in column binary format |
| COLUMN (w) | COL (w) | x | x | x | x | x | x | x | x | Format item | PUT EDIT (A) (COL(10), F (10)); Specifies absolute horizontal spacing for PRINT file |
| COMPILE-TIME | | | | | | | x | x | | Built-in function | DATE_TIME = COMPILETIME; The preprocessor returns a character- |

| Name | Abbreviation | | | | | | | | Category | Description |
|------|------|---|---|---|---|---|---|---|------|------|
| | | | | | | | | | | string containing the data and time of compilation |
| COMPLETION (event) | CPLN | | X | | | X | X | X | Built-in function, pseudo-variable | IF COMPLETION (EV) THEN . . . ; Returns a '1'B if event has completed, otherwise '0'B |
| COMPLEX | CPLX | X | | X | | X | X | X | Attribute | DCL A COMPLEX; Specifies that A is to be stored in the form a + bi, a real part and an imaginary part |
| COMPLEX (a, b) | CPLX (a,b) | X | | X | | X | X | X | Built-in function, pseudo-variable | C = CPLX (A, B); Combines A and B into the complex form A + B; A and B must be real |
| CONDITION (name) | COND (name) | X | | X | | X | X | X | Condition | SIGNAL CONDITION (PRIVATE); Defined by the programmer; SIGNAL causes interrupt and takes action specified by ON CONDITION (PRIVATE); |
| CONDITION | COND | | | X | | X | X | X | Attribute | DCL UNDERFLOW CONDITION; Specifies that UNDERFLOW is to be interpreted as a condition; used when name has been used for other purposes |
| CONJG (x) | | X | | | | X | X | X | Built-in function | A = CONJG (B + 41); Returns the conjugate of a complex number; the conjugate of a + bi is a − bi |
| CONNECTED | CONN | | | X | | X | X | X | Attribute | DCL A (*) CONNECTED; Specifies that A is an array occupying contiguous storage locations; thus, can be used in record I/O, overlay-defining |
| CONSECU-TIVE | | X | X | X | | X | X | X | Option of ENVIRONMENT attribute | DCL F FILE ENV (CONSECUTIVE); Specifies that the organization of data records is tapelike |
| % CONTROL | | | | | | | X | X | Listing control statement | % CONTROL (FORMAT); % CONTROL (NOFORMAT); Activates or deactivates the FORMAT option; ignored by the optimizing compiler |

*Note:* **x** = feature available; **\*** = feature planned but not implemented at time of publication of this text; blank = feature not available.

| Keyword | Abbreviation | PL/C | Series/1 | PL/I-D | DRI's PL/I-G | DOS PL/I optimizer | OS PL/I optimizer | PL/I checkout | ANS PL/I | Use of keyword | Examples and other information |
|---|---|---|---|---|---|---|---|---|---|---|---|
| CONTROLLED | CTL | x | x | x | | x | x | x | x | Attribute | DCL A CTL; ALLOCATE A; Specifies that A is of the CONTROLLED storage class; A must be allocated before use, later freed by FREE |
| CONVERSION | CONV | x | x | x | | x | x | x | x | Condition | ON CONVERSION CALL ERROR; Raised by illegal conversion from character- or bit-string; standard system action = comment + ERROR condition raised |
| COPY | | x | x | x | x | x | x | x | x | Option of GET statement | GET LIST (A, B, C) COPY; Places a copy of input file on SYSPRINT |
| COS (x) | | x | x | x | x | x | x | x | x | Built-in function | A = COS (B); Returns the cosine of B; B expressed in radians |
| COSD (x) | | x | x | x | x | x | x | x | x | Built-in function | A = COSD (B); Returns the cosine of B; B expressed in degrees |
| COSH (x) | | x | x | | x | x | x | x | x | Built-in function | A = COSH (B); Returns hyperbolic cosine of B; B expressed in radians |
| COUNT (file name) | | x | x | | x | x | x | x | | Built-in function | I = COUNT (PAYROLL); Returns the number of data items transmitted during last GET or PUT on the file PAYROLL |
| COUNTER | | | | | | | x | x | | Built-in function | NUMBER = COUNTER; The preprocessor returns a number 00001 for the first invocation and is incremented by one on each successive invocation |

| Feature | Abbr. | 1 | 2 | 3 | 4 | 5 | 6 | 7 | Classification | Example / Description |
|---|---|---|---|---|---|---|---|---|---|---|
| CTLASA | | | | x | x | x | x | x | Option of ENVIRONMENT attribute | DCL OUT FILE ENV (CTLASA); Specifies that each record transmitted will be preceded by an ASA carriage control character |
| CTL360 | | | | x | x | x | x | x | Option of ENVIRONMENT attribute | DCL OUT FILE ENV (CTL360); Specifies that each record transmitted will be preceded by a machine carriage control character |
| CURRENT-STORAGE (variable) | CSTG | | | | x | x | x | | Built-in function | NO_OF_BYTES = CURRENTSTORAGE (WAREA); Returns the implementation-defined storage required by the specified variable |
| D | | | | | x | x | x | | Option of ENVIRONMENT attribute | DCL A FILE .. ENV (ASCII .. D BLKSIZE (200)); Specifies unblocked variable-length records in an ASCII data set, corresponds to record format V in non-ASCII data sets |
| DATA | | | | x | x | x | x | x | Stream I/O transmission mode | GET DATA; PUT DATA (A, B, C); Specifies that data values and names are to be transmitted |
| DATAFIELD | | | | x | x | x | x | | Built-in function | C = DATAFIELD; Extracts contents of data field that caused the NAME condition to be raised |
| DATE | | x | x | x | x | x | x | x | Built-in function | TODAY = DATE; Returns YYMMDD character-string |
| DB | | | | | x | x | x | | Option of ENVIRONMENT attribute | DCL A FILE .. ENV (ASCII DB BLKSIZE (1200) ..); Specifies blocked variable-length records in an ASCII data set, corresponds to record format VB in non-ASCII data sets |
| % DEACTIVATE | % DEACT | | | | | x | x | | Preprocessor statement | % DEACTIVATE A, B, C; Suspends compile-time action on variables listed |

*Note:* x = feature available; * = feature planned but not implemented at time of publication of this text; blank = feature not available.

| Keyword | Abbreviation | PL/C | Series/1 | PL/I-D | DRI's PL/I-G | DOS PL/I optimizer | OS PL/I optimizer | PL/I checkout | ANS PL/I | Use of keyword | Examples and other information |
|---|---|---|---|---|---|---|---|---|---|---|---|
| DECIMAL | DEC | × | × | × | × | × | × | × | × | Attribute | DCL A DECIMAL; Specifies that A is to have a decimal arithmetic base |
| DECIMAL (a,[,p[,q]]) | DEC | × | × | × | × | × | × | × | × | Built-in function | A = DECIMAL (B, 5, 2); B is to be converted to decimal base precision (5,2) |
| DECLARE | DCL | × | × | × | × | × | × | × | × | Statement | DCL A; Used to state attributes for programmer-defined identifiers |
| % DECLARE | % DCL | | | | | × | × | × | × | Preprocessor statement | % DECLARE A, B; Specifies that A and B are to be compile-time variables; attributes are also specified with % DCL |
| DEFAULT | DFT | | | | | × | × | × | × | Statement | DEFAULT ALL STATIC; Allows programmer control over default rules |
| DEFINED | DEF | × | | × | | × | × | × | × | Attribute | DCL A (10, 10) B (100) DEFINED A; Allows multiple names to refer to the same storage location: e.g. B(11) is same as A(2, 1) |
| DELAY (n) | | × | × | | | × | × | × | | Statement | DELAY (1000); Delays execution of the program for 1000 milliseconds of real time |
| DELETE | | | × | | | × | × | × | × | Statement | DELETE FILE (F) KEY (K); Deletes the record whose key is K from F file; only record files with INDEXED or REGIONAL options |
| DESCRIPTORS | | | | | | × | × | × | | Option of DEFAULT statement | DEFAULT DESCRIPTORS (FIXED); Describes default attributes for parameters |

| Feature | | | | | | | | Category | Description |
|---|---|---|---|---|---|---|---|---|---|
| DIM (x,n) | x | x | x | x | x | x | x | Built-in function | I = DIM (TABLE, 2); Returns the current extent of the second dimension of TABLE |
| DIRECT | x | x | x | x | x | x | x | Attribute | DCL F FILE DIRECT; Specifies that records will be transmitted by key directly to or from file; record files only |
| DISPLAY | | x | x | x | x | x | | Statement | DISPLAY ('THIS IS A MESSAGE'); Displays the string on operator's console |
| DIVIDE (x,y,p[,q]) | x | x | x | x | x | x | x | Built-in function | A = DIVIDE (B,C,8,2); Divides B by C in a field of 8 digits with 2 fractional places |
| DO | x | x | x | x | x | x | x | Statement | DO; . . END; DO I = 1 TO 10; . . . END; DO WHILE (X = 0); . . END; Forms a do-group |
| % DO | | | x | x | x | x | x | Preprocessor statement | % DO; . . . % END; % DO I = 1 TO 10; . . . % END; Forms a preprocessor do-group |
| E (w,d[s]) | x | x | x | x | x | x | x | Format item | PUT EDIT (A) (E(10, 3, 4)); Specifies that values in the I/O stream are in floating-point form; i.e., x.xxxE ± m |
| EDIT | x | x | x | x | x | x | x | Stream I/O transmission mode | PUT EDIT (A) (F(3)); Specifies that data items are to be transmitted according to the specifications in the accompanying format list |
| ELSE | x | x | x | x | x | x | x | Clause of IF statement | IF A = B THEN . . . ; ELSE . . . ; The ELSE clause is executed if the test is false |
| % ELSE | | x | x | x | x | x | x | Clause of % IF statement | % IF A = B % THEN . . . ; % ELSE . . . ; The % ELSE clause is executed if the test is false |
| EMPTY | | | x | x | x | x | x | Built-in function | AREA = EMPTY; Resets the contents of an AREA variable to empty status |

*Note:* **x** = feature available; * = feature planned but not implemented at time of publication of this text; blank = feature not available.

| Keyword | Abbreviation | ANS PL/I | PL/I checkout | OS PL/I optimizer | DOS PL/I optimizer | DRI's PL/I-G | PL/I-D | Series/1 | PL/C | Use of keyword | Examples and other information |
|---|---|---|---|---|---|---|---|---|---|---|---|
| END | | x | x | x | x | x | x | x | x | Statement | A: PROC; . . . END; BEGIN; . . . END; DO; . . . END; Terminates blocks and groups |
| % END | | | x | x | x | | x | x | x | Preprocessor statement | %A: PROC; . . . % END; % DO; . . . % END; Terminates compile-time functions and groups |
| ENDFILE (file expression) | | x | x | x | x | x | x | x | x | Condition | ON ENDFILE (PAYROL) GO TO EOJ; Raised by attempts to read past end-of-file during GET or READ; standard system action: ERROR |
| ENDPAGE (file expression) | | x | x | x | x | x | x | x | x | Condition | ON ENDPAGE (PRNT) GO TO HDNG; Raised by attempt to print past page size; PRINT files only; standard system action: start new page, continue |
| ENTRY | | x | x | x | x | x | x | x | x | Attribute, statement | DCL E ENTRY; F: ENTRY; Attribute specifies that identifier is an EXTERNAL entry point; statement specifies secondary entry point |
| ENVIRONMENT | ENV | x | x | x | x | x | x | x | x | Attribute | DCL F FILE ENV (options); List of options is implementation-defined, specifies file options not included in PL/I language |
| ERF (x) | | x | x | x | x | | x | | x | Built-in function | SUMX = ERF (3); Returns the value of the error function |
| ERFC (x) | | x | x | x | x | | x | | x | Built-in function | SUMX = ERFC (3); Returns 1 − ERF (x), the complement of the error function |

| | | 1 | 2 | 3 | 4 | 5 | 6 | 7 | 8 | | |
|---|---|---|---|---|---|---|---|---|---|---|---|
| ERROR | | x | x | x | x | x | x | x | x | Condition | ON ERROR PUT LIST ('OUCH'); Raised by an error forcing termination; standard system action: raise FINISH condition |
| EVENT | | x | | x | | x | | x | | Attribute, option of CALL, DELETE, DISPLAY, READ, REWRITE, WRITE statements | DCL EV EVENT; CALL X EVENT (EV); WAIT (EV); Specifies that an asynchronous I/O is to be performed, or multitasking |
| EXCLUSIVE | EXCL | x | | x | x | | x | | | Attribute | DCL F FILE EXCLUSIVE; Prevents other tasks from accessing the file F simultaneously |
| EXIT | | x | | x | | x | | x | | Statement | EXIT; Causes termination of the task executing EXIT and all dependent tasks |
| EXP | | x | x | x | x | x | x | x | x | Built-in function | A = EXP (B); Returns $e^x$ |
| EXTENT NUMBER (n) | | x | | x | | x | | | | Option of ENVIRONMENT attribute | DCL F FILE ENV (EXTENTNUMBER (3)); Specifies the number of disk extents for INDEXED and REGIONAL files |
| EXTERNAL | EXT | x | x | x | x | x | x | x | x | Attribute | DCL A EXTERNAL; Specifies that the same storage location is to be used for any variable name A with EXT attribute in other blocks |
| F | | x | x | x | x | x | x | x | x | Option of ENVIRONMENT attribute | DCL A FILE ENV (F(80)); Specifies fixed-length unblocked record form and length |
| F (x[,y[,z]]) | | x | x | x | x | x | x | x | x | Format item | PUT EDIT (A) (F(7,2)); Specifies that value is to be displayed in a field of 7 characters, two of which are to the right of the decimal point |
| FB | | x | x | x | x | x | x | x | x | Option of ENVIRONMENT attribute | DCL F FILE ENV (FB); Specifies fixed-length blocked records |

*Note:* **x** = feature available; * = feature planned but not implemented at time of publication of this text; blank = feature not available.

| Keyword | Abbreviation | PL/C | Series/1 | PL/I-D | DRI's PL/I-G | DOS PL/I optimizer | OS PL/I optimizer | PL/I checkout | ANS PL/I | Use of keyword | Examples and other information |
|---|---|---|---|---|---|---|---|---|---|---|---|
| FBS | | × | × | | | | × | × | × | Option of ENVIRONMENT attribute | DCL F FILE ENV (FBS); Specifies fixed-length blocked spanned records |
| FETCH | | | | | | | × | × | | Statement | FETCH CALCTAX; Indicates that a procedure is on auxiliary storage and needs to be copied into main storage so that it may be executed |
| FILE | | × | × | × | × | × | × | × | × | Attribute, option of OPEN, READ, WRITE, DELETE, GET, PUT, CLOSE statements | OPEN FILE (IN); READ FILE (IN) INTO (A); Specifies the name of a PL/I file, either stream- or record-oriented |
| FILESEC | | | | | | × | | | | Option of ENVIRONMENT attribute | DCL DISKET FILE . . ENV (FILESEC MEDIUM (SYS006, 3540) . .); Indicates file security requires that the operator authorizes any later access to the 3540 diskette |
| FINISH | | × | × | × | × | × | × | × | × | Condition | ON FINISH PUT LIST ('EOJ'); Raised before termination of program by execution of any statement causing end; i.e., STOP, RETURN |
| FIXED | | × | × | × | × | × | × | × | × | Attribute | DCL A FIXED; Specifies that variable is to have arithmetic fixed-scale values |
| FIXED (x[,p[,q]]) | | × | × | × | × | × | × | × | × | Built-in function | FX = FIXED (FL, 5, 2); Returns a fixed-scale value of precision (5, 2); base is the same as base of first argument |
| FIXEDOVER-FLOW | FOFL | × | × | × | × | × | × | × | × | Condition | ON FOFL GO TO OVF_ER; Raise when result of arithmetic operation on fixed-scale data exceeds implementation maximum |

| Feature | | | | | | | | Type | Description |
|---|---|---|---|---|---|---|---|---|---|
| FLOAT | x | x | x | x | x | x | x | Attribute | DCL FL FLOAT; Specifies that variable is to have floating scale |
| FLOAT (x[,pl]) | x | x | x | x | x | x | x | Built-in function | FL = FLOAT (FX,6); Specifies that scale of first argument to be converted to float with precision 6 |
| FLOOR (x) | x | x | x | x | x | x | x | Built-in function | I = FLOOR (A); Returns largest integer not exceeding A |
| FLOW | x | | | x | x | x | | Statement | FLOW; Causes information about the transfer of control during the execution of a procedure to be written to SYSPRINT |
| FLOW (n) | x | | | x | x | x | x | Option of PUT statement | PUT FLOW (50); Causes a comment for each of the last (n) transfers of control to be written into the SYSPRINT file stream |
| FORMAT (list) | x | x | x | x | x | x | x | Statement | FR: FORMAT (SKIP,A); PUT EDIT (X) (R(FR)); Specification of remote format list, referred to with R format item; must be labeled |
| FORTRAN | | | | x | x | x | | Option of OPTIONS attribute/option | DCL FRTRN ENTRY OPTIONS (FORTRAN); Specifies that associated entry point is a program compiled by a FORTRAN compiler |
| FREE | x | | x | x | x | x | x | Statement | FREE A; Specifies that storage previously allocated for a BASED or CTL variable is to be released |
| FROM | x | | x | x | x | x | x | Option of READ and REWRITE statements | WRITE FILE (F) FROM (A); Specifies the variable from which data is to be transmitted to a record I/O file |

*Note:* x = feature available; * = feature planned but not implemented at time of publication of this text; blank = feature not available.

| Keyword | Abbreviation | ANS PL/I | PL/I checkout | OS PL/I optimizer | DOS PL/I optimizer | DRI's PL/I-G | PL/I-D | Series/1 | PL/C | Use of keyword | Examples and other information |
|---|---|---|---|---|---|---|---|---|---|---|---|
| FS | | | x | x | | | | | | Option of ENVIRONMENT attribute | DCL F FILE . . ENV (FS BLKSIZE (120) . .); Specifies unblocked records and on direct access devices that every track except the last will be filled to capacity |
| FUNCTION | | | | | x | | | | | Option of ENVIRONMENT attribute | DCL UNITR FILE . ENV (FUNCTION (R,1) MEDIUM (SYS012, 2560) . .); Specifies the operation that is to be performed on the IBM 2560, IBM 5425, or IBM 3525, (i.e., read, punch, or print) |
| GENERIC | | x | x | x | x | | | | | Attribute | DCL E GENERIC (A WHEN (FIXED), B WHEN (FLOAT)); Specifies a family of entry points; one to be chosen on basis of attributes of arguments |
| GENKEY | | | x | x | x | x | | | | Option of ENVIRONMENT attribute | DCL F FILE ENV (GENKEY); Specifies for indexed files that records are to be read using only high-order portion of the key |
| GET | | x | x | x | x | x | x | x | x | Statement | GET LIST (A, B, C); Specifies an input operation on a stream file |
| GO TO | GOTO | x | x | x | x | x | x | x | x | Statement | GO TO ST #10; Specific transfer of control to named statement |
| % GOTO | % GOTO | | x | x | x | | | | x | Preprocessor statement | % GO TO LBL; Transfers control of preprocessor scan to LBL |

| | | | | | | | | | |
|---|---|---|---|---|---|---|---|---|---|
| HALT | | | | | | x | x | Statement | HALT;<br>Causes conversational mode program to be interrupted and control passed to the terminal |
| HBOUND (x,n) | | x | x | x | x | x | x | Built-in function | I = HBOUND (TBL,2);<br>Returns the high bound of the nth dimension of the first argument |
| HIGH (i) | | x | x | x | x | x | x | Built-in function | KEY = HIGH (5);<br>Returns a string, i characters long, of the high collating value; in S/370 implementations, hex FF |
| HIGHINDEX | | | x | x | x | | | Option of ENVIRONMENT attribute | DCL F FILE ENV (HIGHINDEX (2314));<br>Specifies device type on which high-level index of indexed file resides |
| IF | | x | x | x | x | x | x | Statement | IF A = B THEN . . . ; ELSE . . . ;<br>Specifies that the logical expression is to be evaluated; if true THEN, if false ELSE |
| % IF | | | | x | | x | | Preprocessor statement | % IF A = B % THEN . . . ; % ELSE . . . ;<br>Specifies that the logical expression is to be evaluated; if true THEN, if false ELSE |
| IGNORE (n) | | x | x | x | x | x | x | Option of READ statement | READ FILE (F) IGNORE (10);<br>Indicates that 10 records are to be skipped |
| IMAG (x) | | x | | x | x | x | x | Built-in function, pseudo-variable | R = IMAG (CPX);<br>Extracts the imaginary part of a complex number |
| IN (area-variable) | | | x | x | x | x | x | Option of ALLOCATE and FREE statements | ALLOCATE X IN (AR);<br>Specifies the area in which a based variable is to be allocated or freed |
| % INCLUDE | | x | x | x | x | x | x | Preprocessor statement | % INCLUDE PAYROLL;<br>Requests that text from an external file is to be included during preprocessor scan |

*Note:* x = feature available; * = feature planned but not implemented at time of publication of this text; blank = feature not available.

| Keyword | Abbreviation | PL/C | Series/1 | PL/I-D | DRI's PL/I-G | DOS PL/I optimizer | OS PL/I optimizer | PL/I checkout | ANS PL/I | Use of keyword | Examples and other information |
|---|---|---|---|---|---|---|---|---|---|---|---|
| INDEX (string, config) | | x | x | x | x | x | x | x | x | Built-in function | I = INDEX (STR, 'ABC'); Returns the position within first argument at which first occurrence of second argument begins |
| INDEXAREA [(size)] | | | x | x | | x | x | x | | Option of ENVIRONMENT attribute | DCL F FILE ENV (INDEXAREA (10000)); Requests high-level index of indexed file be made resident in main storage |
| INDEXED | | x | x | x | x | x | x | x | | Option of ENVIRONMENT attribute | DCL F FILE ENV (INDEXED); Specifies that the organization of the file is indexed sequential |
| INDEXMULTI-PLE | | | x | x | | x | | | | Option of ENVIRONMENT attribute | DCL F FILE ENV (INDEXMULTIPLE); Specifies that a multiple-level index is to be created for an indexed file |
| INITIAL | INIT | x | x | x | x | x | x | x | x | Attribute | DCL A INITIAL (123.4); Specifies an initial value for a variable |
| INPUT | | x | x | x | x | x | x | x | x | Attribute | DCL F FILE INPUT; Specifies that a file is to be input with GET or READ statements |
| INTER | | | | x | x | x | x | x | | Option of OPTIONS attribute | DCL E ENTRY OPTIONS (INTER); Specifies that PL/I is not to handle interrupts in called entry point |
| INTERNAL | INT | x | x | x | x | x | x | x | x | Attribute | DCL A INTERNAL; Limits the scope of the name to procedure containing declaration and internal procedures |
| INTO (variable) | | x | x | x | x | x | x | x | x | Option of READ statement | READ FILE (F) INTO (AR); Specifies location to which record is to be transmitted |

| Keyword | Abbrev | | | | | | | | Category | Description |
|---|---|---|---|---|---|---|---|---|---|---|
| IRREDUCIBLE | IRRED | | | | x | | x | x | Attribute | DCL E ENTRY IRREDUCIBLE; An optimization specification; different values will be returned by E each time it is invoked |
| KEY (file expression) | | x | x | x | x | x | x | x | Condition | ON KEY (FILEX) BEGIN; . . . . Raised by improper presence or absence of key in KEYED record file |
| KEY (x) | | x | x | | x | x | x | x | Option of READ, DELETE, and REWRITE statements | READ FILE (X) INTO (Y) KEY (K); Identifies the record to be read from named file |
| KEYED | | x | x | x | x | x | x | x | Attribute | DCL F FILE KEYED; Specifies that each record in the file has a key; record files only |
| KEYFROM (x) | | x | x | x | x | x | x | x | Option of WRITE and LOCATE statements | LOCATE X KEYFROM (K); Specifies the key of the record to be written; record files only |
| KEYLENGTH (n) | | x | | | x | | x | | Option of ENVIRONMENT attribute | DCL F FILE KEYED ENV (KEYLENGTH (10)); Specifies the length of the key field of a record file |
| KEYLOC (n) | | x | | | x | | x | x | Option of ENVIRONMENT attribute | DCL F FILE KEYED ENV (KEYLOC (5)); Specifies location of key field within each record, starting with 1 |
| KEYTO (x) | | x | x | | x | x | x | x | Option of READ statement | READ FILE (F) INTO (A) KEYTO (K); Specifies location to which key value of record is to be assigned |
| LABEL | | x | x | x | x | x | x | x | Attribute | DCL L LABEL, L = ST#10; GO TO L; Specifies that L is to take on as values the address of statement labels |
| LBOUND (x,n) | | x | x | | x | x | x | x | Built-in function | I = LBOUND (TABLE,3); Returns the current lower bound of the third dimension of TABLE |

*Note:* **x** = feature available; ***** = feature planned but not implemented at time of publication of this text; blank = feature not available.

| Keyword | Abbreviation | PL/C | Series/1 | PL/I-D | DRI's PL/I-G | DOS PL/I optimizer | OS PL/I optimizer | PL/I checkout | ANS PL/I | Use of keyword | Examples and other information |
|---|---|---|---|---|---|---|---|---|---|---|---|
| LEAVE | | x | | | | x | x | x | | Option of ENVIRONMENT attribute | DCL F FILE ENV (LEAVE)- Requests that tape is to remain at end of data after reading for quick reread BACKWARDS |
| LEAVE | | x | | | | x | x | x | | Statement | LEAVE Causes an exit from a DO group to the first executable statement following the END |
| LENGTH (string) | | x | x | | x | x | x | x | x | Built-in function | I = LENGTH (STR); Returns the current length of the string argument |
| LIKE | | x | | | | x | x | x | x | Attribute | DCL 1 ST2 LIKE ST1; Specifies that the elements of ST2 are to be identical to those in ST1 |
| LINE (n) | | x | x | | x | x | x | x | x | Format item; option of PUT statement | PUT EDIT (A) (LINE (3), F (5)); Specifies absolute vertical spacing for a PRINT file |
| LINENO (file expression) | | x | x | | x | x | x | x | x | Built-in function | IF LINENO (PRT) > 50 THEN . . . ; Returns the current line number of the named PRINT file |
| LINESIZE (w) | | x | x | | x | x | x | x | | Option of OPEN statement | OPEN FILE (F) LINESIZE (120); Specifies the number of character positions in a line of print on file F |
| LIST | | x | x | x | x | x | x | x | x | Stream I/O transmission mode | PUT LIST (A, B, C); Specifies list-directed stream I/O |
| LOCATE | | | | x | | x | x | x | x | Statement | LOCATE AREA FILE (F) SET (P); Allocates a record buffer and transmits previously *located* record to the file; for full language, SET option need not be coded |

| Feature | | | | | | | | Category | Description |
|---|---|---|---|---|---|---|---|---|---|
| LOG (x) | x | x | x | x | x | x | x | Built-in function | A = LOG (B); Returns the logarithm of x to the base e; error if x <= 0 |
| LOG2 (x) | x | x | x | x | x | x | x | Built-in function | A = LOG2(B); Returns the logarithm of x to the base 2; error if x <= 0 |
| LOG10 (x) | x | x | x | x | x | x | x | Built-in function | A = LOG10(B); Returns the logarithm of x to the base 10; error if x <= 0 |
| LOW (i) | x | x | x | x | x | x | x | Built-in function | S = LOW (5); Returns the low collating value in a string of length i; for S/370 implementations hex 00 |
| MAIN | x | x | x | x | x | x | x | Option of OPTIONS attribute/option | A: PROC OPTIONS (MAIN); Specifies this procedure to be primary entry point for program execution |
| MAX (x₁,x₂,...,xₙ) | x | x | x | x | x | x | x | Built-in function | A = MAX (B, C, D, E); Returns the value of the greatest of the arguments |
| MEDIUM (device name, device type) | x | x | | | | | | Option of ENVIRONMENT attribute | DCL F FILE ENV (MEDIUM (SYS005, 2314)); Specifies device-dependent type, logical unit name |
| MIN (x₁,x₂,...,xₙ) | x | x | x | x | x | x | x | Built-in function | A = MIN (B, C, D, E); Returns the value of least of the arguments |
| MOD (x,x₂) | x | x | x | x | x | x | x | Built-in function | A = MOD (B, C); Returns the positive remainder after division of B by C |
| MULTIPLY (x,y,p[q]) | x | x | x | x | x | x | x | Built-in function | A = MULTIPLY (B, C, 10, 5); Equivalent to B * C in a field of 10 digits, 5 of which are fractional |
| NAME (file expression) | x | x | x | x | x | x | x | Condition | ON NAME (INPT) BEGIN; Raised when unrecognizable name encountered during GET DATA; standard system action: comment and continue |

*Note:* x = feature available; * = feature planned but not implemented at time of publication of this text; blank = feature not available.

| Keyword | Abbreviation | ANS PL/I | PL/I checkout | OS PL/I optimizer | DOS PL/I optimizer | DRI's PL/I-G | PL/I-D | Series/1 | PL/C | Use of keyword | Examples and other information |
|---|---|---|---|---|---|---|---|---|---|---|---|
| NCP (n) | | | x | x | | | | | x | Option of ENVIRONMENT attribute | DCL F FILE ENV (NCP (5)); Specifies the number of outstanding I/O requests maximum for asynchronous I/O |
| NOCHECK [(name list)] | | x | x | x | x | | | | x | Condition prefix | (NOCHECK (A, B, C)): X: GO TO Y; Specifies that CHECK condition to be disabled for scope of statement |
| NOCHECK | | | x | x | | | | | x | Statement | NOCHECK (A, X, QUANTITY); Suppresses the CHECK condition for the specified variables |
| NOCONVERSION | NOCONV | x | x | x | x | | | | x | Condition prefix | (NOCONVERSION): A = B + C; Disables conversion condition for scope of statement |
| NOFEED | | | | | x | | | | | Option of ENVIRONMENT attribute | DCL DISKET FILE . . ENV (NOFEED MEDIUM (SYS014,3540) . .); Specifies that the diskette on the IBM 3540 remains in position so that it may be accessed without operator intervention |
| NOFIXED-OVERFLOW | NOFOFL | x | x | x | x | | x | x | x | Condition prefix | (NOFOFL): A = B * C; Disables FIXEDOVERFLOW condition for scope of statement |
| NOFLOW | | | x | x | | | | | x | Statement | NOFLOW; Suppresses the action of the previously executed FLOW statement |
| NOFORMAT | | | x | x | | | | | | Option of % CONTROL statement | % CONTROL (NOFORMAT); Deactivates the FORMAT compiler option of the checkout compiler; ignored by the optimizing compiler |
| NOLABEL | | | | | x | | x | | x | Option of ENVIRONMENT attribute | DCL F FILE ENV (NOLABEL); Specifies that tape data set has no label |

| Feature | | | | | | | Category | Description |
|---|---|---|---|---|---|---|---|---|
| NOLOCK | | | | | x | x | Option of READ statement | READ FILE (F) INTO (A) KEY (K) NO-LOCK; Specifies that exclusive use of record with key K is not required |
| NOMAP | | | | x | x | x | Option of OPTIONS attribute/option | DCL E ENTRY OPTIONS (COBOL NOMAP); Prevents the manipulation of data aggregates in the interface between a PL/1 and COBOL program |
| NOMAPIN | | | | x | x | x | Option of OPTIONS attribute/option | DCL E ENTRY OPTIONS (FORTRAN NOMAPIN); Prevents the manipulation of data aggregates in the interface between a PL/1 and FORTRAN program |
| NOMAPOUT | | | | x | x | x | Option of OPTIONS attribute/option | DCL E ENTRY OPTIONS (FORTRAN NOMAPOUT); Prevents the manipulation of data aggregates in the interface between a PL/1 and FORTRAN program |
| NOOPTIMIZE | | | | x | | | Compiler option | *PROCESS NOOPTIMIZE Requests that the compilation be as fast as possible |
| NOOVER-FLOW (NOOFL) | x | x | | | x | x | x | Condition prefix | (NOOVERFLOW): A = B * C; Disables the OVERFLOW condition for the scope of the statement |
| % NOPRINT | | | | | x | x | Preprocessor Listing control statement | % NOPRINT; Suspends printing of the source and in-source listings |
| NORESCAN | | | | x | x | x | Option of % ACTIVATE statement | % ACTIVATE A NORESCAN; Specifies that after replacement of A, text is not to be rescanned for further replacement |
| NOSIZE | x | x | | | x | x | x | Condition prefix | (NOSIZE): BEGIN: . . . ; Disables the SIZE condition for the scope of the statement |

*Note:* x = feature available; * = feature planned but not implemented at time of publication of this text; blank = feature not available.

| Keyword | Abbreviation | PL/C | Series/1 | PL/I-D | DRI's PL/I-G | DOS PL/I optimizer | OS PL/I optimizer | PL/I checkout | ANS PL/I | Use of keyword | Examples and other information |
|---|---|---|---|---|---|---|---|---|---|---|---|
| NOSTRING-RANGE | NOSTRG | x | x | | | x | x | x | x | Condition prefix | (NOSTRINGRANGE): A = SUBSTR (B, 10, N); Disables the STRINGRANGE condition for the scope of the statement |
| NOSTRING-SIZE | NOSTRZ | | x | x | | x | x | x | x | Condition prefix | (NOSTRINGSIZE); ST = SUBSTR (B, 3); Disables the STRINGSIZE condition for the scope of the statement |
| % NOTE (msg, code) | | | | x | | x | x | x | | Preprocessor statement | % NOTE ('MY MESSAGE',0); Allows generation of a user-specified diagnostic message |
| NOSUB-SCRIPT-RANGE | NOSUBRG | x | x | | | x | x | x | x | Condition prefix | (NOSUBRG): A = B (I + 10); Disables the SUBSCRIPTRANGE condition for the scope of the statement |
| NOTAPEMK | | | | x | | x | | | | Option of ENVIRONMENT attribute | DCL F FILE ENV (NOTAPEMK); Specifies that file located on magnetic tape is not preceded by a tape mark |
| NOUNDER-FLOW | NOUFL | x | x | x | | x | x | x | x | Condition prefix | (NOUNDERFLOW): A = B/C; Disables the UNDERFLOW condition for the scope of the statement |
| NOWRITE | | | | | | x | x | x | | Option of ENVIRONMENT attribute | DCL F FILE ENV (NOWRITE); Requests space optimization when no records will be added to an indexed file |
| NOZERO-DIVIDE | NOZDIV | x | x | x | | x | x | x | x | Condition prefix | (NOZERODIVIDE): A = B/C; Disables the ZERODIVIDE condition for the scope of the statement |
| NULL | | x | x | x | x | x | x | x | x | Built-in function | P = NULL; Returns a null locator value |
| OFFSET (area name) | | | | | | x | x | x | x | Attribute | DCL R OFFSET (AR); Specifies that R will contain the address |

| Keyword | C1 | C2 | C3 | C4 | C5 | C6 | C7 | Type | Description |
|---|---|---|---|---|---|---|---|---|---|
| OFFSET (p, a) | | | | | x | x | x | Built-in function | R = OFFSET (P, AR); Converts a pointer to an offset value from beginning of second argument AR variable |
| OFLTRACKS (n) | | | | x | | x | x | Option of ENVIRONMENT attribute | DCL F FILE ENV (OFLTRACKS (2)); Specifies that n tracks per cylinder are to be reserved for new records |
| OMR | | | | x | | x | x | Option of ENVIRONMENT attribute | DCL MARK FILE . . ENV (OMR . . MEDIUM (SYS007,3505)); Specifies that an 80-column card with optical marks is to be read from the IBM 3505 |
| ON | x | x | x | x | x | x | x | Statement | ON ENDPAGE (F) . . . ; Specifies the on-unit to be executed when condition named is raised |
| ONCHAR | | x | x | x | x | x | x | Built-in function, pseudo-variable | ER_CHAR = ONCHAR; Returns character that caused conversion condition to be raised; the ONCHAR may only appear in the conversion on-unit |
| ONCODE | | | x | x | x | x | x | Built-in function | I = ONCODE; Returns an implementation-defined value that uniquely designates the error encountered; valid only in an on-unit |
| ONCOUNT | | | | x | x | x | | Built-in function | I = ONCOUNT; Returns the number of interrupts pending |
| ONFILE | | x | x | x | x | x | x | Built-in function | C = ONFILE; Returns the name of the file that encountered an error; valid only in an on-unit |
| ONKEY | | | x | x | x | x | x | Built-in function | C = ONKEY; Returns the value of the key, causing the KEY condition to be raised |

Note: x = feature available; * = feature planned but not implemented at time of publication of this text; blank = feature not available.

| Keyword | Abbreviation | PL/C | Series/1 | PL/I-D | DRI's PL/I-G | DOS PL/I optimizer | OS PL/I optimizer | PL/I checkout | ANS PL/I | Use of keyword | Examples and other information |
|---|---|---|---|---|---|---|---|---|---|---|---|
| ONLOC | | x | x | | | x | x | x | x | Built-in function | C = ONLOC;<br>Returns the name of the entry point containing the statement whose execution caused an interrupt |
| ONSOURCE | | x | x | x | x | x | x | x | x | Built-in function, pseudo-variable | C = ONSOURCE;<br>Returns the value of the field containing the character causing the conversion condition to be raised |
| ONSYSLOG | | | | x | | | | | | Option of OPTIONS option of PROCEDURE statement | A: PROC OPTIONS (ONSYSLOG);<br>Specifies that error messages are to be produced on the operator's console |
| OPEN | | x | x | x | x | x | x | x | x | Statement | OPEN FILE (F);<br>Prepares a file for processing |
| OPTIONS (list) | | x | x | x | x | x | x | x | x | Option of PROCEDURE statement | A: PROC OPTIONS (MAIN);<br>Specifies implementation-defined information |
| OPTIONS (list) | | x | | | x | x | x | x | x | Option of ENTRY statement, attribute | DCL E ENTRY OPTIONS (COBOL);<br>Specifies interlanguage communication between PL/I and COBOL or FORTRAN modules |
| ORDER | | x | x | | x | x | x | x | | Option of PROCEDURE and BEGIN statements | BEGIN ORDER;<br>Optimization specification requesting strict sequencing of computation be maintained |
| OTHERWISE | OTHER | | | | | | x | x | | Clause of select group | SELECT (CODE);<br>  WHEN ('I') CALL ISSUE_RTN;<br>  WHEN ('R') CALL RECEIPTS_RTN;<br>  OTHERWISE  CALL  ERROR_CODE;<br>END;<br>  If no WHEN clause "unit" is executed, the "unit" after the OTHERWISE is executed |

| Feature | | | | | | | | | Attribute | Description |
|---|---|---|---|---|---|---|---|---|---|---|
| OUTPUT | x | x | x | x | x | x | x | | | DCL F FILE OUTPUT;<br>Specifies that data is to be transmitted to file using PUT, WRITE, or LOCATE statements |
| OVERFLOW   OFL | x | x | x | x | x | x | x | | Condition | ON OVERFLOW . . . ;<br>Raised when exponent of floating-scale variable exceeds limit |
| P'picture specification' | x | x | x | x | | x | x | | Format item | PUT EDIT (A) (P'ZZ,ZZZ');<br>Allows editing of output or input variables using picture specification characters |
| PAGE | x | x | x | x | x | x | x | | Format item option of PUT statement | PUT PAGE;<br>Specifies positioning of PRINT file at the beginning of a new page |
| % PAGE | | | x | x | x | x | x | | Listing control statement | % PAGE;<br>Causes the following statement to be printed at the top of the next page of the source program listing |
| PAGESIZE (w) | x | x | x | | x | x | x | | Option of OPEN statement | OPEN FILE (F) PAGESIZE (50);<br>Specifies the number of lines to be printed before ENDPAGE condition raised; may only be specified for STREAM PRINT files |
| PARMSET (x) | | | | | x | x | x | | Built-in function | SET_PARM = PARMSET (ARG);<br>Returns a one or zero bit depending on whether the parameter (x) was set when the preprocessor procedure was invoked |
| PASSWORD (password specification) | | | | x | x | x | x | | Option of ENVIRONMENT attribute | DCL VSAM FILE . . ENV (VSAM PASSWORD (HALEI));<br>Specifies the password associated with a VSAM file. It must match the password associated with the file when it was created in order to read and update the file |
| PENDING (file expression) | | | x | | x | x | x | | Condition | ON PENDING BEGIN; . . . ;<br>Raised when a READ on a TRANSIENT file finds that no records are currently in the file |

*Note:* x = feature available; * = feature planned but not implemented at time of publication of this text; blank = feature not available.

| Keyword | Abbreviation | PL/C | Series/1 | PL/I-D | DRI's PL/I-G | DOS PL/I optimizer | OS PL/I optimizer | PL/I checkout | ANS PL/I | Use of keyword | Examples and other information |
|---|---|---|---|---|---|---|---|---|---|---|---|
| PICTURE | PIC | x | | x | | x | x | x | x | Attribute | DCL A PIC'999V99', B PIC'(5)ZV.99'; Specifies base, mode, scale, and precision of numeric data items; also editing characters |
| PLIRETV | | | x | | x | | x | x | | Built-in function | CODE_VALUE = PLIRETV; Obtains the current value of the PL/I return code; see RETCODE |
| POINTER | PTR | x | x | | | x | x | x | x | Attribute | DCL A POINTER; Specifies that A will take on as values the location addresses of other variables; used in list processing and locate mode I/O |
| POINTER (n,a) | PTR (n,a) | | x | x | | x | x | x | x | Built-in function | P = POINTER (OFST,AR); Returns a pointer value representing the sum of the address of the area AR and the value of the OFFSET variable OFST |
| POLY (a,x) | | | | | | x | x | x | | Built-in function | A = POLY (B,X); If B and X are vectors, then POLY returns the polynomial value formed by using the B as coefficients and the $\pi x$ as independent variables |
| POSITION (expression) | POS | x | x | | | x | x | x | x | Attribute | DCL A CHAR (10), B CHAR (5) DEF A POSITION (6); Specifies that B is to occupy the same location as the last half of A |
| PRECISION (x.p[q]) | PREC | x | x | x | | x | x | x | x | Built-in function | A = PRECISION (B, 7, 5); Returns the value of B with precision (7, 5); same base, scale, mode |
| PRINT | | x | x | x | x | x | x | x | x | Attribute | DCL F FILE PRINT; Specifies that the final destination of the file will be the printed page |

| Feature | | | | | | | | | Category | Description |
|---|---|---|---|---|---|---|---|---|---|---|
| % PRINT | | | | | x | x | x | | Listing control statement | % PRINT;<br>Causes printing of the source and in-source listing to be resumed if it has been suspended |
| PRIORITY (x) | | | | | x | x | x | | Option of CALL statement | CALL T PRIORITY (−2);<br>Assigns a priority to a task relative to calling task |
| PRIORITY (task name) | | | x | | | x | x | | Built-in function, pseudo-variable | A = PRIORITY (T);<br>Returns priority of task T relative to invoking task |
| PROCEDURE | PROC | x | x | x | x | x | x | x | Statement | A: PROCEDURE;<br>Specifies beginning of a procedure block, defines primary entry point |
| % PROCEDURE | % PROC | | | | x | x | x | | Preprocessor statement | % A: PROC;<br>Specifies beginning of compile-time procedure; must be invoked via compile-time function reference |
| PROD (x) | | x | | x | x | x | x | | Built-in function | A = PROD (B);<br>B is an array; returns the product of all elements of B |
| PUT | | x | x | x | x | x | x | x | Statement | PUT DATA (X, Y, Z);<br>Stream output statement; specifies transmission of data elements contained in data list |
| R (x) | | x | x | x | x | x | x | x | Format item | PUT EDIT (A, B, C) (R(FMT));<br>Specifies that format list is remote (R); name in parentheses must be label of FORMAT statement |
| R (max-rec-size) | | | | | | | | x | Option of ENVIRONMENT attribute | DCL TP FILE TRANSIENT (R(100));<br>Specifies for teleprocessing files that logical records of max-rec-size maximum are to be transmitted |

*Note:* **x** = feature available; * = feature planned but not implemented at time of publication of this text; blank = feature not available.

| Keyword | Abbreviation | ANS PL/I | PL/I checkout | OS PL/I optimizer | DOS PL/I optimizer | DRI's PL/I-G | PL/I-D | Series/1 | PL/C | Use of keyword | Examples and other information |
|---|---|---|---|---|---|---|---|---|---|---|---|
| RANGE | | | x | x | x | | | | x | Option of DEFAULT statement | DEFAULT RANGE (A: H) SYSTEM; Specifies the range of identifiers to be affected by the DEFAULT specification |
| RCE | | | | | x | | | | | Option of ENVIRONMENT attribute | DCL CARD_COL FILE . . ENV (RCE . . MEDIUM (SYS008,3505)); Specifies that only selected columns will be read from an IBM 3525 or IBM 3505 |
| READ | | x | x | x | x | x | x | x | x | Statement | READ FILE (F) INTO (A) Transfers a record from a record file into main storage |
| REAL | | x | x | x | x | x | x | x | x | Attribute | DCL A REAL; Specifies that the variable will contain only real arithmetic values, *not* complex |
| REAL (x) | | x | x | x | x | | | x | x | Built-in function, pseudo-variable | A = REAL (C); REAL (C) = B; Returns or accepts the real portion of the complex argument |
| RECORD | | x | x | x | x | x | x | x | x | Attribute | DCL F FILE RECORD; Specifies that the file will consist of discrete records to be transmitted with READ or WRITE statements |
| RECORD (file name) | | x | x | x | x | | x | x | x | Condition | ON RECORD (F) BEGIN; . . . . Raised size of record variable is not compatible with actual record size |
| RECSIZE (expression) | | x | x | x | x | | | x | | Option of ENVIRONMENT attribute | DCL F FILE ENV (RECSIZE (100)); Specifies logical record length |
| RECURSIVE | | x | x | x | x | x | | x | x | Option of PROCEDURE statement | A: PROC RECURSIVE; Specifies that the procedure may invoke itself |

| | RED | | | | | | | |
|---|---|---|---|---|---|---|---|---|
| REDUCIBLE | | | | x | x | x | Attribute | DCL E ENTRY REDUCIBLE; Specify that the compiler is allowed to optimize by reducing the number of references to the entry point |
| REENTRANT | | | | x | x | x | Option of OPTIONS option of PROCEDURE statement | A: PROC OPTIONS (REENTRANT); Specifies that the procedure may be invoked for asynchronous execution with previous invocations |
| REFER | | | | x | x | x | Option of BASED attribute | DCL 1 A BASED, 2 B, 2 C (D REFER (B)); Used to declare varying-length arrays or strings in a BASED structure |
| REGIONAL (1) | | x | x | x | x | x | Option of ENVIRONMENT attribute | DCL F FILE ENV (REGIONAL (1)); Specifies data set organization; records are to be transmitted via relative record number |
| REGIONAL (2) | | | | x | x | x | Option of ENVIRONMENT attribute | DCL F FILE ENV (REGIONAL (2)); Specifies data set organization; records are to be transmitted via relative record plus a recorded key |
| REGIONAL (3) | | | x | x | x | x | Option of ENVIRONMENT attribute | DCL F FILE ENV (REGIONAL (3)); Specifies data set organization; records are to be transmitted via relative track plus a recorded key |
| RELEASE entry-constant | | | | x | x | x | Statement | RELEASE INITIAL_ROUTINE; Releases the main storage occupied by the specified procedures and frees it for other purposes |
| REORDER | | x | | x | x | x | Option of PROCEDURE and BEGIN statements | A: PROC REORDER; Optimization specification; allows compiler to reorder the evaluation of expressions for optimum speed |
| REPEAT (string, i) | | x | | x | x | x | Built-in function | A = REPEAT (B,'7'); Specifies that B is to be concatenated to itself 6 times (7 B's altogether) and returned to the point of invocation |

*Note:* x = feature available; * = feature planned but not implemented at time of publication of this text; blank = feature not available.

| Keyword | Abbreviation | ANS PL/I | PL/I checkout | OS PL/I optimizer | DOS PL/I optimizer | DRI's PL/I-G | PL/I-D | Series/1 | PL/C | Use of keyword | Examples and other information |
|---|---|---|---|---|---|---|---|---|---|---|---|
| REPEAT | | x | x | x | x | x | | | | Option of the DO statement | DO INDEX = 1 REPEAT INDEX * 3 WHILE (INDEX < 100); An alternative to the BY and TO option for specifying the modification to the control variable. To specify a terminal condition use the WHILE or UNTIL option. |
| REPLY (c) | | | x | x | x | | x | | | Option of DISPLAY statement | DISPLAY (A) REPLY (B); Specifies variable to which operator response is to be assigned |
| REREAD | | | x | x | | | | x | | Option of ENVIRONMENT attribute and CLOSE statement | DCL F FILE ENV (REREAD); Specifies that tape file is to be rewound in preparation for reading again |
| RESCAN | | | x | x | x | | | | | Preprocessor Option % ACTIVATE statement | % ACTIVE A RESCAN; Specifies that the value of A is to be re-scanned by the preprocessor for further replacement |
| RETCODE | | | x | x | | x | x | x | | Option of the OPTIONS attribute | DCL SUBPROG ENTRY (X, Y, Z) OPTIONS (ASM INTER RETCODE); Enables the non-PL/I routine to pass a return code to PL/I; see PLIRETV |
| RETURN | | x | x | ·x | x | x | x | x | x | Statement | RETURN; Returns control to the point of invocation |
| RETURNS | | x | x | x | x | | | | x | Attribute, option of PROCEDURE and % PROCEDURE statements | A: PROC RETURNS (CHAR); Specifies the attributes of the value to be returned by the entry point after function reference DCL FUNCT RETURNS FIXED; % FUNCT: Proc; Specifies the attributes of the function to be invoked |

| Feature | | | | | | | Type | Description |
|---|---|---|---|---|---|---|---|---|
| REUSE | | | x | x | x | x | Option of ENVIRONMENT attribute | DCL VSAM FILE OUTPUT . . ENV (VSAM REUSE); Specifies the VSAM OUTPUT file as a workfile, to be treated as if it were empty each time it is opened |
| REVERT | | x | x | x | x | x | Statement | REVERT ZERODIVIDE; Causes the action specified for stated condition in the encompassing block to be activated |
| REWRITE | | x | x | x | x | x | Statement | REWRITE FILE (F) FROM (A); Specifies that a record is to be returned to the file; valid for RECORD UPDATE files only |
| ROUND (x,n) | x | x | x | x | x | x | Built-in function | A = ROUND (B, 2); Returns the value of B rounded at the second place to the right (+2) of decimal point |
| SAMEKEY (x) | | | | x | x | x | Built-in function | DCL VINDEX FILE KEYED SEQUENTIAL RECORD ENV (VSAM); IF SAMEKEY (VINDEX) THEN CALL READ_AGAIN; Returns a bit '1' if the next record after an I/O operation on a KEYED SEQUENTIAL VSAM INDEXED data set has the same key |
| SCALARVARYING | | | | x | x | x | Option of ENVIRONMENT attribute | DCL F FILE ENV (SCALARVARYING); Specifies the inclusion of a length field with record indicating length of varying string |
| SELECT | | | x | x | x | x | Statement | SELECT (CODE); WHEN ('I') CALL ISSUES_RTN; WHEN ('R') CALL RECEIPTS_RTN; OTHERWISE CALL ERROR_RTN; END; Allows the selection of one or two or more alternative actions based on a test. |

*Note:* x = feature available; * = feature planned but not implemented at time of publication of this text; blank = feature not available.

| Keyword | Abbreviation | PL/C | Series/1 | PL/I-D | DRI's PL/I-G | DOS PL/I optimizer | OS PL/I optimizer | PL/I checkout | ANS PL/I | Use of keyword | Examples and other information |
|---|---|---|---|---|---|---|---|---|---|---|---|
| SEQUENTIAL | SEQL | x | x | x | x | x | x | x | x | Attribute | DCL F FILE SEQUENTIAL; Specifies that data is to be transmitted according to physical order of data set |
| SET (pointer) | | | x | x | x | x | x | x | x | Option of ALLOCATE, LOCATE, and READ statements | READ FILE (F) SET (P); Sets pointer value to indicate start of area allocated or record in buffer |
| SIGN (x) | | x | x | x | x | x | x | x | x | Built-in function | I = SIGN (X); Returns −1 if X < 0, 0 if X = 0, and +1 if X > 0 |
| SIGNAL | | x | x | x | x | x | x | x | x | Statement | SIGNAL ENDPAGE (PRT); Simulates the occurrence of the stated condition |
| SIN (x) | | x | x | x | x | x | x | x | x | Built-in function | A = SIN (B); Returns the sine of B radians |
| SIND (x) | | x | x | x | x | x | x | x | x | Built-in function | X = SIND (Y); Returns the sine of Y where Y is expressed in degrees |
| SINH (x) | | x | | x | x | x | x | x | x | Built-in function | X = SINH (Y); Returns the hyperbolic sine of Y radians |
| SIS | | | | | | x | x | x | | Option of ENVIRONMENT attribute | DCL VSAMF FILE DIRECT KEYED .. ENV (VSAM SIS); To achieve immediate writing of an addition to a VSAM key-sequenced data set with efficient use of disk space |
| SIZE | | x | x | x | x | x | x | x | x | Condition | ON SIZE BEGIN; . . . ; Raised by assignment of data that causes truncation of high-order significance |

| Statement | 1 | 2 | 3 | 4 | 5 | 6 | 7 | 8 | Description | Example |
|---|---|---|---|---|---|---|---|---|---|---|
| SKIP [(n)] | x | x | x | x | x | x | x | x | Format item, option of GET and PUT statements | PUT LIST (A, B, C) SKIP (2); Specifies relative vertical spacing or beginning of next logical record; assumed 1 if (n) omitted; for PL/I D, (n) maximum is 3 |
| SKIP |  |  | x | x | x |  |  |  | Option of ENVIRONMENT attribute | DCL VSAMF FILE SEQUENTIAL KEYED . . ENV (VSAM SKIP); To improve performance when individual records are to be accessed by key, primarily in ascending key order |
| % SKIP (n) | x | x | x | x |  | x |  |  | Listing control statement | % SKIP (3); Specifies to leave blank 'n' number of lines in the source and insource listings |
| SNAP | x | x | x | x |  | x |  |  | Option of ON statement | ON CONVERSION SNAP; A calling trace is printed on SYSPRINT when condition occurs |
| SNAP | x |  | x | x |  | x |  |  | Option of the PUT statement | PUT SNAP; Causes the current statement number and a list of the currently active on-units and blocks to be placed in the output stream |
| SQRT (x) | x | x | x | x | x | x | x | x | Built-in function | X = SQRT (Y); Returns positive square root; error if argument is less than 0 |
| STACKER (x) |  |  |  | x |  |  |  |  | Option of ENVIRONMENT attribute | DCL CARD FILE . . ENV (MEDIUM (SYS009,3525) STACKER (2)); Specifies the card stacker of an IBM 3525 or IBM 3505 device to which the cards are to be directed |
| STATEMENT | x |  | x | x |  | x |  |  | Option of % PROCEDURE statement | % PRECOMP: PROCEDURE (PARMA, PARMB) , STATEMENT RETURNS (FIXED); Optional word used for documentation in the % PROCEDURE statement |

*Note:* x = feature available; * = feature planned but not implemented at time of publication of this text; blank = feature not available.

| Keyword | Abbreviation | PL/C | Series/1 | PL/I-D | DRI's PL/I-G | DOS PL/I optimizer | OS PL/I optimizer | PL/I checkout | ANS PL/I | Use of keyword | Examples and other information |
|---|---|---|---|---|---|---|---|---|---|---|---|
| STATIC | | x | x | x | x | x | x | x | x | Attribute | DCL A STATIC; Specifies that storage is to be allocated before program execution and remain until termination |
| STATUS (event name) | | | x | | | x | x | x | | Built-in function, pseudo-variable | I = STATUS (EV); Returns the status value of an EVENT variable |
| STOP | | x | x | x | x | x | x | x | x | Statement | STOP; Causes immediate termination of the main task and all subtasks |
| STORAGE (variable) | STG | | | | | x | x | x | | Built-in function | BYTES = STORAGE (WORK_AREA); Returns the number of bytes required by the variable specified |
| STREAM | | x | x | x | | x | x | x | x | Attribute, option of OPEN statement | DCL F FILE STREAM; OPEN FILE (F) STREAM; Specifies that the data on the external medium is to be considered a continuous stream of characters |
| STRING (x) | | x | | x | | x | x | x | x | Built-in function, pseudo-variable | X = STRING (Y); Returns a string representing the concatenation of all elements of a structure or array |
| STRING (string name) | | x | x | x | | x | x | x | x | Option of GET and PUT statements | GET STRING (X) EDIT (A, B, C) (3F(3)); Data is to be transmitted from string X to the variables A, B, and C |
| STRING-RANGE | STRG | x | | | | x | x | x | x | Condition | (STRINGRANGE): X = SUBSTR (Y, 1, I); Raised when arguments of SUBSTR specify substring beyond the range of the first argument |

| Keyword | Abbr. | | | | | | | | Condition / Description | Example |
|---|---|---|---|---|---|---|---|---|---|---|
| STRINGSIZE | STRZ | | x | | x | x | x | x | Condition | (STRINGSIZE): X = SUBSTR (Y, I, J); Raised when longer string assigned to shorter string requiring truncation |
| iSUB | | | x | | x | x | x | x | Dummy variable of DEFINED attribute | DCL A (10, 10), B (10) DEF A (1SUB, 1SUB); Specifies that B (i) is the same element as A (i, i) |
| SUBSCRIPT-RANGE | SUBRG | x | x | x | x | x | x | x | Condition | (SUBRG): A = B (I*J); Raised when subscript exceeds upper bound or lower bound of array dimension |
| SUBSTR (string,i[,j]) | | x | x | x | x | x | x | x | Built-in function, pseudo-variable | A = SUBSTR (B, 1, 5); Returns the portion of the first string argument starting at the ith position for j characters |
| SUM (x) | | x | x | | x | x | x | x | Built-in function | X = SUM (Y); Returns the sum of all elements of an array argument |
| SYSIN | | x | x | x | x | x | x | x | Standard PL/I input file name | GET LIST (A, B, C); Exactly equivalent to GET FILE (SYSIN) LIST (A, B, C); |
| SYSIPT | | x | x | x | x | | | | Standard DOS system input logical unit name | DCL C ''»ßBFILE INPUT RECORD ENV (F(80) MEDIUM (SYSIPT,2540); Data will be transmitted from the device assigned to SYSIPT |
| SYSLST | | x | x | x | x | | | | Standard DOS system output logical name unit | DCL F FILE OUTPUT PRINT ENV (F(121) MEDIUM (SYSLST, 1403)); Data will be transmitted to the device assigned to SYSLST |
| SYSPCH | | x | x | x | x | | | | Standard DOS system output logical unit name | DCL PUNCH FILE OUTPUT RECORD ENV (F BLKSIZE (80) MEDIUM SYSPCH, 2540)); Data will be transmitted to the device assigned to SYSPCH |
| SYSPRINT | | x | x | | x | x | x | x | Standard PL/I output file name | PUT LIST (A, B, C); Exactly equivalent to PUT FILE (SYS-PRINT) LIST (A, B, C); |

*Note:* x = feature available; * = feature planned but not implemented at time of publication of this text; blank = feature not available.

| Keyword | Abbreviation | PL/C | Series/1 | PL/I-D | DRI's PL/I-G | DOS PL/I optimizer | OS PL/I optimizer | PL/I checkout | ANS PL/I | Use of keyword | Examples and other information |
|---|---|---|---|---|---|---|---|---|---|---|---|
| SYSTEM | | x | x | x | | x | x | x | | Option of ON statement | ON FOFL SYSTEM; Specifies that standard system action is to take place when condition is raised |
| SYSTEM | | | | | | x | x | x | | Option of DEFAULT statement | DEFAULT RANGE (*) SYSTEM; Specifies that standard PL/I default rules are to be in effect |
| TAN (x) | | x | x | x | x | x | x | x | x | Built-in function | X = TAN (Y); Returns the tangent of the argument expressed in radians |
| TAND (x) | | x | x | x | x | x | x | x | x | Built-in function | X = TAN (Y); Returns the tangent of the argument expressed in degrees |
| TANH (x) | | x | x | x | x | x | x | x | x | Built-in function | X = TANH (Y); Returns the hyperbolic tangent of argument expressed in radians |
| TASK | | | x | | | | x | x | | Attribute, option of PROCEDURE statement | DCL T TASK; Specifies that the associated identifier is the name of a task |
| TASK (task name) | | | | | | x | x | x | | Option of CALL statement | CALL X TASK (T); Specifies that a task named T is to be created by invoking the entry point X |
| THEN | | x | x | x | x | x | x | x | | Clause of the IF statement | IF A = B THEN . . . ; Specifies the action to be taken if the logical expression is true |
| % THEN | | | | | | x | x | x | | Clause of the % IF statement | % IF A = B % THEN . . . ; Specifies the action to be taken if the logical expression is true |

| Keyword | 1 | 2 | 3 | 4 | 5 | 6 | 7 | 8 | Category | Description / Example |
|---|---|---|---|---|---|---|---|---|---|---|
| TIME | x | x | x | x | x | x | x | x | Built-in function | T = TIME; Returns the time of day in the form HHMMSSTTT, where HH is the hour, MM is minutes, SS is seconds, and TTT is milliseconds |
| TITLE (x) | x | x |  | x | x | x | x | x | Option of OPEN statement | OPEN FILE (F) TITLE ('FILE1'); Specifies the DD name to be used to locate and define the data set |
| TO | x | x | x | x | x | x | x | x | Clause of DO statement | DO I = 1 TO 100; Specifies the limit value of the control variable |
| TOTAL |  |  | x |  |  |  | x | x | Option of ENVIRONMENT attribute | DCL A FILE SEQUENTIAL RECORD INPUT ENV (CONSECUTIVE F BLKSIZE (100) TOTAL); Provides in-line code to perform I/O operations, thereby saving the time that would be required for library calls |
| TP (M\|R) | x | x |  | x | x | x | x | x | Option of ENVIRONMENT attribute | DCL F FILE TRANSIENT (TP) (M) RECSIZE (200); Specifies that teleprocessing data is to be transmitted in record (R) or message (M) form |
| TRANSIENT |  |  | x |  |  | x | x |  | Attribute | DCL F FILE TRANSIENT; Specifies a teleprocessing file |
| TRANSLATE (s,r,p) | x | x | x | x | x | x | x | x | Built-in function | A = TRANSLATE (B,'+','.'); Returns B with all + replaced with periods |
| TRANSMIT (file name) | x | x | x | x | x | x | x | x | Condition | ON TRANSMIT (F) BEGIN; . . . ; Raised by a permanent I/O error on named file |
| TRKOFL |  |  | x |  |  |  | x | x | Option of ENVIRONMENT attribute | DCL F FILE ENV (TRKOFL); Specifies that records may overflow the end of a track on a direct-access device |

*Note:* x = feature available; * = feature planned but not implemented at time of publication of this text; blank = feature not available.

| Keyword | Abbreviation | ANS PL/I | PL/I checkout | OS PL/I optimizer | DOS PL/I optimizer | DRI's PL/I-G | PL/I-D | Series/1 | PL/C | Use of keyword | Examples and other information |
|---|---|---|---|---|---|---|---|---|---|---|---|
| TRUNC (x) | | x | x | x | x | x | x | x | x | Built-in function | X = TRUNC (Y); Returns an integer; FLOOR (Y) if Y >= 0; CEIL (Y) if Y < 0 |
| U | | | x | x | x | | x | | x | Option of ENVIRONMENT attribute | DCL F FILE ENV (U); Specifies that records in file are of undetermined length |
| UNALIGNED | UNAL | x | x | x | x | | x | | x | Attribute | DCL X UNAL; Specifies that data item need not be mapped on an integral word boundary |
| UNBUFFERED | UNBUF | | x | x | x | | x | | | Attribute | DCL F FILE UNBUF; Specifies that records need not pass through intermediate storage |
| UNDEFINED-FILE (file name) | UNDF | x | x | x | x | x | x | x | x | Condition | ON UNDEFINEDFILE (F) BEGIN; . . . ; Raised if named file cannot be opened |
| UNDERFLOW | UFL | x | x | x | x | x | x | x | x | Condition | ON UNDERFLOW BEGIN; . . . ; Raised if exponent of floating scale variable becomes too small |
| UNLOAD | | | | | x | | | | | Option of ENVIRONMENT attribute | DCL F FILE ENV (UNLOAD); Causes a tape file to be rewound and unloaded at EOF, EOV, or CLOSE |
| UNLOCK | | | x | x | | | | | x | Statement | UNLOCK FILE (F); Releases exclusive control of a file |
| UNSPEC (x) | | x | x | x | x | x | x | x | x | Built-in function, pseudo-variable | X = UNSPEC (Y); Returns bit-string that is the internal representation of argument |
| UNTIL | | | x | x | x | | x | | | Option of the DO statement | DO UNTIL (END_OF_FILE); Provides for execution of the statements within the DO group as long as the expression in the UNTIL option is "false" |

| Keyword | | Category | Description / Example |
|---|---|---|---|
| UPDATE | x x x x x x x x x x | Attribute, option of OPEN | DCL F FILE UPDATE; OPEN FILE (F) UPDATE; Specifies that the file is to be used for both INPUT and OUTPUT |
| V | x x x x x x x | Option of ENVIRONMENT attribute | DCL F FILE ENV (V(100)); Specifies that file contains variable-length records |
| VALUE | x x x x x | Option of DEFAULT statement | DEFAULT RANGE (*) VALUE (CHAR (10)); Establishes default rules for string length, area size, and precision |
| VARIABLE | x x x x x x x | Attribute | DCL (E ENTRY, F FILE) VARIABLE; Specifies that the associated ENTRY, FILE, or LABEL is to be a variable rather than a constant |
| VARYING | VAR   x x x x x x x | Attribute | DCL C CHAR (100) VARYING; Specifies that the string is to be of varying length; causes maximum required space to be allocated |
| VB | x x x x x x x | Option of ENVIRONMENT attribute | DCL F FILE ENV (VB); Specifies record format to be variable-length blocked |
| VBS | x x x x x x | Option of ENVIRONMENT attribute | DCL F FILE ENV (VBS); Specifies that the record format is variable blocked spanned |
| VERIFY | x x x x x x | Option of ENVIRONMENT attribute | DCL F FILE ENV (VERIFY); Specifies that write disk check be performed by reading and comparing |
| VERIFY (string$_1$, string$_2$) | x x x x x x x | Built-in function | IF VERIFY (S, '0123456789') = 0 THEN . . . ; Returns the position within the first string argument in which a character appears that is not present in the second argument |

*Note:* x = feature available; * = feature planned but not implemented at time of publication of this text; blank = feature not available.

| Keyword | Abbreviation | ANS PL/I | PL/I checkout | OS PL/I optimizer | DOS PL/I optimizer | DRI's PL/I-G | PL/I-D | Series/1 | PL/C | Use of keyword | Examples and other information |
|---|---|---|---|---|---|---|---|---|---|---|---|
| VOLSEQ | | | | | × | | | | Option of ENVIRONMENT attribute | DCL DISKET FILE .. ENV (VOLSEQ MEDIUM (SYS010, 3540) ..); Specifies that sequence checking is to be provided for the volume serial numbers for an IBM 3540 |
| VS | | | × | × | | × | | × | | Option of ENVIRONMENT attribute | DCL F FILE ENV (VS); Specifies that the record format is variable spanned |
| VSAM | | | × | × | × | | | | | Option of ENVIRONMENT attribute | DCL VSAM FILE RECORD .. ENV (VSAM); Specifies that the data set is to have one of the available VSAM organizations. Its structure is specified by the DEFINE command of the Access Methods Services |
| WAIT | | | × | × | × | | | | | Statement | WAIT (EV1, EV2, EV3) (1); The task will wait until one of the list of events has completed |
| WHEN | | | × | × | × | | | | | Clause of the SELECT group | SELECT (PAY_CODE); WHEN ('S') CALL SALARIED; WHEN ('H') CALL HOURLY; OTHERWISE CALL BAD_CODE; END; Specifies an expression to be evaluated and a "unit" to be executed (depending on the result of the evaluation) |
| WHEN | | | × | × | × | | | | | Used with GENERIC attribute | DCL E GENERIC (E1 WHEN (FIXED), E2 WHEN (FLOAT)); Specifies the selection criteria for entry point selection |

| Feature | | | | | | | | Category | Description |
|---|---|---|---|---|---|---|---|---|---|
| WHILE | x | x | x | x | x | x | x | Option of DO statement | DO WHILE (P ¬= NULL); Specifies iterative processing as long as WHILE clause is true |
| WRITE | x | x | x | x | x | x | x | Statement | WRITE FILE (F) FROM (A); Specifies output data transmission for record files |
| WRTPROT | | | | x | | | | Option of ENVIRONMENT attribute | DCL DISKET FILE OUTPUT . . ENV (. . MEDIUM (SYS011,3540) WRTPROT); Specifies that the data set written on the IBM 3540 be flagged as a read-only data set |
| X (w) | x | x | x | x | x | x | x | Format item | PUT EDIT (FIELDA, FIELDB) (A, X(5), A); Controls spacing of the data items in the stream, on input spacing over characters, on output inserting blanks |
| ZERODIVIDE ZDIV | x | x | x | x | x | x | x | Condition | ON ZERODIVIDE BEGIN; Raised when an attempt to divide by zero is made |

*Note:* x = feature available; * = feature planned but not implemented at time of publication of this text; blank = feature not available.

# APPENDIX D

# IBM Data
# Formats

This appendix summarizes the forms in which data may be represented in IBM's computers. Some instructions in the hardware's instruction set are designed to operate on certain data formats only. Most of the data types are implemented in the PL/I language. The PL/I processor translates source code into the appropriate hardware instructions, the selection depending on the format of the data and the operations required.

Figure 3.1 in Chapter 3 on data types and the assignment statement contains an overview of the data formats and the attributes that signal their implementation in PL/I. In the following discussions, each rectangle in the diagrams represents one byte, which is the basic unit of storage. A byte (for BinarY TErm) consists of eight bits. A byte or combination of contiguous bytes may be used to store a data item.

## Bit

From one to eight bits require one byte of storage. With most PL/I implementations, bit-strings are stored eight bits to a byte. For example, the bit-string 101110011 (nine bits) would require two bytes of storage:

| First byte | Second byte |
|------------|-------------|
| 10111001   | 10000000    |

→ Notice that PL/I bit-strings are left-justified and that zeros are padded to the right of the string to fill out the second byte

| Decimal | Binary | Hexadecimal |
|:---:|:---:|:---:|
| 0 | 0000 | 0 |
| 1 | 0001 | 1 |
| 2 | 0010 | 2 |
| 3 | 0011 | 3 |
| 4 | 0100 | 4 |
| 5 | 0101 | 5 |
| 6 | 0110 | 6 |
| 7 | 0111 | 7 |
| 8 | 1000 | 8 |
| 9 | 1001 | 9 |
| 10 | 1010 | A |
| 11 | 1011 | B |
| 12 | 1100 | C |
| 13 | 1101 | D |
| 14 | 1110 | E |
| 15 | 1111 | F |

FIGURE D.1 Binary and hexadecimal equivalents for the decimal values 1 to 15.

## Hexadecimal

Hexadecimal is a number system with a base of 16 utilizing the symbols 0 through 9 and A through F. Figure D.1 compares the counting notation for three number systems: binary (base 2, two symbols 0 and 1), decimal (base 10, 10 symbols 0 – 9) and hexadecimal (base 16, 16 symbols 0 – 9 and A – F).

The hexadecimal number system is used internally to represent floating-point numbers, whether BINARY FLOAT or DECIMAL FLOAT. Hexadecimal is also used as a convenient shorthand for representing binary numbers or a pattern of bits. Note from the chart in D.1 that each of the possible combinations of four bits (binary column) may be represented by one hexadecimal character. The converse is also true that each single hexadecimal character is represented by a four-bit combination.

To convert the hexadecimal numbers to their decimal equivalents, the chart shown in Figure D.2 may be used.

To find the decimal number, locate the hexadecimal number and its decimal equivalent for each position. Add these to obtain the decimal number. To find the hexadecimal number, locate the next lower decimal number and its hexadecimal equivalent. Each difference is used to obtain the next hexadecimal number until the entire number is developed.

To calculate the number of storage locations required by a routine, the addresses of the first byte and the last byte may be converted to decimal before subtracting, or the subtraction may be done in hexadecimal and the result converted to decimal.

When required to display the contents of storage, by means of a storage **dump,** the operating system output routine will show the contents of each byte by printing two hexadecimal characters. Every possible bit pattern may be represented and the volume that must be output is greatly reduced. For example, AE04 will be printed instead of 1010111000000100.

| BYTE | | | | BYTE | | | | BYTE | | | |
|---|---|---|---|---|---|---|---|---|---|---|---|
| 0123 | | 4567 | | 0123 | | 4567 | | 0123 | | 4567 | |
| HEX | DEC | HEX | DEC | HEX | DEC | HEX | DEC | HEX | DEC | HEX | DEC |
| 0 | 0 | 0 | 0 | 0 | 0 | 0 | 0 | 0 | 0 | 0 | 0 |
| 1 | 1,048,576 | 1 | 65,536 | 1 | 4,096 | 1 | 256 | 1 | 16 | 1 | 1 |
| 2 | 2,097,152 | 2 | 131,072 | 2 | 8,192 | 2 | 512 | 2 | 32 | 2 | 2 |
| 3 | 3,145,728 | 3 | 196,608 | 3 | 12,288 | 3 | 768 | 3 | 48 | 3 | 3 |
| 4 | 4,194,304 | 4 | 262,144 | 4 | 16,384 | 4 | 1,024 | 4 | 64 | 4 | 4 |
| 5 | 5,242,880 | 5 | 327,680 | 5 | 20,480 | 5 | 1,280 | 5 | 80 | 5 | 5 |
| 6 | 6,291,456 | 6 | 393,216 | 6 | 24,576 | 6 | 1,536 | 6 | 96 | 6 | 6 |
| 7 | 7,340,032 | 7 | 458,752 | 7 | 28,672 | 7 | 1,792 | 7 | 112 | 7 | 7 |
| 8 | 8,388,608 | 8 | 524,288 | 8 | 32,768 | 8 | 2,048 | 8 | 128 | 8 | 8 |
| 9 | 9,437,184 | 9 | 589,824 | 9 | 36,864 | 9 | 2,304 | 9 | 144 | 9 | 9 |
| A | 10,485,760 | A | 655,360 | A | 40,960 | A | 2,560 | A | 160 | A | 10 |
| B | 11,534,336 | B | 720,896 | B | 45,056 | B | 2,816 | B | 176 | B | 11 |
| C | 12,582,912 | C | 786,432 | C | 49,152 | C | 3,072 | C | 192 | C | 12 |
| D | 13,631,488 | D | 851,968 | D | 53,248 | D | 3,328 | D | 208 | D | 13 |
| E | 14,680,064 | E | 917,504 | E | 57,344 | E | 3,584 | E | 224 | E | 14 |
| F | 15,728,640 | F | 983,040 | F | 61,440 | F | 3,840 | F | 240 | F | 15 |
| | 6 | | 5 | | 4 | | 3 | | 2 | | 1 |

FIGURE D.2    Hexadecimal conversion chart.

It is up to you to interpret these characters by correlating the bit pattern to the data and the data type you know should be in the specific location. By using the many debugging aids available in PL/I, this exercise may be avoided.

In writing PL/I code, you need not be concerned with hexadecimal notation. Data is normally output in character, decimal, or as a bit pattern.

## Character

One or more bytes of storage is used to represent a string of characters. One byte of storage is used to represent each alphanumeric character in a string. In PL/I, the characters may be any of those allowable on a particular computer. They may be any of the 256 EBCDIC[1] character set. As an example, to represent KENT, WASH. 98031, 16 bytes are needed:

| K | E | N | T | , | | W | A | S | H | . | 9 | 8 | 0 | 3 | 1 |

Figure D.3 is a chart showing the EBCDIC character codes used in IBM mainframe computers. Figure D.4 shows the ASCII[2] codes used on many minicomputers and all micro- or personal computers. About half of these characters will be familiar to you (e.g., A, a, B, b, C, . . .). These symbols and other graphics appear in the third column in Figure D.3. The familiar characters may be entered into the computer via a keyboard or other special input device and are entered in single-character form (i.e., one position or one typewriter character). A number of *control symbols* (e.g., NUL, DEL, ENQ) are defined on p. 590. These symbols require multiple keystrokes because the character is not represented on a standard keyboard. Some of these control characters are represented on a keyboard (e.g., EOT) but have no corresponding graphic output. Many of the 256 characters would not be applicable to all I/O devices.

The various symbols in Figures D.3 and D.4 are defined on the following pages.

---

[1] Extended Binary Coded Decimal Interchange Code (EBCDIC).
[2] American Standard Code for Information Interchange (ASCII).

| DEC | HEX | Symbol | DEC | HEX | Symbol | DEC | HEX | Symbol | DEC | HEX | Symbol |
|---|---|---|---|---|---|---|---|---|---|---|---|
| 0 | 00 | NUL | 64 | 40 | SP | 128 | 80 |  | 192 | C0 |  |
| 1 | 01 | SOH | 65 | 41 |  | 129 | 81 | a | 193 | C1 | A |
| 2 | 02 | STX | 66 | 42 |  | 130 | 82 | b | 194 | C2 | B |
| 3 | 03 | ETX | 67 | 43 |  | 131 | 83 | c | 195 | C3 | C |
| 4 | 04 | PF | 68 | 44 |  | 132 | 84 | d | 196 | C4 | D |
| 5 | 05 | HT | 69 | 45 |  | 133 | 85 | e | 197 | C5 | E |
| 6 | 06 | LC | 70 | 46 |  | 134 | 86 | f | 198 | C6 | F |
| 7 | 07 | DEL | 71 | 47 |  | 135 | 87 | g | 199 | C7 | G |
| 8 | 08 |  | 72 | 48 |  | 136 | 88 | h | 200 | C8 | H |
| 9 | 09 |  | 73 | 49 |  | 137 | 89 | i | 201 | C9 | I |
| 10 | 0A | SMM | 74 | 4A | ¢ | 138 | 8A |  | 202 | CA |  |
| 11 | 0B | VT | 75 | 4B | . | 139 | 8B |  | 203 | CB |  |
| 12 | 0C | FF | 76 | 4C | < | 140 | 8C |  | 204 | CC |  |
| 13 | 0D | CR | 77 | 4D | ( | 141 | 8D |  | 205 | CD |  |
| 14 | 0E | SO | 78 | 4E | + | 142 | 8E |  | 206 | CE |  |
| 15 | 0F | SI | 79 | 4F | \| | 143 | 8F |  | 207 | CF |  |
| 16 | 10 | DLE | 80 | 50 | & | 144 | 90 |  | 208 | D0 |  |
| 17 | 11 | DC1 | 81 | 51 |  | 145 | 91 | j | 209 | D1 | J |
| 18 | 12 | DC2 | 82 | 52 |  | 146 | 92 | k | 210 | D2 | K |
| 19 | 13 | TM | 83 | 53 |  | 147 | 93 | l | 211 | D3 | L |
| 20 | 14 | RES | 84 | 54 |  | 148 | 94 | m | 212 | D4 | M |
| 21 | 15 | NL | 85 | 55 |  | 149 | 95 | n | 213 | D5 | N |
| 22 | 16 | BS | 86 | 56 |  | 150 | 96 | o | 214 | D6 | O |
| 23 | 17 | IL | 87 | 57 |  | 151 | 97 | p | 215 | D7 | P |
| 24 | 18 | CAN | 88 | 58 |  | 152 | 98 | q | 216 | D8 | Q |
| 25 | 19 | EM | 89 | 59 |  | 153 | 99 | r | 217 | D9 | R |
| 26 | 1A | CC | 90 | 5A | ! | 154 | 9A |  | 218 | DA |  |
| 27 | 1B | CU1 | 91 | 5B | $ | 155 | 9B |  | 219 | DB |  |
| 28 | 1C | IFS | 92 | 5C | * | 156 | 9C |  | 220 | DC |  |
| 29 | 1D | IGS | 93 | 5D | ) | 157 | 9D |  | 221 | DD |  |
| 30 | 1E | IRS | 94 | 5E | ; | 158 | 9E |  | 222 | DE |  |
| 31 | 1F | IUS | 95 | 5F | ¬ | 159 | 9F |  | 223 | DF |  |
| 32 | 20 | DS | 96 | 60 | - | 160 | A0 |  | 224 | E0 |  |
| 33 | 21 | SOS | 97 | 61 | / | 161 | A1 |  | 225 | E1 |  |
| 34 | 22 | FS | 98 | 62 |  | 162 | A2 | s | 226 | E2 | S |
| 35 | 23 |  | 99 | 63 |  | 163 | A3 | t | 227 | E3 | T |
| 36 | 24 | BYP | 100 | 64 |  | 164 | A4 | u | 228 | E4 | U |
| 37 | 25 | LF | 101 | 65 |  | 165 | A5 | v | 229 | E5 | V |
| 38 | 26 | ETB | 102 | 66 |  | 166 | A6 | w | 230 | E6 | W |
| 39 | 27 | ESC | 103 | 67 |  | 167 | A7 | x | 231 | E7 | X |
| 40 | 28 |  | 104 | 68 |  | 168 | A8 | y | 232 | E8 | Y |
| 41 | 29 |  | 105 | 69 |  | 169 | A9 | z | 233 | E9 | Z |
| 42 | 2A | SM | 106 | 6A |  | 170 | AA |  | 234 | EA |  |
| 43 | 2B | CU2 | 107 | 6B | , | 171 | AB |  | 235 | EB |  |
| 44 | 2C |  | 108 | 6C | % | 172 | AC |  | 236 | EC |  |
| 45 | 2D | ENQ | 109 | 6D | _ | 173 | AD |  | 237 | ED |  |
| 46 | 2E | ACK | 110 | 6E | > | 174 | AE |  | 238 | EE |  |
| 47 | 2F | BEL | 111 | 6F | ? | 175 | AF |  | 239 | EF |  |
| 48 | 30 |  | 112 | 70 |  | 176 | B0 |  | 240 | F0 | 0 |
| 49 | 31 |  | 113 | 71 |  | 177 | B1 |  | 241 | F1 | 1 |
| 50 | 32 | SYN | 114 | 72 |  | 178 | B2 |  | 242 | F2 | 2 |
| 51 | 33 |  | 115 | 73 |  | 179 | B3 |  | 243 | F3 | 3 |
| 52 | 34 | PN | 116 | 74 |  | 180 | B4 |  | 244 | F4 | 4 |
| 53 | 35 | RS | 117 | 75 |  | 181 | B5 |  | 245 | F5 | 5 |
| 54 | 36 | UC | 118 | 76 |  | 182 | B6 |  | 246 | F6 | 6 |
| 55 | 37 | EOT | 119 | 77 |  | 183 | B7 |  | 247 | F7 | 7 |
| 56 | 38 |  | 120 | 78 |  | 184 | B8 |  | 248 | F8 | 8 |
| 57 | 39 |  | 121 | 79 |  | 185 | B9 |  | 249 | F9 | 9 |
| 58 | 3A |  | 122 | 7A | : | 186 | BA |  | 250 | FA |  |
| 59 | 3B | CU3 | 123 | 7B | # | 187 | BB |  | 251 | FB |  |
| 60 | 3C | DC4 | 124 | 7C | @ | 188 | BC |  | 252 | FC |  |
| 61 | 3D | NAK | 125 | 7D | ' | 189 | BD |  | 253 | FD |  |
| 62 | 3E |  | 126 | 7E | = | 190 | BE |  | 254 | FE |  |
| 63 | 3F | SUB | 127 | 7F | " | 191 | BF |  | 255 | FF |  |

FIGURE D.3   EBCDIC character code chart.

| DEC | OCT | HEX | Symbol | DEC | OCT | HEX | Symbol | DEC | OCT | HEX | Symbol | DEC | OCT | HEX | Symbol |
|---|---|---|---|---|---|---|---|---|---|---|---|---|---|---|---|
| 0 | 000 | 00 | NUL | 32 | 040 | 20 | SP | 64 | 100 | 40 | @ | 96 | 140 | 60 | |
| 1 | 001 | 01 | SOH | 33 | 041 | 21 | ! | 65 | 101 | 41 | A | 97 | 141 | 61 | a |
| 2 | 002 | 02 | STX | 34 | 042 | 22 | " | 66 | 102 | 42 | B | 98 | 142 | 62 | b |
| 3 | 003 | 03 | ETX | 35 | 043 | 23 | # | 67 | 103 | 43 | C | 99 | 143 | 63 | c |
| 4 | 004 | 04 | EOT | 36 | 044 | 24 | $ | 68 | 104 | 44 | D | 100 | 144 | 64 | d |
| 5 | 005 | 05 | ENQ | 37 | 045 | 25 | % | 69 | 105 | 45 | E | 101 | 145 | 65 | e |
| 6 | 006 | 06 | ACK | 38 | 046 | 26 | & | 70 | 106 | 46 | F | 102 | 146 | 66 | f |
| 7 | 007 | 07 | BEL | 39 | 047 | 27 | ' | 71 | 107 | 47 | G | 103 | 147 | 67 | g |
| 8 | 010 | 08 | BS | 40 | 050 | 28 | ( | 72 | 110 | 48 | H | 104 | 150 | 68 | h |
| 9 | 011 | 09 | HT | 41 | 051 | 29 | ) | 73 | 111 | 49 | I | 105 | 151 | 69 | i |
| 10 | 012 | 0A | LF | 42 | 052 | 2A | * | 74 | 112 | 4A | J | 106 | 152 | 6A | j |
| 11 | 013 | 0B | VT | 43 | 053 | 2B | + | 75 | 113 | 4B | K | 107 | 153 | 6B | k |
| 12 | 014 | 0C | FF | 44 | 054 | 2C | , | 76 | 114 | 4C | L | 108 | 154 | 6C | l |
| 13 | 015 | 0D | CR | 45 | 055 | 2D | − | 77 | 115 | 4D | M | 109 | 155 | 6D | m |
| 14 | 016 | 0E | SO | 46 | 056 | 2E | . | 78 | 116 | 4E | N | 110 | 156 | 6E | n |
| 15 | 017 | 0F | SI | 47 | 057 | 2F | / | 79 | 117 | 4F | O | 111 | 157 | 6F | o |
| 16 | 020 | 10 | DLE | 48 | 060 | 30 | 0 | 80 | 120 | 50 | P | 112 | 160 | 70 | p |
| 17 | 021 | 11 | DC1 | 49 | 061 | 31 | 1 | 81 | 121 | 51 | Q | 113 | 161 | 71 | q |
| 18 | 022 | 12 | DC2 | 50 | 062 | 32 | 2 | 82 | 122 | 52 | R | 114 | 162 | 72 | r |
| 19 | 023 | 13 | DC3 | 51 | 063 | 33 | 3 | 83 | 123 | 53 | S | 115 | 163 | 73 | s |
| 20 | 024 | 14 | DC4 | 52 | 064 | 34 | 4 | 84 | 124 | 54 | T | 116 | 164 | 74 | t |
| 21 | 025 | 15 | NAK | 53 | 065 | 35 | 5 | 85 | 125 | 55 | U | 117 | 165 | 75 | u |
| 22 | 026 | 16 | SYN | 54 | 066 | 36 | 6 | 86 | 126 | 56 | V | 118 | 166 | 76 | v |
| 23 | 027 | 17 | ETB | 55 | 067 | 37 | 7 | 87 | 127 | 57 | W | 119 | 167 | 77 | w |
| 24 | 030 | 18 | CAN | 56 | 070 | 38 | 8 | 88 | 130 | 58 | X | 120 | 170 | 78 | x |
| 25 | 031 | 19 | EM | 57 | 071 | 39 | 9 | 89 | 131 | 59 | Y | 121 | 171 | 79 | y |
| 26 | 032 | 1A | SUB | 58 | 072 | 3A | : | 90 | 132 | 5A | Z | 122 | 172 | 7A | z |
| 27 | 033 | 1B | ESC | 59 | 073 | 3B | ; | 91 | 133 | 5B | [ | 123 | 173 | 7B | { |
| 28 | 034 | 1C | FS | 60 | 074 | 3C | < | 92 | 134 | 5C | \ | 124 | 174 | 7C | \| |
| 29 | 035 | 1D | GS | 61 | 075 | 3D | = | 93 | 135 | 5D | ] | 125 | 175 | 7D | } |
| 30 | 036 | 1E | RS | 62 | 076 | 3E | > | 94 | 136 | 5E | ^ | 126 | 176 | 7E | ~ |
| 31 | 037 | 1F | US | 63 | 077 | 3F | ? | 95 | 137 | 5F | _ | 127 | 177 | 7F | DEL |

FIGURE D.4    ASCII codes.

## Zoned Decimal

From one to sixteen bytes may be specified for a sequence of decimal digits representing an arithmetic value.   Each decimal digit requires one byte of storage.

### Special Graphic Characters

| | | | |
|---|---|---|---|
| ¢ | Cent sign | − | Minus sign, hyphen |
| . | Period, decimal point | / | Slash |
| < | Less Than sign | , | Comma |
| ( | Left parenthesis | % | Percent |
| + | Plus sign | _ | Underscore |
| \| | Logical OR | > | Greater Than sign |
| & | Ampersand | ? | Question mark |
| ! | Exclamation point | : | Colon |
| $ | Dollar sign | # | Number sign |
| * | Asterisk | @ | At sign |
| ) | Right parenthesis | ' | Prime, apostrophe, single quote mark |
| ; | Semicolon | = | Equal sign |
| ¬ | Logical NOT | " | Quotation mark |

*Control Character Representations*

| | | | |
|---|---|---|---|
| ACK | Acknowledge | IGS | Interchange group separator |
| BEL | Bell | IL | Idle |
| BS | Backspace | IRS | Interchange record separator |
| BYP | Bypass | IUS | Interchange unit separator |
| CAN | Cancel | LC | Lowercase |
| CC | Cursor control | LF | Line feed |
| CR | Carriage return | NAK | Negative acknowledge |
| CU1 | Customer use 1 | NL | New line |
| CU2 | Customer use 2 | NUL | Null |
| CU3 | Customer use 3 | PF | Punch off |
| DC1 | Device control 1 | PN | Punch on |
| DC2 | Device control 2 | RES | Restore |
| DC4 | Device control 4 | RS | Reader stop |
| DEL | Delete | SI | Shift in |
| DLE | Data link escape | SM | Set mode |
| DS | Digit select | SMM | Start of manual message |
| EM | End of medium | SO | Shift out |
| ENQ | Enquiry | SOH | Start of heading |
| EOT | End of transmission | SOS | Start of significance |
| ESC | Escape | SP | Space |
| ETB | End of transmission block | STX | Start of text |
| ETX | End of text | SUB | Substitute |
| FF | Form feed | SYN | Synchronous idle |
| FS | Field separator | TM | Tape mark |
| HT | Horizontal tab | UC | Uppercase |
| IFS | Interchange file separator | VT | Vertical tab |

The zoned decimal format is actually a subset of the character data format. The digit characters 0 through 9 are specified in EBCDIC.

| 0 | | 1 | | 2 | | |
|---|---|---|---|---|---|---|
| 1111 | 0000 | 1111 | 0001 | 1111 | 0010 | ⟶ Bit pattern |
| F | 0 | F | 1 | F | 2 | ⟶ Hexadecimal notation |
| | 0 | | 1 | | 2 | ⟶ Graphic symbol |

The leftmost four bits of the rightmost byte are used to represent the sign:

A '1100' represents a plus sign.
A '1101' represents a minus sign.
A '1111' is unsigned but is treated as a plus sign by the computer.

| 0 | | 1 | | + | 2 | |
|---|---|---|---|---|---|---|
| 1111 | 0000 | 1111 | 0001 | 1100 | 0010 | ⟶ Bit pattern |
| F | 0 | F | 1 | C | 2 | ⟶ Hexadecimal notation |
| | 0 | | 1 | | B | ⟶ Graphic symbol |

| 0 | 1 | — 2 |
|---|---|---|

1111 0000 1111 0001 1101 0010 ⟶ Bit pattern
F 0 F 1 D 2 ⟶ Hexadecimal notation
0 1 K ⟶ Graphic symbol

Note that the rightmost digit may appear as an alphabetic character when punched into a card or as a 12 or 11 *zone* punched over a digit.

No arithmetic operations may be performed *directly* on data in this format. Data identified as zoned decimal must be converted to one of the coded arithmetic data formats (packed decimal, fixed-point, or floating-point) when arithmetic is to be performed. (In PL/I the conversion is automatic.)

## Packed Decimal

From one to sixteen bytes may be used to store a sequence of decimal digits representing an arithmetic value. A pattern of four bits is defined for each decimal digit. Since a byte consists of eight bits, up to two decimal digits may be *packed* into one byte. In addition, one half of a byte is reserved for the algebraic sign (+ or −) of the number. For example, to represent +5, one byte is needed:

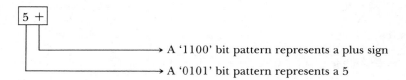

Notice that the bit pattern of each group of four bits is actually a binary representation of the decimal digit. Each decimal digit is internally coded in the same way as a four position binary number (see Figure D.1). However, only the coding for values equivalent to a decimal 0 through 9 is valid.

To represent −12, two bytes are used:

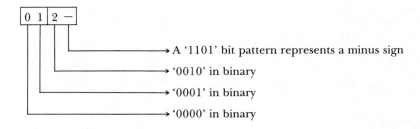

Notice how the sign of the number always appears in the rightmost four bits of the right-hand byte. Also notice, in the above example, how a leading zero was filled in on the left when an even number (e.g., 2, 4, 6, 8, etc.) of digits are to be represented in the packed decimal data format. In the following example, notice that only two bytes are needed to represent a three-digit number:

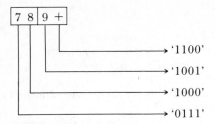

$\rightarrow$ '1100'

$\rightarrow$ '1001'

$\rightarrow$ '1000'

$\rightarrow$ '0111'

Although S/360 or S/370 provides for a maximum of 16 bytes (or 31 decimal digits) for the packed decimal data format, a maximum of eight bytes, which can contain 15 decimal digits, is allowed in most PL/I compilers.

### Fixed-Point

This format represents data in the binary numbering system; that is, base 2. Two or four contiguous bytes may be used to represent this type of data. When two bytes are combined to represent fixed-point binary data, the result is said to be *halfword binary*. Four contiguous bytes constitute a *word*, but the word's address must begin on a "fullword" boundary. This simply means that the starting storage address of the four contiguous bytes must be evenly divisible by four. (Halfwords of binary data must have even-numbered storage addresses.) As a PL/I programmer, you generally do not have to be concerned that this type of data will be properly placed in main storage (i.e., on a fullword boundary), since assigning data to proper storage addresses is automatically done for you by the PL/I compiler.

Here is an example of the value $+65$ as it would appear in fixed-point binary format:

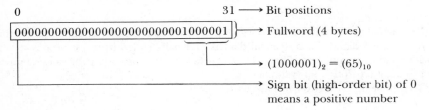

0       31 $\longrightarrow$ Bit positions

00000000000000000000000001000001 $\}\rightarrow$ Fullword (4 bytes)

$\rightarrow (1000001)_2 = (65)_{10}$

$\rightarrow$ Sign bit (high-order bit) of 0 means a positive number

Generally, it is not important that you understand how negative numbers are represented in fixed-point binary. An example of $-5$ is shown below. (Fixed-point binary numbers are represented in two's complement form.)

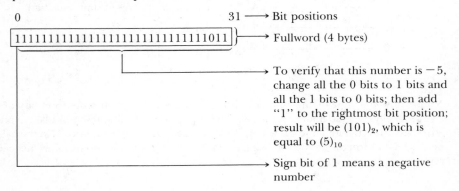

0       31 $\longrightarrow$ Bit positions

11111111111111111111111111111011 $\}\rightarrow$ Fullword (4 bytes)

$\rightarrow$ To verify that this number is $-5$, change all the 0 bits to 1 bits and all the 1 bits to 0 bits; then add "1" to the rightmost bit position; result will be $(101)_2$, which is equal to $(5)_{10}$

$\rightarrow$ Sign bit of 1 means a negative number

| Positive Binary Values | | Powers of 2 | Absolute Values | | Negative Binary Values |
|---|---|---|---|---|---|
| **Bit Positions** 11 1111 1111 2222 2222 2233 0123 4567 8901 2345 6789 0123 4567 8901 | | | Decimal Notation Base - 10 | Hexadecimal Notation Base - 16 | **Bit Positions** 11 1111 1111 2222 2222 2233 0123 4567 8901 2345 6789 0123 4567 8901 |
| 0000 0000 0000 0000 0000 0000 0000 0000 | | – | 0 | 0 | No negative zero |
| 0000 0000 0000 0000 0000 0000 0000 0001 | | 0 | 1 | 1 | 1111 1111 1111 1111 1111 1111 1111 1111 |
| 0000 0000 0000 0000 0000 0000 0000 0010 | | 1 | 2 | 2 | 1111 1111 1111 1111 1111 1111 1111 1110 |
| 0000 0000 0000 0000 0000 0000 0000 0100 | | 2 | 4 | 4 | 1111 1111 1111 1111 1111 1111 1111 1100 |
| 0000 0000 0000 0000 0000 0000 0000 1000 | | 3 | 8 | 8 | 1111 1111 1111 1111 1111 1111 1111 1000 |
| 0000 0000 0000 0000 0000 0000 0001 0000 | | 4 | 16 | 10 | 1111 1111 1111 1111 1111 1111 1111 0000 |
| 0000 0000 0000 0000 0000 0000 0010 0000 | | 5 | 32 | 20 | 1111 1111 1111 1111 1111 1111 1110 0000 |
| 0000 0000 0000 0000 0000 0000 0100 0000 | | 6 | 64 | 40 | 1111 1111 1111 1111 1111 1111 1100 0000 |
| 0000 0000 0000 0000 0000 0000 1000 0000 | | 7 | 128 | 80 | 1111 1111 1111 1111 1111 1111 1000 0000 |
| 0000 0000 0000 0000 0000 0001 0000 0000 | | 8 | 256 | 100 | 1111 1111 1111 1111 1111 1111 0000 0000 |
| 0000 0000 0000 0000 0000 0010 0000 0000 | | 9 | 512 | 200 | 1111 1111 1111 1111 1111 1110 0000 0000 |
| 0000 0000 0000 0000 0000 0100 0000 0000 | | 10 | 1,024 | 400 | 1111 1111 1111 1111 1111 1100 0000 0000 |
| 0000 0000 0000 0000 0000 1000 0000 0000 | | 11 | 2,048 | 800 | 1111 1111 1111 1111 1111 1000 0000 0000 |
| 0000 0000 0000 0000 0001 0000 0000 0000 | | 12 | 4,096 | 1,000 | 1111 1111 1111 1111 1111 0000 0000 0000 |
| 0000 0000 0000 0000 0010 0000 0000 0000 | | 13 | 8,192 | 2,000 | 1111 1111 1111 1111 1110 0000 0000 0000 |
| 0000 0000 0000 0000 0100 0000 0000 0000 | | 14 | 16,384 | 4,000 | 1111 1111 1111 1111 1100 0000 0000 0000 |
| 0000 0000 0000 0000 1000 0000 0000 0000 | | 15 | 32,768 | 8,000 | 1111 1111 1111 1111 1000 0000 0000 0000 |
| 0000 0000 0000 0001 0000 0000 0000 0000 | | 16 | 65,536 | 10,000 | 1111 1111 1111 1111 0000 0000 0000 0000 |
| 0000 0000 0000 0010 0000 0000 0000 0000 | | 17 | 131,072 | 20,000 | 1111 1111 1111 1110 0000 0000 0000 0000 |
| 0000 0000 0000 0100 0000 0000 0000 0000 | | 18 | 262,144 | 40,000 | 1111 1111 1111 1100 0000 0000 0000 0000 |
| 0000 0000 0000 1000 0000 0000 0000 0000 | | 19 | 524,288 | 80,000 | 1111 1111 1111 1000 0000 0000 0000 0000 |
| 0000 0000 0001 0000 0000 0000 0000 0000 | | 20 | 1,048,576 | 100,000 | 1111 1111 1111 0000 0000 0000 0000 0000 |
| 0000 0000 0010 0000 0000 0000 0000 0000 | | 21 | 2,097,152 | 200,000 | 1111 1111 1110 0000 0000 0000 0000 0000 |
| 0000 0000 0100 0000 0000 0000 0000 0000 | | 22 | 4,194,304 | 400,000 | 1111 1111 1100 0000 0000 0000 0000 0000 |
| 0000 0000 1000 0000 0000 0000 0000 0000 | | 23 | 8,388,608 | 800,000 | 1111 1111 1000 0000 0000 0000 0000 0000 |
| 0000 0001 0000 0000 0000 0000 0000 0000 | | 24 | 16,777,216 | 1,000,000 | 1111 1111 0000 0000 0000 0000 0000 0000 |
| 0000 0010 0000 0000 0000 0000 0000 0000 | | 25 | 33,554,432 | 2,000,000 | 1111 1110 0000 0000 0000 0000 0000 0000 |
| 0000 0100 0000 0000 0000 0000 0000 0000 | | 26 | 67,108,864 | 4,000,000 | 1111 1100 0000 0000 0000 0000 0000 0000 |
| 0000 1000 0000 0000 0000 0000 0000 0000 | | 27 | 134,217,728 | 8,000,000 | 1111 1000 0000 0000 0000 0000 0000 0000 |
| 0001 0000 0000 0000 0000 0000 0000 0000 | | 28 | 268,435,456 | 10,000,000 | 1111 0000 0000 0000 0000 0000 0000 0000 |
| 0010 0000 0000 0000 0000 0000 0000 0000 | | 29 | 536,870,912 | 20,000,000 | 1110 0000 0000 0000 0000 0000 0000 0000 |
| 0100 0000 0000 0000 0000 0000 0000 0000 | | 30 | 1,073,741,824 | 40,000,000 | 1100 0000 0000 0000 0000 0000 0000 0000 |
| 0111 1111 1111 1111 1111 1111 1111 1111 No positive equivalent | | – | 2,147,483,647 | 7F,FFF,FFF | 1000 0000 0000 0000 0000 0000 0000 0001 |
| | | 31 | 2,147,483,648 | 80,000,000 | 1000 0000 0000 0000 0000 0000 0000 0000 |

FIGURE D.5 Powers-of-two table.

Figure D.5 shows a powers-of-two table that should be helpful in conversions between binary and decimal numbers. It may also aid in determining the maximum decimal values that can be represented in varying precisions of fixed-point binary numbers.

## Floating-Point

A floating-point format often represents data in a more compact form than does a fixed-point format. This is generally the case when a large number of zeros are required to fix the location of the decimal or binary point in a fixed-point format. For example, the fixed-point decimal fraction 0.000000009 requires eight zeros to establish the location of the decimal point. In floating-point format the zeros are not needed, because the location of the decimal point is specified by an integer exponent appearing within the floating-point data item.

There are three forms of floating-point data: short form, long form, and extended form.

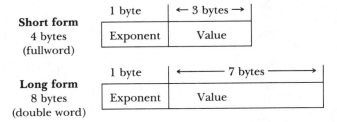

**Short form**
4 bytes
(fullword)

| 1 byte | ← 3 bytes → |
|---|---|
| Exponent | Value |

**Long form**
8 bytes
(double word)

| 1 byte | ←——— 7 bytes ———→ |
|---|---|
| Exponent | Value |

| Extended form 16 bytes (two double words) | 1 byte | ← 7 bytes → |
|---|---|---|
| | Exponent | High-order value |
| | **Unused** | Low-order value |

The primary difference between each form lies in the longer form being able to contain more digits of significance. For example, the number 742682.1130 could not be contained in the short-form floating-point number. The closest that we could come would be 742682, truncating the fraction because of too few bits in the value field. In order to provide a more precise representation of the above number, we must choose a form supplying longer precision (either long or extended).

The *values* of the numbers we can represent in the various forms are, for all practical purposes, the same, because the exponent field determines the magnitude of the number stored in the value field. But the precision maintained in each type is different: for short form, up to six decimal digits; for long form, up to 16 decimal digits; and for extended form, up to 33 decimal digits. Not all PL/I compilers implement all forms of floating-point data. Check the specifications of the compiler you are using for the maximum precision allowed.

As an example of how a decimal number would look in floating-point format inside the computer, consider the decimal value 22.5, which would be written in binary as follows:

16 8 4 2 1 . ½ ¼ ⅛ → Binary place values

1 0 1 1 0 . 1 0 0 → Binary equivalent of 22.5

Floating-point data values are represented in hexadecimal. Thus, the binary value 10110.1 would be represented as follows:

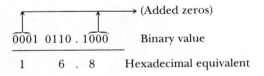

Notice how it was necessary to "pad" with zeros both to the right and to the left of the straight binary value to yield the hexadecimal equivalent. Inside the computer, there is no way to physically record the position of the hexadecimal (or decimal or binary, for that matter) point. The position of the *point* is recorded in the form of an exponent. To relate this back to decimal, we know that:

$$22.5 \quad \text{is equivalent to} \quad .225 \times 10^{+2}$$

where $10^{+2}$ is the exponent. It follows, then, that the hexadecimal value

$$16.8 \quad \text{is equivalent to} \quad .168 + 16^{+2}$$

Recall the short-form floating-point format:

| Exponent | Value |
|----------|-------|
| 1 byte | ←——— 3 bytes ———→ |

To show how the hexadecimal value would be represented in this format, we begin with the following:

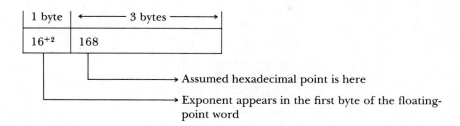

| 1 byte | ←——— 3 bytes ———→ |
|--------|------|
| $16^{+2}$ | 168 |

→ Assumed hexadecimal point is here

→ Exponent appears in the first byte of the floating-point word

Actually, the first byte of the floating-point data item is called a **characteristic.** Characteristic is the preferred term, because it is made up of the exponent plus another factor that is a constant. The constant value is a hexadecimal 40. For example, if the characteristic is $40_{16}$, then it is assumed that the fractional value (which is called the *mantissa*) is scaled at $16^0$; for a characteristic of $41_{16}$, the mantissa is scaled at $16^1$; for a characteristic of 3F the mantissa is scaled at $16^{-1}$. As a further illustration, then, we would have the following:

| *Hexadecimal Characteristic* | *Equivalent Exponent* |
|------------------------------|-----------------------|
| . | . |
| . | . |
| . | . |
| 43 | $16^3$ |
| 42 | $16^2$ |
| 41 | $16^1$ |
| 40 | $16^0$ |
| 3F | $16^{-1}$ |
| 3E | $16^{-2}$ |
| 3D | $16^{-3}$ |
| . | . |
| . | . |
| . | . |

Thus, the decimal value 22.5 is represented in its hexadecimal equivalent, which is 16.8. Because floating-point values are assumed to be fractions, we will say that the value is $0.168 \times 16^2$. The exponent 2 will be added to the hexadecimal constant 40 to give us the characteristic. All of this may be depicted in the following bit structure:

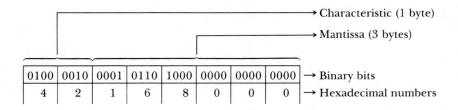

→ Characteristic (1 byte)

→ Mantissa (3 bytes)

| 0100 | 0010 | 0001 | 0110 | 1000 | 0000 | 0000 | 0000 | → Binary bits |
|------|------|------|------|------|------|------|------|-----|
| 4 | 2 | 1 | 6 | 8 | 0 | 0 | 0 | → Hexadecimal numbers |

The high-order bit of the floating-point number is used to represent the sign of the mantissa, 0 for a positive number, 1 for a negative. Thus, the previous discussions have assumed that the numbers being represented were positive. The depiction of a $-16.8$ in floating-point notation would require the alteration of only 1 bit of the previous bit structure.

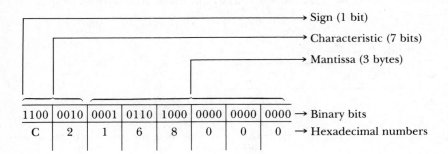

# APPENDIX E

# Glossary of PL/I Terms

Following are definitions of a number of PL/I terms as well as general terms used in data processing. The author wishes to thank IBM for permission to use the PL/I definitions as supplied in 1971 by the PL/I Mission Publications group, IBM United Kingdom Laboratories Limited, Hursley Park, England. The terms marked with an asterisk are IBM definitions.

**ABEND** abnormal end of task

**abnormal end of task** termination of a task prior to its completion because of an error condition that cannot be resolved by recovery facilities while the task is executing

**access** to reference or retrieve data

**access method** the combination of an access technique and a given file or data set organization

*** activate (a block)** to initiate the execution of a block; a procedure block is activated when it is invoked at any of its entry points; a begin block is activated when it is encountered in normal flow of control, including a branch

*** activation (of a block)** (1) the process of activating a block; (2) the execution of a block

*** additive attributes** attributes for which there are no defaults and which, if required, must always be added to the list of specified attributes or be implied (i.e., they have to be added to the set of attributes, if they are required)

**address** an identification for a register, location in storage, or other data source or destination; the identification may be a name, label, or number

**algorithm** a prescribed set of rules for the solution of a problem in a finite number of steps

**aggregate** *see* data aggregate

*** aggregate expression** an array expression or a structure expression

**\*alignment**  the storing of data items in relation to certain machine-dependent boundaries

**allocate**  to grant a resource to, or reserve it for, a job or task; e.g., to grant main storage to a PL/I program when there is a request for the storage (usually during object program execution)

**\*allocated variables**  a variable with which internal storage has been associated and not freed

**\*allocation**  (1) the reservation of internal storage for a variable; (2) a generation of an allocated variable

**\*alphabetic character**  any of the characters A through Z of the English alphabet and the alphabetic extenders #, $, and @ (which may have different graphic representation in different countries)

**alphameric character**  an alphabetic character, a digit, a blank, or a special character

**\*alternative attribute**  an attribute that may be chosen from a group of two or more alternatives; if none is specified, a default is assumed

**\*ambiguous reference**  a reference that is not sufficiently qualified to identify one and only one name known at the point of reference

**\*ANSI**  *American National Standards Institute,* an organization sponsored by the Business Equipment Manufacturers Association (BEMA) for the purpose of establishing voluntary industry standards

**\*argument**  an expression in an argument list as part of a procedure reference

**\*argument list**  a parenthesized list of one or more arguments, separated by commas, following an entry name constant, an entry name variable, a generic name, or a built-in function name; the list is passed to the parameters of the entry point

**\*arithmetic constant**  a fixed-point constant or a floating-point constant; although most arithmetic constants can be signed, the sign is not part of the constant

**\*arithmetic conversion**  the transformation of a value from one arithmetic representation to another

**\*arithmetic data**  data that has the characteristics of base, scale, mode and precision; it includes coded arithmetic data, pictured numeric character data, and pictured numeric bit data

**\*arithmetic operators**  either of the prefix operators + and −, or any of the following infix operators: +, −, *, /, **

**\*arithmetic picture data**  decimal picture data or binary picture data

**\*array**  a named, ordered collection of data elements, all of which have identical attributes; an array has dimensions specified by the dimension attribute, and its individual elements are referred to by subscripts; an array can also be an ordered collection of identical structures

**\*array expression**  an expression whose evaluation yields an array value

**\*array of structures**  an ordered collection of identical structures specified by giving the dimension attribute to a structure name

**\*assignment**  the process of giving a value to a variable

**\*asynchronous operation**  the overlap of an input/output operation with the execution of statements, or the concurrent execution of procedures using multiple flows of control for different tasks

**\*attribute**  (1) a descriptive property associated with a name to describe a characteristic of items that the name may represent; (2) a descriptive property used to describe a characteristic of the result of evaluation of an expression

**\*automatic storage allocation**  the allocation of storage for automatic variables

**\*automatic variable**  a variable that is allocated automatically at the activation of a block and released automatically at the termination of that block

**auxiliary (peripheral) equipment**  equipment not actively involved during the processing of data, such as input/output equipment and auxiliary storage utilizing punched cards, magnetic tapes, disks, or drums

**base**  the number system in which an arithmetic value is represented: decimal or binary in PL/I

**\*base element**  the name of a structure member that is not a minor structure

**\*base item**  the automatic, controlled, or static variable or the parameter upon which a defined variable is defined.  The name may be qualified and/or subscripted

**\*based storage allocation**  the allocation of storage for based variables

**\*based variable**  a variable whose generations are identified by locator variables; a based variable can be used to refer to values of variables of any storage class; it can also be allocated and freed explicitly by use of the ALLOCATE and FREE statements

**batch processing**  a system approach to processing where similar input items are grouped for processing during the same machine run

**\*begin block**  a collection of statements headed by a BEGIN statement and ended by an END statement that is a part of a program that delimits the scope of names and that is activated by normal sequential flow of control, including any branch resulting from a GO TO statement

**binary**  (1) the number system based on the number 2; (2) pertaining to a choice or condition where there are two possibilities

**\*bit**  a binary digit (0 and 1); a contraction of the term *binary digit*

**\*bit-string**  a string composed of zero or more bits

**\*bit-string operators**  the logical operators $\neg$ (not), & (and), and | (or)

**blank**  a code character to denote the presence of no information rather than the absence of information

**block**  (1) a begin block or procedure block; (2) a physical record consisting of more than one logical record; i.e., a group of records handled as one unit

**\*block heading statement**  the PROCEDURE or BEGIN statement that heads a block of statements

**blocking**  the grouping of logical records to form one physical record to be stored on a DASD or tape device

**block length**  physical record length as contrasted with logical record length

**Boolean algebra**  an algebra named for George Boole (1815–1864); Boolean algebra is similar in form to ordinary algebra, but it deals with logical relationships rather than quantifiable relationships

**\*bounds**  the upper and lower limits of an array dimension

**branch**  (1) a sequence of instructions executed as a result of a decision instruction; (2) to depart from the usual sequence of executing instructions in a computer; synonymous with jump or transfer

**\*buffer**  intermediate storage, used in input/output operations, into which a record is read during input and from which a record is written during output

**bug**  a mistake or error (typically in a program)

**\*built-in function**  a function that is supplied by the language

**byte**  a contiguous set of eight binary digits operated upon as a unit; a contraction of the words *binary term*

**\*call** (1) (verb) to invoke a subroutine by means of the CALL statement or CALL option; (2) (noun) such an invocation

**card code** the combinations of punched holes representing characters (letters, digits, special characters) in a punched card

**card column** one of the vertical lines of punching positions on a punched card

**card punch** a device to record information in cards by punching holes in the cards to represent letters, digits, and special characters

**card reader** a device that senses and translates into internal form the holes in punched cards

**carriage control** the process of directing the movement of paper through a line printer from a program

**carriage control characters** standard characters (CTLASA or CTL360) used by a program to affect the movement of paper through a line printer

**carriage tape** a special 12-channel tape, usually made of Mylar®, with punches that direct the movement of paper through a line printer

**case structure** a form in a structured program for representing that a series of tests is to be made and one of many alternate paths taken depending on the results of the tests

**central processing unit (CPU)** the unit of a computing system containing the circuits that calculate and perform logic decisions based on a program of operating instructions

**character** an element of a character set

**characteristic** in S/360 and S/370 data, that part of a floating-point number that contains the exponent

**\*character set** a defined collection of characters; *see* data character set and language character set

**character-string** a string composed of zero or more characters from the complete set of characters whose bit configuration is recognized by the computer system in use; for S/360 and S/370 implementations, any of the 256 EBCDIC characters can be used

**\*character-string picture data** data described by a picture specification which must have at least one A or X picture specification character

**checkout** the process of locating errors in a program by testing the program with sample data

**choice structure** a form in a structured program indicating that a test is to be made and one of two alternate paths taken depending on the results of the test. Also called IF-THEN-ELSE

**clear** to put a storage or memory device into a state denoting zero or blank

**closing (of a file)** dissociating a file definition from a data set

**COBOL** *CO*mmon *B*usiness *O*riented *L*anguage; a data processing language that resembles business English

**coded arithmetic data** arithmetic data stored in a form that is acceptable, without conversion, for arithmetic calculations (i.e., FIXED BINARY, FIXED DECIMAL, FLOAT BINARY, FLOAT DECIMAL)

**coding** (1) (verb) process or act of writing program statements or instructions; (2) (noun) program language statements or instructions

**coding form** a preprinted page onto which program statements or instructions are written

**collating sequence** the sequence in which letters, numbers, and special characters are ranked; the ranking of the alphanumeric data is taken into account when data is to be sorted

**comment** an expression that explains or identifies a step in a program but has no effect on the execution of the program; a string of characters, used for documentation, preceded by /* and terminated by */

**\*commercial character** the following picture specification characters: (1) CR (credit); (2) DB (debit); (3) T, I, and R, the overpunched-sign characters, which indicate that the associated position in the data item contains, or may contain, a digit with an overpunched sign, and that this over-punched sign is to be considered in the character-string value of the data item

**common data area** *see* global variables

**comparison** the examination of the relationship between two similar items of data; usually followed by a decision

**\*comparison operators** infix operators used in comparison expressions; they are $\neg <$ (not less than), $<$ (less than), $<=$ (less than or equal to), $\neg =$ (not equal to), $=$ (equal to), $>=$ (greater than or equal to), $>$ (greater than), and $\neg >$ (not greater than)

**compile** to convert a source-language program such as PL/I to a machine-language program

**compiler** a program that translates source statements to object form

**compile-time** the time during which a source program is translated into an object module; in PL/I, it is the time during which a source program can be altered (preprocessed), if desired, and then translated into an object program

**compile-time statements** *see* preprocessor statement

**\*complex data** arithmetic data, each item of which consists of a real part and an imaginary part

**\*composite operators** an operator composed of two operator symbols, e.g., $\neg >$

**\*compound statement** a statement whose statement body contains one or more statements

**\*concatenation** the operation that joins two strings in the order specified, thus forming one string whose length is equal to the sum of the lengths of the two strings; it is specified by the operator ‖

**\*condition** *see* on-condition

**\*condition list** a list of one or more condition prefixes

**\*condition name** a language keyword (or condition followed by a parenthesized programmer-defined name) that denotes an on-condition that might arise within a task

**\*condition prefix** a parenthesized list of one or more language condition names, prefixed to a statement; it specifies whether the named on-conditions are to be enabled

**console** the unit of equipment used for communication between the operator or service engineer and the computer

**\*constant** an arithmetic or string data item that does not have a name and whose value cannot change; an unsubscripted label prefix or a file name or an entry name

**\*contained text** all text in a procedure (including nested procedures) except its entry names and condition prefixes of the PROCEDURE statement; all text in a begin block except labels and condition prefixes of the BEGIN statement that heads the block; internal blocks are contained in the external procedure

**\*contextual declaration** the appearance of an identifier that has not been explicitly declared, in a context that allows the association of specific attributes with the identifier

**\*control format item** a specification used in edit-directed transmission to specify positioning of a data item within the stream or printed page

**\*controlled parameter** a parameter for which the CONTROLLED attribute is specified in a DECLARE statement; it can be associated only with arguments that have the CONTROLLED attribute

**controlled storage allocation**  the dynamic allocation of storage for variables that have the CONTROLLED attribute

\* **controlled variable**  a variable whose allocation and release are controlled by the ALLOCATE and FREE statements, with access to the current generation only

\* **control variable**  a variable used to control the iterative execution of a group; *see* iterative do-group

\* **conversion**  the transformation of a value from one representation to another to conform to a given set of attributes

**core storage**  a form of magnetic storage that permits high-speed access to information within the computer; *see* magnetic core

\* **cross section of an array**  the elements represented by the extent of at least one dimension (but not all dimensions) of an array; an asterisk in the place of a subscript in an array reference indicates the entire extent of that dimension

**DASD**  *D*irect *A*ccess *S*torage *D*evice, such as a disk, drum, or data cell

**data**  representation of information or value in a form suitable for processing (*also see* problem data)

\* **data aggregate**  a logical collection of two or more data items that can be referred to either collectively or individually; an array or structure

\* **data character set**  all of those characters whose representation is recognized by the computer in use

**data conversion**  the process of changing data from one form of representation to another

\* **data-directed transmission**  the type of stream-oriented transmission in which data is transmitted as a group, ended by a semicolon, where each item is of the form:

$$name = constant$$

\* **data format item**  a specification used in edit-directed transmission to describe the representation of a data item in the stream

**data item**  a single unit of data; it is synonymous with *element*

\* **data list**  a parenthesized list of expressions or repetitive specifications, separated by commas, used in a stream-oriented input or output specification that represents storage locations to which data items are to be assigned during input or values which are to be obtained for output

**data management**  a general term that collectively describes those functions of the control program that provide access to data sets, enforce data storage conventions, and regulate the use of input/output devices

\* **data set**  a collection of data external to the program that can be accessed by the program by reference to a single file name

\* **data specification**  the portion of a stream-oriented data transmission statement that specifies the mode of transmission (DATA, LIST, or EDIT) and includes the data list (or lists) and, for edit-directed mode, the format list (or lists)

\* **data stream**  data being transferred from or to a data set by stream-oriented transmission, as a continuous stream of data elements in character form

\* **data transmission**  the transfer of data from a data set to the program, or vice versa

**debug**  to detect, locate, and remove mistakes from a routine or malfunctions from a computer. Synonymous with troubleshoot.

**deblocking**  the action of making the first and each subsequent logical record of a block available for processing, one record at a time

\* **decimal digit character**  the picture specification character 9

**\*decimal picture data** arithmetic picture data specified by picture specifications containing the following types of picture specification characters: (1) decimal digit characters; (2) the virtual point picture character; (3) zero-suppression characters; (4) sign and currency symbol characters; (5) insertion characters; (6) commercial characters; (7) exponent characters

**decimal point alignment** *see* point alignment

**decision** the computer operation (directed by programming) of determining if a certain relationship exists between data items

**\*declaration** (1) the establishment of an identifier as a name and the construction of a set of attributes (partial or complete) for it; (2) a source of attributes of a particular name

**\*default** the alternative attribute or option assumed, or specified for assumption by the DEFAULT statement, when none has been specified

**\*defined item** a variable declared to represent part or all of the same storage as that assigned to another variable known as the base item

**\*delimiter** all operators, comments, and the following characters; percent, parentheses, comma, period, semicolon, colon, assignment symbol, and blank; they define the limits of identifiers, constants, picture specifications, and keywords

**descriptor** *see* parameter descriptor

**device independence** the ability to request input/output operations without regard to the characteristics of the input/output devices

**diagnostic routine** a programming routine designed to locate and explain errors in a computer routine or hardware components

**digit** one of the characters 0 through 9

**digital data** information expressed in discrete symbols

**\*dimensionality** the number of bounds specifications in an array declaration

**diode** an electronic device used to permit current flow in one direction and to inhibit current flow in the opposite direction

**direct access** *see* random access

**\*disabled** the state in which a particular on-condition will not result in an interrupt

**disk storage** a storage device that uses magnetic recording on flat rotating disks

**documentation** written descriptions, program listings, flowcharts, diagrams, charts, operator's guides, and sample test data, that explain the way in which a computer application is solved

**\*do-group** a sequence of statements headed by a DO statement and ended by its corresponding END statement, used for control purposes

**do-loop** *see* iterative do-group

**DOS/VS** *D*isk *O*perating *S*ystem/*V*irtual *S*torage

**downtime** the elapsed time when a computer is not operating correctly because of machine or program malfunction

**\*drifting characters** *see* sign and currency symbol characters

**drum storage** a method of storing information in code, magnetically, on the surface of a rotating cylinder

**\*dummy argument** temporary storage that is created automatically to hold the value of an argument that is (1) a constant, (2) an operational expression, (3) a variable whose attributes differ from those specified for the corresponding parameter in a known declaration, or (4) an argument enclosed in parentheses

**dump** to copy the contents of all or part of a storage device, usually from a central processing unit into an external storage device

**dynamic storage** storage that is allocated during the execution of an object program

**dynamic storage variable** *see* automatic variable

**EBCDIC** *E*xtended *B*inary *C*oded *D*ecimal *I*nterchange *C*ode, án 8-bit code used to represent a maximum of 256 unique letters, numbers, or special characters

**edit** to arrange information for machine input or output; may involve deleting unwanted
data (truncation), inserting decimal points for printed output, or supressing leading zeros
on printed or punched values

*** edit-directed transmission** the type of stream-oriented transmission in which data appears as a continuous stream of characters and for which a format list is required to specify
the editing desired for the associated data list

*** element** a single item of data as opposed to a collection of data items such as an array; a
scalar item

*** element expression** an expression whose evaluation yields an element value

*** element variable** a variable that represents an element; a scalar variable

*** enabled** that state in which a particular on-condition will result in a program interrupt

*** end-of-file mark** a code which signals that the last record of a file has been read

**end-of-tape marker** a marker on a magnetic tape used to indicate the end of the permissible recording area; for example, a photoreflective strip, a transparent section of tape, or a
particular bit pattern

*** entry name** an identifier that is explicitly or contextually declared to have the ENTRY
attribute or has an implied ENTRY attribute

*** entry point** a point in a procedure at which it may be invoked; *see* primary entry point and
secondary entry point

*** epilogue** those processes that occur automatically at the termination of a block

**evaluation** reduction of an expression to a single value (which may be an array or structure value)

**event** an activity in a program whose status and completion can be determined from an
associated event variable

**event variable** a variable with the EVENT attribute that may be associated with an event;
its value indicates whether the action has been completed and the status of the completion

**exceptional condition** an occurrence that can cause a program interrupt or an unexpected situation—such as an overflow error—or an occurrence of an expected situation
—such as an end-of-file—that occurs at an unpredictable time

**execute** to carry out an instruction or a program

*** explicit declaration** the appearance of an identifier in a DECLARE statement, as a label
prefix, or in a parameter list

**exponent** (1) a number placed at the right and just above a symbol in typography to
indicate the number of times that symbol is a factor; i.e., 10 to the fourth power ($10^4$)
equals $10 \times 10 \times 10 \times 10$ or 10,000; (2) in a floating-point constant, a decimal integer
constant specifying the power to which the base of the floating-point number is to be raised

*** expression** a notation, within a program, that represents a value; a constant or a reference appearing alone, or combinations of constants and/or variables with operators

*** extent** the range indicated by the bounds of an array dimension, the range indicated by
the length of a string, or the range indicated by the size of an area

**external declaration** an explicit or implicit declaration of the EXTERNAL attribute for
an identifier; such an identifier is known in all other procedures for which such a declaration exists

**external name** a name (with the EXTERNAL attribute) whose scope is not necessarily
confined only to one block and its contained blocks

**external procedure** a procedure that is not contained in any other procedure

**external storage** a storage device outside the computer that can store information in a
form acceptable to the computer

**factoring (of attributes)**   enclosing names (in a DECLARE statement) having the same attributes in parentheses; following the parenthesized list is the set of attributes that apply, in order to eliminate repeated specification of the same attributes for more than one name

**\*field (in the data stream)**   that portion of the data stream whose width, in number of characters, is defined by a single data or spacing format item

**\*field (of a picture specification)**   any character-string picture specification or that portion (or all) of a numeric character or numeric bit picture specification that describes a fixed-point number

**\*file**   a named representation, within a program, of a data set; a file is associated with a single data set for each opening

**\*file attribute**   any of the attributes that describe the characteristics of a file

**\*file constant**   a name declared for a file and for which a complete set of file attributes exists during the time that the file is open

**file declaration**   associating attributes with a file name in a program

**file maintenance**   the activity of keeping a file up to date by adding, changing, or deleting data

**\*file name**   a name declared for a file

**\*fixed-point constant**   *see* arithmetic constant

**flip-flop**   a circuit or device containing active elements capable of assuming either one of two stable states at a given time

**floating-point constant**   *see* arithmetic constant

**flowchart**   (1) system flowchart depicts flow of data from outside the computer to the computer; explains or illustrates various job steps; (2) program flowchart diagrams the sequence in which the computer is to carry out instructions

**flow of control**   sequence of execution of PL/I blocks

**\*format item**   a specification used in edit-directed transmission to describe the representation of a data item in the stream (data format item) or to specify positioning of a data item within the stream (control format item)

**\*format list**   a parenthesized list of format items required for an edit-directed data specification

**FORTRAN**   *FOR*mula *TRAN*slation; a data processing language that closely resembles algebraic notation

**\*fully qualified name**   a qualified name that includes all names in the hierarchical sequence above the structure member to which the name refers, as well as the name of the member itself

**\*function**   (1) a function procedure (programmer-specified or built-in); a procedure that is invoked by the appearance of one of its entry names in a function reference and returns a value to the point of reference; (2) the change that takes place from the time the module is entered until it completes its action

**\*function reference**   the appearance of an entry name or built-in function name (or an entry variable) in an expression

**generic key**   character-string that identifies a class of keys; all keys that begin with the string are members of that class; for example, the recorded keys 'ABCD', 'ABCE', and 'ABDF' are all members of the classes identified by the generic keys 'A' and 'AB', and the first two are also members of the class 'ABC'; the three recorded keys can be considered to be unique members of the classes 'ABCD', 'ABCE', and 'ABDF', respectively

**global variables**   data common to a number of modules often referred to as a data pool; the variables are typically resident in main memory at all times and made available to various modules referencing them; the modules may or may not be brought into memory as overlays

**\*group** a do-group; it can be used wherever a single statement can appear, except as an on-unit

**hard copy** a printed copy of machine output, e.g., printed reports, listings, documents, etc.

**hardware** the physical computer equipment, such as the card reader, console printer, and CPU; any data processing equipment

**heading** an alphameric message that precedes an output report

**hexadecimal** base-16 number system

**hexadecimal digits** 0, 1, 2, 3, 4, 5, 6, 7, 8, 9, A, B, C, D, E, F

**hierarchy chart** a structure of program functions to be performed consisting of modules and submodules such that every submodule may only call another module on the level immediately below its level and must return to the module that called it

**high-level language** a programming language that is not restricted by the computer on which it will be used; a language that is not machine-dependent and more closely resembles our own language, allowing the programmer to concentrate on how to solve a problem and not how to solve a problem within the framework of a specific computer; e.g., PL/I

**Hollerith card code** punch card code named after its developer, Herman Hollerith

**housekeeping** operations in a routine that do not contribute directly to the solution of a problem but do contribute directly to the execution of a program by the computer

**\*identifier** a string of alphameric and, possibly, break characters, not contained in a comment or constant and is preceded and followed by a delimiter; the initial character must be alphabetic

**imaginary number** a number whose factors include the square root of $-1$

**\*implicit declaration** the establishment of an identifier, which has no explicit or contextual declaration, as a name; a default set of attributes is assumed for the identifier

**\*implicit opening** the opening of a file as the result of an input or output statement other than the OPEN statement

**inactive block** a procedure or begin block that has not been activated or that has been terminated

**inclusive OR** a logical operation specified by the stroke symbol (|) in PL/I

**\*infix operator** an operator that appears between two operands

**initialize** to set program counters or program switches to a predetermined value, usually at the beginning of a program

**initial value** value assigned to a variable at the time storage is allocated to it

**\*input/output (I/O)** the transfer of data between an external medium and internal storage

**\*insertion picture character** a picture specification character that is, on assignment of the associated data to a character-string, inserted in the indicated position; When used in a P-format item for input, an insertion character serves as a checking picture character

**instruction** a statement that calls for a specific computer operation

**\*internal block** a block that is contained in another block

**\*internal name** a name that is not known outside the block in which it is declared

**\*internal procedure** a procedure that is contained within another block

**\*internal text** all of the text contained in a block except text that is contained in another block; thus, the text of an internal block (except its entry names) is *not* internal to the containing block

**\*interrupt**  the redirection of flow of control of the program (possibly temporary) as the result of the raising of an enabled on-condition or attention

**\*invocation**  the activation of a procedure

**\*invoke**  to activate a procedure at one of its entry points

**\*invoked procedure**  a procedure that has been activated at one of its entry points

**\*invoking block**  a block containing a statement that activates a procedure

**iterate**  to repeat, automatically, under program control, the same series of processing steps until a predetermined stop or branch condition is reached; to loop

**\*iteration factor**  an expression that specifies: (1) in an INITIAL attribute specification, the number of consecutive elements of an array that are to be initialized with a given constant; (2) in a format list, the number of times a given format item or list of items is to be used in succession (*also see* repetition factor)

**\*iterative do-group**  a do-group whose DO statement specifies a control variable and/or a WHILE option

**job**  a group of one or more tasks (subjobs) that are to be performed by the computer under the direction of the operating system

**K**  *see* kilo

**\*key**  data that identifies a record within a direct access data set; *see* recorded key and source key

**keyfield**  generally, a numeric or alphameric field within a record that makes that record unique from all other records in a given file; it is the identifying field by which a given record or records is located

**keypunch**  (1) (verb) to punch holes manually in cards or paper tape as contrasted with output from a computer program causing holes to be punched in cards or tape; (2) (noun) a key-driven device

**\*keyword**  an identifier that, when used in the proper context, has either a language-defined or an implementation-defined meaning in the program

**\*kilo (K)**  a prefix meaning one thousand; e.g., 16K means 16,000, although on a binary machine it also means the power of two that is closest to 16,000; e.g., 16,384

**\*label**  a name used to identify a statement other than a PROCEDURE or ENTRY statement; a statement label

**\*label constant**  an unsubscripted name that appears prefixed to any statement other than a PROCEDURE or ENTRY statement

**\*label prefix**  a label prefixed to a statement

**\*label variable**  a variable declared with the LABEL attribute and thus able to assume as its value a label constant

**\*language character set**  a character set which has been defined to represent program elements in the source language (in this context, character-string constants and comments are not considered as program elements)

**\*leading zeros**  zeros that have no significance in the value of an arithmetic integer; all zeros to the left of the first significant integer digit of a number

**\*level number**  an unsigned decimal integer constant in a DECLARE or ALLOCATE statement that specifies the position of a name in the hierarchy of a structure; it precedes the name to which it refers and is separated from that name only by one or more blanks

**\*level one variable**  a major structure name; any unsubscripted variable not contained within a structure

**library routine** a special-purpose program that may be maintained in storage for use when needed

**line printer** an output unit that is capable of printing an entire line at a time, as contrasted with a typewriter that prints a character at a time

**list-directed transmission** the type of stream-oriented transmission in which data in the stream appears as constants separated by blanks or commas and for which formatting is provided automatically

**list items** single variable names, array names, or structure names listed in a GET or PUT statement (also called *data list items*)

**list processing** a method of processing data in the form of lists. Usually, chained lists are used so that the logical order of items can be changed without altering their physical locations

**\*locator variable** a variable whose value identifies the location in internal storage of a variable or a buffer

**\*logical level (of a structure member)** the depth indicated by a level number when all level numbers are in direct sequence, that is, when the increment between successive level numbers is one

**\*logical operators** the bit-string operators ⌐ (not), & (and) | (or)

**logical record** (1) ANSI—a collection of items independent of their physical environment. Portions of the same logical records may be located in different physical records. \*(2) a record from the standpoint of its content and function, and use, rather than its physical attributes; that is, one that is defined in terms of the information it contains

**loop** the repeated execution of a series of instructions for a fixed number of times or a sequence of instructions that is repeated until a terminal condition exists

**\*lower bound** the lower limit of an array dimension

**machine instruction** an instruction that the particular computer can recognize and execute

**machine language** a language that is used directly by a given computer

**machine operator** the person who manually controls a computer

**macro instruction** a single instruction that causes the computer to execute a predetermined sequence of machine instructions

**magnetic core (main storage)** a configuration of tiny doughnut-shaped magnetic elements in which information can be stored for use at extremely high speed by the central processing unit

**magnetic disk** a flat circular plate with a magnetic surface on which data can be stored by selective magnetization

**magnetic drum** a circular cylinder with a magnetic surface on which data can be stored and retrieved

**merge** (1) to combine items from two or more similarly ordered sets into one set that is arranged in the same order; \*(2) a program or routine that performs this function

**microsecond (μsec)** a millionth of a second

**millisecond (ms)** a thousandth of a second

**\*minor structure** a structure that is contained within another structure; the name of a minor structure is declared with a level number greater than one

**\*mode (of arithmetic data)** a characteristic of arithmetic data: real or complex

**\*multiple declaration** two or more declarations of the same identifier internal to the same block without different qualifications, or two or more external declarations of the same identifier with different attributes in the same program

**multiprocessing**  (1) the parallel execution of two or more computer programs or sequences of instructions by a computer or computer network

* **multiprogramming**  the use of a computing system to execute more than one program concurrently, using a single processing unit

* **multitasking**  the concurrent execution of one main task and one or more subtasks in the same partition or region

* **name**  an identifier appearing in a context where it is not a keyword

* **nesting**  the occurrence of (1) a block within another block; (2) a group within another group; (3) an IF statement in a THEN clause or an ELSE clause; (4) a function reference as an argument of a function reference; (5) a remote format item in the format list of a FORMAT statement; (6) a parameter descriptor list in another parameter descriptor list; (7) an attribute specification within a parenthesized name list for which one or more attributes are being factored

**null statement**  represented by a semicolon; indicates that no action is to be taken

* **null string**  a string data item of zero length

**number system**  a system of counting; e.g., decimal (base-10) number system, hexadecimal (base-16) number system, or binary (base-2) number system

**numeric character data**  *see* decimal picture data

**object program**  the output from a compiler

* **on-condition**  an occurrence, within a PL/I task, that could cause a program interrupt; it may be the detection of an unexpected error or of an occurrence that is expected, but at an unpredictable time

* **on-unit**  the specified action to be executed upon detection of the on-condition named in the containing ON statement

* **opening (of a file)**  the association of a file with a data set and the completion of a full set of attributes for the file name

**operand**  an expression to whose value an operator is applied

**operating system**  an organized collection of techniques and procedures combined into programs that direct a computer's operations

**operation expression**  an expression containing one or more operators

**operator**  a symbol specifying an operation to be performed; *see* arithmetic operators, bit-string operators, comparison operators, and concatenation

**optimist**  a programmer who codes in ink

**option**  a specification in a statement that may be used to influence the execution or interpretation of the statement

**OR**  *see* inclusive OR

**output**  (1) (verb) to print, punch, or display data from a computer program or to write data onto tape or DASD; (2) (noun) results from a computer program

**overflow**  in PL/I, occurs when the characteristic in a floating-point value exceeds (as a result of algebraic computation) $10^{+75}$

**packed decimal**  internal representation of a fixed-point decimal data item

**padding**  one or more characters or bits concatenated to the right of a string to extend the string to a required length; for character-strings, padding is with blanks; for bit-strings, with zeros

**\*parameter** a name in a procedure that is used to refer to an argument passed to that procedure

**parameter descriptor** the set of attributes specified for a single parameter in an ENTRY attribute specification

**\*parameter descriptor list** the list of all parameter descriptors in an ENTRY attribute specification

**\*partially qualified name** a qualified name that is incomplete, i.e., that includes one or more, but not all, names in the hierarchical sequence above the structure member to which the partially qualified name refers, as well as the name of the member itself

**\*physical record** a record from the standpoint of the manner or form in which it is stored, retrieved, and moved; that is, one that is defined in terms of physical qualities. A physical record may contain all or part of one or more logical records

**picture specification** a character-by-character description of the composition and characteristics of binary picture data, decimal picture data, and character-string picture data

**\*picture specification character** any of the characters that can be used in a picture specification; character-string picture data and decimal picture data

**\*point alignment** alignment of arithmetic data in a variable depending upon the location of the decimal point as specified by the precision attributes

**\*pointer variable** a locator variable with the POINTER attribute, whose value identifies an absolute location in internal storage

**point of invocation** the point in the invoking block at which the procedure reference to the invoked procedure appears

**\*precision** the value range of an arithmetic variable expressed as a total number of digits and, for fixed-point variables, the number of those digits assumed to appear to the right of the decimal or binary point

**predicate** *(p)* any logical expression that may be used for a test

**prefix** a label or a parenthesized list of one or more condition names connected by a colon to the beginning of a statement

**\*prefix operator** an operator that precedes an operand and applies only to that operand; the prefix operators are + (plus), − (minus), and ⌐ (not)

**preprocessed text** the output from the first stage of compile-time activity; this output is a sequence of characters that is altered source program text and serves as input to the processor stage in which the actual compilation is performed

**\*preprocessor** a program that examines the source program for preprocessor statements which are then executed, resulting in the alteration of the source program

**\*preprocessor statement** a special statement appearing in the source program that specifies how the source program text is to be altered; identified by a leading percent sign and executed as it is encountered by the preprocessor (appears without the percent sign in preprocessor procedures, which are invoked by a preprocessor function reference)

**\*primary entry point** the entry point identified by any of the names in the label list of the PROCEDURE statement

**\*problem data** string or arithmetic data that is processed by a PL/I program

**\*procedure** a collection of statements, headed by a PROCEDURE statement and ended by an END statement, that is a part of a program, that delimits the scope of names, and that is activated by a reference to one of its entry names

**\*procedure reference** an entry constant or variable or a built-in function name followed by none or more argument lists; it may appear in a CALL statement or CALL option or as a function reference

**\*processor** a program that prepares source program text (possibly preprocessed text) for execution

**\*program**  a set of one or more external procedures

**\*program control data**  data used in a PL/I program to affect the execution of the program; that is, any data that is not string or arithmetic data

**programming**  the art of reducing the plan for the solution of a problem to machine-sensible instructions

**program switch**  a technique that allows the program to make a choice based on some occurrence or test made at a previous point in the program

**\*prologue**  the processes that occur automatically on block activation

**pseudocode**  a statement of the problem to be solved, gradually refined to specify more precisely the steps the computer must take in solving the problem

**\*pseudovariable**  any of the built-in function names that can be used to specify a target variable

**punched card**  (1) a card punched with a pattern of holes to represent data; (2) a card as in (1), before being punched (slang)


**\*qualified name**  a hierarchical sequence of names of structure members, connected by periods, used to identify a component of a structure; any of the names may be subscripted

**quote mark**  *see* single quote mark


**random access**  a technique for storing and retrieving data that does not require a strict sequential storage of the data nor a sequential search of the data nor a sequential search of an entire file to find a specific record; a record can be addressed and accessed directly at its location in the file

**\*range (of a default specification)**  a set of identifiers, constants, and/or parameter descriptors to which the attributes in a default specification of a DEFAULT statement apply

**read**  (1) to transcribe information from an input device to internal storage; (2) to acquire data from a source

**receiving field**  any field to which a value may be assigned

**record**  (1) a group of related facts or fields of information treated as a unit; contains information to describe an item; (2) the unit of transmission in a record I/O operation in the internal form of a level-one variable

**\*recorded key**  a key recorded in a direct-access volume to identify an associated data record

**record I/O**  the transmission of collections of data, called records, one record at a time; the external representation of the data is an exact copy of the internal representation, and vice versa; there is no arithmetic or character conversion in record I/O

**\*recursion**  the reactivation of an active procedure

**recursive code**  program code that calls itself, making use of the results of the previous call to its own code

**reentrant code**  program code that is written so that it can be executed concurrently by two or more procedures.  For example, task B calls function X.  While X is in progress its execution is suspended temporarily so that task A (a higher priority program than B) may use function X.  After X returns results to A, X continues where it left off in computing results for B.

**\*reference**  the appearance of a name, except in a context that causes explicit declaration

**register**  a high-speed device used in a central processing unit for temporary storage of small amounts of data or intermittent results during processing

**\*remote format item**  the letter R specified in a format list together with the label of a separate FORMAT statement

**\*repetition factor**  a parenthesized unsigned decimal integer constant that specifies: (1) the number of occurrences of a string configuration that make up a string constant; (2) the number of occurrences of a picture specification character in a picture specification

**repetition structure**  a form in a structured program that allows for the repetitive execution of an operation

**\*repetitive specification**  an element of a data list (of GET or PUT statements) that specifies controlled iteration to transmit one or more data items, generally used in conjunction with arrays

**\*returned value**  the value returned by a function procedure to the point of invocation

**round**  (1) to adjust the least significant digits retained in truncation to partially reflect the dropped portion; (2) a built-in function in PL/I

**run**  (1) (noun) a single, continuous performance of a computer or device; (2) (verb) to execute an object program

**\*scalar item**  a single item of data; an element

**\*scalar variable**  a variable that can represent only a single data item, an element variable

**\*scale**  a system of mathematical notation; fixed-point or floating-point

**\*scale factor**  a specification of the number of fractional digits in a fixed-point number

**\*scope (of a condition prefix)**  the portion of a program throughout which a particular condition prefix applies

**\*scope (of a declaration)**  the portion of a program throughout which a particular declaration is a source of attributes for a particular name

**\*scope (of a name)**  the portion of a program throughout which the meaning of a particular name does not change

**\*secondary entry point**  an entry point identified by any of the names in the label list of an ENTRY statement

**\*separator**  *see* delimiter

**sequence structure**  a form in a structured program that indicates control is to flow from one operation to the next

**\*sign and currency symbol characters**  the picture specification characters S, +, −, and $; these can be used (1) as static characters, in which case they are specified only once in a picture specification and appear in the associated data item in the position in which they have been specified; (2) as drifting characters, in which case they are specified more than once (as a string in a picture specification) but appear in the associated data item at most once, immediately to the left of the significant portion of the data item

**single quote mark**  alternative term for apostrophe; surrounds string data

**simulate**  to represent the functioning of a system or process by a symbolic (usually mathematical) analogous representation of it

**software**  a program or set of programs written for a computer

**sort**  to arrange data fields or records in either ascending or descending sequence

**source document**  contains original data; e.g., an employee's time card

**source key**  a character-string referred to in a record transmission statement that identifies a particular record within a direct access data set; the source key may or may not also contain, as its first part, a substring to be compared with, or written as, a recorded key to positively identify the record (*note:* the source key can be identical to the recorded key)

**source language**  a language nearest to the user's usual business or professional language, enabling the user to instruct a computer more easily; FORTRAN, COBOL, ALGOL, BASIC, PL/I are a few examples

**source program**  the program that serves as input to the compiler; the source program may contain preprocessor statements

**space** (1) a blank on a printed line; (2) "line spacing" on a printer — the advancement of the paper in a printer moving up one horizontal line

**stacker** on a card reader or punch, the place into which cards that have been processed are fed

\* **standard file** a file assumed by the processor in the absence of a FILE or STRING option in a GET or PUT statement; SYSIN in the standard input file and SYSPRINT is the standard output file

\* **standard system action** action specified by the language to be taken in the absence of an on-unit for an on-condition

\* **statement** a basic element of a PL/I program that is used to delimit a portion of the program, to describe names used in the program, or to specify action to be taken; a statement can consist of a condition list, a label list, a statement identifier, and a statement body that is terminated by a semicolon

\* **statement body** that part of a statement that follows the statement identifier, if any, and is terminated by the semicolon; it includes the statement options

\* **statement identifier** the PL/I keyword that indicates the purpose of the statement

**statement-label constant** *see* label constant

**statement-label variable** *see* label variable

\* **static storage allocation** the allocation of storage for static variables

\* **static variable** a variable that is allocated before execution of the program begins and that remains allocated for the duration of execution of the program

**storage allocation** association of a storage area with a variable

**stream** data being transferred from or to an external medium represented as a continuous string of data items in character form

**stream-oriented I/O** transmission of data items as a continuous stream of characters that are, on input, automatically converted to conform to the attribute of the variables to which they are assigned and, on output, are automatically converted to character representation

\* **string** a connected sequence of characters or bits that is treated as a single data item

**string operator** the string operator is ‖, denoting concatenation of character-strings or bit-strings

\* **string variable** a variable declared with the BIT or CHARACTER attribute, whose values can be either bit-strings or character-strings

**structure** (1) a form in which logic may be expressed in a structured program; (2) a hierarchical set of names that refers to an aggregate or data items that may have different attributes

\* **structure of arrays** a structure containing arrays specified by declaring individual members' names with the dimension attribute

**structured programming** writing a program in a standardized prescribed manner in order to facilitate testing, documentation, and modification of that program

\* **structure expression** an expression whose evaluation yields a structure value

\* **structure member** any of the minor structures or elementary names in a structure

\* **structuring** the makeup of a structure, in terms of the number of members, the order in which they appear, their attributes, and their logical level (but not necessarily their names or declared level numbers)

\* **subfield (of a picture specification)** that portion of a picture specification field that appears before or after a V picture specification character

\* **subroutine** a procedure that is invoked by a CALL statement or CALL option; a subroutine cannot return a value to the invoking block, but it can alter the value of variables

\* **subscript** an element expression that specifies a position within a dimension of an array; a subscript can also be an asterisk, in which case it specifies the entire extent of the dimension

**substructure**  structure declared one or more levels below the major structure level

**\*synchronous**  using a single flow of control for serial execution of a program

**syntax**  the rules governing sentence structure in a language or statement structure in a programming language

**table**  a collection of data in a form suitable for ready reference; it is frequently stored in contiguous machine locations or written in the form of an array of n dimensions

**\*target variable**  a variable to which a value is assigned

**\*task**  (1) the execution of one or more procedures by a single flow of control; (2) a unit of work for the central processing unit

**\*termination (of a block)**  cessation of execution of a block, and the return of control to the activating block by means of a RETURN or END statement, or the transfer of control to the activating block or to some other active block by means of a GO TO statement

**\*termination (of a task)**  cessation of the flow of control for a task

**time-share**  to interleave the use of a computer to serve many problem-solvers during the same time span

**top-down design**  the development of program modules by the repeated process of extracting subfunctions from the overall function to be performed

**truncation**  the removal of one or more digits, characters, or bits from one end of an item of data when a string length or precision of a target variable has been exceeded (e.g., the reduction of precision by dropping one or several of the least significant digits in contrast to round-off—the value 3.14159265 truncated to five digits is 3.1415, whereas one may round off to five digits giving the value 3.1416)

**two's complement**  the way in which negative fixed-point numbers are represented in binary; to find the two's complement of a positive binary value, change all the ones to zeros and all the zeros to ones, and add one

**underflow**  occurs in floating-point arithmetic operations when the algebraic result would cause the exponent to be less than $10^{-78}$

**unformatted**  no editing of data before an I/O operation is to take place

**update**  to modify a file record with current information according to a specified procedure

**\*upper bound**  the upper limit of an array dimension

**V**  *see* virtual point picture character

**\*variable**  a named entity that is used to refer to data and to which values can be assigned; its attributes remain constant, but it can refer to different values at different times; variables fall into three categories, applicable to any data type: element, array, and structure; variables may be subscripted and/or qualified or pointer qualified

**variable-length record**  a file in which the records are of varying lengths

**\*variable name**  an alphameric name selected by the programmer to represent data; an identifier

**\*virtual point picture character**  the picture specification character V, which is used in picture specifications to indicate the position of an assumed decimal or binary point

**volume**  a standard unit of auxiliary storage, a reel of magnetic tape, a disk, or a drum

**word**  a set of characters with one addressable location and treated as one unit

**\*zero-suppression characters**  the picture specification characters Z, Y, and *, which are used to suppress zeros in the corresponding digit positions

# Index of Programs

## CHAPTER 1

Compute average grade, 6
Compute average grade using CHECK, 8
Compute area of a triangle, 27

## CHAPTER 2

Create master inventory files, 61–62
Stock reorder report, 68

## CHAPTER 3

Inventory audit report, 98
Change pessimist to optimist, 120
Backlog report, 125
Prime number generation, 133

## CHAPTER 4

Center character string on line (subroutine), 145
Prorate first month's rent (subroutine), 148
Convert Gregorian date to Julian (subroutine), 157
Translate military time (subroutine), 163
Loan amortization schedule, 172–173, 174–175, 176

## CHAPTER 5

Sort three values, 188
Translate military time using case structure (subroutine), 193
Debugging example, 214
Validate program, 219–220, 221

## CHAPTER 6

Switch first and last name, 236
Compute the sum of odd-numbered elements in array (subroutine), 245
Compute temperature averages, 252–253
Tag sorting, 263
Binary search for insurance premium, 270

## CHAPTER 7

Create name and address file at terminal, 285–286
Sales history bar chart, 320–321

## CHAPTER 8

List file data using linecount, 330
Record I/O and carriage control, 338
Manipulate arrays in structure, 363
Create book status report, 378–379

## CHAPTER 9

Simulate overlay defining using based variables, 396
Locate mode I/O, 404
Create linear list, 420
Binary tree, 425, 427

## CHAPTER 10

Create ISAM file, 483–484, 485–486
Update ISAM file, 489–490, 491–492

# Index of Special Symbols

$\rightarrow$ Locator qualifier, 417
+ Picture character, 340, 344–345, 350
− Picture character, 340, 344–345, 350
$ Picture character, 349–350
* Picture character, 350–351
*PROCESS statement, 264, 375
/*, 3, 377
%PAGE, 69
%SKIP, 69
%INCLUDE, 216
9 picture character, 340–342, 344–345, 351–353
11-punch, 591
12-punch, 591
48-character set, 11–12, 13
60-character set, 10–12, 13
80/80 list program, record I/O, 327–328

# Index of Subjects

A, format item, 289–290, 292–294, 296–297, 299–303
A, picture character, 351–353
Abbreviations of keywords, 540–583
ABS built-in function, 107, 540
Access techniques, 442
ACOS built-in function, 110, 540
Activation of blocks, 388–391
ADDBUFF option, 540
ADD built-in function, 540
Adding records to file, 443–444, 446–447
Addition, 99
ADDR built-in function, 394–395, 540
Addressing techniques for REGIONAL files, 454–456
After print carriage control operation, 329, 468
Aggregate, *see* Data aggregate
Aggregate length table, 264, 374–375
Aggregate option, 264, 375
Alignment of data, in storage, 592
  on data-directed output, 305–306
  on list-directed output, 24–25, 131, 253–254
  processing data in buffers, 394–395
Alignment of decimal point, in edit I/O, 289, 306
  precision, 81, 82
  V picture character, 340–342, 344, 346–348
ALL built-in function, 245, 524–525, 540
ALL option of PUT, 541
  in PL/C, 529
ALLOCATE statement, 393, 405, 406–407, 416–417, 418, 426, 541
  with BASED storage, 416–417
  with CONTROLLED storage, 406–407

Allocation:
  automatic, 387–390, 391–393
  static, 391–393
ALLOCATION built-in function, 407–408, 541
Alphameric data, 10, 13
AND operation, 11, 12, 13, 194
  in assignment statement, 154, 195–196
  on bit-strings, 195
  in IF statement, 194–195
ANSI, 7, 329
ANS PL/I, 539
ANY built-in function, 245, 524, 541
Apostrophe in character constant, 18
Arctangent built-in function, 110, 342
Arguments, data types allowed, 143–146, 176–177
  in built-in function, 106–108
  definition, 105, 112–113, 142, 143–145
  dummy, 148–155, 177
  examples of, 105, 106, 143–155
  list, 142
  number of, 176–177
  passing of, 143–145, 176–177
  table, 267
Arithmetic:
  conversion, G, 121–123
  data, *see* Attributes
  hierarchy of operations, 99–102, 104
  operations on picture data, 340–341, 345
    and rules, 99–102
  operators, G, 99
Arithmetic built-in functions, 106–109
  ABS, 107, 540
  CEIL, 107, 545
  FLOOR, 107, 555
  MAX, 107, 561
  MIN, 107, 561

Arithmetic built-in functions (*Continued*)
MOD, 108–109, 561
ROUND, 106–108, 573
SIGN, 107, 574
SUM, 245, 252, 521–522, 577
TRUNC, 107, 580
Arithmetic coded data, 80–86, 92–95
in I/O, 373–374
Arithmetic conditions:
CONVERSION, 202, 205, 213, 216, 225,
226, 353, 374, 548
FIXEDOVERFLOW, 203, 204, 205, 206,
554
OVERFLOW, 203, 205, 567
SIZE, 203–204, 205, 366, 574
UNDERFLOW, 203, 205, 580
ZERODIVIDE, 203, 205, 583
Arithmetic data:
base, 80–81, 85–86
binary, 20, 93–95
complex, 84–85, 304
constants, *see* Constants
decimal, 79, 82, 92–93, 94
fixed-point, 85–86, 92–94, 592
floating-point, 94–95, 593–596
in I/O, 339–340, 373–374
mode, 84–85
precision, 81–83
real, 84
S/360 and S/370 data formats, 585–596
scale, 80–81
Arithmetic functions to override conversion
rules:
BINARY, 543
DECIMAL, 550
DIVIDE, 551
FIXED, 554
FLOAT, 555
MULTIPLY, 561
PRECISION, 568
Arithmetic operations, 99, 345
Array:
allocation, 405–407, 409
arguments, 245–246
assignments, 255–256
bounds, 237–238
built-in functions, 244–245, 519–525
cross section of, 258–259
declaration of, 237–238
defined, 237
dimensions, 239–242
expressions, 256–259, 519
in record I/O, 332
in stream I/O, 246–247, 294–295, 311

structures, 361–362
subscripts, 241–244, 311, 362
Array manipulation built-in functions:
ALL, 245, 524–525, 540
ANY, 245, 524, 541
DIM, 244, 519–520, 551
HBOUND, 245, 246, 270, 271, 520–521,
557
LBOUND, 244, 246, 520, 521, 559
POLY, 245, 523, 568
PROD, 245, 522–523, 569
SUM, 245, 252, 521–522, 577
ASCII, 541, 587, 589
ASIN built-in function, 110, 542
Assignment:
array, 255–256
defined, 97
multiple, 99
pointer, 395–396
statement, 5, 97–102
string, 90–91
structure, 364–368
symbol, 5, 97
Assignment statement:
arithmetic operation and rules, 5, 29, 97–
102
bit-string operations, 90–91, 185
comparison operations, 195–196
in data-directed I/O, 309–310
symbol, 5, 97
Asterisks:
as array dimensions, 407
as parameter list, 145–146
in attribute and cross-reference table, 126–
127
as picture character, 350–351
in printed output, 306, 316–317
as symbolic representation of null, 410,
414–415
sales history bar chart, 316–321
as subscripts, 258
ATAN built-in function, 110, 542
ATAND built-in function, 110, 542
ATANH built-in function, 110, 542
Attribute and cross reference table, 126–129
Attribute list, in ENTRY, 151–153
Attributes:
of arguments, 143–146, 152–155
of arithmetic data, 80–86, 92–94
base, 80, 85–86
of bit-string data, 86–88
of character-string data, 86–88
defaults, 81, 85–86, 280, 340
definition, 80–81

dimension, 239–242, 407
factoring of, 136
in OPEN statement, 381–382, 469–470
length, 86–88, 146, 351
mode, 84–85
of picture data, 340–341, 351–352
precision, 81–83, 85–86
scale, 80–81, 85–86
storage classes, 387
in structures, 236–237, 359
Attributes (keywords):
ALIGNED, 540
AREA, 541
AUTOMATIC, 387–391, 392–393, 543
BACKWARDS, 464, 467, 496, 543
BASED, 393–395, 403, 416–417, 543
BINARY, 81–83, 93–95, 543
BIT, 86–88, 95–96, 543
BUFFERED, 398, 400, 463–464, 470, 544
BUILTIN, 104–106, 111, 120, 544
CHARACTER, 87–88, 96, 545
COMPLEX, 84–85, 547
CONDITION, 547
CONNECTED, 547
CONTROLLED, 405–408, 548
DECIMAL, 81–82, 92–93, 94, 550
DEFINED, 88–89, 550
DIRECT, 464, 551
ENTRY, 128, 151–152, 159–160, 168, 552
ENVIRONMENT, 277, 329, 456, 457, 465–
    466, 496, 552
EVENT, 553
EXCLUSIVE, 553
EXTERNAL, 128, 168, 392, 462, 553
FILE, 276–277, 280, 461–462, 554
FIXED, 80–81, 92–94, 554
FLOAT, 81–83, 85–86, 94–95, 555
GENERIC, 556
INITIAL, 89, 90–91, 146, 359, 558
INPUT, 276–277, 282, 462, 470, 558
INTERNAL, 462, 558
IRREDUCIBLE, 559
KEYED, 464, 470
LABEL, 559
LIKE, 364, 560
OFFSET, 565
OUTPUT, 276–277, 282, 462, 470, 567
PICTURE, 339–340, 568
POINTER, 393–394, 395–396, 403, 568
POSITION, 90, 568
PRINT, 277, 278–279, 282, 308, 309, 568
REAL, 84, 570
RECORD, 276, 278, 282, 462, 470, 570
RECURSIVE, 161, 431, 570

REDUCIBLE, 571
RETURNS, 159–160, 162, 572
SEQUENTIAL, 398, 464, 574
STATIC, 391–393, 576
STREAM, 276–277, 278, 282, 312, 462,
    470, 576
TASK, 578
TRANSIENT, 579
UNALIGNED, 580
UNBUFFERED, 463, 470, 495, 580
UPDATE, 276, 462, 470, 581
VARIABLE, 581
VARYING, 87–88, 146, 397, 581
AUTOMATIC attribute, 389–391, 543
Automatic storage allocation, 387–391


B, format item, 304, 307, 543
B, picture character, 349, 352
BACKWARDS attribute, 464, 467, 496, 543
Base attribute, 80–81
BASED attribute, 393–395, 403, 416–417,
    543
Base identifier:
    scalar variables, 89–90
    structures, 359
Before print carriage control operation, 329–
    330, 468, 496
BEGIN block, G:
    as on-unit, 199, 310, 313, 543
    storage allocation, 390
Bidirectional list, 411–412, 423
BINARY:
    attribute, 81, 83, 93–95
    built-in function, 543
Binary constants, 16, 20
Binary data, as output, 586
    fixed-point, 20, 79, 81, 83, 85
    floating-point, 20, 95
    machine language, 7
BINARY FIXED, 79, 81, 83, 85, 93–94, 307,
    315
BINARY FLOAT, 85, 94–95, 307
Binary number system, 592–593
Binary point alignment, 81–83
Binary search technique, 265–271, 409
Binary tree, 412–416, 424–431
BIT attribute, 86–88, 95–96
    built-in function, 114, 543
Bit data format, 79, 86–88, 95, 96, 185, 585
    in edit I/O, 304
    maximum length, 95
Bit-string:
    array, 245

Bit-string (*Continued*)
   built-in functions, *see* String-handling built-in functions
   constant, 17, 19–20
   data, 85–91, 95–96, 185
   defined, 19
   format item, 304, 307
   quote marks in I/O, 23–24
   in structures, 359
Bit switches, 168, 185
BL, 438–440
Blank:
   in edit-directed input, 314–315
   edit I/O repetition factor, 294–295, 301–303
   in list-directed input data, 21–22
   picture character, 349, 352
   in PL/I statements, 12–13
   separating attributes, 81
BLKSIZE (ENV option), 277, 282, 466, 544
Block, activation of, 389–391
   BEGIN, 191, 198–199, 310, 390
   deactivating, 389–391
   external, 166
   internal, 165, 387
   nested, 164–166, 387
   PROCEDURE, 4, 6, 8–9, 569
   of records, 436–437
Blocked records:
   in CONSECUTIVE file, 435–437, 438–440
   in INDEXED file, 449
   processing in buffers, 398–404
Blocking, 436–437
Block length, 277–278, 280, 438–439
   in V-type records, 438–440
BOOL built-in function, 544
Boolean operations:
   ALL function, 540
   ANY function, 541
   BOOL function, 544
Boundary alignment, 395, 592
Bounds, of array, 237–239, 244–245, 256–257
Break character, 11–13
Bubble sort, 259–260
Buffer:
   defined, 437, 463
   determining size, 437
   hidden, 463
   processing in, 398
BUFFERED attribute, 398, 463–464, 470, 544

BUFFERS option, 466, 544
BUILTIN attribute, 104–106, 213, 222, 410–411, 544
Built-in function:
   in argument lists, 148–149
   arithmetic, 106–108
   array manipulation, 244–245, 519–522
   debugging aids, 209–211, 213–214
   defined, 104–105
   mathematical, 109, 110
   string handling, 111–119
Built-in function arguments, 148–149
Built-in function names:
   ABS, 107, 540
   ACOS, 110, 540
   ADD, 540
   ADDR, 393, 395, 540
   ALL, 245, 524–525, 540
   ALLOCATION, 407–408, 541
   ANY, 245, 524, 541
   ASIN, 110, 542
   ATAN, 110, 542
   ATAND, 110, 542
   ATANH, 110, 542
   BINARY, 543
   BIT, 114, 543
   BOOL, 544
   CEIL, 107, 545
   CHAR, 114, 545
   COMPILETIME, 546
   COMPLETION, 547
   COMPLEX, 547
   CONJG, 547
   COS, 110, 548
   COSD, 110, 548
   COSH, 110, 548
   COUNT, 251, 252, 312, 548
   COUNTER, 548
   DATAFIELD, 549
   DATE, 109–111, 149, 156–157, 165, 549
   DECIMAL, 550
   DIM, 244, 519–520, 551
   DIVIDE, 551
   EMPTY, 551
   ERF, 110, 552
   ERFC, 110, 552
   EXP, 110, 553
   FIXED, 554
   FLOAT, 176, 555
   FLOOR, 107, 555
   HBOUND, 245, 270, 271, 520, 557
   HIGH, 557

IMAG, 557
INDEX, 114, 558
LBOUND, 244, 520, 559
LENGTH, 114, 145–146, 560
LINENO, 279, 560
LOG, 110, 561
LOG2, 110, 561
LOG10, 110, 561
LOW, 561
MAX, 107, 561
MIN, 107, 561
MOD, 108–109, 561
MULTIPLY, 561
NULL, 410–411, 419–422, 564
OFFSET, 565
ONCHAR, 210–211, 220, 226, 565
ONCODE, 210, 213–214, 224, 565
ONCOUNT, 565
ONFILE, 474, 565
ONKEY, 474, 565
ONLOC, 213–214, 225, 566
ONSOURCE, 210–211, 213–214, 220, 225, 566
POINTER, 568
POLY, 245, 523, 568
PRECISION, 568
PRIORITY, 569
PROD, 245, 522–523, 569
REAL, 570
REPEAT, 114, 571
ROUND, 106–108, 573
SAMEKEY, 573
SIGN, 107, 574
SIN, 110, 574
SIND, 110, 574
SINH, 110, 574
SQRT, 105, 110, 575
STATUS, 576
STRING, 339, 576
SUBSTR, 111–114, 211–212, 296–297, 300, 577
SUM, 245, 395, 521–522, 577
TAN, 110, 578
TAND, 110, 578
TANH, 110, 578
TIME, 109–111, 163, 193, 579
TRANSLATE, 116–117, 579
TRUNC, 107, 580
UNSPEC, 580
VERIFY, 120, 221, 222, 581
BY NAME option, 366–367
Byte, 585
BY and TO, 229–235

C, format item, 304
CALL:
    option of INITIAL attribute, 545
    statement, 142–145, 148–153, 155–156, 160, 190, 389
Capacity record, 459
Carriage control:
    character, 328–330, 337
    record, 228–330
    stream, see LINE; PAGE; SKIP
Carriage tape, 329
CASE structure, 187–191
CEIL built-in function, 107, 545
CHARACTER attribute, 23, 87–88, 96
Characteristic, 595–596
Character set:
    48-character set, 11–13, 104
    60-character set, 10–13, 104
    defined, 10–13, 587
    EBCDIC, 587
    PROCESS statement, 264, 375
Character string:
    constants, 5–6, 16–19
    conversion of, 121–123, 299
    format item, 289–290, 291–292, 298–299, 306
    pictures, 351–356
    quotation marks in I/O, 23–24
Character-string built-in functions:
    CHAR, 114, 533–534, 545
    INDEX, 114, 558
    LENGTH, 114, 145–146, 560
    REPEAT, 114, 571
    STRING, 339, 576
    SUBSTR, 111–114, 211–212, 296–297, 300, 577
    VERIFY, 120, 121, 122
Character-string format item, see A, format item
Character-string pictures, 351–353
CHAR48/CHAR60, 13–14
CHAR built-in function, 114, 533–534, 545
CHECK condition prefix, 8–9, 430–431, 546
Check protection feature, 350–351
Choice structure, 41–43
Circular list, 411
CLOSE statement, 284
Coded arithmetic data, 80–86
Coding, program, 3–4
Coding form (PL/I), 15–16
Collating sequence charts, 588
Collector symbol, 40
Column, in array, 240

COLUMN format item, 289, 292–295, 301–303, 308, 546

Comma:
  in edit I/O data list, 303
  in ENTRY attribute, 152, 552
  picture character, 348, 352, 354–355
  separating variables in DCL, 136
  in stream input data, 21
  in stream I/O data list, 4

Comments:
  defined, 3
  use of, 3, 377

Commercial programming techniques:
  alternate indexing, 481–483
  binary search, 265–271
  binary tree, 412–416, 424–430
  bubble sort, 259–260
  convert date to Julian day, 156–157
  convert 24-hour time, 162–164, 193
  date validation, 216–222
  file create and update, 479–492
  inventory control, 68, 69–71
  loan amortization schedule, 169–176
  merging of records from two files, 487–492
  modular programming, 35–38, 141, 167–169
  printing CR or DB for + or − amounts, 351
  program switches, 48–50, 185
  randomizing technique for direct files, 455–456
  round-off of floating-point data, 522
  sales commission, 241–242
  sales history bar charts, 316–321
  sequence checking, 216–222
  sorting an array, 259–263
  switching first and last names, 236–237
  tag sort, 259–263
  writing headings:
    using edit output, 300–303
    using list output, 24–25
    using record output, 375, 378–379, 382
  80/80 list, 327–328, 329–331

Common data areas, 167–168

Comparison key, 456–458

Comparison operators:
  in assignment statement, 195–196
  defined, 179
  in IF statement, 179, 180
  symbols, 11

Compilation, 6–7, 141–142

Compiler, 7–8

Compiler diagnostics, 8, 15, 129

COMPLEX attribute, 84–85, 547

Complex data format item, 304

Composite operators, 11, 417

Compound IF, 180–185, 194

Compute mean, 2–6, 8–10

Concatenation:
  defined, 102
  example, 102–103, 112, 330
  REPEAT built-in function, 114, 571
  STRING built-in function, 339, 576

Condition:
  disabling, 204–205
  enabling, 204–205
  names, 197, 199, 203
  nullification of, 201–202, 316
  prefix, 205
  stream file, 313

Conditions:
  CHECK, 8–9, 430–431, 546
  CONVERSION, 199, 202, 208, 213–214, 219–220, 225–226, 284, 304, 314–315, 353, 354, 474, 548
  ENDFILE, 58–59, 197–200, 206, 280, 313–314, 552
  ENDPAGE, 199–201, 308, 313–314, 552
  ERROR, 208, 209, 210, 214–216, 224
  FIXEDOVERFLOW, 202–203, 205, 208, 554
  in iterative DO, 232
  KEY, 471–472, 559
  NAME, 310, 561
  OVERFLOW:
    defined, 203, 208, 567
    in iterative DO, 232
  RECORD, 313, 314, 473, 570
  SIZE, 203–204, 306, 313, 315, 574
  STRINGRANGE, 211–212, 576
  STRINGSIZE, 212–213, 577
  SUBSCRIPTRANGE, 264–265, 272, 577
  TRANSMIT, 313, 314, 579
  UNDEFINEDFILE, 473, 580
  UNDERFLOW, 202, 203, 580
  ZERODIVIDE, 202, 203, 583

CONSECUTIVE (ENV option), 465, 467, 547

Consecutive file organization, 433–444, 446, 449, 459, 462

Constants:
  bit-string, 16, 19–20, 28, 95–96
  character-string, 5, 16, 17, 18–19, 96
  complex, 84–85
  in data-directed output, 312
  in data list, 297
  defined, 5, 96
  fixed-point binary, 16, 20
  fixed-point decimal, 16, 17

floating-point binary, 16, 20
floating-point decimal, 16, 17–18
statement-label, 4
Contextual declaration, 166, 395, 403
Control format item, 290–291, 308–309
CONTROLLED attribute, 405–507, 548
Control option:
  in edit I/O, 308
  in list I/O, 25
  priority of, 25–26
Control variable, in iterative DO, 229–232,
    235
Conversion:
  of arguments, 143, 151–152
  to arithmetic data in subset language, 532
  of data, 121–123, 332–333, 524
  decimal/hexadecimal conversion, 586–587
  of external data, 307
  of picture data, 353, 354
  rules, 121–123
  of unlike data types, 121–123, 202
CONVERSION condition, 202, 204–205,
    213–216, 218, 284, 304, 314–315, 474
COPY option of GET, 23
Cornell compiler, 7, 527
COS built-in function, 110, 548
COSD built-in function, 110, 548
COSH built-in function, 110, 548
COUNT built-in function, 251–253, 312,
    548
Counter, in programming, 328–329, 548
Creating data sets:
  consecutive, 443–444
  example, 476–486
  indexed, 444–451
  master file, 61–62
  regional, 449–459
Credit (CR) picture character, 340, 351
Cross-reference table, 126–128
Cross section of arrays, 258
CTL360, 329–330, 468
CTLASA, 329–330, 337, 468
Currency symbol, 349–350
Current line counter, 26, 200
Cylinder, 441–442
Cylinder index, 445–447

DASD, 441–443
Data:
  alphameric, 18
  bit-string, 86–91, 96, 195
  character set, 10–11
  character-string, 79, 86–91, 96
  coded arithmetic, 80–86, 92–96

conversions, 121–123, 332–333
defaults for, 81, 85–86
editing, see P, format item; PICTURE
    attribute item
format items, see Format items
label, 4, 12–15
name, 12
portability, 461
storage requirements, 79
string, 5–6
transmission, see Data list
Data aggregate:
  array, 237–242
  declaration of, 237–239
  define, 81
  in stream I/O, 294–295, 310–311
  structure, 335–339, 357–373
Data area for record I/O, 328, 331–332, 335–
    336
Data attributes, see Attributes
Data conversion:
  of arguments, 143, 151–152
  defined, 121
  during I/O, 332–333
  internal operations, 121–123, 202
  in STREAM transmission, 284, 307
Data-directed I/O, 207, 209, 309–312
Data format item, 290–292, 303–307
Data formats (S/360), 585–596
Data item in data-directed I/O, 207, 209
Data list:
  data-directed I/O, 309–312
  edit-directed I/O, 289–300
  list-directed I/O, 21–27
Data names, 12–14
Data pool, 167
Data set:
  activities, 276
  defined, 276, 435
  labels, 283
  organizations, 443–449
Data stream, 21–25, 287, 293–295
Data transmission:
  direction, 276–277
  record-oriented, 327–335, 373–375
  stream-oriented, 207, 310–311
    edit I/O, 287
    list I/O, 21–26
  type, 276
Data types:
  bit, 16, 19–20, 79, 96, 195, 585
  character, 5–6, 16, 18–19, 88, 96, 587
  fixed binary, 20, 79, 82, 85–86, 93–94, 307,
    315, 592–593

Data types (*Continued*)
    fixed decimal, 80–82, 85–86, 92–93, 307, 315
    float binary, 85, 94–95, 307, 593–596
    float decimal, 82–83, 85, 94, 135, 307, 593–596
    S/360 and S/370, 585–596
Data validation, 211–212, 216–222
DATE built-in function, 109–111, 149, 156–157, 165, 549
Date editing, 112–113, 349
DD record, 452, 457
Deactivation of blocks, 390–391
Debit (DB) picture character, 340, 351
Deblocking of records, 437
Debug, definition, 7–8
Debugging techniques:
    aggregate length table, 373–375
    attribute and cross reference list, 126–129
    CHECK, 8–9, 430–431, 546
    ONCHAR, ONCODE, ONSOURCE, 210–214, 220, 224–226
    program testing, 62–64
    PUT DATA, 207–209, 312
    SIZE condition, 203–204, 306, 313, 315
    STRINGRANGE, 211–212
    STRINGSIZE, 212–213
    SUBSCRIPTRANGE, 264–265, 272
    suggested approach, 373–375
DECIMAL:
    attribute, 80–83, 85–86, 92–93, 94, 550
    built-in function, 550
Decimal constants:
    fixed-point, 16, 17, 18
    floating-point, 16, 17
DECIMAL FIXED, 80–82, 85–86, 92–93, 307, 315
DECIMAL FLOAT, 82–83, 85, 94, 135, 307
Decimal pictures, 340–351
Decimal point alignment:
    in data, 81–82
    in edit I/O, 288, 304–305, 341–342
    *see also* V picture character
Decimal point picture character, 346–348, 352, 356
Decimal variables:
    fixed-point, 16, 92–93, 591–592
    floating-point, 82–83, 94, 593–596
Decision, *see* IF statement
Decision symbol, 39
Declaration:
    array, 237–238
    contextual, 166, 395, 403
    explicit, 78, 81, 164–166

of files, 276–281, 461–469
    implicit, 80, 81
    with OPEN statement, 281–283, 469–470
    partial, 85–86
    scope of, 164–166
DECLARE statement, 23, 78, 80–96, 135, 276–281, 461–469
Default:
    attributes, 80, 85–86, 134–135, 158–159
    files, 128, 280, 282, 311
    precision, 85–86
DEFAULT statement, 550
DEFINED attribute:
    contrasted with BASED, 394
    introduction to, 88–89
    for scalar variables, 88–89
    in structures, 368–370
Defined item, 89
Define overlay, *see* Overlap defining
Delete byte, 447–448
DELETE statement:
    indexed files, 446, 470
    regional files, 477
Deleting records:
    consecutive, 470
    indexed, 446, 492
    regional, 459, 492
    summary, 477
Developing program, 46–47
Diagnostics, 7–8, 15, 128
DIM built-in function, 244, 519–520, 551
Dimensions, of array, 239–242, 245–246, 258–259, 409, 519–525
Direct access:
    concept, 441–442
    technique, 442
Direct addressing, 454
DIRECT attribute:
    defined, 443, 464
    for INDEXED files, 446, 464
    for REGIONAL files, 449
Direct file organization, 443. *See also* REGIONAL data set
Disable, conditions, 204–205, 325
Disk hardware, 441–442
Disk track, 441–442
Division, 99–100
Division/remainder randomizing method, 455–456
Dollar sign picture character, 349–350
Do-group:
    in IF statement, 180–181
    incrementation in, 229–234, 235
    leaving, 235

nesting of, 234, 274
repetitive specification, 232–233
summary of types, 273
DOS, 528, 539
DO statement:
  group, in IF statement, 180–181
  iterative, 229–234
  REPEAT option, 572
DO UNTIL statement, 227–229, 273
DO-UNTIL structure, 228–229
DO WHILE statement, 43–44, 45, 60, 75,
  227, 230, 233, 273
DO-WHILE structure, 43–44, 229, 236–237
Drifting characters:
  characters allowed, 385
  defined, 349
DSA, 389–392
Dummy argument, 149–155
Dummy record, 447, 458–459, 480
Dump program, 586
Dynamic storage allocation, 389–392


E, format item, 290, 304–305, 307
EBCDIC, 588–589
Edit-directed I/O, 289–300
  A format item, 289–290, 291–294, 301–
    304, 307
  array I/O, 295–296
  B format item, 304, 308
  C format item, 304
  compared with list I/O, 287
  COLUMN, 289, 292–295, 302–303, 308,
    546
  data transmission, 287–289, 292
  E format item, 290, 304–305, 307
  F format item, 289–290, 305–306
  GET, 288–289, 556
  LINE, 200, 278–279, 308–309, 560
  PAGE, 279, 308–309, 312, 567
  P format item, 354–356
  PUT, 288–289, 569
  R format item, 290
  Rounding output data, 306
  SKIP, 302–303, 308, 309, 575
  STRING, 298–300, 567
  structure I/O, 360–364
  X format item, 293, 303, 306
Editing characters, 339–340, 346, 349
Editing data:
  P format item in edit I/O, 354–356
  for printed output, 345–351
  simulating P format, 532–534
Editing of date, 111–112, 349

Element:
  of array, 237–238
  of structure, 337, 358–359
Elementary name (item), 337, 358–359
ELSE clause:
  in compound IF, 180–184, 190, 551
  null, 41–42, 183–184
  pairing with IF, 182–185
Enable, 204–205
End-of-file, 52–53, 56, 58, 70, 198–199
ENDFILE condition, 58–59, 75, 198–200,
  206, 280, 313–314, 552
End-of-file mark, 49–50, 284
ENDPAGE condition, 199–201, 308, 313–
  314, 552
END statement, 3, 6, 144, 180–181
  with SELECT, 191–193, 552
E-notation, 17–18, 304–305
ENTRY:
  attribute, 128, 151–153, 159, 552
  statement, 168
ENTRY name, see Subprogram, names
Entry point, 168
Entry-sequenced data set, 443, 449, 459–460
ENVIRONMENT attribute, 277–284, 465,
  552
ENVIRONMENT option:
  ADDBUFF, 468, 540
  BLKSIZE, 277–278, 282, 544
  BUFFERS, 466, 544
  COBOL, 546
  CONSECUTIVE, 443–444, 449, 467, 547
  CTLASA, 329–330, 468, 549
  CTL360, 329–330, 468, 549
  EXTENTNUMBER, 553
  F, 279, 466, 553
  FB, 466, 554
  FBS, 554
  GENKEY, 556
  HIGHINDEX, 557
  INDEXAREA, 467, 558
  INDEXED, 444–449, 467, 558
  INDEXMULTIPLE, 558
  KEYLENGTH, 456–458, 467, 559
  KEYLOC, 467, 559
  LEAVE, 467, 560
  MEDIUM, 561
  NOWRITE, 564
  OFLTRACKS, 565
  PASSWORD, 461, 567
  RECSIZE, 277, 466, 570
  REGIONAL, 449–450, 451, 453–456, 571
  REGIONAL (2), 449, 450, 451–452, 453,
    457, 459, 467, 571

ENVIRONMENT option (*Continued*)
REGIONAL (3), 449, 450, 452, 453–457, 459, 467, 571
REREAD, 467, 572
U, 466, 580
V, 278, 280, 466, 581
VB, 466, 581
VBS, 581
VS, 582
VSAM, 467, 582
Epilogue, 391
ERF built-in function, 110, 552
ERFC built-in function, 110, 552
Equal sign, 5, 97–99, 136–137
ERROR condition, 198, 208, 209, 213–216, 553
Error handling built-in functions, 207–211
ONCHAR, 210–211, 220, 565
ONCODE, 210, 213, 565
ONLOC, 210, 213, 566
ONSOURCE, 210–211, 213, 220, 566
ESDS, 443, 449, 459–460
Execution of program, 6–7
EXIT statement, 381, 389
EXP built-in function, 110, 553
Exponent, 17
Exponential expression, 101–102
notation, 17–18
Exponentiation, 11, 99, 101–102, 593–596
Expression:
arithmetic, 5
array, 256–259, 519
definition, 5, 99
element, 519
evaluation of, 99
example, 5
exponent, 101
in PUT statement, 25, 297
structure, 357, 365
subscript, 244
Extended binary coded decimal interchange code, 587, 588
Extended form floating-point, 94, 594
Extent, of array, 237–238
EXTENTNUMBER (ENV option), 553
External:
name length, 13, 143
procedure, G, 13, 143, 166
storage, G, 275
subprogram names, 14
EXTERNAL attribute, 128, 168, 392, 462
External block, 166
External data:
data-directed I/O, 309–313

edit-directed I/O, 287–290, 290–294
list-directed I/O, 21–23

F, format item, 289–292, 305–306, 553
fixed-length record format, 278
fixed-length record specification in ENV, 277–279, 280
Factoring, of attributes, 136
single identifiers, 136
FB (ENV option), 277, 553
F BLKSIZE, 277–279, 280
FBS (ENV option), 554
F (ENV option), 277, 279, 280, 553
File:
access techniques, 443
attributes, 277–281, 284
create program, 476–492
declaration of stream, 276–281
definition, 275, 435
explicit, 275–276, 280
implicit, 24, 277, 280
input, 277
maintenance, 446–447, 461
name, 276–277
opening of, 281–283
organizations, 443–461
output, 277
record files example, 328–331, 468–469
standard, 280–281, 282–283, 311
stream files example, 277, 287–289, 294, 300–303, 316–322
update, 443–444, 446–448
update program, 476–492
FILE attribute, 277, 280, 462, 554
File create program, 479–480
File declaration, charts:
records, 327–328
stream, 276–281
File label, 283
File names, 12–13
FILE option:
in GET or PUT, 275–276, 288–289, 554
in OPEN or CLOSE, 281–284
File update program, 487
FIXED:
attribute, 79, 80–81, 85–86
built-in function, 554
FIXED BINARY, 79, 81, 83, 85, 93–94, 307, 315
FIXED DECIMAL, 80–82, 85–86, 92–93, 307, 315
Fixed-length record, 278–279, 437, 450, 451, 452

FIXEDOVERFLOW condition:
  in addition, 203–204
  defined, 203–204
  in iterative DO, 232
  in multiplication, 203–204
Fixed-point (binary) data format, 79, 83, 85–
      86, 93–94, 592–593
Fixed-point data:
  binary, 79, 83, 85–86, 93–94, 592–593
  decimal, 79, 80–81, 85–86, 92–93, 591–592
  default precision, 81, 85–86
  internal representation of, 592
  maximum precision of, 83
  in record I/O, 373–375
  in stream I/O, 307–308
Fixed-point format item, see F, format item
Flags, 16, 19
FLOAT:
  attribute, 79, 81, 82–83, 94–95, 555
  built-in function, 555
FLOAT BINARY, 94–95, 307
FLOAT DECIMAL, 79, 81, 82, 83, 94, 307
Floating-point constants, 16–18, 20
Floating-point data:
  binary, 83, 94–95
  decimal, 79, 81–82, 94
  default precision, 81, 85–86
  in edit I/O, 304–305
  external representation of, 16–17, 94–95,
      304–305
  internal representation of, 593–596
  maximum precision of, 94–95, 594
  range of binary exponents, 94–95
  range of decimal exponents, 94
Floating-point data format, 16–18, 79, 82–83,
      593–596
Floating-point format item, see E, format item
FLOOR built-in function, 107, 555
Flowchart, 1, 2, 53–54, 58
Flow of control, 36–37
Format:
  of data-directed data, 309–312
  of edit-directed data, 287–289, 370–371
  of list-directed data, 21–27, 287
  of records, 437–440, 466
Format items:
  A, 289–290, 291–293, 300–303, 303–304,
      540
  B, 304, 307, 543
  C, 304, 545
  COLUMN, 289, 292–295, 301–302, 308,
      546
  E, 290, 304–305, 307, 551
  F, 290–292, 305–306, 553

LINE, 200, 278–279, 308–309, 560
P, 307, 567
PAGE, 200, 278–279, 301, 303, 309, 567
R, 290, 569
SKIP, 302–303, 308–309, 575
X, 293, 303, 306, 583
Format list, 288–290, 301–309
FORMAT statement, 290, 555
Formatting the IF, 181–182
FORTRAN, 276
F RECSIZE, 277
Freeing of storage, 410
Free space, 460–461
FREE statement, 405–406, 408, 416–417, 555
FROM option, 328, 332, 398, 477, 555
Full language, 7
Fullword boundary, 592
Function:
  attributes of returned values, 105–106,
      157–159
  built-in, 104–119, 209–211, 244–245, 279,
      312–313, 519–525
  defined, 104–105, 141
  names, 128
  of modules, 35, 47
  procedure, 157–161
  recursive, 160–162
  reference, 144
  termination of, 157–159, 161, 162–164
  see also Built-in function
Function subprogram arguments, see
      Arguments, data types allowed

Gap, 436–437, 441
GE symbol, 13, 104, 179
GET statement:
  data-directed, 310–311, 312–313
  edit-directed, 288–289, 290–295, 298–299,
      307
  list-directed, 4, 12, 15, 21–26
Global variables, 167
GO TO less programming, 44–45
GO TO statement, 44, 556
GT symbol, 13, 104, 179

Halfword, 592
HALT statement, 557
HBOUND built-in function, 245, 270, 271,
      520, 557
Headings:
  in edit-directed, 301–303
  in list-directed, 24–25, 102–103
  in record output, 379, 380–381

Hexidecimal:
 binary equivalence chart, 586
 conversion chart, 587
 number system, 586–587
Hierarchy:
 of invoking of built-in functions, 113, 148–149
 of PL/I operations, 99–102, 104
 in programming, 35, 47, 72, 73
HIGH built-in function, 557
HIGHINDEX option, 557
Hollerith card code, G, character code charts, 588–589

IBG, *see* Interblock gap
Identifier:
 defined, 12–14
 length of, 12, 86, 87, 351–352
 limiting scope of, 164–165
 partially declared, 85–86
IF statement, 179–185
 bit-string operators, 185, 194–195
 compound, 180
 examples and explanation, 179–185, 190, 194–195
 formatting, 181–182
 nesting of, 182–183, 190
 null ELSE, 42, 183–185
IF-THEN-ELSE structure, 41–43, 180–181, 182, 187–189
IMAG built-in function, 577
Imaginary number, 84
Implied attributes, *see* Attributes, defaults
%INCLUDE, 216
Incrementing in DO loop, 230–231, 247–248
Indentation unit, 15–16
Identical keys, 451–452
INDEXAREA, 467, 558
INDEX built-in function, 558
INDEXED (ENV option), 443–449, 467, 558
Indexed sequential file organization, 443–449
Index marker, 441–442
INDEXMULTIPLE, 558
Index searching, 454–455
Indicators, 185
Indirect addressing, 454–456
Infix:
 array operator, 256–257
 scalar operator, 101
Information retrieval, 19–20
INITIAL attribute:
 for arrays, 239–241, 248–250, 558
 in parameters, 146
 for scalar variables, 89, 90–91

 for STATIC variables, 391
 for structures, 359
Initialize:
 STATIC *vs.* AUTOMATIC variables, 392–393
 string data, 249
 *see also* INITIAL attribute
Initial procedure, G, *see* Main procedure
Initial value, 89, 90–91, 239, 359
INPUT attribute, 277, 280, 282, 462, 469–470, 558
Input buffer processing, 397–404
Input data items:
 data-directed, 309–311
 edit-directed, 287–290, 294–297
 list-directed, 21–24, 287
Input file, *see* File
Input/output steps, 276
Insertion characters, 346–349
Interactive communication, 285–286
Interblock gap, 436–437, 438, 441
INTERNAL attribute, 462, 558
Internal block, 165
Internal name, 149–155
Internal procedure, 12–14, 50, 165
Internal representation:
 of bits, 585
 of character data, 587–589
 of fixed-point data:
  binary, 592–593
  decimal, 591–592
 of floating-point data, 593–596
Inventory control example, 34–36
Invoked procedure, G, 143–145
Invoking procedure, 143–145
I/O and arrays, 246–247
I/O conditions:
 CONVERSION, 199, 202, 205, 208, 213–214, 219–220, 225–226, 284, 304, 314–315, 353, 354, 474, 548
 ENDFILE, 58–59, 197–200, 206, 280, 313–314, 552
 ENDPAGE, 199–201, 308, 313–314, 552
 KEY, 471–472, 559
 RECORD, 313, 314, 473, 570
 SIZE, 203–204, 306, 313, 315, 574
 TRANSMIT, 313, 314, 579
 UNDEFINEDFILE, 473, 580
I/O statements, summary, 470–472. *See also* CLOSE statement; GET statement; OPEN statement; PUT statement; READ statement; REWRITE statement; WRITE statement
Iterative DO, 227, 229–235

JCL (job control language), 7, 10, 278, 283
Julian date, 155–157

K, *see* Kilo
Key, 435–436, 442, 451, 452–454, 456–458
    duplicate, 452
    primary and secondary, 476–492
    sequence for INDEXED files, 464
KEY CONDITION, 471–473
KEYED attribute:
    defined, 464, 470
    in indexed files, 464
    in regional files, 452–454
Keyfield, 436
KEYFROM option, 456–458, 471
KEYLENGTH option:
    for indexed files, 467
    for regional files, 451, 458, 467
KEYLOC option, 467
KEY option of READ or REWRITE, 442,
        452–454, 456–458, 471
Key sequence, 446, 493
Key-sequenced data sets, 443, 449, 459–461
KEYTO option, 472
Keywords:
    abbreviations, 79, 540–583
    available in various PL/I compilers, 540–
        583
    defined, 13–14
Kilo, 607
KSDS, *see* Key-sequenced data sets

Label:
    attribute for arrays, 237, 248–250
    of data set, 283
    definition and examples, 4, 12–14
LABEL attribute, 559
LBOUND built-in function, 244, 519–520,
        521
Leading zeros, 346
LEAVE option, 467
LEAVE statement, 235
Leaving DO, 235
Length attribute:
    data item, 86–88, 351
    identifiers, 86–88
    strings, 86–88
    summary, 135
LENGTH built-in function, 114–115, 145–
        146, 560
LE symbol, 13, 179
Level number, 336, 358–359
Level one identifier, 336, 358–359
LIFO, 406

LIKE attribute, 364, 384
LIMCT, 452
Limiting scope of identifiers, 164–165
Limit value in iterative DO, 229–230, 231–
        232
LINE:
    control option in PUT EDIT, 200, 308–
        309
    control option in PUT LIST, 25–26
    format item in PUT EDIT, 279, 308–309,
        318
Line counter in PL/I, 26, 200
Line printer:
    carriage control, 200, 279, 282–283, 308–
        309, 328–330
    COLUMN, 289, 292–294, 301–303, 308
    control options, 25, 308
    CTLASA, 329–330, 337, 468
    CTL360, 329–330, 468
    file declaration, 278–279
    format items, 290–291, 303–309
    LINE, 25–26, 200, 278–279, 308–309, 560
    PAGE, 24, 25–26, 278–279, 301, 308–309,
        312, 567
    SKIP, 25–26, 200, 302–303, 308–309, 575
    variable-length records, 278, 280
Line-skipping, *see* CTLASA; CTL360; SKIP
Linear list:
    defined, 409
    examples, 410–411, 418–424
    pointer variables in, 409
    sequence in, 411–412
    structures in, 409
LINENO built-in function, 279, 560
LINESIZE option, 281, 282, 560
Link, 411. *See also* Pointer variable
Linkage editor, 142
List argument, 142
List-directed I/O:
    contrasted with edit I/O, 287
    COPY option, 23, 548
    input, 21–24, 287
    I/O stream data format, 21–26, 287
    output, 24–26, 253–254
    output alignment, 131
    PAGE/SKIP, 25–26
    tab positions, 5, 24
List items, G, 409
    contrasted with arrays, 408–409
List processing, G, 408–417, 418–424
    concepts, 408–412
    contrasted with arrays, 408–409
    using BASED to facilitate, 418–424
Literal, *see* Constants

Locate mode, 398, 401–403
LOCATE statement, 402–403
Locator qualified reference, 417, 421–423
LOG built-in function, 110, 561
LOG2 built-in function, 110, 561
LOG10 built-in function, 110, 561
Logical end, 6. *See also* RETURN statement
Logical operation, *see* AND operation; BOOL
    built-in function; OR operation
Logical operators in IF, 194–195
Logical record, 336–337, 399–400
Logical relationships of data, 336
Long form floating-point, 593–594
Loop, 251–272
LOW built-in function, 561
Lower bound, of array, 238
LT symbol, 12, 179

MACRO option, 67
Magnetic tape, 437–438, 462
MAIN attribute, 4, 141–143
Main procedure, 4, 141–143
Main storage, 7
Maintainability, of program, 141–142, 167–
    169
Major structure, 336–337, 358, 364
Manipulating bits, 195
Mantissa, 595–596
Master index, 444–445, 467, 468
Mathematical built-in functions, 104–107, 110
MAX built-in function, 107, 561
MEDIUM option, 534, 561
Merging of records, 433–444
MIN built-in function, 107, 561
Minor structure, G, 358, 364–365
MINUS sign picture character, 340, 345–346,
    352
Miscellaneous built-in function:
    DATE, 109, 111, 149, 156–157, 165, 375,
      549
    TIME, 109–111, 163, 193, 579
Mixed data types, 121–123
Mixed expression, 121–123
MOD built-in function, 108–109, 561
Mode attribute, 84–85
Modular programming, 141–142
Module design, 167–169
Module development, 35–37, 47–48
Move mode, 398–400, 401, 403
Move operations, *see* Assignment statement
Multiple:
    assignment, 97, 98
    declaration, 90–91
    dimensions of array, 246–247

entries, 168–169
    specification in DO, 232–233
Multiplication, 99
Multiply built-in function, 561

NAME condition, 310
Name(s), 12–14
    data, 12
    external, 12–14, 141
    file, 12–14, 276–277
    function subprogram, 128, 158–159
    internal, 12–14, 150, 153–154
    procedure, 12, 142–143
    qualified, 360–361
    subscripted, 241–244, 362
    unique in structures, 337, 339
Negative numbers, in binary, 592
Nested DO, 234–235
Nested IF statement, 182–183
Nested procedures, 50, 181, 565
Nesting, effect on scope, 164–165
    of blocks, 50, 164–165, 166
    of DO statements, 234–235
    of factored attributes, 136
    of IF statements, 42, 182–185, 188, 190
    of repetitive specifications, 294–295
    of SELECT groups, 193
NE symbol, 12, 179
N factorial, 160–161
NG, NL symbols, 12, 179
NOLABEL option, 562
NOT:
    operation, 194, 195, 223
    symbol, 12
NOTAPEMARK option, 563
Null, action, 201–202
    ELSE, 41, 183–185
    on-unit, 201–202
    statement, 184
    string, 88
    value in list, 410, 414, 419
NULL built-in function, 410–411, 419–422,
    464
Number systems:
    binary, 592–593
    hexadecimal, 586–587
Numeric character picture data, *see* Decimal
    pictures

Object program, 7
Object-time, 7
OFLTRACKS option, 565
ONCHAR:
    built-in function, 210–211, 220, 226, 565

pseudo-variable, 210–211, 220
ONCODE built-in function, 210, 213–214, 224, 565
ON condition, *see* Conditions, 198–201, 310
ONCOUNT built-in function, 565
One-dimensional array, 237–239
ONFILE built-in function, 474, 565
ONKEY built-in function, 474, 565
ONLOC built-in function, 213–214, 225, 566
ONSOURCE built-in function, 210–211, 213–214, 220, 225, 566
  pseudo-variable, 210–211, 220
ON statement, 565
On-units, 198, 280, 471–472
OPEN statement, 469–470, 566
OPEN statement attributes, 281–283, 469–470, 566
Opening of files:
  explicit, 281–283, 469–470
  implicit, 281
Operating system, 7
Operations:
  arithmetic, 99–102
  array, 256–259
  bit-string, 185
  comparison, 179, 195–196
  concatenation, 102–103
  logic, 194–196
  priority of, 99–101, 104
  string, 102–103, 111–112
  structure, 364–368
Operator, arithmetic, 99
  bit-string, 185
  comparison, 179
  concatenation, 102–103
  infix, 100–101
  prefix, 100–101
  string, 102–103
Optimist, 120
Optimizing complier, vii, 539
Option, 14
OPTIONS attributes:
  ASSEMBLER, 542
  MAIN, 4, 561
  RETURNS, 159–160, 162, 177, 572
OR operation, 194–195, 223
  on bit strings, 196, 223
OS, vii
OS JCL options, 278, 283, 452, 457, 470
OTHERWISE clause, 191–193, 566
OUTPUT attribute, 277–278, 279, 462, 470, 567
Output data item:
  data-directed, 311–312

edit-directed, 297, 301–303
list-directed, 24–26
Output file, *see* File
Output processing in buffer, 401–404
Overflow:
  fixed-point data, 203–204
  floating-point data, 203–204, 205
  in iterative DO, 232
  page, 201–202
OVERFLOW condition:
  in arithmetic operations, 203–204, 205
  in iterative DO, 232
Overflow record, 446
Overflow tracks, 446
Overlap, 463
Overlap defining:
  scalar on scalar, 88–89
  scalar on structure, 368
  structure on structure, 368–370
  using BASED instead, 394–397

P, format item, 354–356, 567
P, scaling factor, 307, 567
Packed decimal data, 79, 92–93, 287, 373–375, 591–592
Padding of string data, 86–87, 96
%PAGE, 69
PAGE:
  control option in PUT EDIT, 278–279, 301, 308–309, 312, 567
  control option in PUT LIST, 24, 25–26
  format item, 278–279, 301, 308–309, 312, 567
Page overflow, 278–279, 301, 308–309, 328–329
PAGESIZE option, 26, 200, 281, 282, 567
Pairing ELSEs in IF, 180, 182–183
Parameter:
  asterisks in, 145–146
    attributes of, 142–146
  data types allowed, 143–145
  number of, 176–177
Parentheses:
  in assignment statement, 100–101
  in argument list, 148–149
Partially declared identifiers, 85–86
PASSWORD option, 461, 468, 567
Pattern recognition, 524–525
PENDING condition, 567
Physical device name, 534–535
Physical end, 6
Physical record, 398–399, 436–437
PICTURE attribute:
  for arithmetic operations, 344–345

PICTURE attribute (*Continued*)
  introduction, 339–340
  for numeric data, 340–351
  repetition factor, 341
  specification characters, 341–353
  for string data, 352–353
Picture characters:
  asterisk, 350–351
  blank (B), 349, 352
  character (A,X), 352
  comma (,), 348
  conversion of, 340, 345
  credit (CR) and debit (DB), 340, 351, 354, 356
  decimal digit (9), 341
  decimal point (.), 341–342, 346–348, 352
  dollar sign ($), 349–350
  editing data, 345
  signs (S, −, +), 350
  slash (/), 349
  summary, 385
  virtual decimal point (V), 341
  zero suppression (Z), 346
Picture format item, *see* P, format item
PL/C, 527, 529–531
PL/I compilers, 527–539
PL/I constants, 16. *See also* Constants
PL/I-D, 528
PL/I data attributes, *see* Attributes
PL/I-F, 536
PL/I language comparison charts, 540–583
PL/I language components, 10–11
PL/I statements:
  ALLOCATE, 393, 405, 406–407, 416–417, 418, 426, 541
  assignment, 5, 90–91, 97–102
  BEGIN, 191, 198–199, 310, 313, 543
  CALL, 142–145, 148–153, 155, 160, 389, 545
  CHECK, 8–9, 430–431, 546
  CLOSE, 284, 546
  comments, 3, 377
  DECLARE, 23, 80–91, 276–281, 461–469, 550
  DEFAULT, 550
  DELAY, 550
  DELETE, 446–447, 470–472, 477, 550
  DISPLAY, 551
  DO:
    non-iterative, 180–181
    iterative, 229–235
  DO UNTIL, 227–229, 233–234
  DO WHILE, 43–44, 75, 227, 232–233, 236–237

END, 6, 143, 180–181, 191–193, 389, 552
ENTRY, 168, 552
EXIT, 143, 381, 389, 553
FETCH, 554
FORMAT, 290, 550
FREE, 405, 416–417, 555
GET, 4, 12, 21–26, 288–289, 290–295, 298–299, 310–313, 556
GO TO, 44, 556
HALT, 557
IF, 179–185, 194–195, 557
LOCATE, 393, 402–403, 560
null, 183–185, 201–202, 205
ON, 198, 205–206, 280, 313–314, 565
OPEN, 276–277, 281–283, 469–470, 566
PROCEDURE, 4, 6–7, 144–146, 147–148, 157–161, 569
PROCESS, 128, 264
PUT, 5, 24–26, 288–289, 299–300, 301–303, 308, 311–312, 569
READ, 327–328, 331–334, 336–337, 393, 442, 453, 458, 470–472, 477, 570
RELEASE, 571
RETURN, 158, 160–161, 381, 572
REVERT, 573
REWRITE, 398, 444, 470–472, 477, 573
SELECT, 191–193, 573
SIGNAL, 201, 206, 574
STOP, 143, 389, 576
UNLOCK, 580
WAIT, 582
WRITE, 276, 327–328, 334, 337, 452, 457–458, 470–472, 473, 477, 583
Point alignment, G,:
  decimal, 82–83
  in stream I/O, 288–289, 304–306
  *see also* V picture character
POINTER attribute, 393, 395, 397, 403–404, 409, 568
POINTER built-in function, 568
Pointer variable, 393–395, 397–398, 418–424
POLY built-in function, 245, 523, 568
POSITION attribute, 90, 568
Powers of two table, 593
Precision:
  attribute, 80–83
  defined, 81
  floating-point data, 594
  partially declared identifiers, 85–86
  summary of, 135
PRECISION built-in function, 568
Prefix array operator, 256
Prefix condition, 205
Prefix operator, 100–101

Preformatting regional files, 458–459
Preprocessor statements:
  %ACTIVATE, 540
  %DEACTIVATE, 549
  %DECLARE, 550
  %DO, 551
  %ELSE, 551
  %END, 552
  %GOTO, 556
  %IF, 557
  %INCLUDE, 216, 557
  %PAGE, 69, 567
  %PRINT, 569
  %PROCEDURE, 569
  %SKIP, 69, 575
Primary entry point, 168–169
Prime data area, 446
Prime number, 129–134
PRINT attribute, 278–279, 282, 309
Printer control option, *see* Line printer
PRINT files:
  data-directed, 282, 311–312
  edit-directed, 278–279, 282, 301–303
  list-directed, 278–279, 282
Priority:
  of arithmetic operations, 100–102
  of printer control options, 25, 308
PRIORITY built-in function, 569
Procedure,
  activation of, 142, 157, 388–390
  block, 164–165
  external, 12–14, 50, 143, 166
  internal, 14, 50, 166, 387
  invocation of, 142, 157–158
  function, 141–142, 157–163
  MAIN, 4, 141–143
  name (length of), 12–14, 143
  subroutine, 141–157, 162–164
  termination of, 3, 6, 143–144, 158–160,
    161, 162–164
PROCEDURE statement, 4, 6–7, 144–146,
    147–148, 157–161, 569
PROCESS statement, 67, 128, 264
PROD built-in function, 245, 522–523, 569
Program, 6–7
Program checkout, *see* Debug, definition
Program flowchart, 1, 2, 53–54, 58
Program hierarchy chart, 47–48, 72, 73
Program indicator, 185
Program maintenance, 141–142, 167–169
Program segment, 47–51, 218
Program switch, 16, 19, 48–50, 185
Program testing, 9–10
Program trace, 7–9

Progressive overflow technique, 151–152
Prologue, 391
Pseudocode, 2–3, 56–57, 66–67
Pseudovariables:
  COMPLETION, 547
  COMPLEX, 547
  as data items for edit-directed input, 296
  defined, 113–114
  IMAG, 557
  ONCHAR, 210–211, 213, 220
  ONSOURCE, 210–211, 213, 220
  PRIORITY, 569
  REAL, 570
  STATUS, 576
  STRING, 576
  SUBSTR, 113, 296–297, 300
  UNSPEC, 580
PT symbol, 12
PUT DATA, 207–209
PUT statement:
  data-directed, 207–209, 311–312
  edit-directed, 300, 301–303, 308, 370–371
  list-directed, 5, 24–26

Qualified name:
  example of use, 360–361, 371
  maximum length of, 361
  subscripted, 362
Qualified reference locator, 421–424
Quote marks, 5, 18

R, format item, 290, 569
Random access method, *see* Direct access
Random file organization, 487. *See also*
    Regional data set
Randomizing technique for direct file, 455–
    456
Range:
  of DO, 234
  of floating-point data, 94–95
READ SET statement, 400–401, 403, 404
READ statement:
  for consecutive file, 327–328, 331–334
  for indexed files, 470–472, 477
  for regional files, 453, 458, 470–472
Read-write heads, 441–442
REAL attribute, 84–85, 570
REAL built-in function, 570
Real constant, 84–85
RECORD attribute, 276, 277, 282, 328, 570
Record concept, 435
RECORD condition, 199, 313–314, 316, 570
Recorded key:
  for indexed files, 449

Recorded key (*Continued*)
for regional files, 451, 453–454, 456–457
Record formats, 437–440, 466
Record I/O:
arrays, 332
contrasted to stream, 276, 332–335
I/O data area, 328, 331–332, 335–337, 463
no data conversion, 332–333
READ statement, 331–332
WRITE statement, 332
Record size, 277
Record-skipping format item, *see* SKIP
Record *vs.* stream, 332–335
RECSIZE, 277, 374, 570
RECURSIVE option, 160–162
Recursive procedure, 161, 570
Redeclaration, *see* DEFINED attribute
Refinement, 3, 52–56
REGIONAL data set:
declaring files, 461–469
introduction, 450
preformatting files, 458–459
REGIONAL(1), 449–450, 453, 456–457, 459
REGIONAL(2), 449–450, 451–452, 453, 456–457, 458–459
REGIONAL(3), 449–450, 452, 453–454, 455–456, 459
when to use which type, 453–454
Region number:
maximum, 451, 452
relative record, 450, 451–456
relative track, 450, 455–456
Relative record, 450
Relative record data set, 443, 459–461
Relative structuring, 364–366
Relative track, 449–450
Remainder, how to retrieve, 108–109, 134
Remote format item, 290, 569
REPEAT built-in function, 114, 571
option of DO, 572
Repetition factor:
for arrays of string data, 249
defined, G, 18
in edit I/O format list, 294–295, 302–303
in pictures, 341
for string constants, 18, 102–103
Repetition structure, 43–44, 227–228, 229–232
Repetitive specification, 247–248, 294–295, 302–303
REREAD (ENV option), 467, 572
Reserved keywords, 12–13
Responses to occurrences of conditions, 198

Returned value, G, 159
RETURNS:
attribute, 159, 572
option, 161, 162
RETURN statement, 143, 158, 160–161, 163, 381, 572
REWRITE statement:
consecutive files, 444
indexed files, 470–472
regional files, 470–472
ROUND built-in function, 106–108, 573
Rounding data, floating point, 78, 176
in edit-directed I/O, 305
ROUND built-in function, 106–108, 573
SUM built-in function, 245, 252, 521–522, 577
ROW, in array, 239–240
Row major order, 247, 294
RRDS, *see* Relative record data set

Saving pointer variables, 397, 421
Scalar, 81
Scalar-to-array assignment, 255
Scalar-to-structure assignment, 367–368
Scale attribute, 81
Scientific programming techniques:
N!, 160–162
prime number generation, 129–134
Scope:
of condition prefix, G, 205
of contextual declaration, 166
of explicit declaration, 164, 166
of identifiers, 164–166
Search argument, 266, 409
Secondary entry point, G, 168–169
Segment, 47–51, 185, 218
SELECT statement, 191–193, 573
Semicolon:
in data-directed transmission, 309–311
as PL/I null statement, 183–184, 201–202
in PL/I statements, 4, 11
Sequence checking, 219, 221–222
Sequence structure, 40–42
Sequential access concept, 441
Sequential access method, 442
SEQUENTIAL attribute, 398, 464
Sequential file organization, 443
SET option:
in ALLOCATE, 416–417
in LOCATE, 403
in READ, 400
Short form floating-point, 85–86, 94–95, 593–596
SIGNAL statement, 201, 206

Sign picture characters, 344–345, 346, 350
Simple IF, 180, 194
Simulating conditions, 206–207
Simulating overkey defining, 394
Simulating P format, 532–534
SIN built-in function, 110, 574
SIND built-in function, 110, 574
Single quote mark, 6, 18
SINH built-in function, 110, 574
SIZE condition, 199, 203–204, 306, 313, 315
    366
%SKIP, 69, 129
SKIP:
  in edit I/O, 200, 302–303, 308–309
  in list I/O, 25–26
Sort:
  bubble, 259–260
  program, 479
  tag, 259, 261
  utility, 443
Source key:
  indexed files, 442
  regional files, 453–454, 456–458
Source listing:
  attribute table, 126–128
  formatting of, 67–69
Source program, 7
Space, *see* Blank
Spacing format item, *see* X, format item
Spacing in printed output:
  CTLASA, 329–330, 337
  CTL360, 329–330
  SKIP, 25–26
Special characters, 10–12
S picture character, 344, 346, 350, 351
Square root, built-in function, 105, 110
Stack, 405–406, 434
Standard PL/I files, 128, 280–281, 283, 311
Standard system action, 206, 209, 265
Statement(s):
  format, 4, 15–16
  label, 4
  numbers, 128
  termination of, 4, 15
  *see also* PL/I statements
Static, picture characters, 349, 385
STATIC attribute, 391–393, 576
Static storage allocation, 391–393
STATUS built-in function, 576
Status of conditions, 204–205
Stepwise refinement, 52–56
STOP statement, 143, 389, 576
Storage allocation, G, 387–389, 410, 416–417
STORAGE built-in function, 576

Storage class attributes:
  AUTOMATIC, 387–391, 392–393
  BASED, 393, 397, 400, 403–404
  CONTROLLED, 406–408
  default for, 387–391, 392–393
  STATIC, 391–393
Storage classes, 387
Storage requirements for data, 79, 83, 387–
    389, 391–392, 586
STREAM attribute, 277, 328, 462, 576
Stream file conditions, 313
Stream I/O, conveyed belt analogy, 22–23
  contrasted to record I/O, 276, 332–335
  data-directed, 207–209, 309–313
  defined, 21–22, 287
  edit-directed, 287–309
  list-directed, 21–26
Stream *vs.* record, 332–335
STRING:
  built-in function, 339, 576
  option of GET, 298–300
  pseudovariable, 339
String:
  AND, OR, NOT operations, 223
  assignment, 91
  bit, 16, 19–20, 86–88, 95–96
  character, 18–19, 86–91, 96
  concatenate, 102–103, 330–331
  constants, 5–6, 16, 17–20
  defined, 16, 86
  null, 88
STRING option of GET, 298–300
String-handling built-in function: 245, 524–
    525, 540
  ANY, 245, 524, 541
  BIT, 114, 543
  BOOL, 544
  CHAR, 114, 545
  INDEX, 114, 558
  LENGTH, 114, 145–146, 560
  REPEAT, 114, 571
  STRING, 339, 576
  SUBSTR, 111–114, 211–212, 296–297,
    300, 577
  TRANSLATE, 116–117, 579
  UNSPEC, 580
  VERIFY, 120, 221, 222
STRINGRANGE condition, 202, 211–212
STRINGSIZE condition, 202, 212, 213–214
Stroke character, 11
Structure:
  arrays in and of, 361–362
  assignment, 364–368
  BY NAME, 366–367

Structure (*Continued*)
    defined, 335, 357
    expression, 364–365
    factored attributes, 359
    level numbers, 335, 358–359
    with LIKE attribute, 364
    mapping, 402–403
    overlay defining, 359, 368–370, 394–397
    qualified names, 360–361, 371
    in stream I/O, 357, 370–371
    STRING built-in function, 339, 576
Structured programming, 1, 31–32, 39–40, 73
Structured theorem, 45
Stub, 10, 50–51, 62
Subfunction, 62–64
Subprogram:
    defined, 14, 141
    function, 14, 157–160, 162–164
    names, 14, 128, 143
    subroutine, 142–160, 155–157
Subroutine:
    CALL, 142–145
    definition, 14, 141
    procedure, 142–143
    termination, 143–144
Subroutine arguments, *see* Arguments
Subscript:
    constant, 241
    expression, 244
    in stream I/O, 294–295, 310–311
    variable, 242
Subscripted qualified name, 362
Subscripted subscript, 244
SUBSCRIPTRANGE condition, 244, 264–265, 272
Subset language, 7
SUBSTR:
    built-in function, 111–114, 211–212, 296–297, 300, 577
    pseudovariable, 113, 296–297, 300
Substructure, 358
Subtraction, 99
SUM built-in function, 245, 395, 521–522, 577
Switch, 16, 19, 142, 185
SYSIN default file, 128, 280, 282, 577
SYSIPT option of ENV, 577
SYSLST option of ENV, 577
SYSPCH option of ENV, 577
SYSPRINT default file, 128, 280–281, 282, 311, 577
System action, *see* Standard system action

System dummy records, 447, 458–459
S/360, S/370 data formats, 585–596

Table argument, 266
Table function, 267
Table look-up, 265–266
Tab positions, 5, 23–24, 311
Tag sort, 261–263
TAN built-in function, 110, 578
TAND built-in function, 110, 578
Tangent built-in function, 110, 578
TANH built-in function, 110, 578
Tape, *see* Magnetic tape
Termination:
    of PL/I statement, 4, 15
    of program, 6, 143
Test data, 9–10, 63
Testing, program, 9–10, 63–64
THEN clause, 179–180
Three-dimensional array, 240, 247
Throwaway code, 63
TIME built-in function, 109–111, 163, 193, 579
TITLE option, 469–470
Top-down development, 33–38, 72
Trace feature, *see* CHECK condition prefix
Track, 441–442
Track index, 445–446
TRANSIENT attribute, 579
TRANSLATE built-in function, 579
TRANSMIT condition, 314, 579
TRUNC built-in function, 107, 580
Truncation:
    on assignment, 79, 87, 202
    of bit-string data, 96
    built-in function, 107, 580
    of character-string data, 96
Turning on and off bits, 185
Two-dimensional array, 239–241
Two's complement, 592–593

U BLKSIZE, 466
U (ENV option), 450, 452, 459, 466, 580
UNALIGNED attribute, 580
Unblocked records:
    in consecutive file, 436–437, 437–440
    in indexed file, 449
    in regional file, 450
Unblocking of records, 437
UNBUFFERED attribute, 463–464, 470, 580
Undefined-length records, 439–440
UNDEFINEDFILE condition, 473, 580
UNDERFLOW condition, 202–203, 205, 580

Underline, 13–14
Underscore, 13–14
UNSPEC, built-in function, 580
UNTIL option of DO, 233–234, 580
UPDATE attribute, 462, 470, 581
Updating files:
  consecutive, 444, 462
  indexed, 445–449
  regional, 457–458, 470
  summary, 471–472, 477
Upper bound, of array, 238
Utility program, 481

Validation, *see* Data validation
Variable:
  automatic, 387–390, 391–393
  based, 387, 393–404, 413
  complexity when shared, 168
  definition, G, 4, 97, 98
  determining length dynamically, 146
  name, G, 99
  pointer, 393–404, 409, 416–417
  static, 391–393
  subscript, 242–243
  *see also* Identifier
V (ENV option), 277–278, 280, 450, 452, 459,
    466, 581
Variable-length record, 278, 280, 437–440
VARYING attribute, 87–88, 146, 581

VB (ENV option), 466, 581
VBS (ENV option), 581
VERIFY, built-in function, 118, 222, 381, 581
  option of ENV, 581
Virtual decimal point, *see* V, picture character
Volume, 442, 445
V, picture character, 340–342, 346–348
VSAM, 459–461, 467, 468
VS (ENV option), 581

WAIT statement, 582
WHEN clause, *see* SELECT statement
WHILE clause, 233
Work area, 398, 437
WRITE statement:
  consecutive files, 327–328, 332–334, 337,
    398–399, 470–472, 477
  indexed files, 470–472, 477
  regional files, 451–452, 470–472, 477
Writing headings, *see* Headings

X, format item, 293, 303, 306
X, picture character, 351–353

Z, picture character, 346–347, 348, 349
ZERODIVIDE condition, 202, 203, 205, 583
Zero suppression picture character, 346–347
ZONED decimal data format, 589–591